APPLIED BEHAVIOR ANALYSIS

APPLIED
BEHAVIOR
ANALYSIS

JOHN O. COOPER □ **TIMOTHY E. HERON** □ **WILLIAM L. HEWARD**

Ohio State University

MERRIL
an imprint of PRENTICE HALL
Upper Saddle River, New Jersey   Columbus, Ohio

Cover art by Ann Gates
About the artist: Ann Gates is employed at a sheltered workshop.
She created this painting while involved in art therapy there.
Although she has received awards and recognition for her work,
she insists she is not an artist.

Library of Congress Catalog Card Number: 86-61863

Administrative Editor: Vicki Knight
Developmental Editor: Amy Marsh
Production Coordinator: Rebecca Bobb
Art Coordinator: Mark Garrett
Cover Designer: Cathy Watterson

This book was set in Garamond..

15 14 13 12

ISBN 0-675-20223-X

Prentice-Hall International (UK) Limited, London
Prentice-Hall of Australia Pty. Limited, Sydney
Prentice-Hall Canada Inc., Toronto
Prentice-Hall Hispanoamericana, S.A., Mexico
Prentice-Hall of India Private Limited, New Delhi
Prentice-Hall of Japan, Inc., Tokyo
Simon & Schuster Asia Pte. Ltd., Singapore
Editora Prentice-Hall do Brasil, Ltda., Rio de Janeiro

Credits:
Quotes on pages 3, 4, 20, 143, 516, 543, 544, and 547 are reprinted
with permission of Macmillan Publishing Company from *Science
and Human Behavior* by B. F. Skinner. Copyright 1953, renewed
1981 by B. F. Skinner.

Quotes on pages 5, 6, 144, 159, 164, and 178 are reprinted from
"Current Dimensions of Applied Behavior Analysis" by D. M. Baer,
M. M. Wolf, and T. Risley, 1968, *Journal of Applied Behavior
Analysis, 1*, pp. 92, 93, 94, 95, 96. Copyright 1968 by the Society for
the Experimental Analysis of Behavior, Inc. Reprinted by
permission.

Quotes on pages 17, 18, 107, 110, 120, 144, 145, 146, 148, 150, 151,
153, 154, 169, 206–207, 208, 209, 228, 232, 233, 234, 241, and 242
are reprinted from *Strategies and Tactics for Human Behavioral
Research* (pp. 16, 38–39, 48, 49, 50, 51, 53, 89–90, 91, 120, 221, 226,
227, 228, 229, 250–251, 253, 256, 257, 260, 270, 276–278, 283, 293,
303–304, 327, 338, 348, and 371) by J. M. Johnston and H. S.
Pennypacker, 1980, Hillsdale, NJ: Lawrence Erlbaum Associates, Inc.
Copyright 1980 by Lawrence Erlbaum Associates, Inc. Reprinted by
permission.

Quotes on pages 18, 21, 24, 30, and 31 are reprinted from B. F.
Skinner, *Contingencies of Reinforcement: A Theoretical Analysis,* ©
1969, pp. 7, 114, 127, 130, and 131. Reprinted by permission of
Prentice-Hall, Inc., Englewood Cliffs, NJ.

Quotes on pages 308 and 318 are reprinted from "Stimulus Control
Procedures in the Education of Young Children" by B. C. Etzel, J. M.
LeBlanc, K. J. Schilmoeller, and M. E. Stella in *Behavior
Modification Contributions to Education* (pp. 9–10 and 35) by
S. W. Bijou and R. Ruiz (Eds.), 1981, Hillsdale, NJ: Lawrence
Erlbaum Associates, Inc. Copyright 1981 by Lawrence Erlbaum
Associates, Inc. Reprinted by permission.

We dedicate this book to our wives and children (who agreed to this
honor on the condition that we never write another one)

Bunny, Chris, Sharon, Greg, and Brian Cooper
Marge, Kathy, and Christine Heron
Jill Dardig, Lee and Lynn Heward

PREFACE

Changing behavior can be at once a challenging, perplexing, and frustrating endeavor. The challenge lies in recognizing what to do and how to do it. The perplexity is presented by the huge repertoire of human behaviors, the myriad relationships among them, and the multitude of stimuli that compose the environment. Frustration is experienced when even the most meticulously planned and implemented interventions prove ineffective in changing socially important behavior. Success, however, occurs just often enough. When certain techniques for changing behavior prove effective they are used again and again. Over time these various techniques are refined and give rise to related strategies and tactics.

In order to develop a socially useful technology for changing behavior, the principles and procedures that make up the emerging technology must be conceptualized. Their necessary and sufficient elements must be accurately described, scientifically tested, and effectively taught. Only then will the technology be reliably and successfully implemented by others. For these outcomes to occur, the relationships between the behavior of interest and the intervention designed to change that behavior must be determined. A methodology of technological description, precise measurement, and experimental analysis is needed. Such methods have, and continue to be, developed by a group of people—scientists and practitioners—who refer to themselves as applied behavior analysts.

We have titled our book simply *Applied Behavior Analysis,* but it should be viewed as an introductory text on two counts. First, the reader need not possess mastery of any particular prerequisite subject matter in order to obtain a complete understanding of the text. Second, a full understanding of applied behavior analysis requires considerable study and application beyond this text. However, we wanted to write a book that would provide a more extensive and in-depth presentation of applied behavior analysis than that offered by most introductory texts. Our primary goal is to introduce the student to applied behavior analysis in a reasonably complete, technically accurate, and contemporary manner. As a result, the book's scope and treatment of various principles, procedures, and issues suggest that it is intended for concentrated and serious study.

The book is organized into 11 parts. Part one offers a definition of applied behavior analysis, as well as some basic concepts of science and the scientific study of behavior. Parts two and three examine the elements necessary for an applied behavior analysis. Part two presents considerations, criteria, and procedures for selecting, defining, and measuring *applied behavior*. Part three examines the logic and operation of tactics for the experimental *analysis* of behavior-environment relationships, and some issues in planning, replicating, and evaluating analyses of behavior. Parts four through eight consist of chapter-length treatments of the major principles of behavior and their derivative procedures for increasing the frequency of existing behavior, obtaining desired patterns of stimulus control, developing new behaviors, and decreasing the frequency of behavior. Part nine details the rationale, uses, implementation procedures, and considerations for four special applications of behavior change technology: contingency contracting, token economy, group-oriented contingencies, and self-management. Part ten outlines a group of strategies for producing behavior changes with generality; that is, changes in behavior that are maintained across time, occur in appropriate situations beyond the training setting, and spread to other useful behaviors. The book's final part provides suggestions for sharing the results of behavior change efforts with participants, practitioners, parents, administrators, and the scientific community.

A standard set of technical terms is prerequisite to the meaningful description of any scientific activity. Effective communication about the design, application, and/or outcomes of an applied behavior analysis relies upon the accurate and careful use of the discipline's terminology. We have made an effort to define and use the terminology of applied behavior analysis in a conceptually systematic and consistent manner throughout the text. Learning the technical vocabulary of applied behavior analysis is an important initial step in learning the science, and one we encourage students to pursue with diligence.

The text includes graphs and, in some instances, detailed descriptions of experimental procedures from numerous studies found in the applied behavior analysis literature. The studies chosen for inclusion in the book represent some of the classic experiments in the field, as well as examples of contemporary applied behavior analysis. We had a twofold purpose in including as many studies in the text as we did. First, we desired to illustrate the principles and procedures of behavior change with actual rather than hypothetical applications. Second, by incorporating a liberal number of published studies into the text as we have provided the student with opportunities to learn specific strategies used by researchers and practitioners to solve problems, as well as opportunities to develop his or her skills of visually analyzing graphic displays of data. For similar reasons we have included quotations from key publications, not only for the historical and/or technical authority these passages provide, but also because their inclusion increases the student's exposure to the literature of the field. Again, while our objective was to provide a reasonably complete description of the principles and procedures for systematically changing socially important behavior, mastery of this book represents the beginning, not the completion, of one's study of applied behavior analysis. If our efforts have been successful the student will come away with a fundamentally sound repertoire of knowledge about applied behavior analysis that will serve as the foundation for more advanced training and practice.

ACKNOWLEDGMENTS

We thank Vicki Knight, administrative editor at Merrill Publishing Company, for making the commitment to publish this text. Vicki and Amy Marsh, our developmental editor, worked closely and patiently with us throughout the long process of conceptualizing, writing, rewriting, and production. We also wish to thank Phyllis Chorpenning, who typed much of the manuscript; Mary Benis, who carefully edited the copy; and Rebecca Bobb, who coordinated the book's production. The professionalism, understanding, and support of all these Merrill associates were greatly appreciated. We also thank Vicki and Amy for their wise selection of manuscript reviewers.

The book was improved immeasurably by the thorough, incisive, and intellectually stimulating comments and suggestions of our manuscript reviewers. The quality of the chapter-by-chapter reviews we received was superb. The following persons provided much-appreciated input to this book: Sheila Fox, Western Washington University, R. Douglas Greer, Columbia University, Jerome Ulman, Ball State University, and Bonnie Utley, University of Pittsburgh. Samuel Dietz, Georgia State University, Brandon Greene, Southern Illinois University, and Trevor Stokes, West Virginia University, provided valuable suggestions early in the development of the manuscript. We wish to pay a special tribute to David Gast, University of Kentucky, whose role in the project at times was closer to that of a coauthor than that of a reviewer. During the five years of writing the book, we relied often on David's good judgment and impressive command of the behavior analysis literature. He reviewed each chapter at least three different times and at the end read and critiqued the complete manuscript twice. In addition to being knowledgeable scholars, all of our reviewers demonstrated a deep interest in the teaching of applied behavior analysis. They not only expressed their concern that the book be accurate and presented clearly, they supplied examples, references, arguments, and counterarguments that proved invaluable to our effort. While only we can be responsible for any inaccuracies, omissions, and less-than-clear explanations that may remain, our reviewers warrant significant credit for the other parts.

We appreciate the many hours of hard work put forth by our colleagues Nancy Cooke and David Test, University of North Carolina at Charlotte, and Walter Kimball, University of Tennessee at Martin, in writing the instructor's manual, student study objectives, and test bank that accompany this text. All three are dedicated applied behavior analysts and outstanding teachers; two attributes that make them eminently qualified to author these important supplementary materials. We thank also Tom Stephens, our colleague and department chairperson at Ohio State University, for providing an academic environment in which work of this kind can be accomplished. Finally, we wish to acknowledge the professors who first taught us about applied behavior analysis: Saul Axelrod, Vance Cotter, Todd Eachus, Dick Malott, Jack Michael, Joe Spradlin, Roger Ulrich, and Donald Whaley.

JOC
WLH
TEH
Columbus, Ohio

CONTENTS

3

Selecting and Defining Target Behavior 36

4

Measuring and Recording Behavior 59

5

Planning and Directing Observational Procedures 81

PART THREE
EVALUATION AND ANALYSIS OF BEHAVIOR CHANGE

6

Production and Interpretation of Graphic Data Displays 106

7

Introduction to Analysis 142

8

Reversal and Alternating Treatments Designs 163

24

Token Economy 486

25

Group-Oriented Contingencies 499

26

Self-Management 515

PART TEN
GENERALITY OF BEHAVIOR CHANGE

27

Promoting the Generality of Behavior Change 552

PART ELEVEN
COMMUNICATION

28

Communicating the Results of Behavior Change Efforts 586

PART
ONE

Introduction
and Basic Concepts

We believe that prior to the study of specific strategies and procedures for changing behavior, the student of applied behavior analysis should be introduced to the field's defining characteristics and history, its scientific and philosophical orientation, and its overall goals and limitations. We also believe that a thorough study of behavior analysis is more effective if prefaced by a general introduction of the basic terms, concepts, and principles that serve as the foundation for the science. Part one responds to those two beliefs.

1

Definition and Characteristics of Applied Behavior Analysis

KEY TERMS

Applied behavior analysis

Determinism

Functional relation

Empiricism

Parsimony

Scientific manipulation

Philosophic doubt

Applied

Behavioral

Analytic

Technological

Conceptually systematic

Effective

Generality

Behaviorism

Experimental analysis of behavior

Applied behavior analysis is a discipline devoted to the understanding and improvement of human behavior. But there are other disciplines with similar intent. What sets applied behavior analysis apart? The answer lies in its focus, goals, and methodology. Applied behavior analysis focuses on objectively defined, observable behaviors of social significance; it seeks to improve the behavior under study while demonstrating a reliable relationship between the procedures employed and the behavioral improvement; and it uses the methods of science—description, quantification, and analysis. This chapter further defines applied behavior analysis by describing its characteristics and provides a brief outline of

---

This chapter was written by William L. Heward and John O. Cooper.

the history and development of the field. Since applied behavior analysis is, first of all, applied science, its defining characteristics are best understood in the context of some precepts fundamental to all scientific disciplines.

SOME BASIC CHARACTERISTICS OF SCIENCE

To begin to understand any science, one should look past the trappings—the apparatus and instrumentation that are most readily apparent—and examine the rules that govern all scientific activity. The pursuit of knowledge can be called science when it is carried out according to the procedures and methodologies that define science. The investigative methods of science are guided by an overriding set of assumptions and values that can be considered the attitudes of science (Whaley & Surratt, 1968).

Determinism

Science is most useful when it produces knowledge that can be used to reliably predict and control the phenomena it studies. Evidence of such control is all around us in everyday items we take for granted: radios, televisions, cameras, refrigerators. Reliably predicting and controlling any phenomena requires the identification and manipulation of the factors that cause those phenomena to act as they do. **Determinism** is the belief that the universe is a lawful and orderly place and that all phenomena occur as the result of other events. In other words, things do not just happen willy-nilly; they are caused by other factors, which are themselves physical phenomena amenable to scientific investigation.

> If we are to use the methods of science in the field of human affairs, we must assume behavior is lawful and determined. We must expect to discover what a man does is the result of specifiable conditions and that once these conditions have

been discovered, we can anticipate and to some extent determine his actions. (Skinner, 1953, p. 6)

The ultimate products of science are **functional relations,** statements that describe the occurrence of the phenomena under study as a function of the operation of specific variables (Johnston & Pennypacker, 1980). If the world were governed by accidentalism—a philosophical position antithetical to determinism that holds that events occur by accident or without cause—the scientific discovery and technological use of functional relations would be impossible.

Although most scientists believe in the principle of determinism, it is a philosophical position that does not lend itself to empirical proof or disproof, which would require investigating every phenomenon and every possible cause. Nevertheless, "it is the assumption of determinism that guides the methodological practices of the researcher" (Deitz, 1982, p. 55).

Empiricism

Scientific study requires, above all, **empiricism**—the practice of objective observation. In the prescientific era, as well as in nonscientific disciplines today, knowledge was (and is) often guided by speculation, personal opinion, and the "obvious" logic of common sense. The empirical attitude held by scientists, however, demands objective observation based on thorough description and precise quantification of the phenomena of interest.

As in every science, empiricism is the foremost rule in the science of behavior. Every effort to understand, predict, and improve behavior hinges on the behavior analyst's ability to completely define, systematically observe, and accurately record occurrences and nonoccurrences of the behavior of interest.

Parsimony

The dictionary defines **parsimony** as stinginess, and in a special way this definition accurately relates to the behavior of scientists. As

3

an attitude of science, parsimony requires that all simple, logical explanations for the phenomena under investigation be ruled out experimentally before more complex or abstract explanations are considered. An attitude of parsimony is so critical to scientific explanations that it is often referred to as the Law of Parsimony (Whaley & Surratt, 1968).

Scientific Manipulation

Whaley and Surratt (1968) use this well-known anecdote to introduce the concept of scientific manipulation.

> A man who lived in a suburban dwelling area was surprised one evening to see his neighbor bow to the four winds, chant a strange melody, and dance around his front lawn beating a small drum. After witnessing the same ritual for over a month, the man became overwhelmed with curiosity and decided to look into the matter.
> "Why do you go through this same ritual each evening?" the man asked his neighbor.
> "It keeps my house safe from tigers," the neighbor replied.
> "Good grief!" the man said. "Don't you know there isn't a tiger within a thousand miles of here?"
> "Yeah," the neighbor smiled. "Sure works, doesn't it!" (pp. 23-2 to 23-3)

When events are observed to occur together or in close temporal sequence, a functional relation may exist. To investigate that possibility, **scientific manipulation** must be conducted; that is, a controlled experiment (or better, a series of experiments) must be performed in which the factor(s) suspected of having causal status are systematically controlled and manipulated while the effects on the event under study are carefully observed. The neighbor just described could scientifically determine the effectiveness of his ritual by moving to a neighborhood in which tigers were regularly observed and systematically manipulating the use of his antitiger ritual (e.g., 1 week on, 1 week off, 1 week on) while observing and recording the presence of tigers under the ritual and no-ritual conditions.

Philosophic Doubt

The attitude of **philosophic doubt** requires the scientist to continually question the truthfulness of what is regarded as fact. Scientific knowledge must always be viewed as tentative, and the scientist must constantly be willing to replace with new discoveries even those facts of which he is most certain. In his discussion of the importance of determinism and philosophic doubt in the practice of applied behavior analysis, Deitz (1982) concludes,

> The continuing advancement of applied behavior analysis will be insured by the acceptance of the criteria of experimental determinism and philosophic doubt as bases of a definition for the field. The methodological practices derived from determinism will structure research so that it clearly remains within the boundaries of experimental science. Maintaining doubt will insure that applied behavior analysts continue their search for the variables which determine socially important behavior. Doubt will also keep them from believing too strongly in behavioral facts or theories which are already available. (p. 63)

There are other attitudes and values that guide scientific activity (e.g., honesty, thoroughness, replication), all of which are followed because they have proven beneficial to the progress of science. For as Skinner (1953) writes, "Science is first of all a set of attitudes" (p. 12). However, the five attitudes reviewed here serve as an important backdrop for examining applied behavior analysis further.

DEFINING CHARACTERISTICS OF APPLIED BEHAVIOR ANALYSIS

In 1968 Donald M. Baer, Montrose M. Wolf, and Todd R. Risley published their seminal paper, "Some Current Dimensions of Applied Behavior Analysis." The article served to define the purpose of the new field as well as the criteria by which research in applied behavior analysis would be judged. That paper has been the most widely cited publication in applied behavior analysis and still serves today as the standard description of the discipline. Baer et al. (1968) describe seven characteristics of a study in applied behavior analysis: "Obviously, the study must be *applied, behavioral,* and *analytic*; in addition, it should be *technological, conceptually systematic,* and *effective,* and it should display some *generality*" (p. 92).

Applied

The **applied** in applied behavior analysis is determined by the social significance of the behavior under investigation. To meet this criterion, a study must examine behavior(s) that have immediate importance to the subject(s) of the study. A survey of published research in applied behavior analysis shows studies covering virtually the full range of socially significant human behavior, including academic skills, language acquisition and use, work productivity and performance, marital interactions, child-rearing skills, consumption of electricity, public littering, clothing selection, self-help skills, highway speeding, seat belt usage, exercise, elevator use, and sport and leisure skills. The important criterion here is that the behavior is important to the subject or to society.

Behavioral

At first it may seem superfluous to include such an obvious criterion—of course applied behavior analysis must be **behavioral**. However, Baer et al. (1968) raise three important points relative to the behavioral criterion. First, not just any behavior will do; the behavior chosen for study must be the behavior in need of improvement, not a similar behavior or the subject's verbal description of the behavior. Second, the behavior must be able to be measured; the precise and reliable measurement of behavior is just as critical in applied research as it is in laboratory research. Applied researchers

must meet the challenge of measuring socially significant behaviors in their natural settings, and they must do it without resorting to the measurement of nonbehavioral substitutes. Third, when changes in behavior are observed during an investigation, it is necessary to ask whose behavior has changed. Perhaps it has been the behavior of the observers. "Explicit measurement of the reliability of human observers thus becomes not merely good technique, but a prime criterion of whether the study was appropriately behavioral" (Baer et al., 1968, p. 93). Or perhaps the experimenter's behavior has changed in an unplanned way, making it inappropriate to attribute any observed change in the subject's behavior to the variables that were manipulated. The applied behavior analyst should attempt to monitor the behavior of all persons involved in a study.

Analytic

An applied behavioral study is **analytic** when the experimenter has demonstrated a functional relation between the manipulated events and the behavior of interest. In other words, the experimenter must be able to control the occurrence and nonoccurrence of the behavior. Often, however, society does not allow the repeated manipulation of important behaviors to satisfy the requirements of scientific methodology. Therefore, applied behavior analysts must demonstrate control to the greatest extent possible, given the restraints of the setting and behavior; and then they must present the results for judgment by the consumers of the research. The ultimate issue is believability: has the experimenter shown enough control to demonstrate a functional relation?

Technological

A study in applied behavior analysis is **technological** when all of the procedures used in the study are completely identified and precisely described.

It is not enough to say what is to be done when the subject makes response R_1; it is essential also whenever possible to say what is to be done if the subject makes the alternative responses, R_2, R_3, etc. For example, one may read that temper tantrums in children are often extinguished by closing the child in his room for the duration of the tantrums plus ten minutes. Unless that procedure description also states what should be done if the child tries to leave the room early, or kicks out the window, or smears feces on the walls, or begins to make strangling sounds, etc., it is not precise technological description. (Baer et al., 1968, pp. 95–96)

A good check of the technological adequacy of a procedural description is to have a person trained in applied behavior analysis carefully read the description and then act out the procedure in detail. If the person adds any operations, omits any steps, and/or has to ask any questions to clarify what was included in the written description, then the description was not sufficiently technological and requires improvement.

Conceptually Systematic

Although Baer et al. did not state it explicitly, a defining characteristic of applied behavior analysis concerns the types of interventions used in an effort to improve behavior. Although there are an infinite number of tactics and specific procedures that can be used to alter behavior, almost all are derivatives and/or combinations of a relatively few basic principles of behavior. Thus, Baer et al. recommend that research reports of applied behavior analysis be **conceptually systematic,** describing the procedures for behavior change in terms of the relevant principle(s) from which they were derived.

Baer et al. provide a strong rationale for the use of conceptual systems in applied behavior analysis. First, relating specific procedures to basic principles might enable the reader to derive other similar procedures from the same principle(s). Second, conceptual systems are needed if a technology is to become an inte-

grated discipline instead of a "collection of tricks." Loosely related collections of tricks do not lend themselves to systematic expansion, and they are difficult to learn and to teach in great number.

Effective

An **effective** application of behavioral techniques must improve the behavior under investigation to a practical degree. "In application, the theoretical importance of a variable is usually not at issue. Its practical importance, specifically its power in altering behavior enough to be socially important, is the essential crierion" (Baer et al., 1968, p. 96). Whereas some investigations produce results with theoretical or statistical significance, applied behavior analysis must produce clinical or social significance to be judged effective. How much a given behavior of a given subject needs to change for the improvement to be considered socially important is a practical question. Baer et al. state that the answer is most likely to come from the people who must deal with the behavior; they should be asked how much the behavior needs to change.

The necessity of producing behavioral change that is meaningful to the subject and/or those in the subject's environment has led behavior analysts to search for "robust" variables, interventions that produce large and consistent effects on behavior (Baer, 1977).

Generality

A behavior change has **generality** if it lasts over time, appears in environments other than the one in which the behavioral techniques were applied, or spreads to other behaviors not directly treated by the behavior change techniques. Thus, a behavior change that continues after the original treatment procedures are withdrawn has generality, and when changes in behavior occur in nontreatment settings as a function of treatment procedures, generality is evident. Generality exists, also, when behaviors change that were not the focus of treatment. Generality is usually considered a desirable outcome of an applied behavior analysis program because it represents additional dividends in terms of behavior change. Nonetheless, generality is not an automatic result, and Baer et al. recommend that behavior analysts plan for it rather than expect it or lament its absence.

A BRIEF OUTLINE OF THE DEVELOPMENT OF APPLIED BEHAVIOR ANALYSIS

The science of behavior is comprised of three major components. The philosophical and theoretical foundations of the science constitute **behaviorism.** Basic research is the province of the **experimental analysis of behavior.** Practical application and analysis is the concern of applied behavior analysis. However, applied behavior analysis can be fully understood only in the context of the philosophy and scientific experimentation from which it evolved. A thorough description or historic account of behaviorism and the experimental analysis of behavior is beyond the purpose and scope of this book, but this section intends to provide an elementary description of the basic tenets of behaviorism and to outline a few of the major publications and events that have marked the development of the philosophy and science of behavior. (Additional information on the history of behavior analysis can be found in Fantino & Logan, 1979; Johnston & Pennypacker, 1980; Kazdin, 1978a; Millenson, 1967; Skinner, 1956, 1979; and Tawney & Gast, 1984). Table 1.1 illustrates some of the milestones in the development of the science of behavior. Michael (1980, p. 2) also illustrates the development of behavior analysis in terms of teaching materials and organizations.

The Stimulus-Response Behaviorism of Watson

Psychology in the early 1900s was dominated by the study of states of consciousness, images, and other mental processes. Introspection, the act of carefully observing one's own conscious thoughts and mental images, was the primary method of investigation. Although several texts in the first decade of the century defined psychology as the science of behavior (see Kazdin, 1978), J. B. Watson is widely recognized as the spokesman for a new direction in the field of psychology. In his influential article, "Psychology as the Behaviorist Views It," Watson (1913) wrote:

> Psychology as the behaviorist views it is a purely objective experimental branch of natural science. Its theoretical goal is the prediction and control of behavior. Introspection forms no essential part of its methods, nor is the scientific value of its data dependent upon the readiness with which they lend themselves to interpretation in terms of consciousness. (p. 158)

Watson argued that the proper subject matter for psychology was not states of mind or mental processes but observable behavior. Further, the objective study of behavior as a natural science should consist of direct observation of the relationships between environmental stimuli (S) and the responses (R) they evoke. Watsonian behaviorism thus became known as stimulus-response (S-R) psychology. Although there were few scientific facts to support S-R psychology as a workable explanation for most behavior, Watson was confident that his new behaviorism would indeed lead to the prediction and control of human behavior and that it would allow practitioners to improve performance in areas such as education, business, and law.

Watson (1924) made extreme claims concerning human behavior, as illustrated in this famous quotation:

> Give me a dozen healthy infants, well-formed, and my own specified world to bring them up in

TABLE 1.1. A representative selection of the many books, articles, journals, and organizations that have played a major part in the development of behavior analysis.

	Behaviorism *Philosophy of the Science of Behavior*	Experimental Analysis of Behavior *Basic Research into Principles of Behavior*	Applied Behavior Analysis *Application and Extension of Principles to Socially Significant Behavior*
Pre-1930	1913: *Psychology as the Behaviorist Views It* by Watson		
1930s		1938: *The Behavior of Organisms* by Skinner	
1940s	1948: *Walden Two* by Skinner		1949: Operant Conditioning of a "Vegetative Organism" by Fuller
1950s	1953: *Science and Human Behavior* by Skinner 1957: *Verbal Behavior* by Skinner	1950: *Principles of Psychology* by Keller & Schoenfeld 1957: *Schedules of Reinforcement* by Ferster & Skinner 1958: *Journal of Experimental Analysis of Behavior*	1959: "The Psychiatric Nurse as a Behavioral Engineer" by Allyon & Michael

and I'll guarantee to take any one at random and train him to become any type of specialist I might select—doctor, lawyer, artist, merchant-chief and, yes, even beggar-man and thief, regardless of his talents, penchants, tendencies, abilities, vocations, and race of his ancestors. I am going beyond my facts and I admit it, but so have the advocates of the contrary and they have been doing it for many thousands of years. (p. 104)

It is unfortunate that such claims were made, exaggerating the ability to predict and control human behavior beyond the scientific knowledge available. The quotation just cited has been used to discredit Watson and continues to

be used to discredit behaviorism in general, even though behaviorism today is fundamentally different from the early S-R psychology. Nevertheless, Watson's contributions were significant: he made a strong case for the objective study of behavior as a natural science.

The Experimental Analysis of Behavior

The science of behavior formally began in 1938 with the publication of B.F. Skinner's *The Behavior of Organisms*. The book summarized Skinner's laboratory research conducted from

TABLE 1.1. Continued.

Behaviorism	Experimental Analysis of Behavior	Applied Behavior Analysis
1960s		
1963: *Behaviorism at Fifty* by Skinner	1960: *Tactics of Scientific Research* by Sidman 1961: *The Analysis of Behavior* by Holland & Skinner 1964: Society for the Experimental Analysis of Behavior (Division 25 of the American Psychological Association)	1961: *Child Development* by Bijou & Baer 1965: *Case Studies in Behavior Modification* by Ullman & Krasner *Research in Behavior Modification* by Krasner & Ullman 1968: *Journal of Applied Behavior Analysis* "Current Dimensions of Applied Behavior Analysis" by Baer, Wolf, & Risley *Token Economy* by Allyon & Azrin
1969: *Contingencies of Reinforcement* by Skinner		*Technology of Teaching* by Skinner
1970s		
1971: *Beyond Freedom & Dignity* by Skinner 1973: *Behaviorism* (a journal) 1974: *About Behaviorism* by Skinner		1971: *Elementary Principles of Behavior* by Whaley & Malott 1974: Midwestern Association of Behavior Analysis (MABA) 1977: *Behavior Modification* (a journal) "An Implicit Technology of Generalization" by Stokes & Baer
1978: *Reflections on Behaviorism and Society* by Skinner *The Behavior Analyst* (a journal)		1978: MABA becomes the Association for Behavior Analysis
1980s	1980: *Strategies and Tactics for Human Behavioral Research* by Johnston & Pennypacker	

9

1930 to 1937 and brought into perspective two kinds of behavior. The first Skinner called respondent behavior. Respondents are behaviors that are elicited, or brought out, by stimuli that precede the behavior. Reflexes such as pupil constriction in bright light and the patellar tendon reflex (knee jerk) are examples of respondent behaviors. Respondent behaviors are essentially involuntary and occur whenever the eliciting stimulus is presented.

Skinner called the second type of behavior operant behavior. Operant behaviors are not elicited by preceding stimuli but instead are influenced by stimuli that follow the behavior. Skinner (1938) found that most human behavior could not be accounted for by the S-R, or respondent, paradigm and argued that the analysis of operant behavior "with its unique relation to the environment presents a separate important field of investigation" (p. 438).[1]

Skinner named this new science the experimental analysis of behavior and outlined the methodology for its practice. Skinner's investigative procedures evolved into an elegant methodology that provided for the experimental demonstration of principles of behavior. Simply put, Skinner made repeated observations of a well-defined behavior of a single subject (he initially used white rats and later, pigeons) in a controlled and standardized experimental chamber. When the rat pressed a lever or the pigeon pecked a disc, food was delivered. Using systematic manipulation of the arrangement and scheduling of stimuli that both preceded and followed behavior, Skinner and his colleagues and students conducted thousands of laboratory experiments from the 1930s through the 1950s in which they discovered and verified the basic principles of operant behavior. Description of these basic

FIGURE 1.1 B. F. Skinner (1904–). Photo by Christopher S. Johnson.

principles of behavior—general statements of functional relations between behavior and environmental events—comprises a major portion of this text. Thorough understanding of these principles is prerequisite to the skillful design of applied behavior programs.

The Radical Behaviorism of B. F. Skinner

B. F. Skinner, in addition to being the founder of the experimental analysis of behavior, has written extensively on the philosophy of that science. Without question Skinner's writings have been the most influential both in guiding the practice of the science of behavior and in extending the application of the principles of behavior to new areas (e.g., see Catania &

---

[1]In *The Behavior of Organisms* Skinner called the conditioning of respondent behavior Type S conditioning and the conditioning of operant behavior Type R conditioning, but these terms were soon dropped. In chapter 2 both respondent and operant behavior are further defined and discussed.

Harnad, 1984). In 1948 Skinner published *Walden Two,* a fictional account of how the philosophy and principles of behavior might be used in a utopian community. This was followed by his classic text, *Science and Human Behavior* (1953), in which he speculates on how the principles of behavior might apply to complex human behavior in areas such as education, religion, government, law, and psychotherapy.

Much of Skinner's writing in recent years has been devoted to the development and explanation of his philosophy of behaviorism. Skinner begins his book *About Behaviorism* (1974) with these words:

> Behaviorism is not the science of human behavior; it is the philosophy of that science. Some of the questions it asks are these: Is such a science really possible? Can it account for every aspect of human behavior? What methods can it use? Are its laws as valid as those of physics and biology? Will it lead to a technology, and if so, what role will it play in human affairs? (p. 1)

Many believe that the philosophy of behaviorism rejects all events that cannot be operationally defined by objective assessment. Accordingly, Skinner is thought to reject all data from his system that cannot be independently verified by other persons (Moore, 1984). Moore (1985) calls this operational view "a commitment to truth by agreement" (p. 59). This common view of the philosophy of behaviorism is limited; in reality, there are many kinds of behaviorisms. For instance, there are structuralism, methodological behaviorism, and forms of behaviorism that use cognitions as causal factors (e.g., cognitive behavior modification and social learning theory), in addition to the radical behaviorism of Skinner.

Structuralism and methodological behaviorism do reject all events that are not operationally defined by objective assessment (Skinner, 1974). Structuralists also avoid mentalism by restricting their activities to descriptions of behavior. They make no scientific manipulations; accordingly, they do not address questions of causal factors. Methodological behaviorists dif-

fer from the structuralists by using scientific manipulations to search for functional relationships between events. Methodological behaviorists also usually acknowledge the existence of mental events but do not consider them in the analysis of behavior (Skinner, 1974). The structuralists' and methodological behaviorists' reliance on public events, excluding private events, restricts the knowledge base of human behavior and discourages innovation in the science of behavior (Hake, 1982).

Contrary to popular opinion, Skinner does not object to the philosophy of cognitive psychology in its concern with private events (i.e., events taking place "inside the skin") (Moore, 1984). Skinner (1953, 1974) clearly indicates that it is a mistake to rule out events that influence our behavior because they are not accessible to others. However, he is concerned with the use of cognitive processes, ideas, expectancies, and other mentalistic fictions (i.e., hypothetical constructs) to explain the causes of behavior.

Skinner and the philosophy of radical behaviorism acknowledge the events upon which fictions such as cognitive processes are based. Radical behaviorism does not restrict the science of behavior to phenomena that can be detected by more than one person. In the context of radical behaviorism, the term *observe* implies "coming into contact with" (Moore, 1984). Radical behaviorists consider private events such as thinking or sensing the stimuli produced by a damaged tooth to be no different from public events such as oral reading or sensing the sounds produced by a musical instrument. According to Skinner (1974), "What is felt or introspectively observed is not some nonphysical world of consciousness, mind, or mental life but the observer's own body" (pp. 18–19).

The acknowledgment of private events is a major issue of radical behaviorism. Moore (1980) states it concisely:

> For radical behaviorism, private events are those events wherein individuals respond with respect

to certain stimuli accessible to themselves alone. . . . The responses that are made to those stimuli may themselves be public, i.e., observable by others, or they may be private, i.e., accessible only to the individual involved. Nonetheless, to paraphrase Skinner (1953), it need not be supposed that events taking place within the skin have any special properties for that reason alone. . . . For radical behaviorism, then, one's responses with respect to private stimuli are equally lawful and alike in kind to one's responses with respect to public stimuli. (p. 460)

The principles of behavior and the procedures presented in this text apply equally to public and private events. And the philosophical position underlying the content presented here is radical behaviorism, which is the philosophy of the science of behavior.

Although a detailed explanation of the philosophy of radical behaviorism is beyond our scope, the serious student of applied behavior analysis should devote considerable study to the writings of Skinner and others concerned with that philosophy. Hake (1982) addresses how the philosophy of science that is adopted affects professional practice and research. First, the philosophical decisions to ignore all private events or to use explanatory fictions as the causes of behavior may both produce a similar effect on research and practice. Both positions restrict practice and research even though for different reasons. Methodological behaviorism is restrictive because it ignores areas of major importance for an understanding of behavior. Mentalistic positions are also restrictive, for as noted by Skinner (1974), "Mentalistic explanations allay curiosity and bring inquiry to a stop. It is so easy to observe feelings and states of mind at a time and in a place which make them seem like causes that we are not inclined to inquire further" (pp. 15–16). Second, Hake indicates that scientists and practitioners are affected by their own social context, and institutions and schools are dominated by a mentalistic philosophy. A firm grasp of the philosophy of radical behaviorism, in addition to knowledge of principles of behavior, can help the

scientist and practitioner resist the mentalistic approach of dropping the search for controlling variables in the environment and drifting toward mentalistic fictions in the explanation of behavior.

Applied Behavior Analysis

One of the first studies to report the human application of principles of operant behavior was conducted by Fuller (1949). The subject was an 18-year-old boy with profound mental retardation who was described in the language of the time as a "vegetative idiot." He lay on his back, unable to roll over. Fuller filled a syringe with a warm sugar-milk solution and injected it into the subject's mouth every time the boy moved his right arm (that arm was chosen because he moved it infrequently). Within four sessions the subject was moving his arm to a vertical position at a rate of 3 times per minute.

> The attending physicians . . .thought it was impossible for him to learn anything—according to them, he had not learned anything in the 18 years of his life—yet in four experimental sessions, by using the operant conditioning technique, an addition was made to his behavior which, at this level, could be termed appreciable. Those who participated in or observed the experiment are of the opinion that if time permitted, other responses could be conditioned and discriminations learned. (Fuller, 1949, p. 590)

During the 1950s and into the early 1960s, other researchers used the methodology of the experimental analysis of behavior to determine whether the principles of behavior demonstrated in the laboratory with nonhuman subjects could be replicated with humans. For example, Bijou (1955, 1957, 1958) researched several principles of behavior with both normal and mentally retarded subjects; Baer (1960, 1961, 1962) examined the effects of punishment, escape, and avoidance contingencies on preschool children; and Ferster and DeMyer (1961, 1962; DeMyer & Ferster, 1962) conducted a systematic study of the principles of behavior using autistic children as subjects.

Much of the early research with human subjects was conducted in clinic or laboratory settings. Although the subjects typically benefited from the studies by learning new behaviors, the researchers' major purpose was to determine whether or not the principles of behavior are valid with humans. These early researchers did clearly establish that the principles of behavior are applicable to human behavior, and they set the stage for the development of applied behavior analysis.

The formal beginnings of applied behavior analysis can be traced to the 1959 publication of Allyon and Michael's paper titled "The Psychiatric Nurse as a Behavioral Engineer." The authors describe how direct care personnel in a state hospital used a variety of techniques based on the principles of behavior to improve the functioning of chronic psychotic or mentally retarded residents. During the 1960s many researchers began to apply principles of behavior in an effort to improve socially important behaviors, but these early pioneers faced many problems. Laboratory techniques for measuring behavior and for controlling and manipulating variables were sometimes unavailable, or their use was inappropriate, in applied settings. As a result, the early practitioners of applied behavior analysis had to develop new experimental procedures as they went along. There was little funding for the new discipline, and researchers had no ready outlet for publishing their studies, making it difficult to communicate among themselves their findings and solutions to methodological problems. Most journal editors were reluctant to publish studies using an experimental methodology unfamiliar to mainstream social science, which relied on large numbers of subjects and tests of statistical significance.

Despite these problems it was an exciting period, and major new discoveries were being made regularly. Programs in applied behavior analysis were begun at Arizona State University, Florida State University, Indiana University, the University of Illinois, the University of Kansas,

the University of Oregon, the University of Southern Illinois, the University of Washington, and Western Michigan University, among others. Each of these programs made major contributions to the rapid growth of the field during the 1960s through teaching and research.

Two significant events that occurred in 1968 mark that year as the beginning of contemporary applied behavior analysis. First, the *Journal of Applied Behavior Analysis* (JABA) began publication. It was the first behavioral journal in the United States to deal with applied problems and gave researchers using methodology from the experimental analysis of behavior an outlet for publishing their findings. JABA was and continues to be the flagship journal of applied behavior analysis. Many of the early articles in JABA became model demonstrations of how to conduct and interpret applied behavior analysis, which in turn led to improved applications and experimental methodology.

> In 1977, the *American Psychologist* reported that JABA ranked third out of 57 social science journals on mean citations per published article, topped only by the *American Psychologist* and the *Journal of Verbal Learning and Verbal Behavior.* Subscriptions outnumber all but the largest journals, and are distributed worldwide. Major advances in our science and our profession, first reported in JABA, have affected every aspect of our functioning. (Barlow, 1981, p. 1)

The second major event of 1968 was the publication in the inaugural issue of JABA of Baer, Wolf, and Risley's landmark paper, "Some Current Dimensions of Applied Behavior Analysis." As noted earlier, this paper both defines the criteria for judging the adequacy of research in applied behavior analysis and outlines the scope of work for those in the science.

DEFINITION OF APPLIED BEHAVIOR ANALYSIS

This chapter opened with the statement that applied behavior analysis is concerned with the improvement and understanding of human behavior. After describing some of the attitudes fundamental to scientific inquiry, examining the dimensions of applied behavior analysis described by Baer, Wolf, and Risley (1968), and briefly reviewing the development of the field, we can now offer a definition.

> Applied behavior analysis is the science in which procedures derived from the principles of behavior are systematically applied to improve socially significant behavior to a meaningful degree and to demonstrate experimentally that the procedures employed were responsible for the improvement in behavior.

This definition of applied behavior analysis specifies six key aspects of the field. First, the attitudes and methodology of science guide its practice. Second, the behavior change proce-

dures are described and applied in a systematic, technological manner. Third, not any means of changing behavior qualifies as applied behavior analysis; only those procedures conceptually derived from the basic principles of behavior are circumscribed by the field. Fourth, the focus of applied behavior analysis is socially significant behavior. The fifth and sixth parts of the definition specify the twin goals of applied behavior analysis: improvement and understanding. Applied behavior analysis seeks to make meaningful improvement in important behavior and to produce a functional analysis of the factors responsible for that improvement. The remainder of this text will present a foundation of knowledge and skills that can lead to a full understanding of applied behavior analysis.

SUMMARY

Some Basic Characteristics of Science

1 Determinism is the belief that the universe is a lawful and orderly place in which phenomena occur as a result of other events.
2 Empiricism is the practice of objective observation.
3 Parsimony in science requires that all simpler, more logical explanations be ruled out experimentally before a more complex or abstract explanation is considered.
4 Scientific manipulation requires conducting controlled experiments to determine the existence of a functional relation.
5 Philosophic doubt requires the scientist to continually question the truthfulness and validity of all scientific theory and knowledge.

Defining Characteristics of Applied Behavior Analysis

6 A study is applied only if it investigates socially significant behaviors with immediate importance to the subject(s).
7 A study is behavioral if it entails precise measurement of the actual behavior in need of

improvement and documents that it was the subject's behavior that changed.
8 A study is analytic if it demonstrates experimental control over the occurrence and nonoccurrence of the behavior, that is, if a functional relation is demonstrated.
9 A study is technological if its written description of procedure is sufficiently complete and detailed to enable others to replicate the procedure.
10 A study is conceptually systematic if its procedures are derived from basic principles of behavior.
11 A study is effective if it improves behavior sufficiently to produce practical results for the subject.
12 A study possesses generality if it results in behavior changes that last over time, appear in other environments, or spread to other behaviors.

Outline of the Development of Applied Behavior Analysis

13 J. B. Watson espoused an early form of behaviorism known as stimulus-response psy-

chology, which did not account for most human behavior.

14 B. F. Skinner founded the experimental analysis of behavior with the publication of his book *The Behavior of Organisms* in 1938.

15 The experimental analysis of behavior employs the methods of natural science to discover general principles of behavior.

16 Skinner has written extensively on radical behaviorism, the philosophy of the experimental analysis of behavior. Contrary to the opinion of many people, Skinner and the philosophy of radical behaviorism do not reject either the existence or importance of private events.

17 The first published report of human application of operant behavior was a study by Fuller (1949), in which an arm-raising response was conditioned in a profoundly retarded boy.

18 The formal beginnings of applied behavior analysis can be traced to 1959 and the publication of Allyon and Michael's article, "The Psychiatric Nurse as a Behavioral Engineer."

19 Contemporary applied behavior analysis began in 1968 with the publication of the first issue of the *Journal of Applied Behavior Analysis.*

Definition of Applied Behavior Analysis

20 Applied behavior analysis is the science in which procedures derived from the principles of behavior are systematically applied to improve socially significant behavior to a meaningful degree and to demonstrate experimentally that the procedures employed were responsible for the improvement in behavior.

2

Basic Concepts

KEY TERMS

Behavior

Response

Environment

Stimulus

Respondent behavior

Habituation

Elicit

Reflex

Respondent conditioning

Unconditioned stimulus

Neutral stimulus

Conditioned stimulus

Respondent extinction

Operant behavior

Contingency

Emit

Behavioral consequence

Operant conditioning

Response class

Principle of behavior

Behavior change procedure

Positive reinforcement

Negative reinforcement

Type I punishment

Type II punishment

Unconditioned
reinforcer/punisher

Conditioned
reinforcer/punisher

Extinction

Stimulus control

Antecedent stimuli

Three-term contingency

Setting event

History of reinforcement

This chapter was written by William L. Heward.

This chapter defines the fundamental concepts necessary for a scientific analysis of behavior and introduces some basic principles of behavior discovered in such an analysis. All of the principles presented in this chapter are examined in detail later in the book. However, their early introduction provides the student with background information and a source of reference to facilitate an understanding of the text that precedes the more detailed examination.

The first concept to be examined is the most fundamental of all—behavior. The concepts of environment and stimulus are then defined, for environmental stimuli comprise the controlling variables of primary interest in applied behavior analysis. The chapter then presents several of the most fundamental findings produced by the scientific study of the relationship between behavior and environment. The two major types of behavior are described—respondent and operant—and the basic ways in which environmental stimuli influence each type are introduced. The three-term contingency—a concept for expressing the temporal and functional relationships between operant behavior and environment—and its importance as the focal point in applied behavior analysis are then explained. The chapter ends with a discussion of the complexity of human behavior and the difficulty of analyzing and controlling it in applied settings.

BEHAVIOR

The way in which a scientific discipline defines its subject matter exerts profound influence on the discipline's progress as a coherent field of inquiry. Indeed, the way in which a discipline defines the object of its study in large part determines the methods of measurement and experimental manipulation that are appropriate and possible. Building upon Skinner's (1938) definition of **behavior** as "the movement of an organism or of its parts in a frame of reference provided by the organism or by various external objects or fields" (p. 6), Johnston and Pennypacker (1980) have proposed a definition of *behavior* that offers the most conceptually sound and empirically complete delineation of the concept.

> The behavior of an organism is that portion of the organism's interaction with its environment that is characterized by detectable displacements in space through time of some part of the organism and that results in a measurable change in at least one aspect of the environment. (p. 48)

Johnston and Pennypacker continued by elaborating on the major elements of their definition. The phrase *behavior of an organism* restricts the subject matter to the activity of living organisms, leaving notions such as the behavior of the stock market outside the realm of scientific use of the term.

The phrase *portion of the organism's interaction with the environment* specifies the required necessary-and-sufficient conditions for the occurrence of behavior as:

> (1) the existence of two separate entities, organism and environment; and (2) the existence of a relation between them. Behavior cannot occur in an environmental void, nor can it occur in the absence of living tissue. . . . Independent states of the organism, whether real or hypothetical, do not constitute behavioral events, because no interactive process is denoted. Being hungry or being anxious are examples of states that are sometimes confused with the behavior they are postulated to explain. Neither of these phrases specifies an environmental agent with which the hungry or anxious organism interacts, hence no behavior is implied. Similarly, independent conditions or changes in the environment do not define behavioral occurrences because no interactive process is specified. An animal walking in the rain gets wet, but "getting wet" is not an instance of behavior (Johnston & Pennypacker, 1980, p. 49)

Behavior is movement, regardless of scale; hence the phrase *displacements in space through time*. In addition to excluding all states of the organism, the definition does not include as a behavioral event movement produced by the action of independent physical forces. Thus, being blown over by a strong gust of wind would not be an example of behavior; both organisms and nonliving objects move similarly, given sufficient wind. Behavior can be accomplished only by living organisms.

The measurable characteristics of behavior are also highlighted by the displacement phrase. Behavior must be viewed as a continuous process that occurs through time. "Time becomes a universal parameter of behavior and thus figures prominently in the development of suitable units of measurement" (Johnston & Pennypacker, 1980, p. 50). Johnston and Pennypacker refer to these fundamental dimensions by which behavior can be measured as temporal locus (when in time a specified behavior occurs), temporal extent (the duration of a given behavioral event), and repeatability (the frequency with which a specified behavior occurs across time). The most important and basic dimension of behavior is frequency of occurrence. In experimental analysis the occurrence and nonoccurrence of a behavior must be reliably measured. Without accurate measurement determination of the variables that control the behavior is impossible.

Johnston and Pennypacker (1980) call the last part of their definition, *that results in a measurable change at least in some aspect of the environment,* "the most important qualifier for the conduct of the science of behavior."

Because the organism cannot be separated from an environment and because behavior refers to relations between the organism and the environment, it is impossible for a behavioral event not to influence the environment in some way. This being the case, the environment serves both to anchor one side of the defining relation and to provide the means whereby the relation (behavior) may be detected and measured. In other words, by definition, behavior must be detected and measured by its effects on the environment. (p. 51)

Or, in Skinner's (1969) words,

To be observed, a response must affect the environment—it must have an effect upon an observer or upon an instrument which in turn can affect an observer. This is as true of the contraction of a small group of muscle fibers as of pressing a lever or pacing a figure 8. (p. 130)

The term *behavior* is usually used in reference to a larger set or class of movements holding in common certain dimensions (e.g., hand-flapping behavior) or functions (e.g., study behavior). The term **response** is used to refer to a specific instance of a particular behavior. The manner in which a response is defined takes on paramount importance because specific instances of behavior—i.e., responses—are the focus of observation and measurement in behavioral studies (Skinner, 1969). In other words, the response is the measureable unit of analysis in the science of behavior. For example, in a study of handwriting behavior, the writing of individual letters of the alphabet might be the unit of measurement and analysis.

ENVIRONMENT

The science of behavior seeks to discover laws or statements that describe functional behavior-environment relationships. Johnston and Pennypacker (1980) define **environment** as

the conglomerate of real circumstances in which the organism or referenced part of the organism exists. The term may meaningfully include other parts or aspects of the organism distinct from that which is the object of specific inquiry. Thus, the term appropriately denotes a universe of events that differ from instance to instance. (p. 53)

Stimulus is the general term used to describe specific aspects of the environment that can be differentiated from one another. In a given study the term *stimulus* is usually used in reference to those environmental variables the experimenter is controlling or manipulating in some fashion so as to determine their influence on the behavior under investigation. A stimulus is any condition, event, or change in the physical world. Stimuli have physical dimensions (e.g., size, color, intensity, weight, position) and are described, measured, and manipulated according to those dimensions. Stimuli occur both outside and inside the body, although the stimuli most often studied by applied behavior analysts are those outside the body since they are most accessible to reliable observation and measurement. Stimuli are people, places, and things; light, sound, odors, tastes, and textures. Stimuli occur prior to, during, and after the behavior of interest. Some stimuli exert powerful control over behavior whereas others have no measurable effect. Responses and stimuli are the most fundamental concepts in the analysis of behavior.

RESPONDENT BEHAVIOR AND RESPONDENT CONDITIONING

All intact organisms enter the world with the ability to make responses in the presence of certain stimuli; no learning is required. Moreover, all healthy members of a given species come equipped with the same set, or repertoire, of these unlearned behaviors. The ability to respond automatically to certain stimuli is part of the genetic endowment of each organism. Such behaviors function as protection against certain harmful stimuli (e.g., pupil contraction in bright light) and help regulate the internal economy of the organism (e.g., changes in heart rate and respiration in response to temperature and activity levels); these responses evolved through natural selection because of their survival value to the species. This type of behavior, called **respondent behavior,** provides each organism with a set of built-in responses to specific stimuli; these are behaviors the individual organism would not have time to learn.

Respondent behavior is defined as behavior that is elicited by antecedent stimuli. In other words, a response is brought about, or caused, by a stimulus that precedes the behavior. Nothing else is required to make the response

occur. A bright flash of light in the eyes (antecedent stimulus) causes (elicits) the pupils to contract (respondent). If the necessary body parts are in working order, pupil contraction will occur every time.[1]

The verb **elicit**, meaning "to bring about or cause," is used in conjunction with respondent behavior. Taken together, the eliciting stimulus and the behavior it produces are termed a **reflex.** The human organism comes complete with a number of unconditioned, or unlearned, reflexes, all of which assist in maintaining the internal balance and survival of the individual.

New stimuli can acquire the ability to elicit respondents. Called **respondent conditioning,** this type of learning is associated most with the Russian physiologist Ivan Pavlov.[2] Just after the turn of the century, while studying the digestive system of dogs, Pavlov noticed that his experimental animals salivated every time his laboratory assistant opened the cage door to feed them. Dogs do not naturally salivate at the sound of opening doors, but in Pavlov's laboratory they consistently salivated when the door was opened. His curiosity aroused, Pavlov (1927) designed and conducted a classic and historic series of experiments. The result of this work was the experimental demonstration of respondent conditioning.

Pavlov's procedure was to ring a bell just an instant before feeding the dogs. Food in the mouth, an **unconditioned stimulus** (US), elicited salivation; the sound of a bell, a **neutral stimulus** (NS), did not. However, after

---

[1]If the eliciting stimulus for a respondent is repeatedly presented over a short span of time, the strength or magnitude of the response will diminish, and in some cases the response may not appear at all. This process is known as **habituation.**

[2]Respondent conditioning is also referred to as classical or Pavlovian conditioning. For more on respondent conditioning see Geis, Stebbins, and Lundin (1965); Holland and Skinner (1961); and Mallot, General, and Snapper, (1973). Pavlov was not the first to study reflexes; his work was an extension of others, most notably Ivan Sechenov (1829–1905) (Kazdin, 1978). See Gray (1979) for an excellent and interesting description of Pavlov's research.

FIGURE 2.1 Schematic representation of respondent conditioning and respondent extinction. In the top panel presentation of food, an unconditioned stimulus (US), elicits salivation, an unconditioned reflex (UR). The bell, a neutral stimulus (NS), has no effect on salivation. The second panel shows the respondent conditioning procedure. The bell is rung just prior to, or simultaneously with, presentation of the food. The third panel shows the result of respondent conditioning. After sufficient pairings, the bell, now a conditioned stimulus (CS), elicits salivation by itself, and a conditioned reflex (CR) has been created. The bottom panel represents respondent extinction. After repeated presentations of the CS alone, the CR is no longer elicited and the CS becomes an NS again.

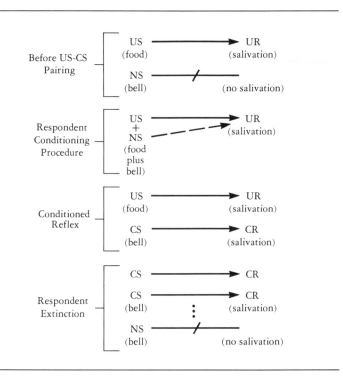

pairing the ringing of the bell with the presentation of food several times, the ring of the bell itself elicited salivation, thus becoming a **conditioned stimulus** (CS). The dogs had learned, or had been conditioned, to salivate in response to a new stimulus, a ringing bell.

Pavlov also discovered that after conditioning, the bell would lose its ability to elicit salivation if it was rung a number of times alone, without being followed by any food. Presenting a conditioned stimulus again and again without the unconditioned stimulus until the conditioned stimulus no longer elicits the conditioned response is called **respondent extinction.** Figure 2.1 shows a schematic representation of respondent conditioning and respondent extinction.

Respondent behavior appears to change little, if at all, during a person's lifetime. There are two exceptions: (1) certain reflexes disappear with maturity, such as that of grasping

an object placed in the palm of the hand, a reflex usually not seen after the age of 3 months (Bijou & Baer, 1965); and (2) a few reflexes develop later in life, such as respondents related to sexual behavior and reproduction. However, during a person's lifetime specific stimuli that were previously neutral (e.g., the high-pitched whine of the dentist's drill) can come to elicit respondents (i.e., increased heartbeat and perspiration). When we look at human behavior, respondents make up only a small percentage of the behaviors of interest to the applied behavior analyst. As Skinner (1953) pointed out,

> Reflexes, conditioned or otherwise, are mainly concerned with the internal physiology of the organism. We are most often interested, however, in behavior which has some effect upon the surrounding world. (p. 59)

It is this latter type of behavior, and the process by which it is learned, that we will now examine.

OPERANT BEHAVIOR AND OPERANT CONDITIONING

When an infant moves her arms through space, setting in motion the mobile dangling in her crib, she is literally operating on her environment. The mobile's movement and sound are stimuli produced by the child's behavior, consequences of her batting at the toy with her hands. If continued observation of the baby reveals an increased rate of arm swinging when the mobile hangs in her crib, her behavior would be described as an operant. The effects or consequences of an **operant behavior** on the environment are responsible for determining the behavior's future rate of occurrence. In addition, the consequences of operant behavior actually function to define the operant in terms of a given set of antecedent conditions. In other words, an operant cannot be defined by describing the topography, or physical shape, of the response (Skinner, 1983). Operants must be defined in terms of their relationship to controlling variables.

> Allowing water to pass over one's hands can perhaps be adequately described as topography, but "washing one's hands" is an "operant" defined by the fact that, when one has behaved this way in the past, one's hands have become clean—a condition which has become reinforcing because, say, it has minimized a threat of criticism or contagion. Behavior of precisely the same topography would be part of another operant if the reinforcement had consisted of simple stimulation (e.g., "tickling") of the hands or the evocation of imitative behavior in a child whom one is teaching to wash his hands. . . . It is not enough to say that an operant is defined by its consequences. The consequences must have had the effect of making a condition of deprivation or aversive stimulation a current variable. . . . Thus, a set of contingencies defines an operant. (Skinner, 1969, pp. 127, 130, 131)

A **contingency**, then, is the complete description of a specific operant. The description of a contingency includes (1) a precise definition of the limits and range of response topographies that will produce (2) a specified consequence and (3) the environmental situation (Skinner's "condition of deprivation or aversive stimulation") in which that consequence influences future probability of response.

Operant behavior is any behavior whose probability of occurrence is determined by its history of consequences. Whereas respondent behavior provides a person with a limited number of automatic responses to certain stimuli and to other environmental events paired with those stimuli, operant behavior enables a person to emit novel, complex responses to an ever-changing world.[3] Operant behavior is dynamic, constantly undergoing change in response to the environment. Table 2.1 contrasts respondent and operant behavior across several dimensions.

Effects of Consequences on Operant Behavior

A **behavioral consequence** is an environmental change (stimulus) that follows a given behavior in a relatively immediate temporal sequence and alters the probability of future occurrences of that behavior.[4] Consequences take one of two forms: (1) a new stimulus is presented or added to the environment; or (2) an already-present stimulus is terminated or removed from the environment. With either operation consequences produce one of two behavioral outcomes when a stimulus event is a controlling variable: (1) the future rate of the behavior will increase, or (2) the future rate of the behavior will decrease.

With our baby and her mobile the behavior of batting the mobile produces new stimuli—

---

[3]The verb **emit** is used in conjunction with operant behavior. Its use fits in well with the definition of operant behavior, allowing reference to the consequences of behavior as the major controlling variables. The verb *elicit* is inappropriate to use with operant behavior because it implies an antecedent stimulus that causes the behavior. Stimuli acquire their ability to control operant behavior because certain consequences have been produced in their presence in the past.

[4]Unless otherwise noted through the rest of the text the term *behavior* will refer to operant behavior.

TABLE 2.1. Some differences between respondent and operant behavior[a].

Dimension	Respondent	Operant
Body parts that produce response	Primarily smooth muscles and glands for most respondents; sometimes striated muscles (e.g., "startle" response); phylogenetically determined.	Primarily striated, or striped, skeletal muscles; sometimes smooth muscles and glands (e.g., biofeedback control of viscera).
Function	To maintain the internal balance of the organism; to provide inborn survival mechanisms that organism probably would not have time to learn.	To enable the individual to interact with the environment; to provide new, more effective ways of coping with an ever-changing environment.
Environmental factors controlling the response	Antecedent stimuli that elicit (or cause) the response; consequences have no effect on the respondent.	Contingencies of reinforcement consisting of (1) antecedent stimulus conditions, (2) the response, and (3) the consequence; consequences of the response primarily determine the probability of its occurring again in the future. Antecedent (discriminative $[S^D]$) stimuli are important also; however, such stimuli acquire control because of and through their association with certain consequences for that response. Therefore, the primary control of operant behavior rests with the consequences, the effects upon the environment, that the behavior produces.
Verb used in reference to behavior's occurrence	*Elicit* ("Tearing was elicited by sand in the eyes.")	*Emit* ("Bobby emitted a high rate of vocalizations.")

movement and musical sounds—that for most infants serve to increase the future rate of hand movements in the direction of the toy. If such an increase in rate occurs, *operant reinforcement* has taken place. In this case the mobile's movement and sounds would be called a reinforcer. If, however, the mobile's movement and musical sounds resulted in a decrease in the baby's rate of playing with the mobile, *punishment* has taken place, and the stimuli produced by her behavior would be called punishers.

The second form that behavioral consequences can take in the environment is the withdrawl or termination of a stimulus event. Let us assume for the purpose of this example that the mobile's movement and sound are reinforcers for the baby. Let us further assume that the mobile turns and plays music automatically but stops whenever the baby bats at it with her arm. In this example hand movements in the direction of the toy would be punished since the behavior results in the termination of a rein-

TABLE 2.1. Continued.

Dimension	Respondent	Operant
Conditioning process	Respondent, classical, or Pavlovian conditioning; through a pairing process stimuli that originally have no effect upon a respondent can acquire the ability to elicit the response (see Figure 2.1).	Operant conditioning; this changes the likelihood that a response will occur in the future by manipulating the consequences for that response.
Behavioral limits	The type and range of respondent behaviors are limited to the survival functions of the organism's reflex structures. All members of the same species possess the same set of reflexes (this assumes a healthy organism). New respondents are not acquired during life, although respondents can be elicited by a wide range of stimuli across members of a given species, depending upon the particular conditioning history of each organism. Repertoire is developed phylogenetically.	Behavior is limited only by the physical condition and genetic structure of the organism. New and more complex operants are acquired continually. Repertoire is developed ontogenetically.
Examples	Pupil contraction/dilation, patellar reflex, startle response, respiration, heartbeat, salivation, glandular secretions, infant grasping and suckling responses to touch.	Reading, writing, speaking, thinking, playing a musical instrument, driving a car, painting, sitting, standing, walking, running.

[a]For additional information on the interrelationship of respondent and operant behavior, see Baldwin and Baldwin (1981); Malott, General, and Snapper (1973); Schwartz and Gamzu (1977); and Skinner (1983).

forcing stimulus. However, if the movement and sounds produced by the mobile were punishers for the baby and if the mobile stopped when she batted it with her arm, that behavior would be reinforced (i.e., increased in rate).

Thus, behavioral consequences are classified as a function of (1) the operation carried out with the stimulus (i.e., it is added to or withdrawn from the environment) and (2) the resultant effect on the future rate of behavior. Figure 2.2 shows the relationship between consequences and their effect on behavior. Each of the four quadrants of Figure 2.2 represents a major principle of behavior, a statement of relationship between an environmental operation (in this case the stimulus change immediately following a behavior) and the future probability of that behavior's occurrence.

FIGURE 2.2 Identification of behavioral processes as a function of stimulus-change operation and resultant effect on behavior. (From W. H. Morse/R. T. Kelleher, "Determinants of Reinforcement and Punishment" in *Handbook of Operant Behavior,* Honig/Staddon eds., © 1977, p. 180. Reprinted by permission of Prentice-Hall, Inc., Englewood Cliffs, NJ.)

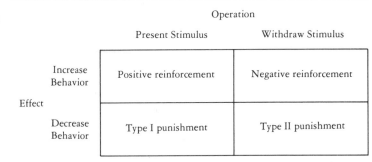

	Operation	
	Present Stimulus	Withdraw Stimulus
Increase Behavior	Positive reinforcement	Negative reinforcement
Decrease Behavior	Type I punishment	Type II punishment

Effect

The term **operant conditioning** encompasses both reinforcement and punishment, which are defined by their effects on behavior. If a behavior is followed by an event that increases the probability of that behavior occurring again in the future, reinforcement has taken place. Conversely, if a behavior is followed by an event that decreases the probability of that behavior's future occurrence, punishment has taken place. Reinforcement and punishment can each be accomplished in two different operations, depending upon what stimulus event is employed and whether the consequence consists of an additive (presentation) or reductive (withdrawal) operation in the environment (Skinner, 1953; Morse & Kelleher, 1977). Some behaviorists (e.g., Michael, 1975) argue that from a functional and theoretical standpoint only two principles are required to describe the basic effects of behavioral consequences—operant reinforcement, or strengthening, and operant punishment, or weakening. However, from a procedural perspective (a critical factor for the applied behavior analyst), there are a number of behavior modification strategies built upon each of the four basic principles represented in Figure 2.2. Several later chapters are devoted to a detailed discussion of each of these basic principles, along with various strategies and the implications for applying them to accomplish socially significant behavior change.

Before reviewing examples of the four basic operant conditioning principles, it is important to understand two facts about how consequences affect behavior. First, consequences can affect only future behavior; the response that produced the consequence is over and gone. A behavioral consequence affects only the probability that similar responses will be emitted again in the future under similar stimulus conditions.

Second, responses emitted because of the effects of reinforcement are likely to differ slightly from the earlier responses but will share enough common elements with the former responses to produce the same consequence. These similar but somewhat different responses comprise a **response class.** It is the response class that is strengthened or weakened by operant conditioning, and the concept of response class is a key to the development and elaboration of new behavior, as will be shown in later chapters.

Reinforcement strengthens responses which differ in topography from the response reinforced. When we reinforce pressing a lever, for example, or saying Hello, responses differing quite widely in topography grow more probable. This is a characteristic of behavior which has strong survival value . . . , since it would be very hard for an organism to acquire an effective repertoire if reinforcement strengthened only identical responses. (Skinner, 1969, p. 131)

BASIC PRINCIPLES AND APPLIED PROCEDURES

A **principle of behavior** describes a basic functional relationship between behavior and its controlling variables. Basic principles of behavior have been demonstrated repeatedly in hundreds, even thousands, of analyses across various species, behaviors, and conditions. A **behavior change procedure** is a method of operationalizing, or putting into practice, a principle of behavior. There are relatively few principles of behavior but many derivative behavior change procedures. To illustrate, reinforcement is a behavioral principle because it describes a lawful relationship between the emission of a behavior, the delivery of a consequence, and the increased probability of the behavior's future occurrence. However, the issuance of check marks in a token economy or the delivery of social praise would both be considered behavior change procedures derived from the more basic principle. To cite another example, punishment is a principle behavior because it describes the established relationship between the emission of a behavior, the presentation of a consequence, and the decreased probability of the behavior's future occurrence. Response cost and time out, on the other hand, are procedures for behavior change; they are two different strategies used by practitioners to operationalize the principle of punishment.

Reinforcement

The most basic and pervasive principle of behavior is that of operant reinforcement. **Positive reinforcement** occurs when a behavior is followed immediately by the presentation of a stimulus and, as a result, occurs more often in the future. For example, the behavior of turning the ignition key to the right to start the car is maintained because the engine has started in the past when the key has been turned to the right. Likewise, a child's independent play is said to be reinforced when it increases as a result of his parents' giving praise and attention when he plays.

Certain stimuli increase the future probability of behavior when they are terminated immediately following a response. This principle is called **negative reinforcement.** When the shower is too hot, the behavior of adjusting the water temperature is reinforced by the termination or withdrawal of the too-hot stimulus. Likewise, the student whose misbehavior in class increases as a result of being sent into the hall when he misbehaves is receiving negative reinforcement for acting out (rather than punishment, which the teacher probably intended). Escape and avoidance contingencies comprise negative reinforcement. By acting out, the misbehaving student escapes (or avoids altogether, depending on the timing of his misbehavior) the punishing (to him) classroom activity.

The concept of negative reinforcement has confused many students of behavior analysis. Much of the confusion can be traced both to the inconsistent early history and development of the term (see Michael, 1975, for an excellent discussion of the problem) and to a significant number of psychology and education textbooks and professors who use the term inaccurately.[5] The principle of negative reinforcement is presented in detail in chapter 11. However, remembering that the term reinforcement always means an increase in response rate and that the modifiers *positive* and *negative* describe the type of stimulus change operation that best characterizes the consequence (i.e., adding or withdrawing a stimulus) should facilitate the discrimination of both the principles and application of positive and negative reinforcement.

---

[5]See Cooke (1984) and Todd Morris (1983) for discussion of the implications of misrepresentation of the principles of behavior and the philosophy of behaviorism in education and psychology textbooks.

Punishment

Although most behaviorists support the definition of *punishment* as a consequence that decreases the probability of subsequent occurrence of the behavior it follows (Azrin & Holz, 1966; Skinner, 1953, p. 185), a variety of terms have been used in the literature to refer to the two types of consequence operations that fit the definition. Some textbooks (Baldwin & Baldwin, 1981; Malott, General, & Snapper, 1973) use the terms *positive punishment* and *negative punishment,* paralleling the terms *positive* and *negative reinforcement.* The modifiers *positive* and *negative* do not connote the intention or desirability of the behavior change produced; they specify only how the stimulus change that served as the punishing consequence was affected—whether it was presented (positive) or withdrawn (negative).

Although the terms *positive* and *negative punishment* are consistent with the terms used to differentiate the two reinforcement operations, they are less clear than the terms introduced by Whaley and Malott (1971) in their classic *Elementary Principles of Behavior.* Whaley and Malott used the phrases "punishment by contingent stimulation" and "punishment by contingent withdrawal of a positive reinforcer" to distinguish between the two punishment operations. This terminology highlights the procedural difference between the two types of punishment. Differences in procedure as well as in the type of stimulus involved—reinforcer or punisher—hold important implications for application when a punishment-based behavior-reduction technique is indicated. The terms **Type I** and **Type II punishment** have been used to differentiate punishment by contingent stimulation and punishment by contingent withdrawal of a positive reinforcer (cf. Foxx, 1982), and these designations have been adopted in this text. However, it should be remembered that they are simply brief substitutes for the more complete terminology introduced by Whaley and Malott.

Just as there were with the two types of reinforcement, there are a number of behavior change procedures that incorporate these two principles of punishment. Some textbooks reserve the term *punishment* for procedures involving Type I punishment and describe separately the behavior change procedures of time out from positive reinforcement and response cost, even though both procedures are derivatives of Type II punishment. Other authors identify time out and response cost as two independent principles of punishment, making a total of three basic types of punishment (e.g., Stumphauzer, 1977). Even though time out and response cost are major strategies and must be a part of the behavior analyst's repertoire, they are behavior change procedures and *not* basic principles of behavior.

Many behavior change procedures, although based primarily on one given principle, actually involve several principles of behavior in application. It is critical for the behavior analyst to have a solid conceptual understanding of the basic principles of behavior. Such knowledge permits better analysis of current controlling variables and better design and assessment of behavioral interventions that recognize the role various principles may be playing in a given situation.

KINDS OF STIMULI THAT REINFORCE AND PUNISH

Some stimuli, even without previous contact, are able to influence the future rate of behaviors they closely follow. If a given stimulus serves to strengthen such behavior, we call the stimulus an **unconditioned reinforcer.**[6] Given appropriate conditions of deprivation, stimuli that support the biological mainten-

---

[6]The terms *unconditioned, primary,* and *unlearned* are all used synonymously to indicate stimuli that affect behavior without prior conditioning. The terms *conditioned, secondary,* and *learned* are synonyms indicating that the effects produced by the stimulus are the result of conditioning.

ance and survival of the organism function as unconditioned reinforcers. Food, water, certain skin temperatures, sleep, and sexual stimulation are examples of unconditioned reinforcers that can strengthen the responses that immediately precede their delivery.

Similarly, an **unconditioned punisher** weakens the responses that precede its delivery even though the recipient has had not prior experience with the stimulus. Unconditioned punishers include those stimuli that cause tissue damage, or that physically harm body cells. Virtually any stimulus to which an organism is sensitive can be intensified to the point that its delivery suppresses behavior (Bijou & Baer, 1965). Bright light, loud sounds, and extreme temperatures, to name a few, are often avoided even though they are below levels that actually cause tissue damage.

> Some rewards and aversives control our actions because of the way our species evolved; we call these unlearned rewards or aversives. We inherit a biological structure that causes some stimuli to be rewarding or aversive. This structure evolved because rewards helped our ancestors survive, while aversives hurt their survival. Some of these unlearned rewards, such as food and fluid, help us survive by strengthening our body cells. Others help our species survive by causing us to produce and care for our offspring—these stimuli include the rewarding stimulation resulting from copulation and nursing. And many unlearned aversives harm our survival by damaging our body cells; such aversives include burns, cuts and bruises. (Malott, Tillema, & Glenn, 1978, p. 9)

Like respondent behaviors, unconditioned reinforcers and punishers are relatively few in number. In fact, very few operant behaviors in the everyday routines of most persons are directly controlled by unconditioned reinforcers and punishers. Even though going to work each day may earn the money that buys the food, the presentation of that food is too far removed in time from the responses that earned it to exert any control over work behavior. Behavior is most affected by its immediate results.

The stimuli that most often serve as reinforcers and punishers are **conditioned reinforcers** and **punishers.** Stimuli that function in this way have been paired in the past with other reinforcers or punishers. Conditioned reinforcers and punishers are not related to any biological need or structure; they are developed as a result of each person's unique experience with her environment. Consequently, the list of conditioned reinforcers and punishers for each person is unique and ever changing: no two people have ever experienced the world in exactly the same way. On the other hand, to the extent that people share similar experiences (e.g., culture, schooling, profession), they are likely to respond in similar ways to many similar conditioned reinforcers and stimuli. Social praise and attention are examples of almost universal conditioned reinforcers in our culture. Because social attention and approval (as well as disapproval) are often paired with so many other reinforcers (and punishers), they exert powerful control over much of human behavior and will receive much attention in later chapters when specific techniques of behavior change are presented.

Because of our similar histories in a common culture, there is considerable generality from one person to the next, prompting the behavior analyst to search for reinforcers and punishers from classes of stimuli that have proven effective with other similar individuals. However, in an effort to establish first an understanding of basic principles of behavior, we have purposely avoided a presentation of many examples of stimuli that may function as reinforcers and punishers. Morse and Kelleher (1977) have made this important point very well.

> Reinforcers and punishers, as environmental "things," appear to have a greater reality than orderly temporal changes in ongoing behavior. Such a view is deceptive. There is no concept that predicts reliably when events will be reinforcers or punishers; *the defining characteristics of reinforcers and punishers are how they change behavior* [italics added]. Events that

increase or decrease the subsequent occurrence of one response may not modify other responses in the same way.

In characterizing reinforcement as the presentation of a reinforcer contingent upon a response, the tendency is to emphasize the event and to ignore the importance of both the contingent relations and the antecedent and subsequent behavior. It is *how* [italics added] they change behavior that defines the terms *reinforcer* and *punisher;* thus it is the orderly change in behavior that is the key to these definitions. It is *not* [italics added] appropriate to presume that particular environmental events such as the presentation of food or electric shock are reinforcers or punishers until a change in the rate of responding has occurred when the event is scheduled in relation to specified responses.

A stimulus paired with a reinforcer is said to have become a conditioned reinforcer, but actually it is the behaving subject that has changed, not the stimulus. . . . It is, of course, useful shorthand to speak of conditioned reinforcers . . . just as it is convenient to speak about a reinforcer rather than speaking about an event that has followed an instance of a specific response and resulted in a subsequent increase in the occurrence of similar responses. The latter may be cumbersome, but it has the advantage of empirical referents. Because many different responses can be shaped by consequent events, and because a given consequent event is often effective in modifying the behavior of different individuals, it becomes common practice to refer to reinforcers without specifying the behavior that is being modified. These common practices have unfortunate consequences. They lead to erroneous views that responses are arbitrary and that the reinforcing or punishing effect of an event is a specific property of the event itself. (pp. 176–177, 180)[7]

The point made by Morse and Kelleher (1977) is of paramount importance to a complete understanding of behavior-environment interactions. Operant reinforcement and punishment are not simply the products of certain stimulus events, which then are referred to as reinforcers and punishers without reference to a given behavior and set of environmental conditions. The terms *reinforcer* and *punisher* are not to be used as a function of an assumed behavioral effect based on a presupposed inherent property of the stimulus event itself. Morse and Kelleher (1977) continue,

> When the borders of the table are designated in terms of stimulus classes (positive-negative; pleasant-noxious) and experimental operations (stimulus presentation–stimulus withdrawal), the cells of the table are, by definition, varieties of reinforcement and punishment. One problem is that the processes indicated in the cells have already been assumed in categorizing stimuli as positive or negative; a second is that there is a tacit assumption that the presentation or withdrawal of a particular stimulus will have an invariant effect. These relations are clearer if empirical operations are used to designate the border conditions. . . . The characterization of behavioral processes depends upon empirical observations. The same stimulus event, under different conditions, may increase behavior or decrease behavior. In the former case the process is called *reinforcement* and in the latter the process is called *punishment.* (p. 180)[8]

Figure 2.2 on page 24 shows the determination of operant reinforcement and punishment processes as a function of stimulus operation and the resultant effect on behavior. At least one of these two processes—reinforcement or punishment—and/or **extinction,** the withdrawal of reinforcement for a previously reinforced behavior, is fundamentally involved in the analysis and modification of all operant behavior.

---

[7]From W. H. Morse/R. T. Kelleher, "Determinants of Reinforcement and Punishment" in *Handbook of Operant Behavior,* Honig/Staddon eds., © 1977, pp. 176–177, 180. Reprinted by permission of Prentice-Hall, Inc., Englewood Cliffs, NJ.

[8]From W. H. Morse/R. T. Kelleher, "Determinants of Reinforcement and Punishment" in *Handbook of Operant Behavior,* Honig/Staddon eds., © 1977, p. 180. Reprinted by permission of Prentice-Hall, Inc., Englewood Cliffs, NJ.

The professor wanted to move on to his next point, but a raised hand in the front row detained him.

Professor: "Yes?"

Student: "You say that operant behavior, like talking, writing, running, reading, driving a car, most everything we do really—you say all of those behaviors are controlled by their consequences, by what comes *after* the response is emitted?"

Professor: "Yes. I believe I said that. Yes."

Student: "Well, I have a hard time with that. When my telephone rings and I go pick up the receiver, that's an operant response, right? I mean, picking up the telephone certainly didn't evolve genetically as a respondent to help us survive, so we are talking about an operant behavior, correct?"

Professor: "Correct."

Student: "All right then. How can you say that my picking up my telephone is controlled by the consequence? I pick up the phone because it is ringing. So does everybody else. Ringing controls the response. And ringing can't be a consequence because it comes before the response."

The professor hestitated with his reply just long enough for the class to sense victory. The student would be the hero, nailing the professor for proposing some theoretical concept with no everyday, real-world validity.

Another Student: "How about stepping on the brake when you see a Stop sign? The sign controls the braking response, and that's not a consequence either."

A Student from the Back of the Room: "Yaah! And take a common classroom example. When a kid sees the addition problem of $2 + 2$ on his worksheet and he writes 4, that response of writing 4 has got to be controlled by the written problem itself. Otherwise, how could we teach kids to write the correct answers to problems?"

Most of the Class: "Yaah!"

Professor: "All of you are absolutely right. And so am I."

Someone Else in the Class: "What do you mean? Explain."

Professor: "That was exactly my next point, and I was hoping you would pick up on it." The professor smiled a thank you at the student who had started the discussion and went on. "All around us, everyday, we react to hundreds, maybe thousands, of stimulus conditions. All of your examples were excellent—excellent examples of what we call **stimulus control.** Stimulus control is a very important and useful phenomenon in the analysis of behavior. It will be the subject of much of our discussion this semester.

"But, and here's the important point, **antecedent stimuli**, those that come before the response of interest, acquire their ability to control that particular response only because they have been associated with certain consequences in the past. So it is not just the ringing of the telephone that causes you to pick up the receiver. It is the fact that in the past picking up the receiver when the phone rang was followed by someone talking to you. It's that someone talking to you, the consequence of picking up the receiver, that really controlled the response in the first place, but you have learned to pick up the phone when you hear it ringing. Why? Because you have learned that it rings only when there's someone on the other end. So we can still speak of consequences as having the ultimate control over operant behavior, but by being associated with various consequences, antecedent stimuli can indicate what kind of consequence is likely. The next concept I am going to introduce will help clarify the issue of what environmental events control the emission of operant behavior. This concept is called the **three-term contingency**, and its understanding, analysis, and manipulation is central to applied behavior analysis."

THE THREE-TERM CONTINGENCY

Operant behavior always occurs as part of a contingency. The universe is a determined, orderly place in which things do not just happen. They happen in relation to other events, and science seeks to discover the relationships among those events. The experimental analysis of behavior has shown that two main sets of environmental events are crucial to our understanding and control of human behavior: antecedents and consequences. The role of consequences has already been discussed.

Antecedent stimuli refer to the state or condition of the environment prior to the emission of a response. There are antecedent stimuli for every response because behavior never occurs in a void. It must be emitted within some environmental context.

> Any stimulus present when an operant is reinforced acquires control in the sense that the rate will be higher when it is present. Such a stimulus does not act as a goad; it does not elicit the response in the sense of forcing it to occur. It is simply an essential aspect of the occasion upon which a response is made and reinforced. The difference is made clear by calling it a discriminative stimulus (or S^D). An adequate formulation of the interaction between an organism and its environment must always specify three things: (1) the occasion upon which a response occurs; (2) the response itself; and (3) the reinforcing consequences. The interrelationships among them are the "contingencies of reinforcement." (Skinner, 1969, p. 7)

Figure 2.3 illustrates the temporal relationship of the components of the three-term contingency. The term *contingency* refers to the interdependency of the three components—antecedent stimulus, behavior, and consequence. If a consequence is said to be contingent upon a particular response, then the response must be emitted before the consequence will occur. For example, a teacher might grant additional recess time only if a certain amount of seatwork is completed within a given time period. The additional recess time is therefore *contingent* upon the seatwork being completed within the given time. The telephone example involves all three elements of the three-term contingency. The consequence of talking to someone is contingent upon the response of picking up the receiver after the antecedent stimulus of the phone beginning to ring.

Virtually everything known about the prediction and control of human behavior is incorporated within the three-term contingency—*a*ntecedent stimuli, *b*ehavior, and *c*onsequences (sometimes called the ABCs of behavior analysis). All applied behavior analysis procedures involve manipulation of one or more components of the three-term contingency. Whether approaching a new behavior change situation or attempting to solve an ongoing program, the behavior analyst should always consider the three-term contingency. Somewhere within it lies the answer.

FIGURE 2.3 Examples of the three-term contingency.

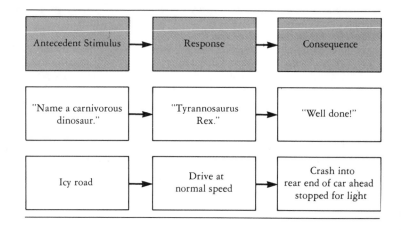

THE COMPLEXITY OF HUMAN BEHAVIOR

Behavior—human or otherwise—remains an extremely difficult subject matter. (Skinner, 1969, p. 114)

The experimental analysis of behavior has demonstrated a number of principles—statements about how behavior works as a function of environmental variables. These basic principles, several of which have been introduced in this chapter, have been demonstrated, verified, and replicated in hundreds and even thousands of experiments; they are scientific fact. The basic principles have also been applied, in a variety of forms, to important human behaviors in everyday settings. In many of these applied behavior analyses impressive results have been obtained. What has been learned from those applications, both the highly successful and the not-so-successful, comprises the bulk of this book.

Yet there is still a great deal more to be done. The science of behavior is a young science with much to discover. And applied behavior analysis, the technological arm of the basic science of behavior, has even further to go (Skinner, 1971). Perhaps the major challenge to behavior analysis lies in dealing with the complexity of human behavior, especially in applied settings where laboratory controls are impossible, impractical, or unethical.

Some Reasons for the Complexity of Human Behavior

Many of the variables contributing to the complexity of behavior stem from three general sources: the complexity of the human repertoire, the complexity of the environment, and individual differences.

Complexity of the Human Repertoire Humans are capable of an incredible range of behaviors. In any given setting concurrent contingencies are vying for control of different behaviors. One aspect of this complexity is that a single event often has multiple effects. For example, the delivery of a punishing stimulus can suppress the response it follows, elicit respondent behaviors, and set the occasion for a response that permits escape from the stimulus to be reinforced—three effects from one event.

Response chains, sometimes of no apparent logical organization, also add to the complexity of behavior (Skinner, 1953). In a response chain, variables produced by one response control the emission of other responses. Returning a winter coat to the attic leads to rediscovering a scrapbook of old family photographs, which sets the occasion for calling Aunt Helen, which sets the occasion for getting out her recipe for apple pie, and so on.

Verbal behavior also lends to the complexity of human behavior (Skinner, 1957). Not only is a problem generated when the difference between saying and doing is not recognized, but verbal behavior itself often produces variables that control a variety of other responses, both motor and verbal.

Complexity of Controlling Variables The environment (i.e., stimulus configurations and their interrelationships) is also complex. Some behaviors are the result of multiple causes; several contingencies can combine to make a behavior more or less likely to occur in a given situation. Perhaps we finally return our neighbor's lawn mower not only because he always invites us in for a cup of coffee, but also because it reduces the self-delivered "guilt" statements over keeping the mower for 2 weeks. Often, variables controlling incompatible responses come into play simultaneously. We cannot go to the movies and finish our homework at the same time.

Some controlling variables, called **setting events,** are more complex than simple stimulus events (Kantor, 1970; Leigland, 1984; Wahler & Fox, 1981).

But, in contrast to stimulus events, setting events are more complicated than the simple presence, absence or change of stimulus (such as turning on a light, a sudden drop in temperature, or a smile from mother). Instead, a setting event is a stimulus-response interaction, which simply because it has occurred will affect other stimulus-response relationships which follow it. (Bijou & Baer, 1961, p. 21)

Bijou and Baer illustrated the possible role of setting events with a hypothetical example of a baby who usually engages in rigorous play in his playpen after his daily nap. When loud noises outdoors prevented the baby from sleeping in his crib and he remained awake and active during his nap time, he later cried and resisted being placed in his playpen and played with. In this example the awake-during-nap-time-in-the-crib interaction served as a setting event with considerable effect on the child's playpen-crying behavior.

Individual Differences People often respond differently to the same set of environmental conditions. The notion of individual differences has been cited as a demonstration that universal principles of behavior based on response-environment interactions do not exist, at least not in reliable form. It is then argued that control of behavior must come from within the person.

In one sense this argument is correct. As each of us experiences varying contingencies of reinforcement (and punishment), our response patterns to those contingencies also vary. Some responses are strengthened (by the contingencies) and others, weakened; this is the nature of operant conditioning. No two people ever experience the world in the same way. Therefore, different people arrive at a given situation with different **histories of reinforcement,** which determine what responses to a particular situation they have in their repertoire at any given time. These are the behaviors that have produced reinforcers or have escaped/avoided punishers in the past.

In the figurative sense that a repertoire of behaviors lies within a person, individual differences can be explained as something a person possesses. However, we only possess those behaviors because of our histories of reinforcement. Differences in responding to current stimulus conditions, then, do not need to be attributed to differences in internal traits or tendencies, but to the orderly result of different histories of reinforcement. Individual differences are also found in sensory and motor deficits (e.g., hearing impairment, cerebral palsy), which the behavior analyst must consider in the design of effective programs (Heward & Orlansky, 1984).

Each of these three sources of complexity will be dealt with both conceptually and strategically as it relates to the implementation of the principles and techniques presented throughout the book.

OBSTACLES TO CONTROL OF BEHAVIOR IN APPLIED SETTINGS

In addition to the difficulty of dealing adequately with the complexity of human behavior in its own right, applied behavior analysts are sometimes prevented from conducting an effective analysis in a given setting because of practical, logistical, financial, sociopolitical, legal, and/or ethical reasons. Most applied behavior analysts work for agencies with limited resources. This may make the data collection required for a more complete analysis impossible. In addition, participants, parents, administrators, and even the general public may at times limit the behavior analyst's options for intervention (e.g., "We don't want our children working for tokens"). Legal or ethical considerations can also preclude determining experimentally the controlling variables for an important behavior.

Each of these practical complexities combines with the behavioral complexities previously mentioned to make the functional analysis of socially important behavior a challenging task. However, the task need not be overwhelming, and few tasks are as rewarding or necessary.

It can always be argued that human behavior is a particularly difficult field. It is, and we are especially likely to think so just because we are so inept in dealing with it.

It is easy to conclude that there must be something about human behavior which makes a scientific analysis, and hence an effective technology, impossible, but we have not by any means exhausted the possibilities. (Skinner, 1971, pp. 6–7)

SUMMARY

Definition of Behavior

1　Behavior is a concept restricted to the movement of living organisms.

2　Behavior is that portion of an organism's interaction with the environment characterized by detectable displacements in space through time of some part of the organism (Johnston & Pennypacker, 1980).

3　Behavior must produce a measurable change in some aspect of the environment.

4　Behavior refers to a set or class of movements holding in common certain dimensions or functions.

5　Response refers to a specific instance of a given behavior.

Definition of Environment

6　Environment is "the conglomerate of real circumstances in which the organism or referenced part of the organism exists" (Johnston & Pennypacker, 1980, p. 53).

7　Stimulus signifies specific aspects of the environment that can be differentiated from one another.

8　Stimuli are described, measured, and manipulated in terms of their physical dimensions.

Respondent Behavior and Respondent Conditioning

9　Respondent behavior is elicited by antecedent stimuli.

10　An unconditioned stimulus and the respondent behavior it elicits (e.g., food and salivation) are called an unconditioned reflex.

11　In respondent conditioning repeated pairing of an unconditioned stimulus (e.g., food) with a neutral stimulus (e.g., bell) results in the development of a conditioned stimulus (the bell), which can by itself elicit the conditioned response (salivation). A conditioned stimulus and its elicited conditioned respondent are called a conditioned reflex.

12　Respondent extinction occurs when a conditioned stimulus is presented repeatedly without being paired with the unconditioned stimulus and thus loses its ability to elicit the conditioned response.

Operant Behavior and Operant Conditioning

13　Operant behavior is behavior for which the probability of occurrence is determined by its history of consequences.

14　A behavioral consequence is an environmental change (stimulus) that follows a given behavior in a relatively immediate temporal sequence and alters the probability of future occurrence of that behavior.

15　Behavioral consequences take one of two forms: (1) a new stimulus is presented or added to the environment or (2) an already present stimulus is terminated or removed from the environment.

16 Operant reinforcement occurs when a consequence increases the future probability of the behavior it follows.

17 Operant punishment occurs when a consequence decreases the future probability of the behavior it follows.

18 Operant conditioning encompasses both reinforcement and punishment processes.

19 Reinforcement and punishment can each be accomplished by two distinct stimulus change operations—the presentation of a stimulus or the removal of a stimulus.

20 Behavioral consequences can affect only the future probability of behavior.

21 Responses emitted because of the effects of reinforcement will usually differ slightly from earlier reinforced responses but will share common elements with the former responses.

22 A response class consists of a group of behaviors that comprise an operant; that is, members of a response class are strengthened or weakened collectively by the process of operant conditioning.

Principles and Procedures

23 A principle of behavior describes a basic functional relationship between behavior and its controlling variables.

24 A behavior change procedure is a method of operationalizing, or putting into practice, a principle of behavior.

25 There are many behavior change procedures derived from relatively few principles of behavior.

26 Positive reinforcement occurs when a behavior is followed immediately by the presentation of a stimulus that increases the rate of the behavior in the future.

27 Negative reinforcement occurs when a behavior is followed immediately by the removal or termination of a stimulus that increases the rate of the behavior in the future.

28 Type I punishment occurs when a behavior is followed immediately by the presentation of a stimulus that decreases the rate of the behavior in the future.

29 Type II punishment occurs when a behavior is followed immediately by the removal or termi-nation of a stimulus that decreases the rate of the behavior in the future.

30 Unconditioned reinforcers and punishers affect behavior without prior conditioning. Primary and unlearned are synonyms for unconditioned.

31 Conditioned reinforcers and punishers affect behavior only after they have been paired with other reinforcers or punishers. Secondary and learned are synonyms for conditioned.

32 Reinforcers and punishers are defined by their effect upon behavior.

33 Stimulus control refers to differential rates of operant responding observed in the presence or absence of antecedent stimuli. Antecedent stimuli acquire the ability to control operant behavior by having been paired with certain consequences in the past.

The Three-Term Contingency

34 Operant behavior is defined by the three-term contingency, which specifies the temporal and functional relationships between antecedent stimuli, behavior, and consequences.

35 All applied behavior analysis procedures involve manipulation of one or more components of the three-term contingency.

The Complexity of Human Behavior

36 Humans possess a huge repertoire of behaviors. In any given setting concurrent contingencies are vying for the control of a large number of behaviors. Response chains and verbal behavior also make human behavior extremely complex.

37 The variables that govern human behavior are often highly complex. Many behaviors have multiple causes, and the effects of setting events are even more complex than those of simple stimuli.

38 Individual differences in histories of reinforcement and organic deficits also help to make the analysis and control of human behavior difficult.

39 Applied behavior analysts are sometimes prevented from conducting an effective analysis of behavior because of practical, logistical, financial, sociopolitical, legal, and/or ethical reasons.

PART TWO

Selection, Definition, and Measurement of Behavior Change Targets

Careful selection of which behaviors are to be modified—the target behaviors to be increased or decreased in frequency or developed as new behaviors—and the systematic measurement and recording of those target behaviors are the foundation of applied behavior analysis. For a behavior change program to be truly applied, it must focus on improvement of socially important behaviors that improve the lives of the clients or students involved in the program. Chapter 3 describes assessment methods used by behavior analysts, issues that should be considered in determining the social significance of potential target behaviors, procedures for prioritizing target behaviors, and the criteria and dimensions by which selected behaviors should be defined to allow for accurate, reliable measurement. Chapter 4 details procedures for implementing the various observation and recording methods used in applied behavior analysis, the advantages and disadvantages of each method, and guidelines for selecting the best measurement method for the target behavior(s) and setting involved. Chapter 5 discusses factors that hinder accurate, reliable measurement of behavior in applied settings, describes methods for combating the influence of those factors, and provides suggestions for cost-effective, practical data collection.

3

Selecting and Defining
Target Behavior

KEY TERMS

Behavioral assessment

Target behavior

Behavior checklist

Anecdotal observation

Ecological assessment

Reactivity

Practice effects

Habilitation

Relevance of behavior rule

Normalization

Social validity

Applied behavior analysis is concerned with producing reliable and predictable improvements in socially important behavior. Although educators and therapists employing other approaches also deal with the behavior of their students and clients, a distinguishing characteristic of the applied behavior analyst is a concern for specifically defined behavior that can be reliably observed and measured. As this chapter shows, the first step in an applied behavior analysis program involves much more than simply identifying a behavior that can be measured.

The chapter begins with a discussion of the role of assessment in behavior analysis, followed by a brief description of the major assessment methods most often used by behavior analysts to determine specific behavior(s) to modify. The next section includes a presentation of important issues that should be considered in determining the social importance of possible target behaviors. The chapter con-

This chapter was written by William L. Heward.

cludes with sections on prioritizing potential target behaviors, writing behavioral definitions, and specifying criteria for evaluating the significance of behavior change.

ROLE OF ASSESSMENT IN APPLIED BEHAVIOR ANALYSIS

Linehan (1977) has offered a succinct and accurate description of the purpose of **behavioral assessment:** "To figure out what the client's problem is and how to change it for the better" (p. 31).

Implicit in Linehan's statements is the idea that behavioral assessment is not simply an exercise in description and classification of behavior. Assessment also involves a functional analysis of behavior with identification of probable antecedent and consequent controlling variables. Additionally, the determination of resources, assets, significant others, competing contingencies, and possible problems related to modifying the behavior(s) of interest are also considered under the rubric of behavioral assessment (Gambrill, 1977; Mash & Terdal, 1976).

Hawkins (1979; Cone & Hawkins, 1977) conceptualizes behavioral assessment as funnel shaped, with an initial broad scope leading to an eventual narrow and constant focus. He describes five phases/functions of behavioral assessment: (1) screening and general disposition (2) definition and general quantification of problems or desired achievement (3) pinpointing the target behavior(s) to be treated (4) monitoring progress and (5) follow-up. Although the five phases form a general chronological sequence, there is often overlap. Part three of this book, "Evaluation and Analysis of Behavior Change," describes the monitoring and follow-up stages of assessment. This chapter is concerned with the preintervention functions of assessment namely, the selection and definition of the **target behavior**—the subject's specific behavior identified for change.

Both knowledge of what constitutes socially important behavior in a given area of human endeavor and skill in using appropriate assessment methods and instruments specific to that discipline are prerequisites for serving as a competent behavior analyst. For instance, the remedial reading specialist must have a thorough understanding of the critical reading behaviors that a competent reader possesses and must be able to determine which of those skills a poor reader needs to master. Likewise, the marriage and family therapist must be able to use assessment methods that accurately describe family dynamics. Numerous additional examples could be provided; the point is that any behavior analyst in human services must be not only competent in applying the principles of behavior, but also trained and experienced in which behaviors to assess. It is well beyond the scope and purpose of this book to discuss the critical behaviors and assessment methods in all of the different human service areas. Instead, methods and issues relevant to all behavioral assessment will be presented.

METHODS AND ISSUES IN GATHERING BEHAVIORAL ASSESSMENT DATA

Four major methods for obtaining assessment information are (1) interviewing the client, (2) interviewing significant others, (3) testing the client, and (4) directly observing the client. Related issues that should be considered are the ecological implications and possible reactive effects of assessment.

Interviewing the Client

Applied behavior analysis relies primarily on direct assessment methods. However, the client interview, which traditionally has been employed as an indirect assessment device and as a treatment technique, is often a first and important step in identifying potential target behaviors that can be verified or rejected by subsequent direct observation. Nevertheless, Peterson (1968) estimated that three-fourths of the information gathered in most assessment interviews could be eliminated with no loss to the client because the information seldom has anything to do with the problem or its treatment. Of course, the interview can be a direct assessment method if certain verbal behaviors of the client are of interest (Hawkins, 1975).

An important difference between the behavioral interview and a traditional interview is the type of information sought and the kinds of questions asked. Gambrill (1977) describes the kind of questions most productive in a behavioral interview.

> A behavioral model focuses on what the client does, in what situations, and how significant others respond, that is, what they do before and after given client behaviors. "What" and "When" questions are used rather than "Why" questions. Asking the clients why they do something presumes they know the answer and is often frustrating to clients, because they probably do not know and it seems that they should (Kadushin, 1972). "Why" questions encourage the offering of "motivational" reasons that are usually uninformative such as "I'm just lazy." Instead, the client could be asked "What happens when . . . ?" One looks closely at what actually happens in the natural environment. Attention is directed toward behavior by questions that focus on it, such as, "Can you give me an example of what he does?" When one example is gained, then another can be requested until it seems that the set of behaviors to which the client refers when he employs a given word have been identified. Information can also be gained by asking what the person complained about would do if he displayed a state opposite to that complained of. A wife could be asked, "What would you do if he loved you?" or "What would he do if he were kind to you?" (p. 153)

Numerous authors have detailed procedures to be used in the behavioral interview (Goldfried & Pomeranz, 1968; Kanfer & Saslow, 1969; Morganstern, 1976), and Kanfer and Grim (1977) provide a framework for organizing information gathered in the interview in order to facilitate target behavior selection.

Clients are sometimes asked to complete questionnaires or needs assessment surveys prior to or during the first interview. Questionnaires have been developed in such areas as marital satisfaction/discord (Stuart & Stuart, 1972) and assertiveness (Gambrill & Richey, 1976) in order to narrow the focus of the interview.

Sometimes as a result of an initial interview, the client is asked to self-monitor particular situations. Self-monitoring can entail immediate written or tape recorded accounts of specific events, structured diary-type recordings in which the client indicates antecedents and consequences of her behavior, or ratings of prescribed behaviors (Mahoney, 1977; Nelson, 1977). Client-collected data can be useful in selecting and defining target behaviors for intervention. For example, Williams (1979) has developed Marital Satisfaction Time Lines, an assessment procedure in which a client records specific pleasant, neutral, and unpleasant behaviors of the marriage partner during each 15-minute time segment the couple is together.

Interviewing Significant Others

Sometimes the behavior analyst either cannot interview the client or desires additional information from others important in the client's life. In such cases interviews of significant others (e.g., parents, classmates, co-workers) are often conducted. Procedures for such interviews are similar to those used in the client interview with what, when, and how questions dominating. Heward, Dardig, and Rossett (1979) give several illustrations of the type of questioning used in interviewing parents.

- During what time of day does Elizabeth seem most uncooperative? What does she do then?

- Are there any parts of the house or certain situations where Jimmy acts like a baby? If so, where, and what does he do?

- How many different ways does Phillip act afraid? Let's make a list of what he does when he's afraid.

□ If Janet were to be more mature and independent as you would like, what would she do differently than she does now? (p. 76)

In addition to seeking help from significant others in target behavior identification, the behavior analyst can sometimes use the interview to determine whether the significant other is willing and able to assist with the soon-to-be implemented behavior change program. Without the assistance of parents, siblings, teacher aides, and staff, many behavior change programs cannot be successful.

Behavior checklists (Walls, Werner, Bacon, & Zane, 1977) and needs assessment surveys (Heward, Dardig, & Rossett, 1979) can also be used with significant others to identify potential target behaviors.

Testing the Client

Literally thousands of tests and standardized assessment devices have been developed to assess behavior (Mitchell, 1985). The vast majority of standardized tests on the market, however, are not conducive to behavioral assessment since the results cannot be translated directly into target behaviors for instruction or treatment. For example, results from standardized tests commonly used in the schools, like the Wide Range Achievement Test (Jastak & Jastak, 1965) or the Iowa Test of Basic Skills (Hieronymus & Lindquist, 1978), might indicate that a child is performing at the third grade level in mathematics. Such information might be useful in determining how the student is doing in math compared to elementary students in general, but it generally does not indicate the specific math skills the child lacks.

Tests are most useful as behavioral assessment devices when they provide a direct measure of the subject's performance of the behaviors of interest. In recent years behaviorally oriented teachers have emphasized the use of criterion-referenced tests that are designed to indicate exactly which skills a student needs to learn and, equally important, which skills he

has already mastered (McLoughlin & Lewis, 1986).

Direct Observation

Direct observation of the client's behavior is the method most often used for determining which behaviors to modify. Two forms of direct observation frequently used for assessment include behavior checklists and direct continuous observations.

Direct Observation with a Behavior Checklist Walls, Werner, Bacon, and Zane (1977) describe 166 behavior checklists, many of which employ direct observation to determine the extent to which an individual demonstrates the behaviors represented on the list. A **behavior checklist** provides descriptions of specific skills (usually in hierarchical order) and the conditions under which each skill should be observed. Some checklists are designed to assess one particular behavior or skill area, like tooth brushing or social skills. Other checklists, like *The Teaching Research Curriculum for Moderately and Severely Handicapped* (Fredericks et al., 1976), can be used to assess a wide range of skill areas including self-help, motor development, oral language, reading, writing skills, and so on. Information provided by good behavior checklists (i.e., those with objectively stated items) can help pinpoint possible target behaviors for intervention.

Anecdotal Observation **Anecdotal observation**, sometimes called ABC recording, an ancedotal report, or a diary record, was first described in the behavioral literature by Bijou, Peterson, and Ault (1968). The aim is to record all behavior as it occurs. With anecdotal observation an observer produces a written narrative of an individual's behaviors throughout a specified period of time and a description of the environmental conditions under which the behaviors were emitted (Cooper, 1981). This technique is often employed to produce behavioral assessment data, which are used in the selection of a target behavior.

Rather than providing data on the frequency of a specific behavior, anecdotal observation is a useful procedure for developing an overall description of a client's behavior patterns. Often a target behavior for intervention can be selected from the information gathered. Anecdotal observation provides a detailed record of the client's behavior within an environmental context, and it permits objective information to be obtained about events that happened just before and after behaviors of interest. This knowledge of antecedents and consequences is extremely helpful in designing planned intervention.

> The real benefits of direct observation, as compared to any other source of information (verbal report, test, etc.), are not only the objectivity and comprehensiveness of information regarding the learner's *behavior,* but also the objectivity and comprehensiveness regarding the *stimulus context* in which the behavior occurs: the general environment, the specific cues, and the consequences. This information is likely to affect one's intervention plan dramatically, because the behavior is seen embedded in a system. (Hawkins, 1986, pp. 344–345)

Anecdotal observation is continuous, requiring the observer to commit full attention to the person being observed. It is not an assessment procedure that can be carried out while engaging in other activities, such as managing a reading group, demonstrating a problem on the chalkboard, or grading papers. In fact, nothing else can be accomplished while engaging in anecdotal observation and recording. But anecdotal observation is usually carried out for relatively short periods of time, probably not more than 20 or 30 minutes at a time, and in those situations where responsibilities can be shifted temporarily (e.g., team teaching).

Some guidelines and suggestions for conducting anecdotal observation include the following:

1 Write down everything the client does and says and everything that happens to the client.

2 Use any kind of homemade shorthand or abbreviations to make recording more efficient, but be sure the notes can be and are accurately expanded immediately after the observation session.

3 Report only action that is seen or heard, not interpretations of that action.

4 Record the temporal relationship of each response noted. Write down what happened just before and just after each response of the client.

5 Record the estimated duration of each instance of the client's behavior. Mark the beginning and ending time of each behavior recorded.

6 Be aware that continuous anecdotal observation is often an obtrusive recording method. Most people behave differently when they see someone with a pencil and clipboard staring at them. Knowing this, observers should try to be as unobtrusive as possible (e.g., staying a reasonable distance away from the subject).

7 Carry out the observations over a period of several days so that the novelty of having someone observe the client will lessen and the repeated observations can produce a truer picture of day-to-day behavior.

8 Use a standard form to record behavior. Figure 3.1 shows a sample form and the results of an anecdotal observation session. This particular form, used in the home by Theresa's teacher, makes it easy to record and later interpret the observed events in proper temporal order. This session's observational record combined with several others showing similar patterns of behavior helped Theresa's parents and teacher agree that "playing alone after dinner" was an important target behavior to increase. The anecdotal record also helped Theresa's parents see that their attention was probably helping to maintain their daughter's whining and hitting.

| Child's Name: Theresa (T) | | Date: June 11 | |
| Observer: Ms. Lewis | | Time of Observation: 6:45–7:15 p.m. | |
Time	Antecedents	Child's Responses	Consequences
6:45	Family clears supper dishes from table.	T follows Mom back and forth.	Mom says, "Don't bother me now. T."
6:51	Dad sponges off table top.	T pulls on Dad's shirt and whines.	Dad says, "Stop it, T."
6:55	Mom and Dad do dishes.	T on kitchen floor playing with blocks.	Mom and Dad talk to each other.
7:00	"	"	"
7:05	"	T holds block and crawls toward Dad's foot.	"
7:07	"	T hits Dad's foot with block.	Dad yells and pushes T away.
7:09	"	T cries.	Mom says, "Quiet T, be a good girl for a change."
7:15	Family watches TV.	T watches TV.	Family watches TV.

FIGURE 3.1 Example of an anecdotal observation recording form. (From *Working with Parents of Handicapped Children,* p. 79, by W. L. Heward, J. C. Dardig, and A. Rossett, 1979; Columbus, OH: Charles E. Merrill. Copyright 1979 by Charles E. Merrill. Reprinted by permission.)

Ecological Implications of Assessment

An ecological perspective regarding human behavior acknowledges complex interrelationships between environment and behavior. An individual can be said to possess a behavioral ecology in the sense that changes in one behavior can affect other behaviors. Also, changes in one aspect of a person's environment can affect the individual's behavior (Rogers-Warren & Warren, 1977). **Ecological assessment** is a response to the complexity of human behavior. In a complete ecological assessment a great deal of information is gathered about the subject and the various environments in which he lives and works. Among the many factors that can affect a person's performance are physiological conditions, physical aspects of the environment (e.g., lighting, seating arrangements, noise level), interaction with other individuals, practitioner-client

interaction, home environment, and past reinforcement history. Each factor represents a potential area for ecological assessment.

Even though a thorough ecological assessment can provide a tremendous amount of descriptive data, the basic purpose of assessment—to identify the most pressing behavior problem and possible ways to alleviate it—should not be forgotten. It is easy to go overboard with the ecological approach, gathering far more information than is necessary. Ecological assessment can be costly in terms of professional and client time, and it also raises the ethical question of the legitimacy of inquiring into diverse areas of a person's life (Hersen & Bellack, 1976). Ultimately, good judgment must be used in determining how much to assess. Gambrill (1977) recommends restricting assessment primarily to the three-term contingency, looking for probable antecedents and consequences of the behaviors of interest. Heron and Heward (1982), writing about the role of ecological assessment for special education teachers, suggest that

> the key to using an ecological assessment is to know *when* to use it. Full-scale ecological assessments for their own sake are not recommended for LD teachers charged with imparting a great number of important skills to many children in a limited amount of time. In most cases, the time and effort spent conducting an exhaustive ecological assessment would be better used in direct instruction. While the results of an ecological assessment might prove interesting, they do not always change the course of a planned intervention. Under what conditions then will an ecological assessment yield data that will significantly affect the course of treatment? Herein lies the challenge. Educators must strive to become keen discriminators of: (1) situations in which a planned intervention has the potential for affecting student behaviors other than the behavior of concern; and (2) situations in which an intervention, estimated to be effective if the target behavior were viewed in isolation, may be ineffective because other ecological variables come into play.
>
> Regardless of the amount and range of information available concerning the student, a teacher must still make instructional decisions based on an empirical analysis of the target behavior. Ultimately, this careful analysis (i.e., direct and daily measurement) of the behavior of interest may be ineffective because other ecological variables come into play. (p. 17)

Reactive Effects of Assessment

Reactivity refers to the effects of an assessment procedure on the behaviors being assessed (Kazdin, 1979). Reactivity can be produced in a variety of ways, including obtrusive observation, practice effects, self-monitoring, and verbal descriptions of operating contingencies. Numerous studies have demonstrated that the presence of observers in applied settings can influence a subject's behavior (Mercatoris & Craighead, 1974; Surratt, Ulrich, & Hawkins, 1969; White, 1977). Also, assessment methods that require an individual to repeatedly perform a specified behavior are susceptible to **practice effects;** in other words, the person's

ability to perform the behavior improves simply because of the opportunities to practice. Perhaps the most obtrusive assessment procedures are those that require the subject to monitor and record her own behavior. Research on self-monitoring shows that the procedure commonly affects the behavior(s) under assessment (Kazdin, 1974; Nelson, 1977). In addition, Gambrill (1977) has suggested that during an assessment interview the behavior analyst's verbal descriptions of contingencies operating on the client's behavior may even be enough to cause some clients to alter those contingencies, thereby altering the behavior.

Reactive effects of assessment are not necessarily negative (e.g., self-monitoring has become as much a treatment procedure as it is an assessment procedure; see chapter 26). But behavior analysts should be aware of possible causes of reactivity in order to either combat those sources by employing unobtrusive measures (Kazdin, 1979) or take the reactive effects into account.

CONSIDERATIONS IN SELECTING A TARGET BEHAVIOR

More often than not, behavioral assessment reveals a wide range of behaviors that might be candidates for modification. Assessment information must be examined to determine which elements of a person's repertoire might yield socially significant target behaviors.

A Definition of Habilitation

Hawkins (1984) suggests that the potential meaningfulness of any behavior change should be judged within the context of **habilitation** (or adjustment), which he defines.

> Habilitation (adjustment) is the degree to which the person's repertoire maximizes short and long term reinforcers for that individual and for others, and minimizes short and long term punishers. (p. 284)

Hawkins (1986) cites these advantages of the definition:

> First, it uses concepts that are already a familiar part of the basic scientific principles from which many of us work, a desirable situation for purposes of parsimony and continued interaction between applied and basic behavioral sciences. Second, it defines the task of treatment—and other education, habilitation, or prevention—fairly clearly and in potentially measurable terms: to change the functional relations between the environment and the repertoire so as to increase the "income" and maintenance of reinforcers for the learner, or others, or to decrease the "income" and maintenance of punishers. Third, it is applicable to all habilitative activities, whether one is parenting a 3-month-old infant, treating an alcoholic, rehabilitating a stroke victim, training a machinist, teaching history to a high school student, or teaching a delinquent youth to tell the truth. Fourth, it deals with both the individual's needs—which have been emphasized almost exclusively by clinicians and by most definitions of abnormality, pathology, or maladjustment—and the needs of the rest of society (cf. Meyerson & Hayes, 1977). Fifth, it does not overemphasize social judgments or social norms, as do many definitions; instead it leaves them as one factor that influences occurrence of punishers or reinforcers. Sixth, it treats adjustment as a continuum and does not emphasize pathology, as many definitions have in the past (Goldiamond, 1974). Seventh, it does not categorize *persons* as adjusted or maladjusted, it calls specific *performances* more or less adaptive. And finally, it is culturally and situationally relative; it incorporates the fact that what is adaptive in China will differ from what is adaptive in California, and what is adaptive with a spouse will differ from what is adaptive with a clerk. (pp. 351–352)

Judgments about how much a particular behavior change will contribute to a person's overall habilitation (adjustment, competence) are difficult to make. In many cases we simply do not know how ultimately useful or functional a given behavior will prove to be (Baer, 1981b, 1982). Applied behavior analysts, however, must place the highest importance upon the selection of target behaviors that are truly useful (Bailey & Lessen, 1984). Examination of each potential behavior change according to the questions/characteristics described here should help clarify its relative importance. Figure 3.2 summarizes these issues in the format of a worksheet/checklist that can be used in evaluating potential target behaviors.

Will the Proposed Change in Behavior Really Help the Client?

Traditionally, if a teacher, therapist, or other human services professional determined that a student's or client's behavior should change, then it followed that the change was beneficial to the individual. This assumption of mutual benefit and goodwill is no longer permissible. Since behavior analysts possess the technology to change explicitly stated behavior in predetermined directions, accountability must be served. Both the goals and the rationale supporting behavior change programs are appropriately open to critical examination by the consumers (clients and their families) and by others affected (society) by the behavior analyst's work.

Criticism has been directed toward the selection of some target behaviors that seemed to have been chosen more for their benefit to others than to the client (e.g., "Be still, be quite, be docile," in Winett & Winkler, 1972) or that were selected in order to maintain the status quo (Budd & Baer, 1976; Holland, 1978). Other target behaviors may have been selected for modification because they piqued the interest of someone in a position to change the behaviors. The following incident is related by Hawkins (1975):

> Recently I was vividly reminded of a problem in applied behavior analysis that I believe has plagued us for years, and one that we need to recognize if we are to conduct ourselves responsibly in the various human services we are trying to perform. A bright, conscientious graduate student was interested in doing his thesis in a program for severely maladjusted children. He wanted to teach cursive writing to a rather bizarre and retarded child. I knew something about the

Client's/Student's Name _____ Date _____

Behavior _____

	Yes	No	Rationale/Comments
Will this behavior really help the client?			
Is this behavior likely to produce reinforcement in the postintervention environment?			
Is this behavior a necessary prerequisite for a more complete or advanced skill that will be directly functional?			
Will this behavior provide access to reinforcement-rich or important learning environments?			
Will this behavior benefit the client by predisposing others to interact in a more reinforcing or supportive manner with him or her?			
Is this behavior age-appropriate?			
Will this behavior enable independent functioning in normalized environments (i.e., is it a complete skill)?			
Does this behavior represent the actual problem/goal, or is it only indirectly related?			
Is the client's verbal behavior an important dimension of the problem/goal?			
If this behavior is to be reduced or eliminated from the client's repertoire, has a desired, adaptive behavior been selected to replace it?			
If the goal is not a specific behavior, will this behavior produce the desired state or goal?			

Summary notes/comments _____

_____

_____

_____

FIGURE 3.2   A worksheet for evaluating the social significance of potential target behaviors.

child and was rather surprised that he selected cursive writing skills since the child could not read (except his name), print, or even reliably identify all the letters of the alphabet. I asked "Who decided that was the problem to work on next?" (p. 195)

Target behavior selection must respond to a more significant rationale than "It would be neat if he could write" (Hawkins, 1975, p. 195).

To determine whether a particular target behavior is of relative benefit to the client, the behavior analyst, significant others, and the client whenever possible should be asking whether the proposed behavior change is functional. Heward, Dardig, and Rossett (1979) suggest assessing a potential target behavior's functionality for the client by asking whether the proposed change in behavior will increase the client's likelihood of experiencing more reinforcement in the near future. Allyon and Azrin (1968) call this the **relevance of behavior rule;** it means that a target behavior should be selected only when it can be determined that the behavior is likely to produce reinforcement in the subject's postintervention or natural environment. The likelihood that a new behavior will result in reinforcement after the formal contingencies of a behavior change program are terminated is the primary determinant of whether or not the new behavior will be maintained, thereby resulting in long-term benefit for the client.

Judging a target behavior's potential to produce reinforcers for the client can also help to clarify whether the proposed behavior change is primarily for the client's benefit or someone else's. Heward, Dardig, and Rossett (1979) provide an example of the parents of a young, mentally retarded boy, who wanted their son to be taught how to make change. Assessment showed that the boy did have some of the prerequisite skills needed to learn how to make change and that a well-designed program would most likely be effective (with a considerable investment of the child's and teacher's time). Results of a behavior checklist and anecdotal observations, however, revealed that the boy lacked many basic self-help and social interaction skills (e.g., personal hygiene and feeding), which he had daily opportunities to perform. Since he lacked the social and verbal skills required for shopping or working as a clerk, making change could not be considered a functional skill for several years. An assessment of the boy's current skills and environment, as well as his likely environments in the near future, showed that making change would be a poor target behavior to select (an example reminiscent of the young man in Hawkins's anecdote being taught to write in cursive).

But the parents disagreed with this conclusion, stating that everyone else their child's age knew how to make change. In effect, the boy's parents were indicating that having their child make change was functional for them. They wanted to be able to say that their child knew how to make change, just like other children his age. After being assured that the goal of making change was neither unreachable nor inappropriate in and of itself but being advised that their son should first learn other behaviors useful to him everyday, the parents agreed to support and participate in a program aimed at improving self-care skills and language development.

Sometimes target behaviors are appropriately selected not because of their direct benefit to the client, but because of an important indirect benefit. Indirect benefits can occur in several different ways. Selecting a target behavior that, in and of itself, is not important but that serves as a necessary prerequisite to learning another functional behavior is one type of indirect yet functional targeting.[1] For example, a reading teacher may require students to master discrimination of long and short vowel sounds, not because such a skill in isolation will ever be useful to students outside the classroom, but because correct identification of vowel sounds is a prerequisite to effective reading.

Hawkins (1986) describes the targeting of "access behaviors" as a means of producing indirect benefits to clients. Special education

---

[1]A target behavior's indirect benefit as a necessary prerequisite for another important behavior should not be confused with indirect teaching. Indirect teaching involves selecting a target behavior different from your true purpose because of a belief that they are related (e.g., having students with poor reading skills practice shape discrimination or balance beam walking). The importance of directness in target behavior selection is discussed later in this section.

students are sometimes taught to complete their workbook pages neatly, interact politely with the regular classroom teacher, and stay in their seats during the teacher's presentation in hopes that these behaviors will increase the probability of their acceptance into the regular classroom and thereby their access to the reinforcement and instructional programs available in that environment.

Another type of indirect benefit occurs when a behavior change objective is of direct, primary interest to a significant other in the client's life; accomplishment of the objective may enable the significant other to behave in a manner more beneficial to the client's interest. For example, a teacher might want the parents of his student Sharon to implement a home-based instruction program, believing that Sharon's language skills would improve considerably if her parents would spend 10 minutes each night playing a vocabulary game with her. In a meeting with Sharon's parents, however, it becomes clear that although Sharon's parents are also concerned about her poor language skills, they have other and in their opinion more pressing needs—Sharon's parents want her to clean her room. Even though Sharon's teacher believes that straightening up a bedroom is not so critical a skill as language development, daily room straightening may indeed be an important target behavior if a sloppy room impedes positive parent-child interactions (such as playing a vocabulary game). In this case daily room straightening should be selected as the target behavior for the direct, immediate benefit of Sharon's parents, with the expectation that they will be more likely and better able to help her with other skill areas if they are happier with her because she straightens her room everyday.

Is the Target Behavior Age-Appropriate?

A number of years ago it was not uncommon to see mentally retarded and other handicapped adults being taught behaviors that nonhandicapped adults would seldom do. It was thought—perhaps as a by-product of the concept of mental age—that a 35-year-old woman with the verbal skills of a 10-year-old should play with dolls. Not only is the selection of such target behaviors demeaning, but their occurrence lessens the probability that other people in that individual's environment will set the occasion for and reinforce more desirable, adaptive behaviors, which could lead to a more normal and rewarding life.

Normalization refers to the use of normal environments, expectations, and procedures "to establish and/or maintain personal behaviors which are as culturally normal as possible" (Wolfensberger, 1972, p. 28). Not a specific technique or procedure, normalization is more a philosophy, which holds as its goal the greatest possible physical and social integration of persons with handicaps into the mainstream of society, regardless of the type or severity of disability.

> Such integration is maximized when all people live in a culturally normative setting in ordinary community housing, can move and communicate in age-appropriate ways and are able to use typical community services such as schools, stores, churches, and physicians. (Madle, 1978, p. 469)

The necessity of selecting age-appropriate target behaviors that are functional under the demands of adult settings has been strongly forwarded, most particularly by authors describing the determination of curricular goals and content for students with severe handicaps (Brown, Bronston, Hamre-Nietupski, Pumpian, Certo, & Gruenewald, 1976; Brown, Falvey, Vincent, Kaye, Johnson, Ferrara-Parrish, & Gruenewald, 1980; Hawkins, 1984; Wilcox & Bellamy, 1982). These writers have stressed the importance of selecting target behaviors that are most clearly related to increased independent functioning by the learner in integrated, normalized environments. In other words, skills that would be functional to an individual in "real-world" vocational, domestic, community, and recreation-leisure environments would have the highest instructional priority. (Bailey & Lessen, 1984, p. 163)

While the concept of normalization grew primarily out of those human service fields that work with handicapped children and adults, it is a principle that should be respected in the selection of target behaviors for all persons.

In addition to the philosophical/ethical reasons for selecting age-appropriate target behaviors, it should be reemphasized that these behaviors are more likely to be maintained than are those behaviors that are not age-appropriate. Instead of teaching a 17-year-old boy how to play with toy trucks and building blocks, instruction in leisure-time skills such as sports, hobbies, and music-related activities would be more appropriate. A 17-year-old who can perform some of these behaviors has a chance to interact in a normal fashion with his peer group, which will help to ensure the maintenance of his newly learned skills and will provide opportunities for learning other adaptive behaviors.

Is This the Behavior Intended for Change?

An all-too-common error in education is teaching a related behavior rather than the behavior of interest. Many behavior change programs have been designed to increase the on-task behavior of an individual when the primary objective has been increased production or work output. On-task behavior is chosen because persons who are productive also tend to be on-task. However, as on-task is usually defined, it is quite possible for a student to be on-task (i.e., in her seat, quiet, looking at or handling academic materials) yet not produce any work.

The targeting of needed prerequisite skills must not be confused with the selection of target behaviors that do not directly represent or fulfill the primary reasons for the behavior analysis effort. Prerequisite skills are not taught as terminal skills for their own sake but as necessary building blocks, or components, of the desired terminal skills. Related but indirect behaviors are not necessary to perform the true objective of the program, nor are they really intended outcomes of the program in and of themselves. In attempting to detect indirectness, behavior analysts should ask two questions: (1) is this behavior a necessary prerequisite to the terminal skill intended, and (2) is this behavior what the instructional program is really all about? If either question can be answered affirmatively, the behavior is eligible for target behavior status.

Is It Just Talk or the Behavior of Interest?

Most nonbehavioral therapies rely heavily on what people say about what they do and why they do it. The client's verbal behavior is considered important because it is believed to be reflective of the client's inner state and the mental processes that govern the client's behavior. Thus, getting a person to talk differently about himself (i.e., in a more healthful, positive, and normal way) is viewed as a significant step in solving the person's problem. Indeed, this change in attitude is considered by some to be the primary goal of therapy.

Behaviorists, on the other hand, distinguish between what people say and what they do (Skinner, 1953). Knowing and doing are not one and the same. Getting someone to understand his behavior by being able to talk logically about it does not necessarily mean that his behavior will change. The compulsive gambler may know that losing money is ruining his life and that his losses would cease if he stopped placing bets. He may even be able to verbalize these facts to a therapist and state quite convincingly that he will gamble no more. He may still continue to bet.

Because verbal behavior can be descriptive of what people do, it is sometimes confused with the actual performance itself. A teacher at a school for juvenile offenders introduced a new math program that included instructional games, group drill, timed tests, and self-graphing. The students responded with many negative comments: "This is stupid," "Man, I'm not writin' down what I do," "I'm not even going to try on these tests." If the teacher had attended only the students' talk about the program, it would probably have been discarded on the first day. But the teacher was aware that negative comments about school and work were expected in the peer group of adolescent delinquents and that many of her students' negative remarks had enabled them in the past to avoid tasks they thought they would not enjoy. Consequently, the teacher ignored the negative comments and attended to and rewarded her students for accuracy and rate of math computation when they participated in the program. In one week's time the negative talk had virtually ceased, and the students' math production was at an all-time high.

There are, of course, situations in which the behavior of interest is what someone says. Helping a person reduce the number of self-effacing comments he makes about himself and increase the frequency of positive self-description is an example of a program in which talk should be the target behavior—not because the self-effacing comments are indicative of a poor self-concept, but because the client's verbal behavior is the problem.

In every case a determination must be made of exactly which behavior is the desired functional outcome of the program: is it a skill or motor performance, or is it verbal behavior? In some cases both doing and talking might be important. The trainee learning to repair lawn mowers may be more likely to get a job if she can describe verbally what she does and if she says that she likes to fix lawn mowers. However, it is possible that she can hold on to a job if she is skilled and efficient in repairing lawn mowers and does not talk about what she does. It is highly unlikely, however, that a person will

last very long on the job if she can talk about fixing lawn mowers but is not able to remove spark plugs or sharpen blades. Target behaviors must be functional.

If the Proposed Objective Is to Reduce or Eliminate a Particular Behavior, What Desirable Adaptive Behavior Will Be Developed to Replace It?

The behavior analyst should never plan to significantly reduce or eliminate a behavior from a person's repertoire without determining which adaptive behavior will take its place and then developing contingencies so that the replacement behavior becomes part of the systematic program of behavior change. Teachers and other human service professionals should be in the business of building positive response repertoires, not merely reacting to and eliminating behaviors they find troublesome (Goldiamond, 1974; Lovitt, 1977). Even though a child's maladaptive behaviors are often exceedingly annoying to others and, in the long run, perhaps damaging to the child himself because the inappropriate behaviors may impede the learning of more positive, adaptive ways of responding, those undesirable responses have proven functional for the child. That is, the maladaptive behavior has worked for the child in the past by producing reinforcers and/or avoiding or escaping punishers. A program that only denies that avenue of reinforcement for the child is a nonconstructive approach. It does not teach the child what adaptive behaviors should be performed in place of the inappropriate behavior.

Some of the most effective and recommended methods for eliminating unwanted behavior focus primarily on the development of desirable replacement behaviors. Goldiamond (1974) recommends that a "constructional" approach be used for analysis of and intervention into behavioral problems, rather than the more expedient "eliminative" approach. Under the constructional approach the "solution to problems is the construction of repertoires (or their reinstatement or transfer to new situations) rather than the elimination of repertoires" (Goldiamond, 1974, p. 14). If a strong case cannot be made for specific, positive replacement behaviors, then a strong enough case has not been made for eliminating the undesirable target behavior. The classroom teacher, for example, who wants a behavior modification program to get students to stay in their seats during reading period must go beyond the simple notion that "they need to be in their seats in order to do the work." The teacher must select materials and design contingencies that facilitate that goal and motivate the students to accomplish their work.

What If the Goal Is Not a Behavior?

Some goals of behavior modification are not in themselves behaviors but are the result or product of certain behaviors. Weight loss is an example. On the surface it might appear that target behavior selection is obvious and straightforward—losing weight. The number of pounds can be accurately and reliably measured; but weight, or more precisely losing weight, is not a behavior. It is not a specific response that can be defined and performed; it is the product or result of other behaviors—most notably reduced food consumption and/or increased exercise. Both eating and exercise are behaviors and can be specifically defined and measured in precise units.

Many otherwise well-designed weight loss programs have not been successful because emphasis was placed on the goal, reduced weight, but not on the behavior necessary to produce the goal. Target behaviors in a weight loss program should be measures of food consumption and exercise level, with intervention strategies designed to modify those behaviors (Stuart & Davis, 1972). Weight should be mea-

sured and charted during a weight loss program, not because it is the target behavior of interest, but because loss of weight gives positive feedback that the program is working.

There are numerous other examples of important goals that are not behaviors but are the end products of behavior. Earning good grades is a goal that must be analyzed to determine what behaviors produce better grades. Dardig and Heward (1981a) describe a contingency contract implemented between a fourth grader, Jeff, and his parents. Jeff wanted to get a better arithmetic grade on his next report card, so he and his parents implemented a contract that required him to study math for one hour each school night before he could watch any television. The contract worked in that the frequency of the target behavior, studying math, increased; but Jeff's arithmetic grade did not improve. It was not until the contract was changed to specify a target behavior directly and functionally related to getting good grades in math that Jeff's goal was met. In order to get a good math grade, a student must correctly solve math problems on quizzes and tests. Although studying may be related to solving math problems, in Jeff's case it proved to be too indirectly related to be functional. When the target behavior in Jeff's program was changed to "correctly solve 15 new math problems each school night," his arithmetic grade improved. The lesson illustrated here is that behavior analysts can better help clients achieve their goals if target behaviors are chosen that are the most directly and functionally related to the client's goal.

Some goals expressed by and for clients are not the direct product of a specific target behavior. These are broader, more general goals: to be more successful, to have more friends, to be creative, to learn good sportsmanship, to develop a good self-concept. Clearly, none of these goals are defined by specific behaviors, and all are more complex in terms of their behavioral components than losing weight or getting a better grade in math. Goals such as creativity represent a class of related behaviors or a general pattern of responding. They are labels that are used to describe people who behave in certain ways. Selecting target behaviors that will help clients or students attain these kinds of goals is even more difficult than their complexity suggests because the goals themselves often mean different things to different people. Weight loss is a clear goal that can be defined in only one way; only the amount of weight to be lost is open for debate or negotiation. However, being a success can entail widely different behaviors. One person may view success in terms of income and job title. For another, success might mean job satisfaction and good use of leisure time. An important role of the behavior analyst during assessment and target behavior identification is to help the client select and define personal behaviors, the sum of which will result in the client and others evaluating her repertoire in the intended fashion.

PRIORITIZING POSSIBLE TARGET BEHAVIORS

In many behavior analysis programs decisions must be made about the relative priority of possible target behaviors. Sometimes the information produced by assessment methods points to one particular aspect of the client's repertoire in need of improvement. More often though, assessment reveals a constellation of related, and sometimes not-so-related, behaviors in need of change. For instance, direct observations of an aggressive child, along with the clinical interview and needs assessment conducted with the child's parents, may produce a long list of possible behaviors to change (e.g., decreasing verbal and physical attacks on others, improving social skills, or better parenting procedures). When more than one potential target behavior remains after consideration of the variables just described, the question

becomes, which behavior should be changed first? Judging each potential target behavior in light of the following nine questions will help determine which behavior deserves attention first.

Does this problem behavior entail any danger? Behaviors that cause harm or pose a serious threat to the client's (or others') personal safety or health must receive first priority.

What is the frequency of this problem, or what would be the opportunities to use this new behavior? A student who consistently writes reversed letters presents more of a problem than does a child who reverses letters only occasionally. Or if the choice is between first teaching a prevocational student to pack his lunch or to learn how to plan his 2-week vacation each year, the former skill takes precedence because the employee-to-be will need to pack his lunch every workday.

How long-standing is this problem or the need for this new skill? A chronic behavior problem or skill deficit should usually take precedence over a more recent problem or need.

Will this new or increased behavior produce higher levels of reinforcement for the client now? If all other considerations are equal, a behavior that will result in a higher level of reinforcement for the client should take precedence over a behavior that will produce little additional reinforcement for the client.

What will be the relative importance of this new or increased behavior in future skill development and independent functioning? Each potential target behavior should be judged in terms of its relation (i.e., prerequisite or supportive) to other critical behaviors needed for optimal learning and development and maximum levels of independent functioning in the future.

Does this behavior targeted for reduction or elimination draw negative attention from others? Some behaviors are not maladaptive because of anything inherent in the behavior itself, but because of the unnecessary problems the behavior causes the client. Some developmentally disabled individuals walk in a way that might appear funny or retarded to the typical person on the street. Thus the walk, while perfectly functional and comfortable to the individual, may reduce certain opportunities for positive interaction and place the handicapped person at a certain disadvantage in public. Granted, education of the public is warranted here, but it would be naive not to consider the negative effects of public reaction, and it may be a disservice to the disabled individual not to help him change his gait. Certain styles of dress, aspects of personal hygiene, and idiosyncratic mannerisms also have potential to become high priority target behaviors when their modification will provide access to more normalized settings or important learning environments.

Will this new behavior produce more reinforcement for significant others in the client's life? Even though an individual's behavior should seldom, if ever, be changed simply for the convenience of others or for maintenance of the status quo (Holland, 1978; Winett & Winkler, 1972), neither should the effect of an individual's behavior change on the significant others in his life be overlooked. This question is usually answered best by the significant others themselves, since persons not directly involved in the individual's life would often have

> no idea how rewarding it is to see your retarded 19 year old acquire the skill of toilet flushing on command or pointing to food when she wants a second helping. I suspect that the average taxpayer would not consider it "meaningful" to him or her for Karrie to acquire such skills. And, although we cannot readily say how much Karrie's being able to flush the toilet enhances her personal reinforcement/punishment ratio, I can testify that it enhances mine as a parent. (Hawkins, 1984), p. 285)

How difficult will it be to change this target behavior? Some behaviors are more difficult to change than others. The behavior analyst can review at least three sources of information to

help assess the level of difficulty or, more precisely, predicting the ease or degree of success in changing a particular behavior. First, what does the literature say about attempts to change this behavior? Most of the target behaviors that confront applied behavior analysts have been the subject of considerable research. The competent professional should be aware and stay abreast of published research reports in her area(s) of application. Not only is such knowledge likely to increase the probability of selecting proven and efficient techniques for modifying certain target behaviors, but it can also help to predict the level of difficulty/chance of success.

Second, how experienced is the behavior analyst? The change agent's own personal competencies and experiences with the target behavior in question should be considered. A teacher who has worked successfully for many years with acting out, aggressive children has an array of effective behavior management strategies ready to employ and might predict success with even the most obnoxious child. However, that same teacher might decide that he is less able to improve a student's written language skills.

Third, to what extent can the client's environment be effectively controlled? Whether or not a certain behavior *can* be changed is not the question. Every bit of experimental research conducted to date indicates that human behavior functions according to empirically determined principles of behavior that describe established behavior-environment relationships. In an applied setting, however, identifying and then consistently manipulating the controlling variables for a given target behavior will determine whether or not the behavior will be changed.

How much will it cost to change this behavior? Cost should be considered prior to implementing any systematic behavior change program. A cost/benefit analysis of several potential target behaviors should not be confused with the position sometimes taken (particularly with severely handicapped students) that if a teaching program is expensive, it should not be implemented. Major court cases have ruled and legislation has required that lack of public funds may not be used as an excuse for not providing an appropriate education to all children regardless of the severity of their handicaps (cf. *Mills v. Board of Education; Wyatt v. Stickney;* P.L. 94–142, The Education for All Handicapped Children Act of 1975). The cost of a behavior change program cannot be determined by simply adding up the dollar amounts that might be expended on equipment, materials, transportation, staff salaries, and the like. Consideration should also be given to how much of the client's time the behavior change program will demand. If, for example, teaching a severely handicapped child shoe tying takes up so much of the child's day that she does not have time to learn other important things—like language, social, leisure, or self-help skills or simply the use of independent time (Orlansky, 1979)—perhaps the shoe-tying objective is too costly.

Total cost in terms of human resources helps to determine the likelihood of success and benefits in a behavior change program. Contrary to the inspirational words typical of motivational speakers, there are several advantages of thinking small.

> Select very small and humble objectives for your behavioral system. If you do, you'll have at least a fighting chance of accomplishing something. But if your objective is to solve all the world's problems, you probably won't get anything accomplished. The world's problems will be solved by taking care of one little problem or objective at a time. There are two reasons why you should select small behavioral objectives: first, you probably have only a limited amount of resources at your disposal. If you concentrate those limited resources on a small number of behavioral objectives, you will be more likely to develop a truly effective behavioral system. And second, the people whose behavior you are trying to modify have only a limited amount of time and energy to devote to your behavior modification system. If they concentrate their time and

effort on a small number of behavioral objectives, they will be much more likely to accomplish something. (Malott, 1973, p. 12–1)

Developing and Using a Target Behavior Ranking Matrix

Assigning a numerical rating to various considerations and issues important in the selection of target behaviors and adding the numbers assigned to each category for each suggested behavior can produce a priority ranking of behaviors. One such ranking matrix is shown in Figure 3.3; it is an adaptation of a system described by Dardig and Heward (1981) for prioritizing and selecting learning objectives for handicapped students' individualized education programs. Each behavior is given a number representing the behavior's value to each of the prioritizing variables (e.g., 0–3 with 0 representing no value or contribution and 3 representing maximum value or benefit).

Persons involved in planning behavior change programs for certain student or client populations will usually want to differentially weigh some of the variables, or require a maximum rating on certain selection variables, and/or add other variables that are of particular importance to their overall goals. For example, professionals planning behavior change programs for senior citizens would probably demand that the immediate benefit of a target behavior be high, and practitioners serving mentally retarded adults would likely insist on maximum age-appropriateness to help promote normalization.

Sometimes there is a goal conflict between the behavior analyst, the client, and/or significant others. Parents may want their teenage daughter in the house by 10:30 P.M. each night, but the daughter wants to stay out later. The school may want a behavior analyst to develop a program to increase students' adherence to dress and social codes. The behavior analyst may believe that these codes are outdated and are not in the purview of the school. Who decides what is best for whom?

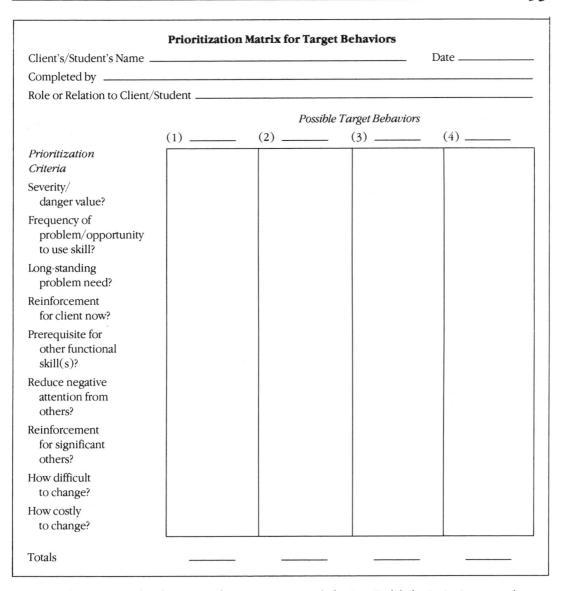

FIGURE 3.3 A numerical ranking matrix for prioritizing target behaviors. Each behavior is given a number representing the extent to which it meets or fulfills each of the prioritization variables. The variables can be differentially weighted, and other variables relevant to a particular program or situation can be added.

One way to minimize and work through conflicts is to require client, parent, and staff/administration participation in the goal determination process. The active participation of parents and, when possible, the student in the selection of short- and long-term goals and treatment procedures is now required by law in the planning of special education services for all school-aged handicapped children (P.L. 94–142). Such participation by all of the significant parties involved in behavior analysis programs goes a long way toward avoiding and resolving goal conflicts, not to mention the invaluable information the participants can provide relative to other aspects of program planning (e.g., identification of likely reinforcers). Reviewing the results of assessment efforts and allowing each participant to give input on the relative merits of each proposed goal or target behavior can often produce consensus on the best direction to go. Program planners should not arbitrarily state beforehand that whatever behavior comes out first in a numerical ranking system will necessarily be considered the highest priority target behavior. However, if the important persons involved in an individual's life go through a rating/ranking process such as the one outlined in Figure 3.3, they are likely to identify areas of agreement and disagreement, thereby leading to further dicussion of target behavior selection and concentration on the critical concerns of those involved.

DEFINING THE TARGET BEHAVIOR

Before a behavior can undergo analysis, it must be specifically defined. A good definition of a target behavior provides an accurate description of the behavior to be changed (and therefore measured), not an inference or an implication of behavior. Asking to be excused from the dinner table is an observable and measurable behavior. By comparison, good manners is not a description of any particular behavior; it merely implies a general class of responses. Hawkins and Dobes (1977) state that behavioral definitions must be explicit rather than implicit, and they describe three characteristics of a good definition.

1 The definition should be objective, referring only to observable characteristics of the behavior (and environment, if needed) or translating any inferential terms (such as "expressing hostile feelings," "intended to help," or "showing interest in") into more objective ones.

2 The definition should be clear in that it should be readable and unambiguous so that experienced observeres could read it and readily paraphrase it accurately.

3 The definition should be complete, delineating the "boundaries" of what is to be included as an instance of the response and what is to be excluded, thereby directing the observers in all situations that are likely to occur and leaving little to their judgment. (p. 169)

These three criteria for behavioral definitions are good ones. A good definition must be objective, assuring that specific instances of the defined target behavior can be reliably observed and recorded. A clear definition is a technological definition that enables others to use and replicate it (Baer, Wolf, & Risley, 1968). A complete definition identifies what is *not* the target behavior as well as what aids observers in discriminating the target behavior from similar responses. It allows accurate recording of noninstances of the target behavior when of interest. In addition, behavioral definitions should be concise.

Role and Importance of Scientific Definition in Applied Behavior Analysis

The field of applied behavior analysis derives its validity from its scientific approach, and scientific validity in its most basic form implies replication. When predicted behavioral effects can be reliably produced again and again, basic principles are confirmed and methods of practice developed. If behavior analysts employ definitions of variables not available to other scientists, replication is not possible. Without replication the usefulness or meaning of data from a given study cannot be determined beyond the specific subjects themselves, thereby foreclosing any orderly development of the discipline as a useful technology (Baer, Wolf, & Risley, 1968).

Explicit, well-written definitions of target behavior are also necessary for the clinical or educational practitioner, who may not be so concerned with replication by others or development of the field. Most behavior analysis programs are not conducted primarily for the advancement of the field; they are implemented by educators, clinicians, and other human service professionals in order to improve the lives of their clients. However, implicit in the application of behavior analysis is an accurate, ongoing evaluation of the target behavior, for which an explicit definition of behavior is a must.

A practitioner concerned only with evaluating his efforts in order to provide optimum service to his clients, might ask, "As long as I know what I mean by [name of target behavior], why must I write down a specific definition?" First, a good behavioral definition is operational. It provides the opportunity to obtain complete information about the behavior's occurrence and nonoccurrence, and it enables the practitioner to apply procedures in a consistently accurate and timely fashion. Second a good definition increases the likelihood of an accurate and believable evaluation of the program's effectiveness. Not only does an evaluation need to be accurate in order to guide ongoing program decisions, but the data must be believable to those with a vested interest in the program's effectiveness. Thus, even though the practitioner may not be interested in demonstrating an analysis to the field at large, she must always be concerned with demonstrating effectiveness (i.e., accountability) to students, clients, parents, and administrators.

Writing Behavioral Definitions

Although it is imperative that objective, precise language be used to define behavior, the name given to a target behavior is not critical. It should identify to those involved in the behavior change program what behavior is under consideration, and it should communicate to others the general class or type of behavior in question. Bryant and Budd (1984) taught behaviorally handicapped preschool children to

share. "Offers to share" occurred when "a child verbally or physically indicated that a peer have, touch, take, manipulate, trade, or cooperatively use a material from the available free play activities or when a child invited a peer to join in a particular activity" (p. 48). Barton, Guess, Garcia, and Baer (1970) helped institutionalized mentally retarded children reduce their "pigging behavior" at mealtime. They defined *pigging* as "eating food spilled on table, floor, clothing, or own tray; and eating food by placing the mouth directly on it (without use of fingers or utensil)" (p. 78).

Morris (1985) suggests testing the definition of a target behavior by asking,

1 Can you count the number of times that the behavior occurs in, for example, a 15-minute period, a one-hour period, or one day? Or, can you count the number of minutes that it takes for the child to perform the behavior? That is, can you tell someone that the behavior occurred "x" number of times of "x" number of minutes today? (Your answer should be "yes.")

2 Will a stranger know exactly what to look for when you tell him/her the target behavior you are planning to modify? That is, can you actually see the child performing the behavior when it occurs? (Your answer should be "yes.")

3 Can you break down the target behavior into smaller behavioral components, each of which is more specific and observable than the original target behavior? (Your answer should be "no.").

In responding to the suggestion that a sourcebook of standardized behavioral definitions be developed because it would increase the likelihood of exact replications among applied researchers and would save considerable time that must be spent in developing and testing situation-specific definitions, Baer (1985) made these observations. Applied behavior analysis programs are implemented because someone (teacher, parent, individual himself) has "complained" that a behavior needs changing. To be valid from an applied perspective, definitions of target behaviors should remain complaint- or situation-specific. Standardization assumes an unlikely similarity across all complainers. A behavioral definition has validity in applied behavior analysis only if it enables observers to capture every aspect of the behavior that the complainer is concerned with and none other.[2]

SETTING CRITERIA FOR BEHAVIOR CHANGE

Subjects, target behaviors, and procedures are chosen for study in applied behavior analysis not because of their relation to theory, but because of their importance to the individuals involved. By definition then, applied behavior analysts attempt to increase the occurrence of adaptive, desirable behaviors and decrease the occurrence of maladaptive, undesirable behaviors. From the beginning the efforts and research of applied behavior analysts have tried to produce something. That something is significant improvement in some important aspect of the client's life or society at large. Behavior analysis efforts that are effective in changing an individual's life in a socially important way are said to have **social validity.** Because of this requirement the field has been characterized, at least implicitly, by an indication before a program begins of what level of behavior is to be produced. Van Houten (1979) makes a good case for specifying the desired outcome criteria before efforts to modify the target behavior begin.

> This step [specifying outcome criteria] becomes as important as the previous step [selecting socially important target behaviors] if one considers that for most behaviors there exists a range of responding within which performance is most adaptive. When the limits of this range are

unknown for a particular behavior, it is possible that one could terminate treatment when performance is above or below these limits. Hence, the behavior would not be occurring within its optimal range. . . .

> In order to know when to initiate and terminate a treatment, practitioners require socially validated standards for which they can aim. (pp. 582, 583)

Van Houten (1979) suggests two basic approaches to determining socially validated performance criteria: (1) use the assessment of individuals judged to be highly competent, and (2) experimentally manipulate different levels of performance to determine empirically which produces optimal results. Van Houten provides guidelines for both approaches. Eaton (1978) describes several factors to consider in selecting desired response rates as instructional objectives for academic skills: the child's previous performance, an adult-to-child proportional formula, peer comparison, functional rates, and normative data guidelines.

Regardless of the method used, specifying treatment goals up-front provides a guideline for continuing or ending treatment and helps eliminate disagreement or bias among those involved in determining whether the program was successful. Unfortunately, an examination of 94 studies that were conducted with school-aged children or handicapped individuals of any age and were published in the *Journal of Applied Behavior Analysis* or *Education and Treatment of Children* during 1980 and 1981 revealed that in only 33% of the reports did the "authors specify any criterion for their terminal behavior along any dimension, and even less frequently (18%) did authors report evaluating the subject's target behavior relative to any other similar populations or a normal group" (Bailey & Lessen, 1984, pp. 165–166). Hopefully, an increasing percentage of applied behavior analysts are determining criteria for behavior change prior to intervention and are reporting these criteria in publications of their research. The importance of social validity in evaluating applied behavior analysis will be described further in chapter 10.

---

[2]The objectivity, clarity, and completeness of a behavioral definition are also judged by the extent to which the definition enables trained observers to conduct reliable measurement of the target behavior. Reliability and validity of measurement are discussed in more detail in chapter 5.

SUMMARY

Role of Behavioral Assessment

1 The purpose of behavioral assessment is "to figure out what the client's problem is and how to change it for the better" (Linehan, 1977, p. 31).

2 Behavioral assessment can be conceptualized as funnel shaped, with an initial broad focus leading to an eventual narrow and constant focus.

3 Behavioral assessment consists of five phases or functions: (1) screening, (2) definition and general quantification of problems or desired achievement, (3) pinpointing the target behavior, (4) monitoring progress during intervention, and (5) follow-up evaluation (Hawkins, 1979).

Methods for Gathering Behavioral Assessment Data

4 The client interview is used to determine the client's description of problem behaviors or achievement goals. What, when, and where questions are emphasized, focusing on the actual behavior of the client and the response of significant others to that behavior.

5 Questionnaires and needs assessment surveys are sometimes completed by the client to supplement the information gathered in the interview.

6 Individuals are sometimes asked to self-monitor certain situations or behaviors. Self-collected data may be useful in selecting and defining target behaviors.

7 Significant others in the client's life can also be interviewed to gather assessment information and, in some cases, to find out whether they will be willing and able to assist in an intervention.

8 Criterion-referenced tests can be useful in identifying specific behaviors (particularly academic skills) that the individual has mastered as well as those that are missing in her repertoire.

9 Direct observation with a behavior checklist that contains specific descriptions of various skills can indicate possible target behaviors.

10 Anecdotal observation, also called ABC recording, an anecdotal report, or a diary, provides a detailed description of an individual's behavior within an environmental context. The observer notes everything the client does or says as well as the events and actions of others that occur before and after each episode of client behavior.

11 Ecological assessment recognizes the complex interrelationships between behavior and the various environments in which most people live. In a complete ecological assessment a large amount of information is gathered concerning the individual's history of reinforcement; family, work, and school variables; health and physical condition; and so on. For most applied problems a complete ecological assessment is neither necessary nor warranted.

12 Reactivity occurs when an assessment or other measurement procedure has an effect on the behavior being monitored.

13 One type of reactivity, called practice effects, occurs when a person's performance of a skill improves simply as a result of opportunities to practice the behavior.

Considerations in Selecting a Target Behavior

14 Target behaviors in applied behavior analysis must be socially significant behaviors that will increase a person's habilitation (adjustment, competence).

15 Habilitation can be defined as "the degree to which the person's repertoire maximizes short and long term reinforcers for that individual and for others, and minimizes short and long term punishers" (Hawkins, 1984, p. 284)

16 A proposed behavior change should be functional for the client; that is, the new behavior should produce increased reinforcement for the individual.

17 The relevance-of-behavior rule requires that a target behavior produce reinforcement for the individual in the postintervention environment.

18 Some target behaviors, although not directly functional in themselves, are appropriate because they are necessary prerequisites for more advanced or complete skills.

19 Some target behaviors are appropriate because they will provide access to reinforcement-rich

environments or environments where important instructional programs are available.

20 Some target behaviors are selected because they will improve the lives of significant others, thereby providing indirect benefit to the individual as the other persons are then predisposed to interact with the individual in a more reinforcing and supportive manner.

21 Target behaviors should be age-appropriate; they should represent the same types of behaviors commonly performed by persons of the same age as the client.

22 The philosophy of normalization requires the selection of target behaviors that are as culturally normal as possible.

23 A target behavior should be, or represent as closely as possible, the actual problem or achievement goal at hand; it should not be an indirect substitute.

24 An individual's verbal behavior should not be confused with actual performance of the skill or behavior of interest. However, there are situations in which the client's verbal behavior should be selected as the target behavior.

25 Whenever a behavior is targeted for reduction or elimination, a desirable, adaptive behavior must be selected to replace it. This represents a constructional approach toward behavior change as opposed to an eliminative approach.

26 When a person's goal is not a specific behavior, a target behavior(s) must be selected that will produce the desired results or state.

Prioritizing Possible Target Behaviors

27 Behavioral assessment often reveals more than one possible behavior or skill area for targeting. Prioritization can sometimes be accomplished by judging each potential target behavior according to the following questions:
   a Does the problem behavior entail any danger?
   b What is the frequency of the problem, or how many opportunities would the individual have to use this skill?
   c How long-standing is the problem or the need for this new skill?
   d Will this behavior produce increased reinforcement for the individual now?

   e How will this behavior aid future skill development?
   f Does this behavior draw negative attention from others?
   g Will this behavior produce more reinforcement for significant others in the individual's life?
   h How difficult will it be to change this behavior?
   i How much will it cost to change this behavior?

28 A numerical ranking matrix can facilitate the prioritization of target behaviors.

29 Participation by the individual whose behavior is to be changed, parents and/or other important family members, staff and administration in identifying and prioritizing target behaviors can help reduce goal conflicts.

Defining the Target Behavior

30 Behavioral definitions should be objective, clear, complete, and concise.

31 A definition of the target behavior is valid if it enables observers to capture every instance of every aspect of the behavior that the complainer is concerned with and none other.

32 A definition of the target behavior is reliable if it enables two or more observers to record the same occurrences and nonoccurrences of behavior.

Setting Criteria for Behavior Change

33 A behavior change has social validity if it changes some aspect of the individual's life in a socially important way.

34 Outcome criteria—which state the level or extent of behavior change desired or needed—should be determined and stated before any intervention of an applied behavior analysis program is begun.

35 Two approaches to determining socially validated performance criteria are (1) using the assessment of individuals judged to be highly competent and (2) experimentally manipulating different levels of performance to determine which produces optimal results.

4

Measuring and Recording Behavior

KEY TERMS

Permanent products

Observational recording

Event recording

Duration recording

Latency recording

Partial-interval recording

Whole-interval recording

Momentary time sampling

Noncontinuous observational control

PLACHECK

Frequency of response

Rate of response

Free operant

Restricted operant

Percentage of response

Trials to criterion

Complexity of task items

Pre- and posttests

Probes

Magnitude of response

Topography of response

Applied behavior analysts stress direct measurement: client responses in actual instruction or treatment situations are observed and recorded as they occur before, during, and after the instruction or treatment procedure. With direct measurement an ongoing assessment of the individual's performance is obtained in the real situation. Indirect measurement, on the other hand, requires that inferences be made concerning the individual's performance. Scores from a math achievement test are one example of an indirect measure because they require an

This chapter was written by John O. Cooper.

inference about actual classroom performance. When a teacher uses a daily direct measurement of a student's math responses during instruction or practice, those scores (e.g., rate correct, percentage correct) do not require an inference about the adequacy of the student's classroom math skills. In addition to direct measurement, applied behavior analysts stress frequent, repeated measurement of target behaviors throughout the treatment process. It is not usually sufficient to measure behavioral occurrences at the beginning and end of an intervention, a procedure that resembles the pre-/posttesting method.

Two errors of judgment are common for interventionists who do not collect direct and frequent measurements of their subject's performance. First, many ineffective intervention programs are continued. The crucial question for continuation of an intervention must be, Is the program actually producing the skill development it claims to produce? As Heward, Dardig, and Rossett (1979) stated, "Without collecting the necessary data to evaluate the program, it might be carried on for months with no measurable learning taking place, thus robbing the child of valuable time in which new skills could be acquired" (pp. 85–86).

Second, many effective programs are discontinued prematurely because subjective judgments find no improvement. For example, teachers who do not use direct and frequent measures might discern little difference between a student's reading 40 words per minute with 60% accuracy and 48 words per minute with 73% accuracy. However, direct and frequent data collected on the rate and accuracy of oral reading would show an improved performance. Decision making in education and treatment must be based upon performance data; the individual's behavior must dictate the proper course of action.

This chapter presents procedures for measuring and recording behaviors. Specifically, it covers the procedures, advantages, and disadvantages of (1) direct measurement of permanent products and (2) direct observational recording. Included is a discussion of frequency, rate, and percentage measures and their use with trials to criterion, complexity of task items, pre- and posttests, and probes. Finally, the chapter presents guidelines for selecting appropriate measurement tactics.

DIRECT MEASUREMENT OF PERMANENT PRODUCTS

Direct measurement of permanent products is used frequently in all the helping professions and is the most common tactic used by classroom teachers. **Permanent products**—such as a written examination, written arithmetic computation, written spelling words, written alphabet letters, coloring, completed puzzles, strung beads, and stacked blocks—result from behaviors that produce tangible items or lasting environmental effects. Measurement of permanent products has been called an ex post facto method of data collection because measurement takes place after the behavior has occurred. Examples of permanent product measurement include metabolic measures (e.g., urine glucose indicator), energy consumption measures (e.g., watt-hour meters), and auto mileage measures (e.g., car odometer). Any performance that is audio- or videotaped, recorded automatically, or written qualifies as a permanent product recording.

Desirable Aspects

The measurement of permanent products has several advantages. First, permanent products are the outcome of important academic and vocational instruction. Second, most instances of behaviors that do not produce permanent products can be measured as permanent products by using audiovisual equipment. Third, practitioners do not have to observe the behavior as it occurs, yet an accurate and reliable measurement of the occurrence can be made at a later time. Fourth, permanent products can be translated into numerical terms.

Considerations

Measuring behavior via permanent products is a convenience for practitioners. However, such measurement should not necessarily be used whenever possible. Some behaviors affect fairly permanent changes in the environment that are not absolutely reliable for the purposes of measurement. Heward et. al. (1979) illustrates this point with the case of an 8-year-old child who engaged in self-injurious behaviors. These behaviors produced long-lasting effects—bruises, welts, and even torn and bleeding skin—that could be measured after the occurrence of the behavior. But accurate measures could not be obtained by examining Amy's body on a regular basis. Certainly discolored skin, abrasions, and other such marks would indicate that the child had been injured. But how or how many times? And were there self-injurious acts that didn't leave observable marks? All of these questions are important in evaluating the effectiveness of any treatment procedure, yet none could be answered with any certainty by relying on the measurement of permanent products.

Two rules should be considered in using permanent products for data collection. *Rule 1:* Measurement of permanent products is desirable when each occurrence of the target behavior results naturally in the same permanent product. Measuring a student's written answers on math worksheets is an appropriate application of the above rule. Each computation naturally produces the same permanent product—a written answer on the worksheet. *Rule 2:* Measurement of permanent products is desirable when the product can be produced only by the target behavior. The only action that could produce written answers on a math worksheet is a student's computation of the problems. The example of the 8-year-old girl with self-

injurious behaviors also illustrates the importance of Rule 2. Even though her bruises, welts, and bleeding skin are permanent products, they could have been produced by actions other than self-injurious behaviors.

Many important behaviors do not naturally produce lasting permanent products unless they are audio- or video-recorded. For instance, oral reading, many social behaviors, and physical activity in individual and group sports do not naturally generate permanet products. In such cases it is sometimes possible, and often desirable, to use special equipment to obtain permanent products. Initiating conversation could be reproduced as a permanent product if tape-recorded. The wheelchair movement of an orthopedically handicapped child could be measured as a permanent product by attaching a bicycle odometer to one of the chair's wheels. A quarterback's passing performance (e.g., number of passes completed, total yardage) could be measured with a film or videotape of the game.

Heward et. al. (1979) identify a number of questions to be answered when considering the use of special equipment to obtain permanent products. "Is the equipment called for . . . available and practical? Will it be easy to collect data from the permanent product? Will the equipment alter the environment in a way that will change the nature of the target behavior? Is such a change desirable?" (p. 87). For example, the use of a tape recorder to produce initiating conversations might encourage the person to talk less or more. The effect of any special equipment should be assessed.

DIRECT OBSERVATIONAL RECORDING

Behavior analysts are concerned with many socially significant behaviors that do not naturally result in permanent products. When it is not convenient or feasible to use special equipment to observe these behaviors, they must be observed and recorded as they occur. When observers look at behaviors and produce records of those behaviors as they occur, they are engaging in direct **observational recording**. A wide variety of techniques have been developed for producing observational recordings. However, the most common procedures used in applied settings are event recording, duration recording, latency recording, interval recording, and momentary time sample recording.

Event Recording

Event recording is a tally or count of behaviors as they occur. Noting the number of times a target behavior occurs is a frequently used observational recording technique. Examples of event recording include a tally of the number of correct and erroneous oral student responses, the number of people car pooling, the number of times a student is tardy, the number of occupational accidents in the operation of an industrial organization.

Trice and Parker (1983) used event recording while working to reduce the use of obscene words by two adolescents in a resource classroom. They recorded all occurrences of six offensive words that were emitted frequently; they wrote down the target words, in order, as they occurred. Although pencil and paper are sufficient for making event recordings, the following items may facilitate the process:

1 Wrist counters. These counters, often used by golfers, can be purchased from sporting goods stores or large department stores. Most wrist counters can record from 0 to 99 responses.
2 Hand-tally digital counters. Hand-tally counters are frequently used in grocery stores to tally purchases made or in cafeterias to tally the number of people served. ~
3 Wrist-tally boards. The wrist-tally board is a note pad encased in a plastic holder on a watch band.

4 Masking tape attached to the wrist or a student's desk on which tallies can be marked.
5 Pennies, buttons, or paper clips that can be moved from one pocket to another each time the target behavior occurs.

Desirable Aspects Event recording has several major advantages. First, it does not interfere with other ongoing activities. A teacher can continue with instruction and at the same time tally the occurrence of a target behavior. Second, event recording is easy. Most people can use tallies to record behavior accurately the first time they attempt it. Finally, event recording always produces numerical products.

Considerations Event recording is an appropriate measurement technique for most behaviors. However, the target behavior must be discrete and have a definite beginning and ending. Event recording is easy to use with target behaviors such as giving an oral response to a question or giving praise to a child. Event recording would be difficult for behaviors such as humming; it would be difficult for observers to agree on when one hum ends and another begins.

Another consideration with event recording is that the target behaviors should not occur at high rates, which make it difficult for an observer to accurately record each discrete occurrence. Behaviors that may be difficult to tally because of their high rates include rocking, rapid jerks of the body, running, and tapping objects.

In addition, the target behavior in event recording should not be one that can occur for extended time periods, such as staying on task, listening, playing quietly alone, being out of one's seat, or thumb sucking. Task-oriented or continuous behavior such as reading is another example of a target behavior for which event recording would not be indicated. Classes of continuous behaviors occuring across time are usually not a terminal concern of applied behavior analysts. For example, reading per se is of less concern than the number of words read correctly and incorrectly per minute or the number of reading comprehension questions answered correctly. Similarly, movements of the client that show that he is utilizing what is being heard are a more important dimension to measure than the act of listening.

As a final consideration, event recording should be expressed as a number of occurrences only if the opportunities to respond and the observation times are constant across sessions (e.g., each observation session is 10 minutes). If these conditions are not constant, rate is the acceptable datum and will be discussed later.

Duration Recording

When a practitioner is concerned with how long a client engages in high-rate, extended, or continuous behaviors, **duration recording** should be used. If a supervisor is concerned with the amount of free time a beginning classroom teacher gives her students, duration recording would be the best way to gather the needed data.

Duration recording can be used to measure target behaviors that are emitted at high rates. Some individuals with severe behavior disorders emit high rates of self-injurious behaviors, (such as face slapping). Since each slap has a distinguishable start and finish, event recording could be used. If slapping occurred at high rates, however, counting each occurrence might be difficult and unreliable. An easier and more reliable method would be to record the total amount of time the individual engaged in face slapping.

Duration measures can be collected using either of two procedures: total duration or duration per occurrence. Total duration measures the total amount of time an individual is engaged in a performance during a period of observation. In contrast, duration per occurrence reports the amount of time for each instance of the behavior during a period of observation.

Goetz, Ayala, Hatfield, Marshall, and Etzel (1983) used the total duration measurement procedure while teaching independence in preschool children. They were concerned with the total amount of time per session spent by the preschool children putting away 50 blocks after free play. Timing started when the teacher assembled the children and said, "Now is the time to pick up the blocks" (p. 254). Timing stopped when the last block was put away.

Duration per occurrence was used by Gaylord-Ross, Haring, Breen, and Pitts-Conway (1984) to measure the duration of social interaction between autistic and nonhandicapped youths. To record, they started a stopwatch at the onset of an interaction and turned it off at the conclusion of the interaction. The time shown on the stopwatch was then recorded at the end of each interaction.

Analysts must be able to determine when event, total duration, and duration per occurrence recording are appropriate for data collection. For instance, a teacher concerned about a student's out-of-seat behavior could use event recording because out-of-seat behavior is discrete and would not occur at such a high rate as to make a tally of occurrences difficult. The teacher could also use total duration recording because one emission of out-of-seat behavior has the potential to occur for an extended time period. However, total duration and event recording measure entirely different dimensions of behavior, and these differences provide the criterion for selection. Event recording establishes the numerical dimension of behavior, whereas duration recording provides the temporal dimension. With out-of-seat behavior, event recording would tell how many times the student left his seat. Total duration recording would indicate how long the student was out-of-seat during the observation period. Because of the relevance of the temporal dimension, total duration recording would be a more appropriate measurement technique in this case. With event recording the teacher might report that the student was out of his seat only one time in a 30-minute observation period.

However, if that one time occupied 29 of the 30 minutes, a different picture of the behavior is obtained. In this situation duration per occurrence would be an even better measurement technique because it establishes both the numerical and temporal dimensions of behavior. By using duration per occurrence, the teacher would know the number of times the student was out-of-seat and the duration of time of each occurrence of this behavior. As a general rule, duration per occurrence is preferable to total duration because it provides more information concerning the target behavior. However, if behavior endurance is the major consideration, then total duration recording may be sufficient (Tawney & Gast, 1984).

The most precise nonautomated instrument for duration recording is a stopwatch. A wall clock or wristwatch can also be used but will probably produce measures less precise than those obtained with a stopwatch. The procedure for recording total duration with a stopwatch is to activate the stopwatch as the behavior starts and stop the timing at the end of the episode. *Without resetting the stopwatch*, the

observer must start it again at the beginning of the second occurrence of the behavior and stop the timing at the end of the second episode. The observer continues to accumulate the durations of time in this fashion until the end of the observation period and then transfers the total duration of time showing on the stopwatch to a record sheet.

The procedure for recording duration per occurrence with a stopwatch is to activate the stopwatch as the behavior starts and stop the timing at the end of the episode. The observer transfers the duration of time showing on the stopwatch to a data sheet and resets the watch. The stopwatch is started again at the beginning of the second occurrence of the behavior and is stopped at the end of the episode. The duration of time is transferred to a data sheet, and the procedure is continued until the end of the observation session. Figure 4.1 illustrates the use of a data sheet for recording duration per occurrence.

Total duration recording is most frequently reported in two ways. One method is a report of the cumulative duration of time that a target

Duration per Occurrence Data Sheet

Subject name: BJC   Observer: Jones
Behavior: Self-stimulating behavior
Date: March 8, 1987
Time start: 10:15 A.M.   Time stop: 10:35 A.M.
Condition: Preinstruction   Session number: 7

Number of Episode	Elapsed Time per Episode (in minutes ['] and seconds ["])
1	1' 17"
2	6' 5"
3	2' 1"
4	3' 35"
	Total: 12' 58"

FIGURE 4.1 Sample data sheet for recording duration per occurrence.

behavior occurred within a specified time period. For example, a kindergarten teacher concerned with isolate behavior could record the cumulative duration of isolate behavior occurring during daily 30-minute free play periods. The kindergarten students might have engaged in a cumulative total of 18 minutes of isolate behavior during one free play period. If the duration of the free play periods varied from day to day, the teacher should report the total duration of isolate behavior as a percentage of time (total duration of isolate behavior ÷ duration of free play period × 100 = % of isolate behavior in one free play period).

Another way to use total duration recording is to keep individual totals of the amount of time required to complete a specific task when no minimum or maximum time criteria are specified. For example, a community planner concerned with the amount of time specific individuals spent in a new recreation center could report individual time durations (e.g., for 4 successive days one individual's daily time in minutes at the center).

Latency Recording

Latency recording is the measurement of elapsed time between the onset of a stimulus (e.g., task direction, cue) and the initiation of a behavior. Latency recording should be used when the major concern is the length of time between an opportunity to emit a behavior and the beginning performance of that behavior. For example, a student may be slow in following teacher directions. The response latency would be the length of time between the end of the teacher's direction and the student's compliance. Concern can also focus on latencies that are too short. For instance, a student may give incorrect answers because she does not wait for the teacher to complete the questions. Brasted and Callahan (1984) used latency recording to measure whether feedback from an electronic fetal monitor (EFM) changed the reported time of contraction onset during

labor. The EFM is used routinely during labor and delivery for detection of fetal distress. However, its use is controversial because some contend that it increases maternal anxiety. Others hold that the EFM has no effect on the psychological process. Brasted and Callahan asked women in labor to press an event button when they felt a contraction. Latency was measured from contraction onset as indicated by the EFM to the women's button press.

The procedure for latency recording is similar to that for duration recording. Both report data on the temporal dimension of behavior, both use the same measurement procedure (e.g., use of some timing instrument such as a stopwatch), and both require a precise identification of the phenomenon to be recorded. Figure 4.2 provides a sample data sheet used for latency recording.

Interval Recording and Momentary Time Sampling

Interval recording and momentary time sampling provide an estimate of the number of occurrences and the duration of behaviors. With these data collection systems the analyst records the number of time intervals within an observation session in which the target behavior has been identified as present or absent. Interval recording and momentary time sampling procedures are most useful with continuous and high-rate behaviors.

Interval recording Interval recording is used to measure the presence or absence of behavior within specific time intervals. The total observation session is divided into brief time intervals of equal size. For example, if the total observation session is 10 minutes and the observer is using 10-second interval measurement, the session would be divided into 60 equal 10-second recording units. The interval size selected should provide the observer with sufficient time to observe and record behavior reliably. Interval size usually ranges from 6 to

---

Latency Recording Data Sheet

Subject name: __BJC__   Observer: __Smith__

Behavior: __Leaves seat to go to teacher when asked__

Date: __March 8, 1987__

Time start: __8:30 A.M.__   Time stop: __11:30 A.M.__

Condition: __Baseline__   Session number: __2__

Number of Stimulus	Elapsed Time per Episode (in minutes ['] and seconds [″])
1	2' 20″
2	3' 58″
3	1' 2″

FIGURE 4.2   Sample data sheet for recording latency.

---

15 seconds, depending on the behavior to be observed. To record the presence or absence of behaviors, the observer can draw a series of ruled boxes on paper, with each box representing one interval. The boxes can be positioned either horizontally or vertically, as shown in Figure 4.3. The observer marks each time interval with a symbol that indicates whether the behavior occurred. Data collected via interval recording are reported as the percentage of intervals in which the target behavior occurred. The data in Figure 4.3 show that the student was on-task during 50% of the intervals.

$$\frac{(\text{intervals on-task) } 6}{(\text{total intervals) } 12} \times 100 = 50\%$$

Interval recording commonly involves the use of pen, paper, clipboard, and stopwatch. The stopwatch can be attached to the clipboard with commercial attachment devices, but rubber bands are also satisfactory. One disadvantage of using the clipboard and stopwatch is that the observer must periodically look away from the subjects to observe the stopwatch, perhaps decreasing the accuracy of measurement. Worthy (1968) describes a miniature device that generates audible signals to be used

for interval recording. This device eliminates the need to monitor a stopwatch. Worthy's description is complete enough that most TV/radio repair shops could build the timing device. Another procedure for generating an audible cue is to use a cassette recorder with an attached ear phone and a tape that signals the elapsed time. For example, at the beginning of the tape the observer might hear the word "Start". At the end of the first 10 seconds a cue such as "Record 1" could be presented, "Record 2" at the end of the second 10 seconds, and so on.

Interval recording can be conducted in two ways. The first and most common procedure is **partial-interval recording,** which requires the observer to record simply whether the behavior was present or absent at any time during the interval. Partial-interval recording is not concerned with how many times the behavior occurred during the interval or how long the behavior was present. Partial-interval recording can be used in all instances when interval recording is the selected measurement system. However, whenever it is important to know whether a class of behaviors is occurring for an extended duration, whole-interval recording

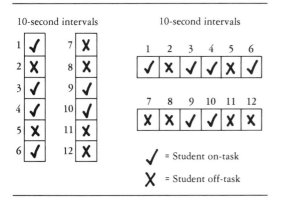

10-second intervals

1	✓	7	✗
2	✗	8	✗
3	✓	9	✓
4	✓	10	✓
5	✗	11	✗
6	✓	12	✗

10-second intervals

1	2	3	4	5	6
✓	✗	✓	✓	✗	✓

7	8	9	10	11	12
✗	✗	✓	✓	✗	✗

✓ = Student on-task

✗ = Student off-task

FIGURE 4.3 Examples of interval recording.

may be preferred. **Whole-interval recording** requires that the behavior be present throughout the entire interval if it is to be considered an occurrence. For example, if attending behaviors were recorded using the whole-interval procedure, a student would need to attend during the full interval to have that interval scored as an occurrence.

Stevenson and Fantuzzo (1984) used partial-interval recording to measure the occurrence and nonoccurrence of disruptive behaviors (e.g., out-of-seat, talking out) of fifth-grade students during 10-minute math drills. They scored fifty 10-second intervals during each drill and recorded the presence of any disruptive behavior during an interval as an occurrence. Lagomarcino, Reid, Ivancic, and Faw (1984) instructed severely and profoundly retarded persons in leisure dance. A whole-interval recording procedure was used for data collection and evaluation of instruction. Their procedure consisted of observing each of two dancers individually for alternating 1-minute periods. They used 10-second intervals, each followed by 5 seconds for recording the presence or absence of appropriate dancing. To be scored as an occurrence, appropriate dancing had to be present during the entire 10 seconds.

Momentary Time Sampling The procedure for **momentary time sampling** is sim-

ilar to that for interval recording but with a noticeable difference. Momentary time sampling is concerned with recording the presence or absence of behaviors immediately following specified time intervals, unlike interval recording, which is concerned with recording behaviors during specified time intervals. If an observer wishes to record the occurrence or nonoccurrence of a behavior, a paper is ruled into squares that represent equal or variable time intervals. A procedure used by Test and Heward (1984) illustrates how variable time periods can be programmed for momentary time sampling.

> A random numbers table was used to generate numbers betwen 1 and 1800, representing the total number of seconds in a 30-minute session. The random numbers were selected and placed on a number line, with the criterion that no two numbers could be less than 10 seconds apart, until 30 observation points had been marked. This list of numbers was then used as a guide for making the variable interval time sampling [recording form]. (p. 181)

To record using momentary time sampling, the observer checks the time intervals in which the behavior was or was not taking place at the moment the interval ended. Behavior is scored only once per interval and is reported as a percentage of intervals. For example, a leader of a summer recreation program for elementary-aged children was concerned with the cooperative play of a child during a 60-minute activity period. The period was divided into 5-minute intervals, permitting the leader to observe and record the child's cooperative play 12 times. Regardless of the cooperative play during the 5-minute interval, the recreation leader recorded only the behavior at the instant the interval ended. Figure 4.4 shows that the child played cooperatively at the end of 67% of the intervals during this 60-minute activity period $\left(\frac{8}{12} \times 100 = 66.66\%\right)$.

The observer can use a wall clock or wristwatch for time sampling. However, giving instructions or working with an individual or

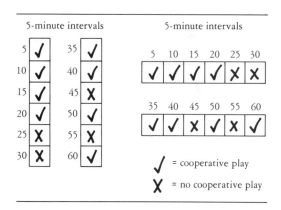

5-minute intervals

5	✓	35	✓
10	✓	40	✓
15	✓	45	✗
20	✓	50	✓
25	✗	55	✗
30	✗	60	✓

5-minute intervals

5	10	15	20	25	30
✓	✓	✓	✓	✗	✗

35	40	45	50	55	60
✓	✓	✗	✓	✗	✓

✓ = cooperative play

✗ = no cooperative play

FIGURE 4.4 Momentary time sampling using 5-minute intervals during a 60-minute period.

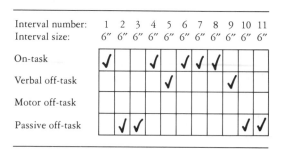

Interval number:	1	2	3	4	5	6	7	8	9	10	11
Interval size:	6″	6″	6″	6″	6″	6″	6″	6″	6″	6″	6″
On-task	✓			✓		✓	✓	✓			
Verbal off-task					✓				✓		
Motor off-task											
Passive off-task		✓	✓							✓	✓

FIGURE 4.5 Interval recording of several behaviors.

group makes it difficult to time intervals without a signaling device. Common kitchen timers have been useful for this purpose.

Using Interval Recording and Momentary Time Sampling with Several Individuals or Several Behaviors

Observers often need to record the same behavior for several individuals in a group or several different behaviors for the same individual. If more than one individual or more than one discrete behavior is to be observed and recorded, the observer can add additional rows for each behavior or individual (see Figure 4.5). The only consideration that limits that number of discrete behaviors or individuals that can be measured simultaneously is the probability of obtaining reliable data. Reliability of recording will probably decrease when the observer simultaneously records more than three or four categories. However, accuracy increases with training and recording experience.

When recording several individuals, observers frequently record only one individual per interval (see Figure 4.6). The data sheet in Figure 4.6 shows that John did not attend during the first 10-second interval, Laura attended during the second 10-second interval, Alice attended during the third 10-second interval, and so on.

Another tactic used with interval recording of several response categories is referred to as **noncontinuous observational control** (Tawney & Gast, 1984). To use this procedure, the observer observes during the first interval, records during the second interval what was observed in the first interval, observes again in the third interval, records in the fourth, and so on (see Figure 4.7). Figure 4.7 shows that the first 6 seconds were used for observation. The observer then used the second interval to record what was observed in the first: the student had been on-task. This process of observe-then-record continues throughout the observation period.

A sampling procedure that is used for scoring group behavior is **PLACHECK**—Planned Activity Check (Doke & Risley, 1972). With PLACHECK a group of individuals is observed at the end of a specified time period. The number of individuals engaged in specified behaviors is tallied and compared to the total number of individuals in the group. For example, Doke and Risley (1972) were interested in comparing group participation in required and optional before-school activity schedules. To provide data, at the end of 3-minute intervals observers tallied the total number of children in either the required or the optional activity area and then the number of children actually participating in an activity in either area. These data were reported as separate per-

FIGURE 4.6 Interval recording of several individuals.

Interval number:	1	2	3	4	5	6
Interval size:	10″	10″	10″	10″	10″	10″

Observation number per student	John (10″)	Laura (10″)	Alicia (10″)	Daryl (10″)	Mary Ann (10″)	Hans (10″)
1	✗	✓	✓	✗	✗	✓
2	✓	✓	✗			
3						
4						

✓ = attending   ✗ = nonattending

centages of children participating in required or optional activities.

Desirable Aspects Interval recording has two major advantages. First, interval recording can provide an estimate of the frequency and duration of the behavior. Second, and perhaps most importantly, interval recording provides an estimate of performance across time intervals, which is not possible with event and total duration recording. Interval recording indicates when a behavior is likely to occur or not occur. For example, interval recording can help ascertain whether a behavior is likely to occur at the beginning, middle, or end of an observation period. Such information is valuable in planning the delivery of antecedent and consequent events.

Momentary time sampling is a useful tactic because numerical estimates of individual or group behavior can be obtained while the observer is involved in instruction or other activities. This is particularly true of variable time sampling and is a key advantage for classroom teachers. In addition, both interval recording and momentary time sampling permit point-to-point (or interval-by-interval) reliability checks, which will be discussed in chapter 5.

Considerations A major disadvantage of interval recording is that it requires the undivided attention of an observer. Therefore, the observer cannot be expected to collect data and also direct other activities.

Another consideration stems from the idea that in applied behavior analysis a recorded change in behavior is more believable when a conservative measurement procedure is selected (Sulzer-Azaroff & Mayer, 1977). Basically, it is preferable to choose the most stringent measurement procedure. For instance, the partial-interval procedure tends to produce a slight overestimate of the presence of the target behavior; the whole-interval procedure, a slight underestimate. As a general rule in interval recording, the partial-interval procedure should be used when the goal is to produce a behavior reduction, and the whole-interval procedure, a behavior increase. For example, if the goal is to increase attending behaviors, the whole-interval procedure should be selected. Since

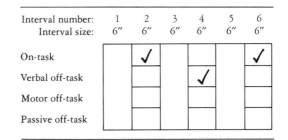

Interval number:	1	2	3	4	5	6
Interval size:	6″	6″	6″	6″	6″	6″
On-task		✓				✓
Verbal off-task				✓		
Motor off-task						
Passive off-task						

FIGURE 4.7 Interval recording with noncontinuous observational control.

that procedure requires the behavior to occur for the full interval before an occurrence is scored, it produces a more conservative tally than the partial-interval procedure, in which any occurrence of the behavior during the interval is scored as an occurrence.

Event, duration, latency, and interval recording and momentary time sampling are the most frequently used observation systems in applied settings. Combined with measurement of permanent products, they provide the observer with a wide range of options for data collection. Table 4.1 contains information relevant to selecting an appropriate measurement procedure.

REPORTING DATA COLLECTED

The purpose of data collection is to provide information for program planning and decision making and for analyzing the effects of environmental arrangements on behavior (see chapters 6, 7, 8, 9, and 10 for a discussion of analysis techniques). To accomplish this purpose, it is necessary to compare performance over time. What an individual produces at a specific point in time is usually not important for decision making or analysis if that performance cannot be compared in order to make a judgment. Simply recording an amount of behavior is usually unacceptable. For example, if John gave correct answers to 60 questions on his physics test, did he understand all 60 out of 60 items or only 60 out of 200 items? Or perhaps Mary called her teacher a derogatory name once, but did she do that once in 5 minutes, 1 week, or a full school year? And if Bill was attentive 2 minutes on Monday, was that 2 minutes out of 5 minutes or out of 2 hours?

Amount of behavior should be converted to other units of measurement to allow for a comparison of behavior across time. The major units of conversion are frequency, rate, and percentage measures. Other relevant dimensions of behavior in applied settings include duration, latency (discussed earlier), topography, and magnitude of response. However, these dimensions must also be converted to frequency, rate, or percentage if they are to communicate meaningful information.

Frequency of Response

Frequency of response is the number of times a specific behavior occurs in some period of time. Tallying, or counting, responses is possible when the behavior is readily observable and when it is discrete; that is, when it can be separated from other responses.

Frequency should be used as a measurement of behavior only when time and opportunity for response are constant. If frequency measures are used without reference to these variables, performance is open to subjective interpretation. For example, frequency would be an appropriate measure if the student, on consecutive sessions, received 30 similar arithmetic problems (the same opportunity to respond each session) with 14 minutes to work on the problems (constant time each session). Frequency would not be appropriate if the number of problems varied from session to session or if the amount of time to work the problems varied from session to session.

Rate of Response

Rate of Response is a frequency measure because it is the number of behaviors occurring in a unit of time. However, rate of response is usually expressed as responses per minute or responses per hour. Rate is calculated by dividing the total number of responses by the amount of time spent producing those responses (rate = number of responses divided by time). Rate of response is considered the basic datum of the science of behavior (Skinner, 1966). Rate measures are sensitive to proficiency of performance. As Kunzelmann (1970)

TABLE 4.1. Information for selecting appropriate measurement procedures.

Permanent Products

Measure: A product that is tangible and can be measured after the behavior has occurred.

Dimension: Usually numerical but can be temporal when taken from audio and video recordings.

Examples: Written spelling; written math problems; video and audio recordings of social interaction; assembly tasks; sorting tasks.

Considerations: (1) Some behaviors effect fairly permanent changes in the environment yet are not absolutely reliable for purposes of measurement. (2) This approach should be used when each occurrence of the behavior results naturally in the same permanent product. (3) This procedure is appropriate when the product can be produced only by the target behavior. (4) Special equipment or apparatus can be used to obtain permanent products when it is available and practical, when data collection from the special equipment is easy, and when the equipment does not adversely alter the environment in a way that will change the nature of the behavior.

Event Recording

Measure: A tally or count of discrete events as they occur.

Dimension: Numerical.

Examples: Number of times arriving at work on time; number of times tattling; number of positive statements.

Considerations: (1) Behavior should be discrete, having a definite beginning and end. (2) Behavior should not occur at very high rates. (3) Behavior should not be a class of responses that can occur for extended time periods.

Duration Recording

Measure: The extent of time a behavior occurs during an observation period.

Dimension: Temporal.

Example: Length of time running.

Considerations: (1) This procedure can indicate how long a client engages in a particular class of behaviors. (2) It can be used with endurance activities. (3) This approach does not have a numerical dimension.

Measure: Duration per occurrence—the extent of time of each occurrence of the behavior.

Dimension: Numerical and temporal.

Examples: Length of time attending, time out-of-seat.

Considerations: (1) This technique provides data on the number of occurrences, duration of each occurrence, and total duration. (2) As a general rule, duration per occurrence provides more information about the target behavior than total duration does.

Table 4.1 continues on p. 72.

TABLE 4.1. Continued.

Latency Recording

Measure: Length of elapsed time between the onset of a stimulus and the occurrence of a behavior.

Dimension: Temporal.

Example: Compliance with teacher's directions.

Considerations: (1) This procedure is appropriate when the major concern is the length of time that occurs between an opportunity to emit a behavior and the beginning performance of that task. (2) Concern can focus on either increasing or decreasing the latency period.

Interval Recording

Measure: Presence or absence of a behavior at any time during the interval.

Dimension: Numerical and temporal estimate.

Examples: Talking out, standing in a particular location.

Considerations: (1) This technique can be used in all instances of interval recording. (2) It will produce a slight overestimation of the presence of the behavior. (3) This method should be used when the goal is to produce a behavior reduction. (4) Interval recording requires the undivided attention of the observer.

Measure: Presence of a behavior throughout the entire interval.

Dimension: Temporal estimate.

Examples: Attending, staying on-task.

Considerations: (1) This approach indicates whether a class of behaviors is continuous. (2) It will produce a slight underestimation of the presence of the behavior. (3) The goal should be to produce a behavior increase. (4) Interval recording requires the undivided attention of the observer.

Momentary Time Sampling

Measure: Occurrence or nonoccurrence of a behavior immediately following specified equal or variable time periods.

Dimension: Numerical estimate.

Examples: Stereotypic behaviors such as rocking, face slapping, and hand flapping.

Considerations: (1) This technique is not appropriate for low-rate behaviors. (2) It is easy to use and will not interfere with other ongoing activities of the observer. (3) This method can be used easily for either individual or group behavior.

states, "The student who worked 10 minutes and got 80 problems correct with a correct rate of eight problems per minute on the 100-item test is much more proficient than the student who took 20 minutes, also got 80 problems correct, but who had a correct rate of four problems a minute" (p. 31). (This statement assumes that the problems were of the same or similar difficulty.) Basically, rate is the only measure of performance that provides information on proficiency, and skill acquisition needs to be expressed in terms of proficiency as well as accuracy. Also, of all measures rate is the most sensitive to the effects of environmental arrangements on performance because it reveals small increments of behavior change.

When a client has the opportunity to emit correct and incorrect responses, the practitioner should compute a rate measure for both variables. This situation is most common during educational instruction (White & Haring, 1980). Two examples of academic behaviors for which rate measures should be computed for both correct and incorrect responses are words read per minute and answers to arithmetic problems per minute. Correct and incorrect rate measures together provide important information to help the teacher evaluate how well the student is progressing. Ideally, the practitioner should observe the correct response rate accelerating toward a terminal criterion and the incorrect response rate decelerating to a low, stable criterion.

Baer and Fowler (1984) state that rate of response is an appropriate measure for all behaviors characterized as free operants but not for restricted operants. They define a **free operant** as any operant behavior that results in minimal displacement of the organism in both time and space. As such, a free operant can be emitted at nearly any time; it is also discrete, does not require much time for completion, and can produce a wide range of response rates. Typical free operant responses used in animal laboratory studies include the bar press and key peck. Many occurrences of academic and social behaviors meet the definition of free operants—for example, number of words read per minute; number of digits counted by ones, twos, threes per minute; number of letter strokes written per minute; self slaps. Each of these examples can be emitted at almost any time, each discrete response does not use much time, and each performance can display a wide range of rates.

On the other hand, Baer and Fowler define **restricted operants** as operant behaviors that do not meet the defining characteristics of free operants. In other words, rates of occurrence of the behaviors are controlled by opportunities to emit each discrete response; in addition, some important clusters of related classes of behaviors are not defined pragmatically as a specific, discrete response incident. Typical restricted operants used in animal laboratory studies include moving from one place to another in a maze or shuttlebox. Typical applied examples of controlled opportunities include waiting for the teacher to present a flash card before a response can be made or providing oral responses to the teacher's reading comprehension questions. In each of these examples the rate of response is controlled by how quickly the teacher presents the problem or question. Each discrete response can be made only when the teacher provides the opportunity to respond. These are restricted operants.

Baer and Fowler (1984) provide an excellent example of restricted operants that are related behaviors with a significant combined effect on the environment.

> For a representative example, consider the case of a preschool teacher reinforcing a child for interacting with peers rather than with adults. In behavioral preschools, that is a very common and effective solution to a consistent problem.
>
> The child's behavior, that of interacting with peers, is a complex class of responses. Some of its prominent members can be described in these terms: the child comes near to other children, looks at them, talks to them, or answers them when they talk. He or she offers any of the materials that the preschool makes available for child work and play, takes materials offered by another child, or manipulates some of those materials for the other children. The child touches the other children, gestures to them, displays facial expressions to them, or does any or all of these actions in any combination, and in any sequence. (p. 154)

As a general rule, rate of response is the preferred measure for free operants because of the sensitivity of the data to behavior change and the precision with which the measurement technique can be defined. Restricted operants, such as opportunity-bound behaviors, demand consideration of other measurement techniques. Proportion of opportunities, often expressed as a percentage, is the measure of choice for restricted operants.

Percentage of Response

Percentage of Response is a ratio that expresses the amount of a behavior as a certain number of responses per every 100 responses. Percentage is obtained by dividing the total opportunities for response (e.g., 25 test items) into the number of correct or incorrect responses (e.g., 17 correct answers) and multiplying that result by 100 $\left(\frac{17}{25} = .68 \times 100 = 68\% \right)$. Ideally, if the total number of response opportunities is less than 100, percentage should not be computed (Guilford, 1965). If a lower limit must be set, Guilford holds that it is unwise to compute percentages when the dividend is less than 20. When the dividend is less than 20, small changes in behavior are greatly over- or underestimated with the percentage measure.

Percentage is an appropriate measure when opportunity to respond is not constant across observation periods and when proficiency is not an issue.

Other Procedures Using Frequency, Rate, and Percentage Measures

Frequency, rate, and percentage measures have been employed with several different measurement techniques by applied behavior analysts. The most common techniques include trials to criterion, techniques for equalizing the complexity of task items across sessions, pre- and posttests, and probes.

Trials to Criterion **Trials to criterion** is the report of the number of times response opportunities are presented before an individual achieves a preestablished level of accuracy or proficiency. For example, the measurement could be reported as 10 trials to achieve 100% accuracy (percentage) or 10 trials to achieve 60 words per minute (rate). Touchette and Howard (1984) used this approach to report the number

of trials required for severely retarded students to achieve a criterion on discrimination tasks.

Measuring trials to criterion is appropriate in an evaluative comparison of two or more kinds of materials or methods of intervention. For example, a teacher might report the number of times the word *that* was presented orally before a student read it independently and might compare that number to the number of times the word *that* was presented in written form for tracing before the student read it independently. Measuring trials to criterion gives a teacher useful information for planning the amount of time that should be allotted for instruction. In the previous example, if trials to criterion are tallied for several different words taught to a student in different ways, the teacher can then compare performance measures to determine whether the student masters words better with one method than another.

In addition, measuring trials to criterion can be important when the intervention is concerned with learning-to-learn phenomena such as acquiring concepts and operations (Tawney & Gast, 1984). Typically, the number of trials needed to reach a response criterion decreases with the presentation of successive exemplars of a concept. With a preschool child learning the concept of redness, for instance, stimulus items representative of that concept may initially require several instructional trials before the child achieves a response criterion. However, as more exemplars of that class of stimuli are taught to a criterion, fewer and fewer instructional trials will be required. The learner is said to have learned the concept of redness when correct responses are emitted on the first trials with novel exemplars of the color red.

Complexity of Task Items The response units suggested for previously discussed measures have been whole units (e.g., whole words read or spelled, finished mathematics problems). Measuring responses in whole units, however, does not take into account the complexity of each possible response. One method for measuring academic responses that does take complexity into account is to count the operations necessary to achieve a correct response. These operations can be reported as frequency, percentage, or rate. For example, in measuring spelling performance, instead of counting a word as correct or incorrect, the teacher might consider the number of letters that are in correct sequence within each word.

Helwig (1973) reported a mathematics response rate calculated on the number of operations sufficient to produce the answer. In each session the student was given 20 multiplication and division problems selected at random from a set of 120 problems. The length of time for each session was recorded by the teacher. All the problems were of two types: $a \times b = c$ and $a \div b = c$. The student was asked to find one of the factors: the product, the dividend, the divisor, or the quotient. The problems required from one to five operations. For example, finding the answer to the problem $55 \times 5 = ?$ requires the student to perform four operations; a correct answer would be scored as four correct responses.

(1) Multiply the ones: $5 \times 5 = 25$.

(2) Record the 5 ones and
carry the 2 tens.

$$\begin{array}{r} \overset{2}{5}5 \\ \underline{5} \\ \mathbf{5} \end{array}$$

(3) Multiply the tens: $5 \times 5(0) = 25(0)$.

(4) Add the 2 tens carried
and record.

$$\begin{array}{r} \overset{2}{5}5 \\ \underline{5} \\ \mathbf{275} \end{array}$$

When there was more than one possible way to find the answer, the mean number of operations was figured for that problem. For example, in the problem $4 \times ? = 164$ the answer by multiplication requires two operations; by division, four. The mean number of operations is three. In Helwig's example each set of 20 problems was checked, and the number of correct

responses and errors was recorded and reported as a rate of response.

Pre- and Posttests One tactic used by teachers to measure students' acquisition of academic skills is pre- and posttesting. The pretest provides an assessment of what the student can do before instruction. The posttest, given after instruction, presumably determines the skills the student has achieved as a function of instruction.

Pre- and posttest measurement can be used in two ways. First, the teacher can report the student's posttest score as a final grade. Second, the teacher can report the student's score as instructional gain from pretesting to posttesting. If a student scored 2 correct out of 20 items on the pretest and 10 correct out of 20 items on the posttest, the teacher would report a gain score (increase) of 8, or 40% ($8 \div 20 = .40$ or 40%).

Since pre- and posttests are most frequently reported as percentage measures, a note of caution is warranted on the use and interpretation of percentages. First, different percentages can be reported from the same set of data and can lead to different interpretations of the outcome. For example, in the illustration just presented, the student had a gain score of 40%. With these same data it is possible to show that the student improved 500%: the student achieved a fivefold improvement—from 2 correct to 10 correct—which equals 500%. This is a completely different interpretation from an improvement of 40 percentage points. In another case, it is possible to show percentage improvement even though incorrect responses are being maintained or even increased. A student might be presented with 20 multiplication facts and answers 10 correctly, showing 50% accuracy. During the next session the teacher might add 10 multiplication problems to the original 20, and the student might answer 20 correctly, showing 67% accuracy. Even with the improved score, the student still has the same number of errors. Problems of interpretation such as these are resolved when frequency/rate measures are reported for correct and incorrect responses. An additional caution is that data gathered during only one session of pretesting can mislead the instructor/therapist because of response variability from session to session.

A major advantage of pretesting is that it provides the teacher with an estimate of student skills in the instructional area. The pretest allows the teacher to modify teaching topics to cover skills that the student has not previously acquired. Another advantage is that pre- and posttests require little teacher time.

An obvious limitation of pre- and posttests is that both measures must be applied only to items that represent exactly the same unit of study and the same level of complexity. Because only two measures are compared, the teacher must be sure that the pre- and posttests are equivalent in the kind and manner of response required. This limitation ceases to be a problem if the teacher combines pre- and posttest measures with some other form of continuous measurement.

Probes An important question of instructional effectiveness is whether the teaching of certain specific items has a generalized effect and improves students' accuracy on similar untaught items. For example, if the teacher specifically teaches several words with a consonant-vowel-consonant pattern, will the student correctly read other untaught words that follow the same pattern? To answer this question, the teacher could periodically present untaught words, or **probes,** as well as the words being taught, and then record correct or incorrect reponses to probes. Probe items should be related in form or function to the items taught. In this context a probe prompts responses to (1) different stimuli, (2) different stimulus configurations, or (3) different stimulus relationships from those presented during instruction (Spradlin & Saunders, 1984).

The advantages of probe measures are similar to the advantages of pretests: both provide

a general estimate of student skills and require little teacher time. Also, probes can tell a teacher whether instruction on selected items affects the student's accuracy on similar items that have not been taught. If accuracy on untaught items increases, the teacher can say that the student has mastered the concept and additional instruction is unnecessary. However, if accuracy on untaught items does not increase, the probe measures can be used as measures of baseline skill prior to teaching those items.

Magnitude and Topography

Two final dimensions of behavior are magnitude and topography of response. **Magnitude of response** is the strength, force, or intensity of each instance of the target behavior. There are some practical applications using magnitude as the unit of measurement. For example, the observer might be interested in the volume of alcohol consumed, the number of pounds a client can lift, or the degree of a student's handwriting pressure. However, these applications are limited. Often magnitude must be recorded with electromechanical devices, which may be too expensive or may not be available or appropriate for applied settings. Even when magnitude is the unit of measure, it must be reported in terms of frequency, rate, percentage, or duration. For instance, Greene, Bailey, and Barber (1981) measured the magnitude of verbal outbursts on a school bus transporting sixth- through eighth-grade students. They used a sound recording device that recorded the number of times outbursts of sound exceeded a specified threshold and the total duration of time these outbursts remained above that threshold.

Topography of response is the form or shape of the behavior. For example, Jack wrote his name within the lines; Sharon reversed the digits in the numbers 12, 13, 14, and 15. Trap, Milner-Davis, Joseph, and Cooper (1978) measured the topography of cursive handwriting by recording the deviation of the students' cursive letters from model letters. Topography is usually reported as frequency, rate, percentage, or duration of response.

Table 4.2 provides a summary of information for reporting data collected with permanent products and observational recording techniques.

TABLE 4.2. Selection of behavioral dimension for reporting data.

Frequency

Definition: Simple count of correct and/or erroneous responses occurring in some period of time.

Application: Simple procedure requiring minimum amount of teacher time; generally does not interfere with ongoing teaching; provides for analysis of errors when used with permanent products; easily understood by parents and children.

Data evaluation: (1) For day-to-day comparisons of data total number of opportunities for response should not vary with assignments. (2) This measure reflects skill efficiency/proficiency.

Rate

Definition: Frequency of a behavior during a certain unit of time (computed by dividing the total number of correct or erroneous responses by the amount of time spent on the task).

Application: Most sensitive measure of behavior (i.e., most likely to show small changes; excellent as criterion for mastery of skills; appropriate for measuring all free operants; may require more teacher time to measure and compute; not always easily understood by parents and children.

Data evaluation: (1) Measures are not comparable if difference in length of sessions is extreme (e.g., rate in a 1-minute sample may be higher than that in a 30-minute sample for some students and some academic responses). (2) Student, not teacher or materials, should control maximum rate of response. (3) This measure accurately reflects proficiency if complexity of tasks remains constant.

Percentage

Defintion: Amount of behavior expressed as a certain number of responses in every 100 (computed by dividing the number of correct or erroneous responses by the total number of opportunities for responses and then multiplying by 100).

Application: Often the measure of choice for restricted operants; easily understood by parents and children.

Data evaluation: (1) Student performance in sessions offering unequal response opportunities can be compared.

Trials to Criterion

Definition: Number of times response opportunities are presented before student achieves a preestablished criterion.

Application: Appropriate for an evaluative comparison of two or more kinds of materials or instructional methods and for learning-to-learn phenomena; use in planning the time to be given to instruction; easily understood by parents and children.

Data evaluation: (1) The criterion set will probably require a measure for each trial; however, only the number of trials to achieve the criterion is usually reported. (2) This measure can show efficiency if criterion is stated as rate.

TABLE 4.2. Continued.

Complexity of Task Items

Definition: Measurement of the number of operations sufficient for a correct response.

Application: Useful when complexity of response varies greatly within one measurement episode or when a fine analysis or response is desired.

Data evaluation: (1) Number of operations may be used to compute frequency, percentage, or rate.

Pre- and Posttests

Definition: Measurement of behavior before and after instruction.

Application: Provides a minimal estimate of skills in an instructional area; requires a minimum of time; can be used to assess what can be done before instruction (pretest); can be reported as a final grade (posttest). Teacher may report instructional gain from pre- to posttesting.

Data evaluation: (1) Measurement at intervals during instruction is critical if time between pre- and posttests is weeks or months.

Probes

Definition: Infrequent measurement of responses to different stimuli, different stimulus configurations, or different stimulus relationships from those presented during instruction.

Application: Indicates whether the teaching of specific items has a generalized effect on similar untaught items; requires minimum of teacher time; provides an estimate of student skills; can be used to measure baseline skill prior to instruction.

Data evaluation: (1) Probe items should be related in form or function to items taught.

Magnitude

Definition: The strength, force, or intensity of each instance of a response.

Data evaluation: (1) Magnitude must often be recorded with electromechanical devices. (2) Magnitude measures are reported in terms of frequency, rate, percentage, or duration.

Topography

Definition: The form or shape of the behavior.

Data evaluation: Topography measures are reported in terms of frequency, rate, percentage, or duration.

SUMMARY

Direct Measurement of Permanent Products

1 Permanent products result from behaviors that produce tangible items or environmental effects that can be measured at some time following the client's responses.

2 Measurement of permanent products is desirable when each occurrence of the target behavior results naturally in the same permanent product.

3 Measurement of permanent products is desirable when the product can be produced only by the target behavior.

4 When target behaviors do not naturally produce permanent products, it is possible and often desirable to use special equipment or apparatus to obtain permanent products.

Observational Recording

Event Recording
5 Event recording is a tally or count of behaviors as they occur.
6 The target behavior should be discrete, with a definite beginning and end; it should not occur at high rates; and it should not be a class of responses that can occur for extended time periods.
7 Event recording can be expressed as a number of occurrences only if the opportunities for response and the observation times are constant across sessions.

Duration Recording
8 When an analyst is concerned with how long a client engages in a particular class of behaviors, duration recording is appropriate.
9 Duration recording can measure target behaviors that are emitted at very high rates.
10 Event recording establishes the numerical dimension of behavior, whereas duration recording establishes the temporal dimension.
11 Duration recording is most frequently used in two ways: one method reports the cumulative duration of behaviors occurring within specified time periods, and the other reports the amount of time taken for each occurrence of a specified behavior.

Latency and Interval Recording and Momentary Time Sampling
12 Latency recording is the measurement of the length of elapsed time between the onset of a stimulus and the occurrence of a behavior.
13 Interval recording and momentary time sampling provide estimates of both the number of occurrences and the duration of a behavior.
14 Interval recording is used to measure the presence or absence of behavior within specific time intervals.
15 Interval recording can be scored as partial-interval recording or whole-interval recording.

16 Momentary time sampling records the presence or absence of behaviors immediately following specified time intervals.
17 With PLACHECK a group of individuals is observed at the end of a specified time period. The number of individuals engaged in specified behaviors is tallied and compared to the total number of individuals in the group.

Reporting Data Collected

18 The purposes of data collection are to provide information for program planning and decision making and for analyzing the effects of environmental arrangements on behavior.
19 The major dimensions of behavior include frequency, rate, percentage, duration, topography, and magnitude of response.

Frequency of Response
20 Frequency of response is the number of times a specific behavior occurs in some period of time.

Rate of Response
21 Rate of response is a frequency measure because it records the number of behaviors occurring in a unit of time. However, rate of response is usually expressed in responses per minute or responses per hour.
22 Rate/frequency is the only measure of performance that will provide information on proficiency.

Percentage of Response
23 Percentage of response is a ratio that expresses the amount of behavior as a certain number of responses per every 100 responses.
24 Ideally, if the total number of response opportunities is less than 100, percentages should not be computed.

Variations on Frequency, Rate, and Percentage Measures

Trials to Criterion
25 Trials to criterion measures the number of times response opportunities are presented before an individual achieves a preestablished level of competence or proficiency.

Complexity

26 A method for measuring academic responses that takes complexity into account is to count the operations necessary to achieve a correct response.

Pre- and Posttests

27 A pretest is used primarily to assess what the student can do before instruction. The posttest is given following instruction.

Probes

28 A probe is an infrequent measurement of responses to different stimuli, different stimulus configurations, or different stimulus relationships from those presented during instruction.

Magnitude and Topography

29 Magnitude of response is the strength, force, or intensity of each instance of the target behavior.

30 Topography of response is the form or shape of the behavior.

5

Planning and Directing Observational Procedures

KEY TERMS

Continuous recording

Sampling procedure

Repeated measures

Variability

Naturalistic observations

Calibration

Observation code

Reliability of observations

Interobserver agreement

Procedural reliability

Accuracy of observation

Interval-by-interval (I-I) method

Scored-interval (S-I) method

Unscored-interval (U-I) method

Reactivity

Observer drift

Complexity of measurement

Observer expectations

This chapter discusses the factors that influence the accuracy and believability of data. Specifically, it can help the behavior analyst interpret the usefulness of reported data and can help the beginning applied researcher avoid measurement practices that might prevent the collection of usable data. The chapter covers the scheduling of continuous and sample observations, selecting times for observation, establishing duration of observation sessions, planning sampling procedures, establishing observation codes, reaching interobserver agreement and

This chapter was written by John O. Cooper.

implementing it, and identifying sources of influence on the agreement and accuracy of measurement.

SCHEDULING CONTINUOUS AND SAMPLE OBSERVATIONS

An observer has two choices in scheduling observations: he can choose to record the occurrence of the behavior continuously or to measure a sample of the behavior. A **continuous recording** of behavior implies that the observer records all possible occurrences of the target behavior. For example, if the target behavior is miscues that occur during a 20-minute oral reading period, all miscues occurring during this period should be recorded. If the target behavior is cooperative play during free time at school, all occurrences of cooperative play during free time should be recorded. On the other hand, when using a **sampling procedure,** only a portion of the occurrences of the behavior is recorded. In the previous example the teacher might sample the occurrences of miscues during the first 2 minutes of oral reading even though the full instructional session is 20 minutes. Likewise, cooperative play could be measured for 5 minutes out of the 35-minute period occurring during the school day.

Ideally, all occurrences of the behavior of interest should be recorded. However, available resources in settings used for treatment or instruction often necessitate the use of sampling procedures. A sampling procedure may be sufficient for decision making and analysis if the samples represent an adequate approximation of the true parameters of the behavior of interest. It is more important to acquire samples of a behavior frequently, producing **repeated measures**, than it is to obtain a single continuous measure of the behavior. Obviously, with repeated measures of the behavior, a pattern or trend will develop to indicate whether the behavior of interest is increasing, decreasing, or remaining constant. As a general rule, observations should be scheduled on a daily or frequent basis, even if for only brief periods.

SELECTING TIMES FOR OBSERVATION

Data collected during observations are compared over time so that trends in the occurrence or nonoccurrence of a behavior will become obvious. Therefore, the times of observation should be standardized. If a teacher is interested in a meaningful comparison of students' attending behavior, the data need to be collected at the same time each day. It would be pointless to compare data collected from 9:00 to 9:10 A.M. on Monday with data collected from 2:00 to 2:10 P.M. on Tuesday because the conditions would be too different for a meaningful comparison to be made. In another illustration a supervisor is interested in the rate of contingent praise provided by a teacher to individual students. On some days the supervisor observes the teacher working with a large group; on other days, with a small group. Unfortunately, because the rate of contingent praise would probably not be the same for both large and small group instruction, a meaningful comparison cannot be achieved. Standardized observation times require (1) an equal opportunity for the occurrence or nonoccurrence of the behavior during each observation session and (2) consistent conditions from one observation session to the next.

Appropriate Samples of Behavior: Representative or Conservative

Behavior is variable. Some behaviors have a greater likelihood of occurring at a particular time than others. Likewise, on some occasions a behavior will occur at high rates; at other times, at low rates. Consequently, **variability**, the degree to which a behavior changes over time, needs to be considered when selecting times for observations. Selection will differ according to the two primary purposes of data collection: to answer naturalistic questions concerning the variability of behavior and to establish an analysis of the effects of treatment or instruction.

Representative   Observational study of human behavior is often undertaken to provide answers to naturalistic questions. For example, Do elementary teachers talk less often to their Hispanic-speaking students than to other students in their rooms? What is the mean number of words read per minute by regular fourth graders? What is the frequency of conversational questions asked by female high school students? **Naturalistic observations** are usually used to provide normative information and, in turn, may become a standard for treatment or instructional goals and criteria. If a training program in conversational skills for adjudicated adolescent females is to be implemented, one measure of success might be based on the naturalistic studies of their nonadjudicated counterparts.

With naturalistic observations it is important to select observation times that are the most representative of the behavior to be observed. Thus, the most typical performance becomes the standard, rather than the best or worst case. White (1975) clearly required naturalistic observation in her study of the natural rates of teacher approval and disapproval in the classroom. To record the most representative samples of existing teacher approval and disapproval, White varied the time of day for observation so that both morning and afternoon classes were included. In addition, observations were made during each of the major instructional subjects but not during special events such as art, music, or gymnastics. Her data show that teacher approval rates dropped across grade levels. With the exception of Grades 1 and 2, rates of teacher verbal disapproval exceeded the rates of teacher approval.

Conservative   When an intervention is planned for a behavior, the most conservative times for observation should be selected. For instance, chronic rumination is a serious problem for some infants. It is defined as "bringing up food without nausea, retching, or disgust. The food is then ejected from the mouth or reswallowed" (Kanner, 1957, p. 484). Rumination may have a greater likelihood of occurring immediately after a meal rather than 3 or 4 hours later. Consequently, the time after meals should be selected for observation because it should provide the best information for evaluating the effects of the planned intervention to reduce the occurrence of rumination. Basically, if an intervention is planned to decrease a behavior, observations should be scheduled when the behavior is likely to be at its highest level. If the goal is to increase a behavior, observations should be scheduled when the behavior will be at its lowest level. A successful intervention will be more believable at these times.

ESTABLISHING THE DURATION OF OBSERVATION SESSIONS

Many beginning analysts have difficulty deciding the length of an observation session. An appropriate duration depends on environmental conditions and the frequency of the behaviors under observation. Nonetheless, some general guidelines for determining the duration of observation sessions may help.

When the observer is responsible for both instruction and data collection, short periods of time for observation and recording can be used. Often classroom teachers become disenchanted with data collection because they make their observation sessions too long. In fact, daily 1- or 2-minute sessions of observation and recording may be sufficient for many academic behaviors, such as reading, writing, and math (White & Haring, 1980). Sometimes, however, the rate of the behavior must determine the duration of the observation. High-rate behaviors can usually be scheduled for 1 to 3 minutes, whereas low-rate behaviors require longer observation times. For example, some severely retarded persons emit self-abusive behaviors at high rates (e.g., face slapping, head banging). Because these behaviors occur so frequently, an observation time of just a few minutes would be appropriate. However, other behaviors of theirs (e.g., verbalizations, eye contact, following directions) may require several hours of observation time.

Observation sessions can be conducted for extended durations when the procedures of measurement do not disturb other concurrent activities, such as instruction, and when an observer is responsible only for data collection. Since observer stress and boredom are common during extended observation sessions, we recommend that observers be given a short break following each 20 to 30 minutes of observation.

PLANNING SAMPLING PROCEDURES

Observers in applied settings are often responsible for collecting data on several subjects or behaviors. Various procedures for observation sampling can be implemented. It is important to select procedures that most accurately estimate the true parameters of the target behavior.

Issues with Time Sampling Observation Techniques

Applied behavior analysts concerned with collecting data on several subjects or behaviors frequently use a time sampling observation technique. *Time sampling* is a generic term for three different observation techniques discussed in chapter 4: whole-interval recording, partial-interval recording, and momentary time sampling.

Powell, Martindale, and Kulp (1975) compared data estimates generated by whole-interval recording, partial-interval recording, and momentary time sampling with data obtained from continuous duration recording (i.e., the true parameter). They found that whole-interval recording consistently underestimated the true parameter, partial-interval recording consistently overestimated the true parameter, and momentary time sampling over- and underestimated the true parameter when time intervals were greater than 2 minutes. With intervals less than 2 minutes, the data estimate from momentary time sampling more closely matched the true parameter. Other experiments (e.g., Simpson & Simpson, 1977; Powell, Martindale, Kulp, Martindale, & Bauman, 1977) support the results reported by Powell et al. (1975), namely, that momentary time sampling with short time intervals (i.e., less than 2 minutes) is superior to whole- or partial-interval recording for estimating the duration of behavior. Nonetheless, Test and Heward (1984) found that momentary time sampling with intervals of 60 seconds still over- and underestimated the true parameter. Also, Test and Heward found that both fixed and variable time intervals over- and underestimated the true parameter.

It seems clear that time sampling produces some artificial variability in data estimates, which must be considered carefully in the interpretation of results. It is recommended that (1) whole-interval recording be used when the goal is to produce a behavior increase since whole-interval may generate an underestimate of the true parameter; (2) partial-interval recording be used when the goal is to produce a behavior decrease since this technique may generate an overestimate of the true parameter; and (3) momentary time sampling be used with time intervals of less than 2 minutes. Test and Heward also recommend, since momentary time sampling is likely to both over- and underestimate the true parameter, that the number of sessions for data collection be greater than might be sufficient for other data collection techniques. The overestimates and underestimates of behavior might cancel each other out across sessions, but Test and Heward qualify this notion by stating that a built-in function to remove artifactual variability is not useful by itself and should be employed with a **calibration** procedure.

> In cases where momentary time sampling is to be used as the primary method of measurement, we recommend calibrating the procedure to determine its accuracy, relative to continuous duration recording. Calibration might include initially selecting a variety of intervals and comparing each with a continuous duration measure. Calibrations should also be made during each phase of the study. Occasionally an intervention may change the duration of behaviors from long to short or vice-versa. A standard momentary time sampling interval may not accurately reflect these changes, and calibrating procedures would help determine the sensitivity of the observation procedure to changes in the target behavior. Data from calibration checks should be included in research reports, providing the readers with a measure of confidence in the observational procedure. (p. 194)

Issues with Sampling Procedures

Thompson, Holmberg, and Baer (1974) demonstrated percentage of artifactual variability in data estimates associated with three different sampling procedures: contiguous, alternating, and sequential. In their study one individual observed four subjects in a preschool setting. A quarter of the observer's total time was assigned to each subject. The total time of each observation session was 64 minutes.

To sample behavior contiguously, the observer recorded the first subject during the first 16 minutes of the session, the second subject during the second 16 minutes, and so on until all four subjects had been observed.

In the alternating mode Subjects 1 and 2 were observed during the first half of the session and Subjects 3 and 4, during the last half. Each subject was observed in alternating 4-minute time periods. For example, Subject 1 was observed during the first 4 minutes, Sub-

ject 2 during the next four minutes, Subject 1 during the next 4 minutes, and so on until the 32 minutes had expired. The same procedure was then used for Subjects 3 and 4.

The sequential approach systematically rotated the four subjects through 4-minute observations. Subject 1 was observed during the first 4 minutes, Subject 2 during the second 4 minutes, Subject 3 during the third 4-minute interval, and Subject 4 during the fourth. This exact sequence was repeated four times to give the total of 64 minutes of observation.

To arrive at the percentage of artifactual variance in the data estimates associated with these three procedures, Thomson et al. continuously recorded each subject without break for the same 64-minute sessions. Observations from 13 to 22 days were used and the results compared. The data clearly showed that the sequential sampling procedure produced results that more closely resembled the data obtained through continuous recording than did the results of the contiguous or alternating procedures.

Different observation sampling procedures produce different results, which can influence decisions and interpretations based on analysis. Therefore, as Thompson et al. concluded, it is preferable to sample the occurrence of the target behavior briefly but repetitively during the entire observation session.

OBSERVATION CODES

Much of the behavioral research and data collection in applied settings has been based on observational recordings. Many observers use codes to record the presence or absence of several simultaneous behaviors. An **observation code** can be defined as a series of symbols or abbreviations used for recording the presence or absence of classes of behaviors or events (Tawney & Gast, 1984). Any symbol or abbreviation can be used in coding behaviors; for example, *T* for teacher, *V* for talking, *C* for child, + for praise, and so on. Coding has been used frequently in observational recording because (1) it can be a reliable system for concurrent data collection on multiple behaviors, (2) it can be a reliable system for data collection with large numbers of subjects, (3) it can show relationships between occurrences of behavior and environmental events, and (4) it can be used with many situations, populations, and behaviors (Bloom & Fisher, 1982).

Developing and Operationalizing Observation Codes

The first step in developing a code is to select and define the classes of behaviors or events to be recorded, following the procedures presented in chapter 3. Then abbreviations are assigned to the defined classes. The *Journal of Applied Behavior Analysis* contains a number of articles that can be reviewed by persons interested in acquiring skills in the actual development of codes (e.g., Bijou, Peterson, & Adut, 1968; Greenwood, Hops, Walker, Guild, Stokes, & Young, 1979; Horner, 1980; Hall, Lund, & Jackson, 1968; Marholin, Touchette, & Steward, 1979; Sanders & Glynn, 1981; Skrtic & Sepler, 1982; Strain, Shores, & Kerr, 1976; Strain & Timm, 1974; Whaler & Fox, 1980). The following abbreviations and definitions are typical of those found in observation codes:

PA (Physical Aggression): Any physical attack on another person is included in this category. Behaviors such as biting, kicking, and pushing are included. Activities such as wrestling as part of play are not included.

P (Productive Activity): An activity in this category is something the teacher has requested or assigned. Examples are working on a reading assignment, reading a library book, or listening to a tape-recorded story. Answering a question in reading group, although it is a productive behavior, is not included here. Instead, it is coded under the interaction category since the student is making a verbal comment.

M (Management): This category includes time devoted to class business and unrelated to instructional activity, such as taking attendance,

discussing the details of a field trip, or announcing a locker room cleanup. A nonexample of management is lecturing about appropriate behavior in the gymnasium, which is coded as organizational instruction.

After the classes of behavior or events have been selected and defined, the next step is to select a measurement procedure. Most codes use interval recording. However, any observational recording procedure—such as event, latency, duration, momentary time sampling, or a combination—can be used.

After a measurement procedure has been selected, the code developer reaches a critical but potentially creative step. A format or data sheet must be prepared for noting the occurrence or nonoccurrence of the behaviors or events. The variety of formats that can be developed is almost unlimited; the only criteria are ease of use and reliable scoring. The format should not require extended observer training or study before it can be used.

Figure 5.1 is a segment of a format for reporting the percentage of intervals spent in various categories during a band rehearsal. The following categories were selected and defined: song number (SN), between numbers (BN), positive playing (PP), negative playing (NP), positive behavior (PB), negative behavior (NB), directing (D), talking (TK), yelling (Y), poor start (PS), dynamics (DY), style (S), intonation (I), rhythm (R), and tone (T). The coding sheet is divided into three segments: group, section, and individual. The code is recorded under the group category when the whole group is the receiver of the director's attention. If the director is talking to just one section, the coding is recorded under the section category. If the director is talking to or instructing an individual, the code is recorded under the individual category. Each behavior emitted during the interval is circled under the appropriate category. For instance, if the director says the clarinets are playing too softly and the rest of the band is too loud, the DY (dynamics) is circled under the group and section category,

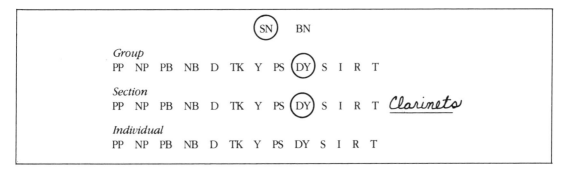

FIGURE 5.1 Sample segment from a format for recording percentage of intervals spent on various categories during band rehearsal. (From "Band Director's Observation Code" by L. D. McCue, 1981, unpublished manuscript, Ohio State University. Reprinted by permission.)

and the name of the section is written on the line provided at the end of the codes in the section category (McCue, 1981).

Figure 5.2 illustrates a format for recording school bus behaviors. The categories selected include appropriate bus behavior (AP), physical restraint (PR), fighting with peer (FP), physical inappropriate seat behavior (PS), cursing or yelling (CY), pestering the driver (PD), and vandalism or destructiveness (VD). With this format each minute of observation is divided into six 10-second intervals per subject. All applicable behavior codes are recorded in each interval. Hypothetical data for three 10-second intervals are presented in Figure 5.2. During the first 10 seconds of observing Subject 1, the student stood up and shouted to a peer, "Ha, ha, I've got your hat!" This was coded as PS (physical inappropriate seat behavior), FP (fighting with peer), and CY (cursing or yelling). During the next 10 seconds the subject sat in his seat but kicked the seat in front of him. This was recorded as PS. During the third 10-second interval the subject made a face at a peer and pointed his finger at him. This behavior was recorded as FP (Shipp, 1979).

Figure 5.3 illustrates a format designed to record most areas of behavior found within the interactions between a medical doctor and patient. It can be used in either an interview or physical examination setting. Categories

selected and defined are medical talk (MT), nonmedical talk (NT), informational talk (IT), interruption (IN), defensiveness (DF), compliance (CO), noncompliance (NC), normativeness (NO), embarrassment (EM), manipulation (MA), resistance (RT), overdramatization (OD), contact-medical (CM), contact-nonmedical (CN), attention (AT), and no response (NR). Observation alternates between doctor and patient in 6-second intervals. During observation of the doctor, the behavior emitted is recorded with a vertical line through the appropriate abbreviation. During observation of the patient, behavior emitted is recorded with a horizontal line through the appropriate abbreviation. Only one behavior is recorded in each interval. In our illustration the doctor walks into the office and says, "Good morning." This is recorded as NT (nonmedical talk). The patient answers, "Hello," and her response is recorded as NT. Next the doctor asks the patient why she is there, recorded as MT (medical talk). The patient explains the problem in detail (IT, informational talk), while the doctor listens (AT, attention) (Matulich, 1982).

A summary sheet needs to be developed for reporting the data collected on the recording form; the recordings need to be organized to facilitate communication. Usually a summary sheet reports a measurement (e.g., percentage of intervals scored) for each category under

Subject	Intervals																	
	1			2			3			4			5			6		
1	AP	PR	(FP)	AP	PR	FP	AP	PR	(FP)	AP	PR	FP	AP	PR	FP	AP	PR	FP
		VD			VD			VD			VD			VD			VD	
	(PS)	(CY)	PD	(PS)	CY	PD	PS	CY	PD	PS	CY	PD	PS	CY	PD	PS	CY	PD

FIGURE 5.2 Sample segment from a format recording school bus behavior. (From "A Code for Recording Bus Behavior" by B. Shipp, 1979, unpublished manuscript, Ohio State University. Reprinted by permission.)

observation. These data are then graphed. An example of a summary sheet is shown in Figure 5.4.

The final step in implementing the code is to write directions for using the code. The directions must be detailed, clear, and specific. A reader should be able to use the code correctly after reading the directions.

In sum, putting a code into operation requires that classes of behavior or events be selected and defined, a measurement procedure selected, a format developed for recording the selected classes of behavior, a summary procedure established for reporting data from the data sheet, and finally directions written for use of the code.

Revising the Code

After the code is developed and applied, revisions may be necessary as its operation is evaluated. Are the observations reliable? Is the code easy to use? Does the code provide information that is valuable in decision making and analysis?

Reliability of observations must be high, or data collected will not be believable. When low reliability is associated with coding, it usually results from inadequately defined classes of behavior or events or an attempt to record too many behaviors in a single observation interval. The most frequent revisions in a code are in the definitions.

Interval	Coding																
1	AT	CM	CN	CO	DF	EM	IN	IT	D̲	MA	MT	NC	NO	NR	N̶T̶	OD	RT
2	AT	CM	CN	CO	DF	EM	IN	IT	P̲	MA	MT	NC	NO	NR	N̶T̶	OD	RT
3	AT	CM	CN	CO	DF	EM	IN	IT	D̲	MA	M̶T̶	NC	NO	NR	NT	OD	RT
4	AT	CM	CN	CO	DF	EM	IN	I̶T̶	P̲	MA	MT	NC	NO	NR	NT	OD	RT
5	A̶T̶	CM	CN	CO	DF	EM	IN	IT	D̲	MA	MT	NC	NO	NR	NT	OD	RT
6	AT	CM	CN	CO	DF	EM	IN	I̶T̶	P̲	MA	MT	NC	NO	NR	NT	OD	RT

FIGURE 5.3 Sample segment from a format for recording interactions between doctor and patient. (From "Behavioral Code: Interactions Between Doctor and Patient" by M. Matulick, 1982, unpublished manuscript, Ohio State University. Reprinted by permission.)

Data Summary Sheet

Student __S. C.__   Observer __Bill Johns__

Date data collected __Feb. 2, 1987__   Condition __Preinstruction__

Total time observed __450 sec.__   Total number of intervals __45__

Total Intervals by Classes of Behaviors		Percentage of Intervals by Classes of Behaviors
Writing	6	13.3
Attending	18	40.0
Interacting with teacher positively	2	4.4
Interacting with peers positively	3	6.7
Interacting with teacher negatively	3	6.7
Interacting with peers negatively	4	8.9
Not attending	9	20.0

FIGURE 5.4   Example of a summary sheet for reporting data obtained from interval recording.

The construction of data sheets is associated with ease of use. Some data sheets are constructed in such a way that observers have difficulty recording their observations. The data sheet may be so busy that observers lose track of where they should be making notations. Figure 5.5 shows two sample formats for a data sheet. In the first the intervals appear undifferentiated. An observer needing to record 200 intervals with this data sheet would have extreme difficulty keeping track of the interval to be recorded. In the second sample horizontal lines have been added between intervals, and every other interval has been shaded. This differentiation helps an observer record in the appropriate place. Also, the clear division between appropriate behaviors and inappropriate behaviors makes recording smoother. The construction or revision of data sheets must be considered an important task.

Even if a code generates reliable observations and is easy to use, revisions may still be necessary. The code must produce information that is valuable in decision making; the data collected must reflect the areas under investigation. For example, in 1976 the authors developed a new code to be used in the supervision of student teachers. The code was reliable and easy to use, yet the data collected on student teacher behaviors were not functional. Supervisors could not use the data to evaluate student teacher performance because the data were so general that feedback to the student teacher was not meaningful. When data generated by a code are not useful, most often the problem lies with the classes of behavior or events selected for inclusion in the code (e.g., overlapping definitions or categories).

Observer Training

Coding systems require that observers identify specific classes of behaviors or events within a group of related classes of behaviors or events.

Observer _____ Date _____

Academic Activity _____

Behavior Codes

Appropriate Behaviors:		Inappropriate Behaviors:	
AP	Approval	DA	Disapproval
CO	Compliance	NC	Noncompliance
AT	Attending	NA	Not attending
OT	On-task	OT	Off-task
PL	Play	LO	Looking around
PI	Peer interaction	PI	Peer interaction

Intervals	Students	Behaviors											
1	Jim	AP	CO	AT	OT	PL	PI	DA	NC	NA	OT	LO	PI
2	John	AP	CO	AT	OT	PL	PI	DA	NC	NA	OT	LO	PI
3	Sue	AP	CO	AT	OT	PL	PI	DA	NC	NA	OT	LO	PI
4	Pat	AP	CO	AT	OT	PL	PI	DA	NC	NA	OT	LO	PI

- -

Intervals	Students	Appropriate Behaviors						Intervals	Inappropriate Behaviors					
1	Jim	AP	CO	AT	OT	PL	PI	1	DA	NC	NA	OT	LO	PI
2	John	AP	CO	AT	OT	PL	PI	2	DA	NC	NA	OT	LO	PI
3	Sue	AP	CO	AT	OT	PL	PI	3	DA	NC	NA	OT	LO	PI
4	Pat	AP	CO	AT	OT	PL	PI	4	DA	NC	NA	OT	LO	PI

FIGURE 5.5 Sample construction of a data sheet for coding behaviors with revised construction shown below dashed lines.

The occurrences of the specific behaviors are then transcribed onto a data sheet. The reliability of such a system is determined by the degree to which independent observers recording the same sequence of behaviors agree on the occurrence or nonoccurrence of the specific behaviors. Therefore, training observers to interpret the system in the same way is essential for the collection of usable data. Observers must learn a common identification of classes of behaviors or events to be recorded, a com-

mon notation system (symbols), and a common set of recording procedures.

During training, observers should have numerous practice sessions with the code before using it in a data collection situation. Hersen and Barlow (1976) recommend that observers continue training until they achieve a minimum of 80% agreement with each other. They note that the 80% agreement criterion is not absolute, however. It will be influenced by the method used for calculating the agreement score, the complexity of the code, and the number of categories and clients being recorded simultaneously.

Several methods are used to train observers, including sample vignettes, longer narrative descriptions of behavior, sequences from videotapes, actors role-playing a script, and actual practice sessions in the environment in which data are to be collected. The practice sessions are especially beneficial because they allow both observer and client to adapt to the novel situation. Each of the procedures listed can be used individually or collectively. The following sequence for observer training is recommended.

Step 1 Trainees should read and familiarize themselves with the coding system. For example, they should know the symbols, the definitions, the way in which observations will be transcribed onto the data sheets, and the use of tools required for obesrvtaion (e.g., stopwatches and other timing devices).

Step 2 Trainees should respond to short behavioral vignettes until they reach an established criterion.

Step 3 Trainees should respond to longer narrative descriptions of behavior until their accuracy of recording reaches an established criterion.

Step 4 Trainees should record from a videotape and/or from the acting out of precoded scripts by live actors.

Step 5 Trainees should receive practice in the actual environment in which data are to be collected. In this final step the trainee should be accompanied by an experienced observer, and both should simultaneously and independently record the behaviors observed. The session should be followed immediately by agreement checks. This training should continue until a preestablished criterion is reached.

INTEROBSERVER AGREEMENT

A major approach to measurement in applied behavior analysis is the use of human observers to record the occurrence or nonoccurrence of specific behaviors. This dependence on human observers has generated interest in procedures for determining and reporting the **reliability of observations** (Harris & Lahey, 1978; Kelly, 1977; Hartmann, 1977; Baer, 1977; Hopkins & Hermann, 1977; Yelton, Wildman, & Erickson, 1977; Kratochwill & Wetzel, 1977; Boykin & Nelson, 1981; Berkimer & Brown, 1979a, 1979b; Hawkins & Fabry, 1979; Kratochwill, 1979). The reliability of observations is usually assessed by comparing the judgments of two independent observers simultaneously measuring the target behavior, to see how closely they agree on the occurrence or nonoccurrence of the behavior. As Hawkins and Fabry (1979) state, the agreement measures help in answering the question, "Is that what I would have seen if I had been there?" (p. 545). These agreement scores are referred to as **interobserver agreement measures** or **interobserver reliability.** We will use the term *interobserver agreement* because the term *reliability* has many different uses in the literature (see Gay, 1981).

Applied behavior analysis has approached the assessment of interobserver agreement with a different view from that which is traditional in the behavioral sciences. Hawkins and Fabry (1979) identify three procedural differences. First, a common practice in the behavioral sciences is to assess observer agreement prior to the study of behavior but not during actual data collection. Hawkins and Fabry speculate that this practice evolved from experiences with standardized tests in which different persons applied the same test to the same subject. Applied behavior analysts, on the other hand, report interobserver agreement measures during the actual data collection. It is important to have interobserver agreement on the actual data from which conclusions will be drawn.

Second, traditional practice often includes reports of interobserver reliability as a single statistic (e.g., a coefficient). In contrast, applied behavior analysts are concerned with how often agreement measures were taken, when they were taken, and how consistent they were over time. Frequently, repeated measures of the independent observers are reported. At the very least the lowest, the highest, and a mean agreement score are reported.

Third, it is not customary in traditional practice to report the methodology used to assess interobserver agreement. Methodology would include the directions and training received by the observers, the method of maintaining the independence of the observers, past experience of the observers, and so on. "Behavior analysts have taken such matters much more seriously even though they often omit some methodological details of importance" (Hawkins & Fabry, 1979, p. 546).

Importance of Interobserver Agreement

Interobserver agreement measures are a necessary component of applied behavior analysis. These measures play a crucial role in the advancement of the science of behavior. Hawkins and Fabry (1979) identify four functions served by interobserver agreement measures.

First, we (especially behavior analysts) are concerned whether the behavior has been defined adequately, where the definitional aspect of measurement is replicable in (generalizable to) other scientists' laboratories. Second, we are concerned with the competency with which those definitions are employed to generate data, especially such factors as the training of observers, their conscientiousness, and their lack of bias. A third concern in any intervention study is whether we can believe the experimental effects show (or not shown). Finally, a fourth concern is whether we can believe the absolute level of the behavior, aside from any effects shown. (p. 547)

The first two concerns are directed toward issues of replication. Since all of science is dependent upon the replication of experimental effects, descriptions of behavior and the methodology of data collection must be specific enough to allow other investigators to apply identical procedures. These first two concerns are directed specifically toward agreement measures on the occurrence or nonoccurrence of the dependent variables (i.e., the behaviors under observation). The third and fourth concerns of Hawkins and Fabry are directed toward the believability of the reported data. When independent observers obtain high agreement regarding the occurrence or nonoccurrence of behavior(s), confidence in the study increases.

Procedural Reliability An additional concern is the collection of interobserver agreement measures on the occurrence or nonoccurrence of the independent variables, which indicate **procedural reliability** (Billingsley, White, & Munson, 1980; Salend, 1984a, 1984b). In other words, was the treatment plan followed as described? Applied behavior analysis requires that both the dependent variables (i.e., target behaviors) and the independent variables (i.e., treatment, intervention) be described completely and assessed reliably.

Interobserver agreement measures have been reported routinely on the dependent variables. However, only a few analysts have directed their attention to procedural reliability (e.g., Billingsley et al., 1980; Peterson, Homer, & Wonderlich, 1982).

A curious double standard has developed in operant technology whereby certain variables—routinely have operational definitions and some measure of observer reliability when the observed behavior is the target response or dependent variable—but no such rigor is applied to the same behaviors when they appear as antecedents or consequences to the target behavior, as independent variables. . . . Either such precautions as definitions and reliability of observation are necessary or they are not. The observational literature clearly suggests that they are. (Peterson et al., pp. 478–479)

Independent variables may be defined in specific, measurable terms, but the analyst may not have applied the treatment plan as described. Assurances must be given that data reflect what actually occurred rather than what was supposed to have occurred.

The major effect of including interobserver agreement measures on independent variables is to require greater specification in the description of the independent variable. In applied behavior analysis the primary deterrent to procedural replication is not the adequacy of behavioral definitions or the competence of observers, but the technological description of the procedure. Technological descriptions of independent variables must include sufficient specification to allow another investigator to apply the procedure as described (Baer, Wolf, & Risley, 1968).

Accuracy of Observation

Accuracy of observation is defined as the agreement between an observer's measurement and some predetermined standard (Hersen & Barlow, 1976). Interobserver agreement measures and accuracy of measurement are different indicators of the quality of data reported. Interobserver agreement measures (i.e., reliability of observations) indicate the believability of the measurement procedure. Accuracy statements indicate the validity of the data collected. High interobserver agreement (e.g., 90%) does not necessarily mean that observations were accurate. Observers may have high agreement between their measurements (i.e., reliable measurement), but the data may be inaccurate. Conversely, observers may have low agreement (i.e., unreliable measurement), but one of the observers may have accurate data.

For instance, two persons may independently score a student's spelling test and have high agreement on the words spelled correctly and incorrectly yet not be accurate. The spelling words would need to be checked against a standard such as a dictionary to determine the accuracy of scoring. If data are accompanied by an accuracy statement, interobserver agreement measures are not necessary. Interobserver agreement measures on the scoring of the spelling test would not add important information about the quality of the data if the scoring was demonstrated to be accurate.

Interobserver agreement measures have been used as the basis for judging the quality of data in applied behavior analysis because of the difficulty in producing a standard against which to measure an observer's accuracy. Accuracy standards for some permanent products such as spelling and math are evident, and the measurement can be calibrated to those standards during the course of an investigation. Calibration for the accuracy of measurement in most direct observational recordings in applied settings is not practical at this time. It is often possible, however, to calibrate the accuracy of observations during observer training. Some techniques include comparing an observer's measurements to machine measurements (i.e., a mechanical, electrical, or electronic device) or to a predetermined script. Another approach is to accept behavioral occurrences that are agreed upon by multiple observers. (For more information on calibration of observers, see Johnson & Pennypacker, 1980.)

ESTABLISHING INTEROBSERVER AGREEMENT

The most common convention for reporting interobserver agreement measures in applied behavior analysis is percentage of agreement between observers. A small number of studies have used correlation coefficients, typically one of the product moment correlations (Kelly, 1977). We will present procedures for establishing percentage of agreement but not correlation coefficients since most behavior analysts have chosen the percentage measure.

Measures of Permanent Products

The following formula is used to establish percentage of agreement among observers measuring permanent products: the number of agreements divided by the total of agreements and disagreements multiplied by 100 equals the percentage of agreement.

$$\frac{\text{agreements}}{\text{agreements} + \text{disagreements}} \times 100 =$$
$$\text{\% of agreement}$$

To illustrate, a teacher is analyzing the effects that a self-contracting program had on mathematics skills. The teacher and an independent observer grade a 25-problem worksheet and report three disagreements. To compute their percentage of agreement, the formula is applied: 22 (number of agreements) divided by 25 (22 agreements + 3 disagreements) multiplied by 100 equals 88%.

Even though agreement among observers measuring permanent products is usually high, there are some problems associated with the procedure. First, and perhaps most important, many cannot accept the logic of requiring interobserver agreement measures for permanent products. They readily agree that it is important for observational recording but find it absurd with permanent products, which are often discrete responses, easy to identify and record. Nonetheless, mistakes do occur in the scoring of permanent products.

Beginning analysts frequently experience problems in maintaining independence of observation while collecting agreement measures for permanent products. Independence of observations is usually violated when one observer is aware of how the other observer has scored the product. Independence of observation would be violated in the earlier illustration if the teacher gave a scored worksheet to the independent observer to grade. To maintain independence, the teacher could give the observer a photocopy of the unmarked worksheet to grade. One observer must be completely unaware of the measurement of the other.

Event Recording

To establish interobserver agreement in event recording, two observers independently but simultaneously record the occurrences of a behavior. Percentage of agreement is computed by dividing the smaller total by the larger total and multiplying by 100.

$$\frac{\text{smaller total}}{\text{larger total}} \times 100 = \text{\% agreement}$$

For example, a child care worker in a residential setting recorded that 9-year-old Billy used profane language 25 times during a 30-minute observation period. A second observer recorded 20 occurrences of the inappropriate verbal behavior during that same time period. The interobserver agreement for that session was 80% $\left(\frac{20}{25} \times 100\right)$.

Percentage agreement with event recording should be interpreted cautiously. Even though the child care worker and the second observer had close agreement on the total number of inappropriate verbal behaviors, the agreement measure cannot provide assurance that the two observers were recording the same behavior. It is possible that the child care worker recorded 16 occurrences during the first 15 minutes of the observation period and 9 occurrences during the last 15 minutes. This may have resulted in overrecording of the target behavior during the first 15 minutes and underrecording during the last 15 minutes. The second observer may have recorded only 4 occurrences in the first 15 minutes and 16 occurrences in the last 15 minutes. The resulting percentage, therefore, would have inflated their actual agreement.

One solution to this problem is to obtain agreement measures from smaller time periods. The 30-minute observation period in the illustration could be broken down into three 10-minute intervals. Percentage of agreement could then be calculated for each 10-minute interval, as shown in Table 5.1. The table suggests that the child care worker and the second observer may not have been observing the same event.

Latency and Duration Recording

Interobserver agreement is established for latency and duration recording in practically the same way that it is for event recording. Two observers independently and simultaneously record the total latency or duration of behavior. Percentage of agreement is computed by dividing the shorter latency or duration by the longer and multiplying by 100.

$$\frac{\text{shorter latency/duration}}{\text{longer latency/duration}} \times 100 = \text{\% agreement}$$

Observers experience three major problems in assessing interobserver agreement in latency and duration recording. First, observers may have difficulty identifying the beginning and end of a target behavior or the onset of a stimulus and the occurrence of a behavior. This problem may be a function of the definition of what is to be observed. A clear, specific definition can overcome this problem. Second, procedures need to be developed to ensure that both observers begin and end the observation period at the same time. One observer could signal the other at the precise moment the observation is to begin, or the timing devices could be started simultaneously prior to the observation session and outside the observation setting with the understanding that the observation would commence when a prearranged time was reached (e.g., the fifth minute). Even a few seconds' difference between observers can greatly distort the percentage of agreement.

Again, as with event recording, interobserver agreement measures for latency and duration recording should be interpreted cautiously. High agreement measures do not necessarily assure that the observers reported the same durations for the same occurrences of behavior.

Interval Recording and Momentary Time Sampling

Interobserver agreement in interval measures is calculated by the number of intervals in which observers agreed or disagreed on the occurrence or nonoccurrence of a behavior.

TABLE 5.1. Obtaining interobserver agreement measures for event recording of smaller time intervals.

Time	Tally of child care worker	Tally of second observer	% Agreement
1:00–1:10	I I I I I I I I I	I	$\frac{1}{9} \times 100 = 11\%$
1:10–1:20	I I I I I I I I I	I I I I I I I I I I I I I	$\frac{9}{13} \times 100 = 69\%$
1:20–1:30	I I I I I I I	I I I I I I	$\frac{6}{7} \times 100 = 86\%$

Each interval in which both observers scored the occurrence of the behavior or the non-occurrence of the behavior is counted as an agreement. Interobserver agreement is computed by dividing the number of agreement intervals by the total number of agreement intervals plus disagreement intervals and multiplying by 100.

$$\frac{\text{agreement intervals}}{\text{agreement} + \text{disagreement intervals}} \times 100$$
$$= \% \text{ agreement}$$

An example follows, showing interobserver agreement of 70%. This record shows that the observers were in agreement for Intervals 2, 3, 4, 5, 7, 9, and 10. Disagreements were scored in Intervals 1, 6, and 8. Thus, $\frac{7}{10} = 70\%$ agreement.

This basic method for calculating interobserver agreement is called the **interval-by-interval (I-I) method** (Hawkins & Dotson, 1975): it uses all intervals in calculating interobserver agreement. Since all intervals are used, the frequency/duration of the behavior greatly influences the percentage of agreement measure. As a control for the influence of the frequency of behavior on the percentage of agreement, Hawkins and Dotson recommend using other calculation methods in addition to the I-I score. Specifically, they suggest using

the scored interval (i.e., occurrence agreement) and the unscored interval (i.e., nonoccurrence agreement). Both the scored- and the unscored-interval methods compute agreement with the same formula: agreement intervals (either scored or unscored) divided by agreement plus disagreement intervals (either scored or unscored) multiplied by 100 equals agreement percentage.

Scored Interval In the **scored-interval (S-I) method** of establishing interobserver agreement, all intervals in which both observers record the nonoccurrence of the behavior are ignored in calculating the agreement score. For example, in the ten 10-second intervals shown earlier, Intervals 4, 7, and 10 would be ignored. Agreement in scored intervals included Intervals 2, 3, 5, and 9; disagreements occurred in Intervals 1, 6, and 8. Therefore, the S-I agreement measure is 57% (4 agreements divided by the sum of 4 agreements plus 3 disagreements × 100 equals 57%). The S-I method is a stringent test of agreement. It usually produces lower agreement scores than are produced by the I-I method. However, when used with high-rate behaviors, S-I calculations produce higher agreement scores. S-I interobserver agreement is recommended for use with low-rate behaviors so that agreement measures are not overestimated.

Unscored Interval In the **unscored-interval (U-I) method** of establishing interobserver agreement, all intervals in which both observers record the occurrence of the behavior are ignored in calculating the agreement scores. An agreement is counted when both observers record the nonoccurrence of the behavior. A disagreement is counted when one observer records the occurrence of the behavior, and the other records its nonoccurrence. Again with the previous illustration, only Intervals 1, 4, 6, 7, 8, and 10 would be considered. Agreement in unscored intervals included Intervals 4, 7, and 10; disagreement occurred in Intervals 1, 6, and 8. Interobserver agreement

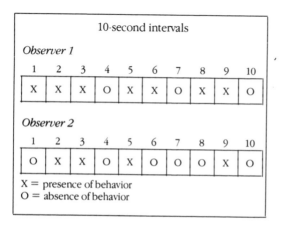

10-second intervals

Observer 1

1	2	3	4	5	6	7	8	9	10
X	X	X	O	X	X	O	X	X	O

Observer 2

1	2	3	4	5	6	7	8	9	10
O	X	X	O	X	O	O	O	X	O

X = presence of behavior
O = absence of behavior

Sample record for computing interobserver agreement.

in this example is 50% (3 divided by the sum of 3 plus 3 $\times$ 100 equals 50%). As with the S-I method, the U-I method is a stringent test of observer agreement and usually produces lower agreement scores than are generated with I-I. An exception is low-rate behavior. U-I agreement is often higher with low-rate behaviors and is consequently recommended for use with high-rate behaviors to avoid an overestimation of the percentage of agreement.

Another method for providing an index of interobserver agreement is to report the mean of the S-I and U-I scores. For instance, the mean of the S-I and U-I scores in our example is 53.5% (57% + 50% divided by 2). With S-I and U-I scores in combination, overestimation or underestimation of agreement scores as a result of rate or duration of behavior should be eliminated or greatly reduced.

In the examples of agreement scores presented here, measures were similar with the exception of the I-I score. This is not always the case. Frequently, these methods of calculation produce wide variance in agreement scores. For this reason it is recommended that each of the agreement scores in interval measures be presented so that the reader can make his own judgment as to the believability of the data.

CONSIDERATIONS IN USING INTEROBSERVER AGREEMENT

There are a number of considerations to be addressed with interobserver agreement measures in applied settings.

How often should interobserver agreement measures be obtained? The frequency of interobserver agreement measures is a compromise between an ideal and a minimum standard. Ideally, these measures should be reported for all recorded responses in each session. Minimally, these measures should be obtained once per condition. For example, with a reversal design (see chapter 8) interobserver

agreement is assessed once during baseline (A¹), intervention (B¹), second baseline (A²), and second intervention (B²). The ideal is difficult to reach because of the availability of observers and the time involved in computing the agreement scores. Most analysts select a procedure that falls between the ideal and the minimum. For instance, they may measure interobserver agreement every third observation session, or once per week. Interobserver agreement can be reported for a preestablished percentage of the sessions, perhaps 20% of the observation sessions. In general, more frequent assessment of interobserver agreement is needed with observational recording than with permanent products.

For what variables should interobserver agreement be reported? Agreement data should parallel the results on dependent variables (i.e., target behaviors). For example, if results are reported for each behavior by each subject, then agreement data should be reported for each behavior by each subject. With interval data interobserver agreement should be reported overall (I-I) and for occurrences (S-I) and nonoccurrences (U-I). With permanent product data interobserver agreement should be reported overall and for correct (occurrence) and incorrect (nonoccurrence) responses. For example, in the measurement of handwriting, Helwig, Johns, Norman, and Cooper (1976) reported an overall agreement measure for all letter strokes. Also, they presented agreement measures on the letter strokes that were scored as meeting criteria (correct responses) and on the letter strokes that were scored as not meeting criteria (incorrect responses).

What is an adequate interobserver agreement measure? A minimum criterion for the acceptability of interobserver agreement is not established at this time (Johnson & Bolstad, 1973). However, the usual convention is to expect independent observers to achieve an average of at least 80% agreement (e.g., Hersen & Barlow, 1976). The 80% criterion is arbitrary and must be interpreted in light of the complexity and quantity of observations. For example, an average interobserver agreement score of 85% for the measurement of permanent products might leave the data suspect. Normally, interobserver agreement measures for permanent products are in the high 90% range. However, an average agreement score of 75% might be considered adequate for data generated by the simultaneous observational measurement of several clients and several different behaviors. The closer the agreement measures are to 100%, the more adequate the interobserver agreement scores become.

How do I communicate interobserver agreement scores to others? There are a number of procedures for reporting interobserver agreement scores. Interobserver agreement can be reported in graphic form, in a table, or as a range of agreement plus the mean or median agreement of all sessions.

One way to report agreement of recording in graphic form is to place the measurement of the second observer on the graph along with the measurement of the primary observer. With this procedure a percentage agreement score is not calculated. In Figure 5.6 the scores of the second observer are reported with a different symbol from that of the primary observer.

Reporting both observers' data in graphic form is a simple procedure for assessing how well the variables under investigation have been defined and whether one observer consistently overestimates or underestimates the measurement. An absence of bias is usually indicated by a random pattern of over- and underestimation. Hawkins and Fabry (1979) comment on a disadvantage of reporting agreement in graphic form: "Because it is graphical rather than numerical, it would be awkward for a secondary source to describe, as when a reviewer of other scientists' research attempts to relate different studies in which different levels or reliability were obtained" (p. 551).[1]

Table 5.2 provides an example of reporting interobserver agreement measures in table form. These data were computed from the measurement of handwriting. The table includes agreement by experimental condition (e.g., Baseline 1, Baseline 2), the number of times interobserver agreement was assessed per condition (i.e., number of samples scored), and the highest and lowest score per condition plus the mean for the listed variables.

---

[1]Individuals interested in the use of graphical aids in reporting interobserver agreement should consult Birkimer and Brown (1979a, 1979b), Hawkins and Fabry (1979), Kratochwill (1979), Hopkins (1979), and Yelton (1979).

FIGURE 5.6 Illustration of measurements of primary and secondary observers presented in graphic form.

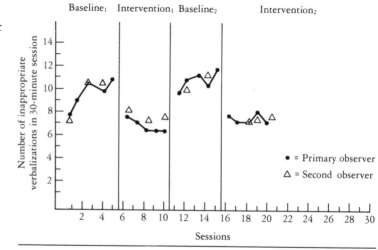

TABLE 5.2. Illustration of reporting interobserver agreement measures in table form.

	Baseline 1 Manuscript (All students)	Baseline 1 Cursive (All students)	Training 1 Manuscript (Students 1, 2, & 3)	Handwriting Conditions			Training 3 Manuscript (Students 8, 9, & 10)	Baseline 4 Cursive (All students)
				Baseline 2 Cursive (All students)	Training 2 Manuscript (Students 4, 5, 6, & 7)	Baseline 3 Cursive (All students)		
Number of samples scored	36	4	6	10	8	10	3	10
Correct stroke agreement								
Mean	97%	90%	99%	92%	98%	93%	100%	94%
Range	82%–100%	75%–100%	95%–100%	75%–100%	87%–100%	75%–100%	100%–100%	86%–100%
Incorrect stroke agreement								
Mean	94%	95%	92%	95%	96%	98%	33%	90%
Range	50%–100%	83%–100%	0%–100%	86%–100%	59%–100%	83%–100%	0%–100%	67%–100%
Overall stroke agreement								
Mean	96%	94%	98%	95%	98%	96%	98%	93%
Range	85%–100%	84%–100%	95%–100%	80%–100%	90%–100%	80%–100%	95%–100%	80%–100%

SOURCE: From "Effects of Training for Manuscript Handwriting on Generalization to Cursive Handwriting" by Esther Kau-To Leung, Pat V. Treblas, John O. Cooper, and Jennifer Trap Porter, p. 316, in *Behavioural Psychotherapy, 10*, 1982, pp. 311–323. Copyright by the British Association for Behavioural Psychotherapy.

The most frequently used approach is to report the lowest and highest agreement scores plus the mean overall agreement in narrative format. For example, agreement measures ranged from 49 to 91% with an overall agreement mean of 84%. However, if a narrative format or a table is used to report interobserver agreement measures, it is important to note when and how often agreement measures were taken. With a graph a common procedure that accomplishes this objective is circling the data point when interobserver agreement is measured. Figure 5.7 shows this example.

SOURCES OF INFLUENCE ON THE AGREEMENT AND ACCURACY OF MEASUREMENT

Human observers are the most frequent source of data collection in applied behavior analysis. A number of environmental conditions can have an impact on observers and influence how well data are collected. Addressing this issue, Kazdin (1977a) identifies reactivity, observer drift, complexity of the measurement system, and observer expectancies and feedback as sources of artifact and bias. In addition, Kazdin makes specific recommendations for eliminating or minimizing the influence of these factors when human observers are employed.

Reactivity

Reactivity in this sense refers to differences in agreement that result from observers' being aware that their observations will be checked. Numerous investigations have demonstrated that mere awareness of a second observer influences observations (e.g., Reid, 1970; Kent, Kanowitz, O'Leary, & Cheiken, 1977). Observers usually sense that their observations will be checked when another observer enters the area or when environmental cues indicate that primary and secondary observers are recording the behaviors of the same client. Reactivity often results in higher interobserver agreement scores and accuracy of observations.

To minimize the chance of reactivity, agreement measures can be unobtrusive or covert. Observers can be informed that all of their observations will be checked. When possible, one-way mirrors can be used for collecting interobserver agreement measures. A further solution is to audio- and/or videotape all sessions and check interobserver agreement only on selected sections of the tape. With this procedure the primary observer never needs to have contact with the secondary observer.

Observer Drift

Observer training seeks to ensure that observers apply a standard definition of behavior and record behavior with a high degree of accuracy. During training, observers are consistently monitored and given feedback concerning their accuracy in applying the definition. Observers frequently receive less feedback and instruction during actual data collection. Research has demonstrated that observers may drift from the standard definition of behavior following training. **Observer drift** occurs when observers change the way they employ the definition of behavior over the course of an investigation. Observer drift does not necessarily result in low interobserver agreement measures. If primary and secondary observers work closely together and communicate, they can develop similar drifts in applying the definition of behavior.

Observer drift can be minimized by providing observer training throughout the investigation. Ongoing training can occur at regular, prescheduled intervals (e.g., every Friday morning) or randomly. Another approach to observer drift is to employ an accuracy criterion, in addition to interobserver agreement measures, during the investigation. Still another

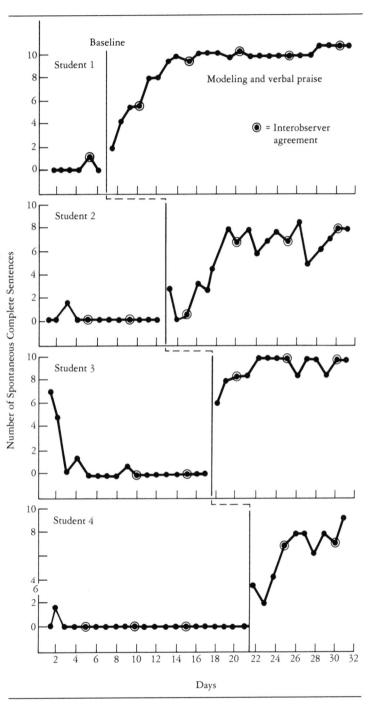

FIGURE 5.7 Example of a graph with data points circled to show when interobserver agreement measures were taken.

possibility is to rotate several observers in assessing interobserver agreement. Finally, observer drift lessens when all sessions are videotaped and interobserver agreement measures are taken from the tapes in random order.

Complexity of the Measurement System

Complexity of measurement is influenced by the number of individuals observed, the number of behaviors recorded, the duration of observations, and the size of the time intervals in interval recording. Therefore, observing several individuals might be more complex than observing fewer individuals: recording several behaviors might be more complex than recording fewer behaviors; and a 5-second interval recording might be more complex than a 10-second interval recording.

Specific recommendations concerning complexity depend upon the specific nature of the study. However, modifications that can be considered are decreasing the number of simultaneously observed individuals or behaviors, decreasing the length of the observation sessions, and increasing the size of the interval.

Observer Expectations and Feedback

Observer expectations concerning an individual's behavior can influence observation. For example, if observers expect posted classroom rules to decrease inappropriate student behaviors, the observers are more likely to observe a decrease in inappropriate behavior. However, it is unlikely that observer expectations alone will influence observations unless they are combined with experimenter feedback. If the observers have expectations but are not given feedback about how the study is progressing, what the intervention is, what phase the investigation is in, and how the individuals are responding, influence on observations will be controlled or minimized.

We recommend using new observers for each phase of analysis. In this way observer expectations are minimized because observers are unaware of what conditions preceded their observations or what conditions will follow. Feedback to observers should be restricted to observer agreement and accuracy of observations.

SUMMARY

Scheduling Continuous and Sample Observations

1 Continuous recording of behavior means that the measurement technique is operative for all possible occurrences of the behavior.
2 A sampling procedure records only a portion of the occurrences of behavior.
3 Ideally, all occurrences of the behavior of interest should be recorded.

Selecting Times for Observation

4 Standardized observation schedules require an equal opportunity for the occurrence or nonoccurrence of the behavior during each observation session and consistent environmental conditions from one observation session to the next.
5 When an intervention is planned for the behavior, the most conservative time for observation should be selected.
6 With naturalistic observations, when no intervention is planned, it is important to select times for observation when the most representative occurrences of the behavior are likely to be present.

Establishing Duration of Observation Sessions

7 Short periods of time for observation and recording can be used when the observer is

responsible for both instruction and data collection.

8 When observers do not set the occasion for the occurrence of the target behavior, the rate of the behavior will determine the duration of the observation time.

Planning Sampling Procedures

9 It is preferable to sample the occurrence of the target behavior briefly but repetitively during the observation session rather than scheduling observation samples in an uninterrupted sequence like that of the continuous or alternating sampling procedures.

Observation Codes

10 The development of a code requires that classes of behavior or events be selected and defined, a measurement procedure selected, a format for recording behaviors developed, a summary procedure established for reporting data from the data sheet, and directions for use written.

11 After the code is developed and applied, revisions may be necessary if the code does not generate reliable observations, is not easy to use, or produces information that is not valuable in decision making.

12 Skills in the actual development of codes can best be acquired by becoming familiar with and using as many existing codes as possible.

13 It is recommended that observers develop codes for specific purposes, outcomes, and situations rather than selecting an existing code for data collection.

14 Methods used in training observers include simple vignettes, longer narrative descriptions of behavior, sequences from videotapes, actors role-playing a script, and actual practice sessions in the environment in which data are to be collected.

Interobserver Agreement

15 The reliability of observations is usually assessed by requiring that at least two observers independently and simultaneously measure the target behavior. The judgments of the two observers are then compared to see how closely they agree on the occurrence or nonoccurrence of the behavior.

16 The most common convention used for reporting interobserver agreement measures in applied behavior analysis is percentage of agreement between observers.

17 Beginning analysts frequently experience problems in maintaining the independence of observers while collecting agreement measures.

18 Ideally, interobserver agreement measures should be reported for all recorded responses of each session. Minimally acceptable is measuring agreement once per condition during analysis.

19 Agreement measures should be presented for each behavior recorded, discussed, and interpreted.

20 The closer the agreement measures are to 100%, the more adequate the interobserver agreement scores.

21 Interobserver agreement can be reported in graphic form, in a table, or as a range of agreement plus the mean agreement of all sessions.

22 Accuracy is defined as the agreement between an observer's measurement and some predetermined standard.

23 Observers may be reliable in their measurement but inaccurate, or they may have accurate but unreliable measurement.

24 Techniques for establishing standards for accuracy of observations include comparing an observer's measurements to machine measurements of the same behavior, to a predetermined script, and to a consensus of multiple observers.

Sources of Influence on the Agreement and Accuracy of Measurement

25 Reactivity, observer drift, complexity of the measurement system, and observer expectations and feedback may be sources of artifact and bias in the measurement of behavior.

PART
THREE

Evaluation and Analysis
of Behavior Change

In Part II we described the criteria for selecting and defining target behaviors and the procedures for observing and recording behavior. But what does the behavior analyst do with the data thus collected? How are the repeated measures of behavior manipulated and interpreted by the behavior analyst to yield the most meaningful information? The next five chapters respond to these questions.

In chapter 6 we explain the basic components of graphic data displays and introduce strategies for objective interpretation of graphic data. An introduction to the experimental investigation of behavior is the topic of chapter 7. The necessary components of such an investigation are explained, as well as the strategies for manipulating and arranging those components to reveal meaningful behavior-environment relations. In chapters 8 and 9 we describe the experimental methods most commonly used in applied behavior analysis to discover functional relations between behavior and its controlling variables. In chapter 10 we cover a wide range of topics necessary for a more complete understanding of behavioral research.

6

Production and Interpretation of Graphic Data Displays

KEY TERMS

Experimental control

Data

Graph

Line graph

Dependent variable

Independent variable

Horizontal axis

X-axis

Vertical axis

Y-axis

Origin

Equal-interval vertical axis

Phase change line

Condition change line

Phase/condition label

Data point

Data path

Figure legend

Bar graph

Cumulative record

Cumulative recorder

Overall response rate

Local response rate

Semilogarithmic chart

Standard Behavior Chart

Hatch/tick mark

Scale break

Visual analysis

Variability

Level

Mean level line

Median level line

Trend

Trend line

Line of progress

Split-middle line of progress

This chapter was written by William L. Heward.

Applied behavior analysis is characterized by the search for and demonstration of experimental control over socially important behavior. **Experimental control** is achieved when a predictable change in an individual's behavior can be reliably and repeatedly produced by the systematic manipulation of some aspect of the person's environment. In order to objectively document and quantify behavior change, direct and repeated measurement of behavior is conducted. The product of these carefully planned and executed observations of behavior, called **data,** is the medium with which the behavior analyst works. In everyday usage the word *data* refers to a wide variety of often-imprecise and subjective information offered as facts. In scientific usage the word *data* means "the quantitative results of deliberate, planned, and usually controlled observation" (Johnston & Pennypacker, 1980, p. 327).[1]

Because behavior change is a dynamic, ongoing process, the behavior analyst must maintain direct and continuous contact with the behavior under investigation. The data produced throughout a scientific study of behavior are the means for that contact; they form the basis on which every important decision is made—to continue with the present procedure, to try something new, or to reinstitute a previous condition. But making valid and reliable decisions from the actual raw data—a series of numbers—is extremely difficult, if not impossible. Only the most obvious changes in performance or no change at all is readily discernible by inspecting a long row of numbers. Important features of behavior change can easily be overlooked.

Three sets of data follow. The first set was collected in successive observations made under two different conditions, A and B.

Condition A	Condition B
120, 125, 115, 130,	114, 110, 115, 121,
126, 130, 123, 120,	110, 116, 107, 120,
120, 127	115, 112

The second set of data is the result of measuring a behavior over consecutive trials.

80, 82, 78, 85, 80, 90, 85, 85, 90, 92

And the third data set was taken on successive school days.

65, 72, 63, 60, 55, 68, 71, 65, 65, 62, 70, 75, 79, 63, 60

What do these numbers tell you? What conclusions can be drawn from each set of data? How long did it take you to reach your conclusions, and how sure of them are you? What if the data sets contained many more measures to interpret? Would other persons be likely to reach the same conclusions by examining each set of data? How could these data be directly and effectively communicated to others?

When presented in a format that displays visually the relationships among a series of measurements, the meaningful features of a set of behavioral data are more immediately apparent. **Graphs,** relatively simple visual formats for displaying data, are the major tool for organizing, storing, interpreting, and communicating the results of applied behavior analysis. The same three sets of hypothetical data are graphically displayed in Figure 6.1. The top graph shows a lower level of responding during Condition B than was measured in Condition A. In the middle graph an upward trend in the response measure over time is evident. The bottom graph reveals a cyclical pattern of responding, characterized by an increasing trend during the first part of each week and a decreasing trend toward the end of each week. The graphs in Figure 6.1 illustrate the fundamental properties of behavior change over time—level, trend, and (cyclical) variability—which will be discussed in detail later

---

[1]Although often used as a singular construction ("This data *is* interesting"), the word *data* is a plural form of Latin origin and is correctly used with plural verbs ("These data *are* new"). *Datum* is the singular form.

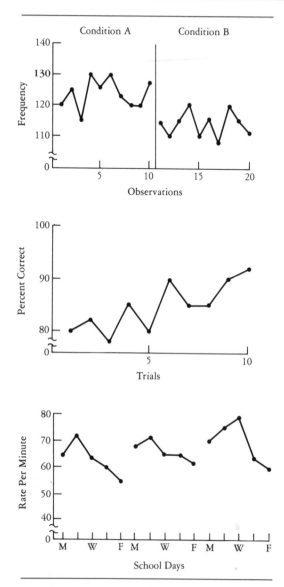

FIGURE 6.1 Graphic displays of three sets of hypothetical data illustrating change in level of responding across conditions (top), trend (middle), and cyclical variability (bottom).

in the chapter. Graphic display of behavioral data has proven the most effective means of detecting, analyzing, and communicating these aspects of behavior change.

BENEFITS OF GRAPHIC DISPLAY OF BEHAVIORAL DATA

Numerous authors have discussed the benefits of using graphs as the primary vehicle for the interpretation and communication of behavioral investigations (Baer, 1977; Johnston & Pennypacker, 1980; Michael, 1974; Parsonson & Baer, 1978; Sidman, 1960; Tawney & Gast, 1984). The major benefits of graphic display and visual analysis of behavioral data are summarized here. First, when each measure of behavior is plotted on a graph immediately after the observational period, the investigator has ongoing access to a complete record of the subject's behavior. Instead of waiting until the investigation or teaching program is complete, behavior change is evaluated continuously, allowing treatment and experimental decisions to be responsive to the subject's performance.

Second, direct and continuous contact with the data enables the researcher to explore interesting variations in behavior as they occur. Some of the most important discoveries about behavior have been made because scientists followed the leads suggested by their data instead of a rigid experimental plan (Sidman, 1960; Skinner, 1956).

Third, like statistical analysis of behavior change, graphs are judgmental aids, devices used to help the experimenter interpret the results of a study (Michael, 1974). In contrast to the statistical tests of inference used in group comparison research, however, visual analysis of graphed data takes little time, requires no special equipment, is relatively easy to learn, imposes no predetermined or arbitrary level for evaluating the significance of behavior change, and does not require the data to conform to certain mathematical properties or statistical assumptions in order to be analyzed.

Fourth, visual analysis is a conservative method of determining the significance of behavior change. A behavior change found to be significant according to the requirements of a test of statistical probability may not be very impressive when the data are plotted graphically and are visually inspected. As a result of visual presentation, variables that produce only weak or unstable effects are not likely to be reported as important findings in applied behavior analysis. Rather, weak or unstable effects are likely to lead to further experimentation in an effort to discover controlling variables that demonstrate the ability to produce meaningful behavior change in a reliable, sustained manner. This screening out of weak variables in favor of robust interventions has enabled applied behavior analysts to develop a useful technology of behavior change (Baer, 1977).[2]

Fifth, the graphic display of data allows and encourages independent judgments and interpretations of the meaning and significance of behavior change. Instead of having to rely on conclusions based on statistical manipulation of the data or on an author's interpretations, the reader of a published report of applied behavior analysis can form her own conclusions because the graph(s) provide direct access to the original data.

Finally, in addition to their primary purpose of displaying the relationship between the independent and dependent variables, graphs can be an effective source of feedback for the person whose behavior is represented on the graph. Graphing one's own performance has also been demonstrated to be an effective intervention for many academic and behavior therapy objectives (Van Houten, 1980).

Parsonson and Baer (1978) have provided one of the best summaries of the purpose of a behavioral graph.

> In essence, the function of the graph is to communicate, in a readily assimilable and attractive manner, descriptions and summaries of data that

enable a rapid and accurate analysis of the facts. (p. 134)

LINE GRAPHS

The simple **line graph,** or frequency polygon, is the most commonly used graphic format for the display of data in applied behavior analysis. The line graph is based on a Cartesian plane, a two-dimensional area formed by the intersection of two perpendicular lines. Any point within the plane represents a specific relationship between the two dimensions described by the intersecting lines. In applied behavior analysis, graphs show the level and change in some quantifiable dimension of the target behavior (**dependent variable**) in relation to a specified point in time and/or environmental condition (**independent variable**).

Parts of a Simple Line Graph

Although graphs vary widely in their construction and final appearance, all share certain elements. The basic parts of a simple line graph described here can be found in Figure 6.2, which displays the data from a study investigating the effects of organized games on the aggressive behaviors of elementary school children on the playground (Murphy, Hutchison, & Bailey, 1983).

1. *Horizontal Axis* The **horizontal axis,** also called the **X-axis,** is a straight, horizontal line that represents the passage of time and the presence, absence, and/or value of the independent variable. A defining characteristic of behavior analysis is the repeated measurement of behavior across time. Time is also the unavoidable dimension in which all manipulations of the independent variable occur. The horizontal axis is marked in equal intervals, each representing an equal passage of time. In Figure 6.2 each interval on the horizontal axis represents successive days on which playground aggression was measured.

---

[2]A comparison of the visual analysis of graphed data and inferences based on statistical tests of significance is presented in chapter 10.

FIGURE 6.2 The major parts of a simple line graph: (1) horizontal axis, (2) vertical axis, (3) phase/condition change lines, (4) phase/condition labels, (5) data points, (6) data path, and (7) figure legend. (From "Behavioral School Psychology Goes Outdoors: The Effect of Organized Games on Playground Aggression" by H. A. Murphy, N. M. Hutchison, and J. S. Bailey, 1983, *Journal of Applied Behavior Analysis, 16,* p. 33. Copyright 1983 by the Society for the Experimental Analysis of Behavior, Inc. Reprinted by permission.)

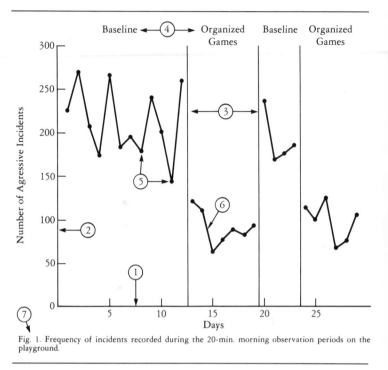

Fig. 1. Frequency of incidents recorded during the 20-min. morning observation periods on the playground.

2. Vertical Axis The **vertical axis,** also called the **Y-axis,** is a vertical line drawn upward from the left-hand end of the horizontal axis. The terms *abcissa* and *ordinate* are commonly used in the social sciences for the horizontal and vertical axes. However, Johnston and Pennypacker (1980) point out that in proper mathematical usage the terms *abcissa* and *ordinate* refer to the values of the first and second elements of a two-dimensional relation. "Thus, the proper terms for describing the perpendicular dimensions of a space are its *axes, horizontal* and *vertical,* and the terms abcissa and ordinate refer to values located thereon" (Johnston & Pennypacker, 1980, p. 338).

The vertical axis represents values of the dependent variable, which in studies of behavior is always some quantifiable dimension of behavior. The intersection of the two axes is called the **origin** and usually, though not necessarily, represents the zero value of the dependent variable. The most common practice is to mark off the vertical axis in an equal-interval scale. As one moves upward from the origin on an **equal-interval vertical axis,** each successive point represents greater value of the dependent variable in an arithmetic or additive function so that equal distances on the axis represent equal amounts of behavior. In Figure 6.2 the vertical axis is scaled to show the number of aggressive incidents by children on the playground.

3. Phase/Condition Change Lines Vertical lines are drawn upward from the horizontal axis at those points in time when changes in the independent variable are executed. **Phase change lines** indicate major changes in the independent variable. In Figure 6.2 phase change lines are drawn to coincide with the introduction or withdrawal of organized games. Sometimes only one component, or value, of the independent variable is changed, while the basic variable or condition remains in effect. When these more minor experimental manipulations are made, they are indicated by **condition change lines,** dashed vertical lines drawn upward at the appropriate points along the horizontal axis. In this way condition changes can be easily distinguished from major phase changes, which are shown by solid lines (see Figure 6.5).

4. *Phase/Condition Labels* Phase or **condition labels,** in the form of single words or brief descriptive phrases, are printed along the top of the graph and parallel to the horizontal axis. These labels identify the experimental conditions (i.e., the presence, absence, or some value of the independent variable) in effect during each phase or condition of the study.

5. *Data Points* Each **data point** on a graph represents two facts: (1) the quantifiable amount of the target behavior recorded during a given measurement interval and (2) the time when and experimental conditions under which that particular measurement was conducted. Using two data points from Figure 6.2 as examples, we can see that on Day 12, the last day of the first baseline condition, approximately 260 aggressive incidents were observed; and on Day 13, the first day of organized games, approximately 120 incidents were recorded.

6. *Data Path* A **data path** is created by connecting successive data points within a given phase or condition with a straight line. The data path, sometimes referred to as a response curve, represents the relationship between the independent and dependent variables and is the primary focus of attention in the interpretation and analysis of graphed data. Because behavior is rarely observed and recorded continuously in applied behavior analysis, the data path represents only an estimate of the actual course taken by the behavior across the time encompassed by the study (Meyers, 1970). The more measurements and resultant data points per unit of time (given an accurate observation and recording system), the more confidence one can place in the story told by the data path.

7. *Figure Legend* The **figure legend** is a concise statement that, in combination with the axis and phase/condition labels, provides the reader with sufficient information to identify the independent and dependent variables. The figure legend should also contain an explanation of any observed but unplanned events that may have affected the dependent variable at specific times of the study (see Figure 6.3) and should point out any potentially misleading or confusing features of the graph.

FIGURE 6.3 Graph using multiple data paths to show effects of independent variable on two dimensions of target behavior. (From "An Analysis and Reduction of Disruptive Behavior on School Buses" by B. F. Greene, J. S. Bailey, and F. Barber, 1981, *Journal of Applied Behavior Analysis, 14,* p. 188. Copyright 1981 by the Society for the Experimental Analysis of Behavior, Inc. Reprinted by permission.)

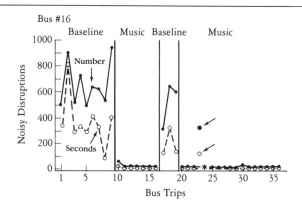

Fig. 5. Frequency and duration (in sec) of noise outbursts above threshold (90 dB SPL). Arrow indicates a trip when students on this bus were stopped at an intersection and a second bus of peers pulled beside them and barraged them with gravel. Asterisk indicates a trip where the Noise Guard was activated by sudden ambient noise after the trip had been successfully completed by students but before observer could record data. Asterisk is set at cutoff criterion.

Variations on the Simple Line Graph: Multiple Data Paths

The line graph is a remarkably versatile vehicle for the display of behavior change. Whereas Figure 6.2 is an example of the line graph in its simplest form—one data path showing the variability of behavior across time and experimental conditions—by the addition of multiple data paths, the line graph can display more complex behavior-environment relations. Multiple data paths can be used to show concurrent measures of (1) two or more dimensions of the same behavior (e.g., frequency and duration), (2) the covariation of two or more different behaviors, (3) the same behavior under different conditions, or (4) the behavior of two or more subjects.

Figure 6.3 shows the results of a study of the effects of contingent music on both the frequency and duration of noisy disruptions by children on a school bus (Greene, Bailey, & Barber, 1981). Had the experimenters recorded only the number of disruptions, it is possible that a significant decrease in frequency could have occurred along with an increase in the duration of disruptions so that the overall social significance of the effect would be minimal. By measuring and plotting both frequency and duration on the same graph, the experimenters were able to analyze the effects of their treatment procedures on the two critical dimensions of the dependent variable.

Both the number of disruptions and their total duration in seconds for each bus trip were plotted against the same vertical axis in Figure 6.3. However, on some multiple data path graphs, a second vertical axis is required to show the proper scaling. Figure 6.4, from the same study, shows an example of a dual-vertical axis graph. The authors used a second vertical axis to scale duration because the

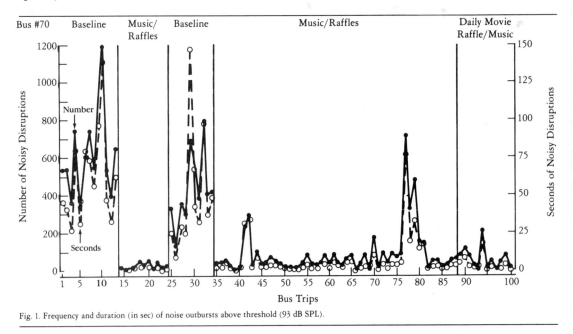

Fig. 1. Frequency and duration (in sec) of noise outbursts above threshold (93 dB SPL).

FIGURE 6.4 Graph with two vertical axes, each showing the scale for one data path. (From "An Analysis and Reduction of Disruptive Behavior on School Buses" by B. F. Greene, J. S. Bailey, and F. Barber, 1981, *Journal of Applied Behavior Analysis, 14,* p. 182. Copyright 1981 by the Society for the Experimental Analysis of Behavior, Inc. Reprinted by permission.)

range of the total duration of disruptions per trip on Bus #70 (0 to 150 seconds) was much less than the range of the number of disruptions per trip (0 to 1200 occurrences). Again, by combining multiple dimensions of the dependent variable on the same graph, visual analysis can be made of both the absolute and relative effects of the independent variable on those dimensions. However, because of the differences in scale, readers of dual-vertical axis graphs must view them with care, particularly when assessing the magnitude of behavior change.

Multiple data paths are also used to facilitate the simultaneous comparison of the effects of experimental manipulations on two or more different behaviors. Determining the covariation of two behaviors as a function of changes in the independent variable is accomplished more easily if both can be displayed on the same set of axes. Figure 6.5 shows the percentage of intervals in which three mentally retarded teenagers exhibited stereotypic responding (e.g., repetitive body movements, rocking) and appropriate behavior (e.g., talking, playing) during a study investigating a procedure in which the subjects received praise for emitting stereotypic responses after a given period of time in which no such responses were emitted (Singh, Dawson, & Manning, 1981).[3] By recording and graphing both stereotypic responding and appropriate behavior, the investigators were able to determine whether reductions in stereotypic responses were accompanied by desired changes in appropriate behavior. Figure 6.5 shows that the spaced responding DRL procedure not only produced substantial reductions in stereotypic responding in all three subjects but also had the concomitant effect of increasing appropriate behavior.

Multiple data paths are also used to represent measures of the same behavior taken under different experimental conditions that alternate throughout an experimental phase. Figure 6.6 shows the percentage of words spelled correctly by a special education student on weekly posttests following traditional and self-correction conditions (McNeish, 1985). Graphing a subject's performance under both conditions on the same set of axes allows direct visual comparisons of differences in absolute levels of responding at any given time as well as relative changes in performance over time.

Multiple data paths can also be used to show the behavior of two or more subjects on the same graph. Generally, a maximum of three different data paths can be displayed effectively on one set of axes. When more than three data paths are displayed on the same graph, the benefits of making additional comparisons are often outweighed by the distraction of too much visual "noise." When more than three data paths must be included on the same graph, other methods of display can be incorporated. Figure 6.7 illustrates an effective use of step charts in combination with conventional data paths to display two child behaviors used as a basis for evaluating two parent behaviors (Issacs, Embry, & Baer, 1982).

OTHER TYPES OF GRAPHS USED IN APPLIED BEHAVIOR ANALYSIS

In addition to the line graph, three other formats for the graphic display of data are used in applied behavior analysis. They are the bar graph, the cumulative record, and the semilogarithmic chart.

Bar Graphs

The **bar graph,** or histogram, is a simple and versatile format for graphically summarizing behavioral data. Like the line graph the bar

---

[3]This procedure, called spaced responding DRL, is included in the general category of differential reinforcement of low rates and is described in chapter 18.

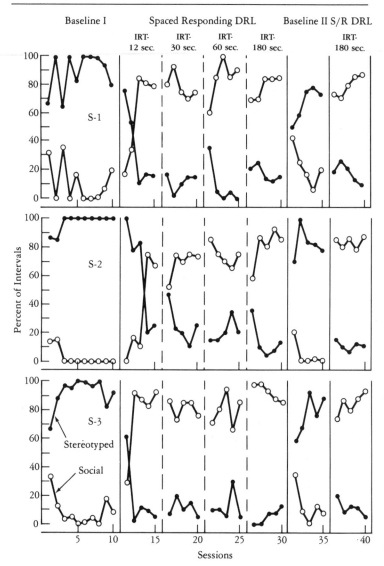

Fig. 1. Percentage of intervals of stereotypic responding and appropriate behavior across experimental conditions.

graph is based on the Cartesian plane and shares most of the line graph's features with one primary difference: the bar graph does not have distinct data points representing successive response measures through time.

Bar graphs serve two major functions in the display of data. First, a bar graph is used when the sets of data to be compared are not related to one another by a common underlying dimension by which the horizontal axis can be

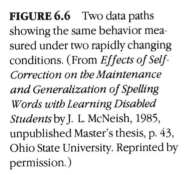

FIGURE 6.6 Two data paths showing the same behavior measured under two rapidly changing conditions. (From *Effects of Self-Correction on the Maintenance and Generalization of Spelling Words with Learning Disabled Students* by J. L. McNeish, 1985, unpublished Master's thesis, p. 43, Ohio State University. Reprinted by permission.)

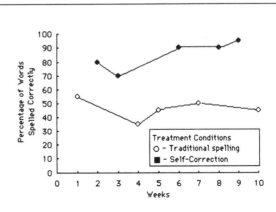

scaled. Figure 6.8 is an example of a bar graph displaying and comparing such discrete data (Haring, 1985).

The second most common use of the bar graph is to give a visual summary of the performance of a subject or group of subjects during the different conditions of an experiment. Figure 6.9 shows two bar graphs that summarize the percentage of male and female juvenile offenders involved in criminal offenses before, during, and after treatment in a teaching family home. The graph also permits comparison of the subjects' incidence of criminal involvement with that of similar youths who received treatment in other group homes (Kirigin, Braukmann, Atwater, and Wolf, 1982).

Although bar graphs can also be used to display range or trend (Parsonson & Baer, 1978), they are typically used to present a measure of central tendency, such as the mean or median score for each condition. A bar graph sacrifices presentation of the variability and trends in behavior (which are apparent in a line graph) in exchange for the efficiency of summarizing and comparing large amounts of data in a simple, easy-to-interpret format.

Bar graphs can take a wide variety of forms to allow a quick and easy comparison of performance across subjects or conditions. How-

ever, bar graphs should be viewed with the understanding that they represent a crude summary that may mask important variability in the data.

Cumulative Records

The **cumulative record** (or graph) was developed by Skinner as the primary means of data collection and analysis in laboratory research in the experimental analysis of behavior. A device called the **cumulative recorder** enables an experimental subject to actually draw its own graph (see Figure 6.10). In a book cataloging 6 years of experimental research on schedules of reinforcement, Ferster and Skinner (1957) described cumulative graphs in the following manner:

A graph showing the number of responses on the ordinate against time on the abscissa has proved to be the most convenient representation of the behavior observed in this research. Fortunately, such a "cumulative" record may be made directly at the time of the experiment. The record is raw data, but it also permits a direct inspection of rate and changes in rate not possible when the behavior is observed directly. . . . Each time the bird responds, the pen moves one step across the paper. At the same time, the paper feeds continuously. If the bird does not respond at all, a horizontal line is drawn in the direction of the

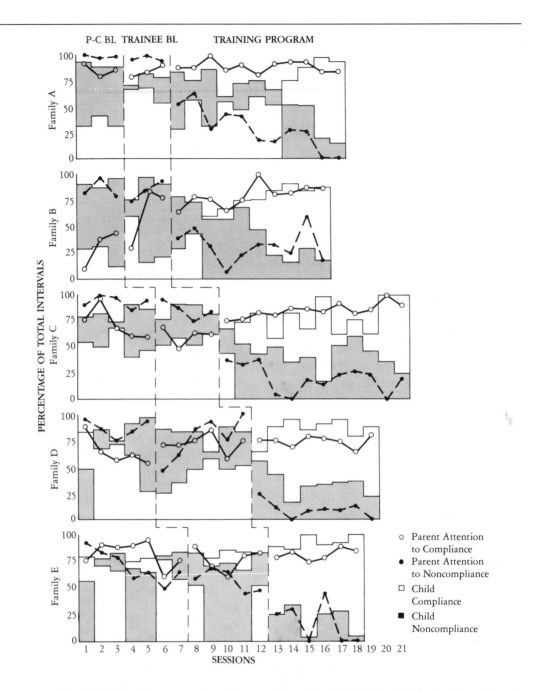

Fig. 4. Percentage of intervals of child compliance/noncompliance and parent attention to these child behaviors for all five families during each experimental condition.

FIGURE 6.7 Graph combining conventional data paths and step charts to effectively display four different behaviors on one set of axes. (From "Training Family Therapists: An Experimental Analysis" by C. D. Issacs, L. H. Embry, and D. M. Baer, 1982, *Journal of Applied Behavior Analysis, 15,* p. 516. Copyright 1982 by the Society for the Experimental Analysis of Behavior, Inc. Reprinted by permission.)

FIGURE 6.8 Bar graph used to summarize and display results of measurements taken under discrete conditions lacking an underlying dimension by which the horizontal axis could be scaled (e.g., time, size of toys). (From "Teaching Between-Class Generalization of Toy Play Behavior to Handicapped Children" by T. G. Haring, 1985, *Journal of Applied Behavior Analysis, 18*, p. 137. Copyright 1985 by the Society for the Experimental Analysis of Behavior, Inc. Reprinted by permission.)

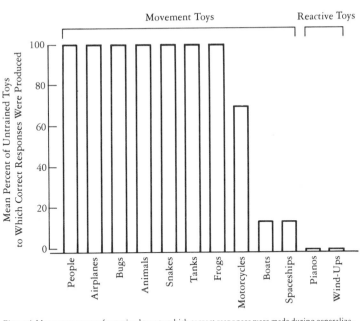

Figure 4. Mean percentage of untrained toys to which correct responses were made during generalization probes with movement toys and reactive toys.

paper feed. The faster the bird pecks, the steeper the line. (p. 23)

When cumulative records are plotted by hand, which is most often the case in applied behavior analysis, the number of responses recorded during each observation period is added (thus the term *cumulative*) to the total number of responses recorded during all previous observation periods. In a cumulative record the Y-axis value of any data point represents the total number of responses recorded since the beginning of data collection. The exception occurs when the total number of responses has exceeded the upper limit of the Y-axis scale, in which case cumulative curves reset to the 0 value of the Y-axis and begin their ascent again. Cumulative records are almost always used with frequency data although other dimensions of behavior, such as duration and latency, can be displayed cumulatively.

Figure 6.11 is an example of a cumulative record from the applied behavior analysis lit-

erature (Neef, Iwata, & Page, 1980). It shows the cumulative number of spelling words mastered by a mentally retarded man under three conditions. The graph shows that Subject 3 mastered a total of 1 word during the 12 sessions of baseline (social praise for correct spelling responses and rewriting incorrectly spelled words three times), a total of 22 words under the interspersal condition (baseline procedures plus the presentation of a previously learned word after each unknown word), and a total of 11 words under the high density reinforcement condition (baseline procedures plus social praise given after each trial for task-related behaviors such as paying attention and writing neatly).

In addition to the total number of responses recorded at any given point in time, cumulative records show the overall and local response rates. Rate is the frequency of responses emitted per unit of time, usually reported as responses per minute in applied behavior

Effects of Group Home Treatment on Percent of Youths
Involved in Offenses

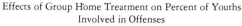

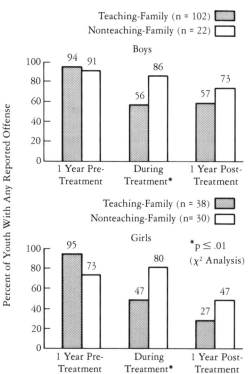

Fig. 1. The percentage of youths involved in offenses one year pretreatment, during treatment, and one year posttreatment.

FIGURE 6.9 Bar graph summarizing and comparing the behavior of different groups of subjects across the conditions of an investigation arranged temporally. (From "An Evaluation of Teaching Family [Achievement Place] Group Homes for Juvenile Delinquents" by K. A. Kirigin, C. G. Braukmann, J. D. Atwater, and M. M. Wolf, 1982, *Journal of Applied Behavior Analysis, 15,* p. 7. Copyright 1982 by the Society for the Experimental Analysis of Behavior, Inc. Reprinted by permission.)

analysis. An **overall response rate** is the average rate of response over a given time period, such as during a specific session, phase, or condition of an experiment. Overall rates are calculated by dividing the total number of responses recorded during the period by the

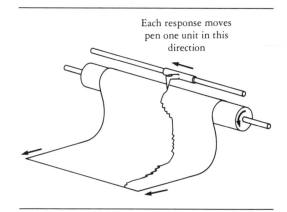

FIGURE 6.10 Diagram of a cumulative recorder. (From *Schedules of Reinforcement,* pp. 24–25, by C. B. Ferster and B. F. Skinner, 1957, Englewood Cliffs, NJ: Prentice-Hall. Copyright 1957 by Prentice-Hall. Reprinted by permission.)

number of observation periods indicated on the horizontal axis. In figure 6.11 the overall response rates are .46 and .23 words mastered per session for the interspersal and high density reinforcement conditions, respectively. (Technically, Figure 6.11 does not represent true rates of response since the number of words spelled correctly was measured and not the rate, or speed, at which they were spelled. However, the slope of each data path does represent the different "rates" of mastering the spelling words in each session within the context of a total of 10 new words presented each day.)

On a cumulative graph, response rates are compared with one another by comparing the slope of each data path. The steeper the slope, the higher the response rate. To produce a visual representation of an overall rate on a cumulative graph, the first and last data points of a given series of observations should be connected with a straight line. A straight line connecting Points a and c in Figure 6.11 would represent Subject 3's overall rate of mastering spelling words during the interspersal condition. A straight line connecting Points a and e

FIGURE 6.11 Cumulative graph of number of spelling words learned by a mentally retarded man during baseline interspersal, and high density reinforcement training. Points a–e have been added to illustrate differences between overall and local response rates. (From "The Effects of Interspersal Training Versus High Density Reinforcement on Spelling Acquisition and Retention" by N. A. Neef, B. A. Iwata, and T. J. Page, 1980. *Journal of Applied Behavior Analysis, 13,* p. 156. Copyright 1980 by the Society for the Experimental Analysis of Behavior, Inc. Adapted by permission.)

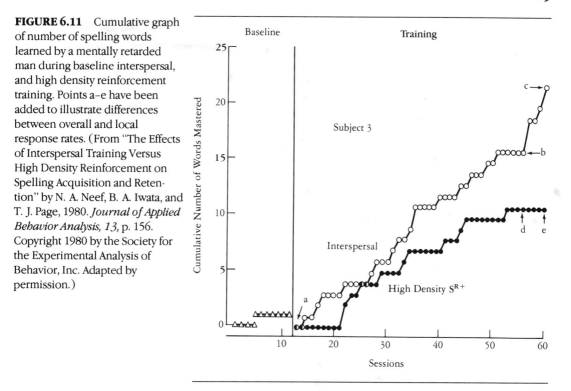

represents his overall rate during the high density reinforcement condition. Relative rates of response can be determined by visually comparing one slope to another; the steeper the slope, the higher the rate of response. Visual comparison of Slopes a-c and a-e shows that the interspersal condition produced the higher overall response rate.

Response rates often fluctuate from moment to moment within a given period. The term **local response rate** refers to the rate of response during periods of time smaller than that for which an overall rate has been given. Over the last 4 sessions of the study shown in Figure 6.11, Subject 3 exhibited a local rate of responding during interspersal training (Slope b-c) that was considerably higher than his overall rate for that condition. At the same time his performance during the final 4 sessions of the high density reinforcement condi-

tion (Slope d-e) shows a lower local response rate than his overall rate for that condition.

A legend giving the slopes of some representative rates can aid considerably in the determination and comparison of relative response rates both within and across cumulative curves plotted on the same set of axes. However, very high rates of responding are difficult to compare visually with one another on cumulative records.

> Although the rate of responding is directly proportional to the slope of the curve, at slopes above 80 degrees small differences in angle represent very large differences in rate; and although these can be measured accurately, they cannot be evaluated easily by [visual] inspection. (Ferster & Skinner, 1957, pp. 24–25)

Even though cumulative records derived from continuous recording are the most directly descriptive displays of behavioral data available (Johnston & Pennypacker, 1980), two other features of behavior, in addition to the comparison of very high rates, can be difficult to determine on some cumulative graphs. One, although the total number of responses since data collection began can be easily seen on a cumulative graph, the number of responses recorded for any given session can be hard to ascertain, given the number of data points and the scaling of the vertical axis. Two, gradual changes in slope from one rate to another can be hard to detect on cumulative graphs (Johnston & Pennypacker, 1980).

Cumulative graphs have been used only rarely in applied behavior analysis. Parsonson and Baer (1978) suggest three reasons that a data display and analytic tool that has proven so valuable in the experimental analysis of behavior has seen such little use in applied work: (1) continuous instrument recording is much less common in applied behavior analysis than it is in the experimental laboratory, (2) persons unfamiliar with cumulative records find them difficult to read, and (3) many applied behavior analysts have little or no background in the experimental analysis of behavior, where the cumulative record originated.

Heward, Dardig, and Rossett (1979) suggest three situations in which cumulative graphs may be preferable to noncumulative line graphs. First, cumulative records are desirable when the total number of responses made over time is important or when progress toward a specific goal can be measured in cumulative units of behavior. The number of new words learned, dollars saved, or miles trained for an upcoming marathon are examples. One look at the most recent data point on the graph reveals the total amount of behavior up to that point in time. Cumulative graphs might also be more effective than noncumulative graphs when the graph is used as a source of feedback for the subject since both total progress and relative rate of performance are easily detected by visual inspection.

In addition, a cumulative record should be used when the target behavior is one that can occur or not occur only once per observation session. In these instances the effects of any intervention are easier to detect on a cumulative graph than on a noncumulative graph. Figure 6.12 shows the same data plotted on noncumulative and cumulative graphs. The cumulative graph clearly shows a relation between behavior and intervention, whereas the noncumulative graph gives the visual impression of greater variability in the data than really exists.

Cumulative records are recommended by Johnston and Pennypacker (1980) for "revealing the fine-grained details of temporal patterning" (p. 348) of single instances or portions of data from an experiment for which the results are otherwise summarized and graphically displayed. Figure 6.13 provides an example of using a cumulative graph to show details of responding not possible to reveal in a graph showing the subject's behavior on a session-by-session basis (Dorsey, Iwata, Reid, & Davis, 1982). The figure shows that in the three sessions for which the results were graphed cumulatively (91, 98, and 107) the subject ceased emitting self-injurious responses earlier in each subsequent session. By plotting the interval-by-interval data cumulatively, the experimenters were able to provide empirical support, in the form of progressively flatter response curves, for the notion that extinction was the principle of behavior underlying the overall decrease in the subject's self-injurious behavior, as shown in a separate noncumulative graph scaled by sessions on the horizontal axis.

Semilogarithmic Charts

All of the graphs discussed so far have been equal-interval graphs on which the distance between any two consecutive points on each axis is always the same. On the X-axis the distance between Session 1 and Session 2 is equal to the distance between Session 11 and

FIGURE 6.12 Same set of hypothetical data plotted on noncumulative and cumulative graphs. Cumulative graphs more clearly reveal patterns of and changes in responding for behaviors that can occur only once during each period of measurement. (From *Working with Parents of Handicapped Children,* p. 100, by W. L. Heward, J. C. Dardig, and A. Rossett, 1979, Columbus, OH: Charles E. Merrill. Copyright 1979 by Charles E. Merrill. Reprinted by permission.)

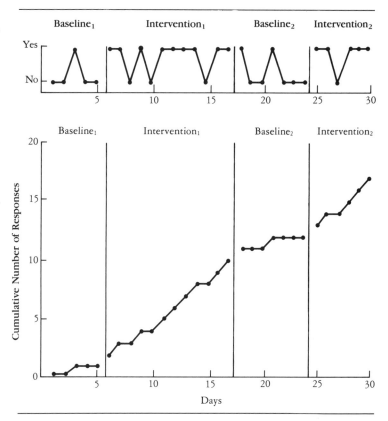

Session 12; on the Y-axis, the distance between 10 and 20 responses per minute is equal to the distance between 35 and 45 responses per minute. On an equal-interval graph equal absolute changes in behavior, whether an increase or decrease in performance, are expressed by equal distances on the Y-axis.

Another way of looking at behavior change is to examine proportional or relative change. Logarithmic scales are well suited to display and communicate proportional change. On a logarithmic scale equal relative changes in performance are represented by equal distances. Since behavior is measured and charted over time, which progresses in equal intervals, the X-axis is marked off in equal intervals, and only the Y-axis is scaled logarithmically. Hence, the term **semilogarithmic chart** refers to

graphs in which only one axis is scaled proportionally.

On semilog charts all behavior changes of equal proportion are shown by equal vertical distances on the vertical axis, regardless of the absolute values of those changes. For example, a doubling of response rate from 4 to 8 per minute would appear on a semilogarithmic chart as the same amount of change as a doubling of 50 to 100 responses per minute. Likewise, a decrease in rate from 75 to 50 responses per minute would occupy the same distance on the vertical axis as a change from 12 to 8 responses per minute.

Figure 6.14 shows the same data graphed on an equal-interval chart (also called arithmetic or add-subtract charts) and on a semilogarithmic chart (also called ratio or multiply-divide

FIGURE 6.13 Cumulative graph used to make a detailed analysis and comparison of subject's self-injurious behavior within selected sessions of an experiment. (From "Protective Equipment: Continuous and Contingent Application in the Treatment of Self-Injurious Behavior" by M. F. Dorsey, B. A. Iwata, D. H. Reid, and P. A. Davis, 1982, *Journal of Applied Behavior Analysis, 15,* p. 229. Copyright 1982 by the Society for the Experimental Analysis of Behavior, Inc. Reprinted by permission.)

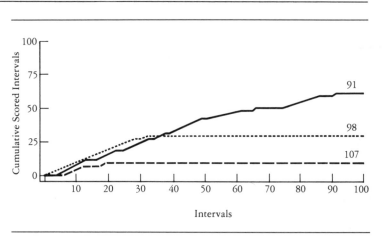

charts). The behavior change that appears as an exponential curve on the arithmetic chart becomes a straight line when plotted on the semilog chart. The vertical axis in the semilog chart in Figure 6.14 is scaled by log-base-2 or X-2 cycles, each cycle on the Y-axis representing a times-2 increase (i.e., a doubling) of the previous behavioral measure.

In the 1960s Lindsley developed the Standard Behavior Chart, a semilogarithmic chart with six X-10 cycles (Lindsley, 1971; Pennypacker, Koenig, & Lindsley, 1972). The Standard Behavior Chart (see Figure 6.15) can accommodate response rates as low as 1 per 24 hours (.000695 per minute) or as high as 1,000 per minute. The horizontal axis is equally divided

FIGURE 6.14 Same set of data plotted on equal-interval, arithmetic scale (left) and on equal-proportion, ratio scale.

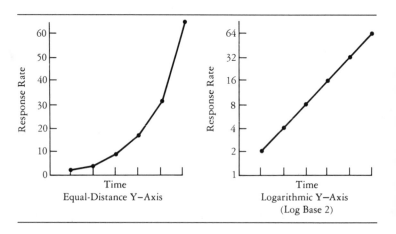

FIGURE 6.15 (opposite page) Standard behavior chart: a standardized, six-cycle semilogarithmic graph paper developed by Lindsley (1971) for charting and analyzing change in response rate over time. (From *Exceptional Teaching,* p. 276, by O. R. White and N. G. Haring, 1980, Columbus, OH: Charles E. Merrill. Copyright 1980 by Charles E. Merrill. And from *Exceptional Children,* p. 131, by W. L. Heward and M. D. Orlansky, 1984, Columbus, OH: Charles E. Merrill. Copyright 1984 by Charles E. Merrill. Adapted by permission.)

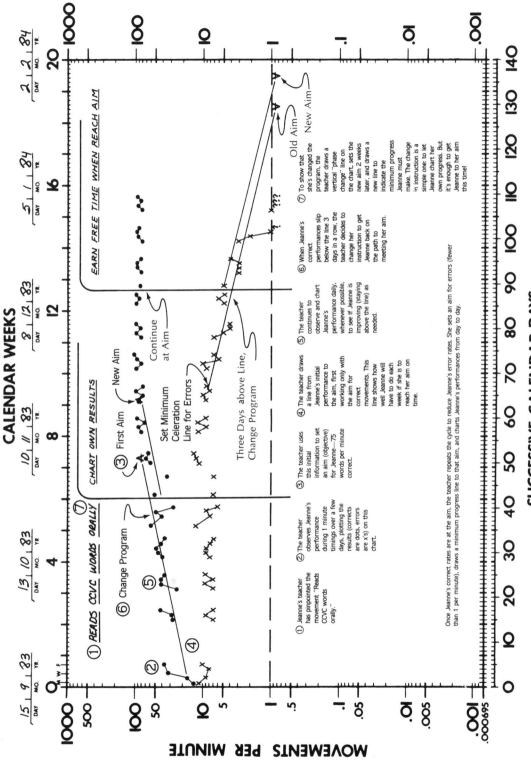

CALENDAR WEEKS

① READS CCVC WORDS ORALLY

EARN FREE TIME WHEN REACH AIM

CHART OWN RESULTS

New Aim

③ First Aim

Continue at Aim

Set Minimum Celeration Line for Errors

⑦ Change Program

⑤

④

②

⑥

Old Aim

New Aim

Three Days above Line, Change Program

???

SUCCESSIVE CALENDAR DAYS

MOVEMENTS PER MINUTE

① Jeanne's teacher has pinpointed the movement "Reads CCVC words orally."

② The teacher observes Jeanne's performance during 1 minute timings over a few days, plotting the results (corrects are dots, errors are x's) on this chart.

③ The teacher uses this initial information to set an aim (objective) for Jeanne—75 words per minute correct.

④ The teacher draws a line from Jeanne's initial performance to the aim, first working only with the aim for correct movements. This line shows how well Jeanne will have to do each week if she is to reach her aim on time.

⑤ The teacher continues to observe and chart Jeanne's performance daily, whenever possible, to see if Jeanne is improving (staying above the line) as needed.

⑥ When Jeanne's correct performances slip below the line 3 days in a row, the teacher decides to change her instruction to get Jeanne back on the path to meeting her aim.

⑦ To show that she's changed the program, the teacher draws a vertical "phase change" line on the chart, sets the new aim 2 weeks later, and draws a new line to indicate the minimum progress Jeanne must make. The change in instruction is a simple one: to let Jeanne chart her own progress. But it's enough to get Jeanne to her aim this time!

Once Jeanne's correct rates are at the aim, the teacher repeats the cycle to reduce Jeanne's error rates. She sets an aim for errors (fewer than 1 per minute), draws a minimum progress line to that aim, and charts Jeanne's performances from day to day.

into 140 calendar days, or 20 weeks. The Standard Behavior Chart provides a standardized means of charting and analyzing change in both absolute and relative rates of response.

An instructional decision-making system, called Precision Teaching, has been developed for use with the Standard Behavior Chart. Figure 6.15 provides a brief overview of the sequence of steps used by precision teachers. Precision Teaching is predicated on the position that (1) learning is best measured as a change in response rate, (2) learning most often occurs through proportional changes in behavior, and (3) past changes in performance can predict future learning.[4]

HOW TO CONSTRUCT GRAPHS

As applied behavior analysis has developed, so have certain stylistic conventions and expectations regarding the construction of graphs. An effective graph presents the facts accurately, completely, and clearly, while maintaining as much simplicity in design as possible. The graph maker must strive to fulfill each of these requirements while remaining alert to any features in the graph's design or construction that might create distortion and might bias either the graph maker's or a future viewer's interpretation of the facts.

Despite the graph's prominent role in applied behavior analysis, there have been remarkably few detailed treatments of the construction of graphs. One notable exception is a chapter by Parsonson and Baer (1978). Cooper (1981) and Tawney and Gast (1984) have also discussed the presentation of graphic data in considerable detail. Recommendations from these sources and others (Johnston & Pennypacker, 1980; *Journal of Applied Behavior Analysis,* 1977, p. 688, and 1982, p. 414; Katzen-

berg, 1975; *Publication Manual of the American Psychological Association,* 1983) were reviewed in the preparation of this section. Additionally, hundreds of graphs published in the applied behavior analysis literature were examined in an effort to discover those features that communicate necessary information most clearly.

Although there are few hard and fast rules for constructing graphs, adhering to the following recommendations should result in clear, well-designed graphic displays consistent in format and appearance with current practice. Although many of the recommendations are illustrated by graphs presented throughout this text, Figures 6.16 and 6.17 have been designed to serve as models for the suggested practices. When a specific figure is not cited for a given recommendation, that feature may be found on both of the model graphs.

Axes

Proportion The relative length of the vertical axis to the horizontal axis, in combination with the scaling of the axes, determines the degree to which a graph will highlight or minimize the variability in a given data set. Published recommendations for the relative length of the vertical axis to the horizontal axis range from a 5:8 ratio (Johnston & Pennypacker, 1980) to a 3:4 ratio (Katzenberg, 1975). On most graphs the vertical axis can be drawn approximately two-thirds the length of the horizontal axis. When multiple sets of axes are to be presented in one figure and/or when the number of observations to be plotted on the horizontal axis is large, the vertical axis can be reduced.

Scaling the Horizontal Axis The horizontal axis should be marked off in equal intervals, each unit representing from left to right the chronological succession of equal time periods or response opportunities in which the behavior was observed and from which an interpretation of behavior change is to be made (e.g.,

---

[4]Readers desiring further information on semilog charts and precision teaching may wish to examine Eaton (1978), Howell (1979), Kunzelmann (1970), White (1974), White and Haring (1980), and the *Journal of Precision Teaching* (1980–1986).

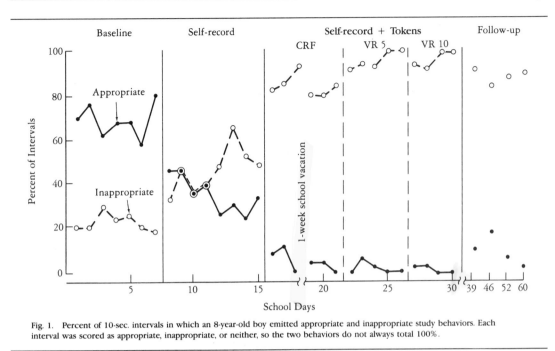

Fig. 1.   Percent of 10-sec. intervals in which an 8-year-old boy emitted appropriate and inappropriate study behaviors. Each interval was scored as appropriate, inappropriate, or neither, so the two behaviors do not always total 100%.

FIGURE 6.16   Hypothetical data illustrating proper techniques of graphic display.

days, sessions, trials). When many data points are to be plotted, it is not necessary to mark each point along the X-axis. Instead, to avoid unnecessary clutter, regularly spaced points on the horizontal axis are marked off with **hatch** or **tick marks** and are numbered by 5's or 10's, making it possible to determine easily the correct location on the axis of any data point.

When multiple sets of axes are stacked one upon another, it is not necessary to number the hatch marks along the horizontal axes of the upper tiers. However, the hatch marks corresponding to those numbered on the bottom tier should be placed on each horizontal axis to facilitate comparison of performance across tiers at any given point in time (Figure 6.17).

Representing the Discontinuity of Time on the Horizontal Axis   Because repeated measures of behavior change take place across time and all experimental manipulations occur in the unavoidable dimension of time, time is a

variable in all experiments and should not be distorted arbitrarily in a graphic display. Each equally spaced unit on the horizontal axis should represent an equal passage of time. A **scale break** is used to indicate discontinuity in the progression of time on the horizontal axis. It can be created by long periods of time in which data are not collected or by a change in the equal scaling of the X-axis (Figure 6.16). Discontinuities of time should be highlighted by identifying each point in time that measurements were made at unequal intervals (see numbering of school days for follow-up data in Figure 6.16).

When measurement occurs across consecutive observations (e.g., stories read, meals, interactions) rather than standard units of time, the horizontal axis still serves as a visual representation of the progression of time since the data plotted against it have been recorded one after the other. The text accompanying such a figure should indicate the real time in which

FIGURE 6.17 Graph illustrating variety of conventions and guidelines for graphic display.

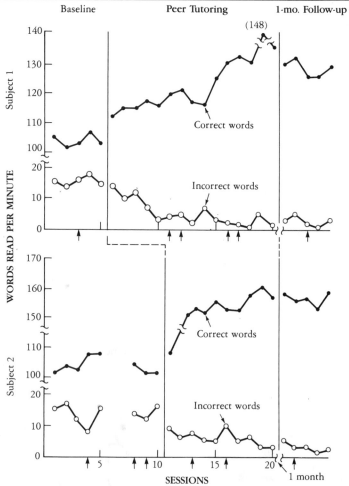

Figure 1. Number of words read correctly and incorrectly during 1-minute probes following each session. Arrows under horizontal axes indicate sessions in which subject used reading material brought from home. Break in data path for subject 2 was caused by 2 days absence.

the consecutive measurements were made (e.g., "Two or three stories were observed each school day"), and discontinuities in that time context should be clearly marked with scale breaks (see vacation break in Figure 6.16).

Labeling the Horizontal Axis The dimension by which the horizontal axis is scaled should be identified in a brief printed label centered below and parallel to the axis.

Scaling the Vertical Axis On equal-interval charts the scale of the vertical axis is the most significant feature of the graph in terms of its portrayal of variability in the data. (Scaling of the vertical axis is standardized on six-cycle semilogarithmic charts so that proportional changes in any response rate appear the same on all charts.) Common practice is to mark the origin at 0 (on cumulative graphs the origin must always be 0) and then to mark off the vertical axis so that the full range of values represented in the data set are accommodated. Increasing the distance on the vertical axis for each unit of measurement magnifies the variability in the data, whereas contracting the units of measurement on the vertical axis minimizes the portrayal of variability in the data set. The graph maker should plot the data set against several different vertical axis scales, watching for distortion of the graphic display that might lead to inappropriate interpretations.

The social significance of behavior change as represented by the vertical axis should be used to guide the selection of appropriate scaling. When small numerical changes in performance are socially significant, the Y-axis scale should reflect a smaller range of values. For example, to most effectively display data from a training program in which an industrial worker's percentage of correctly executed steps in a safety checklist increased from an unsafe range of 80 to 90% to an accident-free 100%, the ordinate should focus on the 80 to 100% range with a scale break indicating the portion of the percent scale not included in the two-dimensional plane. On the other hand, the scaling of the vertical axis should be contracted when small numerical changes in behavior are not socially important and the variability obscured in such a scale is not a significant factor.

Horizontal numbering of regularly spaced tic marks on the vertical axis facilitates use of the scale. The vertical axis should not be extended beyond the hatch mark indicating the highest value on the axis scale. And when the data set includes several measures of 0, the vertical axis should begin at a point slightly above the horizontal axis to avoid having data points fall directly on the axis. This practice results in a neater graph and facilitates discrimination of 0-value measures in data points close to 0 (see Figure 6.16).

When two data paths with widely different and nonoverlapping ranges are displayed against the same Y-axis, a scale break should be used to indicate the range of numbers omitted from the scale (see Figure 6.17).

In multiple-tier graphs equal distances on each vertical axis should represent equal changes in behavior to aid the comparison of data across tiers (Figure 6.17). Also, whenever possible, similar positions on each vertical axis of multiple tier graphs should represent similar absolute values of the dependent variable. When the differences in behavioral measures from one tier to another would result in an overly long vertical axis, a scale break can be used to highlight the difference in absolute values, again aiding a point-to-point comparison of Y-axis positions (see Figure 6.17).

Labeling the Vertical Axis The dimension by which the vertical axis is scaled should be identified with a brief printed label, centered to the left and parallel to the axis. On multiple-tier graphs one label identifying the dimension portrayed on all of the vertical axies can be centered along the axes as a group. Additional labels identifying the source of the data can be printed to the left of each set of axes, parallel to each vertical axis. These individual tier labels should be printed to the right of and in smaller print than the label identifying the dimension of the vertical axes scales (Figure 6.17). Space and design considerations sometimes dictate that labels identifying individual tiers be printed in a conspicuous position above each tier and parallel to the horizontal axis (see Figure 6.5 and 6.9).

Identification of Experimental Conditions

Phase/Condition Change Lines Vertical lines extending upward from the horizontal axis indicate a change in experimental procedures. Phase and condition change lines should be placed beyond the last point on the horizontal axis representing a measurement that was prior to the experimental manipulation signified by the line and before the first measurement of behavior after the change in procedure. In this way data points fall clearly on either side of change lines and never on the lines themselves. Condition changes, representing manipulations of a currently in-place independent variable, are shown by dashed vertical lines, which easily distinguish them from the more major phase changes (Figures 6.5 and 6.16). Condition and phase change lines should be drawn to a height equal to the height of the vertical axis in order to aid the estimation of the value of data points at the top of the vertical axis range.

When the same manipulation of an independent variable occurs at different points along the horizontal axes of multiple-tiered graphs, a dog-leg connecting the change lines of adjacent tiers makes it easy to follow the progression of events in the experiment (Figure 6.17).

Unplanned events that occur during the experiment or minor manipulations that do not warrant a condition change line can be indicated by placing small arrows, asterisks, or other symbols next to the relevant data points (Figure 6.3). On graphs with multiple data path these events can be marked on the X-axis (Figure 6.17). Explanation of any special symbols should always be provided in the figure legend.

Phase/Condition Labels Labels identifying the conditions in effect during each period of an experiment are centered above the space delineated by the phase or condition change lines. Whenever space permits, phase and condition labels should be parallel to the horizontal axis. Labels should be brief but descriptive (e.g., Parental Praise is preferable to Treatment); and the labels should use the same terms or phrases found in the textual discussion of the procedure accompanying the graph. Abbreviations should be used only when space or design limitations prohibit printing the complete label. A single phase label should

span contiguous condition changes with subordinate labels identifying the different conditions within the phase (see Figure 6.16). Numbers are sometimes placed after the labels of repeated conditions (e.g., Baseline 2, Baseline 3) to indicate the number of times the condition has been in effect.

Data Points and Data Paths

Data Points Great care must be taken to place each data point exactly on the coordinates of the horizontal and vertical axis values it represents. Inaccurate placement of data points is an unnecessary source of distortion in graphic displays. Accurate placement is aided by careful selection of graph paper with grid lines sized and spaced appropriately for the data to be plotted. When many different values must be plotted within a small distance on the vertical axis, a graph paper with many grid lines per inch should be used.

Should a data point fall beyond the range of values described by the vertical axis scale, it is plotted just above the scale it transcends, and the actual value of the measurement is printed in parentheses next to the data point. Breaks in the data path leading to and from the off-the-scale data point also help to highlight its discrepancy (see Figure 6.17).

Data points should be marked with bold symbols that are easily discriminated from the data path. When only one set of data is displayed on a graph, solid dots should be used. When multiple data sets are plotted on the same set of axes, a different geometric symbol is used for each set of data. Symbols should be chosen and drawn so that the value of each data point can be determined when data points fall near or upon one another. In most cases three different data sets are the maximum that can be displayed with clarity on a single graph.

Data Paths Data paths are created by drawing a straight line from the center of each data point in a given data set to the center of the next data point in the same set. All data points in a given data set are connected in this manner with the following exceptions:

1 Data points falling on either side of a phase or condition change line are not connected.

2 Data points should not be connected across discontinuities of time in the horizontal axis (see Figure 6.16).

3 Data points should not be connected across a significant span of time in which behavior was not measured. To do so implies that the resultant data path represents the level and trend of the behavior during the span of time in which no measurement was conducted.

4 Data points on either side of a regularly scheduled measurement period in which data were not collected or were lost, destroyed, or otherwise not available (e.g., subject's absence, recording equipment failure) should not be joined together (see baseline phase, bottom graph of Figure 6.17).

5 Data points that fall on either side of a vertical axis scale break should not be connected (see bottom graph, Figure 6.17).

6 Follow-up or postcheck data points should not be connected with one another (see Figure 6.16) unless the measures they represent were taken during successive observations regularly spaced in time in the same manner as measures during the rest of the experiment (see Figure 6.17).

7 If a data point falls beyond the values described by the vertical axis scale, breaks should be made in the data path connecting that data point with those that fall within the described range (see session 19 data point, top graph, Figure 6.17).

When multiple data paths are displayed on the same graph, different styles of lines, in addition to different symbols for the data points, may be used to help distinguish one data path from another (see Figure 6.16). The behavior represented by each data path must be clearly identified, either by printed labels with arrows drawn to the data path (see Figures 6.16 and 6.17) or by a legend that appropriately labels models of the symbols and line styles (see Figures 6.5 and 6.6). Again, in most cases three different data paths are the maximum that should be displayed on a single graph before resorting to other display tactics (e.g., see Figure 6.7). When two data sets travel exactly the same path, the lines should be drawn close to and parallel with one another to help clarify the situation (see the self-record condition of Figure 6.16).

When a cumulative graph displays a data path with various local rates, a legend identifying the rates of several representative slopes found within the data set can aid the viewer in examining the graph most effectively.

Figure Legend

Printed below the graph, the figure legend should give a concise but complete description of the figure. The legend should also direct the viewer's attention to any features of the graph that might be overlooked (e.g., scale changes) and should explain the meaning of any added symbols representing special events.

Some Additional Guidelines and Tips

Graphs should be drawn in only one color—black. Even though the use of color can enhance the attractiveness of a visual display and can effectively highlight certain features, its use is discouraged in the scientific presentation of data. Every effort must be made to let the data stand on their own. The use of color can encourage perceptions of performance or experimental effects that differ from perceptions of the same data displayed in black. Reproduction of graphs and charts in journals and books is another reason for using black only.

The entire figure should be drawn to a size compatible with its intended use. If, for example, the graph is being constructed for publication in a journal, it should be planned to fit the journal's page size.

A variety of graph papers should be kept on hand. Experimenting with several different sizes can help determine the best spacing and number of grid lines for scaling the axes and for accurate plotting of each set of data.

The corners of the graph paper should be taped to a clean, smooth, and well-lighted work space. Initially lines should be drawn in easily erased pencil until the proportions and positioning of the axes and change lines are set. All data points should be plotted in pencil and double-checked for accurate positioning on the grid. Then the entire graph should be drawn in dark black ink or marker. Finally, a plain white sheet of paper (onion skin is easier to see through) should be taped over the graph paper, and the entire figure should be traced in dark black ink. In this way the grid lines of the original graph paper are no longer part of the final display.

Software programs for producing computer-generated graphs are available and are becoming increasingly sophisticated. (Figure 6.6 is an example of a simple graph made by a microcomputer and a dot matrix printer.) More and more computer-generated graphs will no doubt be making their way into the behavior analysis literature. Even though computer graphics programs offer a tremendous time savings over hand-plotted graphs, careful examination should be made of the range of scales available and the printer's capability for both accurate data point placement and precise printing of data paths.

The skills required to construct effective, distortion-free graphic displays are as important as any in the behavior analyst's repertoire. The recommendations given here generally apply to all behavioral graphs. However, each data set and the conditions under which the data were obtained present their own challenges to the graph maker.

HOW TO INTERPRET GRAPHS

When an experimental intervention produces dramatic, replicable changes in behavior that last over time, the effect is readily seen in a well-designed graphic display. Persons with little or no formal training in behavior analysis can correctly read the graph in such cases. Many times, however, behavior changes are not so large, consistent, or durable. Behavior sometimes changes in sporadic, temporary, delayed, or seemingly uncontrolled ways; or behavior may hardly change at all. Graphs displaying these kinds of data patterns often tell equally important and interesting stories about behavior.

In order to interpret graphic data accurately and meaningfully, applied behavior analysts employ a systematic form of examination known as **visual analysis.** Visual analysis of data from an applied behavior analysis study is conducted to answer two questions: (1) Did a meaningful change in behavior take place? (2) To what extent can that change in behavior be attributed to experimental manipulation of the independent variable? Although there are no formalized rules for visual analysis, the dynamic nature of behavior, the scientific and technological necessity of discovering effective interventions, and the applied requirement of producing socially meaningful levels of performance all combine to focus the behavior analyst's interpretive attention on certain properties common to all behavioral data. These fundamental properties of data are (1) the extent and type of variability in the data, (2) the level of the data, and (3) trends in the data. Visual analysis entails an examination of each of these characteristics both within and across the different phases and conditions of an experiment.

Before evaluating the data displayed in a graph, however, the viewer should carefully examine the graph's construction. First, the figure legend, axis labels, and all phase/condition labels should be read carefully. The viewer should then look at each axis, noting its scaling and the location and significance of any scale breaks.

In addition, a visual tracking of each data path should be made to determine whether data points are properly connected. Does each data point represent a single observation, or are the data "blocked" so that each data point is actually a summary of multiple observations? Do the data show performance of an individual subject or the average performance of a group of subjects? If blocked or group data are displayed, is a visual representation of the range or variation of scores provided (e.g., Epstein, Beck, Figueroa, Farkas, Kazdin, Daneman, & Becker, 1981); or do the data themselves allow determination of the amount of variability that was collapsed in the graph? For example, if the horizontal axis is scaled in weeks and each data point represents a student's average score for a week of daily, 5-word spelling tests, data points falling near 0 or at the top end of the closed scale, such as 4.8, pose little problem since they can be the result of only minimal variability in the daily scores for that week. However, scores near the center of the scale, such as 2 to 3, can result from either stable or highly variable performance.

If the viewer suspects distortion produced by a graph's construction, interpretive judgments should be withheld until the data can be replotted on a new set of axes. Distortion due to a loss of important data features in summarizing is not so easily remedied. The viewer must consider the report incomplete and forestall any interpretive conclusions until he has access to the raw data.

Only when the viewer is satisfied that the graph is properly constructed and does not visually distort the behavioral and environmental events it represents, should the data themselves be examined. The data are then inspected to find what they reveal about the behavior measured during each phase or condition of the study.

Visual Analysis Within Phases/Conditions

Data within a given phase or condition are examined to determine (1) the number of data points, (2) the variability of performance, (3) the level of performance, and (4) the direction and degree of any trends.

Number of Data Points and Variability

First, the viewer should determine the quantity of data reported during each phase or condition. This entails a simple counting of data points. As a general rule, the more measurements of the dependent variable per unit of time and the longer the period of time in which measurement occurred, the more confidence one can have in the data path's estimation of the true course of behavior change (given, of course, an accurate observation and measurement system). When **variability** in performance is evident during a given condition, the need is greater for additional data. Variability refers to the extent to which measures of behavior under the same environmental conditions differ from one another. Fewer data points suffice when a high degree of stability is evidenced.

The number of data points needed to provide a believable record of behavior during a given phase or condition also depends on how many times the same phase or condition has been repeated during the study. As a rule, fewer data points are needed in subsequent replications of an experimental condition if the data depict the same level and trend in performance that was noted in earlier applications of the condition.

The published literature of applied behavior analysis also plays a part in determining how much data is sufficient. In general, less lengthy phases are required of experiments investigating relations between previously studied variables if the results are also similar to the previous studies. More data are needed to demonstrate new findings, whether or not new variables are under investigation.

There are other exceptions to this rule of the-more-data-the-better. Ethical concerns do not permit the repeated measurement of certain behaviors (e.g., self-injurious behavior) under an experimental condition in which little or no effort is being made to intervene. Also, there is little purpose in repeated measurement in situations where the subject cannot logically perform the behavior (e.g., measuring long division when concurrent observations indicate that the student has not learned to subtract or multiply). Nor are many data points required to demonstrate that behavior did not occur when in fact it had no opportunity to occur (Horner & Baer, 1978).

Familiarity with the response class measured and the conditions under which it was measured may be the viewer's biggest aid in determining how many data points constitute believability. The quantity of data needed in a given condition is also partly determined by the experimental design employed in a given study. Experimental design tactics are described in chapters 7 to 10.

Level The value on the vertical axis scale around which a set of behavioral measures converge is called **level.** In the visual analysis of behavioral data, level is examined within a phase or condition in terms of its absolute value (mean, median, and/or range) on the Y-axis scale, the degree of stability or variability, and the extent of change from one level to another. Figure 6.18 illustrates the different characteristics of level and variability.

A somewhat common practice in applied behavior analysis has been the addition of **mean level lines** to graphed data. A horizontal line is drawn across a phase or condition at that point on the vertical axis equaling the average value of the response measure during

FIGURE 6.18 Four data paths illustrating (A) a low, stable level of responding, (B) a high, variable level of responding, (C) an initially high, stable level of responding followed by a lower, more variable level of responding, and (D) an extremely variable pattern of responding not indicative of any overall level of responding. Dashed horizontal lines on graphs B, C, and D represent the mean level of responding.

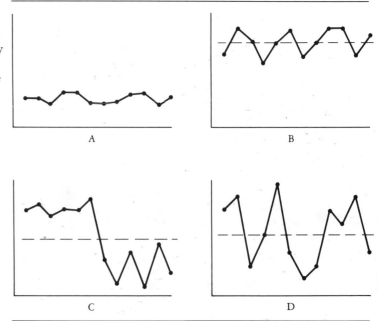

that phase or condition. Mean level lines provide an objective, easy-to-see summary of average performance over a given condition but must be used and interpreted with caution. When the data path is highly stable throughout the condition, mean level lines pose no serious drawbacks. However, the more stability shown by a series of data points, the less need there is for a mean level line. For instance, a mean level line would serve little purpose in Graph A in Figure 6.18. And although mean level lines have been added to Graphs B, C, and D in Figure 6.18, Graph B is the only one of the three for which a mean level line is an appropriate visual summary of level. In Graph C the mean level is not representative of any measure of behavior taken during the phase; the behavior in that graph is best characterized as occurring at two distinct levels. Use of a mean level line in Graph D is also inappropriate because the variability in the data is so great that only 4 of the 12 data points fall close to the mean level line.

Horizontal lines representing the median behavioral measure for each condition are another method for visually summarizing overall level. Since medians give a visual representation of the most typical performance, they are not so influenced by one or two measures that fall far out of the range of the remaining measures. A **median level line** is preferred to a mean level line when representing the central tendency of a series of data points showing considerable variability.

Although there are no standard, mathematical formulas commonly used by behavior analysts for determining stability in graphic data, Tawney and Gast (1984) state that "generally, if 80–90% of the data points of a condition fall within a 15% range of the mean level of all data point values of a condition, applied researchers will consider the data stable" (p. 161). They emphasize that this is a general guideline to be modified by variables such as the overall rate of response and the number of response opportunities per measurement episode.

Change in level within a phase or condition is determined by calculating the difference in absolute value between the first and last data points within the phase or condition and noting whether the change, if any, is in the desired direction. Another method, somewhat less influenced by variability in the data, is to compare the difference between the median value of the first three data points in the condition with the median value of the final three data points in the condition (Koenig & Kunzelmann, 1980).

Trend **Trend** refers to the overall direction taken by a data path. Trends are described in terms of their direction (increasing, decreasing, or zero trend), degree of trend, and extent of variability of data points around the trend. The graphs in Figure 6.19 illustrate a variety of trends and give their general descriptions. The direction and degree of trend in a series of graphically displayed data points can be visually represented with a straight line drawn through the data. There are several methods for calculating such a **trend line,** also called a **line of progress.** One can simply inspect the graphed data and draw a straight line that visually provides the best fit through the data. For this freehand method Lindsley (1985) suggests ignoring one or two data points that fall well beyond the range of the remaining values in a data series and fitting the line of progress to the remaining scores. Although the freehand method is the fastest way of drawing lines of progress, it may not always result in an accurate representation of trend.

Lines of progress can also be calculated with a sophisticated mathematical formula called the ordinary least squares linear regression equation (McCain & McCleary, 1979). Trend lines determined in this fashion have the advantage of complete reliability: the same trend line will always result from the same data set. The disadvantage of this method is the many mathematical operations that must be performed to calculate the trend line. Availability of a computer program to perform the

FIGURE 6.19 Data patterns indicating different combinations of trend direction, degree, and variability: (A) zero trend, high stability; (B) zero trend, high variability; (C) gradually increasing, stable trend; (D) rapidly increasing, variable trend; (E) rapidly decreasing, stable trend; (F) gradually decreasing, variable trend; (G) rapidly increasing trend followed by gradually decreasing trend; (H) no meaningful trend, too much variability and missing data. Split-middle lines of progress have been added to Graphs *C–F.*

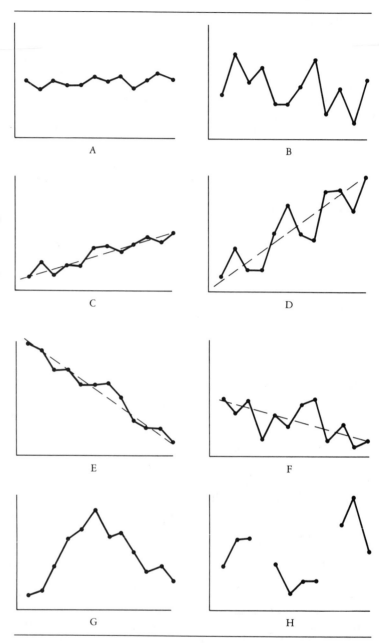

equation can eliminate the time concern in calculating a least squares trend line.

One method of calculating and drawing lines of progress that is more reliable than the freehand method and much less time-consuming than linear regression methods is the **split-middle line of progress,** developed by White (1971). The split-middle technique was developed for use with rate data plotted on semilogarithmic charts, and it has proven an effective technique for predicting future behavior from such data (White, 1974).

Split-middle lines of progress can also be drawn for data plotted against an equal-interval vertical axis, but it must be remembered that such a line is only an estimate that summarizes the overall trend (Bailey, 1984; Tawney & Gast, 1984). Figure 6.20 provides a step-by-step illustration of how to draw split-middle lines of progress. A line of progress cannot be drawn by any method through a series of data points spanning a scale break in the vertical axis and generally should not be drawn across scale breaks in the horizontal axis.

The specific degree of acceleration or deceleration of trends in data plotted on semilogarithmic charts can be quantified in numerical terms. For example, on the Standard Behavior Chart a times-2-celeration means the response rate is doubling each week, and a X-1.25 means the response rate is one-quarter higher each week. A divide-by-2 deceleration means that each week the response rate is one-half of what it was the week before, and a ÷ 1.5 means the response rate is decreasing by one-third each week.

There is no direct way to determine visually the specific rate of acceleration or deceleration in trend from data plotted on equal-interval charts. But visual comparison of trend lines drawn through data on equal-interval charts can provide important information concerning the relative rate of behavior change.

A trend can be highly stable with all of the data points falling on or near the trend line (see Figure 6.19, Graphs C and E). Data paths can also follow a trend even though a high degree of variability is evidenced in the scores (see Figure 6.19, Graphs D and F). Tawney and Gast (1984) suggest that a trend can be considered stable if 80 to 90% of the data points in the condition fall within a 15% range of the trend line.

Visual Analysis Between Phases/Conditions

After inspection of the data within each phase/condition of a study, visual analysis proceeds with a comparison of data across phases/conditions. Drawing proper conclusions entails comparison of the previously discussed properties of behavioral data—level, trend, and stability/variability—between adjacent phases/conditions and across similar phases/conditions.

A phase or condition change line indicates that an independent variable was manipulated at a given point in time. To determine whether an immediate change in behavior occurred at that point in time, one needs to examine the difference between the last data point in the phase/condition preceding the manipulation and the first data point in the subsequent phase/condition.

The data are also examined in terms of the overall level of performance during each condition. In general, when all data points in one condition fall outside the range of values for all data points in an adjacent condition—that is, there is no overlap of data points—a strong case is made that behavior was changed from one condition to the next. When many data points in adjacent conditions overlap one another on the vertical axis, less confidence can be placed in the effect of the independent variable associated with the change in conditions.[5]

Mean or median level lines can be helpful in examining overall level between conditions. However, using mean or median level lines to summarize and compare the overall central tendency of data across phases or conditions poses two serious problems. First, the viewer of such a visual display must guard against letting "apparently large differences among measures of central tendency visually overwhelm the presence of equally large amounts of uncontrolled variability" (Johnston & Pennypacker, 1980, p. 351). Emphasis on mean changes in performance in a graphic display

---

[5]Whether or not a documented change in behavior is interpreted as a function of the independent variable is dependent on the experimental design used in the study. Tactics for experimental design in applied behavior analysis are presented in chapters 7 to 10.

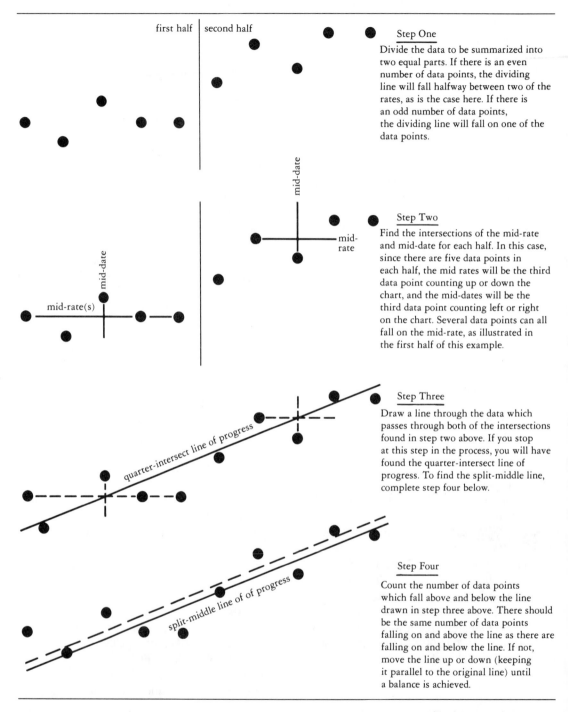

first half | second half

Step One

Divide the data to be summarized into two equal parts. If there is an even number of data points, the dividing line will fall halfway between two of the rates, as is the case here. If there is an odd number of data points, the dividing line will fall on one of the data points.

mid-date

mid-rate

Step Two

Find the intersections of the mid-rate and mid-date for each half. In this case, since there are five data points in each half, the mid rates will be the third data point counting up or down the chart, and the mid-dates will be the third data point counting left or right on the chart. Several data points can all fall on the mid-rate, as illustrated in the first half of this example.

mid-date

mid-rate(s)

quarter-intersect line of progress

Step Three

Draw a line through the data which passes through both of the intersections found in step two above. If you stop at this step in the process, you will have found the quarter-intersect line of progress. To find the split-middle line, complete step four below.

split-middle line of of progress

Step Four

Count the number of data points which fall above and below the line drawn in step three above. There should be the same number of data points falling on and above the line as there are falling on and below the line. If not, move the line up or down (keeping it parallel to the original line) until a balance is achieved.

FIGURE 6.20 How to draw a split-middle line of progress through a series of graphically displayed data points. (From *Exceptional Teaching*, p. 118, by O. R. White and N. G. Haring, 1980, Columbus, OH: Charles E. Merrill. Copyright 1980 by Charles E. Merrill. Reprinted by permission.)

can lead the viewer to believe that a greater degree of experimental control was obtained than is warranted by the data. In the top graph of Figure 6.21 one-half of the data points in Condition B fall within the range of values of the measures taken during Condition A, but the mean level lines suggest a clear change in behavior. Second, measures of central tendency can obscure important trends in the data that warrant interpretations other than those suggested by the central tendency indicators. Although a mean or median line accurately

represents the average or typical performance, neither provides any indication of increasing or decreasing performance. In the bottom graph of Figure 6.21, for example, the mean line suggests a higher level of performance in Condition B than in Condition A, but an examination of trend reveals an entirely different picture of behavioral effects.

A complete visual analysis of behavioral data must also note any changes in level that occur after a new phase or condition has been in place for some time and any changes in level that occur early in a new phase but are later lost. Such delayed or temporary effects can indicate that the independent variable must be in place for some time before behavior changes or that the temporary level change was the result of an uncontrolled variable. In any event more experimentation is called for in an effort to isolate and control the relevant variables.

Visual analysis of data between adjacent phases/conditions includes an examination of the trends exhibited by the data in each phase/condition to determine whether the trend found in the first condition changed in direction or slope during the subsequent condition. In practice, since each data point in a series contributes to both level and trend, the two characteristics are viewed in conjunction with one another. Figure 6.22 presents stylized data paths illustrating four basic combinations of change or lack of change in level and trend between two adjacent conditions. Of course, many other data patterns could display the same characteristics. Idealized, straight-line data paths that eliminate the variability found in most repeated measures of behavior have been used to highlight level and trend.

Visual analysis includes not only an examination and comparison of changes in level and trend between adjacent conditions, but also an examination of performance across similar conditions. Visual analysis is not complete with the identification and description of level, trend, and stability/variability of the data

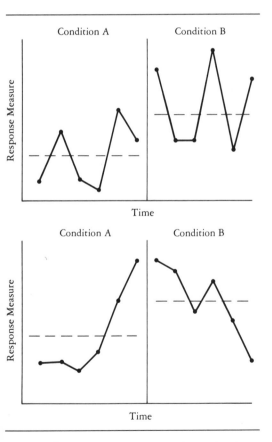

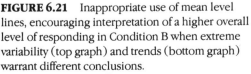

FIGURE 6.21 Inappropriate use of mean level lines, encouraging interpretation of a higher overall level of responding in Condition B when extreme variability (top graph) and trends (bottom graph) warrant different conclusions.

FIGURE 6.22 Stylized data paths illustrating the different combinations of change or lack of change in level and trend between two adjacent conditons: Graphs A and B show no change in either level or trend between the two conditions, Graphs C and D show changes in level and no change in trend, Graphs E and F depict no immediate change in level and a change in trend, and Graphs G and H reveal change in both level and trend. (From "Time-Series Analysis in Operant Research" by R. R. Jones, R. S. Vaught, and M. R. Weinrott, 1977, *Journal of Applied Behavior Analysis, 10,* p. 157. Copyright 1977 by the Society for the Experimental Analysis of Behavior, Inc. Adapted by permission.)

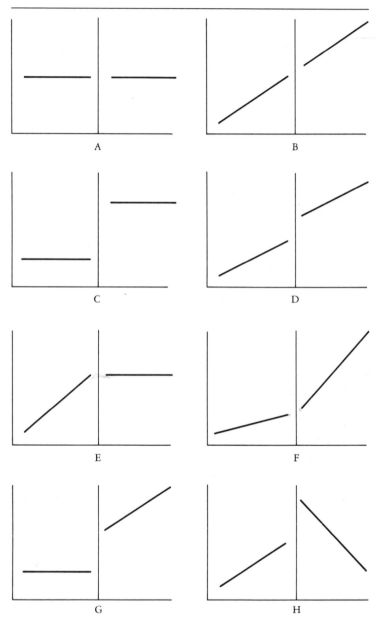

in a given study. When behavior change is demonstrated over the course of a given study, the next question to be asked is, Was the change in behavior a function of the experimentally manipulated variables? The remaining chapters of part three describe tactics of experimental design used by applied behavior analysts in an effort to provide a meaningful answer.

SUMMARY

Benefits of Graphic Display of Behavioral Data

1 Graphing each measure of behavior as it is collected provides a complete, ongoing record of the subject's performance.

2 Direct and continuous contact with the data in a readily analyzable format enables the researcher to identify and investigate interesting variations in behavior as they occur.

3 As a judgmental aid for interpreting experimental results, graphic display is a fast, relatively easy-to-learn method that imposes no arbitrary levels of significance for evaluating behavior change.

4 Visual analysis of graphed data is a conservative method of determining the significance of behavior change; only variables able to produce meaningful effects repeatedly are considered significant, and weak and unstable variables are screened out.

5 Graphic displays of data encourage independent judgments and interpretations.

6 Graphs can serve as an effective source of feedback to those whose behavior is represented on the graph.

Line Graphs

7 Line graphs, the most commonly used format for the graphic display of behavioral data, are based on the Cartesian plane, a two-dimensional area formed by the intersection of two perpendicular lines.

8 Major parts of the simple line graph are the horizontal axis (also called the X-axis), phase/condition change lines, phase/condition labels, the vertical axis (also called the Y-axis), data points, the data path, and the figure legend.

9 Multiple data paths on the same set of axes are used to facilitate comparison of (a) different dimensions of the same behavior, (b) different behaviors of the same subject, (c) measures of the same behavior of the same subject under different, rapidly changing conditions, or (d) the same behavior of different subjects.

10 A second vertical axis is sometimes used to show different scales for multiple data paths.

Other Types of Graphs Used in Applied Behavior Analysis

11 Bar graphs are used for two primary purposes: (a) to display discrete data not related by an underlying dimension that can be used to scale the horizontal axis and (b) to summarize and enable easy comparison of behavior across different conditions of an experiment.

12 Each data point on a cumulative graph, or cumulative record, represents the total number of responses emitted by the subject since measurement began. The steeper the slope of the data path on a cumulative graph, the higher the response rate.

13 Overall response rate refers to the average rate of response over a given time period; a local response rate refers to the rate of response during a smaller period of time within a larger period for which an overall response rate has been given.

14 Cumulative graphs, although not used very often in applied behavior analysis, are especially effective for displaying data when (a) the total number of responses made over time is important, (b) the graph itself is to be used as a source of feedback to the subject, (c) the target behavior can occur only once per measurement period, and (d) a fine analysis of a single

instance or portions of data from an experiment is desired.

15 Semilogarithmic charts are scaled so that changes in behavior that are of equal proportion (e.g., doublings of the response rate) are represented by equal distances on the vertical axis.

16 An instructional decision-making system, called Precision Teaching, has been developed for use with the Standard Behavior Chart, a six-cycle semilogarithmic graph paper that enables the standardized charting of behavior with rates ranging from 1 to 1,000 responses per day.

How to Construct Graphs

17 The vertical axis is drawn to a length approximately two-thirds that of the horizontal axis.

18 The horizontal axis is marked off in equal intervals, each representing from left to right the chronological succession of equal time periods across which behavior was measured.

19 Discontinuities of time are indicated on the horizontal axis by scale breaks.

20 The vertical axis is scaled relative to the dimension of behavior measured, the range of values of the measures obtained, and the social significance of the change in the target behavior.

21 Scale breaks are also used to indicate discontinuities on the vertical axis.

22 Phase/condition change lines are used to indicate manipulations of an independent variable and are drawn to the same height as the vertical axis.

23 Each phase/condition of an experiment should be identified by a brief, descriptive label.

24 Data points should be accurately placed with bold, solid dots. When multiple data paths are used, different geometric symbols are used to distinguish each set of data.

25 Data paths are created by connecting successive data points with a straight line. Successive data points should not be connected when (a) they fall on either side of a phase/condition change line, (b) they span discontinuities of time on the horizontal axis, (c) they span a significant period of time in which behavior was not measured, (d) they span a regularly scheduled measurement period in which data were not collected or were lost or otherwise

unavailable, (e) they fall on either side of a scale break on the vertical axis, (f) they fall in a follow-up or postcheck period that is not regularly spaced in time in the same manner as the rest of the study, and (g) one member of the pair falls outside the range of values described by the vertical axis.

26 The figure legend provides in narrative format a complete description of the graph, giving all of the information needed to interpret the display.

27 Graphs should be drawn only in black and should be sized to fit their intended use.

How to Interpret Graphs

28 Visual analysis of graphed data attempts to answer two questions: did a socially meaningful change in behavior take place, and can the behavior change be attributed to the independent variable?

29 Before beginning to evaluate the data displayed in a graph, a careful examination of the graph's construction should be undertaken. If distortion is suspected from the features of the graph's construction, the data should be re-plotted on a new set of axes before interpretation is attempted.

30 Blocked data and data representing the average performance of a group of subjects should be viewed with the understanding that significant variability may have been lost in the display.

31 Visual analysis of data within a given condition focuses on the number of data points, the variability of performance, the level of performance, and the direction and degree of any trends in the data.

32 As a general rule, the more data in a condition and the greater the stability of those data, the more confidence one can place in the data path's estimate of behavior during that time. The more variability in the behavioral measure during a condition, the greater the need for additional data.

33 Level refers to the value on the vertical axis around which a series of data points converge. When the data in a given condition all fall at or near a specific level, the behavior is considered stable with respect to level; to the extent that the behavioral measures vary considerably from one another, the data are described as showing

variability with respect to level. In cases of extreme variability, no particular level of performance is evidenced.

34 Mean or median level lines are sometimes added to graphic displays to represent the overall average or typical performance during a condition. Mean and median level lines must be used and interpreted with care because they can easily obscure important variability and trends in the data.

35 Trend refers to the overall direction taken by a data path; trends are described in terms of their direction (increasing, decreasing, or zero trend), degree (gradual or steep), and the extent of variability of data points around the trend.

36 Trend direction and degree can be visually represented by drawing a trend line, or line of progress, through a series of data points. Trend lines can be drawn freehand or with the ordinary least squares regression equation or a method called the split-middle line of progress. Split-middle lines of progress can be drawn quickly and reliably and have proved useful in analyzing behavior change.

37 Visual analysis of data across conditions determines whether change in level and/or trend occurred and to what extent any changes were significant.

7

Introduction to Analysis

KEY TERMS

Experimental analysis

Correlation

Functional relation

Analysis

Internal validity

External validity

Confounding variable

Dependent variable

Independent variable

Nonparametric study

Parametric study

Baseline

Stable baseline

Ascending baseline

Descending baseline

Variable baseline

Steady state responding

Baseline logic

Prediction

Practice effects

Affirmation of the consequent

Verification

Replication

This chapter was written by William L. Heward.

Knowledge of the specific arrangements of environmental variables that will produce desired behavior is necessary if a systematic and useful technology of behavior change is to develop. Without this knowledge, behavior change programs could only be considered one-shot efforts, produced by applying procedures randomly selected from a bag of tricks and possessing no generality to other situations. But teachers must be able to teach effective behavior patterns repeatedly to a variety of students; a therapist needs to discover which of several possible treatments will enable a client to behave most appropriately; and a researcher wants to find out whether a procedure shown to be effective with adults can be modified to work with children. These are not farfetched situations but are challenges faced everyday by persons responsible for improving behavior. Basic to all such concerns is a fundamental question that is at the center of every analytic investigation of behavior: How does this behavior work?

Measurement can show whether and when behavior changes, but measurement alone cannot reveal why, or more accurately how, the change came about. An **experimental analysis** must be accomplished to determine how a given behavior functions (works) in relation to specified changes in the environment. This chapter introduces the basic concepts and strategies underlying the analysis of behavior.[1] The first part of the chapter discusses some general conceptions of science and the assumptions about behavior that govern its scientific analysis. The chapter then describes the necessary components of any experiment in behavior and concludes with an explanation

of the logic that guides the experimental methods employed in the analysis of behavior.

THE SCIENTIFIC EXAMINATION OF BEHAVIOR: SOME BASIC CONCEPTIONS AND ASSUMPTIONS

Science

As was discussed in chapter 1, the practice of science is based on a certain philosophy of science that includes assumptions about the nature of natural phenomena (determinism), the kind of information that should be gathered on the phenomena of interest (empiricism), the way in which questions about the workings of nature should be examined (experimental manipulation), and the manner in which the results of experiments are to be judged (with parsimony and philosophic doubt). These attitudes of science apply to all scientific disciplines, including the scientific study of behavior. "The basic characteristics of science are not restricted to any particular subject matter" (Skinner, 1953, p. 11).

In a general sense the goal of science is understanding the phenomena under study—socially important behaviors, in the case of applied behavior analysis. Science produces understanding at three levels: description, prediction, and control. First, systematic observation can enhance the understanding of a given phenomenon by enabling the scientist to describe it accurately. Descriptive knowledge of this type yields a collection of facts about the observed events—facts that can be quantified and classified, as is necessary and important for any scientific discipline.

A second level of scientific understanding occurs when repeated observation shows that two events consistently co-vary. That is, in the presence of one event (e.g., approaching winter) another event occurs with some specified probability (e.g., certain birds fly south). When

---

[1]The scientific study of behavior has benefited immensely from two particularly noteworthy contributions to the literature on experimental methods: Sidman's *Tactics of Scientific Research* (1960) and Johnston and Pennypacker's *Strategies and Tactics of Human Behavioral Research* (1980). Both volumes are essential reading and working references for any serious student or practitioner of behavior analysis, and we acknowledge the significant part both have played in the preparation of this chapter.

systematic co-variation between two events is found, this relationship—termed a **correlation**—can be used to predict the probability that one event will occur, based on the presence of the correlated event.

This ability to predict is a useful result of science; prediction allows preparation. However, the greatest benefits are derived from the third, and highest, level of scientific understanding—control. When experimentation reveals that an event can be made to happen by the manipulation of another event, a **functional relation** is said to exist between the two events. Indeed, the primary question asked by applied behavior analysts is, How can I make this work? (Tawney & Gast, 1984). The understanding gained by the scientific discovery of functional relations is the basis of applied technology in all fields.

> The ultimate product of a natural scientific investigation of the relation between behavior and its determining variables is a statement of the general form: B = F(X1, X2,. . .). Such statements are known as functional relations and state that a certain behavior (or behavior change) is a function of (is determined by) the operation of specific variables X1, X2, and so forth. (Johnston & Pennypacker, 1980, p. 16).

Experimentally determining the effects of environmental manipulation on behavior and demonstrating that those effects can be reliably produced constitute the **analysis** in applied behavior analysis. Reliability in this context is equated with believability that the change in behavior was caused by the variable experimentally manipulated and was not the result of some uncontrolled or unknown factor. The methods of experimentation in any behavioral investigation are selected for their ability to increase the believability of the findings. Analysis of a behavior, then, has occurred when a reliable functional relation between the behavior and some specified aspect of the environment has been demonstrated convincingly.

Baer, Wolf, and Risley (1968) state that analysis of behavior "requires a believable demonstration of the events that can be responsible for the occurrence or nonoccurrence of that behavior. An experimenter has achieved an analysis of a behavior when he can exercise control over it" (p. 94).[2] We have included Baer, Wolf, and Risley's original definition of analysis to highlight an important point. The experimental isolation of a given environmental variable of which a behavior is a function has often been misinterpreted as support for a simplistic conception of the causes of behavior (Johnston & Pennypacker, 1980). The fact that a behavior varies as a function of a given variable does not preclude its varying as a function of other variables as well. Thus, Baer, Wolf, and Risley write of demonstrating that a variable *can* be responsible for the observed behavior change. Even though a complete analysis of a behavior has not been achieved until all of its multiple causes have been accounted for, an applied analysis has been accomplished when the investigator has isolated an environmental variable (or group of variables that operate together as a treatment package) whose manipulation produces predictable and reliable behavior change that is socially significant. An applied analysis of behavior also requires that the target behavior be shown to be a function of an environmental event that can be manipulated effectively (i.e., the presence or absence of the treatment variable can be practically and ethically controlled).

Behavior

Awareness of two facts and two fundamental assumptions about behavior is necessary before one can fully understand either the purpose or methods of human behavioral research. The two facts are that (1) behavior is an individual phenomenon and (2) behavior is a continuous

---

[2] Whether or not a claimed functional relation is believable must, of course, be the judgment of the experimenter's audience. We will explore the believability of research findings further in chapter 10.

phenomenon. The two assumptions are that (1) behavior is determined and (2) behavioral variability is extrinsic to the organism, a logical extension of behavioral determinism.

Behavior Is an Individual Phenomenon

Behavior is defined as an organism's inter-action with the environment. By definition then, a science of behavior is concerned with discovering the laws that govern behavior-environment relations. It also follows that the behavior of individuals must be analyzed in order to examine those relations. Groups do not respond; individuals do.

Measuring the average performance within a group of individuals yields information on the distribution of behavior within the group and, given the methods by which individuals were selected to be in the group, can yield probability statements about the average performance within the larger population represented by the group. However, such methods do not provide information about how any given individual either did perform or might perform in the future. For example, although administrators and taxpayers may be justifiably interested in the average increase in students' reading comprehension from grade level to grade level, such information is of little use to the classroom teacher who must decide how to improve a given student's comprehension skills.

Nonetheless, learning how behavior-environment relations work with many individuals is vital. A technology of behavior change can develop only if it produces functional relations with generality across individuals. The issue is how to achieve that generality. Behavioral scientists believe that discovery of behavioral laws with generality across persons can best be accomplished by replicating with additional subjects the functional relations already empirically demonstrated in individuals. The extent to which both experimentation with single subjects and group-comparison research contribute to the discovery of behavioral laws is discussed in chapter 10.

Behavior Is a Continuous Phenomenon

Just as behavior cannot take place in an environmental void—it must happen somewhere—so must behavior take place at particular points in time. Behavior is neither a state of the organism nor a static event. Instead, behavior takes place in and changes over time. Therefore, single measures, or even multiple measures sporadically dispersed through time, cannot provide an adequate understanding of behavior. Only continuous measurement over time yields a complete record of behavior as it interacts with its environmental influences. Since true continuous measurement is not feasible in most applied settings, systematic repeated measurement of the target behavior has become the hallmark of applied behavior analysis.

Behavior Is Determined

Scientists believe that the universe is a lawful and orderly place, that natural phenomena occur in relationship to other natural events.

> The touchstone of all scientific research is order. The orderliness of relations between variables is at once the operating assumption upon which the experimenter proceeds, the observed fact that permits doing so, and the goal that continuously focuses experimental decisions. (Johnston & Pennypacker, 1980, p. 253)

In other words, the occurrence of events is governed by their functional relations to other events; things have causes and effects and do not just happen. Behavioral scientists believe that human behavior is a natural phenomenon and, like other natural phenomena, is determined.

Although the determinism of behavior must be regarded as an assumption—it cannot logically be proven—it is an assumption based on a tremendous amount of empirical support.

> Data gathered from all scientific fields indicate that *determinism* holds throughout nature. It has become clear that the *law of determinism,* that is, that all things are determined, holds for the behavioral area also. . . . When looking at actual behavior we've found that in situation 1, behavior

is caused; in situation 2, behavior is caused, in situation 3, behavior is caused; . . . and in situation 1001, behavior is caused. Every time an experimenter introduces an independent variable that produces some behavior or some change in behavior, we have further *empirical* evidence that behavior is caused or deterministic. (Malott, General, & Snapper, 1973, pp. 170, 175)

Behavioral Variability Is Extrinsic to the Organism When all conditions during a given phase of an experiment are held constant and repeated measures of the behavior result in a great deal of "bounce" in the data (i.e., the subject is not responding in a consistent fashion), the behavior is said to display variability. One school of experimental methodology—the investigators who use and promote group comparison designs—makes two assumptions about such variability: (1) behavioral variability is an intrinsic characteristic of the organism, and (2) behavioral variability is randomly distributed across individuals in a given population. Two critical methodological implications stem from these two assumptions: (1) experimentally investigating variability is a waste of time—it simply exists, a given; and (2) large groups of subjects are required so that the random nature of variability can be statistically controlled (canceled out).

Both of these assumptions about variability are quite likely false (empirical evidence points in the opposite direction), and both are clearly detrimental to a science of behavior. "Variables are not canceled statistically. They are simply buried so their effects are not seen" (Sidman, 1960, p. 162).[3]

Behavioral researchers approach variability in their data quite differently. The fundamental assumption guiding the science of behavior is that behavioral variability is not intrinsic to the organism but is the result of some uncontrolled aspect of the experiment itself or an uncontrolled or unknown aspect outside the experiment. Thus, instead of attempting to mask variability by averaging the performance of many subjects, the behavior analyst attempts to locate its controlling variables by experimentally manipulating factors suspected of causing the variability. Searching for the causal factors contributes to the understanding of behavior, for experimental demonstration of a source of variability implies experimental control and thus another functional relation. In fact, "tracking down these answers may even turn out to be more rewarding than answering the original experimental question" (Johnston & Pennypacker, 1980 p. 226).

Experimentally tracking down sources of variability is always the preferred approach from a purely scientific viewpoint. However, the applied behavior analyst, with a problem to solve, must often take variability as it presents itself (Sidman, 1960). Sometimes the applied researcher has neither the time nor the resources to experimentally manipulate even suspected and likely sources of variability (e.g., a teacher who interacts with a student for only part of the day has no hope of controlling the many variables outside the classroom). In most settings the applied behavior analyst must seek a treatment variable robust enough to produce a reliable effect on the target behavior that goes beyond the variability produced by uncontrolled variables (Baer, 1977).

Components of Experimental Design

"We conduct experiments to find out something we do not know" (Sidman, 1960, p. 214). That something for the applied behavior analyst is a functional relation between a socially significant behavior and a socially valid treatment. Knowledge of functional relations enables the behavior analyst to reliably alter important behavior in meaningful ways. As stated earlier, demonstration of a functional

---

[3]Some investigators use group comparison designs not just to cancel randomly distributed variability but also to produce what they believe will be results with more generality. Group comparison designs and single-subject methodologies will be compared in chapter 10.

relation requires an analysis of the variables of which the behavior is a function.

Behavior is an interaction between an organism and its environment and is best analyzed by measuring the variability in behavior as a result of imposed variations on the environment. This statement embodies both the goal and the general strategy of behavioral research: to demonstrate that measured changes in the target behavior occur because of experimentally manipulated changes in the environment. Experiments that show convincingly that changes in behavior are a function of the independent variable and are not the result of uncontrolled or unknown variables are said to have a high degree of **internal validity**. A study without internal validity can yield no meaningful statements regarding functional relations between the variables examined in the experiment, nor can it be used as the basis for any statements regarding the generality of the findings to other subjects, settings, and/or behaviors. The term **external validity** commonly refers to the degree to which a study's results are generalizable to other subjects, settings, and/or behaviors. Strategies for assessing and extending the generality of experimentally demonstrated functional relations are discussed in chapter 10.

When initially planning an experiment and while later examining the "live" data from an ongoing study, the investigator must always be on the lookout for threats to internal validity. Variables that are known or suspected to exert an uncontrolled influence on the data pattern are called **confounding variables**. The primary factor in evaluating the strength of an experimental design is the extent to which it eliminates or reduces the effects of confounding variables while still investigating the research questions of interest.

It is impossible to eliminate all sources of variability in an experiment, although the researcher always strives for that ideal. The ideal experimental design would allow the researcher to simultaneously measure and compare the behavior of an individual in both the presence and absence of the treatment variable (Risley, 1969). In reality, the goal of experimental design is to eliminate as many uncontrolled variables as possible and to hold constant the influence of all other variables except the independent variable, which is purposefully manipulated in order to determine its effects.

For our purposes experimental design refers to all of the decisions the investigator must make in planning and executing a study. The essential components and characteristics of any scientific investigation of behavior are (1) a subject, (2) a behavior, (3) a setting, (4) a system for direct and repeated measurement of the behavior, (5) ongoing visual inspection of the experimental data, and (6) an independent variable, the manipulation of which establishes the conditions of the study.

Subjects

The experimental methods used by behavior analysts are most often referred to as single-subject, or N = 1 designs, not because behavior analysis studies are necessarily conducted with only one subject (although some are), but because the strategies for analyzing behavioral changes employ the subject as her own control. In other words, each subject's behavior is measured repeatedly as she is exposed to every condition of the study (e.g., the presence and absence of the treatment variable). During the course of an experiment a subject is often exposed to each different condition several times. Measures of the subject's behavior during each condition of the study serve as the basis for comparing the effects of experimental variables as they are presented or withdrawn in subsequent conditions. Although most studies in applied behavior analysis do involve more than one subject (4 to 8 is common), each subject's data are graphed and analyzed separately. Each subject is treated as an individual experiment.

Sometimes the behavior analyst is interested in evaluating the effect of a treatment variable on group performance—for example, the number of homework assignments completed by members of a fifth grade class. In such cases the total or average number of assignments completed is the behavior of interest, and it is recorded and monitored within a single-subject design. However, it must be remembered that unless each student's data are individually graphed and interpreted, no given student's behavior has actually been analyzed, and the behavior of any given individual cannot be represented by the group results.

Use of a single subject, or a small number of subjects, each of whom is considered an intact experiment, is in sharp contrast to traditional group comparison designs employing large numbers of subjects. Proponents of group comparison designs believe that large numbers of subjects are needed to control for the variability discussed earlier and to increase the generality of any findings to the larger subject population. For now let us leave this issue with a quotation from Johnston and Pennypacker (1980):

> Worse still, the variability imposed by the manipulated independent variable will inevitably be obscured to some degree when it is quantitatively homogenized with intersubject variability; this is perhaps the most dangerous result of comingling inter- and intrasubject variability. That obfuscation is easily averted by insisting that all experimental effects be clearly demonstrated on the behavior of one organism at a time with its single environmental history. The question of the representativeness of the effect for other subjects in the population (subject generality) can then be easily and effectively approached by succeeding investigations with other subjects. (p. 256)

Behavior

The target behavior in a study of applied behavior analysis, or more precisely the target behavior's measurable dimension of interest (e.g., rate, duration), is called the **dependent variable**. The behavior is so labeled because the

experiment is designed precisely to determine whether the behavior is, in fact, dependent upon (i.e., a function of) the independent variable(s) manipulated by the investigator. (An explanation of the criteria and procedures for the selection and definition of response classes that meet the requirements of applied behavior analysis was provided in chapter 3.)

In some studies more than one dependent variable is measured. One reason for using multiple behaviors is to provide data patterns that can serve as a control procedure to evaluate and replicate the effects of an independent variable as it is sequentially applied to each of the behaviors.[4] A second reason for multiple dependent measures is to assess the generality of treatment effects to behaviors other than the response class to which the independent variable was applied. This strategy is used to determine whether the independent variable had any collateral effects—either desired or undesired—on other behaviors of interest. Such behaviors are referred to as secondary dependent variables. The experimenter records regular measures of their rate of occurrence, though perhaps not with the same frequency with which measures of the primary dependent variable are recorded.

Yet another reason for measuring multiple behaviors is to determine whether changes in the behavior of a person other than the subject occur during the course of an experiment and whether such changes might in turn explain observed changes in the subject's behavior. This strategy is implemented primarily as a control strategy in assessing the effects of a suspected confounding variable: the extra behavior(s) measured are not true dependent variables in the sense of undergoing analysis. For example, in a study evaluating the effects of the self-recording of classroom study behavior by a junior high school girl, Broden, Hall, and

---

[4]This is the distinguishing feature of the multiple-baseline design, an experimental tactic widely used by applied behavior analysts. Features of this tactic are presented in chapter 9.

Mitts (1971) observed and recorded throughout the experiment the number of times the girl's teacher paid attention to her. If teacher attention had been found to co-vary with changes in study behavior, a functional relation between self-recording and study behavior would not have been demonstrated. Instead, teacher attention would have been identified as a potential confounding variable, and the next avenue of investigation would have included efforts to experimentally control it (i.e., to hold teacher attention constant) or to systematically manipulate and analyze its effects. In reality, however, the data revealed no functional relation between teacher attention and study behavior during the first four phases of the experiment, when teacher attention was of concern as a highly likely confounding variable.

Setting

Functional relations are demonstrated when observed variations in behavior can be attributed to specific operations imposed on the environment. To properly make such attributions, the investigator must, among other things, control two sets of environmental variables. First, the investigator must control the independent variable by presenting it, withdrawing it, and/or varying its value. Second, the investigator must control, by holding constant, all other aspects of the experimental setting to prevent unplanned environmental variation. These two operations—precisely manipulating the independent variable and maintaining the constancy of every other relevant aspect of the experimental setting—define experimental control.

In basic laboratory research the experimental space is designed and furnished in a manner intended to maximize experimental control. Lighting, temperature, and sound, for example, are all held constant, and programmed apparatus virtually guarantee the presentation of antecedent stimuli and the delivery of consequences as planned. Applied behavior analysis, however, must be conducted in the settings in which socially important behaviors naturally occur—the classroom, home, and workplace. It is impossible to control every feature of an applied environment; and to add to the difficulty, subjects are typically in the experimental setting for only part of each day, bringing with them the influence of ongoing contingencies operating in other settings.

In spite of the complexity and changing nature of applied settings, the behavior analyst must make every effort to hold constant all seemingly relevant aspects. When unplanned variations take place, the investigator must either wait out their effects or try to incorporate them into the design of the experiment. In any event repeated measures of the subject's behavior are the barometer for assessing whether or not unplanned environmental changes are of concern.

A given experiment must, of course, take place in at least one setting, but applied studies can also be conducted in more than one setting. Multiple settings are sometimes used as a control technique to evaluate the effects of an independent variable that is sequentially applied to the target behavior in each setting. In addition, data are often collected in more than one setting to assess whether behavior changes observed in the primary setting also occur in the other setting(s).

Measurement System

Beginning students of behavior analysis are sometimes prone to believe that the discipline is preoccupied with issues and procedures related to the observation and measurement of behavior. They want to get on with the analysis. However, the results of any experiment can be presented and interpreted only in terms of what was measured, and the observation and recording procedures used in the study determine not only what was measured, but how well it was measured (i.e., how representative of the subject's actual behavior is the estimate provided by the experimental data). It is absolutely critical that observation and recording procedures be conducted in a completely standardized manner throughout an experiment. Standardization involves every aspect of a measurement system, from definition of the target behavior to the timing of observations to the manner in which the raw data are transposed from recording sheets to session summary sheets. As detailed in chapter 5, an adventitious change in measurement tactics can result in unwanted variability or confounded treatment effects.

Ongoing Visual Inspection of the Experimental Data

The previous chapter outlined the advantages that accrue to the behavioral researcher who uses continuous visual inspection to maintain direct contact with the experimental data. The behavior analyst must become skilled at recognizing changes in level, trend, and degree of variability as these changes develop in the data. Because behavior is a continuous, dynamic phenomenon, experiments designed to discover its controlling variables must enable the investigator to continuously inspect and respond to the data as the study progresses. Only in this way can the behavior analyst be ready to manipulate features of the environment at the time and in the manner that will reduce the effects of confounding variables.

Independent Variable

Behavior analysts seek reliable relations between behavior and the environmental variables of which it is a function. The particular arrangement of environmental events that the experimenter manipulates during a study is called the **independent variable.** Whereas any changes that must be made in the experimental setting in order to conduct the study (e.g., the addition of observers to measure behavior) are made with the goal of minimizing their effect on the dependent variable, "changes

in the independent variable are arranged by the experimenter in order to maximize . . . its influence on responding" (Johnston & Pennypacker, 1980, p. 260).

In the simplest case from a design perspective but not necessarily from a practical point of view, the independent variable can be manipulated so that it is either present or absent during each time period or phase of the study. When the independent variable is in either of these conditions during a study, the experiment is termed a **nonparametric study**. In contrast, a **parametric study** examines and compares the effects of a range of values of the independent variable. For example, Clark, Rowbury, Baer, and Baer (1973) conducted a parametric study when they used several variable ratio schedules to evaluate the effects of a time-out procedure on the disruptive behavior of a preschool child with mental retardation. Parametric experiments are sometimes used because a functional relation may have more generality if it is based on several values of the independent variable.

Sometimes the investigator is interested in evaluating and comparing the effects of several treatment alternatives. In this case multiple independent variables become part of the experiment. For example, perhaps two separate treatments are evaluated as well as the effects of a third treatment, which represents a combination of both variables. However, even in experiments with multiple independent variables, a simple but fundamental rule of experimental design must be adhered to: *Change only one variable at a time.* Only in this manner can the behavior analyst attribute any measured changes in behavior to a specific independent variable. If two or more variables are altered simultaneously, no conclusions can be made on the extent to which either variable contributed to the change in behavior.

Many of the independent variables evaluated by applied behavior analysts consist of "package interventions" (e.g., rules + praise, self-recording + time-out); but the rule still holds. When manipulating treatment packages, the experimenter must be sure that every component of the package is presented or withdrawn. It is also important to understand that the entire package is being evaluated, not any given component of it. To determine the relative contributions of each part of the package, a component analysis must be carried out. Chapters 8 and 9 describe experimental strategies for component analyses.

Independent variables can be introduced, withdrawn, increased or decreased in value, or combined across behaviors, settings, and/or subjects in an infinite number of ways that produce an infinite number of experimental designs. However, there are only two basic kinds of independent variable changes that can be made with respect to the behavior of a given subject in a given setting.

> Although it seems remarkably simple, there are only two kinds of change that can be arranged with the independent variable: A new condition can be introduced or an old condition can be reintroduced. . . . Experimental designs are merely temporal arrangements of various new and old conditions across behaviors and settings in ways that produce data that are convincing to the investigator and the audience. (Johnston & Pennypacker, 1980, p. 270)

Both Johnston and Pennypacker (1980) and Sidman (1960) warn that there are no set experimental designs available for selection for a given research problem. The investigator must not get locked into design formats that entail a priori assumptions about the nature of the functional relations that are sought and that may be insensitive to unanticipated changes in behavior. Instead, the behavior analyst should select experimental strategies that fit the initial research questions, while standing ever ready to "explore relevant variables by manipulating them in an improvised and rapidly changing design" (Skinner, 1966, p. 21).

Simultaneous with and to a large degree responsible for the growth and success of applied behavior analysis have been the development and refinement of a powerful group of extremely flexible experimental tactics for evaluating behavior-environment relationships. The most widely used tactics and the kinds of research questions for which each is best suited will be presented in chapters 8 and 9. However, to most effectively select, modify, and combine these tactics into convincing experiments, the beginning behavior analyst must first fully understand the reasoning and logic that serves as the foundation of every single-subject investigation.

BASELINE DATA

Behavior analysts discover behavior-environment relationships by comparing data generated by repeated measures of a subject's behavior under the different environmental conditions of the experiment. The basic method of evaluating the effects of a given variable is to impose it on an ongoing measure of behavior obtained in its absence. These original data serve as the **baseline** by which to determine and evaluate any observed changes in behavior. A baseline condition does not necessarily imply the absence of instruction or treatment as such, but rather the absence of a specific independent variable of experimental interest.

Why Establish a Baseline?

The primary purpose for establishing a baseline is to use the subject's performance in the absence of the independent variable as an objective basis for evaluating the effects of the independent variable. In addition, systematic observation of the target behavior before intervention with a treatment variable provides the opportunity to look for and note environmental events that occur just before and just after the behavior. Such empirically obtained descriptive accounts of behavior-environment correlations are often invaluable in planning an effective intervention. The typical example is the baseline observation of a disruptive child whose outbursts are consistently followed by parent or teacher attention. Use of this information in designing an intervention might suggest a combination of planned nonattention following outbursts and contingent attention following desired behavior.

Baseline data are also useful in setting initial criteria for reinforcement, which is a particularly important step when a contingency is first put into effect. (See page 271.) If the criteria are too high, the subject never comes into contact with the contingency; if they are too low, no improvement can be expected.

One final reason for collecting baseline data has to do with the merits of objective observation versus subjective opinion. Sometimes the results of systematic measurement during nontreatment conditions cause significant others to alter their position on the necessity and value of attempting to change the behavior. Perhaps a behavior change target has been chosen be-

cause of several recent and extreme instances or because the behavior's topography attracts undue attention from teachers or parents. Objective measurement over a period of several days might show that the behavior is not, in fact, emitted at a rate significant enough to alter.

Types of Baseline Data Patterns

Figure 7.1 shows four data patterns sometimes generated by baseline measurement. It must be stressed that these hypothetical baselines represent only four examples of the many different baseline data patterns an experimenter can encounter. The potential combinations of different levels, trends, and degrees of variability are, of course, infinite. Nevertheless, in an effort to provide guidance to the beginning behavior analyst, some general statements will be given about the experimental decisions that might be warranted by the data shown in Figure 7.1.

FIGURE 7.1 Data patterns illustrating stable (A), ascending (B), descending (C), and variable (D) baselines.

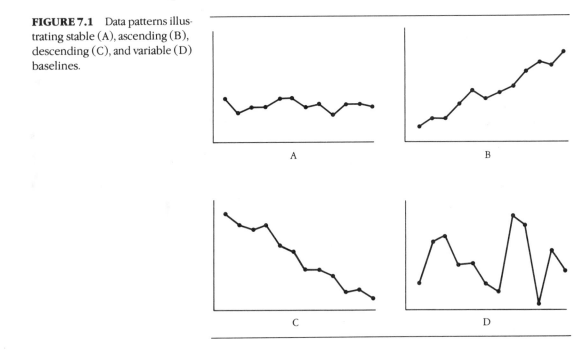

Graph A shows a clearly **stable baseline.** There is no evidence of either an upward or downward trend, and all of the data points fall into a relatively tight range. One can reasonably assume that data such as these form a reliable estimate of the subject's behavior under the prevailing environmental conditions. A stable baseline is the most desirable basis for beginning an experimental analysis. If changes in the behavior are observed when an independent variable is imposed on the baseline shown in Graph A, one can reasonably suspect that those changes are related to the independent variable.

The data in Graphs B and C reveal an **ascending baseline** and a **descending baseline**, respectively. The data path in Graph B shows an increasing trend in the behavior over time, whereas the data path in Graph C shows a decreasing trend. Such trends in baseline data must be treated cautiously by the applied behavior analyst. By definition, dependent variables in applied behavior analysis are selected because they need to be changed. But ascending and descending baselines reveal behaviors already in the process of changing. If the behavior analyst introduces an independent variable, any effects are likely to be obscured or confounded by the variables responsible for the already-occurring change. Yet the investigator needs to change the behavior. The applied perspective can help solve the dilemma.

Whether a treatment variable should be introduced depends upon whether the changing baseline data represent improving or deteriorating performance. If either an ascending or descending baseline represents behavior change in the desired direction, the investigator must withhold treatment and continue to monitor the dependent variable under baseline conditions. When the behavior ceases to improve, as evidenced by stable baseline responding, the independent variable can be applied. If the trend does not level off and the behavior continues to improve, the original problem may no longer be present, leaving no reason

for application of the treatment (although the investigator might be motivated to isolate and analyze the variables responsible for the spontaneous improvement). If an independent variable is applied to an already-improving behavior, it is most difficult, and often impossible, to claim any continued improvement as a function of the independent variable.

Ascending or descending baselines representing significantly deteriorating performance signal an immediate application of the independent variable. From an applied perspective the decision to intervene is obvious: the subject's performance is deteriorating, and a treatment suspected of improving the behavior should be introduced. An independent variable capable of affecting desired behavior change in the presence of other variables working in the opposite direction is most likely a robust and powerful variable, one that will be a welcome addition to the behavior analyst's list of effective treatments. The decision to intervene on deteriorating baselines is also a sound one from an analytic perspective, which will be discussed in the next section.

Graph D in Figure 7.1 shows an **unstable** or **variable baseline**. The data in this graph show just one of many possible patterns of unstable responding. The data points do not consistently fall within a narrow range of values, nor do they give evidence of any clear trend. Introducing the independent variable in the presence of such variability is unwise from an experimental standpoint. Variability is assumed to be the result of environmental variables which, in the case of Graph D, seem to be operating in an uncontrolled fashion. To most effectively analyze behavior, the sources of variability must first be isolated and controlled.

> Establishing stable responding is thus an index of the rigor of experimental control. If sufficiently stable responding cannot be obtained, the experimenter is in no position to add an independent variable of suspected but unknown influence. To do so would be to compound confusion and lead to further ignorance. (Johnston & Pennypacker, 1980, p. 229)

Again, however, applied considerations must be weighed with purely scientific ones. The applied problem may be one that cannot wait to be solved. Or, confounding variables in the subject's environment and the setting(s) of the investigation may simply be beyond the experimenter's control.[5] In such situations the independent variable is introduced with the hope of producing stable responding in its presence. Sidman (1960) agreed that "the behavioral engineer must ordinarily take variability as he finds it, and deal with it as an unavoidable fact of life" (p. 192).

BASELINE LOGIC

Stable responding allows more than a simple before and after comparison of behavior in different experimental conditions. Stable, or **steady state responding**—"in which the behavior of interest exhibits relatively little variation of its measured dimensional quantities" (Johnston & Pennypacker, 1980, p. 227)—enables the behavior analyst to employ a powerful form of inductive reasoning sometimes called **baseline logic.** Baseline logic is an integral feature of all experimental analyses of behavior, whether basic or applied, and entails three elements: prediction, verification, and replication.

Prediction

"**Prediction** may be defined as the anticipated outcome of a presently unknown or future measurement. It is the most elegant use of quantification upon which validation of all scientific and technological activity rests" (Johnston & Pennypacker, 1980, p. 120). Figure 7.2 shows a series of hypothetical data points

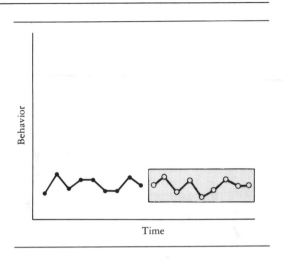

FIGURE 7.2 Solid data points representing the actual measures of behavior that might be generated in a stable baseline; open data points within the shaded box representing the level of responding that would be predicted on the basis of the preceding measures, should the environment remain constant.

representing a stable pattern of responding. The consistency of the first five data points in the series suggests that subsequent measures will fall in the narrow range shown thus far. Indeed, a sixth measure is taken that gives credence to this prediction. The same prediction is then made again, this time with more confidence, and another measure of behavior shows it to be correct. Throughout a baseline or any other experimental condition, an ongoing prediction is made and confirmed until the investigator has every reason to believe that the response measure will not change under the present conditions; in other words, all relevant features of the behavior have been displayed. The shaded portion of Figure 7.2 shows a prediction of future responding under "relatively constant environmental conditions."[6] Given the

---

[5]The applied researcher must guard very carefully against automatically assuming that unwanted variability is a function of variables beyond his capability or resources to isolate and control, and thus failing to pursue investigation of potentially important functional relations.

[6]"The above reference to 'relatively constant environmental conditions' means only that the experimenter is not knowingly producing uncontrolled variations in functionally related environmental events" (Johnston & Pennypacker, 1980, p. 228).

stability of the obtained measures, few experienced scientists would quarrel with the prediction.

How many measures must be taken before an experimenter can use a series of data points to predict future behavior with confidence? Baer, Wolf, and Risley (1968) recommend continuing baseline measurement until "its stability is clear." Even though there are no set answers, some general statements can be made about the predictive power of steady states. All things equal, it is better to have many measurements than few; the longer the condition, the better its predictive power. Also, if the experimenter is not sure whether measurement has produced stable responding, in all likelihood it has not, and more data should be collected before the independent variable is introduced. Finally, the investigator's knowledge of the characteristics of the behavior under constant conditions is invaluable in deciding when to terminate baseline measurement and introduce the independent variable. That knowledge can be drawn both from personal experience in obtaining stable baselines on similar response classes and from familiarity with patterns of baseline responding found in the published literature.

It should be clear by now that guidelines such as "gather baseline data for one week" or "baseline measures taken over two consecutive school weeks are usually sufficient" should not be followed. One or two weeks of baseline measurement may indeed provide a convincing picture of steady state responding. But the question "Are the data sufficiently stable to serve as the basis for experimental evaluation?" can only be answered by ongoing prediction and confirmation by repeated measures in an environment in which all relevant conditions are held constant.

Teachers are often interested in analyzing functional relations between instruction and the acquisition of new skills. In such situations baseline is often assumed to be zero; for example, one would expect repeated observa-tions of a child who has never tied her shoes to yield a perfectly stable baseline of no correct responses. However, casual observations that have never shown a child to emit a particular behavior do not constitute an empirically defensible baseline and cannot be used to justify claims about the effects of any instruction. It might be that if given repeated opportunities to respond, the child would begin to emit the target behavior at a nonzero rate. Improvements in performance resulting from practice opportunities that are necessarily provided in order to obtain repeated measurements are called **practice effects**. For example, attempting to obtain stable baseline data for students performing arithmetic problems can result in improved levels of responding simply because of the repeated practice inherent in the measurement process. Repeated baseline measures must be used either to reveal the existence or to demonstrate the nonexistence of practice effects; otherwise, they will necessarily confound the study, making it impossible to separate and account for the effects of practice and instruction on the subject's final performance. When practice effects are found, baseline data collection must be continued until steady state responding is attained.

The necessity to empirically demonstrate a stable baseline and to control for practice effects does not require applied behavior analysts to withhold needed instruction. Nothing is gained by collecting unduly long baselines of behaviors that cannot reasonably be expected to already be in the subject's repertoire. For example, many behaviors cannot be emitted unless the subject is competent in certain prerequisite behaviors; there is no legitimate possibility of a child's tying his shoes if he currently does not pick up the laces, nor of a student's solving division problems if she cannot subtract and multiply. Obtaining extended baseline data for such behaviors would represent unnecessary pro forma measurement. Such measures would "not so much represent zero behavior as zero opportunity for behavior to occur, and there is no need to document at the level of well-measured data that behavior does not occur when it cannot" (Horner & Baer, 1978, p. 190).

Fortunately, applied behavior analysts have neither to abandon the use of baseline logic nor to repeatedly measure nonexistent behavior at the expense of beginning instruction. The multiple probe technique, described in chapter 9, is an experimental design tactic that enables the use of baseline logic to functionally analyze the relation between instruction and acquisition of behaviors empirically shown to be nonexistent in the subject's repertoire prior to manipulation of the independent variable (Horner & Baer, 1978).

Affirmation of the Consequent

The predictive power of stable baseline responding enables the behavior analyst to employ a kind of inductive logic known as **affirming the consequent** (Johnston & Pennypacker, 1980). When an experimenter decides to apply the independent variable in response to a stable baseline, an explicit assumption has been made: if the independent variable were not applied, the behavior, as indicated by the baseline data path, would not change. The experimenter is also predicting that the independent variable will result in a change in behavior.

The logical reasoning behind affirming the consequent begins with a true antecedent-consequence (if-A-then-B) statement and proceeds like this:

1 If A is true, then B is true.
2 B is found to be true.
3 Therefore, A is true.

The behavior analyst's version is like this:

1 If the independent variable (A) is a controlling factor for the behavior, then the data (B) will show changes in the behavior when the independent variable is present.

2 The data show changes in the behavior when the independent variable is present (B is true).

3 Therefore, the independent variable is a controlling variable for the behavior (therefore, A is true).

The logic, of course, is not completely sound; other factors might be responsible for the truthfulness of A. But, as will be shown, a successful (convincing) experimental design affirms several if-A-then-B possibilities, further reducing or eliminating the likelihood of other factors being responsible for the observed changes in behavior.

Hypothetical data have been plotted in Figures 7.3 to 7.5 to illustrate how the three components of baseline logic—prediction, verification, and replication—are employed in the reversal design, one of the most common and powerful experimental design tactics used by applied behavior analysts (see chapter 8). Figure 7.3 shows a successful affirmation of the consequent. Steady state responding during baseline gave credence to the prediction that continued measurement would produce data similar to those in the shaded portion of the graph if no changes were made in the environment. The independent variable was then introduced, and repeated measurement of the dependent variable during this treatment condition showed that the behavior did indeed change. The difference between the observed level of responding in the presence of the independent variable and the predicted level of responding in the absence of the independent variable represents the extent of the effect of the independent variable. (Using the prediction of behavior measures in the absence of the independent variable represents the behavior analyst's effort to approximate the ideal but impossible simultaneous measurement of the dependent variable in both the presence and

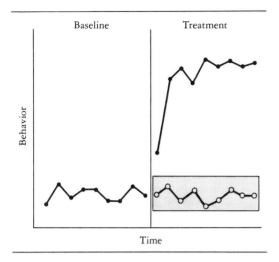

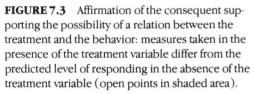

FIGURE 7.3 Affirmation of the consequent supporting the possibility of a relation between the treatment and the behavior: measures taken in the presence of the treatment variable differ from the predicted level of responding in the absence of the treatment variable (open points in shaded area).

absence of the independent variable.) Even though an affirmation of the consequent is demonstrated by the data—a change in the behavior was observed in the presence of the independent variable—asserting a functional relation at this point is unwarranted. The experimental design has not yet ruled out the possibility of other variables being responsible for the change in behavior.

A much more firm statement about the relationship between the treatment and the behavior can be made at this point, however, if changes in the dependent variable are *not* observed in the presence of the independent variable. Assuming accurate measures of the behavior and a measurement system sensitive to changes in the behavior, then no behavior change in the presence of the independent variable constitutes a disconfirmation of the consequent (B was shown not to be true), and the independent variable is eliminated as a controlling variable. However, as Johnston and

Pennypacker (1980) warn, eliminating a treatment from the ranks of controlling variables on the basis of no observed effect presupposes experimental control of the highest order.

However, in the situation illustrated in Figure 7.3, a change in behavior was observed in the presence of the independent variable, revealing at least a correlation between the independent variable and the target behavior. To what extent was the observed behavior change a function of the manipulated variable? To pursue this question, the behavior analyst must employ the next component of baseline logic—verification.

Verification

In order to increase the probability that an observed change in behavior was functionally related to the independent variable, the experimenter must verify its effect. **Verification** is accomplished by demonstrating that the prior level of baseline responding would have remained unchanged had the independent variable not been introduced (Risley, 1969). If that can be demonstrated, this operation verifies the accuracy of the original prediction of continued stable baseline responding and greatly reduces the probability that some uncontrolled (confounding) variable was responsible for the observed change in behavior. Again, the reasoning behind affirmation of the consequent is the logic that underlies the experimental strategy.

Figure 7.4 illustrates the verification of effect in our hypothetical experiment. When steady state responding is evidenced in the presence of the independent variable, the investigator removes the treatment variable, thereby regaining the previous baseline conditions. This strategy allows the possibility of affirming two different consequents (Johnston & Pennypacker, 1980). The first follows this pattern:

1 If the independent variable (A) controls responding, then its removal (B) will

FIGURE 7.4 Verification of a previously predicted level of baseline responding by termination or withdrawal of the treatment variable. The actual data collected during Baseline 2 (solid dots) show a successful verification and a second affirmation of the consequent based on a comparison with the predicted level of responding (open dots in Baseline 2) in the continued presence of the treatment variable.

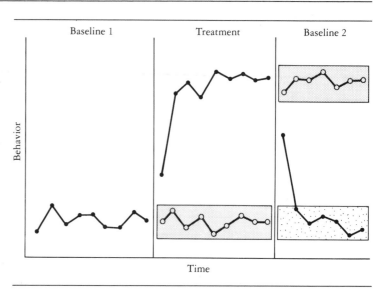

coincide with changes in the response measure.

2 Removal of the independent variable is accompanied by changes in the behavior (B is true).

3 Therefore, the independent variable controls responding (therefore, A is true).

The second follows this pattern:

1 If baseline conditions (A) controlled the behavior before, then similar levels of responding (B) will be revealed when the baseline conditions are returned.

2 When baseline conditions are reinstated, levels of responding similar to those of the previous baseline condition are observed (B is true).

3 Therefore, the baseline conditions controlled the behavior both then and now (therefore, A is true).

The actual data collected during the verification phase of our hypothetical experiment appear in the area shaded with dots under the label Baseline 2 in Figure 7.4. The predicted level of responding if the independent variable had not been removed is represented by the open data points in the shaded area, also under Baseline 2. (The predictive component of baseline logic applies to steady state responding during any condition of an experiment, baseline and treatment phases alike.) The difference between the data actually obtained during Baseline 2 (shaded with dots) and the predicted level of responding during Baseline 2 (just shaded) affirms the first if-A-then-B statement: if the treatment is a controlling variable, then its removal will result in changes in behavior. Similarity between actual responding during Baseline 2 (shaded with dots) and responding during Baseline 1 confirms the second if-A-then-B statement: if baseline conditions controlled the behavior before, reinstating baseline conditions will result in similar levels of responding.

Again, of course, the observed changes in behavior associated with the application and withdrawal of the independent variable are subject to interpretations other than a claim of a functional relation between the two events. However, the case for the existence of a functional relation is becoming stronger. When the independent variable was applied, behavior change was observed; when the independent variable was withdrawn, responding returned to baseline levels. To the extent that the experimenter effectively controls the presence and absence of the independent variable and holds constant all other functionally related variables in the experimental setting, a functional relation appears likely; an important behavior change has been produced and reversed by manipulation of a specified variable. The process of verification greatly reduces the likelihood that some uncontrolled variable was responsible for the change in behavior.

Does this two-step strategy of prediction and verification constitute sufficient demonstration of a functional relation? What if some uncontrolled variable co-varied with the independent variable as it was presented and withdrawn and this uncontrolled variable was actually responsible for the observed changes in behavior? If such was the case, then claiming a functional relation between the target behavior and the independent variable would at best be inaccurate and would, at the worst, preclude a search for the actual controlling variables whose identification and control would help build an effective and reliable technology of behavior change. The appropriately skeptical experimenter (and consumer of experimental research) must question the reliability of effect. How reliable is this verified behavior change? Is the apparent functional relation a fleeting, one-time-only phenomenon, or will repeated application of the independent variable reliably produce the same behavior change? An effective experimental design offers empirical data in response to the questions raised by experimentation. In order to investigate uncertain reliability, the behavior analyst must employ the final, and perhaps the most important, component of baseline logic and experimental design—replication.

Replication

Replication means repeating the previously observed change with further manipulations of the independent variable.[7] Replication within an experiment accomplishes two important goals. First, reproducing the previously observed behavior change reduces the probability that a variable other than the independent variable was responsible for the twice-observed behavior change. Second, replication demonstrates the reliability of the behavior change; it can be made to happen again.

Figure 7.5 adds the component of replication to our hypothetical experiment. After the data during Baseline 2 resemble the level of responding previously noted in Baseline 1, the independent variable is reintroduced; this is the Treatment 2 phase. To the extent that the data generated during the second application of the treatment (shaded with cross-hatched lines) resemble the level of responding observed during Treatment 1, replication has occurred. Our hypothetical experiment has now produced powerful evidence that a functional relation exists between the independent and the dependent variables. The extent to which one has faith in the assertion of a functional relation rests on numerous factors, some of the most important of which are the accuracy and sensitivity of the measurement system, the degree of control maintained by the experimenter over all relevant variables, the length and stability of responding within each phase of the experiment, and the magnitude and consistency of behavior change across conditions. If each of these considerations is satisfied by the experimental design and is supported by the data as displayed within the design, then replication of effect becomes perhaps the most critical factor in claiming a functional relation. "Replication is the essence of believability" (Baer, Wolf, & Risley, 1968, p. 95).

Manipulations of the independent variable in an effort to replicate an observed effect can,

---

[7]Replication also means the repeating of experiments to determine whether their findings can be extended to other subjects, settings, and/or behaviors. The replication of experiments will be examined in chapter 10.

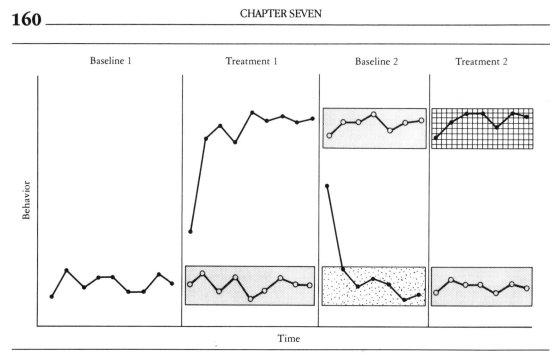

FIGURE 7.5 Replication of experimental effect accomplished by reintroducing the treatment variable. The data collected during Treatment 2 (solid dots shaded with cross hatching) offer a strong case for a functional relation between the treatment variable and the target behavior.

of course, be conducted many times within the design of an experiment. The number of replications required to convincingly demonstrate a functional relation is related to many considerations, including all of those just enumerated, and to the existence of other similar experiments that have produced the same effects. Ultimately, the question of believability must be answered by all those who use the results of a given experiment.

SUMMARY

Introduction

1 Knowledge of specific functional relations between behavior and environment is necessary if a systematic and useful technology of behavior change is to develop.

2 Measurement can show whether and when behavior changes, but measurement alone cannot reveal how the change has come about.

3 An experimental analysis must be performed to determine how a given behavior functions in relation to specific environmental events.

The Scientific Examination of Behavior

4 The basic goal of science is understanding the phenomena under study—socially important behaviors, in the case of applied behavior analysis.

5 Science produces understanding at three levels; description, prediction, and control.

6 A correlation exists when two events systematically co-vary with one another. Predictions can be made about the probability that one event will occur based on the occurrence of the correlated event.

7 Analysis of behavior has been accomplished when a reliable functional relation between the behavior and some specified event in the environment has been demonstrated experimentally.

8 A functional analysis does not eliminate the possibility that the behavior under investigation is also a function of other variables.

9 Behavior is an individual phenomenon. Measuring the average performance within a group of individuals does not provide information about how any individual did behave or might behave.

10 Behavior is a continuous phenomenon; it takes place in and changes through time. Only continuous measurement over time yields a complete record of behavior.

11 The assumption of determinism guides the methodology of behavior analysis.

12 Behavioral variability is extrinsic to the organism; that is, variability is imposed by environmental variables and is not an inherent trait of the organism.

13 Instead of attempting to mask variability by averaging the performance of many subjects, the science of behavior attempts to isolate and experimentally manipulate the environmental factors responsible for the variability.

Components of Experimental Design

14 An experiment with a high degree of internal validity shows convincingly that changes in behavior are a function of the independent variable and not the result of uncontrolled variables.

15 External validity refers to the degree to which a study's results are generalizable to other subjects, settings, and/or behaviors.

16 Confounding variables exert unknown or uncontrolled influences on the dependent variable.

17 In the analysis of behavior, each subject's behavior is measured repeatedly as he is exposed to every condition of the study; in most single-subject experimental designs each subject serves as his own control for confounding variables.

18 There are three major reasons that behavior analysts use multiple-response measures (dependent variables) in some studies: (a) to provide additional data paths that serve as a control procedure for evaluating and replicating the effects of an independent variable that is sequentially applied to each behavior, (b) to assess the generality of treatment effects to behavior other than the response class to which the independent variable was applied, and (c) to determine whether changes in the behavior of a person other than the subject occur during the course of an experiment.

19 In addition to precise manipulation of the independent variable, the behavior analyst must maintain the constancy of every other relevant aspect of the experimental setting.

20 When unplanned events or variations occur in the experimental setting, the behavior analyst must either wait out their effects or incorporate them into the design of the experiment.

21 Observation and recording procedures must be conducted in a standardized manner throughout an experiment.

22 Because behavior is a continuous and dynamic phenomenon, ongoing visual inspection of the data during the course of an experiment is necessary to identify changes in level, trend, and/or variability as they develop.

23 Changes in the independent variable are made in an effort to maximize its effect on the target behavior.

24 A study in which a single-value independent variable is manipulated is termed nonparametric.

25 A parametric study examines and compares the effects of a range of different values of the independent variable.

26 The fundamental rule of experimental design is to change only one variable at a time.

27 Although an infinite number of experimental designs are possible as a result of the many ways in which independent variables can be manipulated and combined, there are only two basic kinds of changes in independent variables: introducing a new condition or reintroducing an old condition.

28 Rather than follow rigid, pro forma experimental designs, the behavior analyst should select experimental tactics suited to the original research questions, while standing ready to "explore relevant variables by manipulating them

in an improvised and rapidly changing design" (Skinner, 1966, p. 21).

Baseline Data

29 The basic method for evaluating the effects of a given variable is to impose it on an ongoing measure of behavior obtained in its absence. Preintervention data serve as the baseline.

30 A baseline condition does not necessarily imply the absence of instruction or treatment per se, but rather the absence of the specific independent variable of experimental interest.

31 In addition to the primary purpose of establishing a baseline as an objective basis for evaluating the effects of the independent variable, there are three other reasons for baseline data collection: (a) systematic observation of the target behavior prior to intervention sometimes yields information about currently operating antecedents and consequences that may be helpful in planning an effective intervention; (b) baseline data are useful in setting effective initial criteria for reinforcement; and (c) sometimes baseline data collection shows that the behavior targeted for change is not, after all, emitted at a rate sufficiently high or low to warrant intervention.

32 Four types of baseline data patterns are stable, ascending, descending, and variable.

33 The independent variable should be introduced when stable baseline responding has been achieved.

34 The independent variable should not be introduced if either an ascending or descending baseline indicates improving performance.

35 The independent variable should be introduced if either an ascending or descending baseline indicates deteriorating performance.

36 The independent variable should not be imposed on a variable, or unstable, baseline.

Baseline Logic

37 Stable, or steady state, responding enables the behavior analyst to employ a powerful form of inductive reasoning, sometimes called baseline logic. Baseline logic entails three elements: prediction, verification, and replication.

38 Prediction of future behavior under "relatively constant environmental conditions" can be made on the basis of repeated measures of behavior showing little or no variation.

39 In general, given stable responding, the more data points and the longer the condition, the more accurate the prediction is likely to be.

40 Practice effects refer to improvements in performance resulting from practice opportunities that must be provided to obtain repeated measures.

41 Extended baseline measurement is not necessary for behavior that has no logical opportunity to occur.

42 The inductive reasoning called affirmation of the consequent lies at the heart of baseline logic.

43 Although the logic of affirming the consequent is not completely sound (some other event may have caused the change in behavior), an effective experimental design confirms several if-A-then-B possibilities, thereby eliminating certain other factors as responsible for the observed changes in behavior.

44 Verification of effect is accomplished by demonstrating that the prior level of baseline responding would have remained unchanged if the independent variable had not been introduced.

45 Replication within an experiment means reproducing a previously observed behavior change by reintroducing the independent variable. Replication within an experiment reduces the probability that a variable other than the independent variable was responsible for the behavior change and demonstrates the reliability of the behavior change.

8

Reversal and Alternating Treatments Designs

KEY TERMS

Reversal design

A-B-A design

A-B-A-B design

Multiple treatment design

Sequence effects

Noncontingent reinforcement reversal design

DRI/DRO reversal design

B-A-B reversal design

Irreversibility

Alternating treatments design

Multiple treatment interference

This chapter describes the reversal and alternating treatments designs, two classes of experimental strategies widely used in applied behavior analysis. In a reversal design the effects of introducing, withdrawing, and reintroducing the independent variable are observed on the target behavior. In an alternating treatments design two or more different interventions are rapidly alternated, and the differential effects on the target behavior are noted. The chapter first presents the kinds of questions about behavior-environment relationships that each design is best suited to answer. The underlying experimental logic is then explained, followed by representative examples from the literature illustrating the major variations of both designs. Guidelines and considerations for selecting and using reversal and alternating treatments designs are also presented.

This chapter was written by William L. Heward.

REVERSAL DESIGNS

Operation and Logic of the Reversal Design

The **reversal design** entails repeated measurement of behavior in a given setting during three consecutive phases of an experiment: (1) a baseline phase in which the independent variable is absent, (2) an intervention phase during which the independent variable is introduced and remains in contact with the behavior, and (3) a return to prior baseline conditions accomplished by withdrawal of the independent variable. The notation system most widely used for describing experimental designs based on the reversal tactic uses the capital letter *A* to denote baseline conditions and *B* to symbolize those periods when the independent variable is present. Thus, an experimental design exploying one reversal is identified as an **A-B-A design.** Although studies using an A-B-A design are sometimes reported in the literature (e.g., Geller, Paterson, & Talbot,

1982; Stitzer, Bigelow, Liebson, & Hawthorne, 1982), the analysis is strengthened tremendously by reintroducing the independent variable in an **A-B-A-B design.**

Figure 8.1 illustrates a graphic prototype of the A-B-A-B reversal design, for which Baer, Wolf, and Risley (1968) provide a description and rationale.

A behavior is measured, and the measure is examined over time until its stability is clear. Then, the experimental variable is applied. The behavior continues to be measured, to see if the variable will produce a behavioral change. If it does, the experimental variable is discontinued or altered, to see if the behavioral change just brought about depends on it. If so, the behavioral change should be lost or diminished (thus the term "reversal"). The experimental variable then is applied again, to see if the behavioral change can be recovered. . . . In using the reversal technique, the experimenter is attempting to show that an analysis is at hand: that whenever he applies a certain variable, the behavior is produced, and whenever he removes this variable, the behavior is lost. (p. 94)

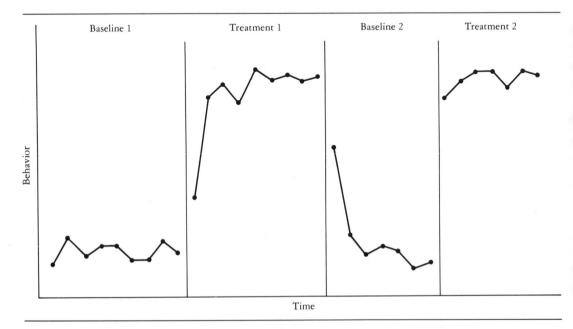

FIGURE 8.1 Graphic prototype of the A-B-A-B reversal design.

Since the reversal design was used in chapter 7 to illustrate baseline logic, a brief review of the role of prediction, verification, and replication in the reversal design should suffice here. Figure 8.2 shows the same data that Figure 8.1 presented with the addition of the open data points representing predicted measures of behavior under continuing conditions. After a stable pattern of responding, or a countertherapeutic trend, is obtained during Baseline 1, the independent variable is introduced. In our hypothetical experiment the behavior observed during Treatment 1, when compared with that of Baseline 1 and the behavior *predicted* by Baseline 1, shows that a behavior change occurred and that the change in behavior coincided with the intervention. After a stable level of responding is reached in Treatment 1, the independent variable is withdrawn, and baseline conditions are reestablished. If the level of responding in Baseline 2

is the same as or closely approximates the measures recorded during Baseline 1, *verification* of the Baseline 1 data is obtained. When withdrawal of the independent variable results in a reversal of the behavior change associated with its introduction, a strong case begins to be made that the intervention is responsible for the observed behavior change. If reintroduction of the independent variable in Treatment 2 reproduces the behavior change observed during Treatment 1, *replication* of effect has been achieved, and a functional relation demonstrated.

The A-B-A-B reversal design is the most straightforward and powerful single-subject design for demonstrating a functional relation between an environmental manipulation and behavior. When a functional relation is revealed (i.e., an analysis has been achieved) with a reversal design, the data tell how the behavior works.

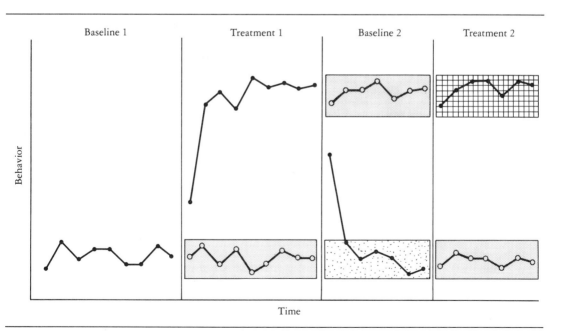

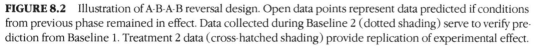

FIGURE 8.2 Illustration of A-B-A-B reversal design. Open data points represent data predicted if conditions from previous phase remained in effect. Data collected during Baseline 2 (dotted shading) serve to verify prediction from Baseline 1. Treatment 2 data (cross-hatched shading) provide replication of experimental effect.

As explanations go, the one offered by the reversal design was not at all a bad one. In answer to the question, "How does this response work?" we could point out demonstrably that it worked like so [see Figure 8.1]. Of course, it might also work in other ways; but, we would wait until we had seen the appropriate graphs before agreeing to any other way. (Baer, 1975, p. 19)

Baer's point must not be overlooked: showing that a behavior works in a predictable and reliable way in the presence and absence of a given variable provides only one answer to the question of how the behavior works. There may be (and quite likely are) other controlling variables for the response class at hand. Whether additional experimentation is needed to explore the other possibilities depends on the social and scientific significance of obtaining a more complete analysis.

In the 1960s and early 1970s the A-B-A-B reversal design was used almost exclusively by applied behavior analysts primarily because of the design's effectiveness. An additional reason was that few alternative designs available at that time included the combined reasoning of prediction, verification, and replication and incorporated the subject as her own control. Indeed, the straightforward A-B-A-B design played such a dominant role in the early years of applied behavior analysis that it came to symbolize the field (Baer, 1975). Today, most studies that incorporate the reversal technique in their experimental design involve variations and extensions of the strategy. However, because of its ability to expose variables for what they are—strong and reliable or weak and unstable—the simple, unadorned A-B-A-B design continues to play a major role in the behavior analysis literature of the 1980s (e.g., Fantuzzo & Clement, 1981; Kelly & Stokes, 1982; Murphy, Hutchison, & Bailey, 1983; Quattrochi-Tubin & Jason, 1980; Van Houten, Nau, MacKenzie-Keating, Sameoto, & Colavecchia, 1982).

A study by Spangler and Marshall (1983) provides an excellent example of the A-B-A-B

design (see Figure 8.3). The experimenters wanted to increase the level of purposeful play activities of a group of 14 institutionalized boys with severe and profound mental retardation. A PLACHEK observational procedure (Doke & Risley, 1972) was used to record at 1-minute intervals the number of children engaged in appropriate activities (e.g., playing or working with a designated task or activity, traveling to or from an activity) or maladaptive behaviors (e.g., stereotyped twirling or rocking, self-injurious behavior). During the first baseline phase, which was a free play condition with toys available and at least two staff members on duty, the group mean appropriate activity levels averaged 13%. Treatment consisted of a unit play manager routine in which a staff member set up the room by placing the toys and games in certain areas of the room and then circulated during playtime, providing prompts, encouragement, and assistance to the boys to play with the equipment. Staff members switched the role of play manager every 30 minutes to avoid fatigue. During the first treatment phase the group mean appropriate activity averaged 70%, dropped to 10% during the reversal phase, and increased again to 79% during the second treatment phase. Inappropriate behavior also changed as a function of the play manager routine, decreasing to an average of 7% and 5% during the two treatment phases. The A-B-A-B design used by Spangler and Marshall enabled a straightforward, unambiguous analysis of overall play behavior of the group of boys as a function of specific staff behavior.

Variations of the A-B-A-B Design

Most studies in applied behavior analysis that employ the reversal technique involve extensions and variations of the A-B-A-B design.

Repeated Reversals Perhaps the most obvious variation is a simple extension of the A-B-A-B design, in which the independent variable is introduced and withdrawn repeatedly: A-B-A-B-A-B, etc. Each presentation and with-

FIGURE 8.3 Example of classic reversal (A-B-A-B) design. (From "The Unit Play Manager as Facilitator of Purposeful Activities Among Institutionalized Profoundly and Severely Retarded Boys" by P. F. Spangler and A. E. Marshall, 1983, *Journal of Applied Behavior Analysis, 16,* p. 348. Copyright 1983 by the Society for the Experimental Analysis of Behavior, Inc. Reprinted by permission.)

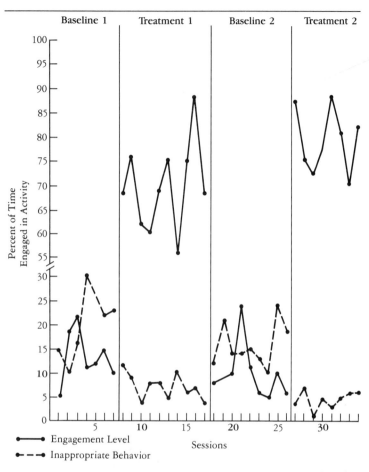

Fig. 1. Percentage of time during 30-min. session in which the group was involved in either a purposeful activity or in maladaptive or inappropriate behavior.

drawal that repeats the earlier effects on behavior increases the likelihood that the behavior change is the result of the experimentally manipulated variable. All other things being equal, a design that incorporates multiple reversals presents a more convincing demonstration of experimental control than does a design with only one reversal. It is possible, though, in a given analysis to reach a point of redundancy beyond which believability is no longer enhanced.

Multiple Treatment Reversal Designs **Multiple treatment designs** include those in which the effects of two or more independent variables are compared to baseline or to one another (e.g., the A-B-A-C-A-D-A-C-A-D design used by Weeks & Gaylord-Ross, 1981; the A-B-C-D-B-D design employed by Bacon-Prue, Blount, Pickering, & Drabman, 1980), and those designs in which the additive or interactive effects of two or more independent variables are investigated (e.g., the A-B-A-B-BC-

B-BC design of Jason & Liotta, 1982). These designs are classified as variations of the reversal design because, when properly conducted, they embody the experimental method and logic of the reversal tactic: each phase serves as a baseline for the subsequent phase (prediction), experimental variables are withdrawn in an attempt to reproduce levels of behavior in a previous phase (verification), and all treatment variables that contribute fully to the analysis are introduced at least twice (replication). Experimental variables can be introduced, withdrawn, changed in value, combined, and otherwise manipulated to produce an endless variety of experimental designs.

Jason and Liotta (1982) employed the reversal tactic in an experiment evaluating the effects of two interventions on the smoking behavior of persons in a no-smoking section of a university cafeteria. Each day during the study the number of smokers and the cumulative amount of time that any smoking occurred were observed and recorded for a 50-minute period during the lunch hour. Following baseline, a sign-prompting condition was implemented in which signs reading "No-Smoking Section for Health and Comfort of Patrons" were placed on each table and four larger signs with the words "No-Smoking Section. Please don't smoke in this section." were placed on the cafeteria walls. After 16 days the signs were removed and baseline conditions were reestablished. The sign prompting condition was then reintroduced, followed by the introduction, removal, and reintroduction of verbal prompting in addition to the signs. In the combined intervention the table and wall signs were displayed; and whenever someone began smoking in the no-smoking area, a university student approached the smoker and said, "I'm concerned about keeping this section for nonsmokers. Would you either stop smoking in this area or move to the smoking area?" After 5 minutes, if the smoker continued to smoke, the student prompter said, "I'd just like to once

again remind you that this is a no-smoking section. Would you please not smoke here?" (p. 574).

Figure 8.4 shows the results of the study, which is best described as an A-B-A-B-BC-B-BC design, since the verbal prompting (C) was added to the sign prompting condition (B) rather than being administered alone. During the two baseline phases smoking occurred during an average of 39 minutes of each 50-minute observational period, and an average of 7.7 persons smoked each day. Overall, an average of 26 minutes of smoking and 5.3 smokers was observed during the sign-prompting phases. The most effective condition was sign-plus-verbal prompting, which resulted in an average of 6.2 minutes of smoking by an average of 1.6 smokers per day. Although it is tempting to interpret the results as showing that verbal prompting was responsible for the large reductions in smoking during the two sign-plus-verbal-prompting conditions, the design does not permit such an unambiguous conclusion. Verbal prompting was not administered in isolation but only in combination with sign prompting; perhaps the signs exerted greater influence on smoking when paired with verbal prompting. Also, because sign prompting alone preceded the sign-plus-verbal-prompting intervention, the results of the combined intervention may have been affected by the earlier introduction of sign prompting alone. The effect of verbal prompting alone can be assessed only by recapturing initial baseline levels of behavior and then manipulating that one variable. Nonetheless, the Jason and Liotta experiment does provide a convincing demonstration of experimental control produced by sign-plus-verbal prompting against a baseline of sign prompting alone.

In most instances extended designs involving multiple independent variables are not planned out in their entirety before the study begins. Instead of following a predetermined, rigid structure that dictates when and how

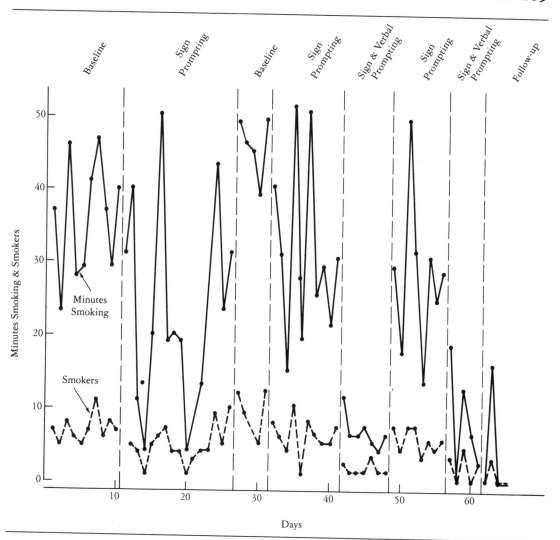

FIGURE 8.4 Example of multiple-treatment reversal design (A-B-A-B-BC-B-BC-follow-up). (From "Reduction of Cigarette Smoking in a University Cafeteria" by L. A. Jason and R. F. Liotta, 1982, *Journal of Applied Behavior Analysis, 15,* p. 576. Copyright 1982 by the Society for the Experimental Analysis of Behavior, Inc. Reprinted by permission.)

experimental manipulations must be made, the applied behavior analyst makes design decisions based on ongoing assessment of the data.

In this sense, a single experiment may be viewed as a number of successive designs that are collectively necessary to clarify relations between independent and dependent variables. Thus, some design decisions might be made in response to the data unfolding as the investigation progresses. This sense of design encourages the experimenter to pursue in more dynamic fashion the solutions to problems of experimental control immediately upon their emergence. (Johnston & Pennypacker, 1980, pp. 250–251)

Students of applied behavior analysis should not interpret this description of experimental design as a recommendation for a completely free-form approach to the manipulation of independent variables. The researcher must always pay the strictest attention to the rule of changing only one variable at a time from one phase to the next and must understand the limitations that a given sequence of manipulations places on the conclusions that can be drawn from the results. In an A-B-A-B-C-B-C design, for instance, comparisons of B to A and C to B can be made, but not of C to A. As was shown in the Jason and Liotta (1982) study, an A-B-A-B-BC-B-BC design permits an evaluation of the additive or interactive effects of BC but does not reveal the independent contribution of C (Hersen and Barlow, 1976).

The major weakness of experiments comparing two or more treatments within the context of a reversal design is the presence of uncontrolled effects on the target behavior caused by the particular sequence of conditions employed in the study. In an A-B-C-B-C design, for example, we can only speak knowingly about the effects of C when it follows B. Recapturing the original baseline performance before introducing the second treatment (as in an A-B-A-C sequence) reduces the threat of **sequence effects** somewhat, as does manipulating the different independent variables in such a way that each one both precedes and follows every other condition in the study. However, in addition to requiring a large amount of time and resources to complete, such extended designs become more accessible to confounding by maturation and other historical variables not controlled by the experimenter. Fortunately, there are other experimental designs available that are better suited for the comparison of multiple treatments.

Noncontingent Reinforcement Reversal Design

With interventions based on positive reinforcement, it can be hypothesized that observed changes in behavior are the result of the subject's feeling better about himself because of the improved environment created by the reinforcement, not because a specific response class has been strengthened through contingent reinforcement. This hypothesis is most often advanced when interventions consisting of social reinforcement are involved: "It doesn't matter *how* the teacher's praise and attention were given; the student's behavior improved because the praise and attention created a warm, loving environment." However, if it can be shown that behavioral improvements produced by contingent reinforcement are lost during experimental conditions when equal amounts of reinforcement are delivered but are not contingent upon emission of the target behavior, a clear demonstration is made of causality between the reinforcement contingency and behavior change. In other words, such a design can show that behavior change is a function of contingent reinforcement, not just a generally enriched environment.

An excellent example of the **noncontingent reinforcement reversal design** is an early study by Baer and Wolf (1970a) on the effects of teachers' social reinforcement on the cooperative play of a preschool child (Figure 8.5). The authors describe quite well the use and purpose of the design.

[The teachers first collected] baselines of cooperative and other related behaviors of the child, and of their own interaction with the child. Ten days of observation indicated that the child spent about 50% of each day in proximity with other children (meaning within 3 feet of them indoors, or 6 feet outdoors). Despite this frequent proximity, however, the child spent only about 2% of her day in cooperative play with these children. The teachers, it was found, interacted with this girl about 20% of the day, not all of it pleasant. The teachers, therefore, set up a period of intense social reinforcement, offered not for cooperative play but free of any response requirement at all: the teachers took turns standing near the girl, attending closely to her activities, offering her materials, and smiling and laughing with her in a happy and admiring manner. The results of 7 days of this noncontin-

FIGURE 8.5 Example of reversal design employing noncontingent reinforcement as a control technique (From "Recent Examples of Behavior Modification in Preschool Settings" by D. M. Baer and M. M. Wolf in *Behavior Modification in Clinical Psychology*, pp. 14–15, edited by C. Neuringer and J. L. Michael, 1970, Englewood Cliffs, NJ: Prentice-Hall. Copyright 1970 by Prentice-Hall. Adapted by permission.)

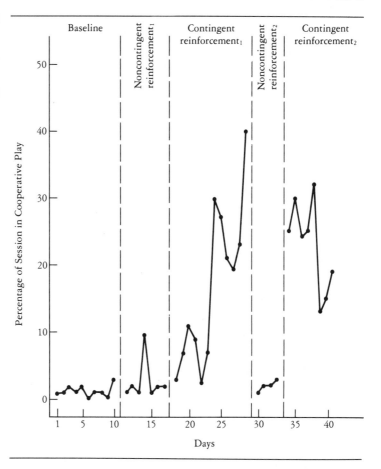

gent extravagance of social reinforcement were straightforward: the child's cooperative play changed not at all, despite the fact that the other children of the group were greatly attracted to the scene, offering the child nearly double the chance to interact with them cooperatively. These 7 days having produced no useful change, the teachers then began their planned reinforcement of cooperative behavior. . . . Contingent social reinforcement, used in amounts less than half that given during the noncontingent period, increased the child's cooperative play from its usual 2% to a high of 40% in the course of 12 days of reinforcement. At that point, in the interests of certainty, the teachers discontinued contingent reinforcement in favor of noncontingent. In the course of 4 days, they lost virtually all of the cooperative behavior they had gained during the reinforcement period of the study, the child

showing about a 5% average of cooperative play over that period of time. Naturally , the study concluded with a return to the contingent use of social reinforcement, a recovery of desirable levels of cooperative play, and a gradual reduction of the teacher's role in maintaining that behavior. (pp. 14–15)[1]

Strictly speaking, using noncontingent reinforcement to demonstrate that the contingent application of reinforcement is requisite to its effectiveness is not a separate variation of the reversal design, but rather an experimental

[1]From Baer/Wolf, "Recent Examples of Behavior Modification in Preschool Settings" in *Behavior Modification in Clinical Psychology*, Neuringer/Michael eds., © 1970, pp. 14–15. Reprinted by permission of Prentice-Hall, Englewood Cliffs, NJ.

control technique based on the reversal procedure. Technically, the noncontingent reinforcement reversal design is a design consisting of multiple treatments; the Baer and Wolf (1970a) study would be described as A-B-C-B-C, with B representing the noncontingent reinforcement conditions and C representing the contingent reinforcement conditions.

The usual procedure is to deliver noncontingent reinforcement on either a fixed or variable time schedule irrespective of the subject's behavior at the time of delivery. A weakness of the noncontingent reinforcement control procedure becomes apparent in cases where a high rate of the desired behavior has been produced during the preceding contingent reinforcement phase. It is highly probable in such situations that at least some of the noncontingent reinforcement, delivered according to a predetermined time schedule, will follow closely in time the subject's performance of the target behavior, thereby functioning as contingent reinforcement. In fact, an intermittent schedule of reinforcement might inadvertently be created that results in even higher levels of performance than those obtained under contingent reinforcement (see chapter 12 for an explanation of the effects of intermittent schedules of reinforcement). In such cases the investigator might consider using either of the two control techniques described next.

DRI and DRO Reversal Designs One way to ensure that reinforcement does not immediately follow the target behavior undergoing analysis is to intentionally deliver it immediately following the subject's performance of behaviors other than the dependent variable. Two methods often used to program reinforcement during a control or reversal condition are (1) differential reinforcement of an incompatible behavior (DRI) and (2) differential reinforcement of other behavior (DRO). In a **DRI reversal design** a specific behavior incompatible with the target behavior (i.e., the two behaviors cannot possibly be emitted at the same time) is identified, and its occurrence is immediately followed by the reinforcement previously delivered contingent on the target behavior. In a **DRO reversal design** reinforcement is delivered following the emission of any behavior other than the target behavior.

Leitenberg (1973) suggests that the term *reversal design* be used only for those experiments in which the treatment contingency is actually reversed, as in a DRI or DRO condition. Leitenberg and a few other writers (e.g., Tawney & Gast, 1984) have maintained a distinction between a reversal design and a true A-B-A-B design, which they term a *withdrawal design*. However, reversal design, as it is most commonly used in the behavioral literature, encompasses both withdrawals and reversals of the intervention, signifying the experimenter's attempt to reverse the direction of the behavior change observed during intervention (Baer, Wolf, & Risley, 1968). Also, withdrawal design sometimes signifies designs in which the treatment variable(s) are sequentially or partially withdrawn after their effects have been analyzed in an effort to promote maintenance of the target behavior (Rusch & Kazdin, 1981).

A study by Goetz and Baer (1973) investigating the effects of teacher praise on preschool children's creative play with building blocks illustrates the use of a DRI control condition. Figure 8.6 shows the number of different block forms (e.g., arch, tower, roof, ramp) built by the three children who participated in the study. During baseline (data points indicated by the letter *N*), "the teacher sat by the child as she built with the blocks, watching closely but quietly, displaying neither criticism nor enthusiasm about any particular use of the blocks" (p. 212). During the next phase (the D data points), "the teacher remarked with interest, enthusiasm, and delight every time that the child placed and/or rearranged the blocks so as to create a form that had not appeared previously in that session's construction(s). . . .

FIGURE 8.6 Reversal design using a DRI control technique. (From "Social Control of Form Diversity and the Emergence of New Forms in Children's Block-building" by E. M. Goetz and D. M. Baer, 1973, *Journal of Applied Behavior Analysis, 6,* p. 213. Copyright 1973 by the Society for the Experimental Analysis of Behavior, Inc. Reprinted by permission.)

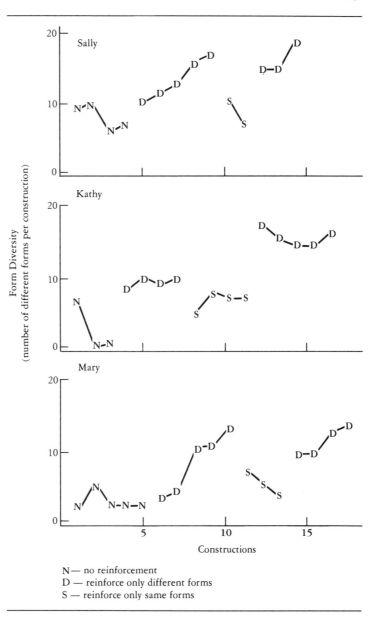

N— no reinforcement
D — reinforce only different forms
S — reinforce only same forms

'Oh, that's very nice—that's different!'" (p. 212).[2] Then, after increasing form diversity was

[2]From "Social Control of Form Diversity and the Emergence of New Forms in Children's Blockbuilding" by E. M. Goetz and D. M. Baer, 1973, *Journal of Applied Behavior Analysis, 6,* p. 212. Copyright 1973 by the Society for the Experimental Analysis of Behavior, Inc. Reprinted by permission.

clearly established, instead of merely withdrawing verbal praise and returning to the initial baseline conditions, the researchers had the teacher provide descriptive praise only when the children constructed the same forms (the S data points). "Thus, for the next two to four sessions, the teacher continued to display interest, enthusiasm, and delight, but only at those times when the child placed and/or rearranged a block so as to create a repetition of a form already apparent in that session's construction(s). . . . Thus, no first usage of a form in a session was reinforced, but every second usage of that form and every usage thereafter within the session was. . . . 'How nice—another arch!' " (p. 212). The final phase of the experiment entailed a return to descriptive praise for different forms. Results show that the children's block-building behavior in terms of form diversity was a function of teacher praise.

By using the DRI condition, Goetz and Baer found that it was not just teacher praise that resulted in more creative block building; teacher praise had to be contingent upon different forms to produce increasing form diversity. (The role of either the attention and praise itself or its descriptive content in producing the increased form diversity was not analyzed in the study—both social reinforcement and information were delivered as a package.) The study is an important one in a long line of research showing the effectiveness of descriptive teacher praise in modifying the behavior of preschool children.

Reynolds and Risley (1968) conducted a study designed to increase the frequency of talking in a 4-year-old girl enrolled in a preschool program for disadvantaged children. After a period of teacher attention contingent upon verbalization, in which the girl's talking increased from a baseline average of 11% of the intervals observed to 75%, a DRO condition was implemented, and the teachers gave their attention to the girl for any behavior other than talking. During the six days of DRO, the girl's rate of verbalization dropped to 6%. Teacher attention was then again given contingent upon talking, and the girl's frequency of verbalization "immediately increased to an average of 51%."

Goetz, Holmberg, and LeBlanc (1975) performed an experiment designed specifically to compare the effectiveness of noncontingent reinforcement and DRO as control procedures in evaluating the effectiveness of teacher proximity and verbal praise in increasing a preschool girl's compliance with teacher requests (see Figure 8.7). They found that both the noncontingent reinforcement and the DRO conditions resulted in decrements in the high percentage of compliance observed during contingent reinforcement but that "DRO yielded a more immediate and dramatic decrease in target behavior" (p. 81). High levels of compliant behavior were quickly regained following both control procedures. The authors suggest that the DRO procedure may have decreased the target behavior faster and more completely because it "enhanced the discrimination" of the behaviors resulting in reinforcement. During noncontingent reinforcement noncompliance was sometimes followed by reinforcement, as was compliance. The importance of this finding, should it prove to have generality to other response classes and other reinforcement-based interventions, is the identification of a procedure that allows the researcher to demonstrate experimental control quickly and thereby return more promptly to conditions designed to strengthen and maintain the desirable target behavior.

B-A-B Reversal Design   In the **B-A-B reversal design** data collection during an initial baseline condition is not carried out; instead the experiment begins with application of the treatment variable. After the initial treatment phase produces stable responding at an acceptable level, the independent variable is removed, and a reversal condition is introduced. If the behavior worsens in the absence of the independent variable (the A condition), the treatment is reintroduced to verify the measures obtained during the first treatment phase.

Compared to the A-B-A design, the B-A-B design is preferable from an applied sense in that the study ends with the treatment variable in effect. However, in terms of evaluating the effects of the independent variable, the B-A-B

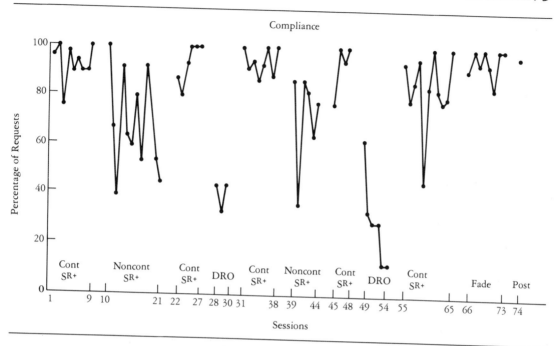

FIGURE 8.7   Results of an experiment comparing noncontingent reinforcement and DRO as control procedures for the compliance behavior of a preschooler. S^{R+} stands for positive reinforcement. (From "Differential Reinforcement of Other Behavior and Noncontingent Reinforcement as Control Procedures During the Modification of a Preschooler's Compliance by E. M. Goetz, M. C. Holmberg, and J. M. LeBlanc, 1975, *Journal of Applied Behavior Analysis, 8,* p. 80. Copyright 1975 by the Society for the Experimental Analysis of Behavior, Inc. Reprinted by permission.)

design is the weaker of the two because it does not enable assessment of the effects of the independent variable on the preintervention, or natural, rate of occurrence of the target behavior. Therefore, the nonintervention condition cannot serve to verify the prediction of a previous nonexistent baseline. Since the design provides no data to determine whether the measures of behavior taken during the A condition represent preintervention performance, sequence effects cannot be ruled out: the level of behavior observed during the A condition may have been influenced by the fact that the treatment condition preceded it. Nevertheless, there are situations in which an initial baseline cannot be collected, and the B-A-B design enables a direct, albeit weak, analysis of effect.

The B-A-B design is most appropriately used with target behaviors that result in physical harm or danger to the subject or others (Tawney & Gast, 1984). In such instances withholding a possibly effective treatment until a stable pattern of baseline responding can be obtained may represent an unethical and inhumane procedure. For example, Murphy, Ruprecht, Baggio, and Nunes (1979) used a B-A-B design in evaluating the effectiveness of a mild punishment procedure combined with reinforcement of other appropriate behavior on the number of self-choking responses emitted by a 24-year-old man with profound mental retardation (Figure 8.8). After the treatment was in effect for 24 sessions, it was withdrawn for 3 sessions during which an

FIGURE 8.8 Example of a B-A-B reversal design used with a self-injurious target behavior. (From "The Use of Mild Punishment in Combination with Reinforcement of Alternate Behaviors to Reduce the Self-Injurious Behavior of a Profoundly Retarded Individual" by R. J. Murphy, M. J. Ruprecht, P. Baggio, and D. L. Nunes, 1979, *AAESPH Review, 4*, p. 191. Copyright 1979 by the *AAESPH Review*. Reprinted by permission.)

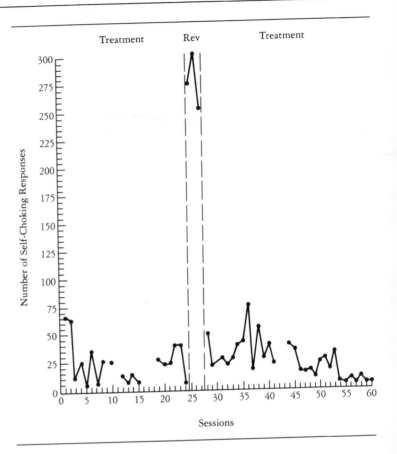

immediate and large increase in self-choking was recorded. Reintroduction of the treatment package resulted in a return to levels of behavior observed during the first treatment phase. The average number of self-chokes during each phase of the B-A-B study was 22, 265, and 24 respectively. Believability in a B-A-B design can be enhanced by repeated brief withdrawals of the independent variable and by the gathering and reporting of any objectively measured data on the level of behavior prior to the first intervention. Although they chose not to collect an initial baseline for ethical and practical reasons, Murphy et al. reported that self-chokes had averaged 434 per day immediately prior to their experiment, when a different procedure had been used by school staff to reduce the self-injurious behavior. Such information in-

creases the believability of the functional relation suggested by their data.

There are other situations in which a B-A-B design might be warranted. For instance, Robinson, Newby, and Ganzell (1981) were asked to develop a behavior management system for a class of 18 hyperactive boys with the stipulation that the program's effectiveness be demonstrated within 4 weeks. Given "the stipulation of success in 4 weeks, a B-A-B design was used" (pp. 310–311).

Considering the Appropriateness of the Reversal Design

The primary advantage of the reversal design is that it provides a powerful statement of a functional relationship between the independent and dependent variables. When an investigator can and does reliably turn the target behavior on and off by presenting and withdrawing a specified variable, a clear and convincing demonstration of experimental control is made. In addition, the reversal design enables quantification of the amount of improvement over the preintervention level of behavior. And the return to baseline provides information on the need to program for maintenance. Furthermore, a complete A-B-A-B experimental design ends with the treatment variable in place. (Additional manipulations in the form of partial or sequential withdrawal of intervention components are made when it is necessary or desirable for the behavior to continue at its improved level in the absence of the complete intervention; see Rusch & Kazdin, 1981.)

However, in spite of its strengths as a tool for analysis, the reversal design entails some real and potential disadvantages, both scientific and social, that must be considered prior to its use. The considerations are of two types: irreversibility, which affects the scientific utility of the design; and social, educational, and ethical concerns over the withdrawal of a seemingly effective intervention.

Irreversibility: A Scientific Consideration

A reversal design is not appropriate in evaluating the effects of a treatment variable that, by its very nature, cannot be withdrawn once it has been presented. Although independent variables involving reinforcement and punishment contingencies can be manipulated with some certainty—the experimenter either presents or withholds the contingency—an independent variable such as information or modeling, once presented, cannot simply be removed. A reversal tactic would not be an effective element in an experimental design investigating the effects of attending a workshop during which participants observed a master teacher use verbal praise. Listening to the rationale for the use of verbal praise and observing the master teacher model the use of praise would have become

part of the practicing teacher's experience and would no longer be susceptible to direct manipulation by the researcher. Such interventions are said to be irreversible.

Irreversibility of the dependent variable must also be considered in determining whether a reversal would be an effective experimental tactic. Behavioral **irreversibility** means that a level of behavior observed in an earlier phase cannot be reproduced even though the experimental conditions are arranged exactly as they were during the earlier phase (Sidman, 1960). Once improved, many target behaviors of interest to the applied behavior analyst remain at their newly enhanced level even when the intervention responsible for the behavior change is removed. Such a state of affairs is desirable from a clinical standpoint: the behavior change is shown to be durable, capable of persisting even in the absence of deliberate treatment. However, irreversibility is a problem if demonstration of the independent variable's role in the behavior change is dependent upon a reversal tactic.

For example, baseline observations might reveal very low, almost nonexistent rates of talking and social interaction for a young child. An intervention consisting of teacher-delivered social reinforcement for talking and interacting could be implemented, and after some time the girl might talk to and interact with her peers at a frequency and in a manner similar to that of her classmates. A reversal technique could then be used: the independent variable, the teacher-delivered reinforcement, could be terminated in an effort to recapture baseline rates of talking and interacting. But it is quite probable that the girl would continue to talk to and interact with her classmates even though the intervention, which may have been responsible for her change in behavior, is withdrawn. In this case a source of reinforcement uncontrolled by the teacher—being talked to and played with by her classmates as a consequence of her increased talking and interacting—would likely maintain high rates of behavior even when teacher-delivered reinforcement is no longer provided. In such instances of irreversibility, a reversal design will reveal little about the existence of a functional relationship between the independent variable and the target behavior.

Nonetheless, one of the major objectives of applied behavior analysis is establishing socially important behavior through experimental treatments so that the behavior will contact naturally occurring "communities of reinforcement" to maintain the behavioral improvement in the absence of treatment (Baer, 1981). In addition to DRO-DRI conditions there are other experimental strategies that can be employed when irreversibility is suspected or apparent, most notably the multiple baseline tactics to be described in chapter 9.

Withdrawing an Effective Intervention: A Social, Educational, and Ethical Consideration

Although it provides a convincing demonstration of experimental control, withdrawal of a seemingly effective intervention in order to evaluate its role in behavior change presents legitimate cause for concern. One must question the appropriateness of any procedure that allows an improved behavior to deteriorate. Numerous concerns have been voiced over this fundamental feature of the reversal design; and although there is considerable overlap, the concerns can be classified as having primarily a social, educational, or ethical base.

By definition, applied behavior analysis is a social enterprise. Behaviors are selected, defined, observed, measured, and modified from, by, and for people. Sometimes the people who are involved in an applied behavior analysis—parents, administrators, teachers, subject(s)—object to the withdrawal of an intervention associated with desirable behavior change. In other words, sometimes a reversal, even though it may provide the most unqualified picture of the behavior-environment relationship under study, is not the experimental

tactic of choice because key participants do not want the intervention to be withdrawn. When a reversal offers the best experimental approach scientifically and poses no ethical problems, the behavior analyst may choose to explain the operation and purpose of the tactic to the persons who are against it. But it is unwise to attempt a reversal without full support of the persons involved, especially those who will be responsible for withdrawing the intervention (Tawney & Gast, 1984). Without their cooperation the procedural integrity of the experiment could easily be compromised (i.e., persons against the withdrawal of treatment could sabotage the return to baseline conditions by implementing the intervention anyway).

Educational or clinical issues concerning the reversal design are often raised in terms of instructional time lost during the reversal phases, as well as the possibility that the behavioral improvement observed during intervention may not be recaptured when treatment is resumed after a return to baseline conditions. We agree with the position of Stolz (1978) that "extended reversals are indefensible." Fortunately, if preintervention levels of performance are quickly reached, reversal phases can be quite short in duration. Sometimes only three or four sessions are needed to show that initial baseline rates have been reproduced; and two or three such brief reversals can provide a convincing demonstration of experimental control. The concern that reversed improvements in behavior will not return when the treatment variable is reintroduced has not been supported by empirical evidence. The behavior analysis literature shows over and over again that a behavior acquired under a given set of environmental conditions can be reacquired rapidly during subsequent reapplication of those conditions. In fact, Baer, Wolf, and Risley (1968) suggest that repeated reversals can even be beneficial from an instructional standpoint by "possibly contributing to the discrimination of relevant stimuli involved in the problem" (p. 94).

A serious ethical concern must be addressed when the use of a reversal design is considered for evaluating a treatment intended to reduce self-injurious or dangerous behaviors. With mildly aggressive actions and mild self-injurious behaviors, short reversal phases, or even one-session baseline probes, can sometimes provide the empirical evidence needed to analyze the relationship between independent and dependent variables (e.g., Luce, Delquadri, & Hall, 1980; Murphy, Ruprecht, Baggio, & Nunes, 1979). One- and two-session reversal conditions were used in a study evaluating an intervention package designed to reduce the pain behavior (e.g., crying, attempting to delay treatment) of severely burned children (Kelley, Jarvie, Middlebrook, McNeer, & Drabman, 1984). Intervention consisted of watching TV cartoons during daily hydrotherapy treatment. Each child was told that "watching TV could help her forget about her pain, help her to feel better, and make the time go by faster" (p. 152). The children were told to pay close attention to the TV during therapy, and they earned stars on a feedback chart for crying less than on previous baseline days. Figure 8.9 shows the results of the experiment.

Nonetheless, with some behaviors it may be determined that withdrawing an intervention associated with improvement for even a few one-session probes would be inappropriate for ethical reasons. In such cases experimental analyses that do not rely on the reversal tactic must be planned

ALTERNATING TREATMENTS DESIGN

One of the most important and most frequently asked questions by teachers, therapists, and others responsible for changing behavior is, Which treatment will be most effective with this subject? In many behavior change situations several possible interventions may be suggested by the research literature, the analyst's own experience, and/or a logical extension of the principles of behavior. Determining which of several possible treatments or a combination of treatments will produce the greatest improvement in behavior is a primary task for applied behavior analysis. The differential effects of two or more treatments can be compared in a multiple treatment design (e.g., A-B-C-B-C); but, as described earlier, such designs are ill-suited for that purpose. Because the different treatments in a multiple treatment design are administered during separate phases sequenced across time, the design is particularly vulnerable to confounding by order effects (i.e., Treatment C may have produced the effect it did only because it followed Treatment B). A second, equally important disadvantage of comparing multiple treatments in an experimental design based on the reversal tactic is the potential length of time required to demonstrate differential effects. Many of the behaviors targeted for change by teachers and therapists are selected because they need immediate improvement. An experimental design that will quickly reveal the most effective treatment among several possible approaches is important for applied behavior analysis.

The alternating treatments design provides both an experimentally sound and an efficient method for comparing two or more treatments. The term **alternating treatments design,** proposed by Barlow and Hayes (1979), communicates most accurately the operation of the design. Various other terms found in the applied behavior analysis literature include *multielement baseline design* (Ulman & Sulzer-Azaroff, 1975), *multiple schedule design* (Hersen & Barlow, 1976), and *simultaneous treatment design* (Kazdin & Hartmann, 1978). A design in which two or more treatments are concurrently or simultaneously presented to the subject and in which by his behavior the subject chooses between treatments is correctly termed a simultaneous treatment design. (Hersen & Barlow, 1976, referred to such a design as a concurrent schedule design.) However, a

FIGURE 8.9 Reversal design with brief return-to-baseline probes to evaluate and verify effects of the independent variable. (From "Decreasing Burned Children's Pain Behavior: Impacting the Trauma of Hydrotherapy" by M. L. Kelley, G. J. Jarvie, J. L. Middlebrook, M. F. McNeer, and R. S. Drabman, 1984, *Journal of Applied Behavior Analysis, 17,* p. 154. Copyright 1984 by the Society for the Experimental Analysis of Behavior, Inc. Reprinted by permission.)

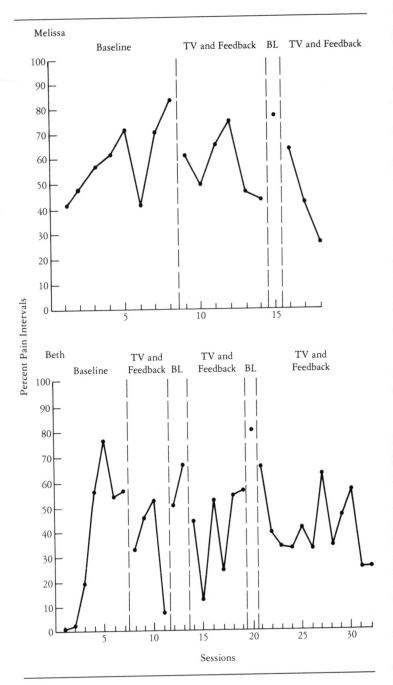

number of studies reported in the literature and identified by their authors as using a simultaneous treatment design have, in fact, employed an alternating treatments design.[3]

Operation and Logic of the Alternating Treatments Design

The alternating treatments design is characterized by the rapid alternation of two or more distinct treatments (i.e., independent variables) while their effects on a single target behavior are noted. In contrast to the reversal design in which experimental manipulations are made only after stability of the dependent variable is achieved in a given phase of an experiment, in the alternating treatments design the different interventions are alternated regardless of the level of behavior. The design is predicated on the behavioral principle of stimulus discrimination (Leitenberg, 1973). A distinct stimulus (e.g., different colored worksheets, a sign, verbal instructions) is associated with each treatment to aid the subject's discrimination of which treatment is in effect during a given observational period.

> The data are plotted separately for each intervention to provide a ready visual representation of the effects of each treatment. Because confounding factors such as time of administration have been neutralized (presumably) by counterbalancing, and because the two treatments are readily discriminable by subjects through instructions or other discriminative stimuli, differences in the individual plots of behavior change corresponding with each treatment should be attributable to the treatment itself, allowing a direct comparison between two (or more) treatments. (Barlow & Hayes, 1979, p. 200)

Figure 8.10 shows a graphic prototype of an alternating treatments design comparing the effects of two treatments, A and B, on the target behavior. In an alternating treatments design the different treatments can be alternated with one another across daily sessions or each treatment can be administered in separate daily sessions or each treatment can comprise only a portion of a single daily session. The days of the week, time of day, order of presentation of the different treatments, persons delivering the different treatments, etc., are counterbalanced to reduce the probability that any observed differences in behavior are the result of variables other than the treatments themselves. For example, assume that each treatment in Figure 8.10 was administered for a 30-minute session each day with the daily order of the treatments randomly determined by a coin flip.

In order for the horizontal axis to accurately reflect the proper time relationship of each observational period, the data points in Figure 8.10 are arranged according to the actual sequence of treatments administered each day. Thus, the horizontal axis is labeled *Sessions*, to identify each consecutive pair of sessions occurring on a given day. Many published

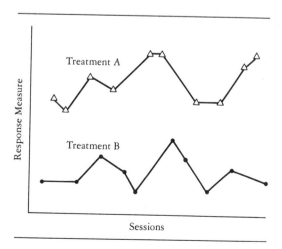

FIGURE 8.10 Graphic prototype of an alternating treatments design comparing the differential effects of two treatments (A and B).

---

[3]See Barlow and Hayes (1979) and Tawney and Gast (1984) for a discussion of the distinction between the simultaneous treatment design and the alternating treatments design. Barlow and Hayes (1979) could find only one true example of a simultaneous treatment design in the applied literature: a study by Browning (1967) in which three techniques for reducing the bragging of a 10-year-old boy were compared.

reports of experiments using an alternating treatments design in which two or more treatments are presented each day plot the behavioral measures recorded under each treatment on a given day (or session) above the same point on the horizontal axis. This practice prohibits the reader from determining the true sequnce of treatment administration and implies that the treatments were administered simultaneously.

The three components of baseline logic necessary for an experimental analysis—prediction, verification, and replication—are found in the alternating treatments design, although each component is not readily identified with a separate phase of the design. In the alternating treatments design each succeeding data point plotted for a specific treatment plays all three roles: (1) it serves as a basis for the *prediction* of future levels of behavior under that treatment, (2) it provides *verification* of previous predictions of performance under that treatment, and (3) it is a *replication* of the differential effect produced by the other treatment(s) that are part of the design.

To understand this logic, the reader should place a piece of paper over all the data points in Figure 8.10 except those representing the first five sessions of each treatment. Each remaining data path provides a basis for predicting future performance under each respective treatment. If the paper is moved to the right to reveal the two data points for the next day, each of the two provides a degree of verification of the previous predictions. As more data are recorded, the prediction of a given level and/or trend of behavior with each treatment is further strengthened by continued verification (assuming, of course, that the additional data are of the same level or trend as their predecessors). In the same way, each time Treatment A is reinstated and measurement shows a difference in performance level from that of Treatment B, a replication of differential effect is made, adding to the investigator's confidence that experimental control is being demonstrated.

Likewise, each reintroduction of Treatment B that results in a difference from Treatment A responding and a similarity with previous Treatment B responding adds another mini-replication that further strengthens the experimental analysis.

In an alternating treatments design visual inspection of the relationship between the data paths representing the different treatments is used to determine the presence and degree of experimental control. Experimental control is defined in this instance as objective, believable evidence that different levels of behavior are predictably and reliably produced by the administration of different treatments. When the data paths for two treatments show no overlap with one another and either stable levels or opposing trends, a clear demonstration of experimental control has been made. Such is the case in Figure 8.10, where there is no overlap of data paths and the picture of differential effects is clear. When some overlap of data paths occurs, a degree of experimental control over the target behavior can still be demonstrated if the majority of data points for a given treatment fall outside the range of values of the majority of data points for the contrasting treatment.

The degree of differential effect produced by two different treatments is determined by the vertical distance between the respective data paths. The greater the vertical distance, quantified by the vertical axis scale, the greater the difference in effect each treatment had on the target behavior. It is possible for experimental control to be shown between two treatments but for the amount of behavior change to be insignificant from an applied viewpoint. The greater the separation of data paths on the vertical axis, the higher the likelihood that the differences are of applied significance.[4]

---

[4]Even though experimental control is not demonstrated between two treatments in an alternating treatments design, both treatments may be effective in changing the target behavior (see the game and game-plus conditions in Figure 8.11).

Data from an experiment comparing the effects of two types of group-contingent reinforcers on the spelling accuracy of fourth grade underachievers illustrate how the alternating treatments design reveals experimental control and quantification of differential effects (Morgan, 1978). The six children in the study were divided into two equally skilled teams of three on the basis of pretesting. Each day during the study a five-word spelling test was administered. The words were given to the students the day before, and a 5-minute study period was provided just prior to the test. Three different treatments were used in the alternating treatments design: (1) in *no game* the students' test papers were immediately graded and returned to them and the next activity in the school day was begun; (2) in *game* the test papers were immediately graded, and each member of the team with the highest total score received a mimeographed Certificate of Achievement and was allowed to stand up and cheer; and (3) in *game plus* the game procedure was followed, and students on the winning team also received a small trinket (e.g., sticker, pencil).

Examination of the results for Subject 3 (shown in Figure 8.11) shows that experimental control over spelling accuracy was obtained between the no-game condition and

both the game and game-plus conditions. Only the first two no-game data points overlap the lower range of scores recorded under the game and game-plus conditions. However, scores for the game and game-plus conditions overlap completely and continuously throughout the study, revealing no difference in spelling accuracy as a function of the difference between the two treatments. The amount of improvement in spelling accuracy between the no-game condition and the game and game-plus conditions is shown by the vertical distance between the data paths. The mean difference between the two game conditions and the no-game condition was 2 words per test. Whether such a difference is significant is, of course, an educational question, not a mathematical or statistical one, although most would agree that an increase of 2 words out of 5 is a socially significant discovery that could contribute to the design of more effective instruction for the student. There was virtually no difference in mean spelling performance by Subject 3 between the game and game-plus conditions. However, even a larger mean difference would not have contributed to the conclusions of the study because of the lack of experimental control between the two treatments.

For Student 6 the game-plus condition produced consistently higher spelling scores than

FIGURE 8.11 Alternating treatments design comparing the effects of three different treatments on the spelling accuracy of a fourth-grade student. (From *Comparison of Two "Good Behavior Game" Group Contingencies on the Spelling Accuracy of Fourth-Grade Students* by Q. E. Morgan, 1978, unpublished master's thesis, Ohio State University. Reprinted by permission.)

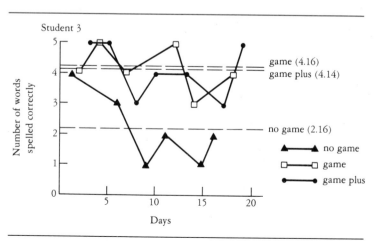

did the game or no-game conditions (see Figure 8.12). Experimental control was demonstrated between the game-plus and the other two treatments, but not between the no-game and game conditions. Again, the degree of difference in behavior change between treatments is measured by the vertical distance between the data paths; in this case there was a mean difference of 1.55 words per test between game-plus and no-game conditions.

Two other important points can be drawn from the data shown in Figures 8.11 and 8.12. First, the study shows how an alternating treatments design can provide the basis for quickly comparing the effects of different interventions. Although the study would have been strengthened considerably by the collection of additional data, after 20 sessions the teacher had sufficient empirical evidence to select and program the most effective consequences for spelling accuracy for each student. Even fewer sessions would probably have identified the most effective intervention if only two conditions had been compared. Second, data for the two subjects reported here underscore the importance of individual analysis. All six children spelled more words correctly under one or both of the game conditions than under the no-game condition. However, Subject 3's spelling accuracy was equally enhanced with either the game or game-plus contingency, whereas only the delivery of a tangible reinforcer resulted in improved spelling scores for Subject 6.

Variations of the Alternating Treatments Design

Although a relatively new experimental tactic in applied behavior analysis, the alternating treatments design is proving to be a versatile and increasingly popular method of comparing the effects of different treatments. The design can also be used to compare one or more treatments to a no-treatment or baseline condition, to assess the relative contributions of individual components of a package intervention, and to perform parametric investigations in which different values of an independent variable are alternated to determine differential effects on behavior change. The three most common ways in which the alternating treatments design is used are (1) a design without an initial baseline; (2) a design consisting of an initial baseline followed by the alternating treatments phase; and (3) the most common application, a design with an initial baseline followed by the alternating treatments phase, which in turn is followed by a final phase administering only the treatment that proved most effective.

FIGURE 8.12 Alternating treatments design comparing the effects of three different treatments on the spelling accuracy of a fourth-grade student. (From *Comparison of Two "Good Behavior Game" Group Contingencies on the Spelling Accuracy of Fourth-Grade Students* by Q. E. Morgan, 1978, unpublished master's thesis, Ohio State University. Reprinted by permission.)

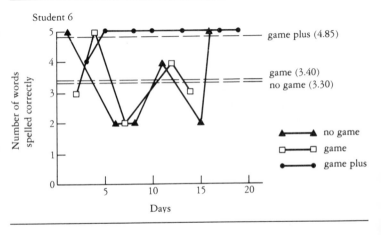

Alternating Treatments Design with No Initial Baseline Phase The alternating treatments design does not require an initial baseline phase. When necessary, the experiment can begin immediately introducing and alternating the different treatments to be compared. Although not a requirement of the design, a baseline condition is usually incorporated into the alternating treatments design as one of the treatments to be compared, as in the Morgan (1978) study (no game, game, and game plus).

Repp, Barton, and Brulle (1983, Experiment 2) also used a three-treatment alternating treatments design to compare the differential effects of baseline (no consequence) and two differ-

ent DRO methods on the rate of disruptive responses by an 8-year-old-boy with moderate mental retardation. All three conditions were presented in random order each day for 20 minutes; colored pieces of paper were taped to the student's desk to serve as discriminative stimuli signaling which condition was in effect. During the momentary DRO condition a treat was delivered to the subject if he was not engaged in disruptive behavior at the precise moment the 5-minute DRO interval ended. During whole-interval DRO the student was required not to have engaged in any disruptive behavior during the entire 5-minute interval in order to receive reinforcement. Figure 8.13

FIGURE 8.13 Example of alternating treatments design with no initial baseline and a no-treatment control condition as one of the alternating variables. (From "A Comparison of Two Procedures for Programming the Differential Reinforcement of Other Behaviors" by A. C. Repp, L. E. Barton, and A. R. Brulle, 1983, *Journal of Applied Behavior Analysis, 16,* p. 441. Copyright 1983 by the Society for the Experimental Analysis of Behavior, Inc. Reprinted by permission.)

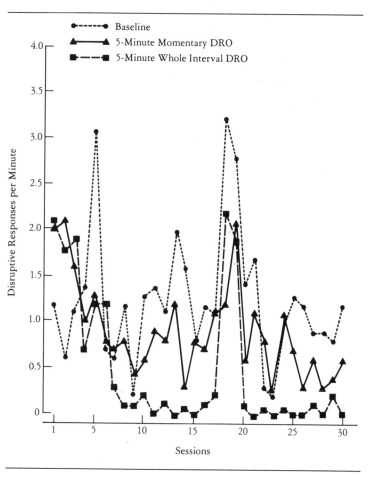

shows the results of this experiment. Although no differential effects were observed between any of the treatments for the first six sessions, from that point on both DRO procedures produced lower rates of disruptive behavior than the baseline condition, with the 5-minute whole-interval DRO producing the greatest reduction in the target behavior. After Session 6 on the graph only a few data points of the three treatments overlap with one another, demonstrating good experimental control between all three conditions.

The use of a no-treatment control condition as one of the alternating variables in an alternating treatments design provides valuable information on the difference in performance under the intervention treatment(s) and no treatment, but such data cannot be taken to represent a preintervention baseline level of behavior. It may be that the levels of behavior observed in the no-treatment condition represent only the level of behavior under a no-treatment condition that is interspersed with the intervention condition(s), an example of a phenomenon known as multiple treatment interference (Barlow & Hayes, 1979), and do not represent the natural level of behavior that existed before the alternating treatments design was begun.

Alternating Treatments Design with Initial Baseline Phase Whenever possible, baseline data should be collected until a stable level of responding or a countertherapeutic trend is evident prior to implementing the alternating treatments phase. A study by Singh and Singh (1985) provides an excellent example of an alternating treatments design incorporating an initial baseline phase. Their experiment evaluated the relative effectiveness of two procedures for reducing the number of oral reading errors committed by adolescents enrolled in a school for mentally retarded children. The first 10 days of the study consisted of a baseline phase in which each student was given a new 100-word passage three times each day and was told, "Here is the story for this session. I want you to read it. Try your best not to make any errors" (p. 66). The experimenter sat nearby but did not assist the student, correct any errors, or attend to self-corrections. If a student requested assistance with new or difficult words, he was prompted to continue reading.

During the alternating treatments phase of the study, three different conditions were presented each day in separate sessions of about 5 minutes each: control (same procedures as those of baseline), word supply, and word analysis. The daily order of the three conditions was randomized, each condition was preceded with specific instructions identifying the procedure to be implemented, and at least a 5-minute interval separated consecutive sessions. These procedures were followed to minimize any sequence or carryover effects from one condition to another. During the word-supply condition each student was instructed, "Here is the story for this session. I want you to read it. I will help you if you make a mistake. I will tell you the correct word while you listen and point to the word in the book. After that, I want you to repeat the word. Try your best not to make any errors" (p. 67). The experimenter supplied the correct word when an oral reading error was made, had the child repeat the correct word once, and instructed the child to continue reading. During the word analysis condition each student was instructed, "Here is the story for this session. I want you to read it. I will help you if you make a mistake. I will help you sound out the word and then you can read the word correctly before you carry on reading the rest of the story. Try your best not to make any errors" (p. 67). When errors were made in this condition, the experimenter directed the child's attention to the phonetic elements of the word, trying to get the child to sound out each part of the word correctly. Then the experimenter had the subject read the entire word at the normal speed and instructed him to continue reading the passage.

The results for all four participants in the study are shown in Figure 8.14. The data points during baseline are the means for the three daily sessions. Although the data are highly variable for each condition during the alternating treatments phase of the study (perhaps because of the varied difficulty of the different passages used), experimental control is evident. All four students committed fewer errors during both the word-supply and the word-analysis conditions than they did during the alternating control condition. Experimental control of oral reading errors, although not complete because of slight overlapping of the data paths, is also demonstrated between the word-supply and the word-analysis conditions, with all four students making fewer errors during the word-analysis condition.

By beginning the study with a baseline phase, the experimenters were able to compare the behavior change produced by each of the treatments with the natural level of performance uncontaminated by the introduction of an intervention. In addition, the initial baseline served as the basis for predicting and assessing the measures obtained during the control sessions of the alternating treatments phase of the study. In the Singh and Singh (1985) study the control data continue the frequency of errors observed during the initial baseline phase, providing evidence that (1) the vertical distance between the data paths for the word-supply and word-analysis conditions and the data path for the control condition represents the true amount of improvement produced by each treatment and (2) the frequency of errors during the control condition is not influenced by reduced errors during the other two treatments (i.e., there is no generalized reduction in oral reading errors from the treated passages to untreated passages).

Alternating Treatments Design with Initial Baseline Phase and Final "Best Treatment" Phase

The most widely used variation of the alternating treatments design consists of three sequential phases: an initial baseline phase, a middle phase comparing alternating treatments, and a final phase in which only the most effective treatment is administered (e.g., Ollendick, Matson, Esvelt-Dawson, & Shapiro, 1980; Singh & Singh, 1984).

Singh and Winton (1985) used this type of design in a study comparing the effects of three components of an overcorrection procedure for the treatment of pica (i.e., the ingestion of nonnutritive or inedible objects) in two institutionalized adult females with profound mental retardation. Pica can lead to lead poisoning and other medical problems, yet one survey found that pica occurred in up to 26% of institutionalized adults with mental retardation (Danford & Huber, 1982). During the initial baseline period data were collected on the rate of pica responses for 15 minutes daily in each of the three settings in which the experiment was carried out (dayroom, sunroom, and dining room). During baseline no treatment contingencies were in effect for pica or any other behavior, but the therapist prohibited subjects from swallowing inedible objects. Following baseline, the three overcorrection components—tidying, oral hygiene, and personal hygiene—were administered in each of the three settings, one treatment randomly assigned to a given setting each day. One therapist (Therapist A) carried out all three treatments during the alternating treatments phase of the study.

The tidying procedure consisted of the therapist's requiring the subject to spit out or throw down the inedible object, pick up the trash can, put the object in the trash can, and empty the trash can. The therapist provided physical guidance in each of the steps whenever necessary. This sequence took approximately 5 minutes to complete. During the oral hygiene condition intervention followed a procedure developed by Foxx and Martin (1975), in which the subject was required to spit out or throw down the object and brush her mouth, teeth, and gums for 5 minutes with

FIGURE 8.14 Example of alternating treatments design with an initial baseline. (From "Comparison of Word-Supply and Word-Analysis Error-Correction Procedures on Oral Reading by Mentally Retarded Children" by J. Singh and N. N. Singh, 1985, *American Journal of Mental Deficiency, 90,* p. 67. Copyright 1985 by the *American Journal of Mental Deficiency.* Reprinted by permission.)

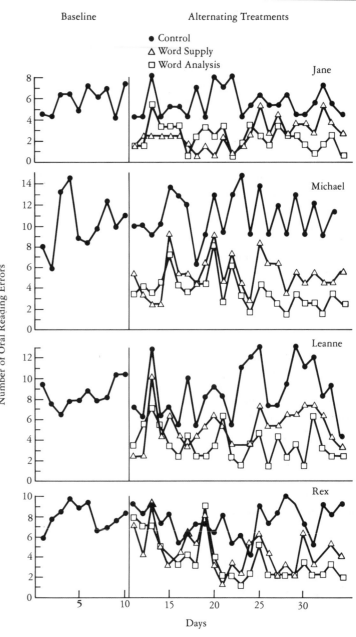

a soft bristle toothbrush that had been soaked in Listerine. The personal hygiene condition (Foxx & Martin, 1975) consisted of requiring the subject to spit out or throw down the object and then wash her hands and scrub her fingernails for 5 minutes. In both hygiene conditions physical guidance was supplied by the therapist as necessary. Time spent in treatment was not included in the 15 minutes of observation and data collection time allocated to each setting.

Results of the study are shown in Figure 8.15. Baseline rates of pica behavior averaged .40 and .70 responses per minute for Subjects 1 and 2, respectively. Rate of pica behavior for both subjects was reduced from baseline levels under all three treatments during the alternating treatments phase, with the oral hygiene procedure producing the greatest decrease in response rate: both subjects averaged only .09 responses per minute under the oral hygiene condition. Visual inspection of the data in the alternating treatments phase shows a clear demonstration of experimental control between the oral hygiene treatment and the other two treatments. No differential effects were observed between the tidying and the personal hygiene treatments. Singh and Winton did not terminate their study at this point, even though a sound comparative analysis had been accomplished. To determine whether the oral hygiene treatment would be as effective in all three settings each day without alternation with the other two treatments, they programmed only the oral hygiene condition for the next seven sessions. The mean rate of pica responses was .06 and .10 for Subjects 1 and 2 during this period. To test the generality of the treatment when applied by different persons, Therapists B, C, and D then administered the oral hygiene procedure during the final phase of the experiment. The study was ended for each subject after 5 consecutive days of no pica behavior during any of the three daily sessions.

The Singh and Winton (1985) study demonstrates use of the alternating treatments design to conduct a component analysis. By separating the original overcorrection procedure of Foxx and Martin (1975) into its parts and manipulating each part as a distinct intervention, the investigators were able to assess the relative effectiveness of each component in isolation. The finding that the oral hygiene procedure alone effectively suppressed pica behavior has important applied implications since less staff and client time are required to administer the treatment (i.e., 5 minutes for the oral hygiene treatment versus 15 minutes for the entire overcorrection routine of Foxx and Martin).

Advantages of the Alternating Treatments Design

The alternating treatments design offers numerous advantages for the experimental evaluation and comparison of two or more independent variables. Most of the benefits cited here were first described by Ulman and Sulzer-Azaroff (1975), who can be credited with bringing the rationale and possibilities of the design to the attention of much of the applied behavior analysis community. Barlow and Hayes (1979) and Kazdin and Hartmann (1978) have also discussed the advantages of the design.

Minimizes Sequence Effects The greatest strength of the alternating treatments design is that, when properly conducted, it minimizes the extent to which an experiment's results are confounded by sequence effects. Sequence effects are a major threat to the validity of any experiment involving multiple treatments. The concern over sequence effects can be summed up in this simple question: Would the results have been the same if the sequence of treatments had been different? Sequence effects are extremely difficult to control in a reversal or multiple baseline design (see chapter 9) that contains two or more independent variables because each experimental variable must remain in effect for a fairly long period of time, thereby producing a specific sequence of events. However, in an alternating

FIGURE 8.15 Example of alternating treatments design with an initial baseline and a final best-treatment-only condition. (From "Controlling Pica by Components of an Overcorrection Procedure" by N. N. Singh and A. S. Winton, 1985, *American Journal of Mental Deficiency, 90,* p. 43. Copyright 1985 by the *American Journal of Mental Deficiency.* Reprinted by permission.)

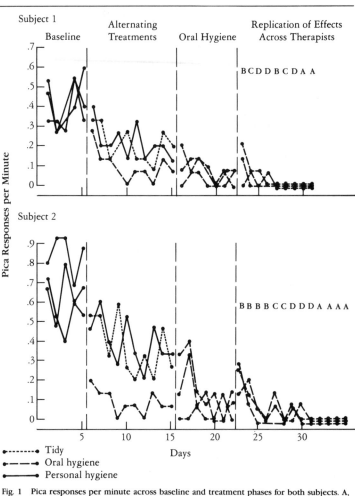

Fig. 1 Pica responses per minute across baseline and treatment phases for both subjects. A, B, C, and D specify the therapist for the day.

treatments design the independent variables are rapidly alternated with one another in a random fashion that produces no particular sequence. Also, each treatment is in effect for short periods of time, reducing the likelihood of carryover effects (O'Brien, 1968). The ability to control sequence effects makes the alternating treatments design a powerful tool for performing complex behavior analyses.

Does Not Require Withdrawal of Treatment Another major advantage of the alternating treatments design is that it does not

require the withdrawal of a seemingly effective treatment in order to demonstrate a functional relationship. Reversing behavioral improvements raises ethical issues that can be avoided with the alternating treatments design. Regardless of ethical issues, however, administrators and teachers may be more likely to accept the alternating treatments design than a reversal design even when one of the alternating treatments is a baseline condition. "It would appear that a return to baseline conditions every other day or every third day is not as disagreeable to a teacher as is first establishing a high level of desirable behavior for a prolonged period, and then reinstating the baseline behaviors" (Ulman & Sulzer-Azaroff, 1975, p. 385).

Speed of Comparison The experimental comparison of two or more treatments can often be made quickly with the alternating treatments design. In one study only 4 days were needed to show the superiority of one treatment over another in increasing the cooperative behavior of a 6-year-old boy (McCullough, Cornell, McDaniel, & Mueller, 1974). When the effects of different treatments become apparent early in an alternating treatments design, the investigator can then switch to programming only the most effective treatment. The efficiency of the alternating treatments design can leave a reseacher with meaningful data even when an experiment must be terminated early (Ulman & Sulzer-Azaroff, 1975). A reversal or multiple baseline design, on the other hand, must be carried through to completion to show a functional relationship.

Minimizes Problem of Irreversibility Some behaviors, even though they have been brought about or modified by application of the independent variable, do not return to baseline levels when the intervention is withdrawn and thus cannot be analyzed in an A-B-A-B design. However, the rapid alternation of treatment and baseline conditions can reveal differences in performance under the two conditions, especially early in an experiment before the baseline condition begins to approximate the treatment level of behavior.

Can Be Used with Unstable Data Determining behavior-environment relationships in the presence of unstable data presents a serious problem for applied behavior analysts. The foundation of baseline logic is the steady state responding used to predict and verify behavioral processes (Sidman, 1960). Yet with many socially important behaviors of interest to applied behavior analysts, obtaining a stable baseline is extremely difficult. Merely providing a subject with opportunities to make a target response can result in gradually improved performance. Practice effects are clearly worthy of empirical investigation because of their applied and scientific importance (Greenwood, Delquadri, & Hall, 1984; Johnston & Pennypacker, 1980), but the unstable baselines they create pose serious problems in the analysis of other variables. Obtaining sufficiently long and stable data patterns for many academic behaviors is also made difficult by the changing levels of task difficulty inherent in curriculum progression.

Since the different treatments are rapidly alternated in the alternating treatments design and since each is presented many times throughout each time period encompassed by the study and since no single condition is present for any considerable length of time, it can be presumed that any effects of practice, change in task difficulty, maturation, or other historical variables will be equally represented across all treatment conditions and will therefore not interfere with a reliable comparison. For example, even though two data paths representing a student's reading performance under two different teaching procedures may both show variable, increasing trends that might be due to practice effects and uneven curriculum materials, any consistent separation and vertical distance between the two data paths can be attributed to differences in the teaching procedures.

Can Be Used to Assess Generalization By alternating various conditions of interest, an experimenter can continually assess the degree of generalization of behavior change from an effective treatment to other conditions of interest. For example, when Singh and Winton (1985) alternated different therapists in the final phase of their study of pica behavior, they were able to determine the extent to which the overcorrection treatment was effective when presented by different persons. In other words, they learned the degree to which the behavioral improvement would generalize to the presence of another stimulus.

***Can Proceed Without an Initial Baseline
Phase*** Even though determining the preintervention level of the target behavior is always
preferable, the clinical necessity of immediately changing some behaviors precludes their
repeated measurement in the absence of intervention. When necessary, the alternating treatments design can be used without an initial
baseline phase.

Considering the Appropriateness of the Alternating Treatments Design

The numerous advantages of the alternating
treatments design are significant. As with all
experimental tactics, however, any specific
arrangement of manipulations presents certain
disadvantages and leaves unanswered certain
questions that can be probed only with additional experimentation.

***Artificial Nature of Rapidly Alternating
Treatments*** The rapid back-and-forth switch-
ing of treatments can be viewed as artificial in
terms of the way that clinical and educational
interventions are usually applied. However,
whether any detrimental effects result from
alternating treatments can be determined only
empirically. In most instances the quick comparison between treatments that is offered by
the alternating treatments design makes up for
any concern over its artificial nature.

Multiple Treatment Interference The fundamental feature of the alternating treatments
design is the rapid alternation of two or more
independent variables irrespective of the behavioral measures recorded under each treatment. Although the rapid alternation minimizes
sequence effects and greatly reduces the time
required to make a comparison between treatments, it raises the important question of
whether the effects observed under any of the
alternated treatments would be the same if
each treatment was implemented alone. **Multiple treatment interference** is the general

term for the confounding of effects observed
under one variable but caused by the presence
of other treatment variables. Multiple treatment
interference must always be suspected in
the alternating treatments design. However, by
following the experimental comparison with
application of only the most effective treatment,
the experimenter can assess the effects of that
treatment when administered in isolation.

Limited Capacity of the Design Although
the alternating treatments design enables an
elegant, scientifically sound method for comparing the effects of different treatments, it is
not an open-ended design in which an unlimited number of possible treatments can be
assessed. In practice, a maximum of three
different treatments can be effectively compared within a single phase of an alternating
treatments design, and in many instances only
two different treatments can be accommodated
(Kazdin & Hartmann, 1978). In an alternating
treatments design each treatment must be carefully counterbalanced across all of the different
conditions of its administration in order to
separate the effects of the treatment from any
effects of administrative variables (e.g., time of
day, order of presentation, settings, administrators). In many applied settings the logistics of
counterbalancing and delivering more than
two or three treatments would be cumbersome
and would cause the experiment to require too
many days to complete. Also, too many competing treatments can decrease the subject's
ability to discriminate between treatments,
thereby reducing the design's effectiveness.

Selection of Treatments Although the alternating treatments design theoretically can be
used to compare the effects of any two treatments as long as they are different in some way,
in reality the design is somewhat more limited.
In order to enhance the probability of discrimination between two treatments (i.e., reliable, measurable differences in behavior), the
various treatments used in an alternating treatments design should embody significant dif-

ferences. For example, an investigator studying the effects of group size on student performance during academic instruction might include conditions of 4, 8, and 20 students in an alternating treatments design. Manipulating alternating conditions of 6, 7, and 8 students, however, is less likely to reveal a functional relation between group size and performance.

In addition, some interventions may not produce important behavior change until and unless they have been consistently implemented for a continuous period of time.

> When a multielement baseline design [alternating treatments design] is employed, overlapping data do not necessarily rule out the possible efficacy of an experimental procedure. The session-by-session alternation of conditions might obscure effects that could be observed if the same condition was presented during several consecutive sessions. It is therefore possible that a given treatment may prove to be effective with a reversal or multiple-baseline design, but not with a multielement baseline design. (Ulman & Sulzer-Azaroff, 1975, p. 382)

The suspicion that a given intervention might be effective if presented in isolation for an extended period can only be explored by experimental manipulation. After an extended application that results in behavioral improvement, the researcher might return to an alternating treatments phase to compare the performance of the original pair of treatments.

SUMMARY

Reversal Design

1 The reversal tactic (A-B-A) entails repeated measurement of behavior in a given setting during three consecutive phases: (1) a baseline phase (absence of the independent variable), (2) a treatment phase (introduction of the independent variable), and (3) a return to baseline conditions (withdrawal of the independent variable).

2 The reversal design is strengthened tremendously by reintroducing the independent variable in the form of an A-B-A-B design. The A-B-A-B design is the most straightforward and powerful single-subject design for demonstrating functional relationships.

Variations of the A-B-A-B Design

3 A more convincing demonstration of a functional relation can sometimes be made by extending the A-B-A-B design with a series of repeated reversals.

4 Variations of the reversal tactic include multiple treatment designs, in which the effects of two or more independent variables are compared to a baseline condition and/or to one another, and designs in which the additive or interactive effects of two or more independent variables are investigated.

5 Multiple treatment designs using the reversal tactic are particularly susceptible to confounding by sequence effects.

6 An experimental design incorporating a noncontingent reinforcement phase as a reversal tactic enables the isolation and analysis of the contingent aspect of reinforcement.

7 Reversal phases incorporating DRO and DRI procedures can also be used to demonstrate the experimental effects of contingent reinforcement.

8 The B-A-B reversal design can be used with target behaviors for which an initial baseline phase is inappropriate for ethical or practical reasons.

Considering the Appropriateness of Reversal Designs

9 An experimental design based on the reversal tactic is ineffective in evaluating the effects of an independent variable that cannot be withdrawn once it has been introduced (e.g., instruction, modeling).

10 Once improved, some behaviors will not reverse to baseline levels even though the independent variable has been withdrawn. Such
behavioral irreversibility precludes effective use
of the reversal tactic.

11 Legitimate social, educational, and ethical concerns are often raised over withdrawing a seemingly effective treatment variable to provide
scientific verification of its function in changing
behavior.

12 Sometimes very brief reversal phases, or even
one-session baseline probes, are sufficient to
demonstrate believable experimental control.

Alternating Treatments Design

13 The alternating treatments design compares
two or more independent variables by rapidly
alternating their presentation and measuring
the effects of each variable on a single behavior.

14 Experimental control is demonstrated in the
alternating treatments design when the data
paths for two different independent variables
show little or no overlap.

15 The degree of differential effect produced by
two different independent variables is determined by the amount of vertical distance between the respective data paths.

Variations of the Alternating Treatments Design

16 An experimental design can consist of an alternating treatments phase implemented without
an initial baseline phase. A no-treatment control condition is often used in such a design as
one of the alternating treatments.

17 Whenever possible, an initial baseline phase
should precede the alternating treatments phase
of an experiment.

18 The variation of the alternating treatments
design that provides the most information is
comprised of three phases: an initial baseline

phase, the alternating treatments phase, and a
final phase in which only the treatment found
most effective is applied.

Advantages of the Alternating Treatments Design

19 The alternating treatments design minimizes
sequence effects.

20 It does not require the withdrawal of treatment.

21 This design can compare the relative effectiveness of two treatments quickly.

22 It minimizes the problem of irreversibility.

23 The alternating treatments design can be used
with unstable data patterns.

24 It can be used to assess generalization of
behavior change.

25 This design can proceed without an initial
baseline.

Considering the Appropriateness of the Alternating Treatments Design

26 Because they are rapidly and randomly alternated, the application of treatments in an alternating treatments design may seem artificial.

27 The alternating treatments design is susceptible
to multiple treatment interference. However,
by following the alternating treatments phase
with a phase in which only one treatment is
administered, the experimenter can assess the
effects of that treatment in isolation.

28 An alternating treatments phase is usually limited to a maximum of three different independent variables.

29 This design is most effective in revealing the
differential effects of independent variables
that are significantly different from one another.

30 The alternating treatments design is not an
effective tactic for assessing the effects of an
independent variable that produces important
changes in behavior only when it is consistently
administered over a continuous period of time.

9

Multiple Baseline and Changing Criterion Designs

KEY TERMS

Multiple baseline design

Multiple baseline across behaviors design

Multiple baseline across settings design

Multiple baseline across subjects design

Multiple probe design

Delayed multiple baseline design

Changing criterion design

This chapter describes two more experimental tactics for analyzing behavior-environment relations—the multiple baseline and the changing criterion designs. In a multiple baseline design the treatment variable is applied sequentially to two or more behaviors, and the effects on each behavior are noted. The changing criterion design is a technique for analyzing improvements in a single behavior as a function of stepwise increments in the response levels required for reinforcement.

MULTIPLE BASELINE DESIGN

The multiple baseline technique has become the most widely used tactic for experimental design in applied behavior analysis. It is a highly flexible technique that enables a researcher or practitioner to analyze the effects of an independent variable across multiple behaviors, settings, and/or subjects without the necessity of withdrawing the treatment variable in order to reverse improvements in behavior.

This chapter was written by William L. Heward.

The implementation, logic, advantages, and limitations of the multiple baseline design, in addition to two derivative experimental techniques, are presented in this section.

Operation and Logic of the Multiple Baseline Design

The **multiple baseline design** was first described in the applied behavior analysis literature by Baer, Wolf, and Risley (1968). They presented the multiple baseline design as an alternative to the reversal design for situations in which the target behavior is likely to be irreversible or in which reproducing baseline levels of performance is undesirable for practical or ethical reasons. Figure 9.1 illustrates Baer, Wolf, and Risley's (1968) explanation of the basic operation of the multiple baseline design.

> In the multiple baseline technique, a number of responses are identified and measured over time to provide baselines against which changes can be evaluated. With these baselines established, the experimenter then applies an experimental variable to one of the behaviors, produces a change in it, and perhaps notes little or no

FIGURE 9.1 Graphic prototype of multiple baseline design.

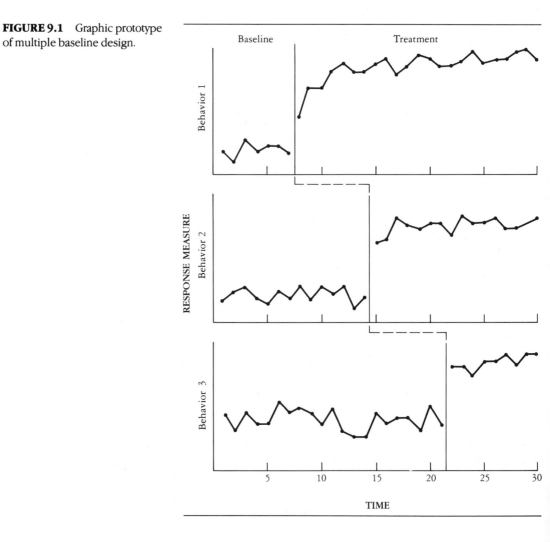

change in the other baselines. If so, rather than reversing the just-produced change, he instead applies the experimental variable to one of the other, as yet unchanged, responses. If it changes at that point, evidence is accruing that the experimental variable is indeed effective, and that the prior change was not simply a matter of coincidence. The variable then may be applied to still another response, and so on. The experimenter is attempting to show that he has a reliable experimental variable, in that each behavior changes maximally only when the experimental variable is applied to it. (p. 94)

Although all of the graphic displays developed or selected for this text as examples of experimental design tactics show data plotted against noncumulative vertical axes, the reader is reminded that repeated measurement data collected within any type of behavioral design can be plotted on both noncumulative and cumulative graphs. For example, Gaylord-Ross, Haring, Breen, and Pitts-Conway (1984) and Wacker, Berg, Wiggins, Muldoon, and Cavanaugh (1985) display the data they collected in multiple baseline design experiments on cumulative graphs. The reader should be careful not to confuse the different techniques for graphic display with procedures for experimental analysis.

The multiple baseline design takes three basic forms: (1) a **multiple baseline across behaviors design**, employing two or more different behaviors of the same subject; (2) a **multiple baseline across settings design**, employing the same behavior of the same subject in two or more different settings; and (3) a **multiple baseline across subjects design**, employing the same behavior of several different subjects. Each of the multiple baseline design's basic forms involves the sequential application of the independent variable across technically different behaviors. That is, in the multiple baseline across settings design, even though the subject's performance of the same target behavior is measured in two or more settings, each behavior-setting combination is treated as a different behavior for analysis. Sim-

ilarly, in a multiple baseline across subjects design, each subject-behavior combination is treated as a different behavior in the operation of the design.

Figure 9.2 shows the same data set as that displayed in Figure 9.1 with predicted data and shading added to illustrate how the three elements of baseline logic—prediction, verification, and replication—are operationalized in the multiple baseline design. When stable baseline responding has been achieved for Behavior 1, the *prediction* is made that continued measurement will reveal similar levels of behavior if the environment is held constant. When the researcher's confidence in such a prediction is high, the independent variable is applied to Behavior 1. The level of responding predicted for Behavior 1 is marked by the open data points within the shaded area plotted within the treatment phase. The actual data collected for Behavior 1 during treatment is shown by the solid data points. These data show a discrepancy with the level of responding predicted if no changes were made in the environment, thereby suggesting the possibility that the independent variable is responsible for the change in behavior. The data collected for Behavior 1 in a multiple baseline design serve the same purpose as the data collected during the first two phases of a reversal design.

Continued baseline measurement of the other behaviors in the experiment offers the possibility of verifying the prediction made for Behavior 1. In a multiple baseline design *verification* of a predicted level of responding for one behavior is made by observing little or no change in the ongoing data patterns of the other behaviors that are still exposed to the conditions under which the prediction was made. In Figure 9.2 the portions of the baseline data for Behaviors 2 and 3 that are shaded with dots verify the validity of the prediction for Behavior 1. Two inferences can be made at this point: (1) the prediction of no change for Behavior 1 in a constant environment was valid because the environment was held constant for

FIGURE 9.2 Graphic prototype of multiple baseline design with shading added to show elements of baseline logic. Open data points represent the prediction of future measures if the environment is held constant. Baseline data shaded with dots for Behaviors 2 and 3 serve as verification of the prediction made for Behavior 1. Behavior 3 baseline data within Bracket A verify prediction made for Behavior 2. Data obtained during the treatment phase for Behaviors 2 and 3 (cross-hatched shading) provide replication of experimental effect.

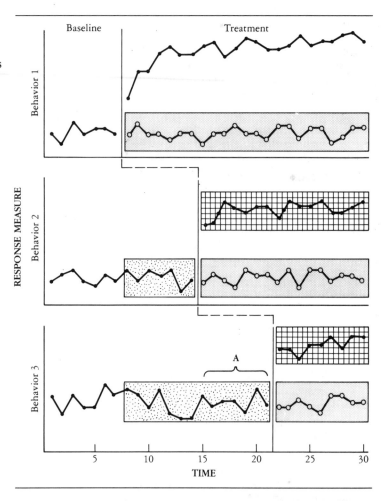

Behaviors 2 and 3 and their levels of responding remained unchanged; and (2) the observed changes in Behavior 1 were brought about by the independent variable because only Behavior 1 was exposed to the independent variable and only Behavior 1 changed.

In a multiple baseline design the independent variable's function in changing a given behavior is inferred by the lack of change in untreated behaviors. Verification of function is not demonstrated directly as it is with the reversal design, thereby making the multiple baseline design an inherently weaker tactic for demonstrating a functional relationship between the independent variable and a target behavior (Hersen & Barlow, 1976). However, this weakness is compensated for somewhat by the multiple opportunities to verify or refute the numerous predictions made within a multiple baseline design. Not only is the prediction for Behavior 1 in Figure 9.2 verified by continued stable baselines for Behavior 2 and 3, but the bracketed portion of the baseline data for Behavior 3 also serves to verify the prediction made for Behavior 2.

When the Behavior 1 level of responding under the treatment condition has stabilized or reached a prestated performance criterion, the independent variable is then applied to Behavior 2. If Behavior 2 changes in the same manner as Behavior 1, *replication* of the independent variable's effect has been achieved (shown by cross-hatched data points). After Behavior 2 has changed maximally, the independent variable is applied to Behavior 3 in an attempt to replicate the effect again. The independent variable is sequentially applied to additional behaviors in this manner until a convincing demonstration of the functional relationship has been established and all of the target behaviors scheduled for improvement have been modified.

As with verification, replication of the independent variable's specific effect on each behavior is not manipulated directly in the multiple baseline design. Instead, the generality of the treatment variable's effect across the behaviors comprising the experiment is demonstrated by applying the independent variable to a series of behaviors. However, assuming accurate measurement and proper experimental control of relevant variables (i.e., the only environmental factor that changes during the course of the experiment should be the independent variable, and its presence, absence, and/or value should be effectively controlled by the experimenter), each time a behavior changes when and only when the independent variable is introduced, confidence in the existence of a functional relationship increases.

How many different behaviors, settings, or subjects must a multiple baseline design include to provide enough replications of effect for a believable experimental demonstration? Baer, Wolf, and Risley (1968) suggest that ultimately the number of replications needed in any design is a matter for the consumers of the research to decide. In other words, to be successful, a multiple baseline design must contain however many replications across behaviors are necessary to convince whoever is being asked to respond to the experiment and to the experimenter's claims (e.g., teachers, administrators, parents, funding sources, journal editors). A multiple baseline design with only two behaviors (i.e., a two-baseline or two-tier

design) is a complete design—all of the elements necessary for experimental analysis are included—and can provide strong support for the effectiveness of the independent variable (e.g., Blount, Drabman, Wilson, & Stewart, 1982; Fleece, Gross, O'Brien, Kistner, Rothblum, & Drabman, 1981; Hamlet, Axelrod, & Kuerschner, 1984; Van Houten & Rolider, 1985). Nevertheless, a minimum of three or four baselines is recommended when applied considerations permit (Hersen & Barlow, 1976; Tawney & Gast, 1984). When the effect of the independent variable is substantial and is reliably replicated, three or four baselines can provide an almost completely convincing demonstration of experimental effect (Cooper, 1981).

Some of the earliest examples of the multiple baseline technique in the literature of applied behavior analysis were the studies by Risley and Hart (1968); Barrish, Saunders, and Wolf (1969, see Figure 25.10); Barton, Guess, Garcia, and Baer (1970); Panyan, Boozer, and Morris (1970); and Schwarz and Hawkins (1970). Some of the pioneering applications of the multiple baseline technique are not readily apparent with casual examination: the authors may not have identified the experimental design as a multiple baseline design (e.g., Schwarz & Hawkins, 1970), and the now-common practice of stacking the tiers of a multiple baseline design one upon the other so that all of the data can be displayed in the same figure was not always used (e.g., Maloney & Hopkins, 1973; Schwarz & Hawkins, 1970).

In 1970 Hall, Cristler, Cranston, and Tucker published a frequently cited paper including three experiments, each an example of one of the three basic forms of the multiple baseline design: across behaviors, across settings, and across subjects. The Hall et al. (1970) paper was important not only because it provided excellent illustrations that still serve today as models of the multiple baseline design, but also because the studies reported were carried out by teachers and parents, indicating that practitioners "can carry out important and significant studies in natural settings using resources available to them" (p. 255). Three recently published studies are included here to illustrate each form of the multiple baseline design.

Multiple Baseline Across Behaviors Design

In the multiple baseline across behaviors design, two or more behaviors of a single individual (or group) are targeted. After steady state responding has been demonstrated under baseline conditions, the independent variable is applied to one of the behaviors while baseline conditions remain in effect for the other behaviors. When steady state or criterion-level performance has been reached for the first behavior, the independent variable is applied to the next behavior, and so on. McGee, Krantz, Mason, and McClannahan (1983) used a multiple baseline across behaviors design to evaluate the effectiveness of a modified incidental-teaching procedure on the acquisition and generalization of receptive language skills by autistic children.

Incidental-teaching procedures take advantage of naturally occurring adult-child interactions to teach language (Hart & Risley, 1974, 1975, 1982). When a child initiates an interaction by asking for an object or commenting on a topic of interest, the teacher requests an elaboration or improvement of the child's request, providing prompts or models as necessary to evoke correct responding from the child, which is then reinforced. However, because many autistic and other severely language-delayed children do not initiate language interactions, modifications of the incidental-teaching procedure are required to take advantage of naturally occurring situations that provide opportunities for language development. Specifically, the teaching adult must begin the language interaction in the context of an on-going functional activity with the child.

McGee et al. (1983) used the daily lunch preparation activity of two autistic children living in a family-style group home, a 15-year-old

girl and a 12-year-old boy, as the occasion to teach object identification. Four sets of three lunch preparation target objects were identified for each subject (e.g., Set 1 for Youth 1 included relish, lettuce, and a baggie plus two distractors—aluminum foil and tuna). Throughout the study, data were collected on the correct object identifications performed by each youth in response to the teaching parent's requests ("Give me _____") made during the preparation of lunches in the kitchen and during a daily generalization test conducted at the dining room table. The location of the objects in relation to one another and the order in which they were requested were randomized to ensure that the youths were discriminating on the basis of the objects themselves and not on the basis of location or order. The incidental-teaching procedure began with the teaching parent making eye contact with the youth and saying, "Give me _____." If the child did not select the requested object, the teaching parent repeated the request, while simultaneously pointing to the correct object. When the subject picked up and delivered the correct object, the teaching parent said, "Good, you gave me the _____," and placed the object back on the kitchen counter. When the object identification tasks had been completed for each set of objects, the youth was allowed to use those objects in the lunch preparation activities. The teaching procedure was applied to the next set of objects when at least 70% accuracy was obtained on the previous set. Each youth prepared three lunches each session so that a total of 36 separate requests were made each session.

Figure 9.3 shows the results of the experiment. Correct object identification increased as a function of the modified incidental-teaching procedure, not only during the lunch preparation sessions themselves (solid data path), but also during the generalization assessment sessions conducted later in the day (dashed data path). Even though receptive language object identification was the overall response class

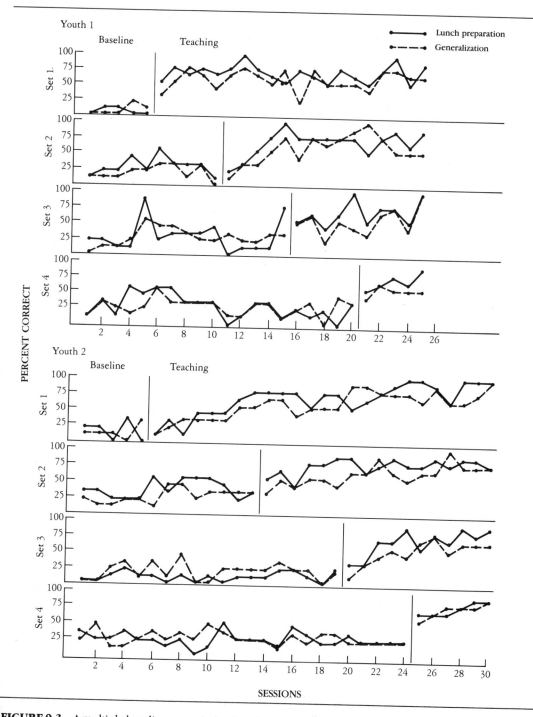

FIGURE 9.3 A multiple baseline across behaviors design showing percent correct, unprompted object identifications achieved by two autistic youths on four sets of objects presented during lunch preparation (solid line) and generalization (dotted line). (From "A Modified Incidental-Teaching Procedure for Autistic Youth: Acquisition and Generalization of Receptive Object Labels", by G. G. McGee, P. J. Krantz, D. Mason, and L. E. McClannahan, 1983, *Journal of Applied Behavior Analysis, 16,* p. 335. Copyright 1983 by the Society for the Experimental Analysis of Behavior, Inc. Reprinted by permission.)

under investigation, each subject's responses to each set of distinct items were separately measured and analyzed as different behaviors within the multiple baseline design.

This study illustrates the fact that the multiple baseline across behaviors design is a single-subject experimental strategy in which each subject serves as her own control. Each subject constitutes a complete experiment, replicated in a second subject in this case. It should be noted that the incidental-teaching strategy was introduced for each set of objects for each subject in response to that subject's performance, not according to a preset schedule of experimental operations. Only in this manner can the experimenter retain the flexibility needed to pursue the behavior-environment relations that are the focus of the science of behavior.

Multiple Baseline Across Settings Design

In the multiple baseline across settings design a single behavior of an individual (or group) is targeted in two or more different settings or conditions (e.g., locations, times of day). After stable responding has been demonstrated under baseline conditions, the independent variable is introduced in one of the settings while baseline conditions remain in effect in the other settings. When maximum behavior change or criterion-level performance has been achieved in the first setting, the independent variable is applied in the second setting, and so on.

Parker, Cataldo, Bourland, Emurian, Corbin, and Page (1984) used a multiple baseline across settings design to determine whether contingent reinforcement could be used to treat orofacial dysfunction. The subject was a 26-year-old woman with moderate mental retardation, congenital spastic quadriplegia, and a history of jaw hyperextension manifested by an open mouth posture. Previous efforts to control the condition with drugs had proved unsuccessful. Two types of mouth closure were targeted for measurement: inappropriate mouth

closure, which was defined as visible contact of the upper and lower teeth with the tongue in between them; appropriate mouth closure, which was defined as any contact of the upper and lower teeth.

All sessions were conducted in a training room with the subject seated in a lounge chair facing a two-way mirror through which observations of her behavior were made. A 20-second whole interval recording procedure was used, with 10 consecutive intervals constituting a trial (some sessions consisted of three trials; others, only one). During the alone condition the subject was by herself in the training room. During the therapist present and mother present conditions, the therapist or the subject's mother sat in a chair about 3 feet from her. Prior to all baseline or treatment sessions the subject was instructed to keep her mouth closed with her upper and lower teeth touching.

The independent variable consisted of reinforcement delivered by an experimenter who observed the subject through the two-way mirror and operated a hand-held microswitch that flashed a panel of red lights about 5 feet away from the subject at eye level. An electromechanical counter outside the training room recorded the cumulative number of light flashes, providing a total point count per session. After each session points were exchanged by the subject for money or social activities. The treatment procedure was first applied in the subject alone condition, with a light flash delivered for each 5-second interval of appropriate mouth closure. This procedure was followed for 12 three-trial sessions (see Figure 9.4). Over the next three sessions the subject was required to sustain appropriate mouth closure for 10 seconds in order to receive a light flash; then the response requirement was raised to 20 seconds. After several trials of 100% appropriate mouth closure in the alone condition, the independent variable was sequentially applied in the therapist present and mother present conditions. The results show that an immediate reduction of inappropriate mouth

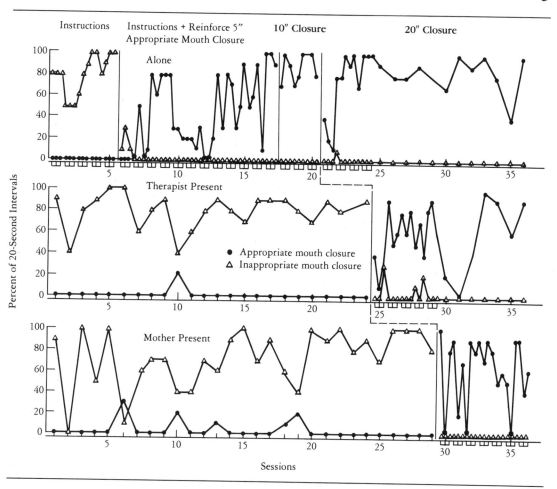

FIGURE 9.4 A multiple baseline across settings design showing percent occurrence of appropriate and inappropriate mouth closures obtained across alone, therapist present, and mother present conditions. (From "Operant Treatment of Orofacial Dysfunction in Neuromuscular Disorders" by L. H. Parker, M. F. Cataldo, G. Bourland, C. S. Emurian, R. J. Corbin, and J. M. Page, 1984, *Journal of Applied Behavior Analysis, 17,* p. 420. Copyright 1984 by the Society for the Experimental Analysis of Behavior, Inc. Reprinted by permission.)

closures to zero or near-zero levels occurred in each of the three conditions (settings) when the independent variable was introduced. Also, appropriate mouth closure increased substantially from zero levels in all three settings when the independent variable was introduced.

This study is interesting for several reasons. First, it illustrates that the multiple baseline across settings design does not require physically separate settings for each tier of the design (e.g., classroom, lunchroom, playground). In this study the presence or absence of other people in the training room constituted the different settings (environments) in which the effects of the independent variable were evaluated. Second, the experiment illustrates how a treatment variable can have differential effects on different behaviors. Although inappropriate mouth closure and appropriate mouth closure were incompatible (i.e., both could not occur at the same time), the subject could still engage in a third behavior, the open mouth posture. Although virtually complete experimental control was evident over inappropriate mouth closure, the treatment was only partially successful in controlling appropriate mouth closure, as shown by the highly variable data patterns. Such variability indicates the operation of functional variables not controlled by the experimenters and suggests the need for further investigation. Third, the study shows that mere instructions to the subject to close her mouth appropriately were ineffective (and the subject had good receptive language skills). Even after high levels of appropriate mouth closure had been attained in the reinforced settings, the subject's behavior showed no changes in the untreated settings. Had the experimenters not included the instructions to the subject to keep her mouth closed as part of the baseline conditions, an appropriate criticism of the study would have been couched in the question, Why not simply tell the subject to keep her mouth closed?

Multiple Baseline Across Subjects Design

In the multiple baseline across subjects design one target behavior is selected for two or more subjects (or groups) in the same setting. After steady state responding has been achieved under baseline conditions, the independent variable is applied to one of the subjects while baseline conditions remain in effect for the other subjects. When criterion-level or stable responding has been attained for the first subject, the independent variable is applied to the second subject, and so on. The multiple baseline across subjects design is the most widely used of all three forms of the design, in part because teachers, clinicians, and other practitioners are commonly confronted by more than one student or client needing to learn the same skill or eliminate the same problem behavior.

Ackerman and Shapiro (1984) used a multiple baseline across subjects design to examine the effects of self-monitoring on the work productivity of sheltered workshop employees. Five mentally retarded adults (mean age of 33 years), whose work productivity ranged from 20 to 40% of the community rate, participated in the study. The target behavior was a 4-step process in which employees packaged bags of six party hats. The number of bags completed per minute served as the dependent variable. Each work day a 1-hour session was divided into two 30-minute segments: an intervention period followed by a generalization period. During baseline the employees were simply given their assigned work and told to work until time was up; no intervention was implemented in either period (see Figure 9.5). In Phase 2 a combination of verbal prompting, verbal praise, and pats on the back were delivered on a variable schedule (20 consequences per employee) contingent on work performance during the intervention period only. During the generalization period in this phase, baseline conditions were in effect, and the trainer sat 10 meters away from the employees, neither responding to their requests nor initiating interaction with them. In Phase 3 the employees used a grocery store counter to self-monitor the number of bags they completed during the intervention period, circling on a chart the number of pieces completed at the end of the period. The self-monitoring counters and charts were removed for the 30-minute generalization period during this phase, thereby reinstating baseline conditions. In the final phase of the study the self-monitoring procedure was implemented during the generalization period also.

Mean productivity rates across the five subjects during baseline were 1.1 and 1.2 during the intervention and generalization periods, respectively. Verbal praise and encouragement (Phase 2) resulted in a mean rate of 1.7 during intervention, but no improvement in productivity during generalization except for Mary,

FIGURE 9.5 A multiple baseline across subjects design showing number of packages completed per minute by each employee during 30-minute intervention and generalization periods. (From "Self-Monitoring and Work Productivity with Mentally Retarded Adults" by A. M. Ackerman and E. S. Shapiro, 1984, *Journal of Applied Behavior Analysis, 17,* p. 406. Copyright 1984 by the Society for the Experimental Analysis of Behavior, Inc. Reprinted by permission.)

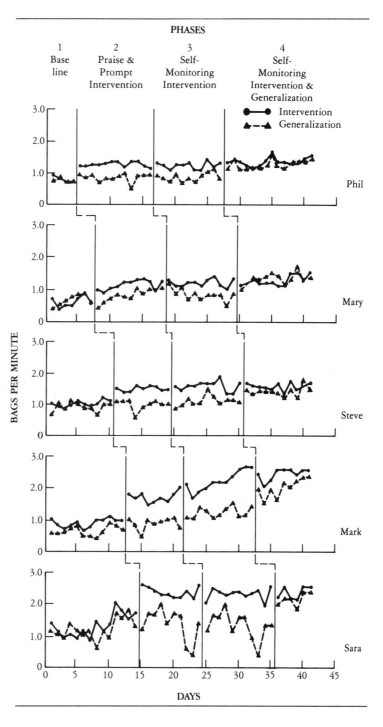

205

whose productivity rate showed an upward trend during that phase. The introduction of self-monitoring in Phase 3 maintained the work rates produced in Phase 2, with Mark's work rate increasing during this phase. Phase 3 performance during the generalization period, when the self-monitoring devices were not available to the employees, was well below that obtained during self-monitoring. When self-monitoring was extended to the second 30-minute work period (Phase 4), productivity approached the levels attained during the initial 30-minute period.

The results show that even though verbal prompts and praise increased work rates during the intervention period, increased performance did not generalize to the next 30-minute work period when praise was not given (with the possible exception of Mary). Self-monitoring maintained the increased work rates (and possibly increased Mark's performance) but did not result in higher productivity rates during the following work period, which was not self-monitored. The study's last phase is interesting in that the results show that self-monitoring can be used to increase work productivity, at least for employees who have successfully used self-monitoring to maintain work rates previously increased by verbal reinforcement. One might be tempted to identify the last two phases of this study as an incorporation of a multiple baseline across settings tactic for each subject: self-monitoring was applied to the first 30-minute work period in Phase 3, and then it was applied to the second 30-minute work period in Phase 4. However, the work rates in the two different settings (i.e., periods) do not serve as equal multiple baselines for this purpose because performance in the intervention period of Phase 3 was previously exposed to the prompting and praising condition. Therefore, sequence effects (which in this case are visible in the changes in work rates between the first 30-minute period of Phase 1 and Phase 2) prohibit the final two phases from being considered a multiple baseline design across settings within the larger multiple baseline across subjects design.

A multiple baseline across subjects design is not a single subject design in the true sense (i.e., each subject does not serve as his own control). Instead, predictions based on one subject's behavior must be verified by the behavior of other subjects, and replication of effect is dependent on the behavior of other subjects. This is both a weakness and a potential advantage of the multiple baseline across subjects design and is discussed further later in the chapter.

Assumptions and Procedural Guidelines for Using Multiple Baseline Designs

Like all experimental strategies the multiple baseline tactic requires the researcher to make certain assumptions about how the behavior-environment relationships under investigation function, even though discovering the existence and operation of those functional relationships is the very reason for conducting the research. In this sense the design of behavioral experiments resembles an empirical guessing game—the experimenter guesses; the data answer. The investigator makes assumptions about behavior and its relation to controlling variables, hypotheses in the informal sense, and then constructs experimental strategies designed to produce data capable of verifying or refuting those assumptions.

The term *hypothesis* as it is used here should not be confused with the formal hypothesis testing models of inferential statistics that are designed to confirm or reject statements deduced from a body of theory. However, as Johnston and Pennypacker (1980) point out,

> More modest hypotheses are constantly being subjected to experimental tests. . . . Whenever an experimenter arranges to affirm the consequent of a particular proposition, he or she is testing a hypothesis, although it is rare to encounter the actual use of such language [in the science of behavior]. Hypothesis testing in this relatively

informal sense guides the construction of experiments without binding the researcher to the importance of unexpected results. (pp. 38–39)

Because verification and replication in the multiple baseline design is dependent upon what happens, or does not happen, to other behaviors as a result of the sequential application of the independent variable, the experimenter must be particularly careful to plan and carry out the design in a manner that will afford the greatest degree of confidence in any relationships suggested by the data. Although the multiple baseline design appears deceptively simple, its successful application entails much more than selecting a group of behaviors and introducing an experimental variable. Adhering to certain guidelines can increase the experimenter's chance of success.

Select Independent yet Functionally Similar Baselines Demonstration of a functional relationship in a multiple baseline design is dependent upon two occurrences: (1) the behaviors still in baseline showing no change in level or trend while behaviors in contact with the independent variable change, and (2) each behavior changing when the independent variable is applied to it. Thus, the experimenter must make two, at times seemingly contradictory, assumptions about the behaviors targeted for analysis in a multiple baseline design. The assumptions are that the behaviors are functionally independent of one another (the behaviors will not co-vary with one another), and yet the behaviors share enough similarity that each will change when the same independent variable is applied to it (Tawney & Gast, 1984). An error in either assumption can result in a failure to demonstrate a functional relationship.

For example, let us suppose that the independent variable is introduced with the first behavior, and changes in level and/or trend are noted, but the other behaviors still in baseline also change. Do the changes in the baseline behaviors mean that an uncontrolled variable is responsible for the changes in all of the behaviors and that the independent variable is an ineffective treatment? Or do the concomitant changes in the untreated behaviors mean that the changes in the first behavior were effected by the independent variable and have generalized to the other behaviors? Or let us suppose instead that the first behavior changes when the independent variable is introduced, but subsequent behaviors do not change when the independent variable is applied. Does this failure to replicate mean that a factor other than the independent variable was responsible for the change observed in the first behavior? Or does it mean only that the subsequent behaviors do not operate as a function of the experimental variable, leaving open the possibility that the change noted in the first behavior was effected by the independent variable?

The answers to these questions can be pursued only by further experimental manipulation. In both kinds of failure to demonstrate experimental control, the multiple baseline design does not rule out the possibility of a functional relationship between the independent variable and the behavior(s) that did change when the variable was applied. In the first instance the failure to demonstrate experimental control with the originally planned design is offset by the opportunity to investigate and possibly isolate the variable robust enough to change multiple behaviors simultaneously. Discovery of variables that reliably produce generalized changes across behaviors, settings, and/or subjects is a major goal of applied behavior analysis (Stokes & Baer, 1977); and if the experimenter is confident that all other relevant variables were held constant before, during, and after the observed behavior changes, the original independent variable is the first candidate for further investigation.

In the second situation, with its failure to replicate changes from one behavior to another, the experimenter can pursue the possibility of a functional relationship between the independent variable and the first behavior, perhaps using a reversal technique, and can hope to discover later an effective intervention for the behavior(s) that did not change. Another possibility is to drop the original independent variable altogether and search for another treatment that might be effective with all of the targeted behaviors.

Select Concurrent and Plausibly Related Multiple Baselines In an effort to ensure the functional independence of behaviors in a multiple baseline design, experimenters should not select response classes or settings so unrelated to one another as to offer no plausible means of comparison. In order for the ongoing baseline measurement of one behavior to provide a logical basis for verifying the prediction of another behavior that has been exposed to an independent variable, two conditions must be met: (1) the two behaviors must be measured concurrently, and (2) all of the relevant variables that influence one behavior must have an opportunity to influence the other behavior. Studies that employ a multiple baseline approach across both subjects and settings often stretch the logic of the design beyond its capabilities. For example, using the stable baseline measures of one child's compliance with parental requests as the basis for verifying the effect of intervention on the compliance behavior of another child living with another family is questionable practice. The sets of variables influencing the two children are surely differentiated by more than the presence or absence of the experimental variable.

> There are some important limits to designating multiple behavior/setting combinations that are intended to function as part of the same experiment. In order for the use of multiple behaviors and settings to be part of the same design and thus augment experimental reasoning, the general experimental conditions under which the two responses (whether two from one subject or one from each of two subjects) are emitted and measured must be ongoing concurrently. . . . Exposure [to the independent variable] does not have to be simultaneous for the

different behavior/setting combinations, [but] it must be the identical treatment conditions along with the associated extraneous variables that impinge on the two responses and/or settings. This is because the conditions imposed on one behavior/setting combination must have the *opportunity* of influencing the other behavior/setting combination at the same time, regardless of the condition that actually prevails for the second. . . . It follows that using responses of two subjects each responding in different settings would not meet the requirement that there be a coincident opportunity for detecting the treatment effect. A treatment condition [as well as the myriad other variables possibly responsible for changes in the behavior of one subject] could not then come into contact with the responding of the other subject, because the second subject's responding would be occurring in an entirely different location. . . . Generally, the greater the plausibility that the two responses would be affected by the single treatment [and all other relevant variables], the more powerful is the demonstration of experimental control evidenced by data showing a change in only one behavior. (Johnston and Pennypacker, 1980, pp. 276–278)

The requirements of concurrency and plausible influence must be met in order for the verification element of baseline logic to operate in a multiple baseline design. However, replication of effect is demonstrated each time a baseline steady state is changed by the introduction of the independent variable, more or less regardless of where or when the variable is applied. Such nonconcurrent and/or unrelated baselines provide valuable data on the generality of a treatment's effectiveness.

This discussion should not be interpreted to mean that a valid (i.e., logically complete) multiple baseline design cannot be conducted across different subjects (or groups), each responding in different settings. Numerous studies using multiple baseline across subjects and settings have contributed to the development of an effective technology of behavior change. Let us consider an experiment designed to analyze the effects of a particular teacher training intervention, perhaps a workshop on using strategies to increase each student's opportunity to respond during group instruction. Concurrent measurement is begun on the frequency of student response opportunities in the classrooms of the teachers who are participating in the study. After stable baselines have been established, the workshop is presented first to one teacher (or group of teachers) and eventually, in staggered multiple baseline fashion, to all of the teachers. In this example even though the different subjects (teachers) are all behaving in different environments (different classrooms), comparison of their baseline conditions is experimentally sound because the variables likely to influence their teaching styles operate in the larger, shared environment in which they all behave (the school and teaching community). Nevertheless, whenever experiments are proposed or published that involve different subjects responding in different settings, researchers and consumers should view the baseline comparisons with a critical eye toward their logical relation to one other.

Do Not Apply the Independent Variable to the Next Behavior Too Soon

Again, in order for verification to occur in a multiple baseline design, it must be clearly established that, as the independent variable is applied to one behavior and change is noted, little or no change is observed in the other, as-yet-untreated behaviors. The potential for a powerful demonstration of experimental control has been destroyed in many studies because the independent variable was applied to subsequent behaviors too soon. Although the operational requirement of sequential application in the multiple baseline tactic is met by introduction of the independent variable even in adjacent time intervals, the experimental reasoning afforded by such closely spaced manipulations is minimal.

> The influence of unknown, concomitant, extraneous variables that might be present could still be substantial, even a day or two later. This problem can be avoided by demonstrating continued stability in responding for the second behavior/

setting combination during and after the introduction of the treatment for the first combination until a sufficient period of time has elapsed to detect any effect on the second combination that might appear. (Johnston & Pennypacker, 1980, p. 283)

Vary the Length of Multiple Baselines Significantly

Generally, the more the baseline phases in a multiple baseline design differ in length from one another, the stronger the design. Baselines of significantly different lengths allow the unambiguous conclusion (assuming an effective treatment variable) that behaviors not only change when the independent variable is applied, but also do not change when the variable has not been applied. If the different baselines are of the same or similar length, the possibility exists that changes noted when the independent variable is introduced are the result of a confounding variable, such as practice or reactivity to observation and measurement, and not a function of the experimental variable.

> Those effects . . . called practice, adaptation, warm-up, self-analysis, etc.; whatever they may be and whatever they may be called, the multiple baseline design controls for them by systematically varying the length of time (sessions, days, weeks) in which they occur prior to the introduction of the training package. . . . Such control is essential, and when the design consists of only two baselines, then the number of points in each prior to experimental intervention should differ as radically as possible, at least by a factor of 2. I cannot see not systematically varying lengths of baselines prior to intervention, and varying them as much as possible/practical. Failure to do that . . . weakens the design too much for credibility. (D. M. Baer, personal communication, June 2, 1978)

Intervene on the Most Stable Baseline First

In the ideal multiple baseline design the independent variable is not applied to any of the behaviors until fully stable responding has been achieved for each. However, the applied behavior analyst is sometimes denied the option of delaying treatment just to increase the strength of an experimental analysis. When intervention must begin before stability is evident across each tier of the design, the independent variable should be applied to the behavior, subject, or setting that shows the most stable baseline. For example, if a study is designed to evaluate the effects of a teaching procedure on the rate of math computation of four students and there is no a priori reason to teach the students in any particular sequence, instruction should begin with the student showing the most stable baseline. However, this recommendation should be followed only when the majority of the baselines in the design show reasonable stability.

Sequential application of the independent variable should be made in order of greatest stability at the time of each subsequent application. Again, however, the realities of the applied world must be heeded. The social significance of changing a particular behavior must sometimes take precedence over the desire to meet the requirements of experimental design.

Variations of the Multiple Baseline design

Two variations of the multiple baseline design are the multiple probe design and the delayed multiple baseline design. The multiple probe design enables the behavior analyst to extend the operation and logic of the multiple baseline tactic to behaviors or situations in which the concurrent measurement of all behaviors comprising the design is unnecessary, potentially reactive, impractical, or too costly. The delayed multiple baseline technique can be used when a planned reversal design is no longer possible or proves ineffective; it can also add additional tiers to an already-operational multiple baseline design.

Multiple Probe Design The **multiple probe design**, first described by Horner and Baer (1978), is a method of analyzing the relationship between the independent variable and the acquisition of a successive approximation or chain sequence. In contrast to the

multiple baseline design—in which data are collected throughout the baseline phase for each behavior, setting, or subject in the experiment—in the multiple probe design intermittent measurements, or probes, provide the basis for determining whether behavior change has occurred prior to intervention. According to Horner and Baer (1978), when applied to a chain or sequence of related behaviors to be learned, the multiple probe design provides answers to four questions: (1) What is the initial level of performance on each step (behavior) in the sequence? (2) What happens when sequential opportunities to perform each step in the sequence are provided prior to training on that step? (3) What happens to each step as training is applied? (4) What happens to the performance of untrained steps in the sequence as criterion-level performance is reached on preceding steps?

Figure 9.6 shows a graphic prototype of the multiple probe design. Although in practice the multiple probe design takes a variety of forms, the basic design has three key features: (1) an initial probe is taken to determine the subject's level of performance on each behavior in the sequence; (2) a series of repeated baseline measures is taken on each step prior to training on that step; and (3) after criterion-level performance is reached on any training step, a probe of each step in the sequence is taken to determine whether performance changes have occurred in any other steps.

The multiple probe design is particularly appropriate for evaluating the effects of instruction on skill sequences in which it is highly unlikely that the subject can improve her performance on later steps in the sequence without acquiring the prior steps. For example, the repeated measurement of the accuracy in solving division problems of a student who possesses no skills in addition, subtraction, and multiplication would add little to an analysis.

> The inevitable zero scores on the division baseline have no real meaning: division could be nothing else than zero (or chance, depending on

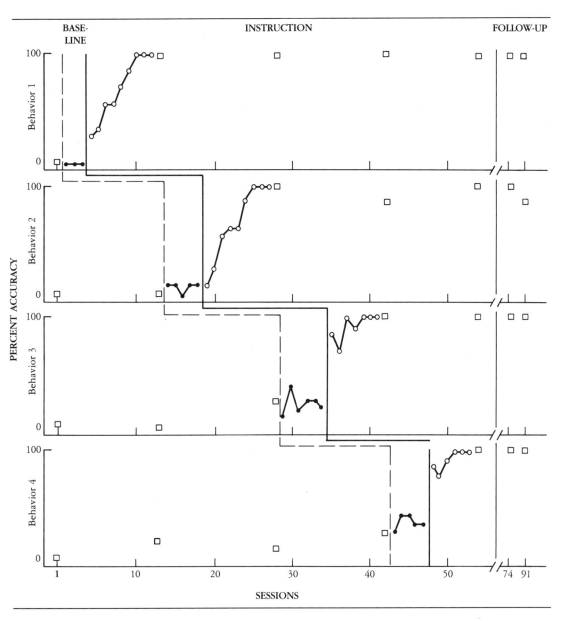

FIGURE 9.6 Graphic prototype of multiple probe design. Square data points represent results of probe sessions in which entire sequence or set of behaviors (1–4) are tested. Other response measures (e.g., rate, duration) could also be used in a multiple probe design.

the test format), and there is no real point in measuring it. Such measures are *pro forma*: they fill out the picture of a multiple baseline, true, but in an illusory way. They do not so much represent zero behavior as zero opportunity for the behavior to occur, and there is no need to document at the level of well-measured data that behavior does not occur when it cannot. (Horner & Baer, 1978, p. 190)

Thus, the multiple probe design avoids the necessity of collecting ritualistic baseline data when the performance of any component of a chain or sequence is impossible or unlikely before acquisition of its preceding component. Thompson, Braam, and Fuqua (1982) used a multiple probe design to analyze the effects of an instructional procedure composed of prompts and token reinforcement on the acquisition of a complex chain of laundry skills by three handicapped students. Observations of people doing laundry resulted in a detailed task analysis of 74 discrete responses that were organized into 7 major components (e.g., sorting, loading washer). Performance was assessed via probe and baseline sessions that preceded training on each component. Probe and baseline sessions began with instructions to the student to do the laundry. When an incorrect response was emitted or when no response occurred within 5 seconds of a prompt to continue, the student was seated away from the laundry area. The trainer then performed the correct response and called the student back to the area so that assessment of the rest of the laundry sequence could continue. The reader can examine Figure 9.7 as the authors explain their scheduling of probe and baseline measurements and the training procedure.

> Probe sessions differed from baseline sessions in two ways. First, a probe measured each response in the entire chain and occurred immediately prior to baseline and training for every component. Baseline sessions occurred following the probe and measured only previously trained components plus the component about to be trained. Baseline data were gathered on a variable number of consecutive sessions immediately prior to training sessions. Second, no tokens or descriptive praise were delivered during probes. During baseline, tokens were delivered for previously trained responses only. . . . Following baseline, each component was trained using a graduated 3-prompt procedure (Horner & Keilitz, 1975), consisting of verbal instruction, modeling, and graduated guidance. If one prompt level failed to produce a correct response within 5 sec, the next level was introduced. . . . When the student performed a component at 100% accuracy for two consecutive trials, he was required to perform the entire laundry chain from the beginning through the component most recently mastered. The entire chain of previously mastered components was trained (chain training condition) until it was performed without errors or prompts for two consecutive trials. (Thompson, Braam, & Fuqua, 1982, p. 179)

Figure 9.7 shows the results for Chester, one of the students. A low percentage of correct responses was made during the probe and baseline sessions, with 100% correct responding occurring only after training was applied to each component. After training, Chester correctly performed 82% of the 74 total responses in the chain during a generalization probe conducted at a community laundromat. An additional five training sessions were needed to retrain responses incorrectly performed during the generalization probe and to train "additional responses necessitated by the presence of coin slots and minor differences between the training and laundromat equipment" (p. 179). On two follow-up sessions conducted 10 months after training, Chester, who had not performed the laundry task for the prior 2 months, performed at 90% accuracy. Similar results were obtained for the other two students.

Thompson et al. added the chain training condition to their study because they believed that components trained as independent skills were unlikely to be emitted in correct sequence without such practice. It should be noted that the experimenters did not begin training a new component until stability had been achieved during the baseline session (see the baseline data for the bottom four tiers of the design).

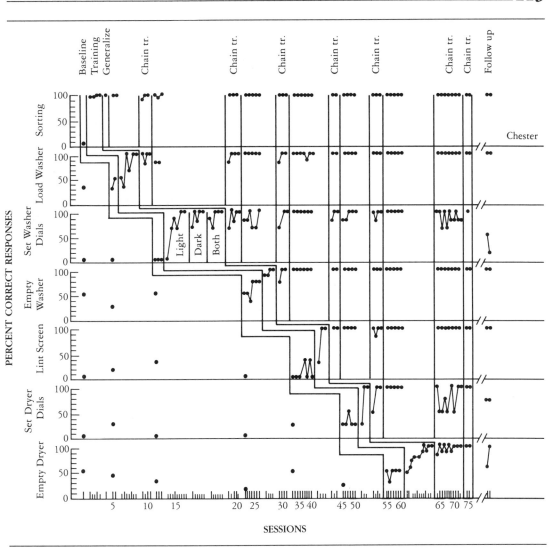

FIGURE 9.7   A multiple probe design showing percent correct responses for each trial on each component of the laundry chain by a young adult male with mental retardation. Heavy vertical lines on the horizontal axis represent successive training sessions; lighter and shorter vertical lines indicate trials within a session. (From "Training and Generalization of Laundry Skills: A Multiple-Probe Evaluation with Handicapped Persons" by T. J. Thompson, S. J. Braam, and R. W. Fuqua, 1982, *Journal of Applied Behavior Analysis, 15,* p. 180. Copyright 1982 by the Society for the Experimental Analysis of Behavior, Inc. Reprinted by permission.)

This patience on the part of the researchers enabled a clear demonstration of a functional relationship between training and skill acquisition. Tawney and Gast (1984) point out that three consecutive probe trials taken immediately prior to the training of each behavior is the absolute minimum necessary to estimate a trend in the data, and they are therefore required for a believable demonstration of experimental control.

In addition to the two uses mentioned here—analysis of the effects of instruction on complex skill sequences and reduction in the amount of baseline measurement for behaviors that have no plausible opportunity to occur—the multiple probe technique is also an effective experimental strategy for situations in which extended baseline measurement may prove reactive, impractical, or costly. The repeated measurement of a skill under nontreatment conditions can prove aversive to some students; and extinction, boredom, or other undesirable responses can occur. Cuvo (1979), in his discussion of multiple baseline designs, suggests that researchers need to recognize that "there is a trade-off between repeatedly administering the dependent measure

to establish a stable baseline on one hand and risking impaired performance by subjecting participants to a potentially punishing experience on the other hand" (pp. 222–223). Furthermore, complete assessment of all skills in a sequence may require too much time that could otherwise be spent on instruction.

Delayed Multiple Baseline Design Heward (1978a) describes a variation of the multiple baseline design that he terms the **delayed multiple baseline design**. The delayed multiple baseline technique is an experimental tactic in which an initial baseline and intervention are begun, and subsequent baselines are added in a staggered or delayed fashion. Figure 9.8 shows a graphic prototype of the delayed mul-

FIGURE 9.8 Graphic prototype of delayed multiple baseline.

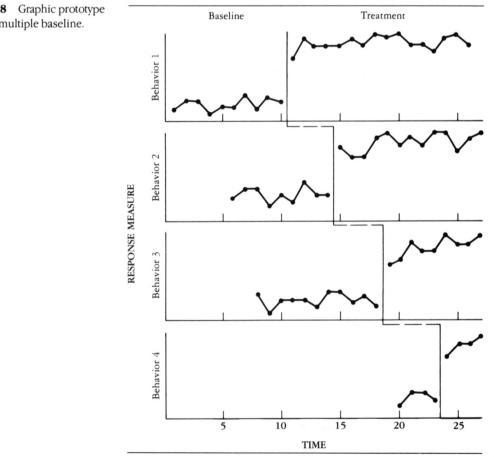

tiple baseline design. The design employs the same experimental reasoning as a full-scale multiple baseline design with the exception that any subsequent baselines begun after the independent variable has been applied to previous behaviors, settings, or subjects cannot be used to verify the truthfulness of predictions based on earlier tiers of the design. In Figure 9.8 baseline measurement was begun early enough with Behaviors 2 and 3 for those data to be used to verify the predictions made for Behavior 1. The final four baseline data points for Behavior 3 also verify the prediction for Behavior 2. However, baseline measurement of Behavior 4 was not begun until after the independent variable had been applied to all of the previous behaviors, thus limiting its role in the design to an additional demonstration of replication.

Use of a delayed multiple baseline design can allow the behavior analyst to conduct research in certain environments in which other experimental designs cannot be carried out. Heward (1978a) discusses three such situations.

1 *A reversal design is no longer desirable or possible.* In applied settings the research environment may shift, negating the use of a previously planned reversal design. Such shifts may involve changes in the subject's environment which make the target behavior no longer likely to reverse to baseline levels, or changes in the behavior of parents, teachers, administrators, the subject/client, or the behavior analyst which, for any number of reasons, make a previously planned reversal design no longer desirable or possible. . . . If there are other behaviors, settings, or subjects appropriate for application of the independent variable, the behavior analyst could use a delayed multiple baseline technique and still pursue evidence of a functional relationship.

2 *Limited resources preclude a full-scale multiple baseline design.* This situation occurs when the behavior analyst only controls resources sufficient to initially record and intervene with one behavior, setting, or subject, and another research strategy is inappropriate. It may be that as a result of the first intervention, more resources become available for gathering additional baselines. This might occur following the improvement of certain behaviors whose pre-treatment topography and/or rate required an inordinate expenditure of staff resources. Or, it could be that a reluctant administrator, after seeing the successful results of the first intervention, provides the resources necessary for additional analysis. Also under this heading would fall the "practical difficulties" cited by Hobbs and Holt (1976) as a reason for delaying baseline measurement in one of three settings.

3 *A "new" behavior, setting, or subject becomes available.* A delayed multiple baseline technique might be employed when another research design was originally planned but a multiple baseline analysis becomes the preferred approach due to changes in the environment (e.g., the subject begins to emit another behavior appropriate for intervention with the experimental variable, the subject begins to emit the original target behavior in another setting, or additional subjects displaying the same target behavior become available.) (pp. 5–6)

Numerous examples of the delayed multiple baseline technique can be found in the applied behavior analysis literature (e.g., Baer, Williams, Osnes, & Stokes, 1984; Copeland, Brown, & Hall, 1974; Hobbs & Holt, 1976; Jones, Fremouw, & Carples, 1977; Risley & Hart, 1968). Poche, Brouwer, and Swearingen (1981) used a delayed multiple baseline design to evaluate the effects of a training program designed to prevent children from being abducted by adults. Three preschool children of normal intelligence and social skills were selected as subjects because, during a screening test, each readily agreed to leave with an adult stranger. The dependent variable was the level of appropriateness of self-protective responses emitted by each child when an adult suspect approached the child and attempted to lure her away with a simple lure ("Would you like to go for a walk?"), an authoritative lure ("Your teacher said it was all right for you to come with me"), or an incentive lure ("I've got a nice surprise in my car. Would you like to come with me and see it?").

Each session began with the child's teacher bringing the child outdoors, then pretending to have to return to the building for some reason. The adult suspect (a confederate of the experimenters but unknown to the child) then approached the child and offered one of the lures. The confederate also served as observer, scoring the child's response on a 0–6 scale, with a score of 6 representing the desired response (saying, "No, I have to go ask my teacher" and moving at least 20 feet away from the suspect within 3 seconds) and a score of 0 indicating that the child moved some distance away from the school building with the suspect. Training consisted of modeling, behavioral rehearsal, and social reinforcement for correct responses.

Figure 9.9 shows the results of the training program. During baseline all three children responded to the lures with safety ratings of 0 or 1. Correct responses to the incentive lure were mastered by all three children in one to three training sessions, with one or two more sessions required for each child to master correct responses to the other two lures. Overall, training took from five to six sessions, or approximately 90 minutes per child. All three children responded correctly when the lures were administered in generalization probes on sidewalk locations 150 to 400 feet from the school.

Although each baseline in this study was of equal length (i.e., had an equal number of data points), contradicting the general rule that baselines should vary significantly in length, there are two good reasons that Poche et al. began training when they did with each subject. First, the almost-total stability of the baseline performance of each child provided an ample basis for evaluating the training program (the only exception to complete susceptibility occurring when Stan only stayed near the adult suspect instead of actually going away with him on his fourth baseline observation). Second, and more imporant, the nature of the target behavior required that it be taught to each

child as soon as possible. While continuing baseline observations for varying lengths across the different subjects is good practice from a purely experimental viewpoint, the ethics of such a practice in this instance would be highly questionable, given the potential danger of repeatedly exposing the children to adult lures while withholding training.

The delayed multiple baseline design presents several limitations (Heward, 1978a). First, from an applied standpoint the design is not a good one if it requires the behavior analyst to wait too long to modify important behaviors, although this problem is inherent in all multiple baseline designs. Second, in a delayed multiple baseline design there is a tendency for the delayed baseline phases to contain fewer data points than are found in a standard multiple baseline design, in which all baselines are begun simultaneously, resulting in baseline phases of considerable and varying length. Long baselines, if stable, provide the predictive power that permits powerful demonstrations of experimental control. Behavior analysts using any type of multiple baseline design must be sure that all baselines, regardless of when they are begun, are of sufficient and varied length to provide a believable basis for comparing experimental effects. A third limitation of the delayed multiple baseline design is that it can mask the interdependence of dependent variables.

The strength of any multiple baseline design is that little or no change is noticed in the other, as yet untreated, dependent variables until, and only until, the experimenter applies the independent variable. In a delayed multiple baseline design, the "delayed baseline" data gathered for subsequent behaviors may represent changed performance due to the experimental manipulation on other behaviors in the design and, therefore, may not be representative of the true, pre-experimental operant level. . . . In such instances, the delayed multiple baseline might result in a "false negative," and the researcher may erroneously conclude that the intervention was not effective on the subsequent behavior(s), when in reality the lack of simultaneous baseline data did not permit the discovery that the

FIGURE 9.9 A delayed multiple baseline design showing the level of appropriateness of self-protective responses during baseline, training, and generality probes in both school and community settings. Closed symbols present data gathered near the school; open symbols, in a location away from the school. (From "Teaching Self-Protection to Young Children" by C. Poche, R. Brouwer, and M. Swearingen, 1981, *Journal of Applied Behavior Analysis, 14,* p. 174. Copyright 1981 by the Society for the Experimental Analysis of Behavior, Inc. Reprinted by permission.)

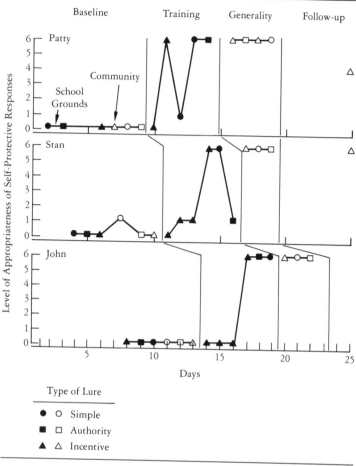

dependent variables covaried. This is a major weakness of the delayed multiple baseline design and makes it a research methodology of second choice whenever a full-scale multiple baseline can be employed. However, this limitation can and should be combated whenever possible by beginning subsequent baselines at least several sessions prior to intervention on previous baselines. (Heward, 1978a, pp. 8–9)

Both the multiple probe design and the delayed multiple baseline design offer the applied behavior analyst alternative tactics for pursuing a multiple baseline analysis when extended baseline measurement is unnecessary, impractical, too costly, or unavailable. Perhaps the most useful application of the delayed mul-

tiple baseline technique is in adding tiers to an already-operational multiple baseline design. Whenever a delayed baseline can be supplemented by probes taken earlier in the course of the study, experimental control is strengthened. As a general rule, the more baseline data, the better.

Considering the Appropriateness of Multiple Baseline Designs

Kazdin (1975) reports that the reversal design was employed in the majority of investigations published in the *Journal of Applied Behavior Analysis* (JABA) from 1968 to 1974. Kazdin also notes that "interestingly, the use of multiple-baseline . . . designs has increased in recent years" (p. 332). An examination of experiments published in JABA from 1981 to 1985 shows that the popularity of the multiple baseline design has continued to increase. During those 5 years the multiple baseline design was used as the primary experimental design element in JABA studies by more than a 2 to 1 margin over the reversal design, the next most used design strategy. Experimental designs combining the multiple baseline and the reversal tactic made up the third most-used analytic approach during this 5-year period. No doubt the significant advantages offered by the multiple baseline design have accounted for its frequent usage. Those advantages, however, must be weighed against the limitations and weaknesses of the design to determine its appropriateness in any given situation.

Advantages of the Multiple Baseline Design Probably the most important advantage of the multiple baseline design is that it does not require withdrawal of a seemingly effective treatment to demonstrate experimental control. With target behaviors that are self-injurious or dangerous to others, this is a most critical consideration. This feature of the multiple baseline design also makes it the most appropriate method for analyzing independent variables that cannot, by their nature, be withdrawn and for investigating target behaviors that are likely to be irreversible. Additionally, because the multiple baseline design does not necessitate a reversal of treatment gains to baseline levels, it may be accepted more readily by parents, teachers, or administrators as a method of demonstrating the effects of an intervention.

The requirement of the multiple baseline technique to sequentially apply the independent variable across multiple behaviors, settings, or subjects complements the usual practice of many practitioners whose goal is to develop multiple behavior changes (Kratochwill & Levin, 1978). Teachers are charged with

helping multiple students learn multiple skills to be used in multiple settings. Likewise, clinicians often need to help their clients improve more than one response class and emit more adaptive behavior in several settings. The multiple baseline design is ideally suited to evaluation of the progressive, multiple behavior changes sought by many practitioners in applied settings.

Because the multiple baseline design entails concurrent measurement of two or more behaviors, settings, or subjects, it is useful in assessing the occurrence of generalization of behavior change. The simultaneous monitoring of several behaviors gives the behavior analyst the opportunity to determine their covariation as a result of manipulations of the independent variable (Hersen & Barlow, 1976). Although changes in behaviors still under baseline conditions eliminate the ability of the multiple baseline design to demonstrate experimental control, such changes reveal the possibility that the independent variable is capable of producing behavioral improvements with desirable generality, thereby suggesting an additional set of research questions and analytic tactics (e.g., Odom, Hoyson, Jamieson, & Strain, 1985).

Finally, the multiple baseline design has the advantage of being relatively easy to conceptualize, thereby offering an effective strategy for experimentation to teachers and parents who are not highly trained in research methodology (Hall, et al., 1970).

Limitations of the Multiple Baseline Design The advantages offered by the multiple baseline design in concurrent measurement of multiple behaviors are offset by a set of related analytic and applied disadvantages. The design entails at least three scientific limitations or considerations. First, a multiple baseline design may not allow a demonstration of experimental control even though a functional relation exists between the independent variable and the target behaviors. Observation of concurrent change in behaviors still under baseline conditions precludes the demonstration of a functional relationship within the original design. Second, from one perspective the multiple baseline design is a weaker method of showing experimental control than is a reversal design; verification of the baseline prediction made for each behavior within a multiple baseline design is not directly demonstrated with that behavior but is inferred from the lack of change in other behaviors. This weakness of the multiple baseline design, however, should be weighed against the design's advantage of providing multiple replications across different behaviors, settings, or subjects. Third, the multiple baseline design provides more information about the effectiveness of the independent variable than it does about the function of any particular target behavior.

> Consistently [the] multiple baseline is less an experimental analysis of the response than of the technique used to alter the response. In the reversal design, the response is made work again and again; in the multiple-baseline designs, it is primarily the technique that works again and again, and the responses either work once each [if different responses are used] or else a single response works once each per setting or once each per subject. Repetitive working of the same response in the same subject or the same setting is not displayed. But, while repetitive working of the response is foregone, repetitive and diverse working of the experimental technique is maximized, as it would not be in the reversal design. (Baer, 1975, p. 22)

Two important applied considerations that must be evaluated in determining the appropriateness of the multiple baseline design are the time and resources required for its implementation. Because the treatment variable cannot be applied to subsequent behaviors, settings, or subjects until the effects of the treatment have been observed in previous behaviors, settings, or subjects, the multiple baseline design requires that intervention be withheld for some behaviors, settings, or subjects, perhaps for a long time. This entails both practical and ethical concerns. Some behaviors simply cannot wait that long for treatment;

their importance makes delaying treatment impractical. And as Stolz (1978) has pointed out, "If the intervention is generally acknowledged to be effective, denying it simply to achieve a multiple-baseline design might be unethical" (p. 33). Second, the resources needed for the concurrent measurement of multiple behaviors must be considered. Use of a multiple baseline design can be particularly costly when behavior must be observed and measured in several settings. However, when the use of intermittent probes during baseline can be justified in lieu of more continuous measurement (Horner & Baer, 1978), the cost of concurrently measuring multiple behaviors can be reduced.

CHANGING CRITERION DESIGN

The changing criterion design can be used to evaluate the effects of reinforcement or punishment contingencies as they are applied in a graduated or stepwise fashion to a single target behavior. The changing criterion design was first described in the applied behavior analysis literature in two papers coauthored by Hall (Hall & Fox, 1977; Hartmann & Hall, 1976).

Operation and Logic of the Changing Criterion Design

The reader can refer to Figure 9.10 as Hartmann and Hall (1976) describe the operation of the **changing criterion design**.

> The design requires initial baseline observations on a single target behavior. This baseline phase is followed by implementation of a treatment program in each of a series of treatment phases. Each treatment phase is associated with a step-wise change in criterion rate for the target behavior. Thus, each phase of the design provides a baseline for the following phase. When the rate of the target behavior changes with each stepwise change in the criterion, therapeutic change is replicated and experimental control is demonstrated. (p. 527)

FIGURE 9.10 Graphic prototype of changing criterion design. The target behavior could also be measured by another dimension (e.g., rate, duration).

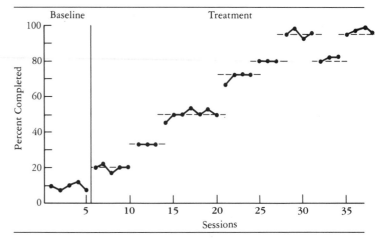

Proper implementation of the changing criterion design requires the careful manipulation of three design factors: length of phases, magnitude of criterion changes, and number of criterion changes. Since each phase in the changing criterion design serves as a baseline for comparing changes in responding measured in the next phase, each phase must be long enough to achieve stable responding. "Each treatment phase must be long enough to allow the rate of the target behavior to restabilize at a new and changed rate; it is stability after change has been achieved, and before introduction of the next change in criterion, that is crucial to producing a convincing demonstration of control" (Hartmann & Hall, 1976, p. 531). Target behaviors that are slower to change therefore require longer phases.

The length of phases in a changing criterion design should also vary considerably to increase the design's validity. In a changing criterion design the target behavior must not only change to the level required by each new criterion in a predictable (preferably immediate) fashion, but must also conform to the new criterion for as long as it is in effect. When the target behavior closely follows successively more demanding criteria that are held in place for varied periods of time, the likelihood is reduced that the observed changes in behavior

are a function of some factor other than the independent variable (e.g., maturation, practice effects).

Similarly, the size of the criterion changes should be varied if a convincing demonstration of experimental control is to be made. When changes in the target behavior occur not only at the time new criteria are implemented but also to the level specified by the new criteria, the probability of a functional relationship is strengthened. In general, a target behavior's immediate change to meet a large criterion change is more impressive than a behavior change in response to a small criterion change. However, if the magnitude of criterion changes is too large, two problems arise. First, from a design standpoint large criterion changes may not permit inclusion of a sufficient number of changes in the design (the third design factor) because the terminal level of performance is reached sooner. The second problem is from an applied view: criterion changes cannot be so large that they contradict good instructional practice. Criterion changes must be large enough to be detectable, but not so large as to be unachievable. Therefore, the variability of the data in each phase must be considered in determining the size of criterion changes. Smaller changes in criterion can be employed with very stable levels of responding, whereas larger criterion changes are required to demonstrate behavior change in the presence of variability (Hartmann & Hall, 1976).

When using a changing criterion design, behavior analysts must be sure not to impose artificial ceilings (or floors) on the rate or frequency of behavior possible in each phase. An obvious mistake of this sort would be to give a student only five math problems to complete when the criterion for reinforcement is five. Although the student could complete fewer than five problems, the possibility of exceeding the criterion has been eliminated, resulting in an impressive-looking graph perhaps, but one that is badly affected by poor experimental procedure.

In general, the more times the target behavior changes to meet a new criterion, the more convincing the demonstration of experimental control. The experimenter cannot, however, simply add any desired number of phases to the design. The number of phases that are possible within a changing criterion design is interrelated with both the length of phases and the size of criterion changes. Longer phases mean that the time necessary to complete the analysis increases; with a limited time to complete the study, the greater the number of phases, the shorter each phase can be.

The operation of two elements of baseline logic—prediction and replication—is clear in the changing criterion design. When stable responding is attained within each phase of the design, a prediction of future responding is made. Replication occurs each time the level of behavior changes in a systematic way immediately after the criterion is changed. Verification of the predictions based on each phase is not so obvious in this design but can be approached in two ways. First, by systematically varying the lengths of phases, a kind of self-evident verification takes place. The prediction is made that the level of responding will not change if the criterion is not changed. When the criterion is not changed and stable responding continues, the prediction is verified.

When it can be shown within the design that levels of responding do not change unless the criterion is changed, regardless of the varied lengths of phases, experimental control is evident. Hall and Fox (1977) suggest another possibility for verification: "The experimenter may return to a former criterion and if the behavior conforms to this criterion level there is also a cogent argument for a high degree of behavioral control" (p. 154). Such a reversed criterion is shown in the next-to-last phase of Figure 9.10. Although a brief interruption of the steady improvement in behavior is required by returning to an earlier criterion level, the tactic strengthens the analysis considerably and should be included in the changing criterion design unless other factors indicate its inappropriateness.

One way to conceptualize the changing criterion design is as a variation of the multiple baseline design. Both Hartmann and Hall (1976, p. 530) and Hall and Fox (1977, p. 164) replotted data from changing criterion design experiments in a multiple baseline format with each tier of the multiple baseline showing the occurrence or nonoccurrence of the target behavior at one of the criterion levels used in the experiment. A vertical phase change line doglegs through the tiers indicating when the criterion for reinforcement was raised to the level represented by each tier. By graphing whether or not the target behavior was emitted during each session at or above the level represented on each tier both before and after the change in criterion to that level, a kind of multiple baseline analysis is revealed. However, the strength of the multiple baseline argument is not quite so convincing since the "different" behaviors represented by each tier are not independent of one another. For example, if a target behavior is emitted 10 times in a given session, all of the tiers representing criteria below 10 responses would have to show that the behavior occurred, and all of the tiers representing criteria of 11 or more would have to show no occurrence of the behavior, or zero responding. The majority of the tiers that would appear to show verification and replication of effect, in fact, could only show these results because of the events plotted on another tier. A multiple baseline design provides its convincing demonstration of experimental control because each behavior in the design is a function of its controlling variables, not an artifact of the measurement of another behavior. Thus, recasting the data from a changing criterion design into a many-tiered multiple baseline format will often result in a biased picture in favor of experimental control.

Even though the multiple baseline design is not completely analogous, the changing criterion design can be conceptualized as a method of analyzing the development of new behaviors. As Sidman (1960) points out, "It is possible to make reinforcement contingent upon a specified value of some aspect of behavior, and to treat that value as a response class in its own right" (p. 391). The changing criterion design can be an effective tactic for showing the repeated production of new rates of behavior as a function of manipulations of the independent variable (i.e., criterion changes).

Other than the experiments included in Hartmann and Hall (1976) and Hall and Fox (1977), there have been few examples of pure changing criterion designs published in the applied behavior analysis literature (e.g., Johnston & McLaughlin, 1982). Some researchers have employed a changing criterion tactic as an element within a larger design (e.g., Schleien, Wehman, & Kiernan, 1981). Figure 9.11 shows the results for one of three subjects in a study by Foxx and Rubinoff (1979) designed to reduce excessive coffee drinking. During baseline the subjects self-recorded daily the amount and types of all beverages containing caffeine that they consumed. At the end of the baseline phase, one of the experimenters converted the daily caffeine intake into milligrams. The treatment goal was to get each subject's consumption of caffeine to no more than 600 milligrams per day (less than five cups of coffee). The

successive criterion levels used for each subject were determined by subtracting 600 from the mean number of milligrams of caffeine consumed by the subject during baseline and dividing by 4 to yield four treatment phases. Each subject deposited $20 with the experimenters, to be earned back in installments by not exceeding the criterion limit for caffeine. Subjects continued to self-record their coffee drinking during the treatment phases, using recording sheets that indicated the amount of caffeine in milligrams in different beverages. The subjects also signed release forms, agreeing to covert observation of their coffee drinking by significant others, which enabled the experimenters to corroborate each subject's self-reports to some degree. At the end of each phase the subjects met with the experimenters to evaluate their progress and receive any deposit money they had earned back.

Figure 9.11 shows that Subject 1 never exceeded the criterion; her daily intake of caffeine decreased from a baseline mean of 1008 to 357 during the fourth and final treatment phase. Her caffeine consumption averaged 298 milligrams on intermittent postchecks taken over a 10-month period. Although the treatment phases varied in length from five to nine sessions, only four criterion changes were implemented, all of the same size. The study would have been strengthened considerably by more criterion changes of various magnitudes. As always, however, the applied behavior analyst must weigh experimental concerns with the need to improve behavior in the most effective and efficient manner. Subject 1's results clearly show that she responded well to the reduced criteria, and there was little applied value in making more gradual reductions in the criterion. If anything, the results suggest that a much larger reduction in the criterion might well have been made in Phase 4. With a lower criterion (e.g., 400 milligrams) Subject 1's caffeine consumption in Phase 4 would have made a more convincing demonstration of experimental control.

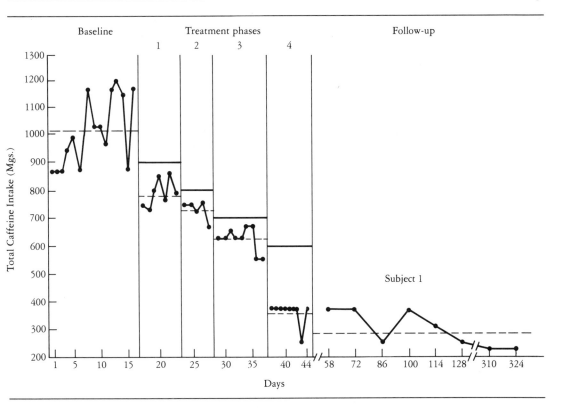

FIGURE 9.11   A changing criterion design showing daily caffeine intake (in milligrams) by a female teacher during baseline, treatment, and follow-up. The criterion level for each treatment phase was 102 mg of caffeine less than the previous treatment phase. Solid horizontal lines indicate the criterion level for each phase; broken lines indicate the mean for each phase. (From "Behavioral Treatment of Caffeinism: Reducing Excessive Coffee Drinking" by R. M. Foxx and A. Rubinoff, 1979, *Journal of Applied Behavior Analysis, 12,* p. 339. Copyright 1979 by the Society for the Experimental Analysis of Behavior, Inc. Reprinted by permission.)

Considering the Appropriateness of the Changing Criterion Design

The changing criterion design is a useful addition to the behavior analyst's set of tactics for evaluating systematic behavior change. Like the multiple baseline design the changing criterion design does not require that improvement in behavior be reversed (although partial reversals to earlier levels of performance enhance the design's capability to demonstrate experimental control); unlike the multiple baseline design only one target behavior is required.

Several characteristics of the changing criterion design limit its effective range of application for functional analysis. The design can be used only with target behaviors that are already in the subject's repertoire and that lend themselves to stepwise modification by the application of consequences. However, this is not as severe a limitation as it might seem. For example, many school children can perform many academic skills to some degree, but not at a useful rate. Many of these skills (e.g., solving math problems, reading) are appropriate for analysis with a changing criterion design.

Although the changing criterion design is sometimes suggested as an experimental tactic for analyzing the effects of shaping programs, it is not appropriate for this purpose. In shaping, a new behavior that initially is not in the person's repertoire is developed by reinforcing responses that meet a gradually changing criterion, called successive approximations, toward the terminal behavior (see chapter 11). However, the changing response criteria employed in shaping are topographical in nature, requiring different forms of behavior at each new level. The multiple probe design (Horner & Baer, 1978) is an appropriate design for analyzing a shaping program because each new response criterion (successive approximation) represents a different response class whose frequency of occurrence is not wholly dependent upon the frequency of behaviors meeting other criteria in the shaping program. The changing criterion design is best suited for evaluation of the effect of instructional techniques on stepwise changes in the rate, frequency, accuracy, duration, or latency of a single target behavior.

The changing criterion design is also limited to contingent reinforcement and/or punishment procedures that can be applied after the target behavior has been emitted at the specified rate, frequency, or accuracy. Again, however, this limitation includes a great many procedures that have proven effective as instructional techniques (e.g., token reinforcement, contingency contracts).

Allowing students to progress as efficiently as possible while meeting the design requirements of changing criterion analysis can be especially difficult. Tawney and Gast (1984) note that "the challenge of identifying criterion levels that will permit the demonstration of experimental control without impeding optimal learning rates" is problematic with all changing criterion designs (p. 298).

SUMMARY

Operation and Logic of the Multiple Baseline Design

1   In a multiple baseline design simultaneous baseline measurement is begun on two or more target behaviors. After stable baseline responding has been achieved, the independent variable is applied to one of the behaviors while baseline conditions remain in effect for the other behaviors. After maximum change has been noted in the first behavior, the independent variable is then applied in sequential fashion to the other behaviors in the design.

2   Experimental control is demonstrated in the multiple baseline design by each behavior's changing when, and only when, the independent variable is applied.

3   The multiple baseline design takes three basic forms: (a) a multiple baseline across behaviors design, employing two or more different behaviors of the same subject; (b) a multiple baseline across settings design, employing the same behavior of the same subject in two or more different settings; and (c) a multiple baseline across subjects design, employing the same behavior of several different subjects.

Assumptions and Procedural Guidelines for Using Multiple Baseline Designs

4   Behaviors comprising multiple baseline designs should be functionally independent of one another (i.e., they do not co-vary) and should share enough similarity with one another that there is a reasonable likelihood each will change when the independent variable is applied to it.

5   Behaviors selected for a multiple baseline design must be measured concurrently and must have an equal possibility of being influenced by the same set of relevant variables.

6   In a multiple baseline design the independent variable must not be applied to the next behav-

7   ior until the previous behavior has changed maximally and a sufficient period of time has elapsed to detect any effect that might appear on behaviors still in baseline conditions.

7   The length of the baseline phases for the different behaviors comprising a multiple baseline design should vary significantly.

8   All other things being equal, the independent variable should be applied first to the behavior showing the most stable level of baseline responding.

Variations of the Multiple Baseline Design

9   The multiple probe design is an effective design for evaluating the effects of instruction on skill sequences in which it is highly unlikely that the subject can improve his performance on later steps in the sequence without instruction or mastery of the earlier steps in the chain. The multiple probe design is also appropriate for situations in which prolonged baseline measurement may prove reactive, impractical, or too costly.

10   In a multiple probe design intermittent measurements, or probes, are taken on all of the behaviors in the design at the outset of the experiment. Thereafter, probes are taken each time the subject has achieved mastery of one of the behaviors or skills in the sequence. Just prior to instruction on each behavior, a series of true baseline measurements are taken until stability is achieved.

11   The delayed multiple baseline design can be used in situations in which (a) a planned reversal design is no longer desirable or possible, (b) limited resources preclude a full-scale multiple baseline design, or (c) a new behavior, setting, or subject appropriate for a multiple baseline analysis becomes available. The delayed mulitple baseline tactic can also be used to add additional tiers to an already-ongoing multiple baseline design.

12   In a delayed multiple baseline design baseline measurement of subsequent behaviors is begun sometime after baseline measurement was begun on earlier behaviors in the design. In a delayed multiple baseline design only baselines begun while earlier behaviors in the design are still under baseline conditions can

be used for verification of the predictions made for the earlier behaviors.

13   Limitations of the delayed multiple baseline design include (a) the behavior analyst may have to wait too long to modify certain behaviors, (b) there is a tendency for baseline phases to contain too few data points, and (c) baselines begun after the independent variable has been applied to earlier behaviors in the design can mask the interdependence (co-variation) of behaviors.

Considering the Appropriateness of Multiple Baseline Designs

14   Advantages of the multiple baseline design include (a) the withdrawal of a seemingly effective treatment is not required in order to show experimental control, (b) sequential implementation of the independent variable parallels the practice of many teachers and clinicians whose task is to change multiple behaviors in different settings and/or subjects, (c) the concurrent measurement of multiple behaviors allows direct monitoring of generalization of behavior change, and (d) the design is relatively easy to conceptualize and use.

15   Limitations of the multiple baseline design include (a) if two or more behaviors in the design co-vary, the multiple baseline design may not demonstrate a functional relationship even though one exists; (b) since verification must be inferred from the lack of change in other behaviors, the multiple baseline design is inherently weaker than the reversal design in showing experimental control between the independent variable and a given behavior; (c) the multiple baseline design is more an evaluation of the independent variable's general effectiveness than an analysis of the behaviors involved in the design; and (d) conducting a multiple baseline design requires considerable time and resources.

Changing Criterion Design

16   The changing criterion design can be used to evaluate the effects of reinforcement or punishment contingencies on the gradual or stepwise improvement of a behavior already in the subject's repertoire.

17 After stable baseline responding has been achieved, the first treatment phase is begun, in which reinforcement (or punishment) is usually contingent upon the subject's performing at a specified level (criterion). The design entails a series of treatment phases, each requiring an improved level of performance over the previous phase. Experimental control is demonstrated in the changing criterion design when the subject's behavior closely conforms to the gradually changing criteria.

18 Three features combine to determine the potential of a changing criterion design to demonstrate experimental control: (a) length of phases, (b) magnitude of criterion changes, and (c) number of criterion changes. The believability of the changing criterion design is enhanced if a previous criterion is reinstated and the subject's behavior reverses to the level previously observed under that criterion.

Considering the Appropriateness of the Changing Criterion Design

19 The primary advantages of the changing criterion design are (a) it does not require a withdrawal or reversal of a seemingly effective treatment, and (b) it provides a functional analysis within the context of a gradually improving behavior, thus complementing the practice of many teachers.

20 Limitations of the changing criterion design include (a) the target behavior must already be in the subject's repertoire, (b) the design is limited to a narrow range of independent variables (primarily reinforcement and certain punishment contingencies), and (c) incorporating the necessary features of the design can actually impede optimal learning rates.

10

Planning, Replicating, and Evaluating Research in Applied Behavior Analysis

KEY TERMS

Double-blind control

Treatment integrity

Treatment drift

Procedural reliability

Direct replication

Systematic replication

Type 1 error

Type 2 error

The previous chapters have outlined considerations in selecting target behaviors, detailed strategies for designing and conducting measurement systems, examined conventions and guidelines for displaying and interpreting behavioral data, and presented tactics for experimental manipulation capable of revealing whether observed changes in a target behavior can be attributed to the independent variable. Although the information described thus far represents a considerable array of strategies and methods for pursuing the demonstration of functional relationships between behavior and its controlling variables, there are many other questions and considerations that must be addressed in the design, replication, and evaluation of behavioral research.

PLANNING RESEARCH IN APPLIED BEHAVIOR ANALYSIS

Importance of Flexibility in Experimental Design

On one level an experimental design is any arrangement of independent variable manipulations that produce data that are interesting

This chapter was written by William L. Heward.

and convincing to the researcher and the audience. An experimental design is interesting and convincing and yields the most useful information for application when it provides an unambiguous demonstration that the independent variable was solely responsible for the observed behavior change. Experiments that demonstrate a clear functional relationship are said to have a high degree of internal validity. The strength of an experimental design must be judged along two lines: first, the extent to which the design demonstrates a reliable effect (i.e., systematic manipulation of the independent variable repeatedly produces a behavior change of consistent form and function) and second, the extent to which the design effectively reduces the plausibility of other explanations for the behavior change (i.e., confounding variables are eliminated).

The word *design* in this context is particularly appropriate as a verb as well as a noun; the effective behavioral researcher must actively *design* each experiment so that each achieves its own unique *design*. There are no readily available experimental designs awaiting selection. The prototype designs presented in the previous two chapters are not experimental designs as such, but rather examples of analytic tactics that afford a form of experimental reasoning and control proven effective in the analysis of a wide range of phenomena of interest to the applied behavior analyst. Johnston and Pennypacker (1980) are clear in their position that the "suspicion some may hold that generic categories of design types exist and should be botanized" (p. 293) is counterproductive to the practice of the science of behavior. Sidman (1960) is even more adamant in his warning regarding the undesirable effects of researchers' believing in the existence of a given set of rules for experimental design.

> The examples may be accepted as constituting a set of rules that must be followed in the design of experiments. I cannot emphasize too strongly that this would be disastrous. I could make the trite statement that every rule has its exception, but this is not strong enough. Nor is the more

relaxed statement that the rules of experimental design are flexible, to be employed only where appropriate. The fact is that *there are no rules of experimental design.* (p. 214)

We agree. The reader must not be led to believe that any of the analytic tactics described in chapters 8 and 9 constitute an experimental design per se.[1] However, we believe that it is important to present the most commonly used analytic tactics in design form for two reasons. First, the vast majority of studies that have advanced the field of applied behavior analysis have based their experimental reasoning on one or a combination of the design tactics described in chapters 8 and 9. Second, we believe that the beginning student of behavior analysis benefits from an examination of specific examples of isolated experimental tactics and their application; it is one step in learning the assumptions and strategic principles that guide the selection and arrangement of individual tactics into meaningful experimental designs (Sulzer-Azaroff, 1983).

Experimental Designs That Combine Analytic Tactics Applied behavior analysis does not, as some critics have suggested, consist largely of the same simple research designs implemented in a "stereotyped or unthoughtful manner." This statement is borne out by examination of the literature. In fact, it is difficult to find studies published in the *Journal of Applied Behavior Analysis* in recent years to serve as straightforward exemplars of the model designs presented in chapters 8 and 9.

To investigate the research questions of interest, an experimenter is often required to build an experimental design that employs a combination of analytic tactics. For example, it is not uncommon for experimenters to analyze multiple treatments by sequentially applying each in multiple baseline fashion (e.g., Van Houten, Malenfant, & Rolider, 1985; Wahler &

---

[1]The analytic tactics presented in chapters 8 and 9 cannot be considered experimental designs for another reason: an experimental design incorporates other elements in addition to the type and sequence of independent variable manipulations (e.g., a measurement system).

Fox, 1980; Yeaton & Bailey, 1983). And by implementing a reversal within each tier of a multiple baseline analysis, researchers are able to determine the existence of a functional relationship between the independent variable and each behavior, setting, or subject of the multiple baseline element and also to analyze the effectiveness of the independent variable across the tiers (e.g., Alexander, 1985; Blew, Schwartz, & Luce, 1985; Carr & Kologinsky, 1983; Dyer, Christian, & Luce, 1982; Heward & Eachus, 1979).

Combining multiple baseline and reversal tactics in an experimental design can also provide the basis for analyzing multiple independent variables (e.g., Greer & Polirstok, 1982). Figure 10.1 shows the results of one of four experiments conducted by Rolider and Van Houten (1985) in evaluating the effectiveness of a procedure they call "movement suppression time-out." The subject was a 17-year-old male with moderate mental retardation who, when conversing with other people, displayed a high rate of poking them in the chest and arms with his index finger. As can be seen in Figure 10.1, the experimental design used to evaluate the treatment variable with this subject embodied both multiple baseline across settings (home and rehabilitation center) and reversal tactics. In addition to comparing movement suppression time-out with a no-treatment baseline condition, the design also enabled comparison with a second treatment, contingent restraint. By counterbalancing the application of the two treatments across settings (when movement suppression was applied in the home on Session 5, contingent restraint was introduced in the rehabilitation center) and reestablishing baseline levels of responding during Baseline 2, the researchers provide a strong case against sequence effects playing a significant role in the behavior changes that occurred. The design shows that movement suppression time-out was effective in reducing the rate of poking, regardless of whether it preceded or followed contingent restraint.

Experimenters have also incorporated alternating treatments into experimental designs containing multiple baseline elements. For example, Bachman and Fuqua (1983) employed an alternating treatments component in a multiple baseline across subjects framework to analyze the effects of several antecedent exercise activities on the inappropriate classroom behaviors of four children with moderate mental retardation. The experimental design used by McGee, Krantz, and McClannahan (1985) to evaluate procedures for teaching language to autistic children incorporated an alternating treatments tactic within a multiple baseline across behaviors element that was nested within an overall multiple baseline across subjects strategy.

Figure 10.2 shows that the experimental design used by Sisson and Barret (1984) to evaluate two language training procedures incorporated a multiple probe across different behaviors component, an alternating treatments analysis, and a final multiple baseline across behaviors implementation of the total communication procedure in isolation. The design produced data that show unequivocally the superiority of the total communication method for these two children, as well as indicating that direct application of the treatment is required for learning to occur on specific sentences. Data for a third subject reveal a functional relationship of the same form and direction as that shown in Figure 10.2, but one not so strongly in favor of the total communication procedure.

Schleien, Wehman, and Kiernan (1981) built a changing criterion phase into an experimental design used to evaluate the effectiveness of an instructional program for teaching handicapped adults an age-appropriate leisure activity (playing darts). Even though numerous other examples could be provided of experimental designs that incorporate multiple analytic elements, the intent is not to present any of these examples as model designs. They are offered instead as illustrations of the infinite number of experimental designs made possible by arranging different combinations and

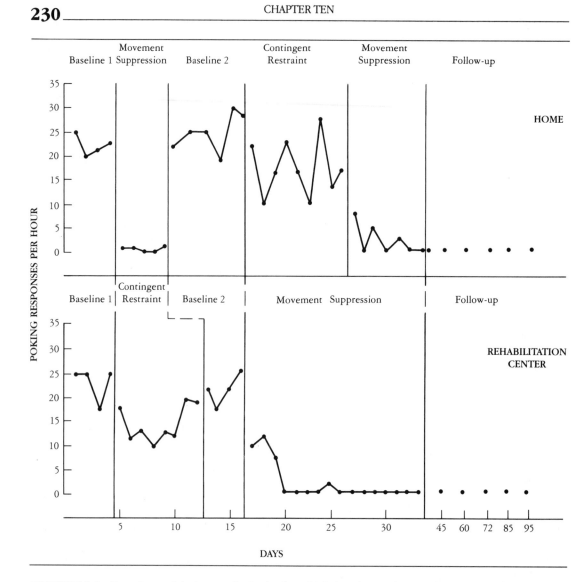

FIGURE 10.1 Experimental design employing both multiple baseline and reversal tactics to analyze the effect of two treatment variables. (From "Movement Suppression Time-Out for Undesirable Behavior in Psychotic and Severely Developmentally Delayed Children" by A. Rolider and R. Van Houten, 1985, *Journal of Applied Behavior Analysis, 18*, p. 286. Copyright 1985 by the Society for the Experimental Analysis of Behavior, Inc. Reprinted by permission.)

sequences of the basic methods of manipulating the independent variable(s). In every instance effective experimental designs are those that use ongoing evaluation of data from individual subjects as the basis for employing the three elements of baseline logic—prediction, verification, and replication.

Importance of the Individual Subject in the Design of Behavioral Experiments

Research in the social sciences traditionally employs experimental designs in which the effects of the independent variable are com-

FIGURE 10.2 Experimental design employing an alternating treatments tactic, a multiple probe, and a multiple baseline across behaviors analysis. (From "Alternating Treatments Comparison of Oral and Total Communication Training with Minimally Verbal Retarded Children" by L. A. Sisson and R. P. Barrett, 1984, *Journal of Applied Behavior Analysis, 17,* p. 562. Copyright 1984 by the Society for Experimental Analysis of Behavior, Inc. Reprinted by permission.)

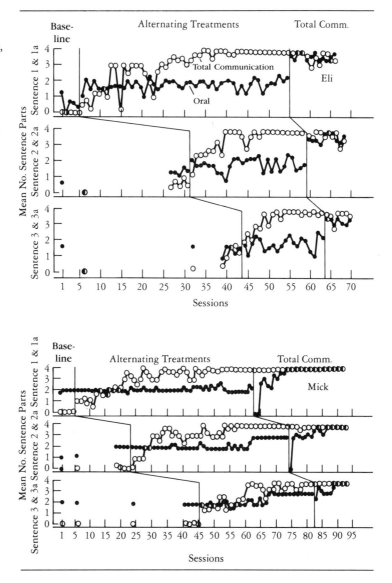

pared across groups of subjects. After intitial measurement of the dependent variable, one group (the experimental group) is exposed to the independent variable, and one group (the control group) is not. Measurement is again conducted and statistical tests are run that enable the researcher to make inferences regarding the likelihood that differences in the performance of the two groups are the result of the independent variable. Designs that use groups

of subjects in this way do so for two primary reasons, both of which were introduced in chapter 7. First, advocates of group designs believe that averaging the performance of many subjects controls for intersubject variability, thereby leaving any changes in performance as the work of the independent variable. The second major reason for group designs is the belief that increasing the number of subjects in such designs gives greater external validity to the results. That is, a treatment variable found effective with the experimental subjects will also have generality with other subjects in the population from which the sample subjects were chosen. This section comments on the first reason given for the use of groups of subjects—to control for intersubject variability. The claim of increased generality of findings is discussed in the section on replication.

A complete response to the many problems posed by the commingling of data from multiple subjects is beyond the scope of this text. Students wishing to study this issue further are encouraged to read more in-depth examinations of the issue (e.g., Johnston & Pennypacker, 1980; Sidman, 1960). Our discussion offers three fundamental concerns with group data that bear heavily on experimental reasoning.

First, by definition applied behavior analysis is concerned with improving the behavior of individuals. Knowing that the average performance of a group changed in a given way tells little about the performance of individual subjects. It is quite possible that the average performance of subjects in the experimental group improved while the performance of some subjects stayed the same and the performance of others deteriorated. In fact, this is almost always the case in large-group studies.

Perhaps in part because the researcher must attend to "the purely logistical demands forced by the management of a battalion of subjects" (Johnston & Pennypacker, 1980, p. 256), group designs are characterized by few measures of the dependent variable (sometimes only a pretest and posttest) and little control over the other variables that might be influencing any individual's behavior. In defense of the method it might be said that no treatment works with everyone, people respond differently, this approach shows that the treatment is generally effective, and so on. But in order for a treatment variable to be useful to the applied behavior analyst, the variables responsible for one subject's improvement and another's lack of improvement must be discovered. The claim that an improved average shows that a treatment is generally effective with most subjects is suspect. It is even possible for the majority of subjects to show no improvement, for some subjects to get worse, and for a few subjects to improve sufficiently to yield an overall average improvement of statistical significance.

The graphs in Figure 10.3 show the individual and average performance of two hypothetical subjects. The left panel suggests the faulty interpretations that are likely to be drawn if only the group's average performance is considered.[2] Concluding that the independent variable has no effect on behavior may be highly erroneous: Subject A's performance improved

---

[2] The posttest data point is reminiscent of the man whose bare feet were in a bucket of ice while his head was stuck inside a hot oven. When asked how he felt, he replied, "On the average, I feel fine."

FIGURE 10.3 Hypothetical data showing that the average performance of a group of subjects may not represent an individual's behavior.

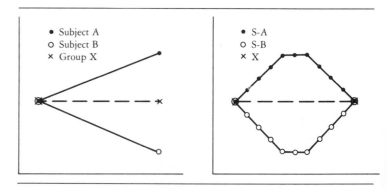

from pretest to posttest; Subject B's behavior deteriorated in that period of time. But what role, if any, the independent variable played in either subject's behavior change over the course of the experiment is unknown. Only by repeatedly measuring the behavior of the individual subjects in the presence and absence of the independent variable can a researcher begin the search for the variables responsible for observed intersubject variability. However, the solution to intersubject variability does not lie in repeated measurement alone (see the right-hand panel in Figure 10.3); the analysis of behavior-environment relationships must still focus on the individual subject.

A second problem associated with the mean performance of a group of subjects is that important sources of variability are lost. The belief that uncontrolled variables in a study can be controlled by statistical manipulations is a faulty one.

> Statistical control is never a substitute for experimental control. . . . The only way to determine whether or not uncontrolled variables are influencing the data is to inspect the data at the finest available level of decomposition, usually point-by-point for each individual subject. No purpose is served by combining the data statistically to obscure such effects. (Johnston & Pennypacker, 1980, p. 371)

If behavior is variable to the extent that socially significant levels of performance are affected, an experimental search for identification and control of the factors responsible for the variation is in order. Attempting to cancel out variability through statistical manipulation neither eliminates its presence in the data nor controls the function of the variables responsible for it. And attributing the effects of unknown or uncontrolled variables in an experiment to the role of chance only serves to remove the researcher even further from identification and analysis of important variables. In his monumental work, *Tactics of Scientific Research*, Sidman (1960) deals repeatedly and forcefully with this critical issue.

To some experimenters, chance is simply a name for the combined effects of uncontrolled variables. If such variables are, in fact, controllable, then chance in this sense is simply an excuse for sloppy experimentation, and no further comment is required. If the uncontrolled variables are actually unknown, then chance is, as Boring (1941) has pointed out, a synonym for ignorance. . . .

One of the most discouraging and at the same time challenging aspects of behavioral science is the sensitivity of behavior to a tremendous array of variables. . . . But variables are not canceled statistically. They are simply buried so that their effects cannot be seen. The rationale for statistical immobilization of unwanted variables is based on the assumed random nature of such variables. . . .

Not only is the assumption of randomness with respect to the uncontrolled variables an untested one but it is also highly improbable. There are few, if any, random phenomena in the behavioral world. (pp. 45, 162–163)

Sidman (1960) also comments on an experimenter's use of statistics in an attempt to deal with troublesome sequence effects.

> He has a neat trick up his sleeve. By averaging together the data for both subjects under Condition A, and again under Condition B, he "cancels out" the order effect, and completely bypasses the problem of irreversibility. By a simple arithmetical operation, two subjects have become one, and a variable has been eliminated.

> It has not, in fact, gone anywhere. Numbers may be made to disappear by adding and subtracting them from each other. Five apples minus three apples are two apples. The numbers are easily changed by a few strokes of the pen, but some eating has to be done before the apples themselves will vanish. (p. 250)

The "eating" that has to be done to control the effects of any variable can be accomplished in only two ways: holding the variable constant throughout the experiment or isolating the suspected factor as an independent variable and manipulating its presence, absence, and/or value during the experiment.

A third weakness of the group-comparison, statistical inference research model is that the power of replicating effects with individual subjects is lost. One of the greatest strengths of single-subject experimental designs is the convincing demonstration of a functional relationship made possible by replication within the design itself. Even though multiple subjects are typically involved in applied behavior analysis research, each subject is always treated as a separate experiment. Although behavior analysts often display and describe the data for all subjects as a group, data from individual subjects are used as the basis for determining and interpreting experimental effects. As Johnston and Pennypacker (1980) warn, "An effect that emerges *only* after individual data have been combined is probably artifactual and not representative of any real behavioral processes." (p. 257).

This discussion should not be interpreted to mean that the behavior of groups of subjects cannot or should not be studied with the strategies and tactics of behavior analysis. There are applied situations in which the overall (average) behavior of a group is socially significant (e.g., actuarial decisions and analyses). In other instances, the behavior analyst may not be able to control the access of subjects to the experimental setting and contingencies or even to identify who all of the subjects are or will be. The dependent variable must then consist of all of the responses made by individuals who enter the experimental setting. Numerous examples of this level of analysis can be found in the so-called community behavior analysis research. For example, such group data have comprised the dependent variable in studies of litter control on a university campus (Bacon-Prue, Blount, Pickering, & Drabman, 1980), car pooling by university students (Jacobs, Fairbanks, Poche, & Bailey, 1982), smoking in a cafeteria (Jason & Liotta, 1982), and driving speed (Van Houten & Nau, 1983). Nevertheless, in behavior analysis experiments such as these, unwanted or unplanned variability in the data is still treated and analyzed directly for what it is: an indication of poor experimental control and the need for further research.

INTERNAL VALIDITY: CONTROLLING POTENTIAL SOURCES OF CONFOUNDING IN AN EXPERIMENTAL DESIGN

Although we have used the term *experimental control* to indicate an experimenter's ability to reliably produce a specified behavior change by manipulating the independent variable, Johnston and Pennypacker (1980) point out that, technically, the phrase "control of *behavior*" is inaccurate because the experimenter really controls some aspect of the subject's *environment*. Therefore, the level of experimental control obtained by a researcher refers to the extent to which she controls all relevant variables in a given experiment. The researcher exerts this control within the context of an experimental design that, even though carefully planned at the outset, takes its ultimate form from the researcher's ongoing examination and response to the data.

As we have said before, an effective experimental design is one that reveals a reliable functional relationship between independent and dependent variables (if one exists), while at the same time minimizing the likelihood that behavior changes are the result of unknown or uncontrolled variables. An experiment has high internal validity when changes in the dependent variable are demonstrated to be a function of the independent variable only. The majority of changes made by an experimenter during the course of a study are made in an effort to control for, or expose, the effects of confounding variables.

In the science of behavior, the quest for and use of steady state responding is the primary means of both attaining and assessing experimental control. Separating the effects of the independent variable from those of other variables requires clear, empirical evidence that the potentially confounding variables either are not present or are being held constant; the demonstration of steady state responding provides that evidence (Johnston & Pennypacker, 1980). Any experimental analysis can be invaded by a virtually unlimited number of potential confounds; and as with every aspect of experimental design, there are no set rules to which an experimenter can turn for identification and control of confounding variables. However, common and likely sources of confounding can be identified as well as tactics that can be considered as possible controls. Confounding variables can be viewed as related primarily to one of four elements of an experiment: subject, setting, measurement of the dependent variable, and independent variable.

Some Sources of Subject Confounding

A variety of subject variables can confound the results of a study. In one sense the ultimate confounding occurs when a subject is lost to the experiment (e.g., he moves away, withdraws consent to participate), and at that point there is little the experimenter can do. Since the possibility of subject attrition exists in any experiment, the experimenter should begin a study, whenever possible, with enough subjects so that the loss of one or two will not completely disable the investigation. At first this suggestion may not seem fully consistent with the stated goals of applied behavior analysis: subjects should participate in studies of applied behavior analysis because of the social importance of changing the target behavior. In an investigation that truly has a single subject, one cannot simply get more subjects who are appropriate for the experiment; the loss of the subject means the end of the study. However, whenever conditions permit, the behavior analyst should select a sufficient number of subjects so that the loss of one or two will not place the investigation in jeopardy.

Maturation, which refers to changes that take place in a subject over the course of an experiment, is another potential confounding variable. For example, maturation could be responsible for a subject's improved performance during the later phases of a study, the result of physical growth or social development unrelated to the experiment and any

manipulations of the independent variable. Experimental designs that incorporate rapidly changing conditions or multiple introductions and withdrawals of the independent variable usually control effectively for maturation.

In virtually all research in applied behavior analysis, a subject is in the experimental setting and is responding under the influence of the contingencies implemented by the investigator for only a portion of the day. For example, a study of the mathematics behavior of elementary school children might take place for only a 30-minute session each weekday. The subjects' behavior during any given session, although ostensibly under the control of the contingencies in effect during the experimental session, can also be influenced by events that have occurred outside the experiment (e.g., a child is involved in a fight on the playground just prior to math period, and his completion and correct rates decrease substantially from previous sessions). Although the experimenter may be aware of some events that are likely causes of variability during a study, many other occurrences go undetected. Repeated measurement is both the control for and the means of detecting the operation of such variables. The uncontrolled variables responsible for a subject's having an off day or an unusually good day are particularly troublesome in research designs with few and/or widely spaced measurements of the dependent variable. This is one of the major weaknesses of using pretest-posttest comparisons as a means of evaluating the effects of an intervening treatment program.

The concern that a subject is odd or unrepresentative of other subjects is generally not an issue in applied behavior analysis. First, a subject should participate because she will benefit if the target behavior is successfully changed. Second, the external validity of results from a single-subject analysis is not dependent upon the extent to which the subject(s) share certain characteristics with other persons. The extent to which a functional relation has generality to other subjects can be established only by replicating the experiment with different subjects.

Setting Confounds

Most studies in applied behavior analysis take place in natural settings. Because a great many aspects of natural settings are beyond the control of the experimenter, such studies are more prone to confounding by uncontrolled events operating within the experimental setting than are studies conducted in the laboratory. When an experimenter observes an unplanned event that coincides with changes in the data, he should hold all possible aspects of the experiment constant until repeated measurement again reveals stable responding. If the unplanned event is of interest and is amenable to experimental manipulation, it should be treated as an independent variable and its possible controlling effects systematically explored.

Researchers must also be observant of "bootleg" reinforcers both within and outside the experimental setting. If subjects have ready access to the consequences being employed as potential reinforcers in the experiment, the effectiveness of those consequences can be diminished.

Potential Confounding Related to Measurement of the Dependent Variable

Chapters 4 and 5 present the many considerations that must go into the design of an accurate and nonreactive measurement system. Numerous sources of confounding exist within any measurement system. Research into behavioral measurement has clearly shown that data showing changes in behavior may simply be an artifact of observer drift, the influence of the experimenter's behavior on observers, and/or observer bias (e.g., Kazdin, 1977a). Although sometimes difficult to accomplish in applied settings where observers often see the independent variable being implemented, keeping observers "blind" to the conditions and ex-

pected outcomes of an experiment reduces the potential for nonrandom observer error (e.g., Rose, 1978). And when observers score permanent products, the products should not contain any identifying marks that indicate who produced each product and under what experimental conditions. Having observers score papers in a randomized order with baseline and treatment papers mixed together also reduces the likelihood of observer drift or bias affecting only the products in the later treatment phases.

Unless a completely unobtrusive measurement system is devised, reactivity of the dependent variable to the measurement procedure must always be considered a possible confound. The experimenter must maintain baseline conditions long enough for any reactive effects to run their course and for stable responding to be obtained. If reactivity to measurement produces undesirable effects (e.g., aggressive behavior, cessation of productivity) and a more unobtrusive measurement procedure cannot be devised, intermittent probes should be considered. When the levels of responding observed in the presence of the independent variable are suspected of resulting from an interaction between the measurement system and the independent variable, Johnston and Pennypacker (1980) recommend varying certain aspects of the measurement procedure while reintroducing the treatment variable.

Practice, adaptation, and warm-up effects can also exert some control over responding, especially during the initial stages of baseline. Again, the proper procedure is to continue baseline conditions until stable responding is obtained or variability is reduced to minimal levels. Intermittent baseline probes should not be used when practice effects are expected.

Potential Confounding Related to the Independent Variable

Many, if not most, independent variables are multifaceted; that is, there is often more to a treatment variable than the specific element in which the investigator is interested. For example, the effects of a token economy on the academic productivity of school children can be confounded by variables such as the personal relationship between the subjects and the teacher delivering the tokens, the social interaction involved in delivering and exchanging tokens, the expectation of both teacher and students that performance will improve when the token system is implemented, and so on. If the intent is to analyze the effects of token reinforcement per se, these potentially confounding variables must be controlled.

When medical researchers use a placebo control (e.g., a pill containing an inert substance), they are attempting to separate the effects produced by the subject's expectations of improvement from any effects actually produced by the drug being tested. Rose (1978) used a placebo control in a study evaluating the effects of artifical food coloring on the classroom behavior of two 8-year-old girls. After an initial baseline phase the girls were given a yellow cookie to eat with breakfast each morning. However, neither the subjects, their parents, nor their classroom teachers knew which cookies contained the artificial food coloring. It was impossible therefore for the subjects, as well as any significant others who interacted with them throughout the day, to expect certain effects. The observers in the classroom were also blind to the presence and absence of the independent variable; they did not know when the subjects had eaten artificially colored cookies and were unaware of the actual purpose of the study. This type of control procedure, called a **double-blind control**, eliminated subject expectations, parent and teacher expectations and possible differential treatment, and observer bias.

A study by Schwarz and Hawkins (1970) provides another good example of a control procedure designed to identify which aspects of a treatment variable are responsible for behavior change. Schwarz and Hawkins evaluated the effects of token reinforcement on three maladaptive behaviors of an elementary student. During treatment the therapist and the girl met after school each day and viewed a videotape that had been made of the subject's classroom behavior earlier that day. The therapist also gave tokens contingent on the girl's videotaped behavior displaying progressively fewer instances of target behaviors. If improvement occurred as a function of this type of treatment, the question would remain whether the child's behavior had improved simply because the attention and rewards improved the girl's self-concept, which in turn changed her symptomatic behavior in the classroom. One could not be certain whether the token rewards contingent upon changes in behavior played an important role in changing the behavior. The procedure used by Schwarz and Hawkins to control for this concern was a simple and direct one. Following baseline measurement, they conducted a phase in which the therapist met with the girl each day after school, giving contingent token reinforcement for improvements in handwriting. The three target behaviors—face touching, posture, and voice volume—showed no change during this control phase, thereby increasing one's confidence that improvements during the later intervention phases were due to the token reinforcement of the girl's behavior. Noncontingent reinforcement, discussed in chapter 8, is another procedure for separating the effects of receiving reinforcers and receiving contingent reinforcement.

Treatment Integrity An experimenter must make every effort to ensure that the independent variable is applied exactly as planned and that no other unplanned variables are inadvertently administered along with the planned treatment. The term **treatment integrity** refers to the extent to which the independent variable is implemented or carried out as planned. When the treatment integrity is low, a major source of confounding enters into the experiment, making it difficult, if not impossible, to interpret the results with confidence. Conclusions based on the effects observed in an experiment in which the independent variable was improperly, inconsistently, partially, or overly applied may, depending upon the results obtained, represent either a false positive or a false negative. If a functional relationship is apparent in the data, one cannot be sure whether the treatment variable as described by the experimenter was responsible or whether the effects were a function of extraneous, uncontrolled elements of the intervention as it was actually applied. On the other hand, it may be equally incorrect to interpret the failure to produce significant behavior change as evidence that an independent variable is ineffective; had the independent variable been implemented as planned, it might have been effective.

There are numerous threats to treatment integrity, particularly in applied settings (Billingsley, White, & Munson, 1980; Peterson, Homer, & Wonderlich, 1982; Salend, 1984a, 1984b). Experimenter bias can cause the researcher to administer the independent variable in such a way that it enjoys an unfair advantage over the baseline or comparative conditions. **Treatment drift** occurs when the independent variable applied during later stages of an experiment only approximates the application earlier in the study (Peterson et al., 1982). Treatment drift can result from the complexity of the independent variable, which can make it difficult for practitioners to implement all of the elements consistently over the course of an experiment. Contingencies influencing the behavior of those responsible for implementing the independent variable can also result in treatment drift. A teacher, for example, might implement only those aspects of a procedure that she likes best and might implement the intervention fully only on those occasions when the experimenter is present.

When planning experiments, researchers should place a high priority on the simplification and standardization of the independent

variable and on adequate training and practice for those who will be responsible for its application. Treatments that are simple, precise, and short and require little effort are more likely to be delivered with consistency (Salend, 1984b). Simple, easy-to-implement techniques are also likely to possess more social validity; they have a higher probability of being accepted and used by practitioners in applied settings. Simplicity is, of course, a relative concern, not a mandate; some socially important behaviors may require intense, complex, and long interventions. However, all things being equal, a simple treatment will probably be applied more consistently than a complex one.

To ensure the consistent presentation of the independent variable, experimenters should standardize as many of its aspects as cost and practicality allow. Standardization of treatment can be accomplished in a variety of ways. When a treatment variable requires a complex and/or long sequence of behavior, a script for the person administering the treatment might increase the accuracy and consistency with which the independent variable is applied. For example, Heron, Heward, Cooke, and Hill (1983) used overhead transparencies and a scripted lesson to ensure that a peer tutoring training program was implemented in the same way for different groups of children.

Whenever the desired nature of the intervention will not be compromised by automation, researchers should consider "canning" the independent variable so that an automated device can be used for its delivery. In the Heron et al. (1983) study a videotaped tutor training presentation would have eliminated the potential confounding created by the teacher's slightly different presentation of the lesson from group to group, but it would also have greatly reduced the desired interactive and personal aspect of the training program. Some treatment variables are well suited to automated presentation in that automation neither limits the desirability of the treatment nor seriously reduces its social validity in terms of acceptability or practicability (e.g., use of videotaped programs to model residential energy conservation).

Whenever possible, training and practice in properly administering the independent variable should be provided to the person(s) who will be responsible for implementing the treatment variable. The researcher should never assume that general competence and experience in the experimental setting guarantees correct and consistent application of an experimental variable.

Procedural Reliability Although simplification, standardization, and training help increase the degree of treatment integrity, they do not guarantee it. When reasonable doubt concerning the correct and consistent application of the independent variable remains, investigators should provide data on the reliability of the independent variable (Billingsley, White & Munson, 1980; Peterson, Homer, & Wonderlich, 1982). **Procedural reliability** is a measure of the extent to which the actual application of the independent variable over the course of an experiment matches its description in the method section of a research report.

Even though the effective control of the presence and absence of the independent variable is a fundamental requirement of proper experimentation, applied behavior analysts have not always made sufficient efforts to assure the integrity of the independent variable. In a review of studies published in the *Journal of Applied Behavior Analysis* from 1968 to 1980, Peterson et al. (1982) found that the majority of articles did not report data assessing the degree to which the independent variable was properly and consistently applied. They noted that a "curious double standard" seemed to develop in applied behavior analysis: observational reliability data were required in order for data on the dependent variable to be accepted as believable, but such data were seldom provided for the independent variable.

Peterson et al. (1982) suggest that the technology developed for increasing the accuracy

and believability of measures of the dependent variable (chapter 5) is fully applicable to the collection of procedureal reliability data. Importantly, observation and recording of the independent variable provides the experimenter with data indicating whether calibration of the treatment agent is necessary (i.e., bringing the treatment agent's behavior in agreement with the true value of the independent variable). Observation and calibration gives the researcher ongoing ability to use retraining and practice to ensure treatment integrity over the course of an experiment.

This overview of some sources of potential confounding variables is, of course, incomplete. A complete inventory of all possible threats to the internal validity of experimental research would be impossible to compile. And presenting such a list might suggest that one need only control for the variables listed and not worry about anything else. In truth, the potential confounding variables are unique to every experiment. The effective researcher is one who constantly questions and probes the influence of as many relevant variables as possible. No experimental design controls for all potential confounds; the challenge is to eliminate or identify the influence of as many extraneous variables as possible.

EXTERNAL VALIDITY: THE ROLE OF REPLICATION IN APPLIED BEHAVIOR ANALYSIS

External validity refers to the degree to which a functional relationship found reliable and valid in a given experiment is considered meaningful under other conditions. A behavior change technique that works only under a circumscribed set of conditions and proves ineffective if any variable in the original experiment is altered makes a limited contribution to the development of a reliable and useful technology of behavior change. When an independent variable has been shown to produce reliable and socially significant improvements in the target behavior of a given subject, a whole series of important questions should then be asked: Will this same procedure be as effective if it is applied to other behaviors? Will the procedure continue to work if it is changed in some way (e.g., applied at a different time of the day, by another person, on a different schedule)? Will it work in a different setting? Will it work with other subjects? The questions concerning external validity are not abstract or rhetorical; they are empirical questions that can be addressed only by empirical methods.

A functional relationship with external validity, or generality, will continue to operate under a variety of conditions. External validity is not an all-or-nothing property, but a matter of degree. A functional relationship that cannot be reproduced under any conditions other than the exact set of original variables (including the original subject) possesses no external validity. At the other end of the continuum, a procedure that is effective at any time, under any conditions, in any setting, with any behavior, and for any subject has complete generality (an improbable situation). Most functional relationships fall somewhere along this continuum, and those with the higher degrees of generality make the greater contribution to the field of applied behavior analysis. Researchers who use the methods of group design approach the issue of external validity quite differently from the way researchers who employ the strategies and tactics of the science of behavior approach it.

External Validity and Group-Design Research

As stated earlier, practitioners of group-comparison experimental designs claim two advantages for the use of large groups of subjects. In addition to their belief that combining the data of a group of subjects controls for intersubject variability, researchers who employ group designs contend that the involvement of many subjects in an experiment increases the external validity of any results that are obtained. On

the surface this is perfectly logical, and on one level it is also true. The more subjects for which a functional relationship is shown to operate, the more likely it is that the functional relationship will also be effective for other subjects who share similar characteristics. And in fact, demonstrating a functional relation with various subjects in different settings is the way applied behavior analysts pursue the problem of external validity.

However, the investigator who claims that the results of a group-comparison investigation are generalizable to other individuals in the population from which the experimental subjects were chosen is violating both a fundamental premise of the group-comparison method and a definitional characteristic of behavior. The proper inferences that can be made from a group-design study are from the sample to the population, not from the sample to the individual (Fisher, 1956). The careful methods of random sampling used in group-design research are followed because they ensure a heterogeneous sample of subjects in which all relevant characteristics in the population are represented. Indeed, the better the sample represents the population from which it is drawn, the less meaningful are the results for any individual subject. "The only statement that can be made concerns the average response of a group with that particular makeup which, unfortunately, is unlikely to be duplicated again" (Hersen & Barlow, 1976, p. 56).

The second problem inherent in trying to extend the results obtained in a group-comparison study to other individuals (or even to a subject who participated in the study, as illustrated in Figure 10.3) is that the group-design experiment does not demonstrate a functional relationship between the behavior of an individual and some aspect(s) of the environment. In other words, from the standpoint of the science of behavior, there is nothing in the results of a group-design experiment that can have external validity; there is nothing to generalize. Johnston & Pennypacker (1980) make this point well.

The problem lies in the generality of groups comparisons to the individual case. Because behavior is a phenomenon that occurs only at the individual level, the science of behavior must have as its goal the understanding of the individual organism's interaction with its environment. Once that is accomplished, the question of generalizing the results from one or a few individuals to a larger number can be properly addressed. . . .

A science of behavior must obviously be able to account for differences in behavior that are observed among individuals, and to do so will require that the generality of its basic functional relations be explored, established, and specified. This requires that the functional relations must first be discovered, a task made all but impossible by premature insistence on the type of artificial generality that is believed furnished by experimentation on large groups of subjects.(pp. 91, 221)

For over 30 years the group-design/statistical-inference model has been the dominant paradigm for research in psychology, education, and the other social sciences. The extent to which this research paradigm has directly contributed to an effective technology of behavior change is highly questionable (Baer, 1977; Birnbrauer, 1981; Michael, 1974). The field of education is perhaps the most telling example of the inability of group-design research to provide data that lead to improved practice (Greer, 1983; Lovitt, 1977). Instructional methods in the classroom are often influenced more by fad and the personal style of individual teachers than by the cumulative knowledge and understanding available from rigorous and sustained experimental analysis of the variables of which learning is a function. The methodology of group-design experimentation is inappropriate for answering the questions of primary interest to the applied behavior analyst—empirical questions that can be pursued only by analysis of repeated measures of individual behavior under all relevant conditions. We agree with Johnston and Pennypacker (1980):

We find the reasoning underlying all such procedures alien to both the subject matter and the goals of a natural science of behavior and regard the utility of group comparisons as extremely limited, no matter how elegant the mathematical treatment of data they afford. . . . [group comparison experimentation constitutes] a process of scientific inquiry that is almost totally inverted; instead of using questions about natural phenomena to guide decisions about experimental design, models of design are allowed to dictate both the form and content of the questions asked. Not only is this antithetical to the established role of experimentation in science, the types of questions allowed by groups comparison designs are largely inappropriate or irrelevant to gaining an understanding of the determinants of behavior. (pp. 89–90)

However, our discussion of the inherent weaknesses of group designs for the science of behavior should not be confused with the position that statistical inference and group designs have no value as knowledge-seeking activities. On the contrary, the methods of statistical inference are appropriate and effective tools for seeking answers to the kinds of questions for which they were devised. The control group/experimental group paradigm is necessary to answer with some degree of confidence the questions involved in many large-scale evaluations. For example, a governmental body is less interested in the effects of a new regulation on any individual person (and even less interested in whether there is a functional relationship between the regulation and an individual's behavior) than it is in the probability that some given percentage of the population will be affected in one way or another. The former concern is a behavioral one, and the experimental methods of the natural science of behavior provide the means to address it. The latter concern is an actuarial one, and it is best pursued with the methods of random sampling, group comparison, and statistical inference.

External Validity and the Analysis of Behavior

The generality of research findings in applied behavior analysis can be assessed, established, and specified only through the replication of experiments. Replication in this context means repeating a previous experiment. Johnston and Pennypacker (1980) point out a distinction between the replication of an experiment and reproduction of the experiment's results.

> Replication does not refer to the reproduction of the results originally observed; thus, the quality of the replication refers only to the extent to which equivalent environmental manipulations associated with earlier observations are duplicated. . . . the term *reproduction* is used to denote duplication of the dependent effect. Thus, one replicates procedures in an effort to reproduce effects. (pp. 303–304)

However, when most researchers report a failure to replicate, they mean that the results of the replication did not match those obtained in the earlier research (e.g., Friedling & O'Leary, 1979).

Direct Replication Sidman (1960) identifies two major types of scientific replication—direct and systematic. In a **direct replication** the researcher makes every effort to duplicate exactly the conditions of an earlier experiment. If the same subject is used in a direct replication, the study is an intrasubject replication. An intersubject direct replication maintains every aspect of the earlier experiment except that different, although similar, subjects are involved (i.e., same age, similar repertoires). Intrasubject replication is one of the defining characteristics of behavior analysis research and is the primary tactic for establishing the reliability of a functional relationship. However, only through intersubject replication can the generality of an experimental finding be determined.

Because of the many uncontrolled variables operating in natural settings, direct replication of experiments is virtually impossible outside the laboratory (Tawney & Gast, 1984). And although there are single-subject research studies that do involve a single subject (e.g., O'Brien, Riner, & Budd, 1983), intersubject replication is the rule rather than the exception in the applied behavior analysis literature. Although uncontrolled variables make it diffi-

cult to directly replicate an experiment across time in applied settings, the vast majority of published studies in behavior analysis do provide evidence of direct intersubject replication because each subject is usually considered an intact experiment. For example, five intersubject replications are provided by a behavior analysis study in which the independent variable is manipulated in exactly the same way for six subjects in the same setting.

Systematic Replication Direct replication of experiments is necessary to demonstrate the reliability of a functional relation, but the generality of that finding to varied conditions can be established only through repeated experimentation in which the conditions of interest are purposefully and systematically varied. Thus, **systematic replication**, when successful in reproducing the results of previous research, not only demonstrates the reliability of the findings but adds to the external validity of the treatment effect by showing that it can be obtained under varying conditions. In a systematic replication any aspect of the replicated experiment can be slightly changed: subjects, setting, administration of the independent variable, target behaviors. The generality of a given treatment is enhanced when it produces similar effects in widely varying conditions.

However, even though systematic replication offers greater potential rewards than direct replication because it can provide new knowledge about the variables under investigation, it does not come without some risk.

> But this procedure is a gamble. If systematic replication fails, the original experiment will still have to be redone, else there is no way of determining whether the failure to replicate stemmed from the introduction of new variables in the second experiment, or whether the control of relevant factors was inadequate in the first experiment.

> On the other hand, if systematic replication succeeds, the pay-off is handsome. Not only is the reliability of the original finding increased, but also its generality with respect to other organisms

and to other experimental procedures is greatly enhanced. Furthermore, additional data are now available which could not have been obtained by a simple repetition of the first experiment. (Sidman, 1960, pp. 111–112)

Sidman goes on to explain that economic husbandry of limited resources must also play an important role in the scientist's determination of how a research program should proceed. Direct replication of a long and costly experiment can provide data on only the reliability of a functional relation, whereas systematic replication can provide information on the reliability and generality of the phenomena under investigation, as well as new information for additional experimentation.

In the group-design/statistical-inference research paradigm, external validity is viewed as an inherent characteristic of a given experiment, something that can be directly assessed by examining the methods used to conduct the study (e.g., sampling procedures). If that logic is extended to single-subject experiments, then single-subject experiments cannot be said to have any external validity. But as Birnbrauer (1981) points out, external validity is not something part of a study *has*. Instead, external validity can be pursued only through an active process of systematic replication.

> Generality is established, or more likely limited, by accumulating studies which are internally valid *and* by placing the results into a systematic context, i.e., seeking out the principles and parameters that particular procedures appear to be enunciating. The most informative studies ask *how* can an earlier positive result be repeated in the present circumstances, with the present problem? (Birnbrauer, 1981, p. 122)

The literature of applied behavior analysis contains many systematic replications of earlier research. Indeed, one might persuasively argue that almost any applied behavior analysis study constitutes a systematic replication of some aspect of earlier research; even when the authors have not pointed it out, virtually every published experiment reveals significant procedural similarity with previous experiments.

However, as we are using the term here, systematic replication refers to concerted and directed efforts to establish and specify the generality of a functional relation over time. For example, Hamlet, Axelrod, and Kuerschner (1984) found a functional relationship between demanded eye contact (e.g., "[Name], turn around") and compliance with adult instructions in two 11-year-old school children. Included in the same published report were the results of six replications conducted by the same researchers over a period of 1 year with nine students aged 2 to 21 years. Similar results were reproduced in eight of the nine replication subjects. Although some might consider this an example of direct intersubject replication, the Hamlet et al. replications were conducted in various settings (classroom, home, institution) and therefore represent a series of systematic replications that demonstrate not only the reliability of the results but also considerable generality across subjects of different ages in different settings.

Some systematic replications are attempts to reproduce the results obtained by another researcher in a slightly different situation or context. For example, Saigh and Umar (1983) successfully reproduced in a Sudanese classroom the positive results originally reported with the Good Behavior Game (Barrish, Saunders & Wolf, 1969; see Figure 25.10). The authors report that a "considerable degree of support for the cross-cultural utility of the game was established" (p. 343). Bittle (1975) reports a novel and effective study conducted with the students and parents of a regular second-grade classroom. By calling a special number parents could access a telephone answering machine and hear prerecorded messages from their child's teacher. Results showed that parents used the system frequently, that students' scores on daily spelling tests improved when the messages included the next day's spelling words (under baseline conditions the words were sent home with the children), and that parents complied with teacher requests of a nonacademic nature (e.g., "Please have your child bring a shoe box to school tomorrow for a special art project"). Heward and Chapman (1981) produced similar results in a systematic replication conducted in a self-contained classroom for primary-aged children with learning disabilities.

Researchers sometimes report multiple experiments that serve as systematic replications investigating the variables influencing a given functional relationship. For example, Carr, Newsom, and Binkoff (1980) conducted four successive experiments designed to identify variables controlling the severely aggressive behavior of two boys with mental retardation; Van Houten et al. (1982) reported four experiments in which they investigated the effectiveness of social reprimands on the behavior of school children; and Rolider and Van Houten (1985) performed four experiments that demonstrated the general effectiveness of movement suppression time-out in reducing the self-injurious, self-stimulatory, and aggressive behaviors of three different children.

Systematic replication is also evident when a research team pursues a consistent line of research by conducting a series of related studies over time. Two examples of this type of replication can be found in the work of Van Houten and Nau and their colleagues on variables influencing highway speeding and driver safety (e.g., Van Houten & Nau, 1981, 1983; Van Houten, Nau, & Marini, 1980; Van Houten, Malenfant, & Rolider, 1985) and in the line of research by Repp and Deitz and colleagues on the effectiveness of differential reinforcement of other behavior (see chapter 18) in reducing undesirable behavior (e.g., Dietz, Repp, & Deitz, 1976; Repp, Barton, & Brulle, 1983; Repp & Deitz, 1974; Repp, Deitz, & Deitz, 1976; Repp, Deitz, & Speir, 1975).

In most instances the systematic replications necessary to develop a major line of research require the efforts of a number of researchers who, although aware of one another's work, function as independent investigators. Johnston and Pennypacker (1980, chapter 21) provide a review of 58 studies on time out from reinforcement as an example of systematic replication. A similar review of several other areas within the experimental and applied behavior analysis literature (e.g., token reinforcement, extinction) also reveals the role of systematic replication in the science and technology of behavior change. Systematic replications occur in both planned and unplanned ways through the work of many experimenters in a given area, and they result in a body of knowledge with significant scientific integrity and technological value.

The Need for More Thorough Analyses of Socially Important Behavior

Even though no behavior analyst would argue the necessity of systematic replication and the central role it plays in the development of an effective technology of behavior change and even though the literature provides evidence that at least a loose form of systematic replication is commonly practiced, a more critical examination of the literature suggests the need for more thorough analysis of the functional relationships under study. Several behavior analysts have commented in recent years on the importance of stressing the analytic side of applied behavior analysis as much as the applied side (e.g., Birnbrauer, 1979, 1981; Deitz, 1978, 1982; Hayes, Rincover, & Solnick, 1980; Michael, 1980; Pennypacker, 1981; Pierce & Epling, 1980). After examining the majority of the experimental articles published in the first 10 volumes of the *Journal of Applied Behavior Analysis* (1968 to 1977), Hayes, Rincover, and Solnick (1980) conclude that a technical drift is occurring in the field away from conceptual analyses and toward an emphasis on client cure. They warn of a likely loss of scientific understanding as a result of focusing purely on the technical aspects of improving behavior in applied settings, and they recommend an increased effort to perform more thorough analyses of behavior.

The importance of component analyses, parametric analyses, and other more sophisticated analytic attempts are often to be found less in "control" (in an immediately applied sense) and more in "understanding" (in a scientific sense). One may easily control, say, aggressive behavior through the use of punishment without having contributed significantly to an understanding of aggression. . . . For example, if one has a package program that is effective, there may be little obvious value in doing a component analysis. But these more complicated analyses may increase our knowledge of the actual functional variables and subsequently increase our ability to generate more efficient and general behavioral programs. Perhaps, we have gone too far in our attempt to be *immediately* applied at the expense of being *ultimately* more effective, in failing to encourage more analogue and analytical studies that have treatment implications. (Hayes, Rincover, & Solnick, 1980, pp. 282–283)

It is possible to reliably reproduce an important behavior change while at the same time not fully understand which variables are responsible for the observed functional relation. Sidman (1960) differentiates this kind of simple reliability from "knowledgeable reproducibility," a more complete level of analysis in which all of the important factors have been identified and are controlled. The extent of a phenomenon's generality is known only when all of the necessary and sufficient conditions for its reproducibility have been specified. Only when all of the variables influencing a functional relation have been identified and accounted for can an analysis be considered complete. Even then, the notion of a complete analysis is highly misleading: "Further dissection or elaboration of either variable in a functional relation inevitably reveals fresh variability, and analysis proceeds anew. . . . the analysis of behavior can never be complete" (Pennypacker, 1981, p. 159). Pennypacker (1981) comments further on what he perceives to be a cursory level of analysis found in much of the applied behavior analysis literature.

We seem content to demonstrate, with the aid of a simple reversal or multiple baseline design, that the phenomenon of interest is susceptible to alteration by the application of some totally unanalyzable treatment package or procedure. If the resulting relation resembles a functional relation described in a basic text on behavior principles, we attach the appropriate descriptive term (reinforcement, extinction, generalization, etc.), delude ourselves and the public into believing that something of explanatory substance has been wrought, and claim another victory for behavior analysis.

Successful analysis . . . is a long-term, often cumulative, process that is merely launched, not completed, by a crude demonstration of controllability in a natural setting. (p. 160)

Deitz (1982) gives a similar call for more thorough analysis, particularly when the independent variable consists of a multiple-component treatment package.

In using treatment packages today's behavior analysts follow the same pattern. Several complex, multifaceted procedures are combined, and success is claimed if some general category of socially important behavior is increased or decreased. . . . The end results of such programs may satisfy their clients and the public, but through these methods . . . little is learned about which part of the treatment aided a cure, which part hindered, or which part did nothing at all.

A more careful analysis of these treatment packages is required. . . . A scientific applied behavior analysis is not satisfied that a package produced a cure. It suggests not only an analysis of the effects of each component of a package, but also an analysis of the effect of different parameters of those components. (p. 63)

We agree with the need for more sophisticated, thorough analysis of the variables controlling socially important behavior. Fortunately, examination of the recent literature reveals more than a few examples of the component and parametric analyses that are the necessary steps to a more complete understanding of behavior; an understanding that is prerequisite to development of a thoroughly effective technology of behavior change. Several of the studies cited earlier as examples of systematic replication incorporate component and parametric analyses. As one example Van Houten and Nau (1983) in their research on highway speeding conducted five experiments in which they systematically compared and varied the components of posted feedback to reduce driver speed. The increasing frequency of sophisticated experimentation of this type marks an important maturing of applied behavior analysis.

It is important to remember that although some research in applied behavior analysis can rightfully be criticized as superficial since it adds little to a conceptual understanding of behavior, studies in which meaningful target behaviors are improved to a socially valid level by the application of a socially valid treatment variable (whether a package or not) are never superficial to the subject and the significant others who share his environment.

EVALUATING RESEARCH IN APPLIED BEHAVIOR ANALYSIS

If one were to write down all of the expectations and characteristics of good research in applied behavior analysis, the list would be long. Thus far in this text we have specified a substantial number of requirements for good applied behavior analysis. Our purpose now is to summarize those requirements in a sequence of questions one might ask in evaluating the quality of published research in applied behavior analysis. Those questions fall under four headings: functional relationship issues, social validity, generality issues, and scientific significance.

Functional Relationship Issues

To determine whether an analysis of behavior has been made, the reader of a research report in applied behavior analysis must decide whether a functional relationship has been demonstrated. This decision requires close examination of the measurement system, the experimental design, and the researcher's control of confounding variables, as well as careful visual analysis and interpretation of the data.

Definition and Measurement of the Dependent Variable The first task is to examine the measurement system to determine whether the reported data can be accepted as a valid representation of the rate, frequency, duration, and/or latency of the target behavior over the course of the experiment. Some important issues that play a major part in this determination are included in the following questions: Was the dependent variable precisely defined? Were the most relevant, measurable dimensions of the target behavior specified (e.g., rate, duration)? Were important concomitant behaviors also measured? Were the methods of observing and recording appropriate for the target behavior? How believable are the data in terms of accuracy and reliability? Have the authors provided sufficient information on the training and calibration of observers? What procedures were in place to determine the accuracy of measurement? Are interobserver agreement percentages reported at the level for which the results are being presented (e.g., by subject and condition)? Were observations of the target behavior numerous enough and spaced closely enough in time to provide a convincing estimate of behavior change over time? Were there any contingencies operating in the experimental setting that may have influenced the observers' behavior? Is there any expectation or indication that the dependent variable may have been reactive to the observation and measurement system? If so, were procedures taken to assess and/or control reactivity?

Steady States If the data do accurately represent the dependent variable over the course of the experiment, the reader should next assess the extent of stability of the target behavior during each phase of the study. Before evaluating the stability of the data paths, however, the reader must look for any sources of distortion contributed by the graphic display. If the graphic display is suspected of encouraging interpretation unwarranted by the data, the results should be replotted on a new set of axes that are scaled more honestly. In an assessment of the stability of the dependent variable within the different phases of an experiment, the length of the phase or condition must be considered as well as the presence of trends in the data path. The consumer should ask whether the experimental conditions in effect during each phase were conducive to practice effects. If so, were these effects allowed to play themselves out before experimental variables were manipulated?

Representativeness of Baseline Conditions If stable responding during baseline phases is evident, the representativeness or fairness of the baseline conditions as the basis for evaluating performance in the presence of the independent variable should be assessed. In other words, were the baseline conditions meaningful in relation to the target behavior, setting, and research questions addressed by the experiment? For example, let us consider an experiment designed to answer this research question: How would the performance of students on daily spelling tests be affected by giving parents access to prerecorded telephone messages that included the next day's spelling words and a request that parents help their children learn them (Heward & Chapman, 1981)? Baseline measurement is conducted under conditions in which parents have not been asked to help their children prepare for the daily spelling quizzes and they do not have access to the next day's words; low and stable scores are obtained. Then, prerecorded telephone messages are implemented, and students' spelling scores improve considerably. Even though a clear functional relation is demonstrated, a consumer should question the importance of such results: Why go to all the trouble of purchasing a telephone answering machine, recording messages, and asking parents to call a special number each evening when parents could simply be asked to help their children practice the next day's spelling words that are brought home from school each day on a piece of paper? In order to make base-line conditions represent a meaningful, or fair, comparison in just such a study, Heward and Chapman (1981) telephoned and wrote parents prior to baseline, asking them to help their children learn each day's spelling words. Then, during baseline and for each day throughout the study, each student took a list of her words home. Thus, the effect of the independent variable could be meaningfully compared to baseline behavior.

Experimental Design The experimental design should be examined to determine the type of experimental reasoning it affords. What elements of the design enable prediction, verification, and replication? Is the design appropriate for the research questions being addressed? Does the design effectively control for confounding variables? Does the design provide the basis for comparative, component, and/or parametric analyses if such questions are warranted?

Visual Analysis and Interpretation As discussed in chapter 7, visual analysis is the primary means of determining the presence and reliability of experimental effect in applied behavior analysis. The level, trend, and variability of the data must be evaluated within and across each phase of the experiment. The reader should judge the rate, amount, and durability of behavior change evidenced in each phase. These judgments must, of course, be made in conjunction with a determination of the social validity of any apparent behavior changes; the objective is to decide on the presence or absence of a functional relationship.

Although various statistical methods of determining the existence of experimental effect in single-subject designs have been recommended (e.g., Gentile, Rhoden, & Klein, 1972; Hartmann, 1974; Hartmann et al., 1980; Jones, Vaught, & Weinrott, 1977; Kazdin, 1976; Shine & Bower, 1971), visual inspection remains the most commonly used, and we believe the most appropriate, method for analyzing data in applied behavior analysis. We will briefly present four factors that favor visual analysis over tests of statistical significance in applied behavior analysis. For a more in-depth discussion of this issue the reader is referred to Michael (1974) and Baer (1977), whose papers provide strong arguments for the continued use of visual inspection.

First, applied behavior analysts have little interest in knowing that a behavior change is statistically significant. Applied behavior analysis is concerned with producing socially significant changes in behavior: "If a problem has been solved, you can *see* that; if you must test for statistical significance, you do not have a solution" (Baer, 1977a, p. 171).

Second, visual analysis encourages the development of an effective technology of behavior change because it is more likely to identify variables that produce strong, large, and reliable effects, while overlooking weak, unreliable variables. Two types of errors are possible when determining experimental effect: a **Type 1 error** is made when the scientist affirms that a variable is a functional one, when in truth it is not; a **Type 2 error** is made when a truly functional variable is discarded as ineffective. Baer (1977a) points out that the behavior analyst's reliance on visual inspection to determine experimental effects results in a low incidence of Type 1 errors but increases the commission of Type 2 errors. The researcher who relies on tests of statistical significance to determine experimental effects makes many more Type 1 errors than the behavior analyst but misses few, if any, variables that might produce some effect.

> Scientists who commit relatively many Type 1 errors are bound to memorize very long lists of variables that are supposed to affect diverse behaviors, some predictable portion of which are not variables at all. By contrast, scientists who commit very few Type 1 errors have relatively short lists of variables to remember. Furthermore, and much more important, it is usually only the very robust, uniformly effective variables that will make their list. Those who will risk Type 1 errors more often will uncover a host of weak variables. Unquestionably, they will know more, although some of that more is wrong, and much of it is

tricky. . . . Those who keep their probability of Type 2 errors low do not often reject an actually functional variable, relative to those whose Type 2 error probability is higher. Again, unquestionably, the practitioner with the lower probability of Type 2 errors will know more; but again, the nature of that more is seen often in its weakness, inconsistency of function, or its tight specialization. . . . Individual-subject-design practitioners . . . necessarily fall into very low probabilities of Type 1 errors and very high probabilities of Type 2 errors, relative to their group-paradigm colleagues. As a result, they learn about fewer variables, but these variables are typically more powerful, general, dependable, and—very important—sometimes actionable. These are exactly the variables on which a technology of behavior might be built. (Baer, 1977a, pp. 170–171)

A third reason not to rely on statistical methods in determining functional relations is that efforts to experimentally determine the factors causing variability might be disbanded.

> The situation where a significance test might seem helpful is typically one involving sufficient uncontrolled variability in the dependent variable that neither the experimenter nor his readers can be sure that there is an interpretable relationship. This is evidence that the relevant behavior is not under good experimental control, a situation calling for more effective experimentation, not a more complex judgmental aid. (Michael, 1974, p. 650)

Fourth, statistical tests of significance can be applied only to data sets meeting certain predetermined criteria. If statistical methods for determining experimental effects were to become highly valued in applied behavior analysis, researchers might begin to design experiments so that such tests could be computed. The resultant loss of experimental flexibility would be counterproductive to the continued development of the science of behavior (Johnston & Pennypacker, 1980; Michael, 1974).

Social Validity

The social validity of a published study in applied behavior analysis should be assessed in three areas: the social significance of the target behavior, the appropriateness of the procedures, and the social importance of the results (Wolf, 1978).

Target Behavior Chapter 3 detailed the many considerations that guide the proper selection of target behaviors in applied behavior analysis. The reader of an applied behavior analysis study should judge the appropriateness of the dependent variable in light of those considerations. Ultimately, all of the issues relative to target behavior selection point to one factor: Will an increase or decrease in the measured dimension of this behavior result in an improvement in the subject's life, either directly or indirectly?

Procedures The independent variable in a published study should be evaluated not only in terms of the effects it produces in the dependent variable, but also in terms of its social acceptance, complexity, practicality, and cost. Regardless of their possible effectiveness, treatment variables that are unacceptable or undesirable to practitioners, parents, and/or subjects are not likely to contribute to a technology of behavior change because they will not be used (and in the case of unethical procedures, should not be used). The same can be said of independent variables that are extremely complex and thus difficult to learn, teach, and apply. Similarly, treatment procedures that require large amounts of time and/or money to implement are less socially valid than procedures that can be more quickly and/or inexpensively applied.

Results Even though a behavior change is clearly visible on a graphic display, it may not represent a socially valid improvement for the subject and/or significant others in the subject's environment. In evaluating the results of an applied behavior analysis study, the reader should ask questions such as these: Is the subject (or significant others) better off now that the behavior has changed? Will this new level of performance result in increased reinforce-

ment for the subject now or in the future? In some instances it is relevant to ask whether the subject (or significant others) believe that his behavior has improved (Wolf, 1978).

Generality Issues

Evaluating the generality of the results obtained in an applied behavior analysis experiment entails assessment of two types of generality: the external validity of the study to other subjects, settings, and behaviors and the maintenance and generality of the behavior change effected in the experimental subjects.

External Validity As was shown earlier in this chapter, assessment of the generality of the findings of a given experiment to other subjects, settings, and behaviors cannot be based solely on inherent aspects of the study itself. The generality of a functional relation can be established only through the active process of systematic replication. Therefore, the reader of an applied behavior analysis study must compare the study's results with those of other published research with which it shares relevant features. The authors of a published report identify in the paper's introduction the experiments that they believe are most relevant. To make an effective judgment of the external validity of the data from a given study, the reader must often locate in the literature and compare the results of those studies and the current experiment.

Even though external validity should not be considered a characteristic of a study per se (Birnbrauer, 1981), various features of an experiment suggest to the reader an expected, or likely, level of generality for the results. For example, an experiment that demonstrated a functional relation of similar form and degree with many subjects of different ages and backgrounds would indicate a high probability of generality to different subjects. Similarly, if the experiment was conducted in various settings and a number of different people administered the independent variable, additional confidence in the external validity of the results is warranted.

Maintenance and Generality of Behavior Change Improvements in behavior are most beneficial when they are long-lasting, appear in other appropriate environments, and spill over to other related behaviors. Producing these kinds of effects is a major goal of applied behavior analysis. (Chapter 27 is devoted to an examination of strategies designed to facilitate the maintenance and generality of behavior change.) Consumers of applied behavior analysis research should consider the maintenance and generality of behavior change in their evaluation of a study. An impressive behavior change that does not last or is limited to a specialized training setting may not be a socially significant behavior change. Do the experimenters at least report the results of assessment of maintenance and generality through follow-up observations and measurement in nontraining environments? Better yet, if maintenance and/or generality are not evident in such follow-up observations, do the experimenters modify their design and implement procedures in an attempt to produce and analyze the occurrence of maintenance and/or generality? Additionally, the reader should ask whether response generality—the improvement in other related behaviors as a function of change in the target behavior(s)—is an appropriate concern in a given study. If so, do the experimenters attempt to assess, analyze, or discuss this phenomenon?

Scientific Significance

A published experiment should also be evaluated in terms of its scientific merit. It is possible for a study to clearly demonstrate a functional relationship between the independent variable and a socially important target behavior and thus be judged significant from an applied perspective yet contribute little to the advancement of the field. Evaluation of

scientific significance takes into consideration such things as the authors' technological description of the experiment as well as their interpretation of the results. Are the procedures described in sufficient detail so that at least the unique aspects of the study can be replicated?[3]

Readers should question the level of conceptual integrity displayed in an experimental report. Have the authors respected the difference between basic principles of behavior and applied techniques? Does the literature review reveal a careful integration of the study with previous research? Does the literature review provide sufficient justification for the study's research questions? Are the authors' conclusions based on the data obtained in the study? Do the authors speculate beyond the data without making it clear that they are doing so? Does the study provide clear direction for additional research to further analyze the problem studied? Is the study important for reasons other than the results actually obtained? For example, an experiment can contribute to the advancement of the field by demonstrating a new measurement technique, investigating a new dependent or independent variable, or incorporating a novel tactic for controlling confounding variables.

Numerous criteria are involved in evaluating the "goodness" of a published study in applied behavior analysis. Although all are important on one level or another, it is unlikely that any one experiment will meet all of the criteria. And, in fact, it is unnecessary for an experiment to do so in order to be considered good. Nevertheless, the incorporation of as many of these considerations as possible facilitates both the social significance and the scientific progress of applied behavior analysis.

---

[3]Ideally, published procedural descriptions should be sufficiently detailed for an experienced investigator to replicate the study. Unfortunately, space limitations of most journals prohibit such detail. The common and recommended practice in replicating the published research of others is to request complete experimental protocols from the original experimenter(s).

SUMMARY

Planning Research in Applied Behavior Analysis

1 Experiments that demonstrate a clear functional relationship are said to have a high degree of internal validity.

2 The strength of an experimental design must be judged along two lines: the extent to which the design demonstrates a reliable effect and the extent to which the design effectively reduces the plausibility of other explanations for the behavior change.

3 To investigate the research questions of interest, an experimenter is often required to build an experimental design that employs a combination of analytic tactics.

4 It is quite possible that the average performance of subjects in an experimental group will improve while the performance of some subjects will stay the same and the performance of others will deteriorate.

5 In order for a treatment variable to be useful to the applied behavior analyst, the variables responsible for one subject's improvement and another's lack of improvement must be discovered.

6 Attempting to cancel out variability through statistical manipulation neither eliminates its presence in the data nor controls the function of the variables responsible for it.

7 Attributing the effects of unknown or uncontrolled variables in an experiment to the role of chance serves only to remove the researcher even further from identification and analysis of important variables.

8 One of the greatest strengths of single-subject experimental designs is the convincing demonstration of a functional relationship made possible by replication within the design itself.

Internal Validity: Controlling Potential Sources of Confounding

9 The phrase "control of behavior" is technically inaccurate because the experimenter really controls some aspect of the subject's environment.

10 In the science of behavior, the quest for and use of steady state responding is the primary means of both attaining and assessing experimental control.

11 Confounding variables can be viewed as related primarily to one of four elements of an experiment: subject, setting, measurement of the dependent variable, and independent variable.

External Validity: The Role of Replication

12 External validity refers to the degree to which a functional relationship found reliable and valid in a given experiment is considered meaningful under other conditions.

13 External validity is not an all-or-nothing property, but a matter of degree.

14 Demonstrating a functional relation with various subjects in different settings is the way applied behavior analysts pursue the problem of external validity.

15 The proper inferences that can be made from a group-design study are from the sample to the population, not from the sample to the individual.

16 From the standpoint of the science of behavior, there is nothing in the results of a group-design experiment that can have external validity; there is nothing to generalize because the group-design experiment does not demonstrate a functional relationship between the behavior of an individual and some aspect(s) of the environment.

17 The extent to which the group-design/statistical-inference model has directly contributed to an effective technology of behavior change is highly questionable.

18 The generality of research findings in applied behavior analysis can be assessed, established, and specified only through the replication of experiments.

19 In a direct replication the researcher makes every effort to duplicate exactly the conditions of an earlier experiment.

20 In a systematic replication the researcher purposefully and systematically varies the conditions of an earlier experiment.

21 Systematic replications occur in both planned and unplanned ways through the work of many experimenters in a given area, and they result in a body of knowledge with significant scientific integrity and technological value.

Evaluating Research in Applied Behavior Analysis

22 A substantial number of requirements for good applied behavior analysis have been specified. They fall in four areas that should be assessed: functional relationship issues, social validity, generality issues, and scientific significance.

PART FOUR

Increasing Existing Behavior

In chapter 11, "Operant Reinforcement," we describe the roles of genetic inheritance and environment with respect to behavior. Also, we elaborate on the principle of reinforcement as the primary way by which behavior is increased. The chapter addresses two reinforcement operations as well as the types and selection of reinforcers. Influencing factors and guidelines for using reinforcement successfully are also detailed.

Chapter 12 describes the environmental arrangements between behavior and reinforcement. It addresses the rules that describe the relationship between reinforcement and the future probability of behavior.

10:10

chap 11
12
17 378-86
18
14 328-333
13 299-303
318-323
15 339-341

1

...nforcement

KEY TERMS

History of reinforcement

Operant reinforcement

Automaticity

Positive reinforcement

Positive reinforcer

Differential reinforcement

Negative reinforcement

Negative reinforcer

Escape

Avoidance

Primary/unconditioned reinforcer

Secondary/conditioned reinforcer

Tangible reinforcer

Activity reinforcer

Social reinforcer

Generalized reinforcer

Satiation

Reinforcer sampling

Premack Principle

This chapter was written by Timothy E. Heron.

Prior to a comprehensive discussion of operant reinforcement, several terms introduced in chapter 2 need to be examined in more detail. Terms such as *stimulus, behavior,* and *response* were defined for both respondent and operant conditioning, and we indicated that respondent (reflexive) behavior comprises only a small portion of an individual's total behavioral repertoire. On the other hand, we indicated that operant behavior accounts for a significant portion of an individual's behavioral repertoire. This chapter expands our description of operant reinforcement. The chapter begins with a discussion of the role of genetic inheritance and then focuses on how operant reinforcement is defined and used in clinical, therapeutic, and educational programs.

THE ROLE OF GENETIC INHERITANCE

All living organisms inherit biological characteristics through natural selection. Natural selection is the process by which an organism, through genetic mutation, develops and transmits features that increase its chances of survival. Humans do not inherit specific operant behaviors through genetic transmission. What they seem to inherit is the capacity to learn new behavior. As Skinner (1981) states,

Human behavior is a joint product of (i) the contingencies of survival responsible for the natural selection of the species and (ii) the contingencies of reinforcement responsible for the repertoires acquired by its members, including (iii) the special contingencies maintained by an evolved social environment. (Ultimately, of course, it is all a matter of natural selection, since operant conditioning is an evolved process, of which cultural practices are special applications.) (p. 502)

An individual's behavior develops and becomes more complex because of his repeated experiences and interactions with the environment. But the role of genetic endowment is not ignored by the applied behavior analyst. Skinner (1974) clarifies the relative contribution of genetic endowment and environmental experience.

A person is first of all an organism, a member of a species and a subspecies, possessing a genetic endowment of anatomical and physiological characteristics, which are the product of the contingencies of survival to which the species has been exposed in the process of evolution. The organism becomes a person as it acquires a repertoire of behavior under the contingencies of reinforcement to which it is exposed during its lifetime. The behavior it exhibits at any moment is under the control of a current setting. It is able to acquire such a repertoire under such control because of processes of conditioning which are also part of its genetic endowment. (p. 207)

The genetic endowment acquired by humans that contributes to operant conditioning is the capacity to be reinforced (or punished) by certain events in the current setting. According to Malott, Tillema, and Glenn (1978), humans are endowed with a biological capacity that causes some stimuli to be rewarding or punishing. This capacity evolved because organisms whose behaviors were strengtheneded or weakened by certain stimuli survived.

From a behavioral standpoint each person acts on her environment and, in turn, is altered by the effects of that behavior on the environment (Ferster, Culbertson, & Boren, 1975). Each successive response performed under certain stimulus conditions (e.g., the deprivation state of the individual, the discriminative stimuli present), together with the consequences of the behavior, produces a cumulative set of experiences that are referred to as a **history of reinforcement.** It is a person's genetic endowment and history of reinforcement that determine whether a response is likely to be emitted under any given stimulus condition. The genetic endowment of a living person cannot be altered, but environmental settings can be changed so that behaviors that are—or can be—emitted are followed by stimuli that are likely to increase the behavior in the future.

Parents, teachers, educators, and clinicians are charged with increasing the behavioral repertoire of other individuals. The commitment of applied behavior analysts is to set the occasion for individuals to come into contact with contingencies of reinforcement so that appropriate behavior is increased and inappropriate or nonfunctional behavior is decreased.

DEFINITION OF OPERANT REINFORCEMENT

As defined in chapter 2, **operant reinforcement** is said to have occurred when a behavior is followed immediately by the presentation of some stimulus and, as a result, occurs more often in the future. Operant reinforcement strengthens a response class of behaviors, not just a single behavior.[1] A response class is a set of behaviors related by their functional similarity.

To illustrate the concept of a response class, we might consider the typing behavior of a high school business education student. The downward movement of the keys produces changes in the environment in the form of letters on paper. A single key stroke is part of a response class of key stroking behaviors. The student could hit the key slightly off center, with varying degrees of pressure, or with one finger in a hunt-and-peck method. Even though these behaviors have different topographies, they belong to the same response class because they are functionally equivalent (i.e., they each produce the same effect on the environment).

The relationship between the key stroke and the paper defines the operant (Ferster et al., 1975). In effect, operant reinforcement increases the future likelihood of behavior within a response class, the members of which

must share at least one common characteristic. Skinner (1953) says it succinctly:

> It is not correct to say the operant reinforcement "strengthens the response which precedes it." The response has already occurred and cannot be changed. What is changed is the future probability of responses in the same class. It is the operant as a class of behavior, rather than the response as a particular instance, which is conditioned. (p. 87)

For the business education student any key stroke that produces legible characters on the paper—regardless of finger location or angle on the key itself—will increase in the future. Downward movements of insufficient force or other extraneous finger movements that do not produce marks on the paper will not be strengthened. Thus, the defining characteristic of operant reinforcement can be summarized as follows: a behavior is emitted in the presence of a particular stimulus, the behavior is followed by an event (i.e., a reinforcing stimulus), and the future probability of the behavior increases because the response had this consequence, and not for any other reason (Catania, 1984). Operant reinforcement provides the foundation for applied behavior analysis.

Another key concept related to operant reinforcement is **automaticity.** According to Michael (1970), automaticity means that

> consequences affect behavior in an automatic or mechanistic way. It is not necessary that the learner be able to verbalize about the relation between his behavior and the consequence, or even verbalize that the consequence has occurred. (p. 30)

The individual does not necessarily have to understand that a given behavior is being reinforced or even verbally agree that it is a behavior that should be reinforced. Consequences that follow behaviors contingently affect the future probability of those behaviors under similar stimulus conditions.

In his autobiography, *A Matter of Consequences,* Skinner (1983) provides an interesting example of how reinforcement produces

---

[1]Hereafter, for economy of presentation, we will use the shorter "future probability of behavior" to mean the "future probability of a class of behavior." We recognize that positive reinforcement increases the likelihood of a class of behavior.

an increase in the future occurrence of behavior. He writes of an incident that occurred at a meeting of scholars convened to discuss the role of intention in defining political activity. At one point in the meeting Erich Fromm, one of the guest speakers, said that people were not pigeons. Skinner recounts what happened next.

> I decided that something had to be done. On a scrap of paper I wrote, "Watch Fromm's left hand. I am going to shape [reinforce by successive approximations] a chopping motion" and passed it down the table to Halleck [a member of the group]. Fromm was sitting directly across the table and speaking mainly to me. I turned my chair slightly so that I could see him out of the corner of my eye. He gesticulated a great deal as he talked, and whenever his left hand came up, I looked straight at him. If he brought the hand down, I nodded and smiled. Within five minutes he was chopping the air so vigorously that his wristwatch kept slipping out over his hand. (pp. 150–151)

POSITIVE REINFORCEMENT

Positive reinforcement is the most widely applied principle of behavior; it is one of the cornerstones upon which applied behavior analysts have built the technology of behavior change. Positive reinforcement has been used successfully alone or in combination with other procedures in numerous training and development programs across a wide range of populations, settings, and behaviors (Witt & Adams, 1980; Matson, 1980; Geller, Winett, & Everett, 1982; Sindelar, Honsaker, & Jenkins, 1982; Parker, Cataldo, Bourland, Emurian, Corbin, & Page, 1984; Haring, 1985).

Positive reinforcement, or reinforcement, can be defined as an operation or as a process. As an operation reinforcement refers to the occurrence of a consequence subsequent to a behavior. As a process reinforcement refers to the increase in responding as a function of the occurrence of the consequence (Catania, 1984). Catania recognizes the difficulty of having a term defined in dichotomous ways. His solu-

tion to the problem is to state that the term *reinforcement* is descriptive, not explanatory. According to Catania (1984) three conditions are necessary for reinforcement.

> First, a response must have some consequence. Second, the response must increase in probability (i.e., the response must be more probable than when it does not have this consequence). Third, the increase in probability must occur *because* the response has this consequence, and not for some other reason. For example, if we only knew that a response had become more probable, it would not be appropriate to say that the response must have been reinforced; the response might have been elicited by a stimulus. It would not even be sufficient that the response was now producing some stimulus it had not been producing before. We would still have to know whether responding increased *because* the stimulus was its consequence. (p. 64)

The stimulus, or event, that follows the behavior and is administered contingently is termed the **positive reinforcer.** If a teacher said, "Very good!" immediately after a student completed a math assignment and if her statement alone increased math assignment completion in the future, then her statement would be a positive reinforcer. However, the presentation of that statement in the presence of a student completing a problem is positive reinforcement only if the future occurrence of problem completion increases.

How is the practitioner to know whether a stimulus that seemingly serves as a positive reinforcer (i.e., the behavior increases in the future) is instead an evoking or discriminative stimulus? According to Higgins and Morris (1985) there are at least three control procedures that allow this important determination.

Control Procedures

Response-Dependent Response-Independent A response-dependent response-independent procedure compares the future rates of responses when the controlling stimulus is presented response dependently (i.e., contingently) as well as response independently (i.e., noncontingently). According to Higgins and Morris (1985), "If response-dependent presentations maintain higher response rates than response-independent presentations, then an inference may be made that reinforcement has been demonstrated." (p. 84)

Schedule Control In a schedule control procedure the practitioner compares the effects of a known reinforcer with the effects of the suspected reinforcer. If the presentations of the latter produce similar response patterns to those of the former (cf. Ferster & Skinner, 1957, for a description of these patterns), then a reinforcement process can be inferred.

Multiple Procedures In a multiple procedures design counter controls are initiated to rule out alternative explanations. Specifically, a series of changes occur in the presentation of the stimulus. For example, if a practitioner wanted to determine whether the verbal statement "Very good" was a reinforcer, the first step might be to determine whether the response-dependent (contingent) presentation of this statement increased behavior. Then, response rates might be compared to those in a response-independent (noncontingent) condition. Third, "Very good" might be paired with a smile. If responding eventually ceased in a smile-only condition, it would demonstrate that the smile alone was insufficient to maintain the response. Finally, a differential reinforcement procedure might be initiated whereby responses under one condition produced the reinforcer but responses under another condition did not. These conditions could then be reversed. If the future probability of the behavior changed in accordance with the switch in differential reinforcement, it could be inferred that the stimulus acted as a reinforcer.

In sum, the point of these procedures is to define precisely those conditions that constitute reinforcement and those that do not. For applied researchers accuracy is essential. Otherwise, any statement regarding the relationship between an antecedent, behavior, and consequence is suspect. Table 11.1 shows how the terms *reinforcer, reinforcing, reinforcement,* and *to reinforce* can be defined. According to Catania (1984), these descriptions apply only when the conditions of the definition are met.

Figure 11.1 shows a schematic diagram of positive reinforcement and displays the three-term contingency described in chapter 2. In our earlier example the stimulus that set the occasion for the response (S^D) was the presence of the math assignment, the response (R) was the student's behavior (i.e., writing the answers), and the positive reinforcer (S^{R+}) was the teacher's verbal praise.

According to Morse and Kelleher (1977) it is often incorrectly presumed that the presentation of a positive event or stimulus serves to increase behavior. Whether a stimulus is described as "positive," "desirable," "appetitive," or "good" has nothing to do with its effectiveness as a reinforcer. A positive reinforcer is determined only by function: if a behavior is more likely to occur as a result of the presentation of the stimulus alone, then by definition that stimulus or event is a positive reinforcer.

A final point regarding positive reinforcement is that it is not an intentional process. Merely intending to reinforce a particular behavior does not mean that only that behavior will be reinforced. In fact, all behaviors occurring at the time of reinforcement will be likely to recur more often in the future.

Advantages of Positive Reinforcement

The obvious advantage of positive reinforcement is that it can be used to increase the future probability of a wide range of behaviors. It can be used to produce new behaviors (see chapter 14), or it can be used to refine the topography, frequency, or duration of existing behaviors. The latter procedure is termed **differential reinforcement** because the reinforcer is applied to one member of a response class of behavior and not to other members. The member of the class of behavior to which the reinforcer is applied increases, whereas

TABLE 11.1 The vocabulary of reinforcement. This vocabulary[a] is appropriate if and only if three conditions exist: (1) a response produces some consequence; (2) that response occurs more often than when it does not produce the consequence; and (3) the increased responding occurs *because* the response has the consequence.

Term	Restrictions	Examples
reinforcer (noun)	A stimulus.	Food pellets were used as reinforcers for the rat's lever presses.
reinforcing (adjective)	A property of a stimulus.	The reinforcing stimulus was produced more often than the other, nonreinforcing stimuli.
reinforcement (noun)	As an operation, the delivery of a consequence when a response occurs.	The fixed-ratio schedule of reinforcement arranged food deliveries after every tenth key peck.
	As a process, the increase in responding that results from the reinforcement operation.	The experiment with monkeys demonstrated reinforcement produced by social consequences.
to reinforce (verb)	As an operation, to deliver a consequence when a response occurs; responses are reinforced and not organisms.	When a period of free play was used to reinforce the child's completion of class assignments, the child's grades improved.
	As a process, to increase responding through the reinforcement operation.	The experiment was designed to find out whether gold stars would reinforce cooperative play among first-graders.

[a]A parallel vocabulary is appropriate to punishment (including *punisher* as a stimulus and *punish* as a verb), with the difference that a punishing consequence makes responding occur less rather than more often.
SOURCE: From *Learning* (2nd ed., p. 63) by A. C. Catania, 1984, Englewood Cliffs, NJ: Prentice-Hall. Copyright 1984 by Prentice-Hall. Reprinted by permission.

members not reinforced decrease in probability. Positive reinforcement can be delivered verbally (Hall & Hall, 1980), monetarily (Stitzer & Bigelow, 1984), with points or tokens (Carden Smith & Fowler, 1984) or as part of overall training package (Bryant & Budd, 1984. Additionally, positive reinforcement can be delivered in the form of activities, privileges, or tangible reinforcers (Hall & Hall, 1980).

NEGATIVE REINFORCEMENT

Negative reinforcement has erroneously been thought of as a punishment procedure or a highly aversive reductive procedure when, in fact, it is a procedure for increasing operant behavior. Negative reinforcement is the reduction or termination of an ongoing stimulus, contingent upon a response that results in the increased likelihood of the behavior occurring again under similar stimulus conditions (Skinner, 1953). According to Ferster, Culbertson, and Boren (1975) "the negative reinforcement procedure is called negative only in the sense that the behavior removes a stimulus rather than producing one" (p. 155). The stimulus that is removed is termed the **negative reinforcer.** Closing a window on a cold day, adjusting the flow of hot water in the shower, removing a pair of tight shoes, turning down the television volume are all instances of re-

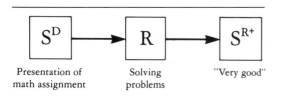

FIGURE 11.1 Schematic diagram of positive reinforcement.

sponses occurring because of past negative reinforcement; the stimulus (e.g., cold air, hot water, pain, noise) is removed contingent upon a response. The result is an increased probability that under similar stimulus conditions in the future, the behavior will occur again. "A negative reinforcer strengthens any behavior that reduces or terminates it" (Skinner, 1974, p. 46).

The distinction between positive and negative reinforcement is not always clear. For instance, in a hot cafeteria the cook might open a window each time the heat reaches a certain temperature. If the window-opening response is not due to any antecedent or discriminative stimulus and if opening the window removes heat, we could consider it negative reinforcement. However, if we say that opening the window presents cooler air to the cafeteria, we could consider that positive reinforcement. It is difficult at times to determine whether reinforcement has been positive or negative. The reader is referred to Michael (1975) for a detailed discussion of this topic.

Contingencies Related to Negative Reinforcement

Escape **Escape** terminates an existing stimulus. A frequent episode in classrooms shows how escape operates. A teacher might be faced with a situation in which two students are name calling loudly in class, and the name calling persists for several minutes. The teacher might tell the students to stop the bickering, and they might do so momentarily. At this point the teacher has been negatively reinforced because his response (telling the students to

stop bickering) terminated the stimulus (the bickering).[2] He escaped the stimulus, making it more likely that he will verbally reprimand the students again the next time they bicker. Figure 11.2 shows a schematic illustration of the escape cited in this example.

Avoidance **Avoidance** occurs when a response avoids, rather than terminates, a stimulus. A student might follow a teacher's verbal directions to avoid having to go to the principal's office. Another student might sit in the back of the bus to avoid being teased by his classmates. A child might walk through a novelty shop with her hands in her pockets to avoid having her mother tell her not to touch things on the shelves. In each case the individual's response avoided the experience of the stimulus.

Escape and avoidance conditioning can be programmed together to produce a desirable outcome. Hansen (1979) used escape and avoidance training in separate investigations to establish enuresis control with two preadolescent children in home settings. Essentially, the procedure relied on a dual-signal device connected to each child's bed but located approximately 4 feet from it. The first signal, at 70 decibels, was activated if the children urinated in the bed. The second signal, at 95 decibels, was activated 7 seconds after the first signal if the children did not switch off the first signal within that time period. At the sound of the first tone, the children were to get out of bed, turn off the signaling unit, go to the bathroom, and put on clean pajamas. The parents had been instructed to go to the child's room, reset the signaling unit, put clean sheets on the bed, and record the occurrence. Although the cumulative number of bedwetting episodes decreased over the course of the 200-day study, the escape and avoidance contingencies explain the increases in the children's getting out of bed to turn off the signaling device. Escape

[2]If the students continue to bicker in the future, the teacher's statement or attention may have served as positive reinforcement for them.

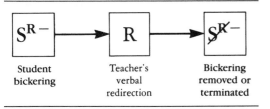

FIGURE 11.2 Schematic diagram of escape.

and avoidance were an integral part of the program: the children's responses within 7 seconds of the first signal terminated the first stimulus (escape) and avoided the sound of the second signal.

Advantages and Disadvantages of Negative Reinforcement

Negative reinforcement shares many of the advantages of positive reinforcement. Foremost is that it can be used to increase the future probability of behavior. However, because the use of negative reinforcement requires a prior worsening of the environment (i.e., stimulus must be present in order to terminate it), negative reinforcement has two disadvantages. First, it is possible that if negative reinforcement is used too often, individuals will simply avoid situations or settings in which "aversive" stimuli are present. Second, aggressive or emotional operants might be directed at the source of the aversive stimulus (e.g., teachers or parents). Either of these undesirable aspects of negative reinforcement can be minimized by using negative reinforcement procedures in combination with positive approaches (e.g., differential reinforcement of other behavior, differential reinforcement of incompatible behavior).

TYPES OF POTENTIAL REINFORCERS

Figure 11.3 shows a schematic diagram of the two major types of reinforcers as well as their associated subcategories.

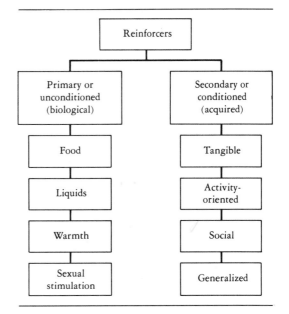

FIGURE 11.3 Types of potential reinforcers.

Primary Reinforcers

Primary or **unconditioned** (unlearned) **reinforcers** are stimuli or events that, by virtue of their biological importance, serve as consequences to increase the probability of behaviors immediately preceding them. Food, water, oxygen, warmth, and sexual stimulation are examples of stimuli that do not have to undergo a conditioning process to serve as positive reinforcers. In a state of deprivation, they reinforce behavior automatically. They are also automatic in the sense that the individual does not have to be aware that the stimulus is a reinforcer.

Primary reinforcers have been used successfully and extensively in applied settings to modify a host of behaviors (see *Journal of Applied Behavior Analysis*, 1968–1985). Wilson, Reid, Phillips, and Burgio (1984) used a contingent snack—a small morsel of food—along with praise, instruction, and modeling to reinforce completion of successive training steps in a family-style dining program. Four adults with developmental disabilities were taught

30 separate steps with premeal, meal, and postmeal components. Although the relative contribution of the snacks in this study was not determined, the overall program proved to be effective, and the authors reported no detrimental weight gain or increase in eating behaviors.

Riordan, Iwata, Finney, Wohl, and Stanley (1984) used "highly preferred food items" as reinforcers to increase the food intake of four inpatient children at a hospital treatment facility. The four children had a history of chronic food refusal. The treatment program consisted of dispensing the high preference food items (e.g. cereal, yogurt, canned fruit, ice cream) contingent upon the consumption of a target food item (e.g., vegetables, bread, eggs). Target food items varied from child to child. Results showed that for three of the four students the contingency was effective: food intake for low preference items increased. For the fourth child the contingency was only mildly effective.

Secondary Reinforcers

Secondary or **conditioned** (learned) **reinforcers** can be defined as those initially neutral stimuli that have acquired reinforcing capability because of being paired with primary reinforcers or established secondary reinforcers. For example, after being repeatedly paired with food when food is delivered as a reinforcer, praise will acquire the reinforcing capability of that food (cf. Skinner, 1953). However, other stimuli present at the time reinforcement occurs can also become conditioned reinforcers. A sound, a color, an odor— any stimulus—can become a conditioned reinforcer by being paired with primary or established reinforcers. In addition, when a behavior is linked to other behaviors (e.g., during chaining, as described in chapter 15), each change in the environment serves as a conditioned reinforcer for the previous step in the chain. There are at least four subcategories of secondary reinforcers identified in the literature.

Tangible Reinforcers A **tangible reinforcer** is an object or activity that increases the future probability of a behavior when the reinforcer is presented subsequent to the emission of that behavior. Trinkets, pins, emblems, marbles, and toys serve as examples of potential tangible reinforcers. Stokes and Kennedy (1980) used a tangible reinforcer along with observation to reinforce cooperative behavior in children receiving dental treatment. The tangible reinforcer was a small dental capsule, individually colored for each child in the study. Delivery of the reinforcer was contingent upon cooperative behavior in the dental chair. The observation component had each child view another child's treatment.

The results of this multiple baseline analysis indicated that the tangible reinforcer and observation reduced the children's uncooperative behavior during dental treatment. Since a component analysis was not performed, it is not possible to say whether the tangible reinforcer or the observation component was the determining factor in the success of the program. According to the anecdotal comments of the children, both treatments were important.

Activity-Oriented Reinforcers An **activity reinforcer** is an event or privilege such as helping the teacher, playing a game, going to the movies, or having lunch with parents. According to Hall and Hall (1980) activity reinforcers can be used in situations where it is inappropriate or impossible to use edibles or tangibles or where the cost of the reinforcement program might be an issue. Many activity reinforcers (e.g., going to the library, visiting friends, attending a recreation center) do not have a cost associated with them.

Pierce and Risley (1974) used recreation activities as a reinforcer for increasing membership and decreasing adolescent disruptions at an urban-based recreation center. During one phase of the study, individuals earned additional recreational time at the community center contingent upon their bringing new members to the center. In this case the center remained open beyond its normal hours. In the second part of the study, incremental units of recreational time were lost when incidences of disruptive behavior were observed. In this case the center closed prior to its scheduled closing time. Minor disruptions (littering the floor) resulted in a 1-minute loss of recreation time. Major disruptions (destroying property) resulted in a 15-minute loss of time. The results of both phases of the study indicated that contingent access to recreational facilities can be used successfully as an activity reinforcer for adolescents in an urban center.

Social Reinforcers **Social reinforcers** can be of three varieties. They can be physical contacts (e.g., hugs, kisses), proximity (i.e., standing or sitting near an individual), or verbal statements (e.g., "Very good"). Verbal statements can be further subdivided into statements of affirmation or information. An example of an affirmative praise statement is "Sue, that is the correct answer." An informational praise statement describes the specific behavior that prompted the praise: "Rich, your lower case letters touched the line as they should." Whereas affirmative verbal praise statements are general in nature, informational verbal praise statements describe a specific behavior.

Even though many studies have used social praise to increase behavior, the classic study continues to be the one conducted by Hall, Lund, and Jackson, 1968. In this study the effects of contingent attention on study behavior were investigated with elementary-aged children. Teachers were initially cued by a classroom observer when students engaged in study or nonstudy behavior. When students engaged in study behavior, the teacher either patted them on the back (physical contact), approached their desk (proximity), or verbally praised them (social praise). Nonstudy behavior was ignored. The results show that when contingent attention was in effect, study behavior increased significantly; when it was not, study behavior decreased. Figure 11.4 shows

the results for one student who participated in the study. During baseline Ken's study behavior averaged 37%. During Reinforcement$_1$ his study behavior increased to 71%. When a reversal condition was introduced, his study behavior decreased to 37%; but when Reinforcement$_2$ was initiated, study behavior recovered to 70% of the observed intervals. The teacher also reported anecdotally that Ken completed his work more consistently and his grades for academic and social behaviors improved.

Generalized Reinforcers According to Ferster and Culbertson (1982) a **generalized reinforcer** "is a type of conditioned reinforcer the effectiveness of which does not depend upon a single kind of deprivation" (p. 371). Tokens and money serve as generalized reinforcers because they provide the individual with access to a wide range of other primary or secondary reinforcers. When tokens—symbols or objects—are delivered subsequent to a behavior, they serve as an interim reinforcer. The token is exchanged for a back-up reinforcer at a later time. A generalized reinforcer can maintain behavior over extended time periods and is less likely to lead to satiation. **Satiation** is the condition that exists when an overabundance of a reinforcer has been provided with a corresponding decrease in the future occurrence of the behavior. In short, the reinforcer has lost its reinforcing properties.

Nelson and Cone (1979) used a token economy with 16 chronic psychiatric patients as a generalized reinforcer for four classes of behavior: personal hygiene, personal management, ward work, and social skills. After defining specific behaviors within each of these classes and assigning a token value to each behavior, ward attendants delivered the token (plus social reinforcement) contingent upon the specified behavior. The tokens (colored cardboard tickets) were exchanged for beverages, personal items, cigarettes, and money that could be used during shopping trips to local stores. The results indicated that the use of the generalized reinforcer, the token, was

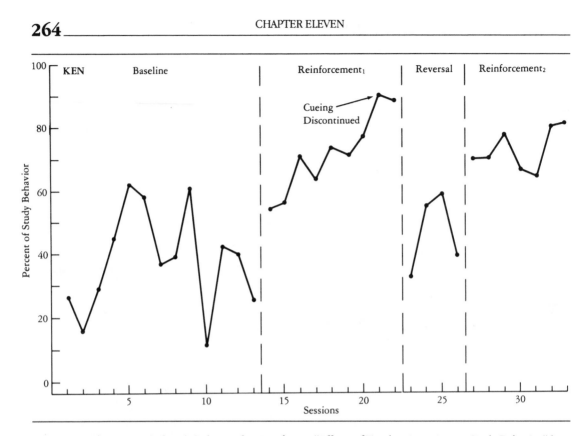

FIGURE 11.4 A record of study behavior for Ken. (From "Effects of Teacher Attention on Study Behavior" by R. V. Hall, D. Lund, and D. Jackson, 1968, *Journal of Applied Behavior Analysis, 1*(1), p. 6. Copyright 1968 by the Society for the Experimental Analysis of Behavior, Inc. Reprinted by permission.)

effective in increasing levels of the specified behaviors within the four target classes for all 16 subjects (see Figure 11.5). Chapter 24 includes a more detailed discussion of how tokens function as generalized reinforcers.

SELECTING POTENTIAL REINFORCERS

According to Hall and Hall (1980) selecting and using an appropriate reinforcer is a basic step in any behavior change program. Unless a suitable reinforcer can be identified, a behavior change program is not likely to be successful. Selection of potential reinforcers can be accomplished in a number of ways: by asking,

observing, sampling, forcing a choice, and trying and seeing.

Asking

The most basic method for determining a potential reinforcer is to ask what the individual prefers. Students, for example, might say that they like free time in class, kickball, time with the teacher, or access to computer games. Adults living in a group home might prefer going shopping, touring a city, or visiting with friends or relatives.

Although asking for an individual preference is relatively simple, the procedure is by no means foolproof. What an individual chooses as a reinforcer may not operate as one, or

FIGURE 11.5 Overall mean percentages of subjects performing personal hygiene, personal management, ward work, and social skills behaviors. (From "Multiple-Baseline Analysis of a Token Economy for Psychiatric Inpatients" by G. L. Nelson and J. D. Cone, 1979, *Journal of Applied Behavior Analysis, 12*(2), p. 268. Copyright 1979 by the Society for the Experimental Analysis of Behavior, Inc. Reprinted by permission.)

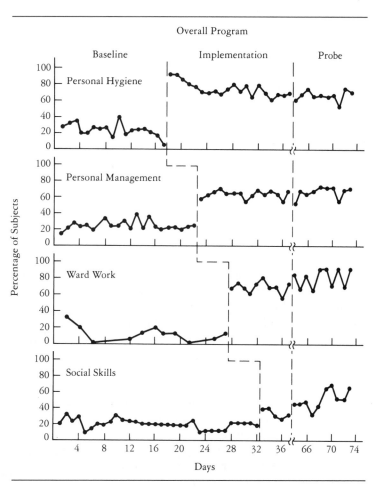

it may function as a reinforcer only under some conditions. For example, a child might say that watching television is a reinforcer, but that may be only the cartoons on Saturday mornings. A menu of reinforcers can ease the practitioner's task in selecting specific reinforcers for individuals.

Practitioners also need to be aware that what an individual identifies as a reinforcer at one time may not function as a reinforcer at another time. Reinforcer preference does change as the individual's age, interest level, and social interactions with peers change (Hall & Hall, 1980). A teacher who uses the asking method in September to determine potential reinforcers

may have to repeat the procedure several times during the year.

Observing

Watching what an individual does on a regular basis can provide a valuable source of information on what activities or events can be used as potential reinforcers. Figure 11.6 shows a weekly summary chart of Mike's after-school activities. These data were collected by observing Mike's behavior without telling him what to do during his free time. Times for scheduled activities (e.g., meals, homework) are not shown.

		M	T	W	R	F
1	Watch TV	4:30–5:00	4:30–6:00	4:30–5:00	4:30–6:00	4:30–5:00
2	Play with toys			5:45–6:00		
3	Play with friends	5:00–5:30		5:00–5:45		5:00–6:00
4	Use telephone	8:00–8:30	8:00–8:30	8:00–8:30	8:00–8:30	8:00–8:30
5	Read	8:30–9:00		8:30–9:00		

FIGURE 11.6 Mike's weekly summary chart of after-school activities.

The chart shows that Mike watched television every day after school for varying amounts of time. Also, 3 days of the week Mike socialized with his friends; he played outdoor games, rode his bike, and played ball. He called his friends on the telephone every evening, and on 2 days of the week he engaged in leisure reading. The only time he played with his toys was a brief time on Wednesday. From these data we see that two activities—watching television and talking on the telephone—occurred the most often and for the longest duration. Presumably these two activities could be considered potential reinforcers. Playing with toys could not be considered a reinforcer since it occurred only once and for just 15 minutes.

Reinforcer Sampling

In **reinforcer sampling** the individual is presented with a sample of the potential reinforcer in order to gain experience with it. The potential reinforcer is not presented contingently; the individual merely experiences it. After this brief exposure, future presentations of the reinforcer are contingent upon the desired behavior. For example, a parent might read the first few pages of an adventure story to his child. Subsequent reading of the story would be contingent upon the child's improved performance with household chores (e.g., cleaning up her room). Reinforcer sampling can also refer to providing the individual with several samples of reinforcers and noting which one(s) are preferred.

The rationale for reinforcer sampling is to give the subject an opportunity to experience an unfamiliar stimulus. If the individual then performs the behavior to earn the reinforcer, it is presumed that the stimulus was a reinforcer.

Forcing a Choice

In a forced choice approach a series of potential reinforcers are made available, and the individual selects one of them from the "menu." For instance, a teacher might present the following contingency: "Dennis, when you finish your math, you can play battleship with Sean, read quietly, or help Mrs. McNeish prepare the social studies project." This procedure for selecting a reinforcer is referred to as a forced choice approach because a limited number of options are available. If Dennis selects working with Mrs. McNeish, it is presumably because her attention is reinforcing to him.

Trying and Seeing

The only way to determine whether any potential reinforcer will actually serve as a reinforcer is to try it and see. However, it is helpful to consider several factors beforehand. Hall and Hall (1980) provide guidelines for selecting age-appropriate reinforcers: the age, interest level, and activity level of the individual should be considered. For instance, coloring would probably be more effective as a reinforcer for primary-aged children than for high school students. Also, it is helpful to try natural reinforcers whenever possible. Natural reinforcers are those that are associated with a particular time, location, or person. Watching television, going to the movies, or using computer games might be associated with specific weekday periods or settings. Extra effort or resources would not be needed for that reinforcer to be delivered.

The Premack Principle

David Premack (1959) hypothesized that reinforcers can be identified by looking at the distribution of behaviors in a free operant situation. Premack believed that behaviors themselves could be used as reinforcers and that the frequency of a response was an important factor in determining how effective a given behavior might be as a reinforcer.

The **Premack Principle,** sometimes called "Grandma's Law," states that access to high frequency behavior is contingent upon the occurrence of low frequency behavior: "You can eat your ice cream" (high frequency behavior) "when you have finished your vegetables" (low frequency behavior). The rationale for the Premack Principle is that a high frequency behavior can serve as a reinforcer for a low frequency behavior. In the example in Figure 11.6, if Mike's parents wanted to use the Premack Principle to increase the frequency of Mike's reading, they might make watching television (a high frequency behavior) contingent upon more frequent reading (a low frequency behavior). Mike's parents might initiate a contingency whereby reading for at least 30 minutes could earn the opportunity to watch TV until bedtime.

Allen and Iwata (1980) used the Premack Principle in a dependent-group contingency (see chapter 25) with 10 mentally retarded adults. In their study, game participation (the high frequency behavior) was made contingent upon exercise completion (the low frequency behavior). The group contingency stated that all the adults had to complete 5 physical exercises before any of them could engage in a game. Figure 11.7 shows the mean percentage of participation for the 10 adults in exercise and game activities; it also shows the session length for exercise. The data suggest that when the Premack contingency was in effect, the mean percentage of exercise increased, the duration of the exercise session decreased, and the mean percentage of game participation remained unchanged. According to Allen and Iwata (1980) the data suggest that the high frequency games were an effective reinforcer for increasing and maintaining the low frequency exercise activity in these adults.

FACTORS INFLUENCING THE EFFECTIVENESS OF REINFORCEMENT

There are at least four sets of variables that affect reinforcement: genetic factors, an individual's history of reinforcement, the current environment, and the deprivation state of the individual. To date, it has not been possible to alter the genetic endowment of individuals; the other three sets of variables can be manipulated to varying degrees.

History of Reinforcement

A person's history of reinforcement refers to the frequency, intensity, and/or duration with which particular responses have been reinforced in the presence of particular stimulus conditions. Each person's history of reinforcement is a cumulative set of experiences and is unique to that person. No two persons have

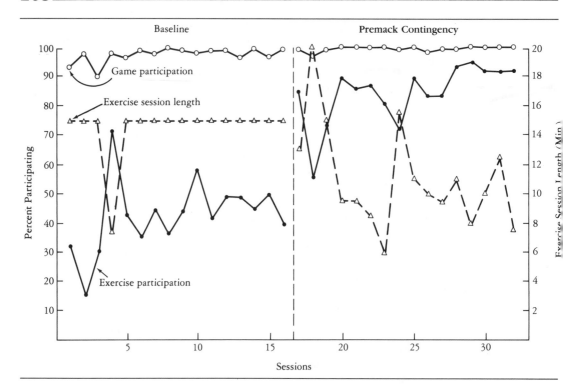

FIGURE 11.7 Daily mean percentage (N = 10) of participation in exercises and games and the exercise session length during baseline and group contingency phases. Participation is scaled on the left ordinate, and exercise session length on the right ordinate. (From L. D. Allen and B. A. Iwata, "Reinforcing Exercise Maintenance: Using Existing High-Rate Activities," *Behavior Modification,* Vol. 4, No. 3 (July, 1980), p. 345. Copyright © 1980 by Sage Publications. Reprinted by permission of Sage Publications, Inc.)

identical histories of reinforcement because no two persons have exactly the same experiences.

A person's history of reinforcement is determined by the schedule of reinforcement for particular responses. Responses that have received continuous reinforcement—each occurrence of the behavior producing reinforcement—are more likely to occur again in the future. On an extinction schedule, where no response produces a reinforcer, future responses are less likely.

How can a person's history of reinforcement be changed? The answer can be seen in an example. If an infant in the presence of any male says, "Girl," and her response produces smiles, laughs, or attention (i.e., reinforcement), then saying "Girl" will soon become a well-established response in the child's repertoire. Can the child's past conditioning with this sequence be changed, or are there other factors that make it impossible to alter the behavior? One way to assess experimentally how the child's past conditioning produces current behavior is to set up a contingency whereby saying "Girl" in the presence of any male does not produce reinforcement and a concurrent contingency whereby saying "Girl" in the presence of any female does produce reinforcement. Through repeated presentations and differential reinforcement of the two situations, the presence of females should set the occasion for saying "Girl," whereas the presence of males should not. If the child's behavior changes, then it would have been demonstrated that responses emitted in the past under particular stimulus conditions can be altered by rearranging the contingencies that produce the reinforcer.

The point here is that a person's past behavior cannot be changed. As soon as a response has been made, it is completed. But current and future responses are amenable to rearrangement using reinforcement. The occasion can be set for a behavior to occur under a specific stimulus condition; then the behavior can be reinforced in the presence of that stimulus condition, but not in its absence.

Current Environment

At least six factors in the current environment influence the effectiveness of reinforcement: timing, consistency, amount, quality, schedule, and novelty.

Timing The timing of reinforcement exists on a continuum: from immediate to delayed. As a general rule, immediate reinforcement is necessary if a behavior is to be increased or maintained (Tarpy & Swabini, 1974; Crow & Mayhew, 1976).

> Delayed reinforcement is not as effective as immediate reinforcement, partially because it allows the organism to emit additional behavior between the response we wish to reinforce and the actual occurrence of the reinforcer. Thus, the intervening behavior is also reinforced, with the result that what is reinforced is the response followed by some other behavior rather than just the response alone. (Reynolds, 1968, p. 29)

Still, delayed reinforcement can be programmed appropriately in applied settings. Mayhew and Anderson (1980) demonstrated that delayed reinforcement was effective in producing higher levels of appropriate behavior in two mentally retarded adults. Essentially,

the procedure involved videotaping the two adults during a classroom session to obtain baseline levels of appropriate work-related behavior (i.e., on-task). Then during delayed reinforcement each adult viewed a 15-minute videotape of the work session just completed. A variable interval schedule of reinforcement was initiated whereby the adults' appropriate behavior on the videotape was reinforced with a token on an average of every 30 seconds (VI 30). These behaviors were reinforced only during the viewing session. Tokens were exchanged at the end of the session for edible reinforcers.

The results of the study showed increased levels of work-related behavior. Also, when the delayed reinforcement condition was reinstituted, even higher levels of performance were noted, indicating that the adults were learning to respond under delayed contingencies. Finally, during phases in the study when extinction was introduced, response maintenance was still achieved.

The practical benefits of using delayed reinforcement with developmentally disabled populations are readily apparent. Although a delayed reinforcement procedure would not be an effective way to establish behavior (Fowler & Baer, 1981), it can be an effective approach to maintain behavior across time and/or settings. In some cases delayed reinforcement might foster generalization to other responses (Baer, Williams, Osnes, & Stokes, 1984).

Consistency To reinforce a behavior with consistency means that the behavior is reinforced according to the requirements of an established schedule of reinforcement. For instance, if a continuous schedule of reinforcement is used, each occurrence of the behavior produces the reinforcer. If a fixed ratio 5 schedule is used (FR 5), every fifth response is reinforced. Regardless of whether the schedule is continuous or intermittent, consistency in delivery of the reinforcer is necessary. Schedules should not be changed in a random, unplanned fashion, especially during the initial stages of learning.

Amount of Reinforcement The amount of a reinforcer that an individual receives also affects the reinforcement program. Walter, an employee for a computer software company, is more likely to develop innovative software if he receives $10,000 for each innovation rather than $1,000. Victor, a developmentally handicapped student, is more likely to complete his homework assignment on time if his father lets him stay up 30 minutes longer each night instead of 5 minutes longer each night. Frances is more likely to type Rose's dissertation if she receives $2.50 per page than if she receives $1.25 per page.

Consideration of how much reinforcement to use should follow the maxim "Reinforce abundantly, but don't give away the store." The consensus (Heward, Dardig, & Rossett, 1979; Hall & Hall, 1980) is that the amount of reinforcement should be proportional to the effort involved in making the response. However, when initiating a behavior change program, additional reinforcement must be used in order to establish the behavior.

Quality The quality of a reinforcer is important to consider in behavior change programs. A toy with lights, changeable components, and movement functions is probably a more powerful reinforcer than a toy without these features. Access to a custom-built sports car is probably a more power reinforcer for an adolescent than the family sedan. The quality of the reinforcer is relative to other reinforcers in the environment and can be used contingently to improve behavior.

Concurrent Schedules A concurrent schedule of reinforcement is one in which two or more intermittent schedules operate independently and at the same time for two or more different behaviors. With a concurrent schedule it is possible that responses receiving a higher

rate of reinforcement will increase, producing a corresponding decrease in the frequency of the other response. Chapter 12, "Schedules of Reinforcement," discusses in more depth how concurrent schedules affect behavior.

Novelty The more varied and different reinforcers are from one another, the more likely it is that they can be used to increase behavior. According to Hall and Hall (1980) persons skilled at using novel or new reinforcers can obtain high rates of behavior. From a behavioral perspective the usefulness of novel reinforcers might be explained in two ways. First, the more novel the reinforcer, the more likely that the person is deprived of the reinforcer. The more deprived the person, the more likely that the stimulus will have a reinforcing effect. Second, the more novel the reinforcer, the less likely that the person will experience satiation Hall and Hall (1980) provide lists of potential novel reinforcers for children in home and school settings.

Deprivation State

For reinforcement to be effective, the subject must experience some level of deprivation prior to delivery of the reinforcer. Food is not as reinforcing to a person who has just had a full meal as it is to an individual who has not eaten in several days. But deprivation is not related only to primary reinforcers. A teacher might arrange a contingency with a high school special education student: "When you are finished with your class assignment, you will earn 15 minutes of free time." If the student has access to free time at other periods during the day or if he has unauthorized access to free time in the class, then it is unlikely that the contingency will be effective. The student simply has not been deprived of the reinforcer, and he may be able to access it with less effort in another environment. The rule to follow is that if a reinforcer is going to be used, the subject should be deprived of it prior to its presentation and should not have access to it in other environments or under other conditions.

GUIDELINES FOR USING REINFORCEMENT

We would like to offer several guidelines to consider when using reinforcement in applied settings. These guidelines come from two main sources—our experiences in developing behaviors and the research literature. They remain guidelines, however, not rules etched in stone. Each situation calling for behavior change is unique, requiring adaptation of existing procedures for implementation.

Establish an Appropriate Criterion for Reinforcement

The first step in establishing a reinforcement schedule is to set the initial criterion. Heward

(1980) devised a formula that uses baseline data to determine the level for reinforcement in an instructional setting.

> For a behavior you wish to increase, set the initial criterion higher than the child's average baseline performance and less than or equal to his best performance during baseline. For a behavior you want to decrease in frequency, the initial criterion for reinforcement should be set at less than the child's average performance during baseline and greater than or equal to his lowest (or best) baseline performance. (p. 7)

Figure 11.8 gives examples of how the formula can be used.

Choose the Appropriate Reinforcer

Hall and Hall (1980) provide several guidelines for choosing an appropriate reinforcer; they recommend that age-appropriate, novel,

---

The criterion-setting formulas are

For increasing behaviors: baseline average	$<$ initial criterion $\le$	highest performance during baseline
For decreasing behaviors: baseline average	$>$ initial criterion $\ge$	lowest performance during baseline

Examples

Target Behavior	Performance Goal	Lowest	Highest	Baseline Average	Range for Initial Criterion
Playing alone	Increase	2 min.	14 min.	6 min.	7–14 min.
Identifying letters of the alphabet	Increase	4 letters	9 letters	5 letters	6–9 letters
Number of leg exercises completed	Increase	0	22	8	9–22
Percentage of math problems correctly solved	Increase	25%	60%	34%	40–60%
Number of typing errors in one letter	Decrease	16	28	22	16–21
Number of calories consumed per day	Decrease	2260	3980	2950	2260–2900

FIGURE 11.8 Using baseline data to individualize an initial criterion for reinforcement. (From "ET Consultant" by W. L. Heward, 1980, *Exceptional Teacher, 1*(9), p. 8. Copyright 1980 by the *Exceptional Teacher.* Reprinted by permission.)

and natural reinforcers be used whenever possible. An earlier statement in this chapter bears repeating: no reinforcement approach is likely to be successful if an inappropriate, nonfunctional reinforcer is used. In addition, practitioners should recognize that the relative strength of a reinforcer can change within a short time period. Although access to toys and dolls might reinforce preschool students one month, wearing grown-up clothes or helping parents might be a more effective reinforcer the next month.

Use Generalized Conditioned Reinforcers

As stated previously, tokens, points, and money make effective reinforcers because the individual can exchange these interim reinforcers for other back-up primary or secondary reinforcers that are scheduled to be delivered at a later time.

Reinforce Appropriate Behavior Immediately

Probably the single most important action of a practitioner attempting to develop new responses is to reinforce the occurrence of the desired behavior immediately after it is emitted. Immediacy of reinforcement is the delivery of the reinforcing stimulus just after the occurrence of the behavior. Implicit in the often-cited phrase "Catch 'em being good" is this notion that the sooner the behavior is reinforced, the more probable the occurrence of the behavior will be in the future. Experimental data indicate that delays in providing reinforcement ultimately affect the performance levels of the individual (Mayhew & Anderson, 1980).

Reinforce Often

Consistent with the practice of reinforcing a behavior immediately after its occurrence is the notion of reinforcing the behavior frequently. In teaching a new behavior, it is imperative to reinforce the behavior frequently. The consensus in the field is that continuous reinforcement is needed to establish a new behavior; intermittent reinforcement is required to maintain behavior (Skinner, 1969).

A common misapplication of this guideline occurs when the practitioner is too stingy with reinforcement, holding that the individual should work for reinforcement. However, it is unreasonable and experimentally unsound to establish a reinforcement contingency in which the criterion is impossible for the subject to achieve. Telling a learning disabled student that she has to complete 12 assignments before going to recess (the reinforcer) when she has never completed more than 4 assignments in the past is a misapplication of reinforcement. It would be better to have the student complete 3 sets of 4 assignments each and be reinforced after each set.

Use Reinforcement Across Settings, Behaviors, and Time

The intent of this guideline is to program for generalization to untrained situations, a tactic called for from the inception of applied behavior analysis (Baer, Wolf, & Risley, 1968). Operationally, practitioners reinforcing appropriate behavior in one setting or time should see to it that occurrences of that behavior are reinforced in other settings or at other times. For example, if a developmentally handicapped student is praised in a resource room for increased social interactions with peers, he should also be praised in the regular classroom, at recess, and in the home setting for appropriate social interaction behaviors.

Use Cues to Prompt Behavior

Practitioners should not hesitate to use supplemental cues to prompt behavior. Visual, verbal, or physical prompts can set the occasion for a behavior to occur and be reinforced. Teachers often use prompts in this way. The teacher's reminder to her students to read and follow the directions before beginning a workbook exercise is a signal that those who do so are likely to be reinforced. Likewise, the caretaker who physically guides the motor movements of a cerebral palsied child is using a prompting technique to set the occasion for a desired behavior, and thereby increasing the likelihood of reinforcement.

SUMMARY

The Role of Genetic Inheritance

1 Humans do not inherit specific operant behaviors through genetic transmission; they inherit the capacity to learn new behavior.
2 An individual's genetic endowment and history of reinforcement determine whether a response is likely to be emitted at any given time.

Definition of Operant Reinforcement

3 Operant reinforcement occurs when a behavior is followed immediately by the presentation of a stimulus and, as a result, occurs more often in the future.
4 Operant reinforcement strengthens response classes, not individual behaviors.

Positive Reinforcement

5 Three components are necessary for positive reinforcement. First, a response must have some consequence. Second, the response must increase in probability. Third, the increase in probability must occur because the response has this consequence and not for some other reason. The stimulus, or event, that follows the behavior and is administered contingently is the positive reinforcer.
6 All positive reinforcers are determined by function, meaning that future occurrences of the behavior must increase subsequent to the presentation of the stimulus.

Negative Reinforcement

7 Negative reinforcement is the removal of a stimulus contingent upon a response that re-sults in the increased likelihood of the behavior occurring again in the future under similar stimulus conditions. The stimulus that is removed is the negative reinforcer.
8 Two contingencies are produced with negative reinforcement—escape and avoidance.

Types of Potential Reinforcers

9 There are two main types of potential reinforcers: primary and secondary. Primary reinforcers are unconditioned (unlearned) reinforcers because they reinforce behavior as a result of their biological importance to the survival of the individual. Secondary reinforcers are conditioned (learned) reinforcers. They are initially neutral and acquire reinforcing capability by being paired with primary reinforcers or other strong secondary reinforcers.
10 Examples of primary reinforcers are food, liquids, warmth, and sexual stimulation. Types of secondary reinforcers are tangible, activity, social, and generalized reinforcers.

Selecting Potential Reinforcers

11 Potential reinforcers can be selected by asking, observing, sampling, forcing a choice, and actually trying the reinforcer.

The Premack Principle

12 The Premack Principle states that access to a high frequency behavior can be made contingent upon the occurrence of a low frequency behavior.

Factors Influencing the Effectiveness of Reinforcement

13 There are four factors that influence the effectiveness of reinforcement. These include: genetic endowment, history of reinforcement, the current environment, and the deprivation state of the individual.

Guidelines

14 An appropriate criterion for reinforcement should be established. It is best to reinforce occurrences of the desired behavior immediately, often, and with an appropriate reinforcer. Also, reinforcement should be generalized across settings, behaviors, and time. Finally, prompts can be used to set the occasion for reinforcement.

12

Schedules of Reinforcement

KEY TERMS

Schedule of reinforcement

Continuous reinforcement (CRF)

Extinction (EXT)

Intermittent schedule of reinforcement (INT)

Schedule thinning

Fixed ratio (FR)

Postreinforcement pause

Variable ratio (VR)

Ratio strain

Differential reinforcement of high rates (DRH)

Differential reinforcement of low rates (DRL)

Interresponse time (IRT)

Fixed interval (FI)

Variable interval (VI)

Limited hold

Concurrent schedules (conc)

Multiple schedules (mult)

Chained schedules (chain)

Mixed schedules (mix)

Tandem schedules (tand)

Alternative schedules (alt)

Conjunctive schedules (conj)

Adjunctive behavior

This chapter was written by John O. Cooper.

A **schedule of reinforcement** is a rule that establishes the probability that a specific occurrence of a behavior will produce reinforcement. Two schedules of reinforcement—continuous reinforcement and extinction—provide the boundaries for all other possible schedules. With **continuous reinforcement (CRF)** an individual is reinforced every time a particular behavior occurs. For example, a teacher using a continuous schedule of reinforcement would praise a student each time she identified a sight word correctly. Examples of behaviors that tend to produce continuous reinforcement include turning on a water faucet (water comes out), answering a telephone after it rings (a voice is heard), and putting money into a vending machine (a product is obtained). The other schedule of reinforcement is called **extinction (EXT)** because no occurrence of the behavior is reinforced. (Extinction is discussed in detail in chapter 16.)

Between continuous reinforcement and extinction a large number of environmental arrangements can be developed in which some occurrences of a behavior will be reinforced and other occurrences of the same behavior will not be. A rule that specifies such an environmental arrangement is called an **intermittent schedule of reinforcement (INT).** A basketball player does not make a basket each time the ball is shot. A door-to-door solicitor does not make a sale at every house. A student does not receive praise after each correct response. Intermittent reinforcement occurs when a reinforcer is delivered on a schedule that is not continuous.

USE OF CONTINUOUS AND INTERMITTENT REINFORCEMENT

Continuous reinforcement is used to strengthen behavior, primarily during the initial stages of acquiring new or developing unused behaviors. For example, Bill, a student in a junior high classroom, does not complete his class assignments even though he has the required skills to do each one. To strengthen assignment completion, the teacher might reinforce him each time he finishes an assignment by allowing him to exercise a classroom privilege. Correspondingly, an elementary school teacher teaching vowel sounds with a CRF schedule would praise her students each time they successfully reproduced the sound.

Intermittent reinforcement is used to maintain established behaviors. In our former example when Bill's assignment completion reaches criterion, his teacher should switch to an intermittent reinforcement schedule to maintain his performance. Whereas previously reinforcers were issued after each completed assignment, the teacher would thin the schedule so that only one out of every two, three, and eventually many more completed assignments would produce reinforcement.

Implementing Intermittent Reinforcement

Schedule thinning from continuous to intermittent reinforcement can be accomplished in two ways. First, verbal instructions or other discriminative stimuli that clearly specify the contingencies will help most individuals make a smooth transition from continuous to intermittent reinforcement (e.g., "Jim, after you have practiced the C, F, and G scales four times each, we can go to the movies"). The verbal instructions set the occasion for higher performance. Admittedly, it is not necessary for an individual to describe the contingent relationship between a behavior and its consequence for effective intermittent reinforcement. However, it is often helpful if clients are aware of what must be accomplished to receive reinforcement. Written rules, directions, and signs can also be used. A rule posted in the classroom can help avoid the erratic behavior that might accompany increased requirements (e.g., "Please note that in this grading period the number of book reports needed for a final grade of *A* has been raised from one to three").

The second way a schedule of reinforcement can be thinned is to gradually extend the schedule; in this case the progression from continuous to intermittent reinforcement is based on the individual's performance. If a student has been solving math problems under a CRF schedule for several weeks, the teacher should adjust the criterion slowly upward from 1 problem (CRF) to 2 or 3 problems (INT) prior to reinforcement. The important point here is that the schedule of reinforcement must be thinned with planning, care, and ongoing evaluation, or the gains made with continuous reinforcement will be lost.

Desirable Aspects of Intermittent Reinforcement

Maintenance of Behavior Maintenance of behavior refers to procedures used to ensure that appropriate changes in behavior will last (Kazdin & Esveldt-Dawson, 1981). Regardless of the type of behavior change technique employed or the degree of success during treatment, behavior analysts must be concerned with sustaining gains after a program is terminated. For example, Mary is in the seventh grade and is enrolled in French, her first foreign language class. After several weeks the teacher informs Mary's parents that she is failing the course. The teacher believes that Mary's problems in French have resulted from lack of daily drill and study. During a parent-teacher conference it is decided that Mary will self-record a tally on a chart kept on the family bulletin board each evening that she studies French for 30 minutes. And on each day that Mary records a tally, her parents are to praise her and offer encouragement. During a follow-up conference 3 weeks later, it is decided that Mary is doing so well that the procedure can be stopped. Unfortunately, a few days later Mary is once again falling behind in French.

In this example a successful program was developed to establish daily study. However, after the program was terminated, the gains were not maintained, primarily because the parents and the teacher did not establish intermittent reinforcement procedures. Let us review what happened and what could have happened. Continuous reinforcement was used correctly to develop daily study behavior. However, after the study behavior was established, gradually fewer and fewer occurrences of the behavior should have been reinforced. The parents should have praised Mary after every second day of daily study, then every fourth day, then once per week, and so on. With intermittent reinforcement Mary would have been more likely to continue daily study after the program was terminated.

Resistance to Extinction Extinction is a procedure in which reinforcement of a previously reinforced behavior is discontinued. The persistence of an individual's response during the period of nonreinforcement is described as resistance to extinction. Several variables determine how long a behavior continues in the absence of reinforcement. In general, though, behaviors with a history of intermittent reinforcement are more resistant to extinction than those with a history of continuous reinforcement.

High Rates of Response Another advantage of intermittent reinforcement is the high response rate that can be produced. The next section will elaborate on this advantage.

Progression to Naturally Occurring Reinforcement A major goal of most behavior change programs is the development of naturally occurring activities, stimuli, or events as reinforcers. It is more desirable for individuals to read because they like to read, rather than to obtain reinforcement from a teacher or parent; to engage in athletics for the enjoyment of the activity, rather than for a grade or because of a physician's directive; to help around the house for the personal satisfaction it brings, rather than to earn an allowance. Intermittent reinforcement is usually necessary for the progression to naturally occurring reinforcement. Even though some individuals spend hours each day practicing a musical instrument because they enjoy the activity, chances are good that this persistent behavior developed gradually. At first the beginning music student needs a great deal of reinforcement to continue the activity: "You really practiced well today," "I can't believe how well you played," "Your mother told me you received a first place in the contest—that's super!" These social reinforcers are paired with other reinforcers from teachers, family, and peers. As the student develops more proficiency in music, the outside reinforcers occur less frequently, intermittently. Eventually, the student spends long periods making music without receiving any reinforcement from others because making music has become a reinforcing activity.

Some might explain the transition of our music student from an externally reinforced individual to a self-reinforced musician as the development of intrinsic motivation, which seems to imply that something inside the individual is responsible for maintaining the behavior. This view is incorrect from a behavioral standpoint. Intrinsic motivation can be described more accurately as reinforcement that is received from the manipulation of the physical environment. Some individuals ride bicycles, go backpacking, read, write, or help others because the manipulation of the environment is reinforcing. When performing an activity is reinforcement, the activity reinforcer has "developed as a function of an individual's environmental or reinforcement history. It does not occur in the absence of intermittent reinforcement" (Sulzer-Azaroff and Mayer, 1977, p. 338).

Control for Satiation If individuals receive too much reinforcement, satiation occurs and response rates decrease. Satiation is more likely to take place on a continuous schedule of reinforcement than on an intermittent schedule. As fewer reinforcers are received in a given period of time—as is the case with intermittent reinforcement—the chances of satiation are decreased. This relationship holds true for both unconditioned and conditioned reinforcers, but it is especially true for unconditioned reinforcers.

Cost Effectiveness Intermittent reinforcement is also more cost effective than continuous reinforcement in terms of the contingency manager's time and effort. For example, in a classroom setting with 25 or 30 students, a teacher can systematically provide intermittent reinforcement for each student. But it is impossible for one teacher to provide continuous reinforcement for every desirable response that she wants to maintain in the classroom.

BASIC INTERMITTENT SCHEDULES OF REINFORCEMENT

Schedules of reinforcement have been carefully studied in laboratory settings. The results of these investigations have yielded some well-established principles regarding the effects of schedules of reinforcement on behavior.

Ratio and Interval Schedules

Ratio schedules and interval schedules are two classifications of frequently used schedules of intermittent reinforcement in applied settings. Ratio schedules require that "a certain number of responses be emitted before one response is reinforced" (Reynolds, 1968, p. 60). If the ratio requirement for a behavior is set at 10 correct responses, the first 9 correct responses go unreinforced. Only the 10th correct response produces the reinforcer. Interval schedules require that "a given interval of time elapses before a response can be reinforced" (Reynolds, 1968, p. 60). The interval of time is usually measured from the delivery of the last reinforcer. In reinforcing accurate math performance on a 5-minute interval schedule, after 5 minutes elapse, the first correct math response is reinforced. Upon delivery of the reinforcer, a new 5-minute interval begins.

Whereas ratio schedules focus on the number of responses emitted by an individual, interval schedules focus on the passage of a specified period of time. With ratio schedules the individual's response rate controls how quickly reinforcement becomes available. The sooner an individual emits the ratio requirements, the sooner the reinforcer will be delivered. With interval schedules the number of responses is irrelevant; emitting high rates of response will not cause time to pass faster. Thus, the rapidity of reinforcer availability is self-controlled with ratio schedules and time-controlled with interval schedules.

Fixed and Variable Schedules

Ratio and interval schedules can be applied on a fixed or variable basis. On a fixed schedule the ratio or interval requirement remains constant. On a variable schedule the ratio or interval requirement varies from one reinforced response to another. The combination of ratio or interval and fixed or variable conditions results in four basic schedules of reinforcement: fixed ratio, variable ratio, fixed interval, and variable interval. The following sections will define and illustrate each of these commonly used schedules.

RATIO SCHEDULES

Fixed Ratio Defined

When a given number of responses must be emitted before reinforcement, a **fixed ratio (FR)** schedule of reinforcement is in operation. For example, an FR 4 schedule means that every 4th correct (or target) response is reinforced; in an FR 15 schedule every 15th correct response is reinforced. Some business and industrial tasks are paid on an FR schedule (e.g., piecework). A worker might receive a pay credit after completing a specified number of tasks (e.g., assembling 15 pieces of equipment, picking a box of oranges). A student might receive either a happy face after learning 5 new sight words or a certain number of points after completing 10 math problems.

Characteristics of FR Performance

Consistency of Performance After an individual has responded for some time under an FR schedule, a typical pattern of behavior is observed. After the first response of the ratio requirement, the remaining required responses are completed with very little hesitation between responses. After reinforcement there is a **postreinforcement pause** (i.e., a period of time after reinforcement in which the subject ceases to respond). The length of the postreinforcement pause is a function of the size of the ratio. A large ratio requirement produces a long pause; a small ratio generates a short pause. The postreinforcement pause can be so short under small ratio requirements that it is indiscernible (Whaley & Malott, 1971). Whaley and Malott (1971) described the FR schedule as an all-or-nothing schedule: the individual goes all out to complete the ratio requirements or does nothing at all (pauses).

Rate of Response Fixed ratio schedules tend to generate high rates of responding. Individuals work rapidly with a fixed ratio because they are reinforced as soon as the ratio requirements are met. Typists who contract their services usually work on an FR schedule; they receive a specified amount for the work contracted. A typist with a 25-page manuscript to complete is likely to type at the maximum rate. The sooner the manuscript is typed, the sooner payment is received, and the more work the typist can complete in a day.

The major factor influencing the rate of response on FR schedules is the size of the ratio. In general, the larger the ratio requirement, the higher the rate of response. However, as soon as the ratio requirements exceed a maximum ratio, the rate of response decreases. The maximum ratio is determined by the past FR history of the individual and the manner in which the ratio has been selected. If ratio requirements are raised gradually over an extended period of time, extremely high ratio requirements can be reached.

In the case of a student whose teacher is reinforcing math performance with an FR schedule, the teacher might reinforce correct math performance with points after every 3rd problem completed (FR 3), and the student might complete 12 problems within the specified time and receive reinforcement four times. However, it is likely that the student would complete more problems in less time if reinforcement was contingent on the completion of 12 correct problems rather than 3. The higher ratio is likely to produce a higher rate of response. Figure 12.1 is a summary of the definition and performance characteristics during ongoing FR reinforcement. An FR schedule can be established with relative ease by gradually increasing the ratio number to the appropriate level.

Variable Ratio Defined

In a **variable ratio (VR)** schedule of reinforcement, the number of correct responses prior to reinforcement varies. VR schedules are described with a number representing the average (mean) number of responses required for reinforcement. In an FR 10 schedule every 10th correct response produces the reinforcer; in a VR 10 schedule on the average every 10th correct response produces the reinforcer. Reinforcement can come after 1 response, 20, 3, or 8, but the average number of responses is 10.

Perhaps the best example of a VR schedule is the operation of a slot machine, the so-called one-armed bandit. These machines are programmed to pay off only a certain percentage of the times they are played; the average is established by the casino. The player cannot predict when the next operation of the machine will pay off. A person might win 2 or 3 times in succession and then not for another 100 or more plays. Other examples of VR schedules of reinforcement include card games and other games of chance, the commission a sales representative receives for each sale, and almost all competitive sports.

Student behaviors are frequently reinforced according to variable ratios. Usually a student cannot predict when the teacher will call on him to give an answer and receive reinforcement. Good grades, awards, promotions, all may come after an unpredictable number of

FIGURE 12.1 Summary of FR performance during ongoing reinforcement.

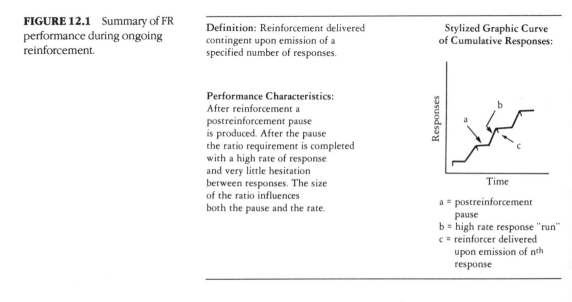

Definition: Reinforcement delivered contingent upon emission of a specified number of responses.

Performance Characteristics:
After reinforcement a postreinforcement pause is produced. After the pause the ratio requirement is completed with a high rate of response and very little hesitation between responses. The size of the ratio influences both the pause and the rate.

Stylized Graphic Curve of Cumulative Responses:

Responses

Time

a = postreinforcement pause
b = high rate response "run"
c = reinforcer delivered upon emission of nth response

responses. And in checking seatwork, the teacher may reinforce a student's work after 10 problems have been completed, another student's work after 3 problems, and so on.

Characteristics of VR Performance

Consistency of Performance Variable ratio schedules produce consistent, steady rates of response; VR schedules do not produce a postreinforcement pause. Lundin (1969) speculates that the absence of any pause in responding is due to the absence of information about when the next response will be reinforced. Responding remains steady because the next response may produce reinforcement.

Rate of Response Like the FR schedule the VR schedule tends to produce high rates of response. Also similar is the major influence of the size of the ratio on the rate of response. The larger the ratio requirements, until some maximum ratio is reached, the higher the rate of response. Also, like FR schedules extremely high ratio requirements can be reached if the ratio requirements for the VR are raised gradually over extended periods of time. Figure 12.2 provides a summary of the definition

and performance characteristics during ongoing VR reinforcement.

Establishing VR Schedules

Behavior analysts frequently reinforce performance on VR schedules. However, the VR schedules used in applied settings are seldom implemented with a planned, systematic approach. In other words, the reinforcer is delivered by chance, hit or miss. This non-systematic application is not the most effective use of variable ratio schedules. They should be selected and preplanned before implementation to provide reinforcement with maximum effectiveness.

Variable ratio schedules can be selected by specifying the maximum ratio to be used (e.g., 15 responses); then a table of random numbers can be consulted to produce the specific ratios. For instance, if the contingency manager selects 15 responses as the maximum, a table of random numbers might generate the following sequence of ratios: 8, 1, 1, 14, 3, 10, 14, 15, and 6. This example would be a VR 8 schedule of reinforcement (on the average each 8th response produces the reinforcer) with a range from 1 to 15 responses.

FIGURE 12.2 Summary of VR performance during ongoing reinforcement.

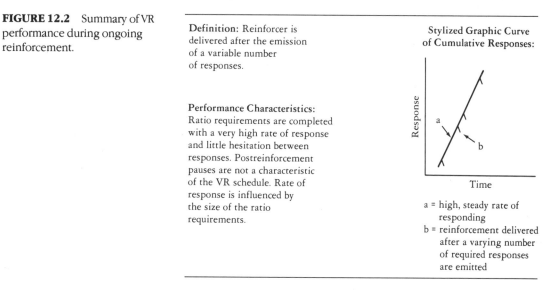

Definition: Reinforcer is delivered after the emission of a variable number of responses.

Performance Characteristics: Ratio requirements are completed with a very high rate of response and little hesitation between responses. Postreinforcement pauses are not a characteristic of the VR schedule. Rate of response is influenced by the size of the ratio requirements.

Stylized Graphic Curve of Cumulative Responses:

Response

Time

a = high, steady rate of responding
b = reinforcement delivered after a varying number of required responses are emitted

Because of the performance generated with a VR schedule (i.e., high and steady rate of response, resistance to extinction), it is a desirable schedule of reinforcement for academic behavior. The following VR procedures are suggested for either academic or social behavior and can be used with either individual or group contingencies of reinforcement.

Tic-Tac-Toe

1 Establish a maximum ratio for the individual student or group.

2 Give the individual or group a tic-tac-toe score sheet.

3 Have the student(s) fill in each square of the score sheet with a number no greater than the maximum ratio. For example, if the maximum ratio is 30, the score sheet might look like this.

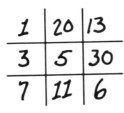

4 Fill a box or some other type of container with numbered slips of paper (with numbers no higher than the maximum number). Include each number several times; for example, five ones, five twos, five threes.

5 Contingent upon the occurrence of the desired behavior, permit the student(s) to withdraw one slip of paper from the box. If the number on the paper corresponds with a number on the score sheet, instruct the student(s) to mark out that number on the score sheet.

6 When the student has marked out three numbers in a row—horizontally, vertically, or diagonally—deliver the reinforcer.

For example, the student(s) might withdraw one slip of paper for each homework assignment completed. The reinforcement might be to select an activity from the class job board (e.g., teacher's helper, collecting milk money, running the projector).

Classroom Lottery

1 Have each student write her name on an index card after completing a specified task or behavior.

2 Instruct the student to drop the card into a box located on the teacher's desk.

3 After an established interval of time (e.g., one week), draw a card from the box and declare that student the winner. There can be first, second, and third place or any number of winners. The more cards a student gets into the box, the greater the chance that one of her cards will be picked.

The lottery has been used to increase the outside reading of elementary students. For each unit of outside reading completed, the student might fill out a card with his name and the title of the book or article. Every 2 weeks the teacher could draw one card from the box and give the winning student a new book. To make the book an especially desirable reward, the teacher could let the student earn the privilege of returning the book to the school, inscribed with his name, class, and date (e.g., "This book was donated to the High Street Library by Brian Lee, fifth grade, 1994").

Desk Calendar

1 Give each student a desk calendar with loose-leaf date pages secured to the calendar base with metal clips.

2 Remove the loose-leaf date pages from the calendar base.

3 Establish a maximum ratio for each student.

4 Number index cards consecutively from one to the maximum ratio. Include multiple cards for each number (e.g., five ones, five twos). If a large average ratio is desired, include more large numbers;

for small average ratios, use more small numbers.

5 With a paper punch make holes in the index cards so that they can be attached to the calendar base.

6 Shuffle the index cards to randomize the order, and then attach to a calendar base face down.

7 Direct each student to produce his own VR schedule by turning over one index card at a time and completing that ratio before turning over another card.

Students can use the desk calendar base to generate VR reinforcement of math facts. For example, after receiving a math worksheet, Sharon turns over the first card. It has a 5 written on it. After completing five problems, Sharon holds up her hand to signal her teacher that she has completed the ratio requirement. The teacher checks Sharon's work, provides feedback, and reinforces her if the problems are correct. Sharon then turns over the second card; the ratio requirement is 1. After completing that single problem, Sharon receives reinforcement and turns over the third card. This time the ratio is 14. The cycle continues until all of the cards in the stack are used. New cards can then be added and/or old cards, reshuffled to create a new series of numbers. The average of the numbers does not change in the reshuffling.

Considerations with Ratio Schedules

Both FR and VR schedules of reinforcement have two major advantages. First, and perhaps most important, ratio schedules produce high rates of responding. In most situations concerned with the development of skills (e.g., reading, math computation, music performance, sports), a high rate of response is desirable. Second, ratio schedules are easy to use.

However, ratio schedules also have a potential disadvantage: **ratio strain** can result from abrupt increases in ratio requirements. Ratio strain is indicated by avoidance, aggression, and unpredictable pauses in responding. When it is evident, the contingency manager should reduce the ratio requirement, which can be increased gradually after the behavior has recovered. Ratio strain can generally be avoided by programming small, gradual increases in ratio requirements. However, even with gradual increases ratio strain will occur when the ratio becomes so large that the reinforcement cannot maintain the response level or the response requirement exceeds the individual's physiological capabilities.

Schedules of Differential Reinforcement of Rates of Responding

Applied behavior analysts frequently encounter problems in response rate. An individual may perform a behavior too infrequently or too often, and the result may be detrimental to social or academic growth. Procedures for correcting such problems include differential reinforcement schedules. Differential reinforcement of particular rates of behavior is a variation of ratio schedules. Delivery of the reinforcer is contingent upon responses occurring at a rate either higher or lower than some predetermined criterion. The reinforcement of responses higher than a predetermined criterion is called **differential reinforcement of high rates (DRH).** When responses are reinforced only when they are lower than the criterion, the schedule provides **differential reinforcement of low rates (DRL).**

Two definitions of DRH and DRL are used in applied behavior analysis. The first states that reinforcement is available only for responses that are spaced apart from each other by a given time criterion. The amount of time that occurs between two responses is the interresponse time (IRT). IRTs and response rates are functionally related: long IRTs generate low rates of responding, and short IRTs produce high rates of responding. Reinforcement on a DRH schedule is given whenever a response occurs before a stated time criterion has elapsed. If the stated time criterion is 3 minutes, the student receives reinforcement only when the IRT is 3 minutes or less. Under the DRL schedule reinforcement follows responses that occur after a stated time criterion has elapsed. If the stated time criterion is again 3 minutes, the student on a DRL schedule receives reinforcement only when the IRT is 3 minutes or more. The DRH schedule produces a higher rate of responding; the DRL, a lower rate of responding.

This first definition of DRH and DRL as IRT schedules of reinforcement has been used almost exclusively in laboratory settings. There are two apparent reasons for its lack of application in applied settings. First, most applied settings do not have sufficient automated equipment to measure interresponse time. Second, in laboratory settings reinforcement is delivered usually, but not necessarily, following each correct response that meets the IRT criterion. Such frequent reinforcement would disrupt student activity in most instructional settings. However, with increased use of a computer for tutorial and academic response practice, opportunities will become available to use IRT-based schedules of reinforcement to accelerate or decelerate academic responding. The computer can be programmed to monitor the pauses between academic responses and provide consequences for each response meeting the IRT criterion. Consequences can be programmed to provide little disruption in instructional activity.

The second definition of DRH and DRL schedules states that a prescribed number of responses occurring within a specified period of time are reinforced. For example, under a DRH schedule the prescribed number of responses might be 30 within a 10-minute instructional period. If a student emits 30 (or more) responses during the 10 minutes, reinforcement will be delivered.

An illustration of the use of a DRH schedule follows. A student might read with few errors at his assigned reading level, but the number of words read per minute might be so low that it inhibits his academic growth. To differentially reinforce high rates of reading, his teacher can make reinforcement contingent upon reading an average of 50 or more words per minute for 10 minutes. Only if the student reads at an average rate of 50 or more words per minute is he reinforced after the 10 minutes. A reading rate below 50 words per minute does not produce reinforcement. As the student's rate of reading increases, the DRH schedule can be adjusted higher.

INTERVAL SCHEDULES

Fixed Interval Defined

In a **fixed interval** (FI) schedule of reinforcement, the first correct or desired response after a designated and constant amount of time produces the reinforcer (Ferster & Skinner, 1957). On a fixed interval 3-minute schedule (FI 3) the first correct or desired response following the passage of 3 minutes produces the reinforcer. Many practitioners mistakenly assume that the passage of time alone is sufficient for delivery of the reinforcing stimulus with a fixed interval schedule of reinforcement. However, on an FI schedule the reinforcer is available after the time interval has elapsed, but it is not delivered until a correct or desired response is emitted. Therefore, on an FI 3 schedule more than 3 minutes can elapse between reinforcers. When a response does occur after the 3-minute interval, that response is immediately reinforced, and a new 3-minute interval is begun.

Actual examples of FI schedules in everyday life are difficult to find. However, many situations approximate and in reality function as FI schedules. For example, mail is often delivered close to a fixed time each day. An individual can make many trips to the mailbox to check, but only the first response following the mail delivery will be reinforced. Picking up a paycheck is another example. A payment of wages by the hour, day, week, or month is contingent upon the first response of coming to the pay location after the required interval.

FI schedules are relatively easy to use in applied settings. A teacher could reinforce a student on an FI 2 schedule for correct computations on a math worksheet. A kitchen timer could signal the 2-minute interval, after which the student would be reinforced for his first correct solution. The teacher would then reset the timer for another 2-minute interval.

Characteristics of FI Performance

Consistency of Performance Typical performance on an FI schedule consists of a low or zero rate of responding, a postreinforcement pause, during the early part of the interval. Toward the end of the interval an increasing rate of response is evident, usually reaching a maximum just before delivery of the reinforcer. The gradually accelerating rate of response toward the end of the interval is called an FI scallop because of the rounded curves that are shown on a cumulative graph (see Figure 12.3).

The postreinforcement pause and scallop effect can be seen in many everyday situations. When college students are assigned a term paper, they typically do not rush to the library and start to work on the paper immediately. More often they wait a few days or weeks before starting to work. However, as the due date approaches, their work on the assignment increases in an accelerating fashion, and many are typing the final draft just before class. Cramming for a mid-term or final examination is another example of a postreinforcement pause and scallop effect.

Why does an FI schedule generate a characteristic pause and scallop effect? After adjustment to an FI schedule, an individual develops a time discrimination and learns that responses emitted right after a reinforced response are never reinforced. Therefore, responding during the early part of the interval undergoes extinction. As Lundin (1969) states it, "This is based on the fact that a response which closely follows the one reinforced is never paid off" (p. 81).

The effects of FI and FR schedules of reinforcement are similar in that both produce pauses following reinforcement. However, it is

FIGURE 12.3 Summary of FI performance during ongoing reinforcement.

Definition: The first correct response after a designated and constant amount of time produces the reinforcer.

Performance Characteristics: FI schedules generate slow to moderate rates of responding with a pause in responding following reinforcement. Responding begins to accelerate toward the end of the interval.

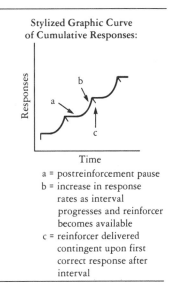

Stylized Graphic Curve of Cumulative Responses:

Responses

Time

a = postreinforcement pause
b = increase in response
     rates as interval
     progresses and reinforcer
     becomes available
c = reinforcer delivered
     contingent upon first
     correct response after
     interval

important to recognize the different character-istics of behavior that emerge under each schedule. Responses under an FR schedule are emitted at a consistent rate until the ratio requirement is completed, whereas responses under an FI schedule begin to accelerate toward the end of each interval.

Competing Responses Since responses are emitted at a low or zero rate during the first part of the interval, an individual may engage in behaviors other than the responses being reinforced on the FI schedule. The implication for behavior analysts is that the FI schedule may set the occasion for off-task behaviors during the early part of each interval.

Rate of Responding Overall, FI schedules usually generate a slow to moderate rate of response. Rate of response and length of post-reinforcement pause can be influenced by manipulation of the size of the time interval. The larger the fixed interval of time, the longer the postreinforcement pause and the lower the overall rate of response. Figure 12.3 summarizes the performance characteristics of FI schedules during ongoing reinforcement. An FI schedule can be established easily by gradually adjusting the interval size to the desired level.

Variable Interval Defined

As in an FI schedule, availability of reinforce-ment in a **variable interval** schedule (VI) of reinforcement is contingent upon the passage of time. The distinguishing feature of VI schedules is that "the intervals between rein-forcement vary in a random or nearly random order" (Ferster & Skinner, 1957, p. 326). Vari-able interval schedules are differentiated by stating the average (mean) interval of time before the opportunity for reinforcement. For example, in a variable interval 5-minute sched-ule (VI 5) the average interval between rein-forcement and the opportunity for subsequent reinforcement is 5 minutes. The actual time intervals in a VI 5 schedule might be 2 minutes, 5, 3, or 10.

An example of VI reinforcement in everyday situations occurs when one individual tele-phones another individual whose line is busy. This is a VI schedule because a variable interval of time is necessary for the second individual to conclude the telephone conversation and hang up so that another call can be connected. After that interval the first dialing of the second person's number will probably produce an answer (the reinforcer). The number of re-sponses (attempts) does not influence the availability of reinforcement in a VI schedule: no matter how many times the busy number is dialed, the call will not be completed until the line is free. And the time interval is unpre-dictable in a VI schedule: the busy signal may last for a short or long time.

Characteristics of VI Performance

Consistency of Performance After adjust-ment to a VI schedule of reinforcement, a constant, stable rate of response is generated. The VI schedule has been described as produc-ing hard and consistent workers (Whaley & Malott, 1971). The slope of the VI schedule on a cumulative graph tends to be uniform with few, if any, postreinforcement pauses (see Fig-ure 12.4). On a VI schedule there is little hesitation between responses. For example, pop quizzes at unpredictable times tend to occasion more consistent study behavior from students than do quizzes scheduled at fixed intervals of time. Furthermore, students are less apt to engage in competing off-task behaviors during instructional and study periods when the occurrence of a pop quiz is likely.

Rate of Responding Variable interval sched-ules of reinforcement generate low to mod-erate rates of response. As with FI schedules, the rate of response during VI reinforcement can be influenced by the average size of the time intervals. The larger the average variable inter-val, the lower the rate of response. Figure 12.4 summarizes the performance characteristics of VI schedules during ongoing reinforcement.

FIGURE 12.4 Summary of VI performance during ongoing reinforcement.

Definition: The first correct response following varying intervals of time produces the reinforcer.

Performance Characteristics: A VI schedule generates a slow to moderate response that is constant and stable. There are few, if any, postreinforcement pauses with VI schedules.

Stylized Graphic Curve of Cumulative Responses:

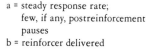

a = steady response rate; few, if any, postreinforcement pauses
b = reinforcer delivered

Generating Variable Intervals

VI schedules are often applied by therapists, clinicians, and teachers in haphazard rather than systematic fashion. Time intervals with a predetermined average are not often specified in advance. A teacher might set a kitchen timer with varied intervals of time ranging from 1 minute to 10 minutes without any prior plan as to which intervals or which order will be used. This set-them-as-you-go selection of intervals meets the basic requirements for a VI schedule; however, it is not the most effective way of reinforcing individuals on a VI schedule. A planned, systematic application of varied intervals of time should increase the effectiveness of a VI schedule.

The recommended procedure is to select the maximum time interval—whether in seconds, minutes, hours, or days—that will maintain performance and still be appropriate for the situation. Clinical judgment or, preferably, a baseline assessment should be considered in selecting that maximum interval. A table of random numbers can then be used to select the varied intervals between zero and the maximum interval. An average for the VI schedule is then calculated. If a larger average interval of time is desired, some of the smaller time intervals can be replaced with larger ones. Conversely, if the average is too large, some of the higher intervals can be replaced with smaller ones.

Consideration with Interval Schedules

Interval schedules generate low to moderate response rates although interval size determines, to a degree, increases or decreases in the rate of responding. Another way to increase the rate of response with interval schedules is to add a **limited hold** (Reynolds, 1968). A limited hold requires that the first response following the appropriate time interval occur within a specified time limit. That is, reinforcement will remain available for only a limited amount of time. If a response is not emitted within that limited amount of time, the opportunity to receive the reinforcer is lost, and a new fixed or variable interval is started. Interval schedules with a limited hold are abbreviated FI/LH (e.g., FI 5 min./LH 30 sec.) or VI/LH (e.g., VI 3 min./LH 1 min.). Limited holds with interval schedules do not change the overall response characteristics of FI and VI schedules

---

General summary of basic schedules of reinforcement

1 A continuous schedule of reinforcement should be used for the acquisition of new behaviors or for strengthening low probability or weak behaviors.

2 All intermittent schedules of reinforcement produce behavior that is more resistant to extinction than that produced by continuous reinforcement. Generally VR and VI schedules of reinforcement are more resistant to extinction than are FR and FI schedules.

3 Ratio schedules of reinforcement produce high rates of response. Interval schedules generate low to moderate rates of response.

4 Postreinforcement pauses are characteristic of both FR and FI schedules of reinforcement.

5 FR schedules produce all-or-nothing behavior. In an FI schedule the rate of responding increases toward the end of the interval.

6 VI and VR schedules are characterized by steady, continuous responding.

---

beyond a possible rate increase. An FI/LH schedule will still produce a postreinforcement pause and a scallop effect; however, the pause will be much shorter. VI/LH schedules will still produce constant and stable responding.

Both fixed interval and variable interval schedules are relatively easy to implement in applied settings. Managers need only monitor the passage of time with a timer, clock, calendar, or any other visual or auditory signal. This process is sometimes more time-efficient than counting responses, which is required with ratio schedules. If a low to moderate rate is appropriate during behavior maintenance, interval schedules may be suitable. However, managers should use caution when applying an FI schedule in a clinical setting since the postreinforcement pause can set the occasion for off-task and other competing responses. In both FI and VI schedules error responses can develop because an individual's behavior during the interval is not part of the reinforcement schedule; only the first correct response following the interval is reinforced.

COMPLEX SCHEDULES OF REINFORCEMENT

Continuous reinforcement, the four simple intermittent schedules of reinforcement (FR, VR, FI, VI), differential reinforcement of various rates of responding (DRH and DRL), and extinction can be combined to produce more complex schedules of reinforcement. The basic schedules can be arranged to occur successively or to operate simultaneously; they can be scheduled with or without discriminative stimuli; and they can be designed so that each component separately or all components together receive reinforcement (Ferster & Skinner, 1957; Thompson & Grabowski, 1972; Reese & Woolfenden, 1973).

Concurrent Schedules of Reinforcement

A **concurrent schedule (conc)** of reinforcement is in effect when two or more of the basic intermittent schedules are operating independently at the same time for two or more different behaviors. In a nonhuman example, a pigeon might be placed in an experimental chamber containing two keys. Responses on the left key are reinforced on an FR 3 schedule; a VI 2 schedule is arranged for responses on the right key. This schedule of reinforcement is identified as conc FR 3 VI 2. In an everyday application, Sharon receives reinforcement from her parents for doing homework and practicing the cello. After school she can choose when to do homework and when to practice the cello, and she can distribute her responses between these two simultaneously available schedules of reinforcement.

Williams (1973) identifies three types of interactions found with concurrent operants. First, when similar reinforcement is scheduled for each of the concurrent responses, the response receiving the higher frequency of reinforcement will increase in rate whereas a corresponding decrease will occur in the response rate of the other behavior. Commenting on this type of interaction, Myerson and Hale (1984) state that applied behavior analysts must plan to use concurrent schedules in practice because there are situations (1) when the teacher cannot control the delivery of reinforcement for inappropriate behavior; (2) when failing to provide reinforcement for the inappropriate behavior is inadvisable because of possible aggressive or emotional behaviors; and (3) when punishment for the inappropriate behavior is ethically unacceptable. If any of these situations exist, behavior analysts can implement a concurrent schedule of reinforcement that provides greater reinforcement for a competing response to decrease the occurrence of the inappropriate behavior.

The second interaction is found when one response produces reinforcement and the other, punishment. By definition, responses associated with punishment will decrease in occurrence. That decrease will often be accompanied by an increased rate of responding for the behavior producing reinforcement.

A third interaction involves a situation in which one response produces reinforcement and the other response results in avoidance of an aversive stimulus. In this situation an increase in intensity or frequency of the aversive stimulus will increase the likelihood of more avoidance behavior and will decrease the occurrence of the other response.

Myerson and Hale (1984) note the practical implications for concurrent schedules in applied settings.

Results obtained with the concurrent schedules procedure are of importance for the analysis of human behavior because of the ubiquitous presence of concurrent schedules in the world outside the laboratory. Reinforcements are often available for more than one response class or from more than one source or both. Thus, concurrent schedules represent a more realistic laboratory analog than do single reinforcement schedules, and the results of concurrent experiments may have corresponding greater relevance to applied settings. (p. 367)

Discrimination Schedules of Reinforcement

The following schedules involve combinations of two or more schedules of reinforcement, one or more behaviors of interest, and a specific stimulus associated with each schedule of reinforcement.

Multiple Schedule A **multiple schedule (mult)** is defined as two or more schedules of reinforcement that are presented in an alternating, usually random, sequence. Only one schedule occurs at a time, and each schedule is correlated with a discriminative stimulus or cue that is present as long as the schedule is in effect. To illustrate with a laboratory example, a pigeon could be presented with alternating green and red lights projected on a response key. In the presence of the green light, the pigeon is reinforced on an FI 5-minute schedule. An FR 100 schedule is in effect in the presence of the red light. This schedule of reinforcement is identified as mult FI 5 FR 100. After several presentations of the multiple schedule the pigeon will develop a stable performance typical of the basic schedule of reinforcement in effect. When the green light is on, the pigeon will show the scalloped pattern of responding associated with the FI schedule. During the red light condition performance will switch to the high rate of responding typical of an FR schedule of reinforcement.

Academic behaviors are often under the control of multiple schedules of reinforcement. For example, a student might be working basic math facts with her teacher and also with a tutor. When the teacher provides math instruction, it is with a small group of students. The tutor then provides individual instruction on the material covered in the small group. This situation follows a multiple schedule because there is one class of behaviors of interest (i.e., math facts), a discriminative stimulus or cue for each contingency in effect (i.e., teacher/tutor, small group/individual), and different likelihood of reinforcement (i.e., less frequent in group instruction). In another everyday illustration of the multiple schedule, Jim helps his mother and father clean house on Friday afternoons and Saturday mornings. Jim cleans his grandmother's bedroom and bathroom on Friday afternoons and the family room and downstairs bathroom on Saturday mornings. Jim receives $2.00 per week for cleaning his grandmother's rooms but does not receive money for cleaning the family room or downstairs bathroom. Again, there is one class of behaviors of interest (i.e., cleaning the house), a cue for each contingency in effect (i.e., grandmother's rooms on Fridays/other rooms on Saturdays), and different schedules of reinforcement associated with the different cues (i.e., $2.00 for grandmother's rooms/no money for the other rooms).

Chained Schedules

A **chained schedule (chain)** is similar to the multiple schedule. Both have two or more basic schedule requirements, only one schedule occurring at a time, and a discriminative stimulus or cue that is correlated with a specific schedule and is present as long as the schedule is in effect. However, there are differences between the multiple and chained schedules. First, the components (i.e., the cues and basic schedules) in a chained schedule are always presented in a specific order or sequence and are never in the random order characteristic of multiple schedules. Second, the behavior of interest may be the same for all components of the chain, or different behaviors may

be required for different components in the chain. Third, reinforcement for responding in the first component is the presentation of the second component; reinforcement for responding in the second component is presentation of the third component, and so on until all components have been completed in a specific sequence. The last component normally produces unconditioned reinforcement in a laboratory setting or unconditioned or conditioned reinforcement in applied settings.

Again, a laboratory example shows us a chained schedule with three components. The discriminative stimulus for the first component is a response key illuminated with a blue light, a green light in the second component, and an orange light in the third component. The 35th response on the blue key is reinforced by having the blue key change to green. The first response on the green key after 1 minute is reinforced by having the green key change to orange. After three responses on the orange key, the pigeon is given access to food reinforcement. This schedule is identified as chain FR 35 VI 1 FR 3. (See chapter 13 for a discussion of how the discriminative stimuli function as conditioned reinforcement for the responses producing the stimulus change.) This example illustrates a chained schedule with one behavior of interest for all components of the chain. Another laboratory example involves more than one behavior of interest. A monkey is placed in a dark experimental chamber in which three pulls of a chain turn on a chamber light. The light sets the occasion for a bar-pressing response. After four bar presses the monkey is reinforced with food. The schedule is chain FR 3 FR 4.

An applied example shows a more elaborate sequence of different behaviors of interest that must be emitted in a specific order. Three times each year Bill services the headset on his bicycle. To do the maintenance, he must complete 13 components in a specific order, each of which is associated with a discriminative stimulus or cue. (1) Disconnect the front brake cable; (2) remove handlebar and stem as a unit; (3) remove front wheel; (4) remove locknut, unscrew counterclockwise; (5) support fork and unscrew adjusting race; (6) lower fork out of frame; (7) inspect the races; (8) grease and replace bearing balls for the lower stack; (9) grease and replace bearing balls for upper race; (10) grease threads of steering column; (11) slide fork into frame and thread the screwed race; (12) return lockwasher; (13) adjust and lock down the headset (Davis, 1984). The final outcome (i.e., a clean, greased, and adjusted bicycle headset) is contingent upon completion of all 13 components.

Nondiscrimination Schedules of Reinforcement

There are two major nondiscrimination schedules of reinforcement: **mixed schedules (mix)** and **tandem schedules (tand)**. The procedure for the mixed schedule is identical to that of the multiple schedule except that the mixed schedule has no discriminative stimuli or cues correlated with the schedule in effect. For example, a mix FR 10 FI 1 is a schedule in which reinforcement sometimes occurs after the completion of 10 responses and sometimes occurs with the first correct response after a 1-minute interval from the preceding reinforcement. The procedure for the tandem schedule is identical to the chained schedule except, like the mixed schedule, the tandem schedule has no discriminative stimuli or cues associated with components in the chain. For instance, a tand FR 15 FI 2 is a schedule in which, after completion of 15 responses, the first correct response following an interval of 2 minutes is reinforced.

Everyday behavioral occurrences, including education and treatment, are almost always correlated with discriminative stimuli or cues. Therefore, it appears that mixed and tandem schedules have little application at this time. They are included here because there is considerable experimental data concerning their

effects on behavior; and as the science of behavior develops over time, it may become more apparent how these schedules can operate in everyday situations as well as in education and treatment.

Schedules Combining Both Number of Responses and Intervals of Time

There are two complex schedules of reinforcement in which basic ratio and interval schedules retain fixed values regardless of preceding behavior.

Alternative Schedules An **alternative schedule (alt)** is in effect whenever reinforcement follows the first completion of either a ratio schedule requirement or an interval schedule requirement. For example, a pigeon might be reinforced after emitting 50 key pecks or after the first response following a 5-minute interval, whichever comes first. This schedule would be an alt FR 50 FI 5; reinforcement would occur when (1) 50 responses have been made, provided the 5-minute interval of time has not elapsed; or (2) the first response has been made after a period of 5 minutes, provided 50 responses have not been made.

Teachers use the alternative schedule of reinforcement frequently during academic instruction. For instance, a teacher might assign 25 math problems with plans to check the student's work after 3 minutes. If the student completes the 25 problems accurately prior to the end of the 3-minute interval, reinforcement should follow. However, if the ratio requirement of 25 math problems has not been completed, the first correct response following a period of 3 minutes should be reinforced.

Conjunctive Schedules A **conjunctive schedule (conj)** of reinforcement is in effect whenever reinforcement follows the completion of requirements for both a ratio schedule and an interval schedule of reinforcement. For example, a pigeon might receive reinforcement when at least 2 minutes have elapsed and

50 responses have been made. This schedule would be identified as conj FI 2 FR 50. With the conjunctive schedule of reinforcement, the first response following the conclusion of the time interval produces reinforcement if a certain number of responses have been completed.

A teacher may be using a conjunctive schedule of reinforcement when a certain number of responses must be completed and a certain period of time must pass before an evaluation of progress is given. For example, on Monday a teacher might tell his students that they now have the opportunity to schedule times for him to hear their independent project reports. On Friday they will be able to present their oral reports to the class for a grade if the teacher has heard the reports first.

Duvinsky and Poppen (1982) found that human performance on a conjunctive schedule is influenced by the ratio and interval requirements. When task requirements are high in relationship to the interval requirements, people are likely to work steadily on the task throughout the time available. However, people are likely to engage in behaviors other than the task requirements when there is a large time interval and a low ratio requirement.

Table 12.1 provides a summary of the characteristics of complex schedules of reinforcement.

Basic Intermittent Schedules of Reinforcement in Human Affairs

Research has produced some well-established principles concerning the effects of basic intermittent schedules of reinforcement on behavior. These effects have been identified in laboratory studies, but they have not been documented clearly in human affairs, such as education and treatment, where many factors influence the behavior of interest. Most of the examples used in this chapter to illustrate the FR, VR, FI, and VI schedules of reinforcement are only approximations of true laboratory basic intermittent schedules of reinforcement.

Poppen (1982), commenting on typical examples of FI schedules of reinforcement in human affairs (e.g., receiving a paycheck, meeting a term paper deadline, studying for an examination), notes that these examples contain many more variables than a simple FI schedule of reinforcement. Several of the variables he identifies can influence all of the basic intermittent schedules of reinforcement in human affairs. Such variables include (1) instructions given by the teacher and self-instructions; (2) environmental aids, such as calendars and clocks; (3) past histories of responding to intermittent schedules of reinforcement; (4) current schedules of reinforcement available in almost all human situations; and (5) the sequential reponse required in many applications of basic intermittent schedules of reinforcement in human affairs. Thus, most applied schedules of reinforcement are more analogous to complex schedules than to basic intermittent schedules.

Poppen (1982) gives caution to the extrapolation of principles of schedule performance produced in basic research because of gaps in our knowledge of human performance.

> The reader should remember that experimental laboratory analysis restricts many classes of variables so that the operation of a few may be systematically observed. Extrapolating from the laboratory to other situations is a risky business in that the presence of many more variables and their interactions are likely to obscure the relationships observed under controlled conditions. (p. 128)

ADJUNCTIVE BEHAVIOR

This chapter has stressed the effects of schedules of reinforcement on specific behaviors. In any given situation many other behaviors will be emitted at the same time as the behavior of interest. Millenson and Leslie (1979) refer to these other behaviors as the natural behaviors a subject brings to a situation—behaviors that are not considered to be under the control of

TABLE 12.1. Summary and comparison of basic dimensions defining complex schedules of reinforcement.

	Schedule Name						
Dimension	*Concurrent*	*Multiple*	*Chained*	*Mixed*	*Tandem*	*Alternative*	*Conjunctive*
Number of basic schedules of reinforcement in effect	2 or more	2 or more	2 or more	2 or more	2 or more	2 or more	2 or more
Number of response classes involved	2 or more	1	1 or more	1	1 or more	1	1
Discriminative stimuli or cues associated with each component schedule	Possible	Yes	Yes	No	No	Possible	Possible
Successive presentation of basic schedules	No	Yes	Yes	Yes	Yes	No	No
Simultaneous presentation of basic schedules	Yes	No	No	No	No	Yes	Yes
Reinforcement limited to final component of basic schedule	No	No	Yes	No	Yes	No	Yes
Reinforcement for independent components of basic schedule	Yes	Yes	No	Yes	No	Yes	No

concurrent schedules of reinforcement. Typical examples of such behaviors are normal time fillers, such as doodling and idle talking. If the frequency of these other behaviors increases when a specific behavior is controlled by a schedule of reinforcement, they are called **adjunctive,** or *schedule-induced,* **behaviors.** Foster (1978) defines adjunctive behavior as "a behavior which is maintained indirectly by the typical controlling variables of another behavior, rather than directly by its own typical controlling variables" (p. 545).

The phenomenon of adjunctive behavior is well established in laboratory studies (e.g.,

Falk, 1971; Staddon, 1977) but has been neglected in applied behavior analysis. The topic does not even appear in the cumulative index of the *Journal of Applied Behavior Analysis* from 1968 through 1985. However, common adjunctive behaviors can become excessive; for example, the use of drugs, including tobacco, caffeine, and alcohol; overeating; nailbiting; self-stimulation; and self-abuse. These potentially excessive adjunctive behaviors may be of major importance in applied behavior analysis.

Foster (1978) voices concern that applied behavior analysis does not have a data or knowledge base for adjunctive phenomena. As a result, many professionals may apply interventions directly to adjunctive behaviors rather than to the variables functionally related to their occurrence. These direct interventions may be futile as well as costly in terms of money, time, and effort. Foster illustrates this concern with an observed case involving a young retarded adult.

> A young retarded adult developed a bedwetting problem shortly after entering a sheltered workshop program. This problem occurred several times per week and persisted in spite of several reinforcement procedures applied to it and in spite of the fact that termination from the work placement was not contingent upon bedwetting. The problem ceased only when the client was terminated from the workshop because of poor work performance and enrolled in a day activity center. Absolutely no bedwetting was observed for several months until he began another workshop program, at which point bedwetting

resumed. This problem has persisted in spite of renewed attempts at applying consequences to it, in spite of the fact that his work performance is entirely satisfactory and he expresses a desire to continue at the job, and in spite of the fact that there is still no contingent relation between bedwetting and termination of employment. In many such instances, it has proved more effective to modify the environmental "inducing" variables which originally produced the behaviors . . . , in this case, some as-yet-undetermined time, effort, or consequence property of the work routine. (p. 545)

One of the major areas for future research in applied behavior analysis is the conditions under which adjunctive behaviors are developed and maintained. Such findings will undoubtedly advance the science of behavior and will provide an important foundation for improved practice in education and treatment.

SUMMARY

Definition of Schedule of Reinforcement

1 A schedule of reinforcement is a rule that establishes the probability that a specific occurrence of a behavior will produce reinforcment.

Use of Continuous and Intermittent Reinforcement

2 Continuous reinforcement should be used during the initial stages of learning and for later strengthening of behavior.
3 Intermittent reinforcement should be used to maintain behavior.
4 The transition from continuous to intermittent reinforcement can be smoothed by increasing response requirements gradually and using prompts, cues, or instructions.
5 Intermittent reinforcement has the following desirable aspects: (a) it can be used to maintain behavior; (b) it is resistant to extinction; (c) it generates high response rates; (d) it

assists the move to more naturally occurring reinforcement; (e) it helps to control satiation; and (f) it is cost-effective.

Basic Intermittent Schedules of Reinforcement

6 Schedules of reinforcement can be either ratio or interval and can be applied on either a fixed or a variable basis.
7 In a fixed ratio schedule a constant number of responses must be made before reinforcement is delivered.
8 In a variable ratio an average number of responses must be made before reinforcement is delivered.
9 In a fixed interval schedule the first response following the passage of a specific, constant amount of time produces the reinforcement.
10 In a variable interval schedule the first response following the passage of a specific, average amount of time produces the reinforcement.

11 Each schedule of reinforcement has unique response characteristics that determine the consistency of responding, the rate of responding, and performance during extinction.

Differential Reinforcement of Rates of Responding

12 DRH and DRL are variations of ratio schedules and specify that reinforcement will be delivered contingent upon responses occuring at an established rate criterion.

Complex Schedules of Reinforcement

13 Continuous reinforcement, the four simple intermittent schedules of reinforcement, dif-ferential reinforcement of rates of responding, and extinction can be combined to produce more complex schedules of reinforcement.

14 The complex schedules of reinforcement include concurrent, multiple, chained, mixed, tandem, alternative, and conjunctive schedules.

Adjunctive Behavior

15 If the frequency of other behaviors increases when a specific behavior is controlled by a schedule of reinforcement, these other behaviors are called adjunctive or schedule-induced behaviors.

PART
FIVE

Stimulus Control

Reinforcement of an operant response generates two important effects. First, as a result of reinforcement, the likelihood of the future occurrence of the response is increased. Second, stimuli that immediately precede the response or are present during reinforcement are affected by the reinforcement and acquire some control over the recurrence of the response. Part four addressed the arrangements of stimuli following behavior. Part five addresses the arrangements of stimuli preceding behavior.

13

Stimulus Control

KEY TERMS

Discriminative stimulus (S^D)

Stimulus control

Environmental control

Phylogenetic history

Ontogenetic history

Stimulus generalization

Discrimination

Stimulus generalization gradients

Behavioral process

Simultaneous discrimination

Successive discrimination

Concept formation

Stimulus class

Preattending skills

Opportunity to respond

Salience

Masking

Overshadowing

Response prompts

Stimulus prompts

Fading

Transfer of stimulus control

Errorless learning

Most-to-least prompting

Graduated guidance

Shadowing

Spatial fading

Least-to-most prompting

Time delay

Stimulus fading

Superimposition

Stimulus shaping

Establishing operation

Establishing stimulus

This chapter was written by John O. Cooper.

Reinforcement of an operant response increases the likelihood of the future occurrence of the response and influences the stimuli that immediately precede the response or are present during reinforcement. The stimuli preceding the response (i.e., antecedent stimuli) may acquire some control over the recurrence of that response. In a typical laboratory demonstration of operant conditioning, a rat is placed in an experimental chamber and given the opportunity to press a lever. Contingent on a lever press the rat receives a food pellet. Reinforcement of the lever press increases the probability of recurrence of the response.

This simple demonstration can be made more complex by manipulating other variables. For example, from time to time a buzzer might sound, and lever pressing might then produce a food pellet only when emitted in the presence of the buzzer. The buzzer sound is called a **discriminative stimulus (S^D,** pronounced "S-dee"); it precedes the lever press. With some experience the rat will emit more lever presses in the presence of the buzzer sound (S^D) than in its absence. Behavior that is emitted more often in the presence of the S^D than during its absence is under **stimulus control.** Technically, stimulus control is demonstrated when the characteristic of a response, such as rate or future probability of occurrence, is altered concurrently with a change made in a particular property of an antecedent stimulus (Rilling, 1977). The stimulus change acquires control when a response is followed with reinforcement and the stimulus change is correlated with an increased frequency of reinforcement.

Stimulus control of behavior is not just an interesting oddity for laboratory demonstrations; it is a critical process for everyday behavior, education, and treatment. Most people do not answer the telephone in the absence of a ring; a person driving a car in the city is more likely to stop the car in the presence of a red traffic light than in its absence; an individual may emit some specific complex behavior in the presence of directions but not in their absence.

Some behaviors that are labeled as inappropriate are not necessarily inappropriate in themselves but are not under the stimulus control defined as appropriate by the reinforcing community. Loud talking may be appropriate on the playground but not in the classroom. Arriving 15 to 20 minutes late may be appropriate for a party but not for a job interview. Some behaviors that parents, teachers, clinicians, and society in general may call inappropriate are not behavior problems per se but are problems of emitting behaviors at a time or in a place or circumstance that is deemed inappropriate by others. Such is not a response problem but a problem of stimulus control and a major concern of education and treatment. This chapter addresses the factors related to the development of stimulus control.

ANTECEDENT STIMULI

Environmental control (S^D) of an operant response appears similar to the control of a conditioned stimulus over a respondent behavior. The S^D and the conditioned stimulus both are antecedent stimuli that can influence the occurrence of behavior. However, it is crucial to an understanding of environmental control of operant behavior to distinguish between the function of an S^D for operant behavior and a conditioned stimulus for respondent conditioning. In a typical laboratory demonstration of respondent conditioning, a dog is restrained in a harness, food is presented to the dog, and salivation is *elicited*. In such demonstrations food is an unconditioned stimulus that elicits the unconditioned response—salivation. Later in the demonstration a neutral stimulus (e.g., a buzzer sound) is produced that does not elicit salivation. However, the buzzer sound is paired with the delivery of food and the elicitation of salivation; and after several occurrences of simultaneous presentation, the buzzer sound (a neutral stimulus) becomes a conditioned stimulus that will elicit salivation (a conditioned response) in the absence of food (an unconditioned stimulus).

Laboratory examples of operant and respondent conditioning show that an antecedent stimulus can acquire control over a behavior. A buzzer sounds, and a rat presses a bar. A buzzer sounds, and a dog salivates. Despite the similarities the bar press is an operant behavior, salivation is a respondent behavior, and the manner in which the S^D and the conditioned stimulus acquire their controlling functions is very different. The S^D acquires controlling functions through association with stimuli that occur immediately following behavior. Conversely, the conditioned stimulus acquires controlling functions through association with other antecedent stimuli (i.e., the unconditioned stimulus).

A fixed relationship, called a reflex, is evident between an antecedent stimulus and a respondent behavior. Because of the fixed relationship, antecedent stimuli are said to elicit the behavior. Reflexive behavior is determined by the **phylogenetic history** (e.g., inherited history, genetic background) of the organism. However, the relationship between an antecedent stimulus and an operant behavior is not fixed. Therefore, operant behavior is not elicited but is *emitted*, and the antecedent stimulus (S^D) is said to set the occasion on which a response will be reinforced. **Ontogenetic history** (e.g., an organism's interaction with the environment, unique experiences of an organism) is the major factor in the occurrence of operant behavior, which is much less influenced by phylogenetic history than is respondent behavior (Ferster & Culbertson, 1982).

Stimuli in Environmental Control

The physical environment contains many forms of energy that can be perceived by the individual. Evolutionary adaptation to our physical environment has provided us with anatomical structures (i.e., organ receptors) that utilize these forms of energy. For example, the eye utilizes electromagnetic radiation; the ear, air-pressure vibrations; the tongue and nose, chemical energies; skin receptors, mechanical pressure and thermal changes.

When investigating the effects of stimuli on behavior, stimuli are described in terms of their physical properties. Not all physical properties of a stimulus can affect operant behavior. For instance, ultraviolet radiation is physical energy, but it is not a stimulus for humans because it does not result in any relationship with operant behavior. A stimulus is defined as any form of physical energy that is capable of being used in forming a relationship with behavior (Millenson & Leslie, 1979).

Stimulus Dimensions

Response terms and the terms used to describe the physical dimensions of stimuli are often misused by new students of applied behavior analysis. Stimulus dimensions of the visual environment are described in terms of frequency, amplitude or intensity, and complexity of light waves. Response dimensions of the same environment consider color and brightness. Auditory stimuli are produced by a vibrating object that disturbs the surrounding air and creates waves of pressure differences. Those waves describe the stimulus dimensions of sound. Response dimensions of the auditory environment are expressed in pitch, loudness, and timber. Smell and taste describe the response to chemical structures; temperature is a response to thermal energy; and weight describes quantitative force.

STIMULUS GENERALIZATION

When a response is reinforced in the presence of one stimulus, there is a general tendency to respond in the presence of new stimuli that have similar physical properties or have been associated with the stimulus. This tendency is called **stimulus generalization**. Conversely, **discrimination** is demonstrated when the response is not emitted in the presence of new stimuli. Different degrees of stimulus control are the defining characteristics of stimulus generalization and discrimination. Stimulus generalization reflects a loose degree of stimulus control, whereas discrimination indicates a relatively precise degree of control. In a simple everyday situation stimulus generalization can be observed when a young child who has learned to say "daddy" in the presence of her father says "daddy" in the presence of a variety of other men (stimuli)—a neighbor, a clerk in a store, Uncle Jim. Further conditioning is required to sharpen the degree of stimulus control to one specific stimulus, the father.

Stimulus generalization is more likely to occur when the new stimuli are of similar physical dimension but differ from the original stimulus only in some quantative property of that dimension. For instance, if a response has been reinforced in the presence of a visual stimulus, stimulus generalization is more likely to occur with a new stimulus that is also visual but consists of light waves of different frequency and intensity rather than a new stimulus that is auditory. Also, stimulus generalization is more likely when the new stimuli have other elements (e.g., size, shape) in common with the original stimulus. A student reinforced for making a response to a flash card with a circle on it is more likely to make the same response to a flash card containing an oval shape than to a card with a triangular shape.

The two conditions just cited have important implications for applied behavior analysis. In many training situations stimulus generalization is a desirable outcome. For example, a special education student mainstreamed to a regular classroom is expected to respond to academic and social stimuli in the same way that was demonstrated in the special classroom. An individual who acquired skills in us-

ing money in a training setting is expected to apply those skills in other settings, such as a grocery store and restaurant. Techniques for enhancing stimulus generalization are described in chapter 27; briefly, stimulus generalization is enhanced by the selection of antecedent stimuli in the training setting that are similar to the antecedent stimuli in the setting in which stimulus generalization is to occur. To illustrate, the special education teacher of the student to be mainstreamed into the regular classroom should use S^Ds as similar to those presented in the regular class as possible (e.g., same textbooks, worksheets, and other materials; same procedure for giving directions, oral and written; same requirements for assignments).

Measurement of Stimulus Generalization

Stimulus generalization gradients are used to measure stimulus generalization and discrimination. The generalization gradients show the extent to which responses reinforced in one stimulus condition are emitted in the presence of new stimuli. Figure 13.1 illustrates a typical generalization gradient. When the slope of the gradient is relatively flat, little stimulus control is evident. However, as the slope of the gradient increases, more control is demonstrated.

Many techniques are available for obtaining a stimulus generalization gradient (Rilling, 1977; Fantino & Logan, 1979), and this chapter cannot include examples of them all. However, the classic technique of Guttman and Kalish (1956) is a representative example. Their technique is important because many prior researchers had obtained stimulus generalization gradients by conditioning groups of subjects on the same stimulus value and then testing them individually, each with a different stimulus value. Obviously, this type of technique cannot demonstrate the degree of stimulus control for individual subjects. Guttman and Kalish provided a method of acquiring gradients for each subject and laid the foundation

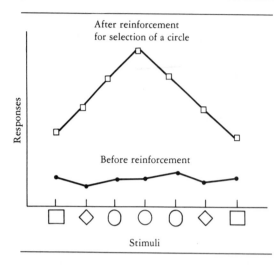

FIGURE 13.1 Hypothetical example of a generalization gradient.

for greater understanding of the principles governing stimulus control.

Guttman and Kalish reinforced pigeons on a VI 1-minute schedule for pecking a disk that was illuminated with a light source appearing yellow-green to humans (i.e., a wavelength of 550 mμ). After the pecking behavior had stabilized, the pigeons were tested under extinction conditions on the original stimulus and a randomized series of 11 different wavelengths never presented during training.

Two conditions in the Guttman and Kalish study were critical in producing their stimulus generalization gradients. The first condition was the selection of a VI schedule of reinforcement for conditioning the discrimination. As discussed in chapter 12, an intermittent schedule of reinforcement is more resistant to extinction than is continuous reinforcement, and the VI schedule generates stable rates of responding. With this conditioning history the subjects emitted enough responses during extinction to produce sufficient gradients for analysis. Also important was the selection of an extinction condition for the test of stimulus generalization. Stimulus generalization is defined as responding in the presence of a new stimulus after a response has been conditioned

in the presence of another similar stimulus. If responding is reinforced during testing for stimulus generalization, it cannot be clear whether responses are influenced by the schedule of reinforcement or by stimulus generalization. Guttman and Kalish avoided this problem of confounding their results by testing their subjects during extinction.

Stimulus Generalization: A Relative Phenomenon

The occurrence of stimulus generalization should be differentiated from the other principles and techniques that result in a behavior change (e.g., reinforcement, extinction, shaping). Stimulus generalization is a relative behavioral phenomenon; it is not a behavioral process. Stimulus generalization is a behavioral occurrence that can immediately follow a behavior change. For example, after a response is conditioned in the presence of one stimulus, other new stimuli may set the occasion for that same behavior to occur without other environmental manipulations or any development over time. The production of a change in behavior over a period of time under a fixed set of environmental conditions defines a **behavioral process**. Time to experience environmental conditions is an important variable in a behavioral process.

DEVELOPMENT OF STIMULUS CONTROL WITH DIFFERENTIAL REINFORCEMENT

An important procedure in applied behavior analysis for producing stimulus discrimination is to use differential reinforcement in the presence of two or more stimuli.

Stimulus Discrimination Training with Differential Reinforcement

The basic paradigm for stimulus discrimination training requires one response and two antecedent stimulus conditions. A response in the presence of one stimulus condition (S^D) is reinforced. A response that occurs in the presence of the other stimulus is not reinforced or receives less frequent reinforcement. That other stimulus is termed S^Δ (pronounced "S-delta"). When this training procedure is applied appropriately and consistently, the probability of a response in the presence of the S^D will come to exceed the likelihood of a response in the presence of the S^Δ. Over time, there will often be no response in the presence of the S^Δ.

Dyer, Christian, and Luce (1982) provide an example of teaching a simple discrimination skill to three autistic children. The first child was taught to discriminate between *his* and *her*. The child was presented simultaneously with two wooden figures, a male and a female, and was told, "Point to his [or her] head." When the child pointed to the appropriate figure's head, she was reinforced. A response to the inappropriate figure was not reinforced. This procedure involved one response (i.e., pointing) and two stimulus conditions—the S^D (i.e., directions plus the appropriate figure) and the S^Δ (i.e., directions plus the inappropriate figure). The second child was taught to describe the function of two common objects. The child was presented with one of two picture cards—a towel or a fork—and asked, "What's this for?" Reinforcement was delivered if the child said "dry with" in the presence of the towel picture or "eat with" in the presence of the fork picture. Other responses were not reinforced. The picture card of the towel was an S^D that set the occasion for the response "dry with"; it was an S^Δ condition for any other response. Similarly, the picture card of the fork set the occasion for the response "eat with"; it was an S^Δ condition for any other response. The third autistic child received training in discrimination between *right* and *left*. This child was directed, "Raise your right [or left] hand." She was reinforced when the appropriate hand was raised. If the inappropriate hand was raised, no reinforcement was delivered. Again, this third example illustrates responses under S^D and S^Δ conditions to develop behavior discrimination.

The basic stimulus discrimination training paradigm is usually described as alternating conditions of reinforcement and extinction. An S^D sets the occasion for a response to occur that will be reinforced. An S^Δ sets the occasion for any response to receive no reinforcement or less frequent reinforcement. An important point in discrimination training with differential reinforcement is this function of the S^Δ. It is used not only to show a condition of zero reinforcement (extinction) but also to denote a condition of less frequent reinforcement (Michael, 1982). For instance, a student could compute answers to math problems under one antecedent stimulus condition associated with an FR 10 schedule of reinforcement (S^D condition) and another stimulus condition associated with an FR 50 schedule of reinforcement (S^Δ condition). The S^D condition would be expected to produce a higher likelihood of response than the S^Δ condition.

Simultaneous and Successive Discrimination

Discrimination training with differential reinforcement can be implemented in one of two ways. First, two or more different stimuli (S^D and S^Δ conditions) can be presented at the same time. This concurrent presentation of multiple stimuli is a procedure of **simultaneous discrimination**. Second, stimulus tasks can be presented in sequence, one condition at a time. The successive presentation of stimuli is a procedure of **successive discrimination**. Usually a new stimulus item is presented only after a prescribed criterion of acquisition has been reached with the initial stimulus. Deciding which way to turn at an intersection on the way to visit a new friend is an example of a simultaneous discrimination; correct and incorrect turns are available simultaneously. Successive discrimination occurs in the attempt to discover which house is the home of the new friend.

Although successive discriminations are often required in everyday experience, most planned discrimination training in applied settings should present stimulus items simultaneously. The simultaneous presentation is preferred because (1) the individual has access to all relevant stimulus cues at one time and (2) an on-the-spot comparison of choices is permitted. In investigation of simultaneous and successive training in applied settings, Schroeder and Baer (1972) and Panyan and Hall (1978) found that the two methods were comparable in acquisition of discrimination. However, both studies reported that the simultaneous procedure produced more generalization than the successive presentations.

CONCEPT FORMATION

The preceding section showed how an antecedent stimulus can acquire control over a response; that is, it can cause a behavior to be emitted more often in its presence than in its absence. A preschool student who has not learned to name the primary colors might be taught these colors with a discrimination training procedure. For instance, to teach the color red, the teacher could use a red object such as a red apple as the S^D and a nonred object such as a yellow apple as the S^Δ. Both apples could be positioned randomly in front of the student, and the teacher could direct the student to point to the red apple. A correct response would be positively reinforced, and an incorrect response would not be reinforced. After a few correct responses the red apple would acquire stimulus control over the student's response, and the student would be able to reliably differentiate the red apple from the yellow apple. However, this simple discrimination may not be sufficient to meet the implied instructional objective of identifying the color red. The teacher may want the student to learn not only a discrimination between apples but also the concept of redness.

    Terms like *concept formation* or *concept acquisition* imply for most people some hypothet-

ical construct of a mental process outside the science of behavior. Yet acquiring a concept is clearly dependent upon responses in the presence of antecedent stimuli and the consequences following those responses. Concept formation is a behavioral process dependent on stimulus generalization and discrimination.

Definition of Concept Formation

Concept formation is a complex example of stimulus control. A concept is defined as both stimulus generalization within a class of stimuli and discrimination between classes of stimuli (Keller & Schoenfeld, 1950). A **stimulus class** is a set of stimuli with a common relationship. An illustration of this definition can be found in the concept of redness. Light waves of different wavelength impinge on the eye and nerves associated with that organ to produce an effect described as color. For example, a red object is called red because the object reflects waves that produce red light when the object is seen in daylight. There is a gradation of wavelengths that generate different colors called red—from light red to dark red. These different shades of the color red share a relationship and are included in the same stimulus class. Therefore the concept of redness requires stimulus generalization from the trained stimulus to many other stimuli within the stimulus class. If the preschool child described earlier had acquired the concept of redness, he would be able to identify the red apple and, without specific training, choose a red balloon, a red toy car, a red pencil, and so on. In addition to stimulus generalization, a concept requires discrimination between classes of stimuli. For example, the concept of redness requires discriminating between red and other colors and irrelevant dimensions, such as shape or size. The concept begins with discrimination between the red apple and the yellow apple but results in discriminating a red dress from a blue dress, a red toy car from a white car, a red pencil from a black pencil.

Teaching Concept Formation

Responses to S^D and S^Δ conditions are fundamental in the acquisition of a concept. Antecedent stimuli representative of a group of stimuli sharing a common relationship (i.e., the stimulus class) and antecedent stimuli from other stimulus classes must be presented. In other words, before a concept can be acquired, exemplars of what the concept is (i.e., the S^D condition) and what the concept is not (i.e., S^Δ condition) must be presented. This approach holds true for all conceptual development, whether the concepts are of red, chair, and triangle or honesty, patriotism, justice, freedom, and sharing, which seem more abstract. Discrimination training is the basic procedure for teaching a concept.

Bryant and Budd (1984) taught six behaviorally handicapped children the concept of verbal and physical sharing. The children were presented with examples of sharing. The teacher told the children why sharing is important and modeled sharing behavior with the children. The teacher also included examples of behaviors that are not sharing. For example, "We can share by giving the other children things when they ask nicely for them. We can also share by asking for toys that other children have. It is not sharing to hit or push other children, take toys they are playing with or tell them they cannot play" (p. 50). The teacher praised and prompted sharing behavior. When children refused to share (e.g., took without asking, opposed play, were aggressive), the teacher followed the behavior with prompts on how to share appropriately. Figure 13. 2 shows data for the six children who received training on the concept of sharing. As can be seen in Figure 13.2, five of the six children may have acquired the concept of sharing, as indicated by their increase in sharing. The data also suggest that there was a decrease in not sharing (i.e., negative behaviors).

The example from Bryant and Budd illustrates how discrimination training with differential reinforcement can be applied directly to teaching a concept. It is also possible to acquire a concept through vicarious discrimination training and differential reinforcement. A simple verbal definition of a concept may be sufficient for concept formation without additional direct training. The definition should include examples of what the concept is and what the concept is not. Literature is frequently written to teach a concept vicariously, as is readily noted in children's literature, where concepts such as good and bad, honest and dishonest, courageous and cowardly are frequent themes.

An actual children's story can illustrate the approach. An owner of a mom-and-pop grocery store wanted to hire a young person to work in the store. The job was to sweep the floor, help bag groceries, and keep the shelves neat. The owner wanted an honest person to work for him, so he decided to test all applicants to see whether they were honest. The first young person who applied was given the opportunity to try the job before the owner made the commitment to hire him. But before the applicant came to work, the owner hid a dollar bill where he knew the young person would find it. At the end of the test period the owner asked the applicant how he had liked working in the store, whether he wanted the job, and whether anything surprising or unusual had happened to him. The applicant replied that he wanted the job and that nothing surpising had happened to him. The grocer told the first applicant that he wanted to consider others who had applied also. The second applicant worked a test period with the same results as the first person. He did not get the job. The third young person to work for the grocer was sweeping the floor, found the dollar bill, and took it immediately to the grocer. The third applicant said he wanted to turn in the dollar bill in case one of the customers or the grocer had dropped it. The grocer asked the applicant whether he liked the job and wanted to work for him. The young person replied that he did. The grocer told the applicant that the job was his because he was an honest person. The grocer also let him keep the dollar bill.

FIGURE 13.2 Individual child levels of sharing behavior and negative interactions as percentages of total intervals observed across 4-day session blocks. Dashed vertical lines indicate introduction of sharing training for successive pairs of children. (From "Teaching Behaviorally Handicapped Preschool Children to Share" by L. E. Bryant and K. S. Budd, 1984, *Journal of Applied Behavior Analysis, 17,* p. 52. Copyright 1984 by the Society for the Experimental Analysis of Behavior, Inc. Reprinted by permission.)

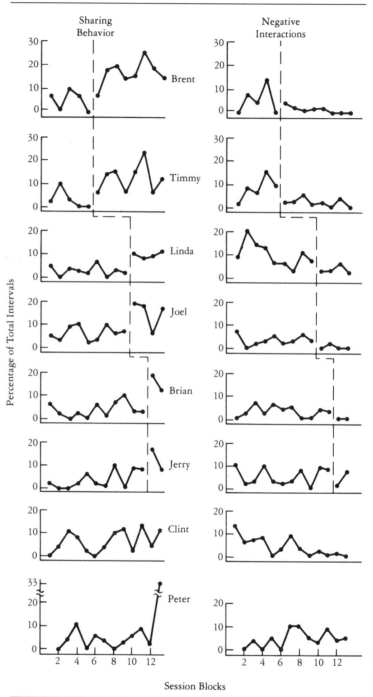

306

This example presents exemplars of behavior that is honest and behavior that is dishonest. The honest behavior is reinforced (i.e., the honest person got the job), and the dishonest behavior is not reinforced (i.e., the first two applicants did not get the job). The story could be used to help teach the concept of honesty vicariously.

Object, Relational, and Heterogeneous Stimulus Classes

Conceptual behaviors are under the discriminative control of a broad class of antecedent stimuli. The stimuli in the class may be held together by a common relationship, often a physical form (i.e., topographical structure) or a spatial arrangement (Millenson & Leslie, 1979). For instance, in the stimulus class of dog, an individual dog will share a common physical form with all other members of that stimulus class. A dog can be differentiated from a horse, cat, cow, and so on. Spatial arrangements and topological structures of stimuli are the common relationships for most object concepts, such as book, table, house, tree, cup, cat, rug, onion, corn, car, and the printed numeral 6. For other concepts a relational, or relative, relationship is established among a broad group of stimuli. Illustrative of these concepts are bigger than, hotter than, higher than, on top of, to the left of. These relational concepts comprise a large portion of our conceptual repertoire. Still other concepts are observed within a broad class of stimuli that appear to lack a common relationship. These stimulus classes are comprised of heterogeneous stimuli. Figure 13.3 is a set of antecedent stimuli that control the same response, entering an appropriate public rest room, even though the stimuli share no common physical relationship.

As demonstrated in Figure 13.3, the apparent lack of a common spatial relationship or topological structure does not preclude the development of control over a given response by a broad class of stimuli. However, the

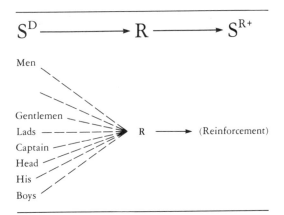

FIGURE 13.3 Stimuli of different physical forms that control the same response. (From "Perception, Language, and Conceptualization Rules" (p. 214) by I. Goldiamond in *Problem Solving: Research, Method, and Theory* by B. Kleinmuntz (Ed.), 1966, New York: Wiley. Copyright 1966 by Wiley. Adapted by permission.)

heterogeneous stimulus class does not produce the degree of stimulus generalization generally found among stimulus classes sharing a common spatial or topological relationship (Millenson & Leslie, 1979). Discrimination training with differential reinforcement is often necessary to expand the number of controlling stimuli in a heterogeneous stimuli class.

The development of conceptual behavior is of major importance in education and treatment, whether stated implicitly or explicitly in the goals and objectives of instruction. Teaching object, relational, and heterogeneous concepts requires different instructional considerations. Teaching selected exemplars of what an object or relational concept is and is not will often be sufficient because of the likelihood of stimulus generalization occurring with these concepts. With heterogeneous concepts, however, the instructional plan should include an identification of all stimuli in the heterogeneous stimulus class that are important to the client's behavior and a schedule for discrimination training of each identified stimulus.

FACTORS AFFECTING THE DEVELOPMENT OF STIMULUS CONTROL

There are least five important factors related to the development of stimulus control: (1) reinforcement, (2) preattending skills, (3) stimulus presentation, (4) salience of the stimuli, and (5) masking and overshadowing.

Reinforcement

Stimulus control is established by more frequent reinforcement of behaviors in the presence of the S^D than in the presence of the S^{Δ}. Effective differential reinforcement requires that reinforcers be identified and used correctly (chapter 11 provides guidelines). Perhaps the major reason some teachers have difficulty in establishing stimulus control is that they do not provide reinforcing consequences for responses made in the presence of the S^D.

Preattending Skills

The acquisition of certain prerequisite skills is important for the development of stimulus control. For academic or social skills the learner should engage in orienting behaviors appropriate to the S^D in the instructional setting. Such behaviors include looking at the instructional materials, looking at the teacher whenever a response is modeled, listening to oral instructions, and sitting quietly for short periods of time. Etzel, LeBlanc, Schilmoeller, and Stella (1981) label these prerequisite skills **preattending skills**. They say that learners without preattending skills are often described as flighty, unsettled, distractible, and preoccupied. Etzel et al. demonstrated that these preattending skills are not necessarily influenced by motivation or task difficulty and presented the following conclusions:

1 Placing the children with inappropriate preattending responses in a very easy learning task—one that they can learn quite readily (or in some instances already know)—does not reduce inappropriate preattending responses or increase appropriate preattending responses.

2 Placing the children in a more difficult learning task tends to increase inappropriate preattending, but returning them to an easier task does not necessarily reduce inappropriate responses. Changing *some* aspect of the environment seemed to be more related to poor preattending than task difficulty per se.

3 Increasing the amount of consequences (reinforcers) that followed correct responses does not reduce inappropriate preattending behaviors or increase correct responses.

4 Using training programs that are errorless with most other children tends to result in more correct answers with these children, but they tend to have more errors than other children on the same programs. Such programs do not alter their inappropriate preattending behaviors. (pp. 9–10)

The implications for teachers are that preattending skills must be assessed prior to instruction. Learners without these skills must be taught them through direct behavioral intervention. Learners must emit behaviors that orient the sensory receptors to the appropriate S^D before stimulus control can be developed.

Stimulus Presentation

The teacher's behavior in presenting the S^D has a major impact on the development of stimulus control. There are three areas of concern: the specificity of directions, the student's opportunities to respond, and the pacing of response opportunities.

Specificity of Directions   Instructional directions should relate directly to the discrimination to be made (Gersten, Carnine, & White, 1984). Teachers often try to help students by providing a set of detailed instructions. However, much of the detailed information is not relevant to the response to be brought under stimulus control. For instance, in teaching a new sight word, some teachers give several examples of how the word can be used (Etzel et al., 1981). If the objective is to identify the word *pig* when the word is presented in simultaneous discrimination training, a teacher might use a set of detailed instructions: "This is the word *pig*. A pig is an animal. Pigs live on farms. Pigs like to play in mud. Point to *pig* and say the word."

A more direct approach would contain minimal distractions from the word to be taught: "This is the word *pig*. Say *pig* and point to the word *pig*." The direct approach usually results in quicker acquisition of stimulus control, possibly because the directions focus on the objective—in this case, saying and pointing to the word *pig* (S^D). Knowing that a pig is an animal that lives on a farm and likes to play in mud may distract the learner from the discrimination to be made.

Opportunity to Respond **Opportunity to respond** is defined by Greenwood, Delquadri, and Hall (1984) as "the interaction between (a) teacher-formulated instructional antecedent stimuli (the materials presented, prompts, questions asked, signals to respond, etc.) and (b) their success in establishing the academic responding desired or implied by the material" (p. 64). The research on opportunity to respond conducted at the Juniper Gardens Children's Project (e.g., Delquadri, Greenwood, & Hall, 1979; Hall, Delquadri, Greenwood, & Thurston, 1982) has clearly established that stimulus control associated with frequent opportunities to respond increases academic achievement.

Opportunity to respond implies that the teacher should arrange antecedent stimuli so that all students can make the desired responses. Greenwood, et al. (1984) reported data showing that in six intercity classrooms, Grades 1 to 4, 75% of the school day was used for academic instruction with the students responding actively to instruction during only 25% of the school day. Students must be provided with many opportunities to practice academic behavior.

A second implication of opportunity to respond is that students should be placed in learning situations in which they can emit high rates of correct responses. Too often students are asked to respond to antecedent stimuli that set the occasion for incorrect responses; the students have not acquired sufficient prerequisite skills to respond correctly. Stephens (1976) recommends that teachers use only instructional antecedent stimuli that occasion student responses that are correct 70 to 90% of the time. He further recommends that these instructional antecedent stimuli be presented only under teacher direction. Independent student response to antecedent stimuli, according to Stephens, should not be systematically planned until student responses are correct at least 90% of the time.

A third implication from the literature on opportunity to respond is the importance of active responding rather than passive responding. Active academic responding includes behaviors such as calculating math facts, reading orally, answering questions, playing academic games, pointing to a word, asking questions. Passive responding includes visual attention to teachers, peers, or materials; specific examples include watching a teacher present a lecture or give directions, watching a peer read orally, raising hand, waiting for teacher help. Greenwood et al. (1984) report that passive responding represents a major portion, as much as 45%, of instructional time in the school day. This research suggests that active responding to antecedent stimuli may be one of the most important correlates of academic achievement. Passive responding is viewed as an important academic survival skill; but in the absence of a high rate of active responding, it may not be an important factor in the development of academic performance.

Pacing of Response Opportunities The pacing of response opportunities appears to affect academic achievement. Pacing has been studied with pigeons (e.g., Holt & Shafer, 1973), preschoolers (e.g., Croll, 1970), elementary-aged students (Carnine, 1976), autistic children (Koegel, Dunlap, & Dyer, 1980), and adults (e.g., Grobe, Pettibone, & Martin, 1973).

The literature suggests that a rapid presentation of antecedent stimuli may produce higher achievement with a lower error rate than a slow rate of presentation. Carnine and Fink (1978) state that a rapid pace of instruction increases the quantity of material taught and maintains the students' attention. Carnine (1976) found that during small group reading instruction rapid presentations produce more achievement in correct letter and word identifications and less disruptive behavior than slow presentations produced. Figure 13.4 presents the data for off-task behavior, answering correctly, and participation for one of Carnine's subjects under alternating conditions of slow- and rapid-paced instruction. As shown in Figure 13.4, the student clearly demonstrated superior performance under conditions of rapid stimulus presentation.

Attention

People attend to some antecedent stimuli more than others. Most often individuals attend more

FIGURE 13.4 Percentage occurrence of off-task behavior, answering correctly, and participation for Subject 1 during phases of slow and fast presentation. The dotted lines indicate when Subject 1 was absent. (From "Effects of Two Teacher-Presentation Rates on Off-Task Behavior, Answering Correctly, and Participation" by D. W. Carnine, 1976, *Journal of Applied Behavior Analysis, 9,* p. 204. Copyright 1976 by the Society for the Experimental Analysis of Behavior, Inc. Reprinted by permission.)

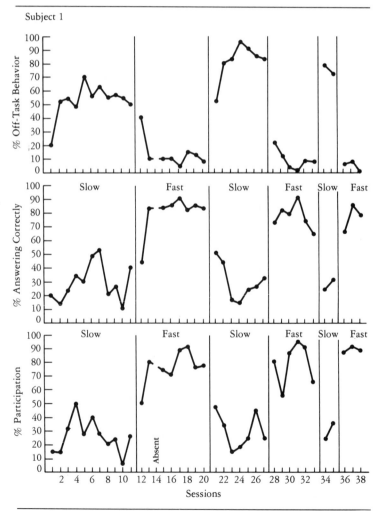

to antecedent stimuli that have been differentially correlated in the past with reinforcement or other consequences. Motorists attend to traffic lights. Students attend to test instructions. Children attend to cartoons on television. Gamblers attend to the numbers on their lottery tickets. However, factors other than previous differential reinforcement can influence the attention directed to stimuli.

Salience The **salience** of the stimulus is a major factor that influences attention and ultimately the development of stimulus control. Salience refers to the prominence of the stimulus in the individual's environment. That is, will the individual notice and respond to the stimulus dimensions? Depending upon the sensory capabilities of an individual, the past history of reinforcement, and the situation (i.e., stimulus context), some stimuli are more salient than others. For instance, a student may not attend to stimuli written on the blackboard because of poor visual acuity or to the teacher's oral directions because of poor auditory acuity. Because of sensory problems a student may focus attention on other stimuli. Another student may attend to noninstructional stimuli because past responses to instructional stimuli have not been differentially reinforced by the teacher, parents, or peer group. Still another student may fail to attend to instructional stimuli because her attention is focused on a toy in her desk.

The importance of stimulus salience in the development of stimulus control focuses on the modality of stimulus presentation not only because of individual sensory capabilities but also because of unique past experiences with different modalities. Many educational researchers and authorities (e.g., Barbe & Swassing, 1979) have discussed the importance of presenting instructional stimuli in the modality strength of the student. For example, Student A notices and responds to instructional stimuli in the visual modality more than the oral. For Student B the reverse might be true. Accordingly,

modality strength—whether visual, auditory, kinetic, or tactile—may be an important variable in instruction. Thus far, the educational research literature in teaching to modality strength has generated mixed results, which may be a function of measurement procedures and selection of variables rather than an absence of functional relationship.

Two important implications can be drawn from the role of stimulus salience in the development of stimulus control during education and treatment. First, it is important for students to receive comprehensive physical/sensory examinations, and these results must be made known to teachers. If physical/sensory deficits cannot be corrected, teachers must make alternative stimulus modalities available during instruction. Second, because past history influences the salience of stimuli, assessment of modality strengths should be conducted prior to instruction.

Masking and **overshadowing** (Mackintosh, 1977) are conditions that also influence the salience of stimuli. In masking, even though one stimulus has control over behavior, another stimulus blocks that control from being expressed. For example, a student may know the answers to certain instructional stimuli but will not emit the response in the presence of the peer group. With overshadowing, the presence of one stimulus condition interferes with the acquisition of control by another stimulus. Some stimuli are more salient than others. For example, during algebra instruction some male students may be more likely to look out of the window to watch the cheerleaders' practice than to attend to the instructional stimuli presented by the teacher.

Both masking and overshadowing are of concern in instructional settings. Teachers should be aware of these phenomena and try to rule out their effects as much as possible. Three ways to overcome masking and overshadowing are (1) to make changes in the physical environment (e.g., lower the window shade, remove the toy until recess), (2) to make the instructional stimuli as intense and centrally located as possible (e.g., rapid pace of instruction, high rate of opportunity to respond), and (3) to consistently reinforce behavior in the presence of the instructionally relevant stimuli.

RESPONSE AND STIMULUS PROMPTS

Prompts (Billingsley & Romer, 1983; Snell, 1983a) are supplementary stimuli used to increase the likelihood that a student will emit a correct response in the presence of the S^D, which will eventually control the behavior. Prompts are stimuli given before or during the performance of a behavior; they help behavior occur so that the teacher can provide reinforcement. Prompts associated with the response are termed **response prompts**; they include verbal directions, modeling, and physical guidance.

Response Prompts

Verbal Directions   Verbal directions can be used as a supplementary prompt to occasion a response. Verbal prompts can be one word, several words, or even a paragraph in length. The critical feature is that a verbal prompt function as a supplementary stimulus to occasion a correct response.

Verbal directions are used routinely in many settings. For example, in classrooms teachers use verbal prompting when a student's response to the initial S^D is not forthcoming. To illustrate, let us suppose that a student was called on to read this sentence, "Plants need soil, air, and water to grow"; but he read, "Plants need . . . Plants need . . . Plants need . . ." and continued to repeat these first two words. To set the occasion for the student to make a correct response, the teacher might use any number of verbal prompts. She might ask the student,

"Did that make sense?" Or she might use a rhyming word for *soil*, say the first part of the word *soil*, or say the whole word for the student. Numerous other examples of verbal directions can be cited. A parent reminding his daughter to make her bows larger when she ties her shoes is using a verbal prompt. Likewise, the gymnastics coach who tells her students to shift their weight as they begin to swing on the bar is verbally prompting behavior.

Three procedures for verbal prompts are in common use (Cuvo & Davis, 1980). First, the teacher can tell the student what is expected (e.g., remind the student that she is to do the math worksheet). Favell, McGimsey, and Jones (1980) successfully decreased the rapid eating behavior of an institutionalized male by using a combination of reinforcement for pauses and a verbal prompt ("Wait") if the subject failed to pause independently. The second procedure is to ask questions concerning the performance (e.g., "Does *soil* follow *need*?" "What is the next word?") Third, the procedure to follow can be described. For instance, the addition process for $19 + 2$ can be described verbally: "Add 9 and 2. The answer is 11. Carry the 1 to the tens column. Add the tens column. . . ." Telling the student what is expected is a helpful prompt for behaviors that are under the control of natural S^Ds. Asking questions is an appropriate procedure for behaviors only partially mastered. The procedural description is most appropriate when a new skill is being learned.

When using verbal prompts, it is critical that the verbal stimuli used as prompts be in the student's repertoire. Simple words and vocabulary may need to be used, often in conjunction with gestures.

Modeling   A behavior can be modeled by demonstrating the desired behavior so that it can be imitated. Modeling prompts are slightly more intrusive than verbal prompts because the teacher must demonstrate the correct response.

The most notable work on the use of modeling to occasion behavior has been conducted by Bandura (1969). Taken as a whole, his research has shown that modeling can be an effective way to prompt behaviors if certain conditions are met. For example, the effectiveness of modeling may be increased when the sex, age, and characteristics of the model closely resemble those of the imitator. Also, the likelihood of success may be increased by the prestige of the model. However, modeled responses are not limited to human performances. The model can be presented through visual illustration (e.g., words on a printed card to be copied, a series of pictures to be imitated).

The use of models to assist in the development of appropriate academic and social behavior has been demonstrated repeatedly. O'Leary and O'Leary (1977) cite three studies in which modeling was used alone or in combination with other procedures to improve child interactions, question asking, and teacher-student interactions.

Modeling tends to be most effective when the imitator has some of the component behaviors in place prior to beginning the modeling procedure. It is easier, more practical, and more successful to use a modeling procedure to prompt a student to shoot a basketball through a hoop if he already is able to hold the ball, raise it over his head, and push the ball away from his body. Few practitioners would use modeling to teach a severely handicapped child to tie her shoes if she could not hold the laces in her hands. In addition, visual attending skills are important because the student must see the model to imitate the performance. Finally, modeling as a prompt should be used only with students who have already developed imitative skills (see chapter 16 for a more complete discussion of modeling and imitation).

Physical Guidance With physical guidance an individual is bodily assisted through an action. For example, a parent using physical guidance to prompt his athetoid cerebral pal-

sied child to eat would place his hands on top of the child's, scoop up a spoonful of food, and raise the child's hand to her mouth. All of the performance is under the direction of the parent.

Physical guidance is the most intrusive of the three response prompts mentioned thus far. It requires that the teacher be involved directly with the student. Physical response prompts provide little opportunity for the student to emit the behavior without the direct assistance of the teacher. However, for some individuals physical guidance may be the only prompt possible for occasioning responses; that is, the degree of physical handicap may be so severe that verbal or model prompts are ineffective. Physical guidance is not restricted in its use to the physically handicapped. Speech therapists helping students make correct sounds, physical education teachers helping students through a gymnastics routine, or parents helping their children dress might all use physical guidance during the initial stages of behavior acquisition.

Snell (1983a) refers to physical guidance as "putting the learner through" the performance and stresses of the important difference between that and doing it for the learner. "For example, complete manual guidance during dressing may mean standing behind a child, taking the back of his hands and moving his fingers to grasp the top of his pants and pulling upward. The child's pants are not simply pulled up for him" (p. 125).

Stimulus Prompts

Stimulus prompts are stimuli used in conjunction with the task stimuli or instructional materials. Stimulus prompts are cues to help the student emit a correct response. Snell (1983a) identifies three cue techniques for prompting a behavior. First are movement cues. For instance, a student learning to discriminate a penny from a dime might be helped with movement cues; the teacher might point to, tap, touch, or look at the coin to be identified. Second are position cues. In the coin discrimination task the teacher could use a position cue and place the correct coin closer to the student. Third are redundancy cues. Redundancy cues occur when one or more stimulus/response dimensions (e.g., color, size, shape) are paired with the correct choice. For instance, the teacher might place the correct coin on a white sheet of paper. M. E. Skinner (1978) used redundancy cues to vary the size of instructional stimuli in teaching number discrimination of numbers with the same digits to elementary-aged students with learning disabilities. (e.g., 17, *71* ; 12, *21*).

TRANSFER OF STIMULUS CONTROL

Response and stimulus prompts are supplementary antecedent stimuli that should be introduced during only the acquisition phase of instruction. As soon as the behavior is occurring, response and stimulus prompts must be removed so that stimulus control can be transferred to the natural stimulus. **Fading** is a technique to gradually change the antecedent stimulus: stimuli are faded in or out; that is, they are presented or removed gradually. Eventually the response will be occasioned by a partially changed or new stimulus. Fading response and stimulus prompts is the technique used for **transfer of stimulus control** from the prompts to the natural stimulus, which minimizes the number of error responses occurring in the presence of the natural stimulus.

Terrace's (1963a, b) research in the transfer of stimulus control using fading and superimposition of stimuli provides classic illustrations of this procedure. In these studies Terrace taught pigeons to make red-green and vertical-horizontal discriminations with a minimum of errors. His use of techniques for gradually transferring stimulus control was called **error-**

less learning. To teach the red-green discrimination, the S^{Δ} (red light) was presented before the pigeon's responses to the S^D (green light) were under stimulus control. The initial introduction of the red light was with low illumination and for brief time intervals. During successive presentations of the stimuli, Terrace gradually increased the intensity of the red light and the duration of time it was illuminated until it differed from the green light only in hue. With this procedure Terrace taught the pigeon to discriminate red from green with only a minimum number of errors (responses to the S^{Δ}).

Terrace further demonstrated that stimulus control acquired with red and green lights could be transferred to vertical and horizontal lines with a minimum number of errors (i.e., responses in the presence of the S^{Δ}). His procedure consisted of first superimposing a white vertical line on the green light (S^D) and a white horizontal line on the red light (S^{Δ}). Then the pigeons were given several presentations of the two compound stimuli. Finally, the intensity of the red and green lights was reduced gradually until only the vertical and horizontal lines remained as stimulus conditions. The pigeons showed almost perfect transfer of stimulus control from the red-green lights to the vertical-horizontal lines. That is, they emitted responses in the presence of the vertical line (S^D) and seldom responded in the presence of the horizontal line (S^{Δ}).

Following Terrace's work, other researchers produced landmark studies showing that the transfer of stimulus control with few S^{Δ} responses was possible with children (e.g., Bijou, 1968; Moore & Goldiamond, 1964; Sidman & Stoddard, 1966). Martin and Pear (1983) present several reasons for using procedures that result in fewer student errors. First, errors decrease the time available for instruction. Second, when an error occurs, it is likely to be repeated. Third, the lack of reinforcement may result in inappropriate emotional behaviors, such as tantrums and aggressive behavior.

Transfer of Response Prompts

Wolery and Gast (1984) describe four procedures for transferring stimulus control from response prompts to natural stimuli. They describe these procedures as most-to-least prompts, graduated guidance, least-to-most prompts, and time delay.

Most-to-Least Prompts The procedure of **most-to-least prompting** has been employed extensively with persons demonstrating severe developmental disabilities. Wolery and Gast (1984) recommend this procedure for performances such as motor imitation, self-feeding, dressing, instruction following, vocational task assembly, and manual guidance. To transfer stimulus control from the response prompt to the natural stimuli, the teacher initially guides the student physically through the entire performance. The teacher then gradually reduces the amount of physical assistance provided as training progresses from session to session. Usually this procedure moves from physical prompts to visual prompts and, last, to verbal directions (Billingsley & Romer, 1983). Csapo (1981) transferred stimulus control using the most-to-least procedure in a discrimination task with severely handicapped students. First, complete physical guidance and a verbal direction were given. After three correct responses complete physical guidance was faded to partial physical guidance, such as touching the arm. Partial physical guidance was removed after three correct responses and was replaced with a gestural prompt. In the last step only verbal directions were used to occasion the response.

Graduated Guidance Like most-to-least prompts, **graduated guidance** is a fading procedure used frequently in instructing persons with severe developmental disabilities. Wolery and Gast consider graduated guidance to be appropriate for the same types of performances that were indicated for most-to-least prompts (e.g., feeding, toileting, dressing). The procedure for graduated guidance requires the teacher to provide a physical prompt only when it is needed, and then it is faded immediately whenever the student responds correctly. Foxx and Azrin (1973a) recommend using shadowing and spatial fading with the graduated guidance procedure as soon as the student is performing the skill independently. **Shadowing** has the teacher following the student's movements with her hands very near but not touching the child. The teacher then gradually increases the distance of her hands from the student. Shadowing provides the opportunity for an immediate physical prompt if the student is not responding correctly. **Spatial fading** involves gradually changing the location of the physical prompt. For example, if the physical prompt is used for a hand movement, the teacher can move the prompt from the hand to the wrist, to the elbow, to the shoulder, and then to no physical contact.

Least-to-Most Prompts **Least-to-most prompting** is an appropriate fading procedure for most skill development. With this procedure the student is given the opportunity to perform the response with the least amount of assistance on each trial. Greater degrees of assistance are provided as successive opportunities are required. This procedure requires that a latency interval (frequently 5 seconds) occur between the presentation of the natural S^D and the opportunity to emit the response. If the response does not occur within the specified time, a response prompt of least assistance is provided (i.e., a verbal prompt). If after the specified latency period no correct response is emitted again, another prompt is given providing additional assistance (e.g., a gesture). Partial or full physical guidance can be provided if the student has not responded to lesser assistance. The following scenario illustrates the procedure for least-to-most prompts.

Tutor: Joe, point to the numeral 8 [the natural S^D] on the number line in front of you.

Joe: (He spends 5 seconds without a response.)

Tutor: Joe, point to the numeral 8 on your number line. It's the one between 7 and 9. [verbal prompt]

Joe: (Again, he spends 5 seconds without a response.)

Tutor: Joe, watch me point to the numeral 8 on your paper. [gestural prompt] Now you point to the numeral 8.

Joe: (He points to the 9.)

Tutor: Joe, point to the numeral 8. (During the verbal direction the tutor places his hand on top of Joe's and moves Joe's hand close to the numeral 8.) [partial physical prompt]

Joe: (Again, he points to the 9.)

Tutor: Joe, point to the numeral 8. (During the direction the tutor guides Joe's finger to the numeral 8.) [full physical prompt]

Wolery and Gast (1984) list four basic guidelines to be followed when using least-to-most prompts. First, the natural S^D to which stimulus control will be transferred is presented at each prompt level. Second, a constant latency interval (e.g., 5 seconds) follows the presentation of each natural S^D or prompt, within which time the student has an opportunity to respond without additional assistance. Third, increased assistance is presented at each prompt level. Fourth, each correct response is positively reinforced even if prompted. The advantages of this fading procedure are that it allows the student to respond in the presence of the natural S^D on each trial and permits the student's behavior to determine the level of prompting needed for a correct response.

Time Delay **Time delay** transfers stimulus control from a prompt to the natural stimulus by delaying the presentation of the prompt after the natural stimulus has been presented. Most-to-least prompts, graduated guidance, and least-to-most prompts rely on gradual changes in the form, position, or intensity of the response prompts to produce a transfer of stimulus control. In contrast, time delay uses only variations in the time intervals between presentation of the natural stimulus and the response prompt to produce the transfer of stimulus control.

Snell and Gast (1981) describe two time delay procedures—progressive and constant. The progressive time delay procedure starts with a zero time delay between the presentation of the natural stimulus and the response prompt: the two are presented simultaneously. Usually, several trials of zero time delay are presented before variations are programmed. The number of trials depends upon the task difficulty and the functioning level of the student. Following simultaneous presentation, the time delay is gradually and systematically increased, usually in 1-second intervals. The time delay can be increased after a specific number of presentations, after each session, or after a specific number of sessions. Table 13.1 illustrates progressive time delay by sessions.

TABLE 13.1. Illustration of the progressive time delay procedure.

Session	Delay in Seconds	Operation
1	0	Natural S^D and response prompt are presented simultaneously.
2	1	Response prompt is provided if response does not occur within 1 second after presentation of the natural S^D.
3	2	Response prompt is provided if response does not occur within 2 seconds after presentation of the natural S^D.
4	3	Response prompt is provided if response does not occur within 3 seconds after presentation of the natural S^D.

(Time delay continues to increase)

The constant time delay procedure, like the progressive time delay, begins with several trials using a zero time delay. Then, for all other trials the response prompt is delayed for a fixed time interval (e.g., 4 seconds) after the presentation of the natural stimulus.

Transfer of Stimulus Control with Stimulus Manipulations

The focus of the preceding sections was on stimulus prompts that can be used without making variations in the task stimuli or materials. In the stimulus manipulation procedures discussed here, the task stimuli or materials are changed systematically to prompt a response. These stimuli are then faded in or out as soon as the prompt has occasioned the response so that stimulus control is transferred from the prompt to the natural stimulus. Stimulus manipulation procedures include stimulus fading and stimulus shaping (Etzel et a., 1981). Superimposition of stimuli is used frequently with both procedures.

Stimulus Fading **Stimulus fading** involves highlighting a physical dimension (e.g., color, size, position) of a stimulus to increase the likelihood of a correct response. The highlighted or exaggerated dimension is faded gradually in or out. The following series illustrates stimulus fading during handwriting instruction:

A A A A A A

This is an example of stimulus fading because the stimulus prompt, the letter *A*, is faded out systematically. The following series gives an example of stimulus fading in arithmetic:

$$4 + 5 = 9, 4 + 5 = 9, 4 + 5 = 9, 4 + 5 = 9.$$

These examples have shown how stimulus prompts can be faded out. M. E. Skinner (1978) faded a stimulus prompt in and out while teaching elementary-aged students. He varied the size of numbers on a series of flash cards to teach numeral discrimination between numbers with the same digits (e.g., 17, 71). The first card in the sequence had the largest difference between pairs of stimuli, whereas the last card in the sequence showed pairs of the same size. Figure 13.5 gives an example of the cards used by Skinner.

Frequently **superimposition** of stimuli is used with stimulus fading. In this procedure two specific classes of stimuli are presented to prompt a response. In one instance the transfer of stimulus control occurs when one stimulus is faded out; in another application one stimulus is faded in as the other stimulus is faded

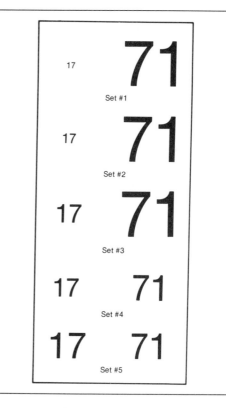

FIGURE 13.5 Illustration of a stimulus fading-in-and-out procedure using one pair of similar numerals. (From "Using Fading to Remediate Number Reversals" by M. E. Skinner, 1978, *The Directive Teacher, 1,* p. 10. Copyright 1978 by *The Directive Teacher.* Reprinted by permission.)

out. The study by Terrace (1963a, b) demonstrating the transfer of stimulus control from a red-green discrimination to a vertical-horizontal discrimination shows superimposition of two specific classes of stimuli and the fading out of one stimulus class. The lines were superimposed on the colored lights; then the lights were gradually faded out, leaving only the vertical and horizontal lines as the discriminative stimuli. Figure 13.6 provides an applied example of superimposition and stimulus fading procedures used by Terrace. The figure shows a series of steps from an arithmetic program to teach $7 - 2 =$ ___.

The other procedure used frequently fades in the natural stimulus and fades out the stimulus prompt. Figure 13.7 illustrates this superimposition procedure, in which the prompt is faded out and the natural stimulus $8 + 5 =$ ___ is faded in.

Stimulus Shaping **Stimulus shaping** occurs when the overall configuration or topography of the stimulus is changed (Etzel, et al. 1981). Figure 13.8 illustrates the difference between stimulus shaping and stimulus fading in teaching circle-ellipse discrimination.

In stimulus shaping it is necessary to select an initial stimulus shape that will prompt the correct response. For example, in teaching number recognition a stimulus shaping program could include the following steps (Johnston, 1973):

The shape of the stimulus prompt must change gradually so that the student continues to respond correctly. In teaching word identification, stimulus shaping could include the following steps (Johnston, 1973):

Figure 13.9 shows how superimposition of stimuli can be used with stimulus shaping in arithmetic instruction. The $+$ and $=$ signs are superimposed on the stimulus shaping program and are gradually faded in.

In summary, a wide variety of procedures exist for transferring stimulus control from response and stimulus prompts to natural stimuli. Currently, procedures for transferring stimulus control of response prompts are more practical in teaching situations because of the greater skill and time required for material preparation in stimulus fading and shaping. However, if commercial publishers produce more tested instructional materials that use stimulus manipulations to improve student performance, major advances will be seen in education and treatment in the future. "It stands to reason that *any procedure* that allows stimuli in the child's conceptual environment to control the child's responding more quickly and with fewer errors would be welcome into the technology of education" (Etzel, et al., 1981, p. 35).

DISCRIMINATIVE AND MOTIVATIONAL FUNCTIONS OF STIMULI

Discriminative and motivational functions of variables are different and need to be distinguished to improve the technological description and understanding of stimulus control. Three conditions are sufficient for the demonstration of stimulus control. First, a response characteristic, such as probability of occurrence, is altered whenever a change is made in a particular property of an antecedent stimulus (e.g., S^D to S^Δ conditions). Second, a response in the presence of an antecedent stimulus is followed

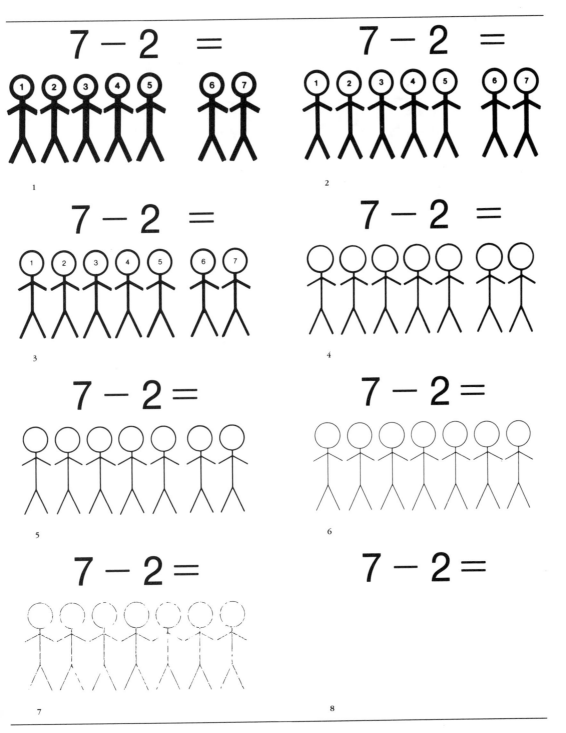

FIGURE 13.6 Illustration of two classes of superimposed stimuli with one class then faded out. (From *Addition and Subtraction Math Program with Stimulus Shaping and Stimulus Fading* by T. Johnson, 1973, unpublished project, Ohio Department of Education. Reprinted by permission.)

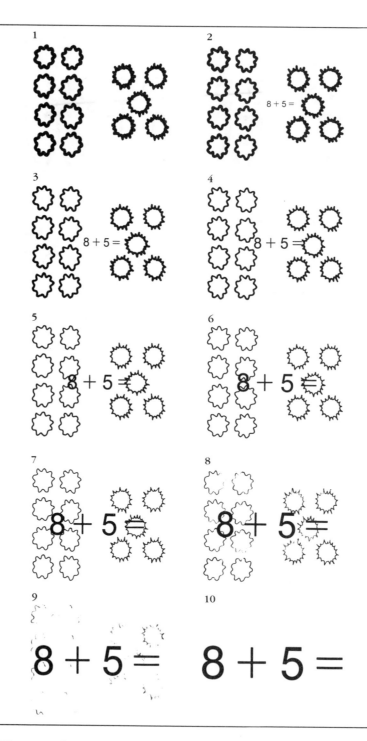

FIGURE 13.7 Illustration of superimposition and stimulus fading to fade in the natural stimulus and fade out the stimulus prompt. (From *Addition and Subtraction Math Program with Stimulus Shaping and Stimulus Fading* by T. Johnson, 1973, unpublished project, Ohio Department of Education. Reprinted by permission.)

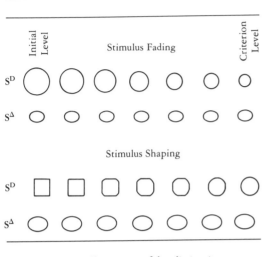

FIGURE 13.8 Illustration of the distinction between fading and shaping in gradual stimulus manipulation. (From "Stimulus Control Procedures in the Education of Young Children" by B. C. Etzel, J. M. LeBlanc, K. J. Schilmoeller, and M. E. Stella in *Behavior Modification Contributions to Education*, p. 23, by S. W. Bijou and R. Ruiz (Eds.), 1981, Hillsdale, NJ: Lawrence Erlbaum. Copyright 1981 by Lawrence Erlbaum. Reprinted by permission.)

with reinforcement. Third, the S^D condition is correlated with an increased frequency of reinforcement. The third condition is crucial but is often taken for granted. Alteration of rate or probability of response occurrence in the presence of an S^D is determined by the momentary effectiveness of reinforcement. If an individual has reached satiation with the reinforcer relevant to the S^D, generally the rate or probability of response occurrence will not be altered. The third condition implies a history of an increased frequency of reinforcement in the S^D condition and a decreased frequency of reinforcement in the S^Δ condition. This history of differential reinforcement is, again, crucial for the development of discriminative functions of stimuli.

In some situations a stimulus change alters the rate or probability of response occurrence and appears to have an S^D effect; however, there is no evidence of a history of effective differential reinforcement correlated with the altered response probability. These situations are probably related to motivational operations such as deprivation or aversive stimulation (Skinner, 1957) rather than stimulus control. For example, deprivation can be used to generate two different response effects.

> Operant behavior can thus be increased in frequency (evoked) in two different ways. Consider, for example, an organism that is at least somewhat water deprived and for which some class of responses has a history of water reinforcement. Assume further that the current stimulus conditions have been associated with a low, but nonzero frequency of water reinforcement for those responses. Such responses can be made momentarily more frequent (1) by further depriving the organism of water, or (2) by changing to a situation where they have been more frequently followed by water reinforcement (the S^D effect). (Michael, 1982, p. 150)[1]

Michael uses the terms *establishing operations* and *establishing stimuli* to distinguish the discriminative and motivational functions of stimuli.

Establishing Operations

Michael (1982) defines an **establishing operation** (E^O) as "any change in the environment which alters the effectiveness of some object or event as reinforcement and simultaneously alters the momentary frequency of the behavior that has been followed by that reinforcement" (pp. 150–151).[2] Michael suggests using this more general term in place of

---

[1] From "Distinguishing Between Discriminative and Motivational Functions of Stimuli" by J. Michael, 1982, *Journal of the Experimental Analysis of Behavior, 37,* p. 150. Copyright 1982 by the Society for the Experimental Analysis of Behavior, Inc. Reprinted by permission.

[2] From "Distinguishing Between Discriminative and Motivational Functions of Stimuli" by J. Michael, 1982, *Journal of the Experimental Analysis of Behavior, 37,* pp. 150–151. Copyright 1982 by the Society for the Experimental Analysis of Behavior, Inc. Reprinted by permission.

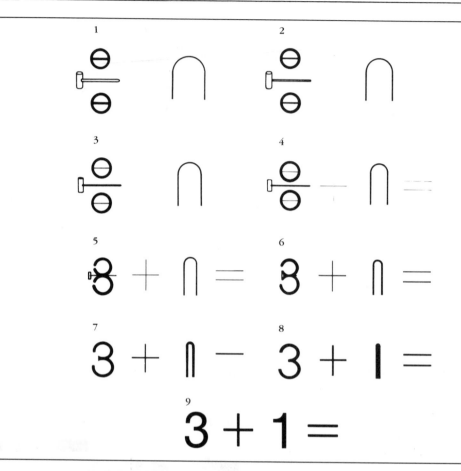

FIGURE 13.9 Illustration of superimposition of stimuli and stimulus shaping. (From *Addition and Subtraction Math Program with Stimulus Shaping and Stimulus Fading* by T. Johnson, 1973, unpublished project, Ohio Department of Education. Reprinted by permission.)

terms to describe motivation—such as deprivation, satiation, motive, and drive—because of similar effects produced by different stimulus operations. For instance, salt ingestion, perspiration, and blood loss produce similar response effects to those of water deprivation but cannot be called water deprivation.

The value of the general term *establishing operation* goes beyond the mere convenience of a descriptive term. Most importantly, its use clarifies the conditions under which responses are under stimulus control, and Michael stresses this point in an excellent example. In a typical

shock-escape procedure an animal is placed in an experimental chamber. Shock is administered until a response removes the shock for a designated period of time. Then the shock is reintroduced until it is again terminated with a response, and so on. An experienced animal removes the shock immediately. In such a situation some would say that the shock serves as an S^D: shock, an antecedent stimulus, sets the occasion for a response, which is reinforced (shock removed). Also, there exists a high probability of response occurrence in the presence of the shock. However, in this situation shock does not function as an S^D. A response in the presence of an S^D must produce more frequent reinforcement than it does in its absence. Even though the animal receives reinforcement by removing the shock, the absence of shock does not constitute a state of lower frequency reinforcement. Before the response can be reinforced, the shock must be on. Shock in this example is functioning as an establishing operation because it changes what functions as reinforcement.

This example can show the difference between an establishing operation and stimulus control if the experimental conditions are changed so that a buzzer is sounded at different periods of time throughout the session and the shock can be removed only when a response is made while the buzzer is sounding. A response would be unreinforced in the absence of the buzzer (i.e., the shock would not be removed), the buzzer would function as an S^D, and stimulus control would be demonstrated. In this modified example the characteristics of the response would be different in the presence and absence of the buzzer, and the buzzer would be correlated with an increased frequency of reinforcement.

In summary, the term *establishing operation* is a convenient way to consider stimuli that influence the momentary effectiveness of reinforcement and consequently make responses that have produced that type of reinforcement in the past momentarily more frequent. Most importantly, the use of the term may increase the likelihood of an accurate description of stimulus control.

Establishing Stimulus

Establishing operations alter the effectiveness of both unconditioned and conditioned reinforcement. Directions to a glass of water (conditioned reinforcement for asking for water) becomes effective reinforcement in the presence of water deprivation (unconditioned reinforcement). However, Michael states that there are common situations in which a stimulus change produces a second stimulus change, in the presence of which the effectiveness of conditioned reinforcement is altered but not the effectiveness of unconditioned reinforcement. If there is increased likelihood of the occurrence of behavior that in the past has produced the conditioned reinforcement associated with the second stimulus change, an **establishing stimulus** (S^E) has been produced. An establishing operation is similar to but different from an establishing stimulus. An establishing operation alters the effectiveness of reinforcement for all members of a species. It does not depend on individual history. Water deprivation alters the effectiveness of water reinforcement for all humans; food deprivation alters the effectiveness of food reinforcement for all humans. In contrast, an establishing stimulus does depend on individual history in altering the effectiveness of reinforcement. An establishing stimulus does not affect all members of a given species in the same way.

Before a stimulus change can be termed an establishing stimulus, four conditions must exist. First, a discriminative stimulus (S_1) must be present to occasion a response (R_1). Second, the conditions must be such that the response cannot be made and reinforced until another stimulus change (S_2) is produced. Third, the second stimulus change must be effective conditioned reinforcement. Fourth, the second stimulus change must occasion behavior (R_2) that in the past has produced the second stimulus change. Under these conditions S_1 functions as a discriminative stimulus for R_1 and as an establishing stimulus for R_2.

For example, a teacher might tell students to complete Math Worksheet 4. The teacher's directions constitute a discriminative stimulus (S_1) to occasion student responses to the problems on the worksheet (R_1), which will receive reinforcement from the teacher. However, one student cannot complete the worksheet because she has lost her copy of it (S_2). So the student asks the teacher for another copy of the

FIGURE 13.10 Conditions for an establishing stimulus and the relationship between an S^D and an S^E. (From "Distinguishing Between Discriminative and Motivational Functions of Stimuli" by J. Michael, 1982, *Journal of the Experimental Analysis of Behavior, 37,* p. 152. Copyright 1982 by the Society for the Experimental Analysis of Behavior, Inc. Adapted by permission.)

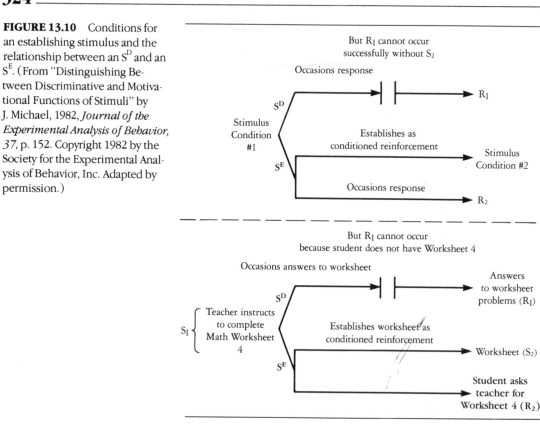

worksheet (R_2). The teacher's directive has functioned as an S^E for this one student. Figure 13.10 shows the relationship between the discriminative stimulus and the establishing stimulus.

> Much more common [than reinforcing events called unconditioned] are those stimulus changes which alter the reinforcing effectiveness of events ordinarily referred to as conditioned reinforcement, and which evoke the behavior

that has previously produced this reinforcement. We do not have a convenient way of referring to such stimulus changes, and because of this they may be subsumed under the heading of discriminative stimuli. (Michael, 1982, p. 154)[3]

---

[3]From "Distinguishing Between Discriminative and Motivational Functions of Stimuli" by J. Michael, 1982, *Journal of the Experimental Analysis of Behavior, 37,* p. 154. Copyright 1982 by the Society for the Experimental Analysis of Behavior, Inc. Reprinted by permission.

SUMMARY

Antecedent Stimuli

1 Stimulus control is demonstrated (a) when the characteristics of a response are altered whenever a change is made in a particular property of an antecedent stimulus, (b) when a response is followed with effective reinforcement, and (c) when the stimulus change is correlated with an increased frequency of reinforcement.

2 In an investigation of the effects of stimuli on behavior, stimuli are described in terms of their physical properties.

3 Stimuli are defined as any form of physical energy capable of a relationship with behavior.

4 The terms used to describe the physical dimensions of stimuli and responses are often confused.

Stimulus Generalization

5 When a response is reinforced in the presence of one stimulus, there is a general tendency to respond in the presence of new and similar stimuli. This response tendency is called stimulus generalization.

6 Discrimination is demonstrated when a response is not emitted in the presence of new stimuli.

7 Stimulus generalization reflects a loose degree of stimulus control, whereas discrimination indicates a relatively precise degree of control.

8 Stimulus generalization gradients are used to measure stimulus generalization and discrimination.

Stimulus Discrimination Training with Differential Reinforcement

9 The basic paradigm for stimulus discrimination training requires one response and two antecedent stimulus conditions. A response in the presence of one stimulus condition (S^D) is reinforced. A response in the presence of the other stimulus (S^Δ) is not reinforced or receives less frequent reinforcement.

Concept Formation

10 A concept is defined as stimulus generalization within a class of stimuli and discrimination between classes of stimuli.

11 A stimulus class is a set of stimuli with a common relationship.

12 Before a concept can be acquired, exemplars of what the concept is and is not must be presented.

Factors Affecting the Development of Stimulus Control

13 There are at least five important factors related to the development of stimulus control: (a) reinforcement, (b) preattending skills, (c) stimulus presentation, (d) salience of the stimuli, and (e) masking and overshadowing.

14 Salience of a stimulus refers to its prominence in the individual's environment.

15 In masking, even though a stimulus has control over behavior, another stimulus blocks that control.

16 With overshadowing, the presence of one stimulus condition interferes with the acquisition of control by another stimulus.

Response and Stimulus Prompts

17 Prompts are supplementary stimuli used to increase the likelihood that a correct response will be emitted in the presence of the natural S^D, which will eventually control the behavior.

18 Response prompts are associated with the response; they include verbal directions, modeling, and physical guidance.

19 Stimulus prompts are cues used in conjunction with the task stimuli or instructional materials.

Transfer of Stimulus Control

20 Fading is a technique to gradually change the antecedent stimulus. After fading, the response will be occasioned by a partially changed or new stimulus.

21 Fading response and stimulus prompts is the technique for transferring stimulus control from prompts to the natural stimuli.

22 Four procedures for transferring stimulus control from response prompts to natural stimuli include (a) most-to-least prompts, (b) graduated guidance, (c) least-to-most prompts, and (d) time delay.

23 Stimulus fading involves a physical dimension of a stimulus highlighted to increase the likelihood of a correct response. The highlighted or exaggerated dimension is faded gradually in or out.

24 Superimposition of stimuli is used with stimulus fading and stimulus shaping.

25 Stimulus shaping is a prompt in which the overall configuration or topography of the stimulus is changed.

Discriminative and Motivational Functions

26 In some situations a stimulus change alters the rate or probability of response occurrence and appears to have an S^D effect without any history of effective differential reinforcement correlated with the altered response probability. These situations probably relate to motivational operations.

27 Establishing operations and establishing stimuli can help distinguish the discriminative and motivational functions of stimuli.

PART
SIX

Developing New Behavior

Part six contains three chapters related to developing new behavior in an individual. Chapter 14 discusses behavioral shaping; it provides specific examples of how to reinforce successive approximations and how to shape new behavior within and across response topographies. The chapter also includes procedures for increasing the efficiency of behavior shaping and guidelines for implementing it in applied settings.

Chapter 15 demonstrates how discrete responses can be linked in behavior chains to form more complex behaviors. Procedures for a task analysis are provided, and the chapter addresses the varied uses of chaining, in addition to the factors affecting the performance of behavior chains.

Chapter 16 discusses imitation—different types of models, the characteristics of imitative behavior, procedures for developing an imitative repertoire, and training techniques.

14

Behavioral Shaping

KEY TERMS

Behavioral shaping

Differential reinforcement

Response differentiation

Successive approximation

The process by which one systematically and differentially reinforces successive approximations to a terminal behavior is termed **behavioral shaping.** Behavioral shaping is used in many everyday situations. For example, language therapists use behavioral shaping when they differentially reinforce speech by first reinforcing lip movements, then sound production, and finally word and sentence expression. Residential staff caring for individuals with severe mental retardation shape social interaction when they differentially reinforce eye contact, one-word greetings, and conversational speech. A basketball coach shapes the foul shooting behavior of his players when he differentially reinforces accurate shooting from positions farther from the basket and nearer to the foul line.

Behavioral shaping can require many steps, and improvement is seldom immediate or linear. If a systematic approach is used, however, progress can almost always be measured. Although behavioral shaping can be time-consuming, it represents a practical approach to teaching new behaviors, especially those behaviors that cannot easily be learned by physical cues or verbal prompts.

This chapter further defines behavioral shaping and discusses the essential role of differential reinforcement in the behavioral shaping process. The chapter also presents examples of how to shape behavior across and within re-

---

This chapter was written by Timothy E. Heron.

ponse topographies and includes suggestions for improving the efficiency of behavioral shaping. The chapter concludes with guidelines to consider in implementing a behavioral shaping procedure.

DEFINITION AND ILLUSTRATION OF BEHAVIORAL SHAPING

Behavioral shaping is defined as the differential reinforcement of successive approximations to a desired behavior. According to Panyan (1980), "Shaping fosters the gradual development of a new behavior by repeatedly reinforcing minor improvements or steps toward that behavior. Instead of waiting for a new behavior to occur in its final form, we reinforce every resemblance of that new behavior" (p. 1). There are two key aspects of the definition that warrant clarification. First, what does differential reinforcement mean in the context of behavioral shaping? Second, what constitutes a successive approximation to a terminal behavior?

According to Holland and Skinner (1961), **differential reinforcement** means that one member of a response class is reinforced while other previously emitted members of the same response class are not. With differential reinforcement a member of a response class changes, becomes differentiated. At the same time the future probability of occurrence of one member of a response class increases, and that of other members of the response class decreases. In essence, **response differentiation** results.

Figure 14.1 provides an illustration of differential reinforcement used to teach an emotionally disturbed preschooler who was in danger of losing his eyesight to wear corrective glasses (cf. Wolf, Risley, & Mees, 1964). The step-by-step progression of training shows that the first behavior reinforced was touching glasses. When that was established, picking up glasses was reinforced, and touching glasses was placed on

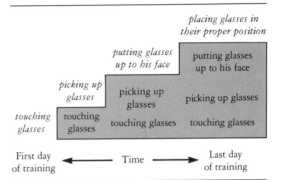

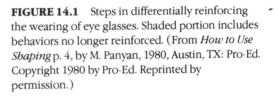

First day of training ← Time → Last day of training

FIGURE 14.1 Steps in differentially reinforcing the wearing of eye glasses. Shaded portion includes behaviors no longer reinforced. (From *How to Use Shaping* p. 4, by M. Panyan, 1980, Austin, TX: Pro-Ed. Copyright 1980 by Pro-Ed. Reprinted by permission.)

extinction (see shaded portion of figure). Next, putting glasses up to his face was reinforced, and the two previously emitted behaviors were placed on extinction. Training continued until the final step, placing glasses in their proper position, was emitted, and all previous behaviors were placed on extinction.

Differential reinforcement can be applied across topographies of behavior. For instance, a student's vocal participation can be differentially reinforced across whispers, conversational speech, and shouts. Differential reinforcement can also be applied within a response topography. For instance, within conversational speech the voice intensity, duration, and amount of speech can be shaped. More will be presented later on this topic.

In response to the second key question, What constitutes a successive approximation? A **successive approximation** to a desired behavior can be considered any intermediate behavior that is either a prerequisite component of the final behavior or a higher order member of the same response topography as the final behavior. An intermediate prerequisite behavior is one in which the topography of the response is necessary for the final perfor-

329

mance of the behavior. If the final behavior is conversational speech, then lip movement, sound production, word utterances, and phrase or sentence expression are all necessary prerequisites. Each of these behaviors would be differentially reinforced to achieve conversational speech.

A higher order member of a similar response topography is one in which the form of the behavior is the same; but the intensity, amount, or duration of the behavior is not. For example, let us suppose a behavior analyst is working with an individual whose verbal participation during class is evident but whose intensity of production is inadequate. In essence, the student cannot be heard from the back of the room. A successive approximation to 65 decibels (dB)—the intensity of normal conversational speech—might be 45, 55, and ultimately 65 dB. These higher order production behaviors can be acquired by differentially reinforcing higher intensity levels. When 45 dB is achieved, verbal production intensities of a lower magnitude are placed on extinction. Likewise, when 55 dB and finally 65 dB are achieved, all previous lower levels of intensity are not reinforced (i.e., they are placed on extinction). Thus, each higher order intensity level (45, 55, 65 dB) is shaped by differentially reinforcing successive approximations until the terminal behavior is emitted consistently.

Fleece, Gross, O'Brien, Kistner, Rothblum, and Drabman (1981) used a behavioral shaping procedure to increase the voice volume of two children enrolled in a private preschool for students with physical and/or developmental disabilities. Baseline data were collected on voice volume production in the regular classroom. Voice volume was measured on a 0- to 20-point scale with 0 indicating that the child's voice level was usually inaudible, 10 indicating normal voice volume, and 20 indicating a screaming level. The behavioral shaping procedure consisted of having the children recite a nursery rhyme aloud in the presence of a voice-activated relay device. Increased levels of voice

volume activated a light display. The intensity of the light corresponded to increased levels of voice volume: higher voice volume produced an intense light, and lower voice volume produced a dim light. The teacher shaped voice volume by increasing the sensitivity threshold of the relay device. Whereas in the beginning stages of training, a low voice was sufficient to activate the dim light, in later stages a much higher volume was needed to produce the same effect. The children were given performance feedback ("You did not light the light that time"), but they were not given positive verbal praise for increased voice volume.

Measures of the children's performance using a multiple baseline design across students indicated that the voice volume increased in the classroom setting as a function of treatment (see Figure 14.2). Also, the data indicated that voice volume remained high after a 4-month period. Anecdotal information provided by school staff indicated that the children's higher voice volume generalized to other settings beyond the classroom.

From a practical standpoint measures of increased dB production could be obtained with a voice-sensitive tape recorder or an audiometric recording device that emits a signal (light or sound) only when a specific threshold level is achieved (cf. Fleece et al, 1981). Productions below the criterion level would not activate the recording device.

Figure 14.3 (upper panel) shows how a teacher or parent might measure progress during a behavioral shaping procedure designed to teach independent tricycle riding. The four steps in the riding program were shaped within 15 sessions. Figure 14.3 (lower panel) shows how the data from the riding program might be graphed.

Advantages of Behavioral Shaping

First, behavioral shaping is a positive procedure. Reinforcement is delivered consistently upon the occurrence of successive approxima-

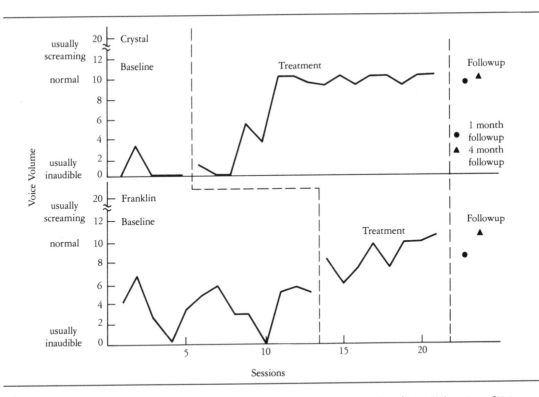

FIGURE 14.2 Average voice volume levels per session in the classroom setting. (From "Elevation of Voice Volume in Young Developmentally Delayed Children via an Operant Shaping Procedure" by L. Fleece, A. Gross, T. O'Brien, J. Kistner, E. Rothblum, and R. Drabman, 1981, *Journal of Applied Behavioral Analysis, 14*(3), p. 354. Copyright by the Society for the Experimental Analysis of Behavior, Inc. Reprinted by permission.)

tions to the desired behavior: other behaviors that are emitted are placed on extinction. Punishment or other aversive procedures are not involved. Second, behavioral shaping can be used to teach new behaviors. Since shaping is systematically and gradually implemented, the end goal is always in sight. And behavioral shaping can be combined with other established behavior change or behavior-building procedures (e.g., fading, chaining).

Disadvantages of Behavioral Shaping

Behavioral shaping is time-consuming. The practitioner must be prepared for the possibility of extended training before the final goal

is achieved. Second, progress is not always linear: the individual does not always proceed from one behavior to the next in a continuous, uninterrupted flow. Often the individual's progress is erratic: a considerable time might elapse after a behavior is demonstrated before the next approximation of the desired behavior is emitted. If too much time passes, that step may need to be further reduced into substeps, allowing for more reinforcement and progress. A final disadvantage of behavioral shaping is its need for a knowledgeable practitioner to consistently monitor the individual to detect subtle indications that the next step in the sequence has been performed. Many practitioners are not able to monitor behavior with sufficient frequency to note

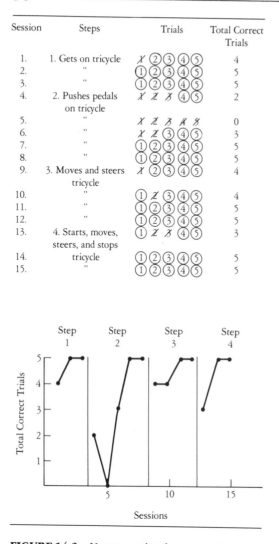

Session	Steps	Trials	Total Correct Trials
1.	1. Gets on tricycle	̶1̶ ②③④⑤	4
2.	"	①②③④⑤	5
3.	"	①②③④⑤	5
4.	2. Pushes pedals on tricycle	̶1̶ ̶2̶ ̶3̶ ④⑤	2
5.	"	̶1̶ ̶2̶ ̶3̶ ̶4̶ ̶5̶	0
6.	"	̶1̶ ̶2̶ ③④⑤	3
7.	"	①②③④⑤	5
8.	"	①②③④⑤	5
9.	3. Moves and steers tricycle	̶1̶ ②③④⑤	4
10.	"	① ̶2̶ ③④⑤	4
11.	"	①②③④⑤	5
12.	"	①②③④⑤	5
13.	4. Starts, moves, steers, and stops tricycle	① ̶2̶ ̶3̶ ④⑤	3
14.	"	①②③④⑤	5
15.	"	①②③④⑤	5

FIGURE 14.3 Upper panel: A four-step behavioral shaping procedure to teach tricycle riding. Lower panel: Graph of total correct trials during the 15-session program. Criterion for advancement to the next step was 5 correct trials for 2 sessions in a row. (From *How to Use Shaping*, p. 20, by M. Panyan, 1980, Austin, TX: Pro-Ed. Copyright 1980 by Pro-Ed. Reprinted by permission.)

these minute changes. Consequently, behavioral shaping may be conducted inappropriately or, at least, inefficiently. On a related issue, obtaining suitable reliability measures may be difficult with a behavioral shaping procedure. Agreement on what constitutes the next approximation may be impossible with many complex behaviors.

BEHAVIORAL SHAPING ACROSS AND WITHIN DIFFERENT RESPONSE TOPOGRAPHIES

Shaping behavior across different response topographies means that select members of a response class are differentially reinforced, and members of other response classes are not reinforced. Lip movement, guttural sounds, one-word utterances, and phrase/sentence production represent different topographies within one response class of speaking behaviors; they are the prerequisite behaviors of speaking. When shaping behavior across different response topographies, the practitioner gradually increases the criterion of performance before reinforcement is delivered.

One classic study that shows how behaviors are shaped both across and within response topographies was reported by Isaacs, Thomas, and Goldiamond (1960). In their study they successfully shaped the verbal behavior of a man diagnosed as a catatonic schizophrenic. "Andrew" had not spoken for 19 years, despite the efforts of his caretakers to encourage speech production. Essentially the behavioral shaping procedure was initiated when an astute psychologist noticed that Andrew's usually passive expression had changed slightly when a package of chewing gum was inadvertently dropped on the floor. The psychologist realized that gum might be used as a reinforcer to build behaviors in the response class of talking, so he selected speech production as the terminal behavior.

The next step in the behavioral shaping process was to select the initial behavior to reinforce. Lip movement was chosen because the psychologist noted that slight lip movements had occurred in the presence of the pack of gum and, more importantly, lip movement was in the response class of fluent speech.

As soon as lip movement was established by differential reinforcement, the psychologist waited for the next approximation of the terminal behavior. During this phase lip movement alone was no longer reinforced; only lip movement associated with sound emission produced the reinforcement. As soon as Andrew was able to utter a guttural sound, vocalizations were differentially reinforced. Then the guttural sound itself was shaped (differential reinforcement within a response topography) until Andrew said the word *gum.* After the 6th week of behavioral shaping, the psychologist asked Andrew to say *gum,* to which Andrew responded, "Gum, please." During that session and afterwards Andrew went on to converse with the psychologist and others at the institution about his identity and background. Isaacs et al. (1960) provided a powerful demonstration of behavioral shaping. After selection of the terminal behavior and the initial starting point, each member of the response class was shaped by differential reinforcement of successive approximations to the terminal behavior.

Shaping a behavior within a response topography means that the form of the behavior remains constant, but differential reinforcement is applied to a dimension of the behavior (e.g., frequency, intensity, duration, rate). To illustrate, let us suppose that a physical education teacher is instructing a class of high school–aged students in water safety. Specifically, she is teaching them how to throw a life preserver a given distance to a person struggling in the water. Since the important skill in this activity is to throw the life preserver near the person, the physical education teacher might shape accurate tossing behavior by reinforcing successive approximations to a toss of a given distance. In other words, each toss that is near the person (e.g., within a 4-foot distance) will be praised, whereas tosses outside that range will not be. As students become more accurate, the area can be further reduced so that the final behavior is a toss within 2 feet of the person. In this case the magnitude or intensity of the behavior within a response class is being shaped; the form of the toss remains the same.

Another illustration of shaping a behavior within a response topography is the parent who attempts to increase the duration of her child's piano practice. The criterion for success in this particular program might be to have the child practice for 30 minutes three times per week (e.g., Monday, Wednesday, and Friday). To accomplish her objective, the parent must shape progressively longer periods of practice, perhaps beginning with just one night per week. During the first phase of this program the parent might reinforce 12, 15, 20, 25, and ultimately 30 minutes of practice just on Mondays. No contingency would be in effect for the other two days. As soon as an intermediate criterion level is reached (e.g., 20 minutes), reinforcement is no longer delivered for less than 20 minutes of practice unless performance stalls at a higher level and progress is impeded.

During the next phase of behavioral shaping, the process is repeated for Monday and Wednesday nights. Now the child must meet the criterion on both days before reinforcement is delivered. Finally, the sequence is repeated for all three nights. It is important to remember that the behavior being shaped is not piano playing. The child is able to play the piano; the topography of that response class has been learned. What is being shaped by differential reinforcement is a dimension of behavior within the response class, namely, the duration of piano practice.

INCREASING THE EFFICIENCY OF BEHAVIORAL SHAPING

The Isaacs et al. (1960) study illustrates another aspect of behavioral shaping—efficiency. During the early stages of the program the psychologist waited for the next approximation of the behavior to appear before delivering the reinforcer, but waiting can be time-consuming and wasteful. Isaacs et al. improved their efficiency by using a verbal statement, "Say *gum*," after the sixth training session. Presumably, if the psychologist had not used a verbal prompt, several additional sessions would have been necessary before a successful outcome was achieved.

Foxx (1982) suggests several ways to improve the efficiency of behavioral shaping. First, a discriminative stimulus (S^D) should be combined with shaping. For example, when attempting to shape hand shaking as a greeting skill for an adult with developmental disabilities, the teacher might say, "Frank, hold out your arm." Second, physical guidance can be provided; the teacher might manually assist Frank in holding out his arm. Third, the teacher might use an imitative prompt to demonstrate arm extension (e.g., "Frank, hold out your arm like this"). Obviously, any prompt that is introduced would later be faded.

GUIDELINES FOR SELECTING AND IMPLEMENTING BEHAVIORAL SHAPING

The practitioner must consider many factors before deciding to use a behavioral shaping procedure. The nature of the behaviors to be learned and the resources available should be assessed. For example, a fifth-grade teacher might be interested in increasing the number of math calculation problems performed by a student with learning disabilities. Perhaps the student is currently able to work 5 problems per math period, with a range of 0 to 10 problems. If the student is able to work and check her performance independently at the end of the period, a behavioral shaping procedure could be implemented in which the number of completed math problems would be differentially reinforced. Reinforcement might be presented for 5, 7, 9, and then 11 or more problems per period. In this case solving the math problem is within a specific response topography, and the teacher can use the stu-

dent herself to monitor her own performance. If the individual is unable to monitor her own performance and if staff or other resources are in short supply, another procedure should be considered (e.g., DRO, DRI).

In addition, since many behavioral shaping procedures require multiple steps and since a linear progression cannot be predicted beforehand, the practitioner is advised to estimate the total amount of time available to accomplish the goal. Time estimates can be determined by asking other practitioners how long it took them to shape similar behaviors, or by differentially reinforcing a few behaviors and extrapolating from that experience the total amount of time needed for all of the behaviors. These two procedures are likely to yield only rough estimates because any number of unforeseen factors can accelerate or decelerate progress. However, if it appears that more time is needed than can be arranged, the practitioner should abandon the strategy. Some behaviors seem to preclude the use of shaping as a behavior-building technique. For instance, if a high school English teacher is interested in increasing the public speaking repertoires of his students, prompting, modeling, or peer tutoring might be more efficient than behavioral shaping. Telling or showing the students how to use gestures, inflection, eye contact, and metaphors would be much faster than trying to shape each of these distinct response classes alone.

After the decision has been made to use a behavioral shaping procedure, the following guidelines can assist the practitioner in implementing the procedure in applied settings.

Select the Terminal Behavior

Practitioners often have to teach individuals who have multiple behaviors to change. Consequently, it is important that the highest priority behavior be identified quickly. The ultimate criterion in this decision is the individual's expected independence after the behavior change, that is, the likelihood of her earning additional reinforcers from the environment (Bailey & Lessen, 1984). For example, if a student with severe behavior disorders frequently roams the classroom poking other students, taking their papers, and verbally harrassing them, a behavioral shaping procedure might best begin with a behavior incompatible with roaming around the room because of the utility it would have for the individual and the other students. In addition, if in-seat behavior is developed, it is likely that it will be noticed and reinforced by the staff with whom the student interacts. In this case behavioral shaping should differentially reinforce longer durations of in-seat behavior.

It is also important to define the terminal behavior precisely. For example, a behavior analyst might want to shape the appropriate sitting behavior or an individual with severe retardation. The analyst might define that sitting behavior as being located upright in the chair, facing the front of the room with buttocks against the bottom of the chair and back against the chair rest during a 15-minute morning activity. With this definition the analyst can determine when the behavior is achieved. He can also determine what does not constitute the behavior, an important discrimination if behavioral shaping is to be conducted efficiently. In our illustration the analyst would be able to identify instances of nonsitting as well (e.g., the student might be half in and half out of the seat, or the student might be in the seat but turned toward the back of the room).

Decide the Criterion for Success

Immediately after the terminal behavior is identified, the criterion for success should be specified. In other words, the practitioner must decide how accurate, fast, intense, durable, or generalizable the behavior must be before it can be considered learned. There are several measures that can be applied to establish a criterion of success. Some of the more common include rate, frequency, percentage, magnitude, and duration. Depending upon the terminal behavior, any or all of these can be used to assess achievement. Norms for success can be determined by measuring the behavior in a similar peer group or consulting established norms in the literature.

In the earlier illustration the criterion for success could be the student's sitting in her seat appropriately 90% of the time during the morning activity for 5 consecutive days. In this example two criteria are specified: the first is the percentage of acceptable sitting behavior per session (i.e., 90%); the second is the number of days that this criterion must be met to establish the behavior (i.e., 5 consecutive days). Foxx (1982) sums up the situation accurately: "Clear-cut levels for success at each step or stage must be specified. An acceptable level of performance of the target behavior should also be specified so that you know when the behavior shaping process is complete" (p. 73).

Conduct an Analysis of the Response Class

The purpose of conducting an analysis of the response class is to identify the discrete behavioral units, or steps, in the shaping sequence. When these component behaviors are known, the practitioner can plan for each behavioral topography that needs to be learned.

An analysis of the relevant component behaviors across or within a response class can be accomplished in several ways. First, the practitioner can consult experts in the field to determine their views on the proper sequence of steps for a given behavior (Van Houten, 1979; Snell, 1983). Teachers who have taught three-digit multiplication for several years should be able to state the series of prerequisite behaviors needed to perform the activity. Second, normative data can be used to provide an estimate of the steps involved. Third, a videotape can be used to analyze the component behaviors. Finally, the practitioner can perform the behavior himself, noting the discrete behavioral components as he enacts them.

The ultimate determination of the steps that need to be taken and their order, the length of time that reinforcement should be delivered at a given step, and the criteria for skipping or repeating steps must be the judgment of the practitioner. The individual's performance should dictate when step size should be increased, maintained, or decreased.

Identify the First Behavior to Reinforce

Two criteria are suggested as a means to identify the initial behavior for reinforcement. First, the behavior should already occur at some minimum level; and second, the behavior should be a member of the targeted response class. The first criterion reduces the practitioner's need to wait for the occurrence of the initial behavior. As stated previously, waiting for a behavior to be emitted can be therapeutically counterproductive and is usually unnecessary. The second criterion sets the occasion for the practitioner to reinforce an already existing behavioral component that has one dimension in common with the terminal behavior. For example, if the terminal behavior is expressive speech, as it was in the case of Andrew, lip movement could be a good first choice.

Eliminate Interfering or Extraneous Stimuli

The practitioner should eliminate other sources of distraction during a behavioral shaping session. For example, if a parent is interested in shaping one dimension of his daughter's morning dressing behavior (e.g., the rate of dressing) and he decides to begin the behavioral shaping procedure in a room where and at a time when cartoons are shown on the television, it is unlikely that the behavioral shaping

program will be successful. The cartoons will compete for the girl's attention. It would be more efficient for the parent to choose a time when and a location where sources of distraction can be reduced or eliminated.

Proceed in Gradual Stages

It cannot be overemphasized that progress toward the terminal goal should proceed in gradual stages. The practitioner should anticipate changes in the rate of progress and should be prepared to go from step to step as the individual's behavior dictates. Each new occurrence of a successive approximation to the terminal behavior needs to be recognized and reinforced. If it is not, behavioral shaping will proceed haphazardly and will require a much longer period of time. Furthermore, a behavior's emission and reinforcement at a given step does not mean that the next behavior in the sequence will be immediately produced. Figure 14.4 shows the results of a study by Horner (1971), which illustrates that successful completion of trials at one criterion level does not mean that initial success will occur at the next step in the sequence. The data from this six-step training program to teach a spina bifida child to walk with the aid of a parallel bar show that the number of successful trials decreased after the criterion was reached on the previous step. That is, after successfully completing the trials at Step 0, the child experienced a decrease in the number of successful trials at step 1. With the exception of Step 3 and the reinstatement of Step 5 after extinction, all initial sessions within the various steps show a decreasing pattern of performance (Horner, 1971).

The practitioner must also be aware that many trials may be required at a given step before the subject can advance to the next step. Figure 14.4 illustrates this point as well. On the other hand, only one trial may be required. The practitioner must watch carefully and be prepared to reinforce many trials at a given step or rapid movement toward the terminal objective.

FIGURE 14.4 Actual number of trials meeting the criterion of each step within a successive approximation sequence establishing the use of parallel bars through baseline, acquisition, extinction, and reacquisition conditions. (From "Establishing Use of Crutches by a Mentally Retarded Spina Bifida Child" by R. D. Horner, 1971, *Journal of Applied Behavior Analysis*, *4*(3), p. 186. Copyright 1971 by the Society for the Experimental Analysis of Behavior, Inc. Reprinted by permission.)

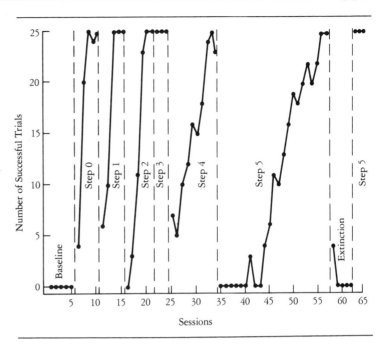

Limit the Number of Steps at Each Level

Just as it is important to proceed gradually from step to step, it is equally important that progress not be impeded by offering too many trials at a given step. The behavior may become too firmly established, and extinction of that step will have to be completed before progress can begin again (Ferster & Culbertson, 1982). The longer reinforcement is delivered at a given step, the more resistant the behavior becomes to extinction. In general, if the individual is progressing steadily, reinforcement is probably being delivered at the correct pace. If too many mistakes are being made, behavioral shaping is probably proceeding too quickly. Finally, if the individual's performance appears to be stabilizing at a particular level, behavioral shaping is probably going too slowly. Sometimes all three of these conditions appear

before a behavioral shaping procedure is completed. Foxx (1982) suggests, "If you reinforce one level of performance (approximation) too long, that behavior will become so rigidly established that it will be very difficult to motivate the student to move to the next performance level. On the other hand, the student's new behavior may extinguish if you attempt to make her progress too rapidly because she will not have had time to associate the new behavior with reinforcement" (pp. 73–74).

Continue Reinforcement When the Terminal Behavior Is Achieved

When the final behavior is demonstrated and reinforced, it is necessary to continue to reinforce it. Otherwise the behavior will be lost, and performance will return to a lower level. Reinforcement must continue until the criterion for success is achieved and a maintenance schedule of reinforcement is established.

Link the Behavior to Other Behaviors

If possible, the shaped behavior should be one that can be linked to other behaviors. For instance, after completing the 15-step program to teach tricycle riding, the teacher or parent might link this behavior to other recreational or social activities (e.g., talking to other children while riding). Chapter 15 describes in detail how behaviors can be linked to form more complex responses.

SUMMARY

Definition and Illustration of Behavioral Shaping

1 Behavioral shaping is defined as the differential reinforcement of successive approximations to a desired behavior.

2 Differential reinforcement means that one member of a response class is reinforced, while other members of the response class are not.

3 A successive approximation is any intermediate behavior that is either a prerequisite component of the terminal behavior or a higher order member of the same response topography as the terminal behavior.

Behavioral Shaping Across and Within Different Response Topographies

4 Shaping behavior across different response topographies means that select members of a response class are differentially reinforced and members of other response classes are not reinforced.

5 Shaping a behavior within a response topography means that differential reinforcement is applied to dimension of the behavior (e.g., intensity, duration, rate, or amount) while the form of the behavior remains constant.

Increasing the Efficiency of Behavioral Shaping

6 The efficiency of behavioral shaping can be increased by using a discriminative stimulus, a physical prompt, or an imitative prompt.

Guidelines for Selecting and Implementing Behavioral Shaping

7 Before deciding whether to implement a behavioral shaping procedure, the practitioner should consider the nature of the behavior and the available resources and time.

8 After a decision is made to implement a behavioral shaping procedure, the practitioner should select the terminal behavior, determine the criterion for success, conduct an analysis of the response class, identify the first behavior to reinforce, eliminate interfering stimuli, proceed in gradual steps, limit the number of steps at each level, continue to reinforce the terminal behavior, and link the behavior to other behaviors.

15

Behavior Chains

KEY TERMS

Behavior chain

Chaining

Task analysis

Forward chaining

Total task presentation

Backward chaining

Backward chaining with leap aheads

Behavior chain with a limited hold

This chapter defines a behavior chain, provides a rationale for establishing behavior chains in applied settings, and discusses the importance of task analysis in behavior chain training. The chapter then presents a procedure for constructing and validating a task analysis, along with procedures for assessing individual mastery level. Subsequently, forward chaining, total task presentation, backward chaining, and backward chaining with leap aheads are addressed. Then guidelines are given for deciding which behavior chain procedure to use in applied settings, and behavior chains with limited holds are described. Techniques for breaking an inappropriate chain are also addressed, and the chapter concludes with an examination of factors affecting the performance of a behavior chain.

DEFINITION OF A BEHAVIOR CHAIN

A **behavior chain** is defined as a specific sequence of responses, each associated with a particular stimulus condition. Each discrete

---

This chapter was written by Timothy E. Heron.

response and the associated stimulus condition serve as an individual component of the chain. When individual components are linked together, the result is a behavior chain. In a chain the stimulus conditions (i.e., the discriminative stimuli and conditioned reinforcers) operate so that each response produces a conditioned reinforcer that simultaneously serves as a discriminative stimulus (S^D) for the next response. Thus, the stimulus linking the components together serves a dual function: it is an S^D and a conditioned reinforcer.

A technical example of a chain is contained in Figure 15.1, which shows four responses (R_1, R_2, R_3, and R_4) with a specific stimulus condition (S_1, S_2, S_3, and S_4) associated with each response. The blue light (S_1) serves as an S^D to occasion the first response (R_1). That response in the presence of the blue light terminates the blue light and produces the onset of the green light (S_2). The green light serves as conditioned reinforcement for R_1 and as an S^D for R_2. That response (R_2) terminates the green light and produces the onset of the red light (S_3). The process continues until all components of the chain are completed and the final reinforcing stimulus is delivered.

A classroom example of a behavior chain is found in Table 15.1 and Figure 15.2. In preparing a class of preschool students for recess, the teacher might say to one student, "Please put on your overcoat." The teacher's statement would serve as the S^D (S_1) to occasion the student's first response (R_1), obtaining the coat from the closet. That response in the presence of the teacher's statement terminates the teacher's statement and produces the onset of the coat in the student's hands (S_2). The coat in the student's hands serves as conditioned reinforcement for obtaining the coat from the closet (R_1) and as an S^D (S_2) for putting one arm through a sleeve (R_2). That response, putting one arm through the sleeve in the presence of the coat in both hands, terminates the stimulus condition of the coat in the student's hands and produces the onset of (S_3), one arm in a sleeve and one arm out. That stimulus serves as conditioned reinforcement for putting one arm through a sleeve and as an S^D (S_3) for placing the second arm through the other sleeve (R_3). That response terminates the condition of one arm in a sleeve and one arm out and produces the S^D (S_4) of the coat being completely on. The coat being fully on serves as a conditioned reinforcer for putting the second arm through the other sleeve and serves as an S^D for zippering it (R_4). Zippering the coat in the presence of the coat being fully on produces teacher praise.

It is important to note three things about a behavior chain: (1) a behavior chain involves the performance of a specific series of discrete responses; (2) the performance of each behavior in the sequence changes the environment in such a way as to produce conditioned reinforcement for the preceding response as well as to serve as an S^D for the next response;

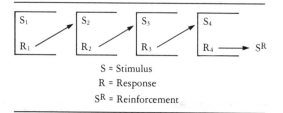

S = Stimulus
R = Response
S^R = Reinforcement

FIGURE 15.1   Illustration of a behavior chain with the following stimulus conditions: blue light (S_1), green light (S_2), red light (S_3), and white light (S_4).

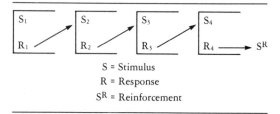

S = Stimulus
R = Response
S^R = Reinforcement

FIGURE 15.2   Illustration of a behavior chain with the stimulus conditions and responses shown in Table 15.1.

TABLE 15.1. Delineation of the relationship between each discriminative stimulus, response, and reinforcement in a sample behavior chain.

Discriminative Stimulus		Response		Conditioned Reinforcement
S_1	Teacher statement	R_1	Obtain coat from closet	Coat in hands
S_2	Coat in hands	R_2	Place one arm in sleeve	One arm in sleeve
S_3	One arm in sleeve/ one arm out	R_3	Place second arm in sleeve	Coat on
S_4	Coat on	R_4	Zipper the coat	Teacher praise

and (3) the behaviors must be performed in the correct order, preferably in close temporal succession to one another.

Whereas a behavior chain connotes the result of the performance of a sequential series of behaviors, the term **chaining** refers to the way in which these behaviors are linked together. In forward chaining, behaviors are linked together beginning with the first behavior in the sequence. In backward chaining, the behaviors are linked together beginning with the last behavior in the sequence. Both of these procedures and their variations are discussed in detail later in the chapter.

RATIONALE FOR USING CHAINS

A behavior analyst should be skilled in building a behavior chain. According to Gruber, Reeser, and Reid (1979), an important aspect of the education and teaching of individuals, especially those with developmental disabilities, is increasing independent living skills (e.g., self-grooming, travel skills, socialization abilities). The more these skills can be developed, the more likely it is that the individual can function within the least restrictive alternative placement (e.g., a group home instead of an institution) or participate in activities without adult supervision. Gruber et al. (1979) used chaining to teach institutionalized individuals with profound retardation to go from a living area within the institution to a school on the grounds, thereby increasing the residents' level of independence.

In addition, chaining can provide the means by which a series of discrete behaviors can be combined to form a more complex series of responses, which occasion the delivery of positive reinforcement. Essentially, chaining is a procedure that can be used to add behaviors to an existing behavioral repertoire. For example, an individual with a developmental disability might consistently seek assistance from a sheltered workshop teacher in the process of completing an assembly task. The workshop teacher could use a chaining procedure to lengthen the number of responses that must be performed before reinforcement is delivered. The teacher might give the individual a written or pictorial list of the mechanical parts that must be assembled to complete the job. When the first portion of the task is finished, the individual crosses off the first word or picture on the list and proceeds to the second task. In behavioral terms the first word or picture on the list serves as the S^D to occasion the response of completing the first task. That response, in the presence of the word or picture on the list, terminates the initial stimulus and produces the onset of the next stimulus, the second word or picture on the list. The completion of the second task serves as conditioned reinforcement for completing the task and produces the onset of the third S^D. In this way the chaining procedure enables simple behaviors to be combined into a longer series of complex responses.

Chaining can also be used as part of an overall behavior change procedure. Azrin and Foxx (1971) used chaining as part of a procedure to teach toileting skills.

> The distinctive feature of this training procedure was its consideration of proper toileting as a complex and lengthy chain of responses that includes social, physical, and physiological stimuli and requires strong positive and negative operant consequences for its maintenance in that chain, rather than considering it as a simple associative muscular reflex to internal stimuli.... Recognition of continence as a lengthy operant chain of toilet behaviors suggested that intensive concern should be given to the resident's skill in dressing as a major contributing factor as well as to his unprompted approach behavior to the toilet and for the absence of competing reinforcers of inactivity." (p. 98)

Included in Foxx and Azrin's program to teach appropriate toileting skills were several response prompting strategies (e.g., verbal and physical as well as auditory). These response prompts were later faded after the behavior was established. Chaining, however, was the overall behavior-building procedure.

TASK ANALYSIS

Before the components of a chain can be linked together in practice, it is necessary to (1) assess and validate the components of the behavioral sequence (i.e., construct a task analysis; (2) assess the mastery level of the individual with respect to these behaviors (i.e., conduct a task analysis assessment); and (3) teach the individual to perform the behaviors in order and in close temporal succession (i.e., chain training). A **task analysis** involves breaking a complex skill or series of behaviors into smaller, teachable units. A task analysis is important because it allows the practitioner to determine the content and sequence of instruction, the starting point for intervention, and the next skill(s) to teach in the series (Axelrod, 1983). ABC analysis and latticing are alternate forms of task analysis. In ABC analysis all environmental events before, during, and after the behavior are listed, and the behavior analyst attempts to identify causal relationships between stimulus events and responses. In latticing the skill components and the sequence of steps for each skill are listed; each skill component has one or more steps associated with it.[1]

According to Gold (1976), a system of task analysis should include not only the content (i.e., the steps to be learned), but also the process (i.e., the instructional strategy to be used). Bailey and Wolery (1984) also consider task analysis to be a process and a product. As a process they state that task analysis is a way in which complex behaviors are broken down into smaller steps. As a product task analysis is the "written series of learner behaviors sequenced by difficulty" (Bailey & Wolery, 1984, p. 45).

Constructing and Validating a Task Analysis

The purpose of constructing and validating a task analysis is to determine the sequence of critical behaviors an individual must perform to complete a given task efficiently. As Tucker and Berry (1980) note, when teaching severely multiply handicapped individuals to wear a hearing aid, the sequence of behaviors that one individual needs to perform might not be the identical sequence that another individual needs to perform to achieve the same outcome. Task analysis must be individualized.

Table 15.2 shows the hearing aid program task analysis that Tucker and Berry used in their study. Of the 31 potential steps that they identified in the total sequence, Susan needed to complete only 13 steps; Tom, 14

---

[1]For additional information on these variations the reader is referred to White (1971) and Smith, Smith, and Edgar (1976).

TABLE 15.2. Task analysis of a hearing aid program.

Component	Step	Susan	Tom	Matthew	Billy	Randy	Steve
Universal	1. Open container	1	1	1	1	1	1
	2. Remove harness (or other)	2	2	2	2	2	2
Commercial	3. Harness over head	3		3			
Harness	4. Fasten side strap 1	4		4			
	5. Fasten side strap 2	5		5			
Modified	6. Arm 1 though strap 1		3		3		3
Harness	7. Arm 2 though strap 2		4		*		4
	8. Harness over head		5		4		5
	9. Fasten harness		6		5		6
T-shirt	10. Pull T-shirt over head					3	
	11. Arm 1 through sleeve 1					4	
	12. Arm 2 through sleeve 2					5	
	13. Pull hem down to waist					6	
Vest	14. Wrist 1 through hole 1						
	15. Vest to shoulder						
	16. Wrist 2 through hole 2						
	17. Vest to shoulder						
	18. Fasten vest						
Universal	19. Unsnap pocket	6	7	6	6	7	7
	20. Remove aid from container	7	8	7	7	8	8
	21. Insert aid into pocket	8	9	8	8	9	9
	22. Snap pocket	9	10	9	9	10	10
Body-type	23. Pick up earmold	10	11		10		11
Air Aid	24. Insert earmold into ear	11	12		11		12
Body-type	25. Pick up headband			10		11	
Bone Aid	26. Place headband on head			11		12	
Ear Level	27. Pick up aid & earmold						
Aid	28. Place aid behind & over ear						
	29. Insert earmold into ear						
Universal	30. Turn on aid	12	13	12	12	13	13
	31. Set gain control	13	14	13	13	14	14

*Billy's harness contained only 1 strap to accommodate an orthopedically impaired arm.
Source: From "Teaching Severely Multihandicapped Students to Put on Their Own Hearing Aids" by D. J. Tucker and G. W. Berry, 1980, *Journal of Applied Behavior Analysis, 13*(1), p. 69. Copyright by the Society for the Experimental Analysis of Behavior, Inc. Reprinted by permission.

steps; Matthew, 13 steps; and so on. And even though Susan and Matthew each had to perform 13 steps, they were not the same steps. The discrepancy in the number and sequence of steps is related to individual behavioral characteristics—motor, physical, and language repertoires (Robinson & Robinson, 1983). According to Snell and Smith (1983), "The order of the steps or the actual method of performing the task may change, depending upon the student's additional physical or sensory impairments" (p. 88).

There are at least five process methods available to determine whether the task analysis is properly sequenced. In the first method the behavioral components of the sequence are developed after observations and/or pilot studies are conducted of a variety of competent individuals performing the desired sequence of behaviors (Bailey & Wolery, 1984; Cuvo, Leaf, & Borakove, 1978; Foster & Keilitz, 1983; Horner & Keilitz, 1975; Moyer & Dardig, 1978; Thompson, Braam, & Fuqua, 1982; Tucker & Berry, 1980). For example, Horner and Keilitz (1975) produced a task analysis of toothbrushing by observing staff members brushing their teeth and viewing videotapes of three mentally retarded individuals brushing their teeth. Horner and Keilitz identified these toothbrushing steps.

1   Pick up and hold the toothbrush.
2   Wet the toothbrush.
3   Remove the cap from the toothpaste.
4   Apply the toothpaste to the brush.
5   Replace the cap on the toothpaste.
6   Brush the outside surfaces of the teeth.
7   Brush the biting surfaces of the teeth.
8   Brush the inside surfaces of the teeth.
9   Fill the cup with water.
10 Rinse the mouth.
11 Wipe the mouth.
12 Rinse the toothbrush.
13 Rinse the sink.
14 Put the equipment away.
15 Discard the disposables. (p. 303)

Certainly, some of the steps in the Horner and Keilitz (1975) task analysis could appear in a different order or be combined differently. For instance, Step 5, replacing the cap on the toothpaste, could conceivably be the last step in the sequence; or a 16th step "Turn off the restroom light," could be added. Absolute rules for determining step order, number, or sequence do not exist. However, Snell (1983b) provides a guideline.

As with all task analyses, the number and order of the behaviors as well as the actual behaviors themselves will vary if one teacher's task analysis is compared to another's. . . . the number of components and their subdivision depends upon the method selected to perform the task and the amount of detail imposed. (p. 363)

A second method of validating a task analysis is consultation with experts or persons skilled in performing the task (Cronin & Cuvo, 1979; Schleien, Wehman, & Kiernan, 1981; Wilson, Reid, Phillips, & Burgio, 1984). For instance, when teaching mending skills to five mentally retarded adolescents attending a public school, Cronin and Cuvo (1979) consulted with two home economics teachers and one special education teacher who taught sewing. Based on this expert evaluation, a 20-step task analysis was produced that was later used as a basis for training.

A third method of validating the sequence of behaviors in a task analysis is to actually perform the behaviors (Moyer & Dardig, 1978; Snell, 1983). An individual interested in teaching shoe tying could repeatedly tie her own shoes, noting the discrete, observable steps necessary to achieve a correctly tied shoe. Bellamy, Horner, and Inman (1979) state that the advantage of self-performing the task is the opportunity for contact with the task demands of the sequence prior to training, which should provide a clearer notion of the behaviors to be taught and the associated S^Ds necessary to occasion each behavior. Furthermore, they state that self-performing the task several times allows refinement of the response topography to include the most efficient movements.

Table 15.3 shows how an initial 7-step sequence for tying a shoe might be expanded to 14 steps after self-performing the behavior (cf. Bailey & Wolery, 1984). Bailey and Wolery (1984) refer to this process as logical analysis, which means that the behaviors needed to perform the skill are identified and written down in order. Logical analysis is completed more efficiently when the behavior analyst is well grounded in the scope and sequence of the curriculum and is able to match or adapt

TABLE 15.3. Initial and expanded steps for teaching shoe tying.

Shorter Sequence[a]	Longer Sequence[b]
1. Partially tighten shoe laces.	1. Pinch lace.
2. Pull shoe laces tight— vertical pull.	2. Pull lace.
3. Cross shoe laces.	3. Hang lace ends from corresponding sides of shoe.
4. Tighten laces—horizontal pull.	4. Pick up laces in corresponding hands.
5. Tie laces into a knot.	5. Lift laces above shoe.
6. Make a bow.	6. Cross right lace over the left to form a tepee.
7. Tighten bow.	7. Bring left lace toward student.
	8. Pull left lace through tepee.
	9. Pull laces away from each other.
	10. Bend left lace to form a loop.
	11. Pinch loop with left hand.
	12. Bring right lace over the fingers—around loop.
	13. Push right lace through hole.
	14. Pull loops away from each other.

[a]*Source:* Santa Cruz County Office of Education, *Behavioral Characteristics Progression.* Palo Alto, California: VORT Corporation. 1973.

[b]*Source:* Smith, D. D., Smith, J. O., and Edgar, E. Research and application of instructional materials development. In N.G. Haring and L. Brown (Eds.), *Teaching the Severely Handicapped* (Vol. 1). New York: Grune & Stratton. 1976.

Source: From *Teaching Infants and Preschoolers with Handicaps,* p. 47, by D. B. Bailey and M. Wolery, 1984, Columbus, OH: Charles E. Merrill. Copyright 1984 by Charles E. Merrill. Adapted by permission.

the curriculum to the subject's unique needs.

On a related topic, a systematic trial-and-error procedure can assist the behavior analyst in producing a task analysis. Basically, in a systematic trial-and-error method an initial task analysis is generated and then refined and revised as it is tested. With revisions and refinements obtained through field tests, a more functional and appropriate task analysis can be achieved (Foster, Billionis, & Lent, 1976; Foster & Keilitz, 1983). When Foster, Billionis, and Lent (1976) taught women with developmental disabilities to use sanitary napkins appropriately, the original task analysis contained 20 steps. When the revised task analysis was completed by Foster and Keilitz (1983), it contained a total of 35 steps (see Figure 15.3).

A fourth method of sequencing behaviors is to consider the temporal order of the skills to be mastered (Bailey & Wolery, 1984). In other words, the behaviors are listed and taught in the exact order in which they will ultimately be performed. When the behavior analyst is going to link the behaviors together, temporal order task analysis can be an effective strategy to consider.

Original Task Analysis		Revised Task Analysis
	Added →	1. Push down your pants
1. Pick up belt —— Redefined →		2. Pick up the belt
	Added →	3. Sit down
		4. Put on the belt
2. Put on the belt —— Divided		5. Center the belt
		6. Straighten the elastic
3. Pick up napkin →		7. Pick up the napkin
4. Turn blue line away →		8. Turn the blue line away from your body
5. Twist end of short tab →		9. Twist the end of the short tab
6. Hold top of front clip →		10. Hold the top of the front clip
7. Fasten short tab to clip —— Divided		11. Put the short tab through the front clip
		12. Fasten the tab
8. Twist end of long tab →		13. Twist the end of the long tab
9. Hold top of back clip →		14. Hold the top of the back clip
10. Fasten long tab to clip —— Divided		15. Put the long tab through the back clip
		16. Fasten the tab
	Added →	17. Stand up
		18. Turn the blue line away from your body
11. Adjust napkin and belt —— Divided		19. Pull the belt up
		20. Straighten the elastic
12. Push belt down from hips →		21. Push the belt down from your hips
13. Sit down →		22. Sit down
14. Hold top of front clip →		23. Hold the top of the front clip
15. Remove short tab from clip —— Divided		24. Pull the tab to the center of the clip
		25. Push the tab out
16. Hold top of back clip →		26. Hold the top of the back clip
17. Remove long tab from clip —— Divided		27. Pull the tab to the center of the clip
		28. Push the tab out
18. Fold napkin in middle →		29. Fold the napkin in the middle
19. Wrap napkin —— Redefined →		30. Wrap the napkin in paper
20. Discard napkin →		31. Throw the napkin away
	Added →	32. Take off the belt
	Added →	33. Stand up
	Added →	34. Adjust your clothing
	Added →	35. Wash your hands

FIGURE 15.3 A comparison of an initial and a final task analysis for a program of sanitary napkin usage. (From "Empirical Bases for Program Revisions of Task Analysis" by C. D. Foster and I. Keilitz, 1983, *Journal of Special Education Technology*, p. 20. Copyright 1983 by Utah State University. Reprinted by permission.)

Finally, behaviors in a task analysis can be sequenced by response difficulty. According to Bailey and Wolery (1984), sequencing behaviors by response difficulty is more appropriate for conceptual skills that do not necessarily involve related tasks that need to be performed in sequence. For instance, teaching traffic signs to high school students with mental retardation might proceed from discriminating the size and color of signs to verbally naming and then identifying the behavior associated with each sign. These skills are arranged according to difficulty, but they are not sequenced so that a sign discrimination response serves as a conditioned reinforcer or produces the onset of the next stimulus. Consequently, this final method of task analysis is not appropriate for building behavior chains.

Regardless of the method used to put the steps in sequence, Bellamy et al. (1979) recommend that "the trainer should identify and list the stimulus that should function as the S^D for each functional response unit" (p. 76). In their view being able to perform a response is not sufficient. The individual must be able to discriminate the conditions under which that response should be performed. Listing the responses with their associated discriminative stimuli assists the trainer in determining that similar S^Ds do not set the occasion for different or multiple responses. This topic will be discussed in greater detail later in the chapter. Bellamy et al. (1979) illustrate how a task analysis sequence that specifies the S^Ds and associated responses for an assembly task can be used to produce a task analysis data sheet (see Figure 15.4).

Assessing the Mastery Level of Individuals

The purpose of assessing the mastery level of individuals is to determine which components of the task analysis the person is able to perform independently. According to Snell and Smith (1983), there are two principal ways to assess an individual's mastery level of task analysis behaviors prior to training—the single opportunity method and the multiple opportunity method.

Single Opportunity Method The single opportunity method is designed to assess an individual's mastery of behaviors in the task analysis as they are performed in correct sequence. Specifically, a plus (+) or minus (−) is registered for those behaviors correctly or incorrectly emitted. Figure 15.5 provides a hypothetical example of a recording form for the single opportunity method of assessment, using Tucker and Berry's (1980) study as the exemplar.

Assessment in this example began when the teacher said, "Tom, put on your hearing aid." Tom's responses to the steps in the task analysis were then recorded. The figure shows Tom's data for the first 4 days of assessment. On Day 1 Tom opened the hearing aid container and removed the harness; these tasks were performed correctly, independently, sequentially, and within the 6-second time limit. However, Tom then attempted to put the hearing aid harness over his head (Step 5) without first doing Steps 3 and 4. Because he continued to perform this behavior for more than 10 seconds, the teacher stopped the assessment and scored Steps 3 and 4 and all remaining steps as incorrect. On Day 2 Tom was stopped after Step 1 because he performed a step out of order. On Days 3 and 4 the assessment was discontinued after Step 4 because Tom took longer than 6 seconds to perform Step 5. Given a criterion for mastery of 100% accuracy within 6 seconds over three consecutive probes, the data indicate that Tom met the criterion for Step 1 only (the three pluses for Step 2 were not consecutively recorded).

Multiple Opportunity Method The multiple opportunity method of task analysis assessment is designed to assess the individual's level of mastery across all of the behaviors in the task analysis. If an incorrect behavior is

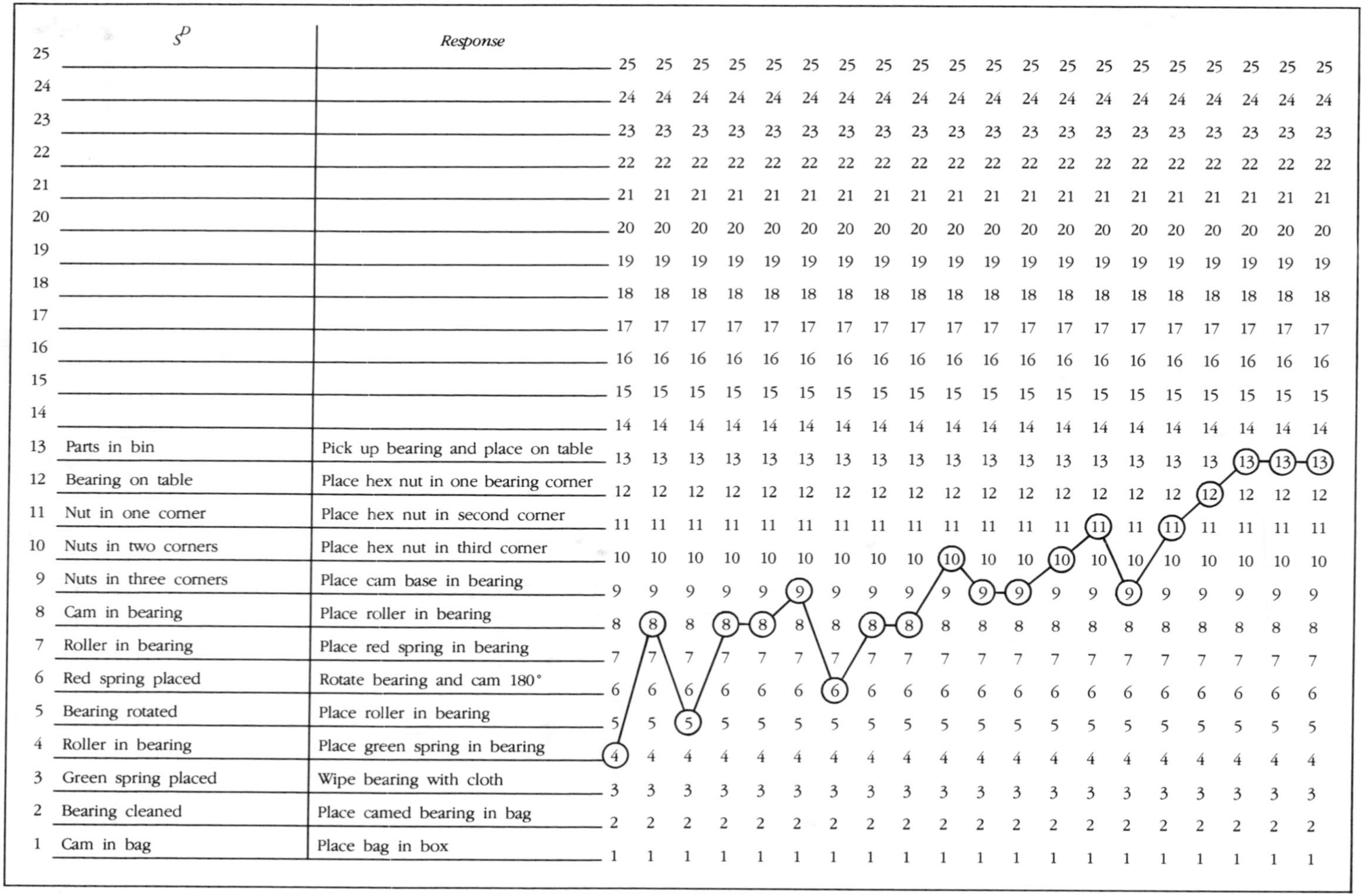

FIGURE 15.4 A task analysis data sheet indicating task acquisition across 20 training problems. (From *Vocational Habilitation of Severely Retarded Adults*, p. 75, by G. T. Bellamy, R. H. Horner, and D. P. Inman, 1979, Austin, TX: Pro-Ed. Copyright 1979 by Pro-Ed. Reprinted by permission.)

**Task Analysis Assessment of
Inserting a Hearing Aid**

Instructional cue: "Put on your hearing aid"
Teacher: Christine
Assessment method: Single opportunity
Student: Tom

		Date			
	Step Behavior	10/1	10/2	10/3	10/4
1	Open container	+	+	+	+
2	Remove harness	+	−	+	+
3	Arm 1/Strap 1	−	−	+	+
4	Arm 2/Strap 2	−	−	+	+
5	Harness over head	−	−	−	−
6	Fasten harness	−	−	−	−
7	Unsnap pocket	−	−	−	−
8	Remove aid from container	−	−	−	−
9	Insert aid into pocket	−	−	−	−
10	Snap pocket	−	−	−	−
11	Pick up earmold	−	−	−	−
12	Insert earmold into ear	−	−	−	−
13	Turn on aid	−	−	−	−
14	Set the control	−	−	−	−
	Percentage of Steps Correct	14%	7%	28%	28%

Materials: Hearing aid container, harness, earmold
Response latency: 6 seconds
Recording key: + (correct) − (incorrect)
Criterion: 100% correct performance for 3 consecutive days

FIGURE 15.5 Task analysis data sheet showing single opportunity assessment of inserting a hearing aid. (From "Teaching Severely Multihandicapped Students to Put on Their Own Hearing Aids" by D. J. Tucker and G. W. Berry, 1980, *Journal of Applied Behavior Analysis, 13*(1), p. 69. Copyright 1980 by the Society for the Experimental Analysis of Behavior, Inc. Adapted by permission.)

performed, a behavior is performed out of sequence, or the time limit for performing the behavior is exceeded, the behavior analyst completes that step for the individual and then positions him for the next step. Thus, any behaviors performed correctly are scored as correct responses.

Figure 15.6 shows that Kathy, after receiving the instructional cue, did not perform the first step in the sequence (opening the container), and a minus was recorded. The teacher then opened the container and positioned Kathy in front of it, at which time Kathy removed the harness (Step 2) and placed her arm through the strap (Step 3). A plus was recorded for each of these behaviors. Because 6 seconds passed before Step 4 was completed, the teacher did it for Kathy, scored a minus, and positioned her to do Step 5. Kathy performed Step 5, and the rest of the assessment continued in this fashion.

The key to performing a task analysis assessment with a multiple opportunity method is to ensure that teaching is not commingled with assessment. It is important for the teacher to do

Task Analysis Assessment of Inserting a Hearing Aid

Instructional cue: "Put on your hearing aid"
Teacher: Marge
Assessment method: Multiple opportunity
Student: Kathy

	Step Behavior	10/1	10/2	10/3	10/4
			Date		
1	Open container	−	+	+	+
2	Remove harness	+	−	+	+
3	Arm 1/Strap 1	+	−	+	+
4	Arm 2/Strap 2	−	−	+	+
5	Harness over head	+	−	+	−
6	Fasten harness	−	+	−	+
7	Unsnap pocket	+	−	+	+
8	Remove aid from container	+	−	−	+
9	Insert aid into pocket	+	+	−	+
10	Snap pocket	+	−	+	−
11	Pick up earmold	+	−	+	−
12	Insert earmold into ear	−	−	−	+
13	Turn on aid	−	−	−	−
14	Set the control	−	−	−	−
	Percentage of Steps Correct	57%	21%	57%	64%

Materials: Hearing aid container, harness, earmold
Response latency: 6 seconds
Recording key: + (correct) − (incorrect)
Criterion: 100% correct performance for 3 consecutive days

FIGURE 15.6 Task analysis data sheet showing multiple opportunity assessment of inserting a hearing aid. (From "Teaching Severely Multihandicapped Students to Put on Their Own Hearing Aids" by D. J. Tucker and G. W. Berry, 1980, *Journal of Applied Behavior Analysis, 13*(1), p. 69. Copyright 1980 by the Society for the Experimental Analysis of Behavior, Inc. Adapted by permission.)

any unperformed step for the student; if the teacher physically guides or models the step, an accurate assessment cannot be obtained.

Although both single opportunity and multiple opportunity methods can be effective ways to determine mastery of initial skills intended to be performed in sequence, it is readily apparent that the single opportunity method is the more conservative measure. It also provides less information to the teacher once instruction is initiated; but it is probably quicker to conduct, especially if the task analysis is long, and it reduces the likelihood of learning taking place during assessment (Snell & Smith, 1983). The multiple opportunity method, on the other hand, may take more time to complete, but it provides the behavior analyst with more information. The teacher could learn which individual skills or small cluster of skills in the task analysis the individual has already mastered. In deciding which of these assessment methods to use, the behavior analyst might follow the guidelines of Snell and Smith (1983).

To select the most suitable method of task analytic assessment, you should consider the particular task, the testing time possible, and the amount and type of assessment information needed to evaluate performance before and during instruction as well as after instruction has ended and skill maintenance or generalization needs to be assessed. (p. 100)

BEHAVIOR CHAINING PROCEDURES

After the task analysis has been constructed and validated and both the criterion for success and the data collection procedures have been determined, the next step is to decide which specific behavior chaining procedure to use to teach the new sequence of behavior. The behavior analyst has four options: forward chaining, total task presentation, backward chaining, and backward chaining with leap aheads.

Forward Chaining

In **forward chaining** the sequence of behavior identified in the task analysis is taught in temporal order. Specifically, reinforcement is delivered when the predetermined criterion for the first behavior in the sequence is achieved. Thereafter reinforcement is delivered for criterion completion of Steps 1 and 2. Each succeeding step requires the cumulative practice of all previous steps in the proper order.

For example, a child learning to brush her teeth according to the task analysis presented earlier would be reinforced when the first step, picking up and holding the toothbrush, is performed accurately three consecutive times. Thereafter, reinforcement would be delivered when that step and the next one, wetting the brush, are performed to the same criterion. Then, removing the cap from the toothpaste would be added, and all three steps would have to be performed before reinforcement is delivered. Ultimately, all 15 steps in the

task analysis should be performed in a similar manner, although at any given training step a variety of prompting strategies might be employed to occasion the response (see Horner & Keilitz, 1975; Schelein et al., 1981).

Longer chains of behaviors can be broken down into smaller chains or skill clusters, and these clusters can be taught in a manner similar to that used with a single response unit. That is, when one skill cluster is mastered, it is linked to the next skill cluster. The final response in the first skill cluster sets the occasion for the first response in the second skill cluster. Essentially, in this variation skill clusters become the analogue for units of behaviors, and these clusters are linked. According to Bellamy et al. (1979),

> Operant chains can be considered to be discrete response units. . . , and as such can be consequated with reinforcement like any other behavior. Therefore, the chain as a whole [or skill cluster] is modifiable because the probability of the entire chain [or skill cluster] is affected by the consequences following the terminal response. These characteristics make it apparent that an operant chain [or skill cluster] can in fact be perceived as a response unit. . . . It suggests that principles of reinforcement that aptly predict the frequency of individual responses may also be useful when applied to the performance of operant chains [or clusters]. (pp. 35–36)

Wilson et al. (1984) combined skill clusters in forward chaining to teach family-style eating to four institutionalized adults with developmental disabilities. After a task analysis of mealtime responses, 12 premeal, 9 meal, and 9 postmeal skill clusters were identified, socially validated, and taught. The instructional procedure involved teaching behaviors one at a time in temporal sequence and breaking the complex behaviors into smaller chains. Training began when the individual was escorted to the dining room and told that it was time to eat. If the individual did not complete the first step in the sequence within 3 seconds, the trainer manually guided the individual's movements to complete the step. Reinforcement in the form of contingent snacks or praise was then provided. When the individual demonstrated the training step twice without manual guidance, the second step in the sequence was introduced. All previous training steps were practiced when new steps were added.

When the first skill cluster was mastered, the second skill cluster was introduced, followed by the final cluster. The results of the study indicate that the forward chaining procedure was effective in teaching the residents family-style eating. By the end of the training sessions, all of the residents were totally, or almost totally, independent in preparing and eating their meals with peers (see Figure 15.7).

The study by Wilson et al. (1984) illustrates several advantages of forward chaining. First, forward chaining can be used to link smaller chains into larger ones. Second, teaching trainers to use a forward chaining procedure is relatively easy, and a trained staff is likely to continue to use the procedure. In addition, behaviors learned in a forward chaining procedure are maintained through follow-up observations, decreasing staff supervision time and increasing individual self-reliance.

Total Task Presentation

Total task presentation is a variation of forward chaining in which the individual receives training on each step in the task analysis during every session. Trainer assistance is provided with any step that the individual is not able to perform, and the chain is trained until the individual is able to perform all of the behaviors in the sequence to the predetermined criterion (Gold, 1976; Snell, 1983; Bellamy et al., 1979).

Horner and Keilitz (1975) used a total task presentation procedure to teach eight mentally retarded residents of a state institution to brush their teeth. Training began with the first step in the sequence and proceeded through the

remaining steps using four levels of prompts: no help, verbal instruction, demonstration and verbal instruction, and physical guidance and verbal instruction. In this program all steps identified in the task analysis were trained each session, and prompts were introduced in successive levels after a 5-second waiting period. Thus, demonstration plus verbal instruction, for example, was used only if verbal instruction alone did not occasion the correct response within 5 seconds. Likewise, physical guidance plus instruction was used only if demonstration plus instruction did not result in a correct response within 5 seconds. As the individual gained skills, the number of prompts used at any given training step was faded.

In a similar study Albin (1977) used a total task presentation format to teach the use of spoon, fork, and bread plate to three individuals with profound retardation. Only one step in the sequence was taught at a time, and the learner was prompted and assisted through the remaining steps. At each step the individual had the opportunity to perform the behavior within 2 seconds. If the behavior was performed, tactile and verbal praise was delivered. If the behavior was not performed within the 2-second period, verbal cues plus firm hand control were used to assist the individual. Later, as the individual gained skill, verbal prompts plus gentle wrist control were used, and finally all manual assistance was faded. Results show that the individuals learned to perform the behaviors.

Spooner (1984) speculates that learning may be enhanced under the total task presentation procedure because individuals have an increased number of stimulus presentations— each link in the sequence is practiced during every session—enabling faster mastery of the behavior chain. Spooner further suggests that the total amount of behavior change may counterbalance the increased amount of training time required to practice every step during every session.

FIGURE 15.7 Percentage of steps in three mealtime skill clusters completed independently by each of four residents during all experimental conditions (From "Normalization of Institutional Mealtimes for Profoundly Retarded Persons: Effects and Non-effects of Teaching Family Style Dining" by P. G. Wilson, D. H. Reid, J. F. Phillips, and L. D. Burgio, 1984, *Journal of Applied Behavior Analysis, 17*, p. 198. Copyright 1984 by the Society for the Experimental Analysis of Behavior, Inc. Reprinted by permission.)

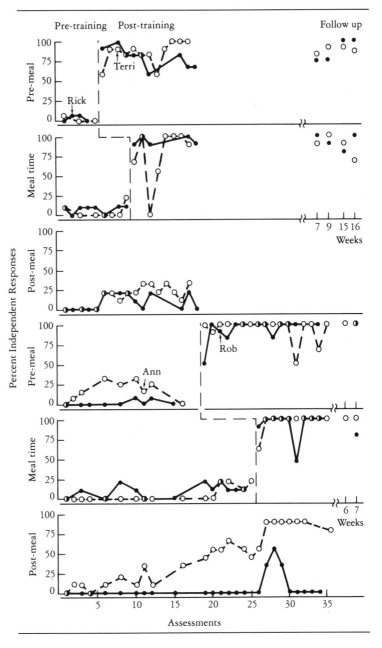

Backward Chaining

Technically speaking, when a **backward chaining** procedure is used, all of the behaviors identified in the task analysis are first completed by the trainer, except for the final behavior in the chain. When the subject performs the final behavior in the sequence at the predetermined criterion level, reinforcement is delivered. Thereafter, reinforcement is delivered when both the last and the next-to-last behaviors in the sequence are performed to criterion. Subsequently, reinforcement is delivered when the last three behaviors are performed to criterion, and this sequence proceeds backward through the chain until all of the steps in the task analysis have been introduced in reverse order and practiced cumulatively.

A classic demonstration of backward chaining was reported by Pierrel and Sherman at Brown University (1963), using a white rat named Barnabus. Barney became so famous for his behavioral performance that he acquired the reputation of being "the rat with a college education." Essentially, what Pierrel and Sherman did was to teach Barney to climb a spiral staircase, push down and cross a drawbridge, climb a ladder, pull a toy car by a chain, enter the car and pedal through a tunnel, climb a flight of stairs, run through an enclosed tube, enter an elevator, raise a miniature replica of the university flag, exit the elevator, and finally press a bar for which he received a pellet of food. This series of 11 responses was trained by initially conditioning the last response in the sequence (i.e., the bar press) in the presence of a buzzer sound, which was established as the S^D for the bar press. Then the next-to-last reponse in the sequence was conditioned (i.e., exiting the elevator) in the presence of the elevator at the bottom of the shaft. Each behavior was added in turn so that a discrete stimulus served as the S^D for the next response and as the conditioned reinforcer for the preceding response.[2]

To illustrate backward chaining in a classroom-related example, let us suppose that a preschool teacher wants to teach a student to tie his shoes. First, the teacher conducts a task analysis of shoe tying and puts the component behaviors in logical sequence.

1 Cross over laces on the shoe.
2 Tie a knot.
3 Make a loop with the lace on the right side of the shoe, and hold it in the right hand.
4 With the left hand wrap the other lace around the loop.
5 Use index or middle finger of the left hand to push the left lace through the opening between the laces.
6 Grasp both loops, one in each hand.
7 Draw the loops snug.

Then she begins with the last step in the sequence, Step 7, and trains that step until the student is able to complete it without mistakes three consecutive times. After each correct trial, reinforcement is delivered. The teacher then introduces the next-to-last step, Step 6, and begins training that step. Reinforcement is contingent upon the emission of Steps 6 and 7. Step 5 is introduced next and the process is repeated, making sure that the training step and all previously learned steps (i.e., Steps 6 and 7) are executed prior to reinforcement. The teacher can use supplemental prompts to set the occasion for the performance of a behavior at any step. However, any prompts— verbal, pictorial, or physical—that are introduced during training have to be faded later in the program. In a backward chaining procedure the tasks are simply arranged in the order in which they occur; then the last step is trained first, and the procedure moves backward. It may be helpful to rearrange the steps in reverse order to avoid confusion.

The rationale for using backward chaining is that the first behavior the individual performs independently produces immediate reinforcement: the shoe is tied. The next-to-last response produces the onset of a stimulus condition that

---

[2]For additional information on this experimental demonstration consult Pierrel and Sherman (1963).

reinforces that step and serves as an S^D for the last behavior, which is now established in the repertoire of the individual. This reinforcing sequence is repeated for the remainder of the steps.

Gruber et al. (1979) used a backward chaining procedure to teach four institutionalized individuals with profound retardation to walk independently from their living area to school without engaging in inappropriate behavior. Their study was conducted in four phases. During the baseline condition the residents were allotted 10 minutes to walk the 1000 feet from their living area to the school. If an inappropriate behavior occurred (e.g., self-injury, hitting, masturbation) or if course deviation took place enroute, timing was stopped, and the individual was returned to the living area.

During the next condition a trainer, standing with the resident in the living area, verbally prompted the individual to go to school. Then the trainer walked with the resident, reinforcing appropriate walking behavior and reprimanding inappropriate behavior. Upon reaching the school, the individual received reinforcement from the school staff.

During travel training probes, the next phase in the program, assessments were made of the individual's ability to complete 25, 50, 75, and 100% of the trip. The purpose was to determine how much of the route the individual was able to complete without assistance. Then, during intensive training a backward chaining procedure was used. Each resident was ordered to walk to school from a short distance (e.g., immediately outside the door of the school). Then the order was repeated for a slightly greater distance. Each successful completion of a training step or cumulative steps produced an edible reinforcer. Whenever the resident did not perform the behavior as required, the trainer issued a verbal or physical prompt. Training continued at each successive distance until three consecutive attempts were completed without error. Thereafter, a posttraining session was implemented in which the trainer, who had been in close proximity to the indi-vidual on the way to school, began to trail behind at greater and greater distances and eventually remained in the living area.

The results of the study show that the backward chaining procedure was successful in teaching the four individuals to walk independently to school from their living area. An 8-week follow-up indicated that the behaviors were being maintained and that an untrained behavior, walking back to the living area from the school, was also maintained (see Figure 15.8).

The primary advantage of backward chaining is that the individual comes into contact with the contingencies of reinforcement immediately, and the functional relationship begins to develop (Bailey & Wolery, 1984). As a direct outcome of reinforcement, the stimulus that is present at the time of reinforcement increases its discriminative properties. The repeated reinforcement of all behaviors in the chain increases the discriminative capability of all the stimuli associated with these behaviors and with the reinforcer. According to Bellamy et al. (1979) the main disadvantage associated with backward chaining is that the passive participation of the learner in earlier responses in the chain can limit the total number of responses made during any given training session.

Backward Chaining with Leap Aheads

Spooner, Spooner, and Ulicny (1986) cite a variation of backward chaining called **backward chaining with leap aheads.** It follows essentially the same procedures that are followed in backward chaining, except that not every step in the task analysis is trained. Some steps are simply probed. In the preschool shoe-tying illustration the learner might perform Step 7, the last behavior in the sequence, and then leap ahead to Step 4. It is important to remember, however, that the individual must still perform Steps 6 and 5 correctly and in sequence with the other steps to receive reinforcement.

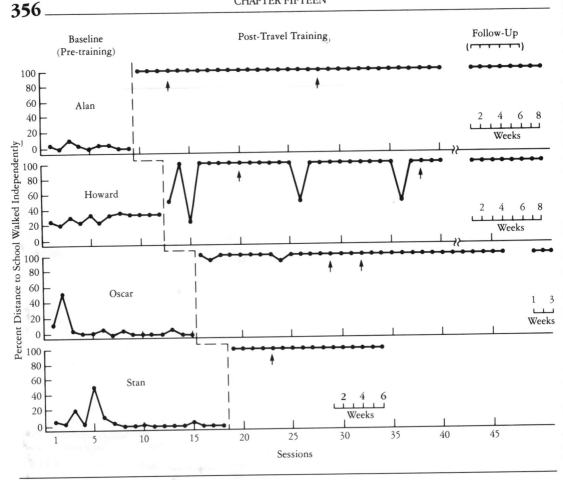

FIGURE 15.8 Percentage of the distance to school walked independently by each resident during posttraining, and follow-up conditions. The first arrow indicates where fading began; the second arrow indicates where maintenance by the living area staff began. For Stan there was no fading, and the arrow indicates where maintenance began. (From "Providing a Less Restrictive Environment for Profoundly Retarded Persons by Teaching Independent Walking Skills" by B. Gruber, R. Reeser, and D. H. Reid, 1979, *Journal of Applied Behavior Analysis, 12(2)*, p. 294. Copyright 1979 by the Society for the Experimental Analysis of Behavior, Inc. Reprinted by permission.)

The purpose of the leap-aheads modification is to speed up the learning of the chain (Liberty & Wilcox, 1981; Spooner, Spooner, Stirewalt, & Ulicny, 1983). In backward chaining the stepwise repetition of the behaviors in the sequence has the potential effect of slowing down the learning process. Because learning can be enhanced if criterion levels are changed (Liberty & Wilcox, 1981) and because the leap-aheads modification has been shown to be effective for some behaviors (Eaton & Wittman, 1982; Lindsley, 1981), the behavior analyst should consider this variation of backward chaining.

Forward or Backward Chaining: Which to Use

Both forward and backward chaining have been shown to be effective with a wide range of self-care, vocational, and independent-living behaviors. Which procedure should be the method of first choice? Unfortunately, a pat answer is not available. Bellamy et al. (1979) summarize the state of the research:

> Although research supports the efficacy of each of these forward and reverse chaining strategies in some training contexts, little is known to date about which strategy is most appropriate in any given situation. Whether one approach leads to more rapid acquisition, fewer errors, or fewer pauses in subsequent performance is still largely a matter of conjecture in applied vocational settings. (p. 34)

The authors of this text agree with Bellamy et al. (1979) but would add that uncertainty in applied settings can be reduced by conducting task analysis assessments, empirically sound data-based studies, and functional evaluations. A systematic approach can determine the appropriate behavior chaining procedure in a given situation.

Behavior Chains with a Limited Hold

A **behavior chain with a limited hold** is a sequence of behaviors that must be performed correctly and within a specific time period if reinforcement is to be presented. Accuracy and proficiency characterize behavior chains with limited holds. An assembly task on a production line exemplifies a chain with a limited hold. In order to meet the production requirements of the job, an individual might have to assemble 30 couplers onto each of 30 shafts within 30 minutes (one per minute). If the coupler is placed on the shaft, the retaining clip is applied, and the unit is forwarded to the next person in line within the prescribed amount of time, reinforcement is delivered. Thus, in a behavior chain with a limited hold the individual must have the prerequisite behaviors in his repertoire but must emit those behaviors in close temporal succession to produce reinforcement.

In describing chains with limited holds the behavior analyst needs to be aware that both accuracy and rate may be essential dimensions. If an individual is able to complete a chain in the correct sequence but his rate is too slow, the behavior analyst must initiate a contingency to increase the rate of performance. One approach is to set a time criterion for the completion of each response within the chain; another approach is to set a designated time criterion for completion of the total chain.

BREAKING AN INAPPROPRIATE BEHAVIOR CHAIN

An inappropriate behavior chain (e.g., nail biting, smoking, encopresis) can be broken if the initial S^D is determined and an alternative S^D is substituted. The first S^D in a chain sets the occasion for the first response, which, in turn, terminates that S^D and produces the onset of the second S^D; and so the chain continues. If the first S^D becomes less likely, the whole chain becomes less likely. However, to break an inappropriate chain, the cues for not emitting the initial behavior in the chain must be stronger than the initial cues that prompted the behavior in the first place (Malott, Tillema, & Glenn, 1978).

Malott et al. (1978) offer several recommendations for reducing the probability of occurrence of the initial behavior in the chain. Let us suppose that Laura engages in nail biting whenever she has to take an examination. First of all, a guilt statement might be substituted at the moment Laura begins to raise her fingers to her mouth ("It is ridiculous for me to bite my nails in this situation"). Thus, by not biting her nails, Laura would escape the consequences of the guilt statement. Second, Laura might restate a rule regarding nail biting. She might say again to herself, "People with clean, well-manicured nails look better." The rule is to remind her of the importance of a good appearance. Third, Laura might use a feedback statement and tell herself that she should resist biting her nails because three of her nails have already grown in, and they look nice. The use of feedback in this manner has been shown to be an effective behavior change procedure (Malott et al., 1978; Van Houten, 1980). Fourth, Laura might establish a reward system whereby she receives reinforcement from others for engaging in self-control. For example, her spouse or a friend might tell her how nice her nails look when they are longer. On the other hand, friends might deliver aversive prompts (e.g., frowns, stares, verbal statements) to cue an individual's own aversive prompts or rules. In this case a friend's aversive comment as Laura's fingers approach her mouth might cue her to issue the self-given rule that "people with clean, well-manicured nails look better." Finally, a combination of these procedures might be needed. According to Malott et al. (1978), at least two, and possibly more, of these recommendations must be followed for the inappropriate behavior chain to be broken. They admit that the process of substituting S^Ds and responses is not foolproof, but it is a place to begin the treatment procedure. The use of added reinforcers or aversives might ensure that self-control cues are maintained over time.

The recommendations of Malott et al. (1978) are more apt to be effective with an individual capable of comprehending instructions, interpreting gestures, or following self-given rules. But what of the person with severe retardation, aphasia, or developmental disabilities? Can an inappropriate chain be broken for such an individual? Let us consider the case of an adult with moderate mental retardation who was trained with the chain shown in Figure 15.9 (upper panel) to bus restaurant tables. Upon completion of the training program the individual was able to perform each of the necessary behaviors in sequence accurately and proficiently. However, on the job site an inappropriate sequence of behaviors began. Specifically, in the presence of the dirty dishes on the

empty table, the individual scraped excess food scraps onto the table itself, instead of placing the soiled items on the food cart. The initial S^D, the empty table with the dirty plates was setting the occasion for a response (dish scraping) that should have occurred later in the chain. To break this inappropriate chain, the behavior analyst should consider several possible sources of difficulty (Bellamy et al., 1979).

Reexamining the S^Ds and Responses

The purpose of reexamining the list of S^Ds and responses in the task analysis is to determine whether the original order of the S^Ds from the training setting is still appropriate in the job placement site. As our earlier discussion made clear, the order of the S^Ds and their associated responses is arbitrary, based primarily on expert opinion, time and motion studies, and practical efficiency. In our example the trainer wants the presence of the soiled dishes on the empty table to occasion the placing of those dishes in the bus cart. Consequently, a rearranged sequence of S^Ds and responses was instituted (see Figure 15.9, lower panel).

Determining Whether Similar S^Ds Cue Different Responses

According to Bellamy et al. (1979), "If two very similar stimuli control different responses, it is likely that the worker will have difficulty determining which response to emit when either stimulus is presented" (p. 70). Figure 15.9 (upper panel) shows two similar S^Ds—dirty dishes on the empty table and dirty dishes on the cart—which perhaps contributed to the scraping of food on the table. In other words, R_2 (scrape dishes) might have come under the control of S_1 (dirty dishes on table). Figure 15.9 (lower panel) shows how the behavior analyst corrected the sequence by rearranging the S^D and their associated responses. Scraping the dishes is now the fifth response in the sequence

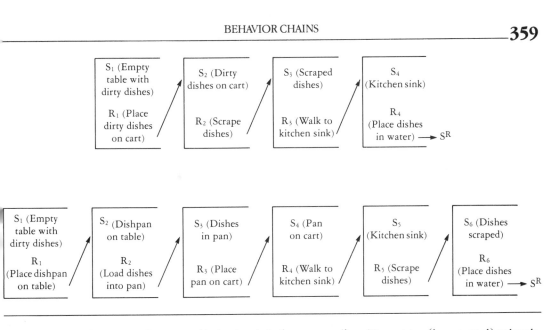

FIGURE 15.9 Illustration of an original behavior chain (upper panel) and its revision (lower panel) to break an inappropriate response sequence.

and is designed to occur in the presence of the kitchen sink, an area away from the restaurant tables. Any potential confusion should now be reduced or eliminated.

Analyzing the Job Setting to Identify Relevant and Irrelevant S^Ds

The behavior analyst should design the training program so that the individual is trained to discriminate the relevant (i.e., critical) components of a stimulus from the irrelevant variations. In Figure 15.9 (lower panel) there are at least two relevant characteristics of S_1: an empty table and the presence of dirty dishes on that table. An irrelevant stimulus might be the location of the table in the restaurant, the number of place settings on the table, or the arrangement of the place settings. A relevant characteristic of S_5, presence of the kitchen sink, would be water faucets, the sink configuration, or soiled dishes. Irrelevant stimuli might be the size and/or location of the sink and the type or style of faucets.

Determining Whether S^Ds in the Job Setting Differ from Training S^Ds

It is quite possible that some variations of the S^Ds cannot be taught during training phases. For this reason many authors recommend conducting the last training sessions in the setting where the behavior chain is expected to be performed (Bailey & Wolery, 1984; Bellamy et al., 1979; Snell, 1983). Any differences that exist can be recognized by the trainer, and subsequent discrimination training can be further refined on site.

Identify the Presence of Novel Stimuli in the Environment

The presence of a novel stimulus, which was unexpected in the original training situation, can prompt the occurrence of an inappropriate chain. In our restaurant example the presence of a crowd might set the occasion for the chain to be performed out of sequence. Likewise, distracting stimuli (e.g., customers coming and going, tips left on the table) might set the occasion for an inappropriate chain. Co-workers also, either unwittingly or cruelly, might give contradictory instructions to the trainee on the job site. In any of these situations, the novel stimuli should be identified and the individual taught to discriminate them along with other S^Ds in the environment.

FACTORS AFFECTING THE PERFORMANCE OF A BEHAVIOR CHAIN

Completeness of the Task Analysis

The more complete, detailed, and accurate the task analysis, the more likely the individual is to progress through the sequence efficaciously. However, if the elements making up the chain are not sequenced appropriately or if the corresponding S^Ds are not identified for each response, then the chain is less likely to be learned.

There are two key points for the behavior analyst to remember in attempting to be accurate with the task analysis. First of all, planning must take place before training. The time devoted to constructing and validating the task analysis is time well spent. And secondly, after the task analysis is constructed, training should begin with the expectation that adjustments in the task analysis may have to be made. As we pointed out with the Foster et al. (1976) study, an original 20-step task analysis was later refined to 35 steps when it became apparent that the initial task analysis was not complete enough to improve performance.

Length or Complexity of the Chain

Longer or more complex behavior chains take more time to learn than shorter or less complex behavior chains. Likewise, if two or more chains are linked, performance of the combined chains may be affected.

> If a worker needs to complete two chains before s/he is reinforced, the amount of behavior required would be substantially different if one chain contained only four responses and the other contained forty responses. The length of the chain contributes to defining the schedule of reinforcement.... While a worker may maintain high performance on a short chain when 20 chains must be completed before reinforcement, s/he may need to be reinforced after completing every chain (or even one-half of a chain) to maintain the same high rate if the chain is exceptionally long. (Bellamy et al., 1979, p. 37)

Schedule of Reinforcement

When a reinforcer is presented subsequent to the performance of a behavior in a chain, it affects each of the responses making up the chain. However, the effect on each response is not identical. Responses performed immediately prior to reinforcement are strengthened more than responses made early in the chain. In short, reinforcement has a reductive effect on earlier responses in the chain; and as the chain becomes longer, this reductive effect can be more pronounced. The behavior analyst is advised to remember two points: (1) a chain can be maintained as a single response if an appropriate schedule of reinforcement is used (see chapter 12); and (2) the number of responses in a chain should be considered when defining the schedule of reinforcement (Bellamy et al., 1979).

Extinction

An individual's performance of a chain during a period of nonreinforcement (extinction) is similar to her performance of a single unit of behavior under extinction. That is, when extinction is introduced, the performance of the chain does not decrease immediately; in fact, it might increase, in a phenomenon known as "extinction burst" (Snell, 1983; Bellamy et al., 1979). As extinction continues, however, responses performed further from the reinforcer (i.e., early responses in the chain) begin to deteriorate. These responses become increasingly less likely as extinction continues; and as they become less likely, the S^Ds they produce and the associated responses become less likely. Ultimately, the performance of the chain deteriorates seriously.

The behavior analyst must be cognizant of the effects of extinction and should not presume that a chain performed correctly once is learned. To forestall the effects of extinction, the complete chain must be practiced repeatedly and in sequence, and the schedule of reinforcement must change from a continuous to an intermittent one.

Stimulus Variation

Bellamy et al. (1979) provide an excellent pictorial representation of how stimulus variation affects the performance of a chain. The upper photograph in Figure 15.10 shows a cam switch bearing before and after placement on a cam switch axle. The lower photograph shows the four different types of bearings that can be used in the assembly process. The response of placing the bearing on the axle must be under the control of the presence of the bearing (S^D); however, the variation of bearings requires that the response be under the control of a class of S^Ds, each sharing a critical component. In the illustration each bearing has a 1.12-cm hole in the center and one or more hex nut slots on a face of the bearing. Stimuli having these features should occasion the response of placing the bearing on the axle, even if other irrelevant dimensions are present (e.g., color, material composition, weight). Stimuli without these features should not occasion the response.

The point is that the behavior analyst should introduce all possible variations of the stimulus item that might be encountered later. Regardless of the behavior chain, presentation of stimulus variations increases the probability that the response will occur in their presence:

in an assembly task, various canisters, and shafts; with dressing skills, different fasteners, zippers, and buttons; with tooth brushing, assorted tubes and pumps.

Response Variation

Often when stimulus variation is introduced, response variation must occur to produce the same effect. Again, Bellamy et al. (1979) provide an illustration with the cam shaft assembly. In the upper left photograph of Figure 15.11 the bearing has been placed on the cam shaft, and the retaining clip is being positioned for placement with a pair of nose pliers. The upper right photograph shows the clip in position. The lower left photograph shows a different bearing configuration (i.e., the S^D is different), requiring a different response. Instead of the retaining clip being lifted over the bearing cap with pliers, it must be pushed over the cap with a wrench-type tool. In effect, the response of lifting or pushing has changed, as well as the response of selecting the appropriate tool. The behavior analyst should be aware that when stimulus variation is introduced, training or retraining responses within the chain may also be required.

Staffing or Supervision Patterns

If the behaviors learned during chain training are to be maintained subsequent to training, the behavior analyst must plan the initial training with the existing staff/supervision pattern in mind. The individual must continue to come into contact with the contingencies of reinforcement often enough to maintain performance, and feedback will be necessary relative to that performance. Errors should be corrected quickly, stimulus or response variation factors should be addressed, and the individual should be observed performing the chain in untrained settings.

In many settings in which chaining might be used to teach a sequence of behaviors (e.g.,

FIGURE 15.10 Upper panel: A cam switch bearing before and after placement on a cam switch axle. Lower panel: Four different types of bearings used in cam switch assembly. (From *Vocational Habilitation of Severely Retarded Adults*, pp. 40 & 42, by G. T. Bellamy, R. H. Horner, and D. P. Inman, 1979, Austin, TX: Pro-Ed. Copyright 1979 by Pro-Ed. Reprinted by permission.)

A. B.

A cam switch bearing before and after placement on a cam switch axle.

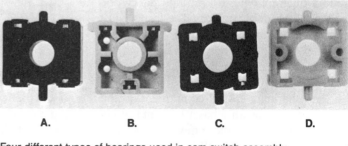

A. B. C. D.

Four different types of bearings used in cam switch assembly.

group homes, sheltered workshops, residential facilities), sufficient staff may not exist. In this situation the behavior analyst might organize the staff along zone patterns. In a zone configuration staff are responsible for individuals within prescribed areas rather than specific individuals whom they monitor from area to area. LeLaurin and Risley (1972) found that when zone patterns were used with school-aged children, their performance was similar to that under a one-to-one pattern. Thus when a one-to-one pattern is impossible, the zone alternative might prove to be a practical staffing option.

FIGURE 15.11 Two ways in which retaining rings are applied to affix bearings to cam axles. (From *Vocational Habilitation of Severely Retarded Adults*, p. 44, by G. T. Bellamy, R. H. Horner, and D. P. Inman, 1979, Austin, TX: Pro-Ed. Copyright 1979 by Pro-Ed. Reprinted by permission.)

Placement with plier tool

Placement with push tool

SUMMARY

Definition of a Behavior Chain

1 A behavior chain is defined as a specific sequence of responses, each associated with a particular stimulus condition. Performance of each discrete response in the presence of the associated stimulus condition serves as an individual component of the chain. In a behavior chain the stimulus condition and the conditioned reinforcer operate so that each response produces a discriminative stimulus for the next response and that S^D simultaneously serves as conditioned reinforcement for the response that preceded it.

Rationale for Using Chains

2 There are at least three reasons that a behavior analyst should be skilled in building behavior chains: they can be used to improve independent-living skills; they can provide the means by which other behaviors are combined into more complex sequences; and they can be used in an overall behavior change program.

Task Analysis

3 A task analysis involves breaking a complex behavior or series of behaviors into smaller, teachable components.

4 The purpose of constructing and validating a task analysis is to determine the sequence of critical behaviors an individual must perform to complete a given task efficiently. Validation can occur in any of five ways: observing the behavior, consulting experts, self-performing the sequence, considering the temporal order of the steps, and analyzing the response difficulty of the sequence.

5 The purpose of assessing the mastery level of individuals is to determine which components of the task analysis can already be performed independently. Assessment can be conducted with the single opportunity or multiple opportunity method.

Behavior Chaining Procedures

6 In forward chaining the first step in the task analysis is trained first, until a predetermined criterion is reached. Subsequent steps are added in sequence and trained to criterion as well. With each successive step reinforcement is delivered contingent upon the performance of all steps trained thus far. Forward chaining can be used to link single units of behaviors or a series of behavior chains.

7 Total task presentation is a variation of forward chaining in which the individual receives training, in sequence from the first step, on every behavior in the task analysis during every session. Trainer assistance is provided with any step that the individual is not able to perform. The chain is trained until the individual is able to perform all of the behaviors in the sequence to criterion.

8 In backward chaining all of the behaviors identified in the task analysis are completed by the trainer, except the last one. When the final behavior in the sequence is performed to criterion, reinforcement is delivered. Thereafter, reinforcement is delivered when both the next-to-last step and the last step are performed. Subsequently, the individual must perform the last three steps before reinforcement is delivered, and the process continues.

9 Backward chaining with leap aheads follows essentially the same procedures that are followed in backward chaining, except that not every step in the task analysis is trained. The leap-aheads modification provides for the probing or assessment of untrained behaviors in the sequence. Its purpose is to speed up training of the behavior chain.

10 The decision to use forward or backward chaining should be based on task analysis assessment, empirically sound data-based studies, and functional evaluation. Both procedures have been shown to be effective.

11 A behavior chain with a limited hold is one in which a sequence of behaviors has to be performed correctly and within a specific period of time in order for reinforcement to be delivered. Accuracy and proficiency are the distinguishing features of chains with limited holds.

Breaking an Inappropriate Behavior Chain

12 An inappropriate chain of behavior can be broken if the initial S^D which sets the occasion for the first behavior in the chain, is recognized and an alternative S^D is substituted. Alternative S^Ds can be determined by reexamining the list of S^Ds and responses in the task analysis, determining whether similar S^Ds cue different responses, analyzing the job setting to identify relevant and irrelevant S^Ds, determining whether the S^Ds in the job setting differ from training S^Ds, and/or identifying the presence of novel S^Ds in the environment.

Factors Affecting the Performance of a Behavior Chain

13 There are at least seven major factors that affect the performance of a chain: (a) completeness of the task analysis, (b) length or complexity of the chain, (c) the schedule of reinforcement, (d) the schedule of nonreinforcement (extinction), (e) stimulus variation, (f) response variation, and (g) staffing/supervision patterns.

16

Imitation

KEY TERMS

Models

Imitative behaviors

Delayed imitation

Learning set

Generalized imitation

The process of acquiring new behaviors through imitation is evident whenever an individual observes a model and then matches the model's behavior by acting similarly under similar conditions. An imitative repertoire is critical in the development of socialization, and imitation may be the key process in and explanation of young children's rapid acquisition of the complex behaviors exhibited by parents, siblings, peers, and influential others. Unquestionably, much normal and abnormal behavior is acquired through imitation. With an understanding of how the process functions, imitation training can be used as a teaching technique to quickly generate new behaviors. If an individual does not imitate, there is little chance for rapid acquisition of new behaviors; and other, more intrusive procedures of instruction must be used.

The process of imitation has received much experimental and theoretical attention. From the results of several studies (e.g., Baer & Sherman, 1964; Brigham & Sherman, 1968; Lovaas, Freitas, Nelson, & Wahlen, 1967; Peterson, 1968; Garcia & Batista-Wallace, 1977; Carr & Kologinsky, 1983) it is now evident that

---

This chapter was written by John O. Cooper.

imitative behaviors are acquired and maintained like other operant behaviors: (1) positive reinforcement increases the probability of imitative behaviors; (2) the probability of similar new behaviors being imitated increases when other imitative behaviors are reinforced; (3) when some imitative behaviors are reinforced, other similar behaviors are imitated without reinforcement; and (4) it is possible to teach some nonimitative children to imitate.

The purpose of this chapter is to define imitative behaviors, describe procedures for imitation training with nonimitative learners, and suggest techniques for imitation training with persons who have existing imitative repertoires.

DEFINITION OF IMITATION

Imitation consists of three environmental arrangements. First, a model is presented that sets the occasion for a response from the learner. Second, following the presentation of the model, the imitative behavior is emitted within a designated response interval (e.g., 10 seconds). Third, the imitative behavior is reinforced.

Imitative Models

A **model** is any antecedent stimulus that is topographically identical to the behavior the trainer wants imitated. The term is often applied to both the individual demonstrating a behavior and the behavior that is demonstrated. Models can be an actual demonstration, or they can be done symbolically (Bandura, 1977). For instance, the trainer of a child with severe mental retardation provides an actual model of appropriate tooth brushing when the child watches the trainer brushing his teeth. Symbolic models are presented in media such as books, movies, or television. A school provides a symbolic model of pedestrian safety when students view a film illustrating appropriate crosswalk behavior. When video or audio

replays are used, self-models can be produced. Dowrick and Dove (1980) used self-models to improve the swimming performance of spina bifida children. They defined a self-model as the "repeated observation of oneself on videotapes that show only desired target behaviors" (p. 15).

Models can be planned or unplanned (Striefel, 1981). Planned models are prearranged for instructional purposes; they are used by trainers to help individuals acquire new skills. A planned model shows a person exactly what should be said or done. Unplanned models, on the other hand, are not specifically used for direct instruction; they are all of the ongoing behaviors in an individual's environment. However, unplanned models often influence the occurrence of behavior because individuals learn from observing the behavior of others (Bandura, 1977). For example, a young person on her first outing on a city bus may observe other boarders to determine how to pay the fare. "Because individuals learn by observing the behavior of those around them, any person's behavior, good or bad, can serve as a model" (Striefel, 1981, p. 1). A model, whether actual or symbolic, planned or unplanned can serve as a discriminative stimulus for continuing to engage in existing imitative behavior or acquiring imitative responses.

Imitative Behaviors

Imitative behaviors cannot be defined as a specific list of discrete behaviors. Any behavior can be considered imitative when certain temporal and topographical characteristics are taken into account. Therefore, an imitative behavior is defined as behavior that immediately follows a model's behavior and has its topography or form controlled by that model's behavior (Baer, Peterson, & Sherman, 1967). An imitative behavior is similar to that of the model but not necessarily identical. It must be systematically controlled by the behavior of the model.

The immediacy requirement in defining imitation is critical when teaching nonimitative persons to imitate. However, much of the imitative behavior occurring in everyday life situations may not be immediate. Imitative behaviors can occur any time after exposure to the model. When an imitative behavior is emitted subsequent to a model presentation but the model is no longer present, it is described as **delayed imitation.** Garcia (1976) demonstrated that delayed imitation can be developed or eliminated by differential reinforcement of the timing of imitative responses. When reinforcement was contingent on some imitative responses that were delayed, other nonreinforced delayed imitative responses also increased in occurrence. On the other hand, when reinforcement was contingent on immediate imitations, other nonreinforced immediate imitations increased in occurrence, and nonreinforced delayed imitations decreased.

Examples of Imitation Training

An Existing Imitative Repertoire Martin (1975) illustrated the use of imitative models and imitative behaviors to increase the use of descriptive adjectives by two children with mild to moderate mental retardation. Both children had an imitative repertoire prior to the study. Their teachers reported that the children seldom used color or size adjectives in their speech, and direct observational recordings supported the teachers' reports. During the observations neither child produced a color adjective modifying a noun; one child produced two size adjectives, and the other produced one size adjective. A pretest demonstrated that both children had receptive use of color and size adjectives.

During imitation training a sentence was counted correct when the child repeated the complete sentence without assistance. A response to the animal pictures was counted correct only if color or size adjectives occurred in an adjective-noun combination. Two types

of sessions were used—imitation training and assessment of generalization. For imitation training the children were asked to imitate 12 sentences modeled verbally for them. Each of the 12 sentences contained one of six animal names that were used in each session. During Phase I (baseline) no color or size adjectives were used (e.g., "I see a bear"). During Phase II both size and color adjectives were used (e.g., "There goes the little white sheep"). Each child was praised for a correct imitation of the sentences, and both were prompted or corrected until all 12 sentences were imitated without errors.

Assessment for generalization consisted of showing the children 12 animal pictures. Only 6 of the pictures were of animals used during imitation training, and big and little animals of the same type were included in each picture. To conduct the session, the experimenter would point to an animal and say, "What is this?" but would give no feedback to the children's verbal responses. The 12 animal pictures were presented twice per session in random order.

During Phase I neither child used color adjectives to describe the animals or size adjectives more than 25% of the time. During Phase II, descriptions including size and color adjectives occurred. It was demonstrated that imitation was sufficient to improve the use of descriptive adjectives with the two children, and the procedure required little time or effort to generate a sizable improvement in the children's verbal behavior. The procedure would be applicable for use in homes, schools, or other applied settings. One child's results are shown in Figure 16.1.

An important aspect of this study is the demonstration of the transfer of effects of imitation training across different tasks, different experiments, and different settings. The procedures for imitation training were effective not only for pictures of animals that were included in the sentences during imitation training but also for novel pictures of animals.

FIGURE 16.1 Percentages of pictured animals described by color and size adjectives by Subject 1 in probe sessions in each of the three phases of the experiment. Squares and solid lines indicate adjectives describing training animal pictures; circles and dashed lines indicate adjectives describing generalization animal pictures. (From "Generalizing the Use of Descriptive Adjectives Through Modeling" by J. A. Martin, 1975, *Journal of Applied Behavior Analysis, 8,* p. 206. Copyright 1975 by the Society for the Experimental Analysis of Behavior, Inc. Reprinted by permission.)

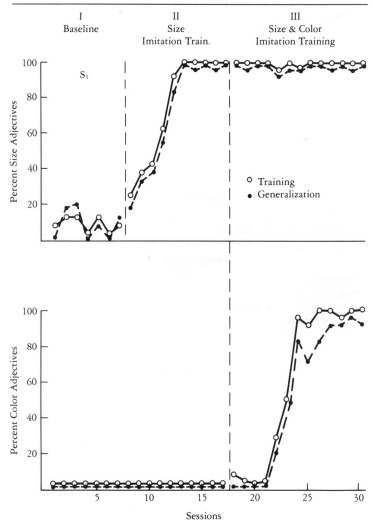

Also, the teacher or nurse, not the experimenter, administered the imitation training; yet when the experimenter assessed for generalization, the children's responses transferred to the experimenter without additional training. In addition, since the teacher and experimenter worked with the children in different settings at different times, transfer occurred to another room and another time of day.

Developing an Imitative Repertoire Baer, Peterson, and Sherman (1967) provide a classic example of teaching nonimitative children to imitate. Three children with severe to profound mental retardation served as subjects. Initially, the children were taught simple matching responses, such as raising an arm after the experimenter said, "Do this," and raised his arm. Shaping, physical guidance, and reinforcement were used to establish the matching response. The experimenter used bits of food to reinforce closer and closer approximation to the model; the physical prompts were gradually faded over several trials. A training series of

130 different matching responses was required before one of the children increased imitation of a new model to 100%. The second child showed similar results: after 130 different matching responses, that child's probability of imitating a new model increased from 0 to 80%. The third child demonstrated imitative behavior more rapidly and imitated the 9th training model on its first presentation.

Baer et al. also presented models in which imitation was never reinforced. These models were different in topography or form and were used as a probe technique to determine whether the children would continue to imitate in the absence of reinforcement. The results show (1) that nonimitative persons were taught to imitate with reinforcement, shaping, and physical prompts; and (2) that when some imitative behaviors were reinforced, other behaviors were imitated without reinforcement. Furthermore, the children demonstrated an effect known as **learning set** (Harlow, 1959), or a learning-to-learn phenomenon, as they progressed through training. In other words, the children acquired imitation of new models faster and faster as training progressed (i.e., fewer trials to criterion).

The Martin (1975) and Baer et al. (1967) studies illustrate several important points concerning imitation training. First, the studies demonstrate the three basic components of imitation training: (1) an imitative model, (2) an imitative behavior matching the topography of the model's behavior, and (3) reinforcement for the learner's imitative behavior. Imitation training is actually discrimination training. The verbal cue ("Do this") and the model serve as S^Ds for an imitative behavior. If the behavior is similar to that of the model, the imitative behavior is reinforced. The model is an S^Δ for responses other than those that closely match the topography of the model's behavior.

A second point illustrated by the studies is that imitative behaviors should be at an appropriate skill level for the learners. Third, physical prompts and verbal cues can be used to occasion the imitative behaviors and can then be gradually faded out. Fourth, performance of new imitative responses can improve as training progresses (i.e., the learning-to-learn phenomenon). Finally, these studies demonstrate **generalized imitation,** which means that imitative behaviors are likely to occur in the absence of specific training and reinforcement of those behaviors. Generalized imitation is the major objective of imitation training—teaching the learner to do what the model does at the verbal cue "Do this," regardless of the behavior modeled. When an individual learns to do what the model does, she is likely to imitate other models that have not been associated with specific training, and those nontrained responses are likely to occur in diverse situations and settings, frequently in the absence of planned reinforcement (Sherman, 1971). Generalized imitation provides for the rapid acquisition of new, complex behaviors that are so characteristic of human endeavors, and it generates those new behaviors without reliance on physical help or previous reinforcement considerations.

IMITATION TRAINING FOR NONIMITATIVE LEARNERS

Most infants and children acquire skills by imitation in incidental interactions between behavior and the environment. Parents and other caregivers do not usually have to apply specific instructional programs to facilitate an imitative repertoire. However, some infants and children, often with severe retardation or behavioral handicaps, fail to develop these skills. Persons without imitative skills will probably never acquire behavioral repertoires beyond the most basic of skills.

It is possible to teach nonimitative children to imitate. Established experimental literature (e.g., Baer, Peterson, & Sherman, 1967) has demonstrated repeatedly an effective teaching method for the acquisition of imitation skill. Striefel (1974) formed this experimental methodology into a training program that can be used by professionals, parents, and caregivers. The central points in Striefel's program are abstracted in the following sections, entitled "Prerequisite Skills for Imitation Training," "Selecting and Defining Behaviors for Training," "Pretesting and Ordering Behaviors for Training'," and "Imitation Training."

Prerequisite Skills for Imitation Training

Imitation relies on attending to the trainer's movements; it is impossible to imitate without attending to the model. Therefore, attending is a prerequisite for imitation training. Striefel defined *attending* as staying seated during instruction, keeping hands in lap, looking at the trainer whenever one's name is called, and looking at objects identified by the trainer. In addition, an attending student does not emit behaviors that interfere with training, such as screaming, making odd hand movements, or lying on the floor.

An assessment of attending skills is essential prior to implementation of training. To assess staying seated, the trainer can seat the student and record the duration of time the student remains seated. To assess looking at the trainer, the trainer can say the student's name in a commanding voice and record whether the student made eye contact and for how long. To assess keeping hands in lap, the trainer can prompt the student to put his hands in his lap and record the duration of time the student's hands remain in that position. To assess looking at objects, the trainer can place several objects on a table and say, "Look at this." Immediately following the command, the trainer should move a finger from in front of the student's eye to one of the objects and should record whether the student looked at the object. The assessment activity should be repeated for a minimum of three sessions. If

the data indicate adequate attending skills (e.g., attending 80%), imitation training can be implemented. If attending skills are not adequate, they must be taught prior to imitation training.

Selecting and Defining Behaviors for Training

Selecting Behaviors The trainer should select about 25 behaviors to be used during initial training. Both gross motor movements (e.g., raising a hand) and fine motor movements (e.g., manual sign language) should be included in the selection. By including both gross and fine motor movements, the student should learn finer and finer differentiation in imitative responses as skill in imitation develops. The initial list should contain one imitative response per occasion rather than a sequence of behaviors. More complex sequences of behavior can be added after the student is imitating simple behaviors. Also, the initial selection should include both movement of body parts and manipulation of physical objects. Some examples of initial motor imitation behaviors include passing a basketball, picking up a glass, bringing hand to mouth, zipping a coat, hopping on one foot.

Defining Behaviors The selected behaviors need to be defined as specified in chapter 3. A clear definition of behavior is essential for consistency of training from session to session.

Pretesting and Ordering Behaviors for Training

Pretesting A pretest of the selected behaviors is necessary to determine which behaviors the student imitates. The pretesting procedure advocated by Striefel consists of one model presentation for each behavior.

> *Step P1:* If objects are involved, place one on the table beside the child and one on the table beside the trainer.

Step P2: Check to see that the child is in the ready position (seated, hands in lap), trainer seated same way.

Step P3: Say the child's name. When child makes eye contact with trainer, say "do this," i.e., *child's name* (pause) "do this."

Step P4: Model the behavior for roughly three seconds (if the behavior is *lift block,* the trainer lifts the block for about three seconds).

Step P5: Allow the child about five seconds to respond.

Step P6: If a correct response occurs, immediately say, "good boy" or something similar and deliver the backup reinforcer (edible) as quickly as possible.

Step P7: Score the child's reponse "+" if he performs the behavior correctly; "−" if it is incorrect; (+) if it is partially correct (if for *lift block* the child touches the block but does not pick it up, it is partially correct (+) because it is an approximation of the correct behavior).

Step P8: Repeat Steps P1–P7 for the next behavior. Repeat the pretest on all the motor imitation items at least three times. Pretesting can usually be completed in three sessions, but for some children it may take longer. If interested in verbal imitation, repeat each of those models three times. The procedure is the same except for Step P3. In place of Step P3, the trainer says "Say _____" ("do this, say ball"). Striefel, 1974, p. 26)

The pretest data are used for program planning. If the student correctly imitates 80% of the motor imitation behaviors, then another program of instruction is recommended; if the 80% criterion is not reached, the student should be scheduled for motor imitation training. If the student imitates correctly 80% of the verbal imitation behaviors, then another program of instruction is recommended; if an 80% criterion for verbal imitation is not met but the student is above 30% correct, verbal imitation training is appropriate.

Ordering Behaviors for Training Pretest data are used also to arrange the order in which imitative behaviors are presented during training. Training behaviors should ascend in order

from the easiest to the most difficult, with levels of difficulty defined by the pretest results. Behaviors imitated correctly on each pretest trial are considered to be learned and are not included during training. The first behaviors in imitation training are those that were imitated correctly on only some pretest trials. Thereafter, behaviors that approximated the model are arranged for training. For example, an approximation would result if the trainer dropped a ball and the student touched the ball but did not drop it. The last behaviors to be introduced in imitation training are those that the student failed to perform or always performed incorrectly.

Imitation Training

Striefel defines four conditions to be used in imitation training: (1) probe sequence, (2) training trials, (3) putting-through procedure, and (4) alternating sequence. The procedures used are the same as those in the eight-step pretest with the exception of when and how often the behaviors are modeled.

Probe Sequence The probe sequence is a short pretest given before each training session. It lets the trainer assess the student's current level of functioning on the behavior to be trained in that instructional session, to determine whether the student is learning to do what the trainer does. The probe sequence procedure consists of three presentations in random order of each of the first three behaviors to be trained. If the student imitates the model on each occurrence of the behavior during the probe sequence, the behavior is considered learned and is not included for training.

Training Trials Training trials are consecutive presentations of one behavior selected from the three behaviors used in the probe sequence. Other than learned behaviors, the behavior most often imitated during the probe sequence is selected first. If the student made approximations only, the behavior with the closest approximations is selected. If no correct imitations or approximations occurred, the first behavior should be determined by the pretest data. The training trials with the selected behavior continue until the student imitates the model correctly on five consecutive trials; then the alternating sequence is implemented. If the student fails to respond for three consecutive trials or makes three consecutive errors, the putting-through procedure is used.

Putting-Through Procedure Physical prompting may be necessary to occasion an imitative response. Striefel calls the physical prompts "putting-through" (see chapter 13 for the procedures of physical prompting and fading). The trainer should begin the putting-through procedure by physically guiding the student's body through the complete imitative movement. This process will get the student used to moving and being reinforced for that specific movement. After physically assisting the complete imitative movement, the trainer should gradually withdraw the physical guidance, letting go of the student's body just before the entire movement is completed. Physical assistance is then withdrawn earlier on each subsequent trial. Eventually the student should be able to initiate and complete the movement without assistance. When the student imitates the model without prompting for five consecutive trials, the alternating sequence is applied.

Alternating Sequence An alternating sequence is used to assess how well a student discriminates between the most recently learned behavior and as many as five previously learned behaviors. In the alternating sequence 10 behaviors are presented in random order. Five of the behaviors are of the most recently learned imitative behavior, and the other five are of previously learned imitative behaviors. The putting-through procedure is used if an error occurs. The most recently learned behavior is removed from training after three sessions of the alternating sequence if the behavior was correctly imitated 14 out of the 15 opportun-

ities. If the student does not reach this criterion, training is continued (Striefel, 1974).

GUIDELINES FOR IMITATION TRAINING

Use Probes in Training

In addition to the probe sequence, approximately five unlearned motor and verbal imitative behaviors should be probed during each training session. These other probes can be presented at the end of the training session or can be intermixed with the training items. The procedure used should follow the routine of pretesting. Probes let the trainer know whether the student is developing generalized imitation skills and starting to imitate verbal behaviors (Striefel, 1974).

Keep Training Sessions Short but Active

The training sessions should be short, typically 10 to 15 minutes. The training sessions should also be active, allowing the learner no more than a few seconds between opportunities for imitative behavior. If possible, more than one training session per day should be scheduled. Two short sessions can be more effective than one long session (Heward, 1978).

Adjust Reinforcement

During the acquisition stages of an imitative repertoire a continuous schedule of reinforcement should be used. That is, each occurrence of an imitative behavior should be reinforced. If a consequence other than social reinforcement is required, it must be able to be given immediately in small amounts and to be quickly consumed. For example, cereal bits, peanuts, or raisins are appropriate. As soon as the putting-through procedure is no longer required, the student should not be reinforced if the imitative behavior does not immediately follow the model (e.g., within 3 seconds). If the student is consistently slow in responding, successive approximations toward shorter response latencies should be reinforced (Heward, 1978b).

Always Pair Reinforcement with Social and Verbal Praise

It may be necessary to use stimuli such as food or liquids for reinforcement when imitation training is begun. But eventually, social stimuli such as verbal praise should be sufficient to maintain imitative behavior. For this reason initial delivery of tangible reinforcers should be paired with social and verbal praise. Social (e.g., patting the student's arm affectionately) and descriptive verbal praise should be presented immediately after each successful imitation, simultaneously with the tangible reinforcement (Heward, 1978b). A student's willingness to participate in imitation training sessions may increase if a game or some other favorite activity follows immediately after each session.

When Progress Breaks Down, Back Up and Work Ahead More Slowly

A trainer must be patient with progress, withdrawing physical prompts gradually and systematically. If the student's progress starts to decrease, the trainer must backtrack and provide more assistance. When performance breaks down, there may be some identifiable reason, such as satiation or distraction; or perhaps the trainer jumped too far ahead and required the student to emit behaviors at too advanced a level. If such a cause is not clear, the trainer should return to an earlier level of successful performance and then work forward again slowly.

Keep a Record

As with all behavior change programs, frequent and direct measurement of the student's behavior is critical. Data should be examined after each session, and the ratio of unsuccessful to successful imitations as well as mastery of new items should be noted. With the use of frequent and direct measurement, objective, well-informed decisions can be made concerning the training program.

Decide When to Terminate Imitation Training

Decisions on terminating imitation training depend on the student's behavior and program goals. One criterion could be to terminate motor imitation training only after the student has learned to do what the trainer does—in other words, when the student imitates each new behavior the first time it is modeled. Another criterion could be to terminate training when the student can imitate a sequence of behaviors (e.g., washing hands, brushing teeth). A final criterion could be to terminate imitation training when the student imitates verbal items (Striefel, 1974).

EFFECTIVE USE OF IMITATION TRAINING WITH ALREADY-EXISTING IMITATIVE REPERTOIRES

Characteristics of the Model

Model Similarity The similarity between the individual providing the model and the individual emitting the imitative behavior can influence the likelihood of imitative behavior occurring (Bandura, 1968). Almost any variable can relate to similarity; for instance, past experience, age, sex, or physical appearance. If imitation is used to teach a teenager how to reduce her use of drugs, a person who has successfully "gone straight" might serve as an effective model. In a weight reduction program a director who previously had a weight problem might be a better model for his clients than an equally competent director who never had a weight problem.

Prestige Bandura, Ross, and Ross (1963) indicate that using a model who is admired or has status or prestige can increase the likelihood of imitative behaviors. These individuals are often leaders. For instance, high school students may imitate the dress or hair styles of their favorite rock star. Young business executives may imitate the social skills and life styles of an established vice president in the company. Peer tutoring programs in schools often select admired class leaders as tutors. The influence of a prestigious model is enhanced further whenever the prestigious model and the imitator have similar characteristics.

Emphasized Models Emphasizing critical aspects of the modeled stimuli can increase the likelihood of imitation. For example, a teacher giving instruction in sight words might hold up a card with the word *blue* written on it and tell the student that the word is *blue*. Then the teacher might tell the student to "say blue." The word *blue* is emphasized by a short pause between *say* and *blue*. Also, the word *blue* is said with more intensity than the word *say*. This technique of emphasis is used in many everyday situations of modeling and imitation. Stimuli to be imitated are stressed by highlighting their characteristics—relevant dimensions such as intensity, motion, color, size, spacing, or any other aspect that can be manipulated to call attention to the behavior to be imitated.

Risley and Reynolds (1970) have contributed to the understanding of the effective use of emphasis in imitation training. The significance of their work is in their demonstration that emphasized stimuli increase the probability of an imitative response and that the likelihood of imitation is an inverse function to the proportion of model stimuli emphasized. In other words, emphasis is an effective technique if it is not used too frequently.

Instructions The effectiveness of a model can be further enhanced in combination with instructions. Instructions such as spoken or printed words are discriminative stimuli that set the occasion for the occurrence of a specific behavior. During imitation training instructions can be used to orient the trainee toward the model and prompt the imitative behavior. For example, the trainer might say, "Sue, look at me. Do this" and then present the model.

Selecting Behaviors to Be Modeled

Appropriate Difficulty Imitation training is a technique that can be used to help students acquire new skills, and it is most effective when the behaviors selected for training are at an appropriate level of difficulty. Selected behaviors must be within the skill level of the trainee (Striefel, 1981), who must have sufficient prerequisite skills to perform the behavior.

Striefel (1981) recommends that trainers do an informal assessment to pinpoint appropriate levels of difficulty. These data allow the trainer to select behaviors that are age-appropriate (e.g., Bunker & Moon, 1983) and are not too complex for the student. Assessment information can be gathered through direct observations, information provided from individuals who know the student (e.g., parents, teachers), or administration of a pretest or baseline.

Positive Reinforcement

Model's Behavior The likelihood of occurrence of an imitative behavior can be increased when the student observes the model's behavior producing reinforcement (also known as observational learning and vicarious reinforcement) (Bandura, Ross, & Ross, 1963). For instance, that same teacher giving instruction in sight words might hold up a flashcard with the word *where* printed on it and say, "John, look at this word. Say the word." If John makes an incorrect response or does not respond, the teacher can intervene in several ways. She can model the behavior (e.g., "John, this word is *where*"; John then says, "Where") and then praise his behavior (e.g., "Fantastic, John! You read *where*"). Or the teacher can structure the activity so that John can watch a peer's behavior produce reinforcement. The teacher might call on another student who knows the sight word: "Bill, say this word." Bill responds, "Where," and the teacher reinforces his response. Then John is given the opportunity to imitate Bill's response. If Bill is a good model for John, there is a good chance that John will learn the sight word. Not only did Bill present an appropriate model, but his behavior was also reinforced.

Attending   Attentiveness to a model is critical for imitation. The skill of attending can be maintained or increased if the observer is reinforced for looking at the model, answering questions that describe the model, and emitting a correct imitation. Attentiveness is an important skill for everyday situations, such as new social situations or emergencies. And it can occasion imitative behaviors that maximize incidents of reinforcement.

CONSIDERATIONS

For an individual with an imitative repertoire, imitation of a model is perhaps the most efficient way to acquire new behaviors. The procedure is quick and requires little effort from the trainer or learner. Alternatives such as shaping and chaining, which rely almost exclusively on reinforcement, require considerable skill on the part of the trainer and are usually slow processes. Because imitation training can result in rapid behavior change with minimal effort, it is appropriate for application in all applied settings, including homes and schools.

Imitating models is inevitable for most individuals. Unfortunately, models can set the occasion for both desirable and undesirable behavior. If punishment, aggression, and self-indulgence are strongly modeled, those actions are likely to be imitated. Consequently, practitioners and parents should provide deliberate models through actual demonstrations or symbolic representations (e.g., television, movies) that promote behaviors important for individual development and cultural survival. "A child can learn blind obedience to authority by modeling the example of his elders as we saw on a mass scale in Hitler's Germany. Knowing the potential power of the modeling process should awaken us to the importance of making available models well calculated to produce thoughtful, rational, and independent citizens" (Krumboltz & Krumboltz, 1972, p. 61).

SUMMARY

Definition of Imitation

1 Three conditions are present during imitation: (a) a model is demonstrated; (b) an imitative behavior follows the model; and (c) the imitative behavior is reinforced.

Imitative Models

2 A model is an antecedent stimulus.
3 A model can be an individual or a demonstrated behavior.
4 Models can be actual demonstrations or symbols.
5 Models can be planned or unplanned.
6 Models can serve as S^Ds for existing imitative behaviors or for totally new behaviors.

Imitative Behaviors

7 An imitative behavior is behavior that immediately follows a model's behavior and has its topography controlled by that model's behavior.

Imitation Training for Nonimitative Learners

8 Prerequisite attending skills should be assessed and developed.
9 Selection and definition of about 25 behaviors for initial training should include both gross and fine motor movements.
10 The selected behaviors should be pretested.
11 Pretest data should be used to arrange the order of behavior presentation during training.

12 Four conditions are used during training: (a) probe sequence, (b) training trials, (c) putting-through, and (d) alternating sequence.

Effective Imitation Training with Already-Existing Imitative Repertoires

Characteristics of the Model

13 The similarity between the individual providing the model and the individual emitting the imitation can influence the likelihood of the imitative behavior occurring.

14 A model with prestige can increase the likelihood of imitative behaviors.

15 Stress or emphasis on the model stimuli can increase the likelihood of imitation.

16 The effectiveness of a model can be further enhanced by instructions.

Selecting Behaviors to Be Modeled

17 Behaviors selected for imitation training should be at an appropriate level of difficulty.

Positive Reinforcement

18 The likelihood of occurrence of an imitative behavior can be increased when the learner observes the model's behavior-producing reinforcers.

19 Attending to the model should be reinforced.

Considerations

20 Imitation skills permit new behaviors to be acquired quickly with little effort expended by the trainer or trainee.

21 Models can set the occasion for desirable or undesirable behavior. Trainers must be aware of the power of modeling and provide models that promote behaviors important for individual development and cultural survival.

PART
SEVEN

Decreasing Behavior I:
Nonpunishment Procedures

Behavior analysts can use several principles and procedures to decrease or eliminate behavior. Two such principles are presented in part seven: extinction and differential reinforcement. In the six schedules of differential reinforcement presented here, the reductive procedures are concerned with building appropriate response repertoires while at the same time generating a decrease in the occurrence of inappropriate behavior. Whenever extinction is the treatment of choice, it is advisable to concurrently provide reinforcement for alternative behaviors so that inappropriate behavior is replaced with functional behavior.

17

Extinction

KEY TERMS

Extinction

Sensory extinction

Forgetting

Spontaneous recovery

Resistance to extinction

This chapter describes how to reduce the occurrence of behavior by withholding reinforcement, a principle known as extinction. Extinction has been demonstrated to be effective in a wide variety of settings, such as homes, schools, and institutions, and with diverse behaviors ranging from severe self-destruction to mild annoyances (e.g., Hall, Grinstead, Collier, & Hall, 1980; Harris, Wolf, & Baer, 1966; Thomas, Becker, & Armstrong, 1968; Rekers & Lovaas, 1974). However, the effectiveness of extinction in an applied setting is dependent primarily on identification of reinforcing consequences and consistent application of the procedure. Extinction does not require the application of aversive stimuli to decrease be-

havior; it does not provide verbal or physical models of punishers being directed toward others. Extinction simply requires the withholding of reinforcement. The chapter defines extinction and describes procedures for applying extinction. Additionally, it discusses extinction behavior and resistance to extinction. Although extinction appears to be a simple process, its application in applied settings can be difficult.

DEFINITION OF EXTINCTION

Extinction is a procedure in which reinforcement of a previously reinforced behavior is discontinued. In this way extinction describes

---

This chapter was written by John. O. Cooper.

a reductive procedure for behaviors previously maintained by positive or negative reinforcement and by naturally occurring sensory consequences.

Extinction with Behaviors Maintained by Positive Reinforcement

Positive reinforcement occurs when a stimulus presented immediately following a behavior results in an increase in the future probability of occurrence of that behavior under similar stimulus conditions. A behavior maintained by positive reinforcement is placed on extinction when the reinforcing stimulus is no longer forthcoming as a consequence of the behavior.

Williams (1959) in a classic study describes the effects of the removal of positive reinforcement (extinction) on the tyrant-like behavior of a 21-month-old boy. The child had been seriously ill for the first 18 months of his life but had completely recovered when the study began. The boy demanded special attention from his parents, especially at bedtime, and responded with temper tantrums when his parents did not provide the attention.

> The parents and an aunt took turns putting him to bed both at night and for S's [subject's] afternoon nap. If the parent left the bedroom after putting S in his bed, S would scream and fuss until the parent returned to the room. As a result, the parent was unable to leave the bedroom until S went to sleep. If the parent began to read while in the bedroom, S would cry until the reading material was put down. The parents felt that S enjoyed his control over them and that he fought off going to sleep as long as he could. In any event, a parent was spending from one-half to two hours each bedtime just waiting in the bedroom until S went to sleep. (p. 269)

Although Williams does not speculate about how the tantrum behavior developed, an explanation is not difficult to imagine. Since the child had been seriously ill for much of his first 18 months, crying had been his signal that he was experiencing discomfort or pain or needed

help. And in effect, his crying was reinforced by his parents' attention. Over the extended illness crying became a high frequency behavior that continued even after the child's health improved. The parents probably realized eventually that their child cried at bedtime to gain their attention and tried to ignore it. But when they did not stay in the room, the crying increased in intensity and emotion. As the days and weeks went by, the child's demand for absolute attention at bedtime grew worse. The parents probably decided again not to stay with the child at bedtime; but the intensity of the crying increased, and some new tantrum behaviors occurred. The parents returned to the room and, by giving in to the tantrum behavior, taught their child to behave like a tyrant.

After 3 months of the tyrant-like behavior, the parents decided that they must do something about their child's tantrums. It seemed clear to them that their attention was maintaining the tantrums; therefore, they planned to apply the principle of extinction. To implement their plan, they put the child to bed in a leisurely and relaxed manner. Then, after bedtime "pleasantries" they left the bedroom and closed the door, timing the duration of screaming and crying from the moment the door was closed. Figure 17.1 shows the duration of the tantrums.

The data show that the child had a tantrum for 45 minutes the first time he was put to bed without his parents' staying in the room. Then the tantrum behaviors gradually decreased until the 10th session, when the child "no longer whimpered, fussed, or cried when the parents left the room. Rather, he smiled as they left. The parents felt that he made happy sounds until he dropped off to sleep" (Williams, 1959, p. 269).

No tantrum behaviors were emitted for approximately 1 week. Then, after his aunt put him to bed, the child screamed and fussed. She reinforced the tantrum by returning to the bedroom and staying with the child until he went to sleep. Tantrum behavior then returned to

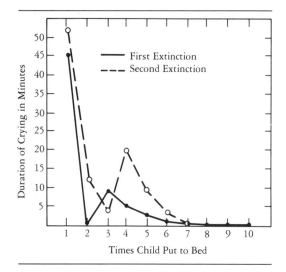

FIGURE 17.1 Two extinction series showing duration of crying as a function of being put to bed. (From "The Elimination of Tantrum Behavior by Extinction Procedures" by C. D. Williams, 1959, *Journal of Abnormal and Social Psychology, 59*, p. 269. Copyright 1959 by the American Psychological Association. Reprinted by permission of the publisher and author.)

the previous high level and had to be decreased a second time.

The data in Figure 17.1 show the duration of tantrums for the 10 days following the aunt's intervention. The data curve is similiar to that for the first removal of parent attention. The duration of the tantrums was somewhat greater during the second removal but reached zero by the ninth session. Williams reports that the child had no further bedtime tantrums during 2 years of follow-up. Clearly, the principle of extinction worked to reduce the future occurrence of a behavior.

Extinction with Behaviors Maintained by Negative Reinforcement

Negative reinforcement occurs when a stimulus terminated immediately following a behavior results in the increased likelihood of occurrence of that behavior under similar stimulus conditions. Behaviors maintained with negative reinforcement are placed on extinction when the stimulus is no longer terminated or removed after the behavior. Carr, Newson, and Binkoff (1980) used extinction to decrease the occurrence of aggressive behaviors maintained by negative reinforcement. The subject was 14 years old, lived in a state institution, and was diagnosed as mentally retarded with autistic features. Even minimal demands, such as being required to sit in a chair during instruction, resulted in his severe aggression toward others. The experimenter wore protective clothing because of the youth's scratching, hitting, kicking, and biting. Prior to implementing the extinction procedure, Carr et al. demonstrated that the youth engaged in aggressive behaviors to terminate aversive demands (e.g., being required to sit in a chair during instruction). Clearly, terminating activities because of the youth's aggression functioned as negative reinforcement for scratching, hitting, kicking, and biting.

The effects of extinction on aggression were analyzed by alternating conditions in which aggression produced escape from treatment (i.e., negative reinforcement) with other occasions during which the learner was not permitted to leave the activity contingent on aggressive behavior (i.e., extinction). When the extinction procedure was in effect, the youth was confined to his chair by a seatbelt across his thighs. The seatbelt eliminated completely any opportunity for escaping from the treatment activity. Figure 17.2 shows the number of aggressive responses per hour under conditions of negative reinforcement and extinction. Carr et al. demonstrated that extinction effectively reduced the aggressive behaviors correlated with instructional demands.

Extinction with Behaviors Maintained by Naturally Occurring Sensory Consequences

Some behaviors are emitted because they produce natural sensory consequences, which can

FIGURE 17.2 Number of aggressive responses per hour during several experimental conditions: extinction (EXT) and negative reinforcement (NEG RFT). From sessions 22 to 39, EXT remained in effect while the experimenter faded out his protective clothing and faded in increasingly greater levels of imitative demands. (From "Escape as a Factor in the Aggressive Behavior of Two Retarded Children" by G. G. Carr, C. D. Newsom, and J. A. Binkoff, 1980, *Journal of Applied Behavior Analysis, 13,* p. 114. Copyright 1980 by the Society for the Experimental Analysis of Behavior, Inc. Reprinted by permission.)

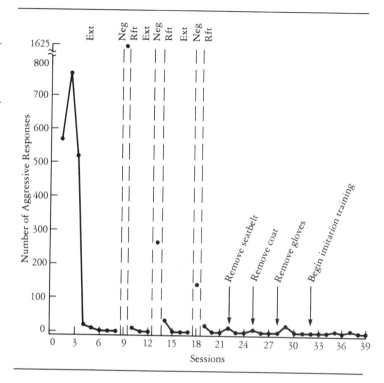

maintain behavior. Rincover (1981) describes these naturally occurring sensory consequences as behavior that "sounds good, looks good, tastes good, smells good, feels good to the touch, or the movement itself is good" (p. 1). Typical behaviors that can be maintained with sensory consequences are labeled self-stimulatory; they are persistent, nonpurposeful, repetitive behaviors (e.g., flipping fingers back and forth in front of the eyes; head rocking; toe walking; manipulating environmental objects such as tissues; hair pulling; grabbing, fondling, and smelling body parts).

Behavior maintained by a naturally occurring sensory consequence is placed on extinction when the sensory consequence is masked or removed. Rincover (1978, 1981) refers to this application as **sensory extinction**. Like all extinction procedures it does not prevent the individual from emitting the behavior. Rather, the environment is arranged so that the sensory consequences are no longer forthcoming.

Rincover (1981) provides numerous examples of the application of sensory extinction. One child persisted in flipping a light switch on and off. The visual sensory consequence was removed by disconnecting the switch. Another child persistently scratched his body until it bled. The tactile (touch) sensory consequence was removed by putting a thin rubber glove on his hand so that he could not feel his skin. Later, the glove was faded by gradually cutting off portions of it. Still another child would ruminate (i.e., throw up and then eat the vomit); the boy liked the taste of his own vomit. The gustatory (taste) sensory extinction procedure consisted of adding lima beans to the vomit. The child did not like lima beans; therefore the vomit did not taste so good, and the positive sensory consequence was masked.

Rincover, Cook, Peoples, and Packard (1979) analyzed the effects of sensory extinction with four children diagnosed as autistic. The children were first observed in order to identify the sensory consequences of their self-stimulating behavior. Larry received kinesthetic stimulation (i.e., stimulation of muscles, tendons, and joints) by holding his arms out to his side and incessantly flapping his fingers, wrists, and arms. Reggie produced auditory stimulation by persistently twirling an object, such as a plate, on a hard surface. Karen repeatedly threw a feather, lint, or small string in the air and waved her hands below it to keep it afloat, producing visual sensory consequences. Janet held her hands in front of her eyes and repetitively rotated her fingers and wrist; she was receiving both visual and kinesthetic stimulation.

To place these behaviors on sensory extinction, Rincover et al. (1979) masked the sensory consequences of Larry's and Janet's finger and arm movements by taping a small vibratory mechanism on the back of their hands. The auditory stimulation from Reggie's plate spinning was masked by carpeting the surface of the table he used for spinning objects. Finally, visual consequences for Janet were removed by placing a handkerchief blindfold over her eyes and for Karen, by turning off overhead lights so she could not see the floating objects (sunlight provided enough illumination for other activi-

ties). Figure 17.3 shows the effects of sensory extinction on the self-stimulatory behaviors of Reggie.

Assessment Procedures for Sensory Extinction Data must be collected prior to applying sensory extinction because not all behavior problems that seem to produce sensory stimulation are maintained by those consequences. For example, in the study by Lovaas and Simmons (1969) self-destructive behaviors such as head banging were demonstrated to be under the control of social consequences. Sensory extinction is appropriate only for behaviors that are maintained solely by sensory consequences; that is, the behaviors are enjoyable for their own sake. Sensory extinction is not appropriate for behaviors, even self-stimulatory behaviors, that are maintained by social consequences.

Guidelines for the Use of Sensory Extinction The first step in the procedure is to assess whether sensory extinction should be used. Data should be collected on antecedent and consequent stimuli that are temporally related to the problem behavior. Does the problem behavior occur more frequently when

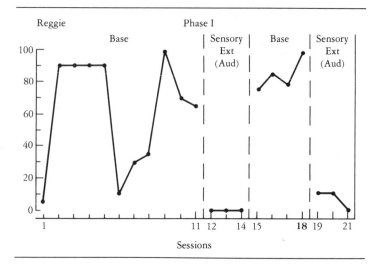

FIGURE 17.3 The effect of sensory extinction (auditory) on Reggie's self-stimulatory behavior. (From "Sensory Extinction and Sensory Reinforcement Principles for Programming Multiple Adaptive Behavior Change" by A. Rincover, R. Cook, A. Peoples, and D. Packard, 1979, *Journal of Applied Behavior Analysis, 12,* p. 227. Copyright 1979 by the Society for the Experimental Analysis of Behavior, Inc. Reprinted by permission.)

something happens in the environment to occasion the behavior? Does the problem behavior occur more frequently when it produces attention from other persons? Or is the frequency of the problem behavior unrelated to antecedent stimuli and social consequences? If the answer to this last question is yes, the individual may be producing behavior only for its sensory consequences. If so, sensory extinction is appropriate.

The second step is to identify the sensory consequences maintaining the behavior. Possible consequences are assessed through direct observation of the behavior and the sensory feedback it produces. The observations should consider tactile, auditory, visual, gustatory, olfactory, and kinesthetic consequences alone or in combination. The final step in the procedure is to develop a method to remove or mask the sensory consequence.

MAINTENANCE OF BEHAVIOR CHANGE

Maintenance of a reduction in behavior generated by an extinction procedure can be arranged by leaving the procedure in effect permanently. A permanent application of extinction with positive and negative reinforcement is frequently the preferred procedure in education and treatment and can often be implemented also with sensory extinction. For example, the carpeting on the table that Reggie used for spinning objects could remain in place indefinitely. However, in many applications of sensory extinction it would be inappropriate and inconvenient to leave the procedure in effect. For instance, it would be both inappropriate and inconvenient to require the child who persistently scratched his body to wear a rubber glove permanently. In such cases it is possible to maintain treatment gains by gradually fading the sensory extinction procedure. The rubber glove in this example was gradually faded by cutting off 1 inch of the glove every 3 to 4 days.

After the glove palm was cut off, the fingers and thumb were removed one at a time.

MISUSE OF TECHNICAL TERM

With the possible exception of negative reinforcement, extinction is the most misunderstood and misused technical term in applied behavior analysis. *Extinction* is a technical term that should be used to describe only the procedure of discontinuing reinforcement for a previously reinforced behavior. Some speak inaccurately of extinction as any decrease in an individual's performance, regardless of what produced the behavior change. But an individual's performance might decrease as a result of a punishment procedure, and to say that "the behavior is extinguishing" would be misleading and incorrect.

Another common misuse of the the technical term is to label as extinction any reduction in behavior that reaches a zero rate of occurrence. For example, if Ray, who smokes two packages of cigarettes per day, decides to stop, he might attend a support clinic once a week where the instructor could use three tactics to help him. First, Ray could receive instructions concerning the harmful effects of smoking. Second, he could be required to graph the number of cigarettes he smokes daily. Third, the instructors and his peers could praise and encourage him for decreases in the number of cigarettes he smokes each day. After 2 months if Ray no longer smokes it would be incorrect to credit extinction. A combination of instructions, self-graphing, and praise probably accounted for the change in smoking behavior.

A final misuse of the term *extinction* occurs when the environment is changed so that no opportunity exists to emit the behavior. For instance, while in high school, Dave developed excellent skills in algebra, geometry, and trigonometry and upon graduation joined the Navy and remained in the service for 8 years. He enrolled in college following his discharge but was shocked to learn that he did so poorly on the college math placement test that he was assigned to a remedial section of Math 100. Dave's math skills did not undergo extinction while he was in the service; he did not have the opportunity to use those skills during that time, and he probably forgot how to compute mathematical functions. In **forgetting**, a behavior is weakened by the passage of time during which the individual does not have the opportunity to emit the behavior. In extinction, behavior is weakened because it does not produce reinforcement (Millenson & Leslie, 1979).

EXTINCTION BEHAVIOR

When a previously reinforced behavior is emitted but is not followed by the usual reinforcing consequences, the occurrence of that behavior should either gradually decrease to its prereinforcement level or stop entirely. Behaviors undergoing extinction are usually associated with predictable characteristics in rate and topography of response.

Initial Increase in Frequency

A general effect of extinction is an immediate increase in frequency of response after the removal of reinforcement; that is, undesirable behaviors placed on extinction usually get worse before they show improvement. To illustrate, if disruptive classroom behaviors are placed on extinction, the teacher should anticipate an initial increase in disruption following the withholding of reinforcement. Thereafter, disruptive behaviors should begin to decrease and should return to their prereinforcement level. The initial increase in behavior usually means the reinforcers that maintained the behavior were successfully identified and withheld; the increase may be an indication that the procedure will be effective. Behavior analysts should be aware of this possible initial increase in response frequency and should be prepared

to withhold the reinforcing consequences on a consistent basis.

Initial Increase in Magnitude

Often an initial increase in the magnitude of the response occurs with an extinction procedure; responses following the removal of reinforcement may become more intense. A child whose bedtime tantrums are ignored for the first time may increase the loudness or magnitude of his screaming and the force of his kicking before the tantrum behaviors begin to decrease.

Gradual Decrease in Frequency and Magnitude

Extinction produces a gradual reduction in behavior. However, when reinforcement is removed abruptly, numerous unreinforced responses can follow. In general, behaviors maintained with negative reinforcement generate an even slower decline in frequency during extinction than do behaviors maintained with positive reinforcement; avoidance responses prevent the individual from experiencing the absence of the negative reinforcers. In other words, avoidance responses are resistant to extinction because they keep the individual from learning that the negative reinforcers are no longer aversive or present.

The extinction procedure is often difficult for teachers and parents to apply because of the initial increase in frequency and magnitude and the gradual decrease in behavior. For example, parents may be unwilling to ignore tantrum behavior for a sufficient amount of time because tantrums are so aversive to parents. Rolider and Van Houten (1984) present a tactic for this practical problem. They suggest teaching parents to ignore gradually increasing durations of bedtime crying. They used baseline data to assess how long the parents could ignore bedtime crying comfortably, before attending to their child. Then, the parents gradually increased their duration of ignoring. Every 2 days they waited an additional 5 minttes before attending to the child until a sufficient total duration of time was achieved.

Spontaneous Recovery

During extinction it is typical for a behavior to continue a decreasing trend until it reaches a prereinforced level or ultimately ceases. However, a phenomenon commonly associated with extinction is the reappearance of the behavior even though it has not been reinforced. This phenomenon is called **spontaneous recovery**. Spontaneous recovery is short-lived and limited if the extinction procedure remains in effect. However, practitioners need to be aware of spontaneous recovery, or they might conclude erroneously that the extinction procedure is no longer effective.

VARIABLES AFFECTING RESISTANCE TO EXTINCTION

Behaviors placed on extinction gradually decrease to prereinforcement levels or cease completely. Continued responding during extinction is termed **resistance to extinction** and is an important consideration for all persons working in the helping professions. Several quantitative measures can be used with resistance to extinction. Reynolds (1968) states that resistance can be measured in terms of "the rate of decline in response frequency, the total number of responses emitted before responding either ceases or reaches some final low level" (p. 33). In addition, resistance to extinction can be described as the duration of time required for a behavior to reach a predetermined criterion. An individual's persistence is determined by experiences (i.e., history of reinforcement) prior to and during extinction.

Schedules of Reinforcement

Chapter 12 discussed the effects of continuous reinforcement (CRF) and intermittent schedules of reinforcement (FR, VR, FI, VI). A general rule describes the effects of extinction on behaviors previously maintained by continuous or intermittent reinforcement: an intermittent reinforcement schedule produces behaviors that are more resistant to extinction than those produced by a continuous reinforcement schedule. If an extinction procedure is applied to behaviors maintained with continuous reinforcement, the effect will be a rapid decrease in behavior. It will take much longer to generate a decrease in behaviors maintained by intermittent reinforcement. Therefore, desirable behaviors should be maintained on intermittent schedules of reinforcement so that they will persist in the absence of reinforcement.

Some intermittent schedules are more resistant than others (Ferster & Skinner, 1957). The two variables schedules (VR and VI) are more resistant to extinction than the fixed schedules (FR and FI). Also, the more sparse the schedule, the greater the resistance to extinction. An interesting example of the effects of intermittent reinforcement on persistence was given by an undergraduate student in one of the authors' introductory class in behavior analysis. About 2 months after a lecture on resistance to extinction, the student shared this experience.

> You know, intermittent reinforcement really does affect persistence. This guy I know was always calling me for a date. I didn't like him and didn't enjoy being with him. Most of the time when he asked for a date I would not go out with him. Occasionally, because of his persistence, I would give in and accept a date. After your lecture I realized that I was maintaining his calling behavior on an intermittent schedule of reinforcement, which could account for his persistence. I decided to change this situation and put him on a continuous schedule of reinforcement. Every time he called for a date, I agreed to go out with him. We spent about 4 evenings a week together for 3 weeks. Then without giving any reason I abruptly stopped accepting dates with him. Since then he's called only three times, and I have not heard from him in 4 weeks.

Number, Amount, and Quality of Reinforcers

The number of times a behavior has been reinforced affects resistance to extinction. Simply stated, a behavior with a long history of reinforcement will be more resistant to extinction than a behavior that has produced few reinforcers. If bedtime tantrums have produced reinforcement for 1 year, they will be more resistant to extinction than they would be if they had been reinforced for 1 week. Also, the amount and quality of the reinforcer has an effect on resistance to extinction. The greater the amount and quality of the reinforcer, short of satiation, the more persistent the behavior during extinction.

Number of Previous Extinction Trials

Successive conditioning and extinction affects the extinction process. Sometimes inappropriate behavior becomes weaker with extinction and then is accidentally strengthened again with reinforcement. When this happens, the behavior analyst can apply the extinction procedure a second time. Typically, decreases in behavior will be more rapid, and there will be fewer total responses during a second application of extinction. And the effect is additive: with each successive application of extinction, decreases in behavior become increasingly rapid until only a single response may be emitted following the withdrawal of reinforcement (Millenson & Leslie, 1979).

Effort

Another variable that can affect resistance to extinction is the effort required to produce the response. If a response requires great effort, it may decrease more quickly during extinction than a response requiring less effort.

GUIDELINES FOR THE EFFECTIVE USE OF EXTINCTION

Combine with Other Procedures

Extinction is an effective procedure, but its effectiveness is increased when it is combined with other procedures. Extinction should always be combined with reinforcement of appropriate behaviors. Like most reductive techniques, extinction teaches what not to do, but not what to do. By combining extinction with reinforcement for appropriate behaviors, the behavior analyst alters the environment to help the individual emit appropriate alternative behaviors. Extinction should not reduce the overall amount of positive consequences received by an individual.

Zimmerman and Zimmerman (1962) used extinction and differential reinforcement with an 11-year-old boy with normal intelligence and severe behavior disorders. Whenever the teacher tested the student on previously studied spelling words, he misspelled most of the words. As a consequence, the teacher asked the student to sound out each word and offered other prompts and cues, and encouragement. Only after the teacher's time-consuming help and attention did the student correctly spell the words. The teacher was certain that the student knew how to spell the words on the test, and she thought there was a good chance that her instruction and encouragement were positive reinforcement for the incorrect spelling responses. Consequently, the teacher intervened by placing incorrect spelling on extinction. She would read a word, and the student would write it on the blackboard. After writing the word incorrectly, the student would glance at the teacher and say, "I can't spell it," or "I can't remember how." The student misspelled the first word 10 times or more while the teacher sat at her desk and completely ignored the student and his incorrect words. Finally, the student correctly spelled the first word. The teacher immediately smiled, praised the correct spelling, and said they could now do the second word. This procedure was continued for the 10 spelling words. Fewer incorrect responses were emitted with each successive word. After 1 month of this procedure, incorrect spelling responses declined to approximately zero per class session.

Identify and Withhold All Sources of Reinforcement for the Target Behavior

A first step in using extinction effectively is to identify and withhold all possible sources of reinforcement that are maintaining the target behavior. In some situations the consequences maintaining the undesirable behavior are obvious. In the Williams (1959) study, for instance, it was probable that parental attention was the only source of reinforcement maintaining the tyrant-like behavior at bedtime. However, behaviors are frequently maintained by multiple sources of reinforcement. The class clown's behavior may be maintained by the teacher's reaction to the disruptive behavior or the attention it generates from peers or a combination of both. Johnny may cry when his mother or father brings him to preschool to avoid school or to keep his parents with him or to occasion his teacher's concern and attention or to achieve some combination of all three. Identifying and withholding only one source of reinforcement may have minimal or no effect if the behavior is maintained by several sources of reinforcement. If teacher and peer attention is maintaining clownish classroom behavior, then withholding only teacher attention will produce little change in behavior. The teacher must withhold her attention and also teach the students to ignore the clownish behavior to effectively apply the extinction procedure.

Withhold Consistently

When the reinforcing consequences have been identified, they must be withheld consistently. Consistency is important to all behavior change procedures; it is absolutely essential to extinction. Lack of consistency is the single most common error in using extinction, and this point cannot be overemphasized.

Use Instructions

The consequences of a behavior affect the future probability of the behavior automati-cally. It is not necessary for an individual to be able to describe the relationship between environmental arrangements and behavior or even to verbalize that a consequence has or has not occurred (Michael, 1970). However, behavior can decrease more quickly during extinction if the individual is informed of the procedure being applied. For example, teachers frequently provide small group or tutorial instruction while other students in the classroom are engaged in independent seat work or learning centers. A common problem with this arrangement occurs when students doing independent work interrupt the small group instruction to ask the teacher questions. Many teachers correct this problem by placing it on extinction; they simply ignore student questions until after the instructional activities are complete. This strategy is often effective. However, the extinction procedure can be more effective if teachers explain to their classes that they are not to be interrupted while working with students and that interruptions will be ignored (i.e., a classroom rule).

Plan for Extinction-Produced Aggression

When behaviors are no longer successful in producing reinforcement, other behaviors that were less likely to occur in the past may be emitted in their place (Ullman & Krasner, 1965); and these behaviors may be aggressive. The changes in response topography and the appearance of mild aggression that sometimes accompany extinction have been interpreted by some as emotional behaviors (Lundin, 1969; Skinner, 1953).

The behavior analyst must plan management strategies for these aggressive behaviors that frequently accompany extinction. It is critical that extinction-produced aggression not be reinforced. A frequent response of teachers, parents, and others in the human service professions is to give in and reinforce the behavior that was placed on extinction, thereby directly reinforcing extinction-produced aggression. For instance, the teacher decides to ignore questions while providing small group instruction. However, when Mary interrupts the teacher with a question and the teacher does not respond, Mary starts disrupting other students. To quiet Mary down, the teacher responds, "Oh, all right, Mary, what did you want to know?" In effect, the teacher is reinforcing not only Mary's interrupting behavior but also the accompanying inappropriate disruption.

Many times extinction-produced aggression takes the form of verbal abuse, and the behavior analyst should be prepared to ignore it completely. If extinction-produced aggression is reinforced, the individual simply learns to perform a new inappropriate behavior. Some aggressive acts and self-injurious behavior cannot or should not be ignored. However, "it is most important that [behavior analysts] prepare for the likelihood of aggressive behavior, know that it is possible to ignore much of it, know exactly what behaviors require additional action, and know exactly how that action will be carried out" (Heward et al., 1979, p. 56).

Increase the Number of Extinction Trials

Whenever possible, the number of extinction trials should be increased for the inappropriate behavior. An extinction trial occurs each time the target behavior is emitted and is not reinforced. In an environment arranged so that the inappropriate behavior can be emitted more frequently, more extinction trials can occur. An increase in the number of extinction trials causes the behavior to be weakened in less time. Heward, Dardig, and Rosset (1979) provide an illustration of this effect.

> Billy's parents are employing an extinction procedure to reduce his tantruming. His parents noticed that Billy had tantrums most often when he did not get his way about staying up late, eating a snack, and going outside. So for the purpose of the program, they decided to set up several additional situations each day in which Billy did not get his way. Billy was then more likely to emit the inappropriate behavior at a higher rate,

thereby giving his parents more occasions to ignore it. As a result, his tantruming decreased more rapidly than it would have if left at its usual rate. (pp. 56–57)

Include Significant Others in Extinction

It is important that other persons in the environment not reinforce the occurrence of the undesirable behavior. A teacher, for example, needs to share extinction plans with other people who might help in the classroom—parent volunteers, grandparents, music teachers, speech therapists, industrial arts specialists—to avoid their reinforcing inappropriate behaviors. All individuals in contact with the learner must apply the same extinction procedure for effective treatment.

Guard Against Unintentional Extinction

Desirable behaviors are often unintentionally placed on extinction. A beginning teacher confronted with one student who is on task and many other students who are not will probably direct most of his attention to the majority and will provide little or no attention to the student who is working. It is common practice to give the most attention to problems—the squeaky wheel gets the grease—and to ignore situations that are going smoothly. However, behaviors must continue to be reinforced if they are to be maintained. All teachers must give attention to students who are on-task.

Know When Not to Use Extinction

Observational Learning Extinction can be inappropriate if the behaviors placed on extinction are likely to be modeled by others. Some behaviors can be tolerated if only one person emits them but become intolerable if a whole group engages in them.

Extreme Behaviors With few exceptions most applications of extinction in applied settings have focused on important but relatively minor behavior problems (e.g., disruptive classroom behavior, tantrums, nonstudy behavior, excessive noise, mild forms of aggression). However, some behaviors are so harmful to self or others (e.g., head banging, arm banging, self-biting) or so destructive to property that they must be controlled with the most rapid and humane procedure available. In such situations extinction is not appropriate.

The use of extinction to decrease severe aggression toward self, others, or property raises ethical concerns. Addressing the issue of ethics, Pinkston, Reese, LeBlanc, and Baer (1973) analyzed the effects of an extinction technique that did not allow an individual to harm himself or his victim. In their approach the aggressor was ignored, but the victim was sheltered from attack. They demonstrated the effectiveness of a safe extinction technique with an extremely

aggressive preschool boy, whose aggressive behaviors included choking, biting, pinching, hitting, and kicking classmates. During the baseline condition the teachers responded to the child's aggression as they had in the past. "Typically, this took the form of verbal admonitions or reproofs such as: 'Cain, we do not do that here,' or 'Cain, you can't play here until you are ready to be a good boy'"(p. 118). During extinction the teachers did not attend to the boy's aggressive behaviors. When he attacked a peer, the teachers immediately attended to the peer. The victim was consoled and provided with an opportunity to play with a toy. In addition, the teachers attended to the boy's positive behaviors. This extinction procedure was effective in greatly reducing aggression. The application of extinction requires sound, mature, humane, and ethical judgment.

SUMMARY

Definition

1 Extinction is a procedure in which reinforcement of a previously reinforced behavior is discontinued.
2 When a behavior is maintained with positive reinforcement, it is placed on extinction when the stimulus, object, or event is no longer produced as a consequence of behavior.
3 Behaviors maintained with negative reinforcement are placed on extinction when a stimulus, object, or event is no longer terminated or removed following the behavior.
4 Behavior maintained by a naturally occurring sensory consequence is placed on extinction when the sensory consequence is masked or removed.

Extinction Behavior

5 Undesirable behaviors placed on extinction usually show an initial increase in frequency; they usually get worse before they show improvement.

6 Responses may initially increase in frequency following the removal of reinforcement; they may also become more intense.
7 Extinction produces a gradual, not an immediate, reduction in behavior.
8 Spontaneous recovery, an event commonly associated with extinction, is the reappearance of the inappropriate behavior after a period of time in which the behavior has not been reinforced.

Variables Affecting Resistance to Extinction

9 Resistance to extinction can be measured in terms of (a) rate of decline in response frequency, (b) total number of responses emitted before responding either ceases or reaches some final low level, and (c) duration of time required for a behavior to reach a predetermined performance criterion.
10 Variables most likely to influence resistance to extinction are schedules of reinforcement;

amount, quality, and number of reinforcers received; number of previous extinction trials; and effort required to make the response.

Guidelines for the Effective Use of Extinction

11 Combine extinction with other procedures.

12 Identify and withhold all sources of reinforcement of the target behavior.

13 Be consistent in withholding reinforcement.

14 Use instructions: behaviors often decrease more quickly during extinction when the subject is informed of the procedure being applied.

15 Plan for extinction-produced aggression.

16 Include other individuals in the extinction plan so that they do not reinforce the occurrence of the undesirable behavior.

17 Increase the number of extinction trials.

18 Do not use extinction for behaviors that are likely to be modeled by others or for behaviors that are harmful to self or others.

18

Decreasing Behavior with Differential Reinforcement

KEY TERMS

Differential reinforcement of incompatible behavior (DRI)

Differential reinforcement of alternative behavior (DRA)

Differential reinforcement of other behavior (DRO)

Fixed DRO

Variable DRO

Differential reinforcement of low rates (DRL)

Full-session DRL

Interval DRL

Spaced-responding DRL

Interresponse time (IRT)

Practitioners have access to effective procedures for decreasing or eliminating maladaptive behaviors. However, ethical and legal issues are raised by the use of some reductive techniques (i.e., extinction, punishment, aversive stimulation, chemical and physical restraints). For example, it is common for communities to debate the ethics of using corporal punishment in school settings. And some treatment procedures are denied to psychiatric patients, persons with mental retardation, and prisoners because the procedures are judged to infringe upon client rights (Budd & Baer, 1976). Because of these concerns applied behavior analysts have sought effective procedures that are judged ethical and humane (e.g., Kazdin, 1980a; Singh & Katz, 1985). These alternative procedures are called positive reductive procedures

---

This chapter was written by John O. Cooper.

(Deitz & Repp, 1983) because they rely on reinforcement to decrease or eliminate behavior rather than the loss of opportunity for additional reinforcement, the removal of acquired reinforcers, or the presentation of a punisher.

Four procedures that use reinforcement to decrease or eliminate inappropriate behavior are differential reinforcement of incompatible behavior (DRI), differential reinforcement of alternative behavior (DRA), differential reinforcement of other behavior (DRO), and differential reinforcement of low rates of responding (DRL). A positive environment is maintained with these procedures, and their application is not likely to raise ethical and legal issues. Society may question why it is important to decrease or eliminate certain behaviors but not how the change is achieved. Included in this chapter are definitions and guidelines for the effective use of differential reinforcement procedures in decreasing inappropriate behavior.

DIFFERENTIAL REINFORCEMENT OF INCOMPATIBLE BEHAVIOR AND ALTERNATIVE BEHAVIOR

Differential reinforcement of incompatible behavior (DRI) is a schedule of reinforcement in which the occurrence of a behavior topographically incompatible with the behavior selected for reduction is followed by reinforcement (Deitz & Repp, 1983). In other words, the behavior selected for differential reinforcement and the behavior selected for reduction cannot be emitted at the same time. For example, if out-of-seat behavior is selected for reduction, in-seat behavior is reinforced because it cannot coexist with out-of-seat behavior. If off-task behavior is to be reduced, on-task behavior is reinforced. Two classes of behavior are mutually exclusive; both cannot be performed simultaneously.

Differential reinforcement of alternative behavior (DRA) and DRI are similar

reductive procedures. DRA reinforces the occurrence of a target behavior that is an alternative to the behavior selected for reduction (Deitz & Repp, 1983). An alternative behavior can be developed to occupy the time that would ordinarily be used for the unwanted behavior. However, the alternative behavior and the unwanted behavior are not topographically incompatible. For example, two students who frequently argue with each other can be assigned to work on a class project together, and reinforcement is made available for the behaviors associated with the project. Working on a class project together and arguing are not topographically incompatible. However, it is likely that the two students will spend less time arguing if cooperative behaviors are strengthened. Deitz, Repp, and Deitz (1976) reinforced appropriate academic work to decrease the in-class sleeping of a 14-year-old student with mild retardation. The teacher attended to and praised the student for her academic performance on the average of every 5 minutes. With another 14-year-old student with mild retardation, Deitz, Repp, and Deitz reinforced appropriate academic work to decrease talk-outs. Again, the teacher attended to the student's appropriate academic performance and ignored his talk-outs. Differential reinforcement was functionally related to both decreased episodes of in-class sleeping and decreased frequencies of talk-outs. These data are presented in Figure 18.1.

Guidelines for the Effective Use of DRI/DRA

DRI and DRA are used frequently in education and treatment. Deitz and Repp (1983) state that these procedures have been used by parents, teachers, employers, and friends throughout time. Nonetheless, even though the practice of DRI/DRA is common, several factors can influence effective use, and suggested guidelines are included here.

First of all, incompatible or alternative behaviors should be selected that are in the

FIGURE 18.1 Upper panel: expisodes of sleeping per 75-minute session for Subject 8 in DRI Experiment 1. Lower panel: frequency of talk-outs per 75-minute session for Subject 9 in DRI Experiment 2. During treatment appropriate academic work was reinforced for both subjects. (From "Reducing Inappropriate Classroom Behavior of Retarded Students Through Three Procedures of Differential Reinforcement" by S. M. Deitz, A. C. Repp, and D. E. D. Deitz, 1976, *Journal of Mental Deficiency Research, 20,* p. 166. Copyright 1976 by the *Journal of Mental Deficiency Research.* Reprinted by permission.)

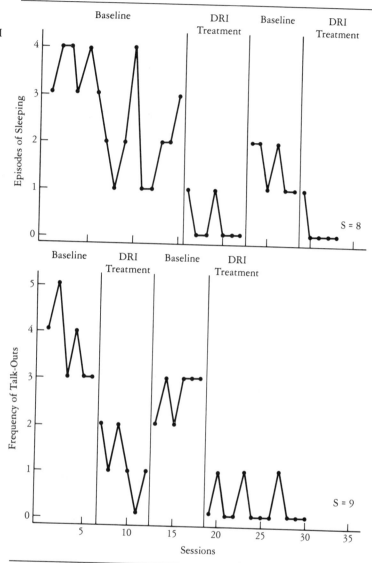

learner's repertoire of responses, that the learner emits with regularity, that will help the learner acquire more skills, and that the learner's natural environment will support after termination of the DRI/DRA intervention. When incompatible and alternative behaviors are selected for their usefulness and relevance to the learner, these behaviors usually continue to be reinforced under natural environmental contingencies. Thus, maintenance in the training setting and transfer to other environments are more likely to occur if this first guideline is followed. Deitz and Repp (1983) comment on usefulness in reference to the earlier example of reinforced academic performance as an alternative to in-class sleeping: "The on-task behavior was reinforced rather than the behavior of simply being awake because [academic] performance was more benefical to the subject than merely remaining awake" (p. 43).

The second guideline is that consequences should be selected from stimuli demonstrated to function as reinforcers and able to be presented contingently, consistently, and immediately following the behavior. Perhaps the greatest threat to the effectivenes of the DRI/DRA (and DRO, DRL) procedure is the use of a stimulus that is only assumed to function as a reinforcer. "When using any reinforcement procedure, not just those programmed to reduce inappropriate behavior, the strength of the reinforcer is an important variable. The reinforcer must be, first of all, effective and, equally as important, durable" (Deitz, Slack, Schwarzmueller, Wilander, Weatherly, & Hilliard, 1978, p. 44). In addition, reinforcers stronger than those maintaining the maladaptive behavior must be identified if the DRI/DRA (and DRO, DRL) procedure is to be functional. Therefore, an assessment should be administered prior to the differential reinforcement procedure to demonstrate that a selected stimulus is indeed a reinforcer.

One assessment procedure first establishes a baseline performance on a simple two-choice task, such as putting 25 marbles in a small box with left and right holes. The subject is simply asked to do the task; no response prompts are given. The holes used to put the marbles into the box are recorded, and the hole used least is the nonpreferred response. Thereafter, the subject is presented with the selected stimulus (i.e., potential reinforcer) immediately after each nonpreferred response. If the subject does not make a nonpreferred response within five opportunities, a response prompt can be given (e.g., "Put the marble in this hole").

Again, the holes used for the marbles are recorded until the nonpreferred hole becomes the preferred hole or until a maximum of three sessions are recorded (25 marbles per session). If the response preference has not changed in three sessions, a different potential reinforcer should be applied. When a change in the response preference is demonstrated, the potential reinforcer is presented immediately after each now-nonpreferred response (i.e., the preferred response during baseline). Again, one response prompt is allowed, and responses are recorded until the response preference changes back to that of baseline or until a maximum of three sessions have been recorded. If after three sessions the response preference has not changed, the entire assessment procedure should be repeated with a different potential reinforcer. Table 18.1 provides an illustration of hypothetical data collected during a reinforcer assessment procedure.

The third guideline for effective use of a DRI/DRA procedure is to establish a schedule of reinforcement (Deitz & Repp, 1983) that initially delivers consequences on a CRF schedule of reinforcement and then provides for a gradually thinning intermittent schedule after the incompatible or alternative behavior is strengthened.

The fourth and final guideline is to combine DRI/DRA with other reductive procedures. Research by Luiselli (1980) and Stokes and Kennedy (1980) provide examples of this guideline. Luiselli (1980) taught parents to apply a treatment package to improve the behavior of their children. One parent reported that his child's excessive running from room to

TABLE 18.1. Illustration of data from an assessment procedure to demonstrate that a consequence is a reinforcer.	*Number of Marbles per Hole*	
	Left Hole	*Right Hole*
Baseline	16	9
Reinforcement$_1$ (right hole)	4	21
Reinforcement$_2$ (left hole)	19	6

room was extremely annoying and disruptive to household activity. The parent differentially reinforced walking from room to room because walking was incompatible with running. The boy's walking was followed with praise statements, such as "Good boy for walking into the kitchen" or "Good, Bobby, you're doing nice walking." This DRI procedure, combined with placing the child on a chair for 3 minutes and using mild reprimands after inappropriate behavior, decreased running in the house from an average of 5½ episodes per hour during baseline conditon to a treatment average of zero episodes. Follow-up at 5,6, and 7 months after termination of the program indicated that the child continued walking in the house rather than running excessively.

Stokes and Kennedy (1980) reported data from 40 grade school children who were part of a governmental dental program. Eight of the children were so disruptive that effective dentistry was not possible. Their uncooperative behaviors involved head and body movements, crying, complaining, and other verbal and motor behaviors that caused delays in dental work. The nurse used praise to differentially reinforce appropriate behaviors of the children. Also, at the end of each session, cooperative children received a small trinket and an opportunity to operate the pneumatic dental chair for the next child scheduled. In addition, the children were told the reasons that they did or did not receive the trinket or the opportunity to operate the chair. All eight children decreased their uncooperative behaviors (see Figure 18.2).

DIFFERENTIAL REINFORCEMENT OF OTHER BEHAVIOR

Differential reinforcement of other behavior (DRO) is a schedule of reinforcement in which reinforcement occurs whenever a specific behavior is not emitted during an interval of time (Reynolds, 1961). Some have

termed the DRO schedule of reinforcement *omission training* (e.g., Sewell, McCoy, & Sewell, 1973; Weiher & Harman, 1975) because reinforcement is for the omission rather than the commission of a behavior. A DRO procedure specifies that any appropriate behavior, other than a behavior selected for reduction, will be followed by reinforcement. Therefore, a reinforcer can follow a very general class of behaviors, for which the only defining characteristic is the absence of the behavior selected for reduction. To apply the DRO procedure (1) an interval of time is set; (2) any appropriate behavior occurring at the end of that interval is reinforced if the target behavior was not emitted during the interval; and (3) any occurrence of the target behavior causes a return to the beginning of the interval.

DRO is a widely used procedure in education and treatment (Deitz & Repp, 1983). Several studies report rapid decreases in selected behaviors (e.g., Ball, McCrady, & Teixeira, 1978; Iwata & Lorentzson, 1976; Peterson & Peterson, 1968; Poling, Miller, Nelson, & Ryan, 1978; Repp, Deitz, & Deitz, 1976; Repp, Deitz, & Speir, 1974). Poling and Ryan (1982) found the DRO procedure to be used most frequently with self-injurious, aggressive, or disruptive behaviors. For example, Allen, Gottseling, and Boylan (1982) used a group DRO procedure to decrease the disruptive classroom behaviors of third-grade students. They used 5-minute time intervals for the reinforcement schedule; a kitchen timer was set and continued to run as long as no disruptive behaviors were emitted. Following the passage of 5 minutes, any appropriate behavior emitted was followed by the accumulation of 1 minute of free time, to be awarded at the end of class time. If a student engaged in a targeted disruptive behavior at any time during the 5-minute interval, the kitchen timer was reset for a new interval. Figure 18.3 shows the decrease of disruptive behaviors during math and language arts instruction.

Repp, Deitz, and Speir (1974) used DRO to decrease the high-rate stereotypic behaviors of

FIGURE 18.2 Percentages of uncooperative behavior for each child. Appointment days are separated by the solid and dotted vertical lines. The shaded bars show the daily mean percentages; the line graph shows behavior during consecutive 10-minute intervals of dental work. The asterisks at the end of some appointments mark the days on which the child was not given the tangible reinforcers. (From "Reducing Child Uncooperative Behavior During Dental Treatment Through Modeling and Reinforcement" by T. F. Stokes, and S. H. Kennedy, 1980, *Journal of Applied Behavior Analysis, 13,* p. 47. Copyright 1980 by the Society for the Experimental Analysis of Behavior, Inc. Reprinted by permission.)

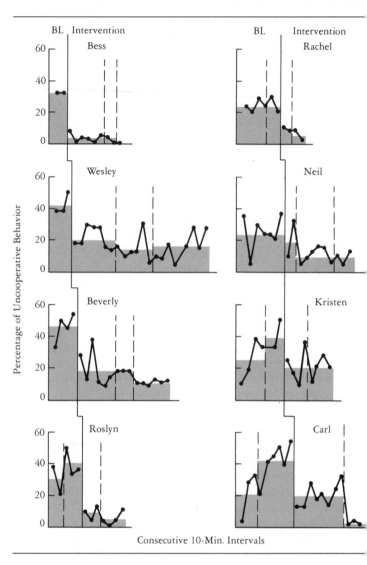

three persons with severe retardation. Behaviors selected for reduction included lip flipping (i.e., a vertical movement of a finger across relaxed lips), rocking, and hand motions (e.g., movement of a hand in a horizontal plane back and forth in front of the face). After an assessment of the response rate during baseline, Repp et al. set an initial DRO time interval of 40 seconds. If the clients did not emit the defined stereotypic behaviors during the inter-

val, they were hugged and verbally praised for 2 to 3 seconds. The DRO schedule reduced stereotypic behaviors to an average of 1% of baseline levels.

In another DRO study the inappropriate behaviors of a 10-year-old retarded student were decreased during bus rides to and from school (Chiang, Iwata, & Dorsey, 1979). The boy's disruptive behaviors included aggression (e.g., slapping, poking, hitting, kicking), being

IGURE 18.3 Daily mean per-
entages of intervals of disruptive
ehavior during baseline and
eatment phases for the entire
roup. (From "A Practical Mechan-
m for Using Free Time as a Rein-
orcer in the Classroom" by L. D.
llen, M. Gottseling, and S. Boylan,
982, *Education and Treatment of
hildren,* 5(4), p. 351. Copyright
982 by *Education and Treatment
f Children.* Reprinted by
ermission.)

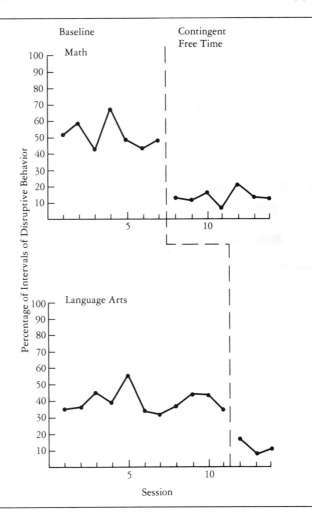

FIGURE 18.3 Daily mean percentages of intervals of disruptive behavior during baseline and treatment phases for the entire group. (From "A Practical Mechanism for Using Free Time as a Reinforcer in the Classroom" by L. D. Allen, M. Gottseling, and S. Boylan, 1982, *Education and Treatment of Children,* 5(4), p. 351. Copyright 1982 by *Education and Treatment of Children.* Reprinted by permission.)

out-of-seat, stereotypic behaviors, and inappropriate vocalizations (e.g., screaming, yelling). This study used a unique procedure for determining the time intervals for the DRO. The bus route was divided into sections designated by landmarks such as stop signs and traffic lights. The bus driver mounted a four-digit hand counter on the dashboard of the bus; the counter was within reach of the driver and within view of the student. At each predetermined landmark the bus driver praised the student and added one point to the hand counter if no disruptive behaviors had been emitted during the interval. Upon arrival (at home or school) the number of points earned was recorded on a card and given to the foster father or teacher. Points were exchanged for access to "toys . . . privileges (e.g., accompanying staff on errands within the school, stopping briefly in another classroom where his father worked to say hello), and small snacks" (Chiang et al., 1979, p. 104). Data show a decrease in disruptive behavior on the bus ride. Before the DRO procedure was applied, disruptive behavior ranged from 20 to 100% with an average of 66.2% for the afternoon rides and 0 to 92% with an average of 48.5% in the mornings. The DRO procedure was first applied only to the afternoon rides; disruptive behavior decreased immediately to an average of 5.1% within a range of 0 to 40%. Disruptive behavior during the morning ride remained unchanged. When the program was applied in the mornings, all disruptive behavior was eliminated.

Variable DRO

Most applications of DRO use a **fixed DRO** (FDRO) schedule of reinforcement in which the interval of time remains the same from trial to trial. When the DRO interval of time is programmed to vary from trial to trial, it is called a **variable DRO** (VDRO) schedule of reinforcement. For example, a variable DRO of 11 seconds means that, on the average, reinforcement follows every 11 seconds of behavior omission. This schedule could use time intervals such as 4, 5, 8, 18, and 20 seconds, arranged to occur in random sequence. Patterson, Jones, Whittier, and Wright (1965) and Topping and Crowe (1974) are among the few who have investigated the VDRO schedule of reinforcement; both groups found the VDRO to be an effective procedure for decreasing behavior.

Guidelines for the Effective Use of DRO

As indicated here, several studies have demonstrated that the DRO procedure effectively decreased behavior. Other studies, however, report that the DRO procedure did not generate a decrease in behavior (e.g., Foxx & Azrin, 1973; Leitenberg, Burchard, Burchard, Fuller, & Lysaght, 1977; Meyers, 1975). The variables that account for the variance in these studies are not clear. However, in addition to the importance of reinforcement, Deitz and Repp (1983) and Repp and Deitz (1979) recommend procedures that can increase the likelihood that the DRO schedule of reinforcement will decrease selected behaviors.

The first suggested guideline is to establish an initial DRO time interval that is consistent with data recorded during the baseline condition; and that allows the subject's behavior to produce frequent reinforcement. There is no commonly accepted rule for setting the initial time interval (Poling & Ryan, 1982); but Deitz and Repp (1983) suggest an initial DRO interval that is less than the baseline mean **interresponse time (IRT)**. To calculate the mean IRT, the total length of all baseline sessions is divided by the total number of responses recorded during the baseline condition. For example, if the subject emitted a total of 30 responses during 5 days of the baseline condition and each baseline session was 10 minutes in length for a total of 50 minutes, then 50 divided by 30 produces a mean IRT interval of $1\frac{2}{3}$ minutes. According to these baseline data, the initial DRO interval could be set for $1\frac{2}{3}$ minutes or less.

The second guideline is to establish procedures for increasing the length of the DRO interval; the procedures should program an increase only after the current DRO interval is effectively controlling behavior and should arrange for small increments in the length of the DRO interval. Poling and Ryan (1982) suggest three possible approaches to increasing the length of the DRO interval. First, intervals can be increased by a constant time. For example, at each opportunity for increase the DRO interval might be increased by 45 seconds. Second, intervals can be increased proportionately. Each time the DRO interval is increased, the length of time is increased by the same percent. Third, based on the learner's performance, the DRO interval can change from session to session. For example, the mean IRT interval from each preceding session can be used as the new DRO interval. If behavior starts to worsen when larger DRO intervals are used, the size of the interval should be decreased until the behavior is again under control. The DRO interval can be lengthened in smaller, more gradual steps after control has been reestablished. Poling and Ryan caution that the magnitude of the DRO consequence may need to be increased as the DRO interval is lengthened.

The third guideline suggests that reinforcement at the end of the DRO interval should be delivered only when the selected behavior did not occur during the interval and no other inappropriate behavior occurred either.

The final guideline recommends that DRO be combined with other reductive procedures. The DRO schedule of reinforcement can be used independently (Poling & Ryan, 1982); however, there is often practical value in combining the DRO schedule with other reductive procedures. Luce and Hall (1981) found that a combination of DRO and contingent exercise (i.e., required exercise after inappropriate behavior) was more effective than DRO alone. Gross, Farrar, and Liner (1982) used a combination of DRO, overcorrection (see chapter 20), and facial screening to decrease chronic hair pulling that resulted in large red bald spots on the head of a 4-year-old child with cerebral palsy. And Rolider and Van Houten (1984b) found that DRO and reprimands were more effective than DRO alone in decreasing physically abusive behaviors that a 4½-year-old girl was directing toward her baby sister. They reported similarly that DRO and reprimands were more effective than DRO alone in decreasing the thumb sucking of a 12-year-old boy. In a third experiment they showed that DRO and reprimands produced greater reductions in bedtime tantrums than DRO and extinction.

DIFFERENTIAL REINFORCEMENT OF LOW RATES OF RESPONDING

In laboratory studies Ferster and Skinner (1957) demonstrated a schedule of reinforcement that produced consistently low rates of responding. This schedule was called **differential reinforcement of low rates (DRL)**. Based on the laboratory procedures for programming DRL schedules, Deitz (1977) labeled and described three types of DRL schedules for application in education and treatment: full-session DRL, interval DRL, and spaced-responding DRL.

Full-Session DRL

A **full-session DRL** is programmed to deliver reinforcement if response during the instructional session is equal to or below a criterion limit (Deitz & Repp, 1983). If the learner emits more than the specified number of responses during the session, the behavior is not reinforced. For example, if the DRL criterion limit is four disruptive acts per hour, the learner's behavior is reinforced at the end of the hour if four or fewer disruptive acts have been emitted.

In an influential paper Deitz and Repp (1973) reported three studies that demonstrated the efficacy and manageability of a full-session DRL schedule of reinforcement in decreasing classroom misbehavior. The first study decreased the talk-outs of an 11-year-old boy with mental retardation. His teacher had considered him the most disruptive student in the class. During 10 days of baseline, the student averaged 5.7 talk-outs during a 50-minute session (an average rate of 0.11 per minute). During the 14 days that the full-session DRL was in effect following the baseline condition, the student was allowed 5 minutes for play at the end of the day when he emitted three or fewer talk-outs during a 50-minute session. Talk-outs during the DRL condition decreased to an average 0.93 (an average rate of 0.02 per minute). A return to baseline slightly increased the talk-outs to an average of 1.5 per session (an average rate of 0.03 per minute), as shown in Figure 18.4.

The second study was a replication of the first, except that the full-session DRL schedule was applied as a group contingency. In this situation the DRL criterion limit for the total class of 10 mentally retarded students was 5 or fewer talk-outs during a 50-minute session. All students received two pieces of candy if the criterion was met. Talk-outs decreased from a

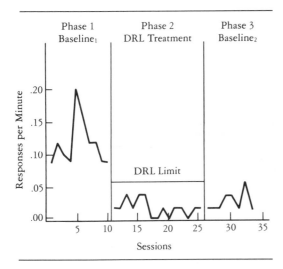

FIGURE 18.4 The rate of talk-outs during baseline and treatment phases for one TMR male. (From "Decreasing Classroom Misbehavior Through the Use of DRL Schedules of Reinforcement" by S. M. Deitz and A. C. Repp, 1973, *Journal of Applied Behavior Analysis, 6*, p. 458. Copyright 1973 by the Society for the Experimental Analysis of Behavior, Inc. Reprinted by permission.)

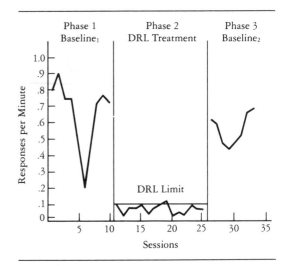

FIGURE 18.5 The rate of talk-outs for a class of TMR children during baseline and treatment phases. (From "Decreasing Classroom Misbehavior Through the Use of DRL Schedules of Reinforcement" by S. M. Deitz and A. C. Repp., 1973, *Journal of Applied Behavior Analysis, 6*, p. 460. Copyright 1973 by the Society for the Experimental Analysis of Behavior, Inc. Reprinted by permission.)

baseline average of 32.7 per 50-minute session (an average rate of 0.65 per minute) to an average of 3.13 per session (an average of 0.07 per minute) while the full-session DRL was in effect. A return to baseline increased the talk-outs to an average of 27.61 per session (an averge rate of 0.54 per minute). Figure 18.5 presents data from this second study.

The third study involved a group DRL contingency applied to 15 high school senior girls enrolled in an office procedures course. Each class session was 50 minutes in length. This third study differed in one dimension from the previous two studies: Deitz and Repp gradually reduced the full-session DRL limit in the third study. During the first 4 days of the full-session DRL condition, the criterion limit was set at five or fewer off-task verbal behaviors during each class session. The DRL criterion limits were then reduced to three or fewer, one or fewer, and zero reponses. The students earned a free

Friday class when they kept off-task verbal behaviors at or below the DRL limit Monday through Thursday. As shown in Figure 18.6, the changing full-session DRL criterion limits generated an orderly effect; the fourth DRL limit eliminated the off-task verbal behaviors.

Interval DRL

An **interval DRL** schedule of reinforcement divides the instructional session into equal intervals of time. Reinforcement is delivered after each interval if responding during the interval was equal to or below a criterion limit. When the learner emits more than the specified number of responses during the interval, the opportunity for reinforcement is postponed, and a new interval of time is begun (Deitz, 1977). For example, if a DRL criterion limit of four disruptive acts per hour is set, the learner's behavior is reinforced after each 15

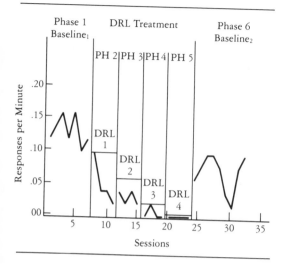

FIGURE 18.6 The rate of subject changes for a class of high school senior girls during baseline and treatment phases with differing DRL limits. (From "Decreasing Classroom Misbehavior Through the Use of DRL Schedules of Reinforcement" by S. M. Deitz and A. C. Repp., 1973, *Journal of Applied Behavior Analysis, 6*, p. 461. Copyright 1973 by the Society for the Experimental Analysis of Behavior, Inc. Reprinted by permission.)

minutes during which no more than one disruptive act is emitted. Whenever a second disruptive act is emitted during the interval, a new 15-minute interval of time is begun. Beginning a new interval postpones the opportunity for reinforcement.

Deitz (1977) initially defined the interval DRL schedule of reinforceemnt with a criterion limit of one response per interval. However, Deitz and Repp (1983) indicate that they have programmed interval DRL with criterion limits above one per interval. "A response which occurs an average of 14 times per hour could be limited to three occurrences per 15-minute interval. The response limit of three could then be lowered to two responses per interval, and then to one response per interval" (Deitz & Repp, 1983, p. 37).

Deitz et al. (1978) illustrated the use of the interval DRL schedule of reinforcement in de-

creasing the disruptive behaviors of a student with learning disabilities. The 7-year-old student emitted a variety of disruptive behaviors in the classroom (e.g., running in the room; shoving, pushing, or hitting; throwing objects). He averaged 19.3 inappropriate behaviors per 30-minute session during 13 sessions of baseline. Then an interval DRL (DRL A in Figure 18.7) was implemented, and the student was given a sheet of paper ruled into 15 blocks, each representing a 2-minute interval. A star was placed in a block each time the student completed 2 minutes at or below the DRL limit. For each star the student was permitted to spend 1 minute on the playground with the experimenter. Each interval was terminated whenever the student emitted more than one disruptive act, and a new 2-minute interval was begun. When the interval DRL was introduced, disruptive behaviors decreased to an average of 5 responses per session; the student met the DRL criterion limit during 98% of the intervals during this condition. Deitz et al. then increased the length of the DRL interval from 2 to 3 minutes and increased the value of each star to 1.5 minutes on the playground (DRL B in Figure 18.7). Disruptive acts decreased to an average of 1.8 behaviors per session under this condition. A return to baseline increased the response to an average of 8.8 disruptive acts per session. When the interval DRL 3-minutes was again reinstated, disruptive acts decreased to an average of 1.2 per 30-minute session. These data are presented in Figure 18.7

Spaced-Responding DRL

A **spaced-responding DRL** schedule is programmed to deliver reinforcement after a behavior that is separated from a prior behavior by a minimum amount of time (Deitz & Repp, 1983). The technical term for the separation of time between two responses is **interresponse time (IRT)**. IRTs and rates of responding are functionally related. Long IRTs generate low rates of responding; short IRTs produce high

FIGURE 18.7 The frequency of inappropriate responses per session during the five phases of the experiment. (From "Reducing Inappropriate Behavior in Special Classrooms by Reinforcing Average Interresponse Times: Interval DRL" by S. M. Deitz, D. J. Slack, E. B. Schwarzmueller, A. P. Wilander, T. J. Weatherly, and G. Hilliard, 1978, *Behavior Therapy*, 9, p. 40. Copyright 1978 by the Association for the Advancement of Behavior Therapy. Reprinted by permission of the publisher and the author.)

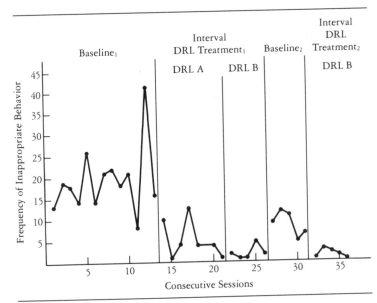

rates of responding. If only long IRTs are differentially reinforced low rates of responding will be developed. For example, a student who asks questions so frequently that the questions interfere with the learning and teaching in the classroom could be placed on a spaced-responding DRL schedule to decrease but not eliminate question asking. A question might be reinforced only if a prior question had not been asked for at least 5 minutes.

Favell, McGimsey, and Jones (1980) used a spaced-responding DRL schedule of reinforcement and response prompts to decrease the rapid eating of four profoundly retarded persons. Favell et al. reinforced short independent pauses (IRTs) between bites of food and then reinforced longer and longer pauses. They also manually prompted a separation between bites and then faded the response prompts.

> Specifically, each time the subject paused independently for at least one or two seconds following a bite, the trainer praised the subject for pausing and then gave him or her a bite of a favorite food. . . . If a subject began to take a bite without pausing for two seconds, the trainer said "Wait," placed his spoon hand on the table, and reinforced the subject with praise and a bite of food.

> For the first five prompts the subject was reinforced even if he or she resisted. . . . After these five prompts, reinforcement was delivered only if the subject complied with the prompt—that is, did not resist. The manual assistance was then quickly faded to the point that only the verbal cue "Wait" was used. Throughout the fading process the subject was reinforced and allowed to take another bite only when he or she had paused for two seconds without being manually restrained. During the fading process the trainer reinforced successively longer independent pauses, until the subject was pausing five seconds before receiving reinforcement. (Favell et al., 1980, pp. 485–486)[1]

Favell et al. no longer reinforced prompted pauses when a minimum of 5-second pauses was occurring independently between about 75% of all bites. Then food reinforcement and praise were gradually thinned. Figure 18.8 shows that the frequency of eating was decreased from an average of 10 to 12 bites per 30

_____

[1]From J. E. Favell, J. F. McGimsey, and M. L. Jones, "Rapid Eating in the Retarded: Reduction by Nonaversive Procedures," *Behavior Modification*, Vol. 4, No. 4 (October, 1980). Copyright © 1980 by Sage Publications. Reprinted by permission of Sage Publications, Inc.

FIGURE 18.8 Rate of eating for subjects 1,2,3, and 4 across baseline and treatment conditions. Solid data points represent data from two daily meals; open data points represent data from a single meal. (From J. E. Favell, J. F. McGimsey, and M. L. Jones, "Rapid Eating in the Retarded: Reduction by Nonaversive Procedures," *Behavior Modification,* Vol. 4, No. 4 (October, 1980). Copyright © 1980 by Sage Publications. Reprinted by permission of Sage Publications, Inc.)

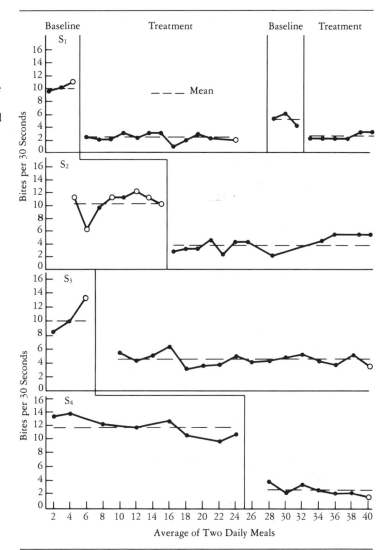

seconds during baseline to the spaced-responding DRL level of 3 to 4 bites per 30 seconds.

Guidelines for the Effective Use of DRL

The applied literature contains an adequate data base for the full-session DRL schedule of reinforcement (e.g., Barrish, Saunders, & Wolf, 1969; Dampf, 1977; Deitz & Repp, 1973; Fishbein & Wasik, 1981; Hall, Willard, Goldsmith, Emerson, Owen, Davis, & Porcia, 1971; Lutzker & White-Blackburn, 1979; Saigh & Umar, 1983). However, few applied researchers have addressed interval DRL and spaced-responding DRL (Deitz & Repp, 1983). Drawing upon the data base for full-session DRL and their investigations of interval and spaced-responding DRL, Deitz and Repp (1983) give several suggestions for increasing the likelihood of effective use of DRL.

First of all, the initial DRL criterion limit should be set at the average, or mean, number of responses emitted during the baseline conditions, or slightly lower than that average, when using the full-session DRL. For example, baseline data of 8, 13, 10, 7, and 12 responses produce an average of 10 responses. Therefore, an initial DRL limit of 8 to 10 responses per session would be appropriate. With interval DRL (Deitz, 1977) and spaced-responding DRL the interval size or interresponse time should be set at the average baseline IRT, or slightly lower than that average. For example, if the baseline average number of responses per 60-minute session is 4, an initial interval DRL criterion limit of 1 response per 15 minutes would be acceptable. For spaced-responding DRL a response would need to be separated from the previous response by a minimum of 15 minutes to earn reinforcement.

The second guideline concerns the gradual decrease of the DRL criterion limit. With a full-session DRL new DRL limits should reflect the average or slightly less than average number of responses emitted during recent sessions under the previous DRL limit. With an interval DRL the number of responses per interval can be gradually lowered if the current limit is more than one response per interval. If the current limit is only one response per interval, the length of the interval can be gradually increased. With a spaced-responding DRL new DRL limits should match the average or slightly less than average IRT emitted during recent sessions under the previous DRL limit. With all DRL variations the criterion limit must be gradually and systematically changed over time.

The third guideline is to establish a decision rule for changing the DRL criterion limit. One possible rule is that the DRL limit is changed whenever the learner does not exceed the limit in three consecutive sessions. Another possibility is that the DRL limit is changed whenever the learner receives reinforcement for at least 90% of the opportunities during three consecutive sessions.

CONSIDERATIONS

A major goal of behavior change programs in applied settings should be the development of an appropriate behavioral repertoire for learners. DRI/DRA meets this goal: strengthening incompatible or alternative behaviors to replace an inappropriate behavior is basic to the DRI/DRA procedure. With proper selection of behaviors, DRI/DRA can promote educational, social, and personal skill development. DRO may also come very close to this major goal. DRO does not specify which behaviors are to be reinforced, but DRO does provide the opportunity for reinforcement of an infinite number of behaviors. Consequently, it is possible for the DRO procedure to develop and strengthen collateral behaviors that are important for learners. The major difference is that with DRI/DRA the analyst is controlling the development of alternative behaviors and can concurrently measure both the inappropriate behavior and the desired replacement behavior. With DRO the learner's behavior, other than the behavior specified for omission, determines which alternate behaviors will be strengthened.

An appropriate behavioral repertoire can also be developed by changing the rate of responding rather than eliminating behaviors. For example, most behaviors are viewed as inappropriate because they occur too often or not often enough. When the rate of response can be adjusted to appropriate levels, often those same behaviors can enhance the development of academic and social skills. Individuals may emit a behavior less frequently if they are told to slow down or are given rules that define an appropriate rate of response. However, when instructions do not decrease the rate of occurrence, consequences are probably needed. DRL is the only reductive procedure that employs consequences yet needs not totally eliminate the occurrence of the behavior. When extinction, DRI/DRA, DRO, or punishment procedures are applied it is quite possible that the inappropriate behavior will no longer occur. For this reason DRL becomes an important reductive strategy: a DRL contingency tells the learner that the behavior is acceptable, but there should be less of it.

DRI/DRA and DRL procedures usually produce a gradual decrease in behavior (Deitz & Repp, 1983). Consequently, they may not be the best procedures to use when it is important to produce a rapid reduction in inappropriate behavior. If the behavior is dangerous to the learner or to others, if it is destructive, or if it interferes with health and safety, DRI/DRA or DRL should probably not be selected as the only reductive technique to be used. It is possible to produce a more rapid change in behavior when DRI/DRA is combined with other reductive procedures (e.g., punishment). DRI/DRA may be slow to gain behavioral control because the procedure does not provide consequences for inappropriate behavior, as does DRO. DRO may be more appropriate for disruptive and aggressive behaviors because behavior can be decreased rapidly with a DRO procedure (Deitz et al., 1976). And as with DRI/DRA, even more rapid change in behavior can be produced when DRO is combined with other reductive procedures.

DRI/DRA, DRO, and DRL can be used in most applied settings. DRI/DRA is the easiest of the three differential reinforcement procedures to implement. And even though DRI/DRA produces a more gradual decrease in behavior than does DRO or DRL, it is often the most appropriate reductive procedure for many varieties of classroom misbehaviors. DRO is the procedure of choice when the objective is to eliminate behavior, not just to decrease it. However, the use of DRO is time-consuming, particularly with small intervals, because it requires constant observation and timing and frequent reinforcement.

DRL is appropriate when some occurrences of the behavior can be tolerated. Interval and spaced-responding DRL are also time-consuming procedures to apply because, like DRO, they require constant observation and timing and frequent reinforcement. Most practitioners, without the help of an outside observer, would have difficulty using the interval and spaced-responding DRL procedure while managing and instructing a full group of learners. Interval and spaced-responding DRL procedures are reasonable for one-on-one settings if the situation does not call for major instructional activity. The research cited earlier in reducing high rates of eating illustrates how a teacher could employ spaced-responding DRL. Full-session DRL is usually not time-consuming to apply and is a practical application for almost all education and treatment settings.

Full-session, interval, and spaced-responding DRL schedules provide different levels of reinforcement for learners. Spaced-responding is the only DRL schedule to directly reinforce specific responses; a response must be emitted after a minimum IRT before reinforcement. With full-session and interval DRL a response does not need to occur for reinforcement. Deitz (1977) recommends spaced-responding DRL if the goal is to decrease the occurrence of a behavior but to maintain it at lower rates. If it is not important to maintain a response, full-session or interval DRL can be selected. Spaced-responding and interval DRL may be more appropriate than full-session DRL for learners with severe learning problems because those two procedures program reinforcement at a higher rate, which permits the learner to come into more frequent contact with the reinforcement contingency.

Full-session, interval, and spaced-responding DRL procedures also provide different levels of feedback for learners. The most accurate feedback comes with spaced-responding DRL because reinforcement follows each response that meets the IRT limit. If the response does not meet the IRT criterion limit, a timer is immediately reset, thereby providing learners with immediate feedback on each response. Interval DRL also provides a high level of feedback, although it is less than that of spaced-responding DRL. "There is a relatively high degree of feedback within short intervals of time. While the first response in an interval receives no feedback [extinction], on the second, the timer is reset, thus informing the subject of its inappropriate nature. At the end of the interval where fewer than two responses occurred, reinforcement is delivered. These three types of feedback all tend to decrease responding and thus cumulatively add to the effectiveness of the Interval DRL procedure" (Deitz et al., 1978, p. 44).

The full-session DRL can be arranged with or without feedback. The usual arrangement is not to provide feedback concerning moment-to-moment accumulation of responses. Deitz (1977) states that with full-session moment-to-moment feedback learners would respond only to the DRL criterion limit: if the limit is exceeded and the opportunity for reinforcement is lost, the learners may then emit high rates of misbehavior. When the schedule is arranged without moment-to-moment feedback, learners usually stay well below the DRL limit. The full-session DRL, without moment-to-moment feedback, may not be as effective for learners with severe learning problems as the spaced-responding and interval DRL; its effectiveness relies heavily on an initial verbal description of the contingencies of reinforcement (Deitz, 1977).

SUMMARY

Differential Reinforcement of Incompatible Behavior and Alternative Behavior

1 DRI is a schedule of reinforcement in which the occurrence of a behavior topographically incompatible with behavior selected for reduction is followed by reinforcement.

2 DRA provides reinforcement for the occurrence of a target behavior that is an alternative to the behavior selected for reduction.

3 Incompatible or alternative behaviors should be selected that are in the learner's repertoire of responses, that the learner emits with regularity, that will help the learner acquire more skills, and that the learner's natural environment will support.

4 Consequences should be selected from stimuli demonstrated to function as reinforcers and able to be presented contingently, consistently, and immediately following behavior.

5 A schedule of reinforcement should be established that initially delivers consequences on a CRF schedule and then provides for a gradually thinning intermittent schedule of reinforcement.

6 DRI/DRA should be combined with other reductive procedures.

Differential Reinforcement of Other Behavior

7 DRO is a schedule of reinforcement in which reinforcement occurs whenever a specific behavior is not emitted during an interval of time.

8 When the DRO interval of time is programmed to vary from trial to trial, it is called a variable DRO schedule of reinforcement.

9 The initial DRO time interval should be consistent with data recorded during the baseline condition and should allow the learner's behavior to produce frequent reinforcement.

10 Procedures should be established for increasing the length of the DRO interval.

11 After the DRO interval has ended, reinforcement should be delivered only when the selected behavior did not occur during the interval and no other inappropriate behavior occurred either.

12 DRO can be combined with other reductive procedures.

Differential Reinforcement of Low Rates of Responding

13 A DRL schedule produces low, consistent rates of responding.

14 A full-session DRL schedule is programmed to deliver reinforcement when responding during an instructional session is equal to or below a criterion limit.

15 With an interval DRL reinforcement is delivered after each interval in which responding is equal to or below a criterion limit.

16 A spaced-responding DRL is programmed to deliver reinforcement after a behavior that is separated from a prior behavior by a minimum amount of time.

17 Interresponse time (IRT) is the technical term for the separation of time between two responses.

18 Baseline data should be used to set the initial DRL criterion limit.

19 The DRL criterion limit should be gradually decreased.

20 A decision rule should be established for changing the DRL criterion limit.

Considerations

21 With proper selection of behaviors DRI/DRA can promote educational, social, and personal skill development.

22 DRO does not specify which behaviors will be reinforced, as does DRI/DRA, but DRO does provide the opportunity for reinforcement of an infinite number of behaviors.

23 DRL is the only reductive procedure that employs consequences yet needs not totally eliminate the occurrence of behavior.

24 DRI/DRA or DRL may not be the best procedure to use when it is important to generate a rapid reduction in behavior.

25 DRO may be more appropriate for disruptive and aggressive behaviors than DRI/DRA or DRL because behavior can be decreased rapidly with DRO.

26 DRO is the procedure of choice when the objective is to eliminate behavior, just not decrease behavior.

27 DRL is appropriate when some occurrences of the behavior can be tolerated.

28 Full-session, interval, and spaced-responding DRL procedures provide different levels of reinforcement and feedback.

PART EIGHT

Decreasing Behavior II: Punishment Procedures

Part VIII contains four chapters. Chapter 19 describes the principle of punishment; chapter 20 describes a corresponding Type I punishment procedure—overcorrection. Type I punishment refers to the application of an aversive stimulus or event subsequent to a behavior. Chapters 21 and 22 describe time out from positive reinforcement and response cost, respectively. These procedures are referred to as Type II punishment, which involves the removal of positive reinforcement.

The sequence of chapters in this part corresponds with our belief that the behavior reduction principle should be described first, followed by the procedures of application. The authors wish to make clear that this order does not correspond with a recommended order of usage. Quite the opposite is true. We subscribe to the least restrictive model of implementation, which means that intervention should begin with the least restrictive contingency and proceed to a more restrictive contingency only as necessary (Gaylord-Ross, 1980; Foxx, 1982; Evans and Meyer, 1985).

19

Punishment by Contingent Presentation of a Stimulus

KEY TERMS

Punishment

Aversive stimulus

Unconditioned aversive stimulus

Conditioned aversive stimulus

Least restrictive alternative

Cruel and unusual punishment

Corporal punishment

Informed consent

Fair Pair Rule

Respondent aggression

Operant aggression

Behavior analysts working in applied settings are sometimes faced with maladaptive or life-threatening behaviors that are resistant to positive reductive approaches. In such cases a quick and effective means of reducing the frequency, duration, or magnitude of the target behavior is necessary. This chapter defines the principle of punishment, cites its rationale, discusses the ethical and legal considerations associated with punishment, and presents a decision-making model for implementing punishment. The chapter also presents methodological guidelines and discusses the undesirable aspects of punishment.

This chapter was written by Timothy E. Heron.

DEFINITION OF PUNISHMENT

For the general public, punishment usually refers to the application of physical pain or psychological hurt following the performance of a behavior. Most lay individuals would probably say that a child spanked for running into the street had been punished. From this point of view, the presentation of a stimulus or event (spanking) after the occurrence of a behavior (running into the street) constitutes punishment. However, **punishment** by the contingent presentation of a stimulus immediately after a behavior is defined technically in terms of its effect on future behavior (Azrin & Holz, 1966). Specifically, a decrease in the future probability of the occurrence of the behavior must be observed before a procedure can be called punishment. If the likelihood of the child's running into the street is not reduced after the spanking, punishment has not occurred. By the same principle, if a teacher says, "Very good" to a student after she completes each of her morning assignments but assignment completion decreases in the future, then punishment has occurred even though the teacher believed he was using a reinforcing statement.

Thus, whether a consequence is "aversive" or not has nothing to do with whether punishment has occurred. Across each of the sensory modalities an aversive stimulus can be described as unpleasant, annoying, or painful. Yet these descriptions are not sufficient; what might be unpleasant, annoying, or painful to one individual might not be to another. To avoid these subjective interpretations, an **aversive stimulus** is technically defined by its effect on behavior: a stimulus is considered aversive when a response is strengthened by its contingent removal or when a response is depressed by its contingent presentation. According to Bailey (1983), aversive stimuli can include sounds, smells, tastes, visual images, or physical sensations (i.e., localized pain or overall discomfort).

An aversive stimulus can be classified as unconditioned (primary) or conditioned (secondary). The inherent properties of an **unconditioned aversive stimulus** generate a reductive effect without the individual's having prior experience with the stimulus. For example, if a blast of a loud tone is applied subsequent to a behavior, a reductive effect can be noted (cf. Flanagan, Goldiamond, & Azrin, 1958).

A **conditioned aversive stimulus** is not inherently noxious or objectionable. This stimulus is initially neutral but becomes aversive by repeated pairing with an unconditioned aversive stimulus or a previously acquired conditioned aversive stimulus. For example, a verbal comment such as "No!" is not inherently aversive. That is, hearing the word does not produce a physiological reaction or necessarily result in decreased behavior. The expression becomes aversive by being repeatedly paired with other aversive stimuli in a respondent conditioning procedure.

To reiterate, punishment is not defined by the action of the punisher but by the effect on the future probability of that class of behavior. In a definition of punishment three conditions are necessary: (1) a behavior must be emitted, (2) the behavior must be followed by a stimulus, and (3) the future probability of the behavior must be reduced because of that stimulus alone.

RATIONALE FOR USING PUNISHMENT

There are two main reasons for using punishment in applied settings. One reason is related to procedural/methodological effectiveness; the other is based on ethical grounds.

Procedural Effectiveness

Punishment can be an effective technique in a behavior reduction program, particularly when the behaviors to be reduced have been resistant to other reductive or behavioral shaping approaches. Several researchers have acknowledged that punishment may produce rapid and lasting suppression of the behavior, reduce the misbehavior of individuals other than the one being punished, and produce positive side effects (Foxx, 1982; Axelrod, 1983; Van Houten, 1983). Even though there are safeguards and undesirable aspects associated with punishment, the practitioner must realize that punishment, by definition, does reduce the future probability of behavior.

Ethical Grounds

From an ethical standpoint it can be argued that since punishment can be used in a therapeutic way to suppress the future occurrence of maladaptive behavior, not using punishment, especially in situations where other procedures have been tried unsuccessfully, withholds a potentially effective treatment and maintains the client in a dangerous or uncomfortable state. Harris and Ersner-Hershfield (1978) indicate that clients have a right to treatment; Baer (1971) is even more specific.

> [Punishment] is a legitimate therapeutic technique that is justifiable and commendable when it relieves persons of the even greater punishments that result from their own habitual behavior. (p. 111)

Several studies illustrate Baer's point. For example, Risley (1968) applied contingent electric shock to reduce the dangerous climbing behavior of a 6-year-old girl who had suffered multiple contusions and had lost two teeth in falls, as well as destroying the furniture in her home. Shock was administered only after time out from positive reinforcement, extinction, and the reinforcement of incompatible behaviors did not reduce the climbing. Shock treatment in a laboratory setting reduced the child's climbing in the laboratory but not in the home. When contingent shock, paired with "No," was applied in the home setting, climbing decreased in that setting as well (see Figure 19.1). Subsequently, the mother spanked the girl in response to climbing. For the 25 days during which this intervention occurred, climbing averaged 2.0 instances per day. However, the mother disliked the spanking procedure, and it was terminated. In its place a time out plus shock avoidance procedure was instituted, whereby the child was told to sit in a chair (10-minute time out) if she climbed. Failure to go, sit, or stay in the chair resulted in shock. Although not as effective as the initial shock treatment, this combination procedure was deemed to more closely approximate normal child-rearing practices.

Shock is not the only type of unconditioned aversive punisher that has been used to reduce

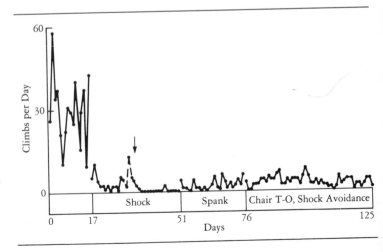

FIGURE 19.1 Graph of the frequency of S's climbing at home. Each dot represents one day. The dotted lines during the shock condition represent days when the shock device was malfunctioning. The device was repaired at the arrow. (From "The Effects and Side Effects of Punishing the Autistic Behaviors of a Deviant Child" by T. R. Risley, 1969, *Journal of Applied Behavior Analysis, 1*(1), p. 29. Copyright 1968 by the Society for the Experimental Analysis of Behavior, Inc. Reprinted by permission.)

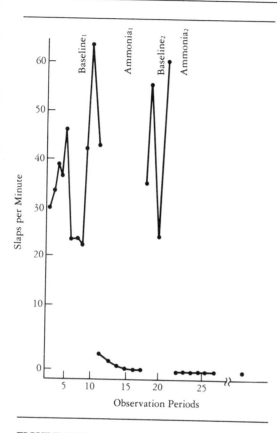

FIGURE 19.2 A record of an autistic woman's face slapping during experimental sessions under baseline and punishment conditions. (From "Punishment of Self-Injurious Behavior Using Aromatic Ammonia as the Aversive Stimulus" by B. A. Tanner and M. Zeiler, 1975, *Journal of Applied Behavior Analysis, 8*(1), p. 56. Copyright 1975 by the Society for the Experimental Analysis of Behavior, Inc. Reprinted by permission.)

self-injurious behavior (SIB). Tanner and Zeiler (1975) demonstrated that aromatic ammonia was sufficient to reduce the slapping behavior of a 20-year-old autistic individual. An ammonia capsule was crushed and placed under the subject's nose after an occurrence of slapping. Once opened, the capsule released a noxious smell that was aversive at close range but only mildly annoying at a distance of 2 feet. The results of this reversal design study indicate that when aromatic ammonia was not

used, slapping averaged 39 occurrences per minute. When the ammonia condition was in effect, slapping averaged .5 occurrences per minute. The authors state that the procedure was effective, could be administered by many staff members, and could be used in situations in which electric shock was restricted (see Figure 19.2).

Dorsey, Iwata, Ong, and McSween (1980) provide another example in which the societal, ethical, or legal sanctions against electric shock are accommodated while the needs of individuals engaged in SIB are served. Their study demonstrated that contingent spraying of a fine mist of water in the face of seven profoundly retarded individuals reduced their self-injurious behaviors. When the mist was not used, the maladaptive behaviors returned to their preintervention level (see Figure 19.3). A second phase of the study demonstrated that pairing "No" with the presentation of the water mist and using a 1-minute DRO schedule of reinforcement reduced the self-injurious behavior of two nonambulatory patients. The data suggest that the verbal "No" acquired the suppressive properties of the mist (See Figure 19.4).

In both studies mentioned here the harmful and/or self-injurious behavior might have continued if the punishment procedure had not been implemented. So from an ethical standpoint it was a legitimate use of punishment.

ETHICAL AND LEGAL CONSIDERATIONS

Griffith (1983) states that practitioners should be aware of the ethical and legal issues related to punishment. First, the practitioner should be able to identify the rationale for the treatment in use; second, the practitioner should be able to discriminate between psychomedical techniques for suppressing behavior (e.g., electroconvulsive shock) and behavioral techniques (e.g., contingent electric shock). Longo, Rotatori, Kapperman, and Heinze (1981) indicate that the practitioner should be well-versed

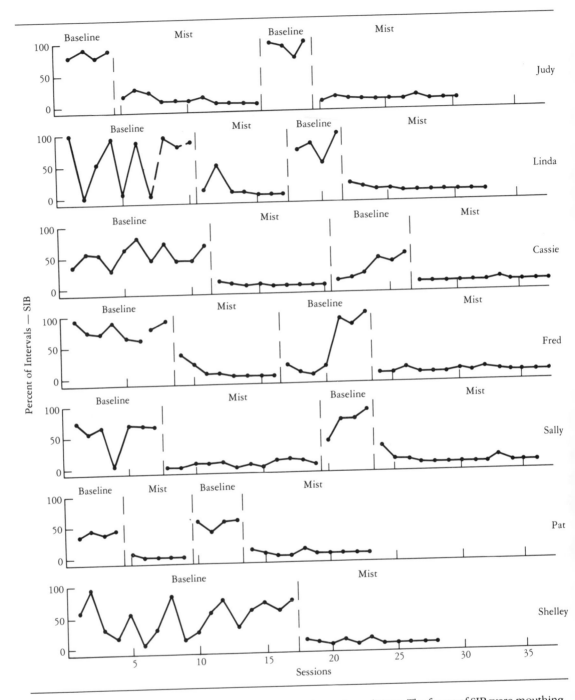

FIGURE 19.3 Percentage of intervals of SIB across experimental conditions. The forms of SIB were mouthing (Judy, Linda, Cassie, and Fred), hand biting (Sally), skin tearing (Pat), and head banging (Shelley). (From "Treatment of Self-Injurious Behavior Using a Water Mist: Initial Response Suppression and Generalization" by M. F. Dorsey, B. A. Iwata, P. Ong, and T. E. McSween, 1980, *Journal of Applied Behavior Analysis, 13*(2), p. 348. Copyright 1980 by the Society for the Experimental Analysis of Behavior, Inc. Reprinted by permission.)

FIGURE 19.4 Percentage of intervals of hand biting for Cindy and Sally across experimental conditions. Open data points represent sessions within a DRO condition in which DRO was not used. The numbers 1 through 5 along the abscissas refer to different experimenters conducting the sessions. (From "Treatment of Self-Injurious Behavior Using a Water Mist: Initial Response Suppression and Generalization" by M. F. Dorsey, B. A. Iwata, P. Ong, and T. E. McSween, 1980, *Journal of Applied Behavior Analysis, 13*(2), p. 350. Copyright 1980 by the Society for the Experimental Analysis of Behavior, Inc. Reprinted by permission.)

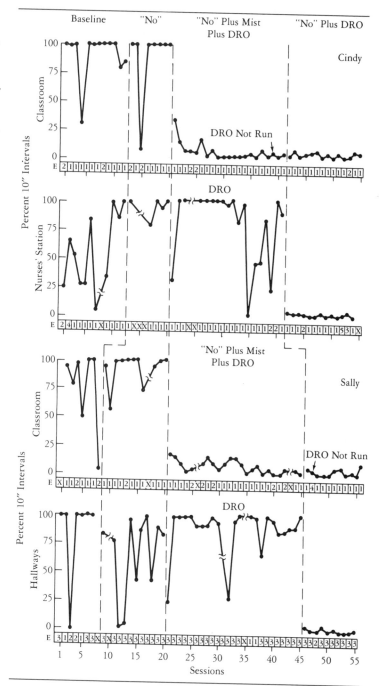

in the doctrine of the least restrictive alternative, issues related to cruel and unusual punishment, and informed consent prior to implementation of a punishment procedure.

Doctrine of the Least Restrictive Alternative

The doctrine of the **least restrictive alternative** (LRA) means that other less intrusive procedures must be considered and/or tried and found to be inappropriate or ineffective before punishment is presented. This doctrine is based on the premise that the intervention approach selected should not unnecessarily limit an individual's access to basic human freedoms (e.g., movement, food, privacy, leisure).[1] This doctrine has been codified by the Association for Persons with Severe Handicaps in their *Resolution on Intrusive Interventions* (1981). According to Evans and Meyer (1985), the resolution states that students "have a right to effective interventions that do not inflict pain, tissue damage, humiliation, discomfort, and stigma as expected side effects accompanying behavior change" (p. 48).

Carr and Lovaas (1983) state that the use of punishment by contingent presentation of a stimulus should not be the method of first choice, even when attempting to reduce self-injurious behavior. They suggest that four less intrusive procedures be tried before a decision is made to use punishment: (1) differential reinforcement of other behavior (DRO), the intent of which is to provide reinforcement for gradually longer periods of time without the maladaptive behavior; (2) DRO combined with extinction so that any social reinforcers maintaining the maladaptive behavior are withheld, thereby reducing the future probability of the behavior; (3) time out from positive reinforcement so that all sources of environmental rein-

forcement are reduced; and (4) DRO combined with positive practice overcorrection, the intent of which is to have the individual practice appropriate, alternative responses. Carr and Lovaas (1983) readily concede that cases arise, particularly in the area of self-injurious behavior, in which the application of one or more of these procedures would require too much time or staff, or the behavior is on an intermittent schedule that renders the techniques inappropriate. However, the point remains: other procedures must be considered before punishment is delivered.

One vehicle for ensuring that other methods have been considered is a written policy statement that outlines all of the conditions for using punishment (Griffith, 1983; Wood & Braaten, 1983). Figure 19.5 outlines a model policy statement. Readers should also consult their local, state, or professional association policy statements regarding the use of punishment. For example, the Association for the Advancement of Behavior Therapy (AABT) provides guidelines that address selection of treatment issues (Favell, et al., 1982). A decision-making model presented later in the chapter details the sequence in which punishment might be introduced.

Cruel and Unusual Punishment

According to Longo et al. (1981) **cruel and unusual punishment** (1) "serves no more effective purpose than a lesser punishment; and (2) is inflicted arbitrarily" (p. 81). Griffith (1983) points out that the Eighth Amendment to the U.S. Constitution provides protection from cruel and unusual punishment, and the Fourteenth Amendment protects individuals from harm. Relative to using punishment procedures in applied settings, several courts have ruled on the protection from harm issues (see Wheeler v. Glass, 1973; *New York Association for Retarded Children v. Carey*, 1975).

Also, the U.S. Supreme Court ruling in *Ingraham v. Wright* (1977) upheld the notion that **corporal punishment**, defined as the

---

[1]The term *least restrictive alternative* usually refers to the use of an intervention. A related term, *least restrictive environment*, refers to the placement or setting in which the intervention is carried out.

A. Policy Statement

1. Description of the place of aversive procedures in a therapeutic education program.
2. Definitions of permitted and prohibited aversive procedures.
3. Citation of relevant local, state and federal laws, regulations and court decisions. (May be omitted or appended.)

B. Procedural Guidelines

1. Promotion of awareness of aversive procedure use and abuse among staff and the public.
2. Staff training requirements.
3. Description of appropriate use of aversive procedures, including specification of roles and settings, necessary preparation, and follow-up.
4. Maintenance and retention of records of use.
5. Procedures followed in handling complaints and appeals.
6. Specific cautions.
7. List of useful resources. (May be omitted or appended.)
8. Procedure for periodic review.

FIGURE 19.5 Outline of a model policy/guideline statement. (From "Developing Guidelines for the Use of Punishing Interventions in the Schools" by F. H. Wood and S. Braaten, 1983, *Exceptional Education Quarterly, 3*(4), p. 72. Copyright 1983 by Pro-Ed. Reprinted by permission.)

contingent paddling or swatting of a student on the buttocks in the presence of witnesses, does not violate constitutional protection against cruel and unusual punishment (Rose, 1983). Despite the lack of empirical evidence of the efficacy of corporal punishment as a behavior reducing procedure, it continues to be a sanctioned management procedure in many applied settings (Rose, 1983).

To lessen the risk of punishment being inflicted arbitrarily, at least three controls should be applied: (1) a review mechanism must be rigorously adhered to before, during, and after the punishment is administered (Griffith & Henning, 1981; Favell et al., 1982; (2) staff should be properly trained and supervised (Wood & Braaten, 1983); and (3) informed consent must be obtained from the individual and parents or guardians (Carr & Lovaas, 1983; Griffith, 1983).

Informed Consent According to Carr and Lovaas (1983), **informed consent** has several levels. First, the individual and parent or guardian should have the opportunity to review material related to the general area of delivering an aversive stimulus to suppress behavior. Second, all persons involved in the treatment should have a chance to discuss the nature of the aversives to be used in the program and the effects and side effects of the proposed punishment procedure. Third, all persons should have the opportunity to experience the aversive treatment themselves. Finally, the public at large should be made aware of the proposed treatment (Carr & Lovaas, 1983).

The consent handbook of the American Association on Mental Deficiency (1977) addresses not only the content of the dialogue but also the manner in which the dialogue should take place. The handbook states that individuals should have procedures explained to them without jargon and in their primary language. Furthermore, the purpose, effect, side effects, and benefits should be explained succinctly.

The issue of informed consent assumes still another dimension when the subject to be punished is incapable of making a decision because she is a minor or is developmentally disabled or mentally incompetent. Before an individual's treatment is decided by a review committee, Griffith (1983) recommends that at least four points be satisfied.

1 The client must be judged to be dangerous to self or others. This is generally a clinical decision, but such a determination is quite typically precipitated by an aggressive or malicious act.
2 There must be a reasonable probability that the proposed treatment will benefit the client; such treatments are usually considered to be professionally acceptable and are reported in major literature sources.
3 Clients should be incapable of making rational decisions concerning treatment.
4 A series of procedural safeguards must be in place to protect the rights of both the client and clinicians who design and implement treatment programs. (p. 320)

Establishing a review committee and obtaining informed consent does not guarantee that the court will ultimately approve any type of punishment. In *Mackey v. Procunier* (1973), for example, an individual had consented to shock treatment but not to an administration of a drug, succinylcholine. The court ruled that the drug procedure was aversive, involved force experimentation, and invaded the patient's mental privacy.

To aid review committees and practitioners with the issue of informed consent, Cook, Altman, and Haavik (1978) provide a model consent form that includes all of the items needed to satisfy recent court rulings and professional standards. Also, their form might help practitioners decide on alternative treatments and/or monitor the proposed punishment program (see Figure 19.6).

A DECISION-MAKING MODEL FOR USING PUNISHMENT

Gaylord-Ross (1980) outlines a decision-making model for implementing punishment that is consistent with the doctrine of least restrictive alternative and that goes beyond Carr

and Lovaas's (1983) suggestion to use only DRO/DRI strategies prior to punishment. The Gaylord-Ross model addresses five areas for reducing aberrant behavior: assessment, reinforcement, ecology, curriculum, and punishment (see Figure 19.7).

Assessment

The purpose of this component of the model is to adequately quantify and qualify the severity of the inappropriate behavior. Various questions should be answered. Is the behavior severe? Is the inappropriate behavior harmful to the individual or to other persons? Does the current behavior lead to restrictions that prohibit the individual from earning reinforcers? Is the problem of such magnitude that it cannot be ignored, and have medical factors been ruled out? If the answer to any of these questions is yes, Gaylord-Ross recommends proceeding to the next component in the model.

Reinforcement

At this stage the practitioner continues assessment, but now the focus is to determine whether the current inappropriate behavior is being maintained by positive reinforcers, negative reinforcers, or the density of reinforcement. If the inappropriate behavior seems to be maintained by any of these factors, appropriate interventions are introduced (e.g., extinction, paced instruction, or differential reinforcement of incompatible behavior. If the problem is not solved at this level, the practitioner progresses to the next component.

Ecology

Gaylord-Ross proposes that changes in the individual's environment—his milieu—may reduce the level of undesirable behavior. For example, crowded or noisy classrooms might be replaced by more spacious and quiet surroundings. Adding sensory objects to the environment (i.e., visual and/or tactile stimuli) might set the occasion for the individual to

[*Name of Facility*]
Informed Consent for Aversive Procedures

Name of client:
Birth date:
Today's date:
Supervisor:
Therapist(s):

1. Description of the behavior to be modified:
2. Description of the procedures that have already been implemented (give outcome):
3. Description of other treatment alternatives (assess effects):
4. Justification for the use of aversive procedures:
5. Description of aversive treatment procedure(s)—include hierarchy of treatment procedures where appropriate:
6. Description of possible side effects:
7. Describe any special precautions to be used in implementing treatment procedure:
8. Data recording procedures (give baseline data):
9. Expected behavioral outcome:
10. List persons who will implement treatment procedures (names and qualifications):
11. List the names of those on the committee for legal and ethical protection:
12. Informed consent:

    As legal guardian for this patient, I, [Name of legal guardian] hereby consent to the use of the treatment procedures described on the previous pages in the treatment of [Name of person to be treated]. I acknowledge that no guarantees have been made to me regarding the results of this treatment. I understand that within the scope of this treatment there is no intent to cause detrimental side effects to the patient. I also understand that the treatment procedures described above will be closely monitored and supervised and in the event of the observation of any detrimental side effects which might be injurious to the patient, the treatment procedures will be immediately terminated. I further understand that the decision to terminate may be made either by me or by the therapist. However, normally the decision will be made jointly. This form has been fully explained to me and I certify that I understand its contents.

(Signed)
(Address)
(City, State, ZIP)
(Phone)
(Relationship)
(Date)
(Witness)
(Signature)
(Address)
(City, State, ZIP)
(Phone)
(Date)

FIGURE 19.6 Model consent form. (From "Consent for Aversive Treatment" by J. W. Cook, K. Altman, and S. Haavik, 1978, *Mental Retardation, 16*(1), pp. 47–48. Copyright 1978 by the American Association on Mental Deficiency. Adapted by permission.)

419

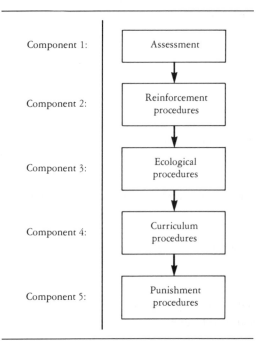

Component 1: Assessment

Component 2: Reinforcement procedures

Component 3: Ecological procedures

Component 4: Curriculum procedures

Component 5: Punishment procedures

FIGURE 19.7 Decision-making model for treating aberrant behavior. (From "A Decision Model for the Treatment of Aberrant Behavior in Applied Settings" by R. Gaylord-Ross in *Methods of Instruction for Severely Handicapped Students,* p. 138, by Wayne Sailor, Barbara Wilcox, and Lou Brown (Eds.) 1980, Baltimore: Paul H. Brookes. Copyright 1980 by Paul H. Brookes. Reprinted by permission.)

engage in appropriate alternative behavior. For additional information on procedures for conducting ecological assessments and interventions, the reader is referred to Rogers-Warren and Warren (1977) and Heron and Heward (1982). If restructuring the ecology does not produce substantial change, the practitioner should proceed to the fourth level of the model.

Curriculum

The purpose of the curriculum component is to ascertain the extent to which an antecedent event (i.e., the task to be completed or the directions issued) affects performance. According to Gaylord-Ross, if the behavior problem co-varies consistently with the type of task to be completed, then alternatives to the curriculum may affect subsequent behavior. Two suggested accommodations relate to changing the level of the instructional task itself and ensuring that the task has a high preference level for the individual. We would add that variations in the design of any instructional materials should also be considered (see Vargas, 1982).

If the first four levels of the model have been considered, implemented, evaluated, and found to be lacking, then the punishment component is investigated.

Punishment

Figure 19.8 shows a detailed schematic of the Gaylord-Ross punishment component. The upper tier is designated for selecting the punishing event, the middle tier is reserved for implementation, and the lower tier refers to evaluation. As stated previously, practitioners using this component of the model must decide whether (1) punishment is the appropriate course of action, (2) any medical conditions contraindicate its use, and (3) the punishment procedure is likely to be successful. To help resolve these areas of concern, practitioners must carefully examine the data on previous interventions, medical records, and the individual's history of reinforcement and/or punishment. For example, using the sharp reprimand "No" might not serve as a conditioned aversive stimulus if it was never paired with previously conditioned or unconditioned aversive stimuli for that individual.

When the preliminary decision has been made to proceed with punishment, the practitioner needs to select the initial punishment procedure (upper tier). If the least restrictive alternative model is used, response cost, time out from positive reinforcement, and overcorrection would be considered in that order. According to Gaylord-Ross, the final decision about which procedure to implement should be based on (1) "the individual characteristics of the student and the behavior problem, (2) the likelihood of the program being carried out

FIGURE 19.8 Flowchart of the punishment component. (From "A Decision Model for the Treatment of Aberrant Behavior in Applied Settings" by R. Gaylord-Ross in *Methods of Instruction for Severely Handicapped Students,* p. 151, by Wayne Sailor, Barbara Wilcox, and Lou Brown (Eds.), 1980, Baltimore: Paul H. Brookes. Copyright 1980 by Paul H. Brookes. Reprinted by permission.)

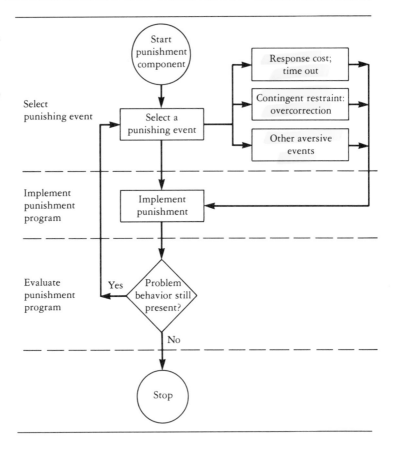

in a consistent manner, (3) the probability of successfully eliminating the behavior, and (4) the ethical and legal legitimacy of using a specific procedure. If one punishment procedure has been implemented and has failed to eliminate the problem behavior, another punishment procedure can be implemented" (p. 153).

The next step in the punishment component is implementation (middle tier). Gaylord-Ross recommends that any punishing event be accompanied by a verbal command such as "No" or "Stop that" so that the reprimand acquires conditioned aversive properties. According to Gaylord-Ross, "a program of such pairing places the student under the verbal control of the teacher and reduces the use of aversive consequences" (p. 153). We would add that any punishment procedure should also include the reinforcement of desirable behavior (e.g., DRI).

From a technical standpoint it is important during implementation to obtain reliability data on the independent variable. In other words, data should be collected on whether the procedure is being implemented as intended. Abandoning a punishment procedure that was not implemented correctly would not serve anyone's best interest. Furthermore, the implementation phase must be given a fair trial. At least 3 to 5 data points should be collected to determine whether the aberrant behavior is increasing, decreasing, or remaining the same.

The last phase of the model addresses evaluation (lower tier). Without question direct and daily measures of the behavior are needed.

Close examination and analysis of the data allow the behavior analyst to determine whether the problem continues to exist or has been eliminated. Where possible, measures of social validity (Wolf, 1978) should also be obtained to determine whether meaningful changes have been observed by other persons with whom the individual interacts.

The Gaylord-Ross decision-making model is an excellent resource for practitioners prior to and during implementation of punishment. Nonetheless, it is not without shortcomings. Merely proposing a least restrictive alternative model does not remove nagging ethical questions. As Barton, Brulle, and Repp (1983) indicate, the least restrictive alternative model presents its own set of ethical and legal problems. For example, treatments presumed to be the least restrictive based on the literature might not be so for a given individual. Also, beginning with a mild aversive and moving toward a major aversive as the former fails to produce results may result in habituation, reducing the overall effectiveness of the stronger aversive. Finally, deciding whether mild aversives should be delivered over a longer period of time or whether a strong aversive should be presented over a shorter period of time is an ethical dilemma. According to Budd and Baer (1977) and Barton, Brulle, and Repp (1983), using increasingly aversive procedures over time may be more restrictive than using the strongest possible aversive initially. Gast and Wolery (1987) provide a guideline on this point when they state: "If the choice of treatments is between procedures that are equally effective, then the least aversive (intrusive) should be selected. If the choice is between a less intrusive but *in*effective procedure and a more aversive but effective procedure, then the effective procedure should be selected."

Although the Gaylord-Ross model must await empirical validation, it does serve as a useful device for deciding when and how punishment should be introduced. Members of review committees should find the model a superb vehicle for documenting all interventions used prior to and during punishment.

METHODOLOGICAL GUIDELINES

The methodological guidelines presented here deal with the actual procedures of implementing punishment and are designed to (1) improve the effectiveness of punishment, (2) reduce the negative side effects of punishment, and (3) increase the likelihood that other forms of treatment or instruction will be used to strengthen appropriate behavior. These guidelines underscore many of the summary remarks of Azrin and Holz (1966).

Decide the Form and Intensity of Punishment

The least aversive, yet most effective, form of punishment should be used. If saying "No" sharply is likely to reduce a maladaptive behavior, it should be used instead of stimuli such as water mist, aromatic ammonia, or hand slaps. Employing such a hierarchical sequence is consistent with the doctrine of least restrictive alternative (Carr & Lovaas, 1983; Barton, Brulle, & Repp, 1983).

The question to answer when deciding on the form of punishment is, Will this form of punishment suppress the behavior? Punishment must be intensive enough to be effective, but not so intense as to cause physical harm to the individual. Punishment is more effective if the aversive stimulus is delivered at its optimum level initially, rather than gradually increasing the level over time (Azrin & Holz, 1966). Thus, the teacher who repeatedly admonishes her students in a mild fashion to "sit down" would be advised instead to state once strongly, "SIT DOWN." When the command is issued once, students are more likely to follow the direction. If the command is given repeatedly, students may quickly adapt to the increased frequency, and the procedure will gradually lose its effect. As Madsen, Becker, Thomas, Koser, and Plager (1968) demonstrated, the repeated use of a reprimand while students were out-of-seat served to increase, rather than reduce, the behavior.

Time the Presentation of Punishment

To be effective, the aversive stimulus must be delivered immediately after the maladaptive behavior occurs. The longer the time interval between the occurrence of the behavior and the delivery of the stimulus, the weaker the procedure becomes. In addition, evidence suggests that punishing an inappropriate behavior as soon as it begins is more effective than waiting until the chain of behavior has been completed (Solomon, 1964). The reason is that once an undesirable behavior is initiated, powerful secondary positive reinforcers associated with the behavior serve to prompt its continuation, thereby counteracting the inhibiting or suppressing efforts of the punishment (Mowrer, 1960). If a teacher is interested in decreasing self-injurious or self-stimulatory behavior, an effective punishment strategy would deliver the aversive stimulus at the onset of these behaviors, rather than at their conclusion. Sulzer-Azaroff and Mayer (1977) extend Mowrer's notion and state that saying no or providing a priori rules of conduct serves as a discriminative stimulus that signals that punishment will be delivered if the undesirable behavior is performed.

Ramey (1974) speculates on why the use of electric shock to reduce the self-abuse of an 11-year-old retarded student failed to produce aggression toward the teacher or other peers: the punishment stopped the beginning of a chain of behaviors and thus suppressed the remaining behaviors as well. Barlow (1972) lends support to Ramey's speculation: "If aver-

sion only is applied to the end of the chain the performance of preliminary behavior outside of treatment may rapidly set the occasion for recurrence of the undesirable behavior" (p. 120).

Experience the Aversive Stimulus Personally

Carr and Lovaas (1983) recommend that the practitioner experience any aversive stimulus herself, before the treatment begins, as a reminder of the technique that is being employed and the physical discomfort that it produces.

Be Consistent

Punish each occurrence of the undesirable behavior. This guideline implies that practitioners can use an aversive stimulus repeatedly, if necessary. Warnings should be minimized: one warning per occurrence is usually sufficient if the client is aware of the behavior that produces punishment.

Use a Combination of Procedures

Punishment should not be used in isolation but should be combined with other behavior change procedures, especially those that focus on the reinforcement of incompatible behaviors. According to White and Haring (1980), the **Fair Pair Rule** should be used whenever punishment is used. The Fair Pair Rule states that the practitioner should choose one or more alternatives to increase for every behavior targeted for reduction. An advantage of this rule is that it focuses the intervention on increasing desirable behavior, setting the occasion for the individual to build a behavior repertoire. The Fair Pair Rule is best operationalized using DRI and/or DRO. According to Walker (1979), punishment is more likely to be successful when reinforcement is delivered for an incompatible behavior. Also, Holz, Azrin, and Ayllon (1963) found that punishment was ineffective in reducing psychotic behavior when that behavior was the only means by which the patients could attain reinforcement. When an alternative response is available, punishment is usually effective in reducing the inappropriate behavior.

Record Effects

Graphing the frequency of the undesirable behavior before, during, and after the presentation of the aversive stimulus helps to establish the effectiveness of punishment. Inspecting the data regularly reminds the punisher of the purpose of the program and directly indicates when punishment should be terminated. When the data indicate that a clinical and significant change has occurred, punishment should not be continued, although an occasional booster session may be required to maintain the suppression of the behavior.

Observe Collateral Behaviors

The suppression of one inappropriate behavior can lead to the increased expression of another. Practitioners should expand their observations to include collateral or parallel behaviors. In other words, if a teacher is attempting to reduce face slapping, she should monitor other self-injurious behaviors as well (e.g., pinching, self-mutilation).

UNDESIRABLE ASPECTS OF PUNISHMENT

Negative Reinforcement of the Punisher

The use of aversive stimulation is widespread and occurs frequently in treatment and society. The primary reason is that it tends to negatively reinforce the person who delivers the punishment; when the punisher applies an aversive consequence that terminates a behavior, the punisher is reinforced by the cessation of that behavior. The next time that behavior occurs, the punisher is likely to apply similar aversive consequences to terminate it.

Emotional or Aggressive Behavior

Several authors (e.g., Azrin & Holz, 1966; Jones & Jones, 1981) have indicated that severe punishment can produce aggressive behavior. If a client is punished, the client may attempt to destroy nearby objects; this action is referred to as **respondent aggression** because the aggression is not directed toward the source of the punishment (Foxx, 1982). Or the client may try to attack, escape, or avoid the punisher; this action is referred to as **operant aggression** because it attempts to terminate the punishment (Azrin & Holz, 1966; Foxx, 1982).

Avoidance and Escape

A student who has been punished for being late to class may avoid coming to class. A psychiatric patient who has been punished for inappropriate eating may avoid the cafeteria. Mayer, Sulzer, and Cody (1968) indicate that avoidance and escape need not always take place in the literal sense of the term. Individuals can escape punishing environments by taking drugs or alcohol, or by simply tuning-out. Bandura (1969) indicates that punishment is most effective when all forms of unauthorized escape can be controlled. Mayhew and Harris (1979) found that squirting citric acid in the mouth of a profoundly retarded 19-year-old after the occurrence of self-injurious behavior greatly reduced the level of that behavior. In their study the subject could not escape the presentation of the citric acid. As noted, other researchers (e.g., Tanner & Zeiler, 1975) have used noxious substances contingently to reduce self-destructive behavior. However, Mayhew and Harris point out that one of the disadvantages of the ammonia procedure is that the fumes have a limited range of effectiveness, approximately 2 feet, so the individual might be able to escape or avoid the aversive stimulus by moving away.

Negative Modeling

Most readers are familiar with the example of the parent who says, while spanking the child, "This will teach you not to hit anyone else!" Unfortunately, the child may be more likely in the future to imitate the parent's action rather than the parent's message. Summarizing the results of several laboratory and field-based studies, Bandura (1969) concludes,

> Anyone attempting to control specific troublesome responses should avoid modeling punitive forms of behavior that not only counteract the effects of direct training but also increase the probability that on future occasions the individual may respond to interpersonal thwarting in an imitative manner. (p. 313)

Unpredictability

It is difficult to predict precisely all of the effects and side effects of punishment prior to a treatment program. When punishment is used, the person presenting the aversive stimulus should be aware that some or all of the undesirable aspects presented here may be observed; and the alternate plan should be available to deal with them. The best advice is to use punishment by contingent presentation of an aversive stimulus only in circumstances where other less aversive procedures have failed or when a life-threatening situation is encountered that requires the immediate suppression of a behavior. Even then, the practitioner should rigorously adhere to ethical and legal sanctions before implementing this reductive approach.

SUMMARY

Definition of Punishment

1 Punishment can be defined as the application of an aversive stimulus immediately after a behavior with the effect of reducing the future occurrence of that behavior.

Rationale for Using Punishment

2 There are two main reasons for using punishment: (1) it has been shown to be effective in reducing behavior; and (2) not using punishment in some situations would be withholding a potentially successful treatment and maintaining the individual in a dangerous state.

Ethical and Legal Considerations

3 Three issues related to the ethical and legal aspects of punishment are (1) the doctrine of the least restrictive alternative (LRA); (2) cruel and unusual punishment; and (3) informed consent.

A Decision-Making Model for Using Punishment

4 A five-component decision-making model for implementing punishment includes assessment, reinforcement, ecology, curriculum, and punishment.

5 The decision-making model is based on the doctrine of the least restrictive alternative and provides a systematic way to select, implement, and evaluate punishment procedures.

Methodological Guidelines

6 Methodological guidelines address the question of how punishment should be delivered.

7 The major methodological guidelines are to (a) decide the form and intensity of punishment, (b) time the presentation of the punishment stimulus, (c) experience the aversive stimulus personally, (d) be consistent, (e) use a combination of procedures and the Fair Pair

Rule, (f) record effects, and (g) observe collateral behaviors.

Undesirable Aspects of Punishment

8 Punishment tends to negatively reinforce the punisher, increasing the likelihood of repeated use by the punisher.

9 It can elicit emotional or aggressive behaviors from the individual who was punished.

10 It can promote avoidance and escape and can also serve as a negative modeling procedure.

11 The effects of punishment are unpredictable.

20

Overcorrection

KEY TERMS

Overcorrection

Restitutional overcorrection

Positive practice overcorrection

Simple correction

Con~~tingent exercise~~

Neg~~ative practice~~

For~~ced movement exercises~~

Habi~~t reversal~~

This chapter discusses the behavior reduction procedure known as overcorrection. Overcorrection is considered a package approach because it involves more than one principle of behavior change. Although it is apparent from a review of the literature that overcorrection has been used to reduce a number of disruptive, annoying, and self-injurious behaviors, it is not readily apparent which elements of overcorrection (e.g., restitution,

positive practice, avoidance, time out, punishment) produce the response-suppressing change. This chapter defines overcorrection, provides a rationale for its use, distinguishes it from other reductive procedures with similar elements, presents two types of positive practice overcorrection, and cites the problems associated with overcorrection. In addition, the chapter includes guidelines for using overcorrection in applied settings.

This chapter was written by Timothy E. Heron.

DEFINITION OF OVERCORRECTION

Overcorrection is a reductive procedure that consists of one or two components: restitutional overcorrection and/or positive practice overcorrection (Foxx & Azrin, 1972; Foxx & Bechtel, 1983). Overcorrection was originally designed to combine the suppressive effects of punishment and the educative effects of positive practice. According to Foxx and Azrin (1973b) **restitutional overcorrection** is defined as "requiring the disruptor to correct the consequences of his misbehavior by having him restore the situation to a state vastly improved from that which existed before the disruption" (p. 2). For example, if a student places a piece of gum underneath his desk, he has to clean not only the undersurface of his own desk, but also all the other desks in the class. **Positive practice overcorrection**, on the other hand, is presumably an educative component insofar as it provides an opportunity to engage in appropriate behavior. To continue the gum example, with positive practice overcorrection the student might practice repeatedly placing his gum in the trash can.

According to Foxx and Bechtel (1983), overcorrection is

> the label given to a set of specifically designed, empirically defined aversive stimuli that are used in applied situations. Accordingly, overcorrection functions as a Type 1 punisher when it reduces the future probability of the behavior it follows and as negative reinforcer when it increases the future probability of behaviors that avoid or terminate it. Thus, overcorrection is not a behavioral principle or a mechanism for explaining procedural effects on behavior. Rather, it represents a strategy for unifying several behavioral principles (Type 1 and Type 2 punishment, extinction, and negative reinforcement), and a socially relevant terminology that is easily understood by the general public. (p. 134)

Still, the practitioner should realize that overcorrection is ultimately based on the principle of punishment, and the effectiveness of the procedure rests on decreasing the future occurrence of the behavior preceding its application. If overcorrection is used subsequent to the occurrence of a behavior and that behavior decreases in frequency in the future, then a functional definition of punishment is evident (cf. Azrin & Holz, 1966).

The reader should be aware that not all behaviors lend themselves to the use of both restitutional and positive practice overcorrection. If the environment is not altered by an inappropriate act, then positive practice overcorrection should be used (Foxx & Azrin, 1973b; Epstein, Doke, Sajwaj, Sorrall, & Rimmer, 1974; Foxx & Bechtel, 1983). Self-stimulatory behavior is an example of a behavior in which no environmental disruption occurs and for which only positive practice overcorrection should be used (Shapiro, Barrett, & Ollendick, 1980; Wells, Forehand, Hickey, & Green, 1977).

RATIONALE AND ASSUMPTIONS FOR OVERCORRECTION

According to Foxx (1982), the basic rationale for overcorrection is that it assists the normalization process; in other words, it relies on consequences that normal individuals apply to themselves subsequent to undesirable social behavior. A negative consequence for letting a cigarette burn a hole in a sofa might be to repair the hole and then have the entire sofa cleaned. Foxx's position is that practitioners should attempt to use procedures that they might use themselves.

Another reason for overcorrection is that the procedure can be directly related to the misbehavior. Unlike other reductive techniques, such as response cost or time out, in which an individual is fined or loses access to reinforcement after an inappropriate behavior, with overcorrection a corrective or educative consequence can be applied directly to the misbehavior (Foxx, 1982). Foxx and Bechtel (1983) state that the term *educative* should be interpreted to mean an increase in desirable behavior as a function of the presentation of overcorrection. The term is not intended to mean that the practitioner structures a program to deliver reinforcement during positive practice overcorrection. In fact, little, if any, reinforcement should be delivered during positive practice overcorrection.[1] If a developmentally handicapped adult upsets all of the chairs in a cafeteria, she might be required with restitutional overcorrection to straighten all of the chairs in the room. Thus, the restitutional activity can be topographically similar and functionally related to the misbehavior. If positive practice overcorrection is employed, the adult might be required to engage in an appropriate behavior while being seated at the table (Foxx & Bechtel, 1983). In either case the consequence that is delivered is usually different from that presented with other reductive procedures.

Also, although it can be argued that some forms of punishment are arbitrary (e.g., loss of 20 minutes of free time), the restitutional overcorrection component is assumed to help the individual experience the effort required by others to restore the damaged environment (Axelrod, Brantner, & Meddock, 1978; Marholin, Luiselli, & Townsend, 1980; Foxx, 1982; Foxx & Bechtel, 1983). It is assumed that the individual will learn not to perform the inappropriate behavior by experiencing the inconvenience of correcting or rectifying the situation (Azrin & Besalel, 1980). For example, an adult with mental retardation who resides in a group home and repeatedly throws food on the floor at dinner time would presumably learn from restitutional overcorrection how much work is required to maintain a sanitary eating environment.

Marholin et al. (1980) state that overcorrection was originally designed as a procedure to teach responsibility to the offender; contingent upon the emission of an undesirable behavior, overcorrection is applied so that the individual experiences the inconvenience produced by the misbehavior. Azrin and Besalel (1980) sum up this part of the rationale: "The important consideration is that the person spend time and effort to realize that he must take responsibility for his actions. Only in that way can he experience the inconvenience suffered by the other person(s) who must correct the disturbance" (p. 17).

A further rationale for overcorrection is that it serves as an alternative to other presumably more intrusive forms of punishment because of its capacity to incorporate a positive practice procedure. Even though the positive practice component may have to be completed with graduated guidance, it is still designed to teach appropriate behavior. And finally, as Epstein et al. (1974) suggest, reductive procedures are needed that are clinically and practically effective (i.e., they are strong, immediate, and lasting), that can be applied across a variety of persons, and that are acceptable to behavior change practitioners. In their view overcorrection meets these criteria.

DISTINGUISHING OVERCORRECTION FROM OTHER SIMILAR REDUCTIVE APPROACHES

The term *overcorrection* is often misused in the literature (Miltenberger & Fuqua, 1981; Foxx & Bechtel, 1983). Procedures with similar components, such as simple correction, contingent exercise, and negative practice, are labeled overcorrection even though they do not meet the criteria of the definition. To help clarify matters, we will examine several similar reductive procedures to distinguish them from the concept of overcorrection presented here.

---

[1]For additional discussion on the educative aspects of overcorrection, the reader is referred to Foxx and Bechtel (1983) and Miltenberger and Fuqua (1981).

Simple Correction

According to Azrin and Besalel (1980), **simple correction** means that, subsequent to an offense, the environment is returned to its previous state. For example, a simple correction procedure is in effect if, subsequent to throwing a piece of litter on the playground, a child is instructed to pick it up. Azrin and Besalel (1980) state that simple correction should be used for those behavior problems that occur infrequently, are not deliberate, and do not interfere with the behavior of other individuals. Simple correction is not an appropriate alternative if the misbehavior produces an irreversible effect (e.g., an item of clothing is destroyed) or if the corrective behavior is beyond the individual's means (e.g., replacing a valuable piece of china).

Contingent Exercise

In **contingent exercise** the individual is required, subsequent to the inappropriate behavior, to perform a response that is not topographically related to the misbehavior (Luce, Delquadri, & Hall, 1980). In one part of the Luce et al. study the number of hitting behaviors of a 6-year-old male were reduced by having him stand up and sit down 10 times after each hitting episode. Initially, the child had to be physically prompted to stand; an assistant held the child's hand while pulling his upper body forward. Physical prompts were accompanied by verbal prompts, such as "Stand up" or "Sit down." If a hitting episode occurred during the contingent exercise, the procedure was reinstated. Figure 20.1 shows that when contingent exercise was in effect, the number of hitting episodes decreased to near zero levels.

Although Luce et al. (1980) have shown that contingent exercise can be used to reduce inappropriate behavior, their procedure does not meet the criterion of overcorrection because standing up and sitting down are not positive practice countermeasures for hitting. They are topographically dissimilar to hitting.

Negative Practice

Negative practice is the opposite of overcorrection because the individual is required to perform the misbehavior repeatedly. Having a student repeatedly tap on her desk as a consequence of desk tapping is an example of negative practice. Azrin, Nunn, and Frantz (1980a) used negative practice to reduce the nervous tics of 22 institutionalized patients. In the negative practice condition the patients were required to perform the tic in front of a mirror for 30-second periods during a 1-hour session while simultaneously saying to themselves, "This is what I am not supposed to do." Even though the negative practice procedure had a beneficial reductive effect for these patients, it was not an overcorrection procedure because there was no attempt to use a positive practice countermeasure.

Quiet Training, Required Relaxation, Relaxation Training

According to Foxx and Bechtel (1983), these procedures are virtually identical: they require an agitated person to lie face down or face up until all forms of the violent or aggressive behavior disappear for a specified period of time. With this criterion these procedures more appropriately resemble time out from positive reinforcement. Although the authors recommend that these procedures be used prior to overcorrection, they are not overcorrection procedures themselves.

TYPES OF POSITIVE PRACTICE OVERCORRECTION

There are two basic types of positive practice overcorrection that have been identified in the literature: forced movement exercises and habit reversal.

Forced Movement Exercises

In **forced movement exercises**, sometimes referred to as functional movement training,

FIGURE 20.1 The number of hits exhibited by a 6-year-old autistic male during 6-hour sessions at school. During baseline the behavior was ignored, and no contingencies were provided for aggressive behavior. Contingent exercise introduced stand-up and sit-on-the-floor exercise contingent on hitting. (From "Contingent Exercise: A Mild but Powerful Procedure for Suppressing Inappropriate Verbal and Aggressive Behavior" by S. C. Luce, J. Delquadri, and R. V. Hall, 1980, *Journal of Applied Behavior Analysis, 13*(4), p. 587. Copyright 1980 by the Society for the Experimental Analysis of Behavior, Inc. Reprinted by permission.)

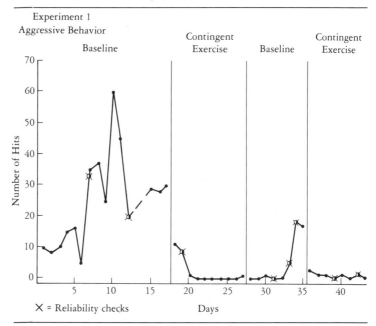

the individual is helped from one movement to another with graduated guidance (i.e., physical guidance plus fading) or shadowing (i.e., close physical proximity without contact) (Foxx & Bechtel, 1983). Typically, forced movement exercises are conducted in three stages: (1) the individual is told to perform a specific behavior, usually topographically related to the target behavior to be learned; (2) the person is guided physically to ensure that he engages in the behavior; and (3) the person performs multiple repetitions of the movements for a specific period of time. According to Miltenberger and Fuqua (1981), forced movement exercises have been used most often to reduce self-stimulatory behavior or self-injurious behavior.

Habit Reversal

A **habit reversal** procedure requires that an individual perform a behavior incompatible with the inappropriate behavior. For example, a behavior incompatible with striking a peer is holding a cup. Azrin, Nunn, and Frantz (1980b) demonstrated that a habit reversal procedure,

teaching nail biters a competing hand-grasping response, successfully reduced nail-biting episodes of 97 institutionalized adults by as much as 99%.

CONSIDERATIONS WITH OVERCORRECTION

Staff Considerations

Adequate staff and supervision are needed for overcorrection (Foxx & Bechtel, 1983; Miltenberger & Fuqua, 1981). Staff members are needed to monitor behaviors continuously and to provide the prompts that might be necessary during either restitution or positive practice. Unfortunately, in many applied settings staff members are spread so thin that it is impossible to use overcorrection.

Also, given the presence of trained staff—which can be a problem in many applied settings—there is no guarantee that the procedure will be maintained when the trainers are gone. As soon as trained staff are reassigned other duties, it is possible that the overcorrection procedure will be abandoned. Axelrod et al. (1978) report on the results of several studies conducted in institutional and home settings; the studies showed that overcorrection produced the intended effect, but it was withdrawn because the procedures were too difficult or required too much staff time or supervision. Unless adequate staff can be provided, overcorrection should not be the intervention of choice.

Length of Program

According to Foxx (1982), if the behavior targeted for reduction occurs at a high rate, reducing it to more manageable levels with overcorrection may take too long. Before using overcorrection, the practitioner should be reasonably certain that she can provide the time needed to implement the procedure consistently. Otherwise, another reductive procedure (e.g., DRI) should be considered (Foxx, 1982).

Client Resistance

Client resistance to overcorrection can take many forms and can occur during either restitutional or positive practice overcorrection. In an attempt to decrease thefts in an institutionalized population, Azrin and Wesolowski (1974) found that clients resisted efforts to return stolen items, although none of the clients became physically abusive.

Resistance can also be manifested in several other ways. For example, the client can engage in tantrum behavior, cry, or whine (Matson, Horne, Ollendick, & Ollendick, 1979; Matson, Stephens, & Horne, 1978) or can engage in disruptive, emotional, or aggressive behaviors (Doleys, McWhorter, Williams, & Gentry, 1977). During the positive practice component of overcorrection, the client can balk at having to complete the appropriate sequence of steps repeatedly. Resistance at this stage

can be physical or verbal also, and graduated guidance or shadowing may be required to complete the necessary steps. If graduated guidance is planned, the practitioner must be physically capable of moving the individual through the movements.

There are several ways to reduce the likelihood of client resistance to overcorrection. First, client resistance should be anticipated; practitioners should not assume that clients will comply with their instructions. Overcorrection is based on the principle of punishment, and practitioners should be prepared to deal with client reactions.

Another way to reduce, or at least minimize, client reaction to overcorrection is to use supplementary verbal prompts. For example, let us suppose that an adult with mental retardation stole a food item from another resident in the cafeteria. If resistance is evident during the restitutional component of overcorrection, the practitioner might say, "Fred, you must return that food to Jane immediately!" The practitioner might also physically guide Fred to Jane's tray to return the stolen food and then guide him through the line again to obtain additional food for her.

Client resistance can also be eliminated by using brief periods of time out. Matson and Stephens (1977) found that a DRI procedure did not substantially reduce the level of behavior from the baseline condition. And during the initial days of overcorrection, physical guidance through the steps was not possible without a struggle. Time out was introduced until the disruptions were reduced, and then the client continued her overcorrection training (See Figure 20.2).

Finally, client resistance can be reduced by applying the overcorrection procedure consistently. Clients soon learn that there is no escaping the consequences, and they are less likely to engage in resistant behavior. Like other behavioral reduction procedures, consistency is necessary for success.

FIGURE 20.2 Mean frequency of object-throwing instances across 2-day blocks for baseline, DRI, and overcorrection phases and across weeks during postchecks. (From J. L. Matson and R. M. Stephens, "Overcorrection of Aggressive Behavior in a Chronic Psychiatric Patient," *Behavior Modification,* Vol. 1, No. 4 (October, 1977) p. 562. Copyright © 1977 by Sage Publications. Reprinted by permission of Sage Publications, Inc.)

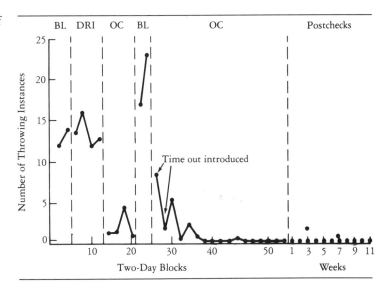

Selection of Restitutional and Positive Practice Activities

Foxx (1982) and Foxx and Bechtel (1983) indicate that the on-the-spot selection of restitutional activities can be difficult for the practitioner. For example, it might be difficult to determine appropriate restitutional activities for institutional residents who frequently give bear hugs and kisses to visitors. Since there is some evidence—although by no means conclusive—to indicate that restitutional activity should be related topographically to the misbehavior (cf. Foxx & Martin, 1975; Epstein et al., 1974), identifying an appropriate restitutional activity may be difficult.

Inadvertent Reinforcement

An overcorrection procedure, although intended to reduce inappropriate behavior, can actually serve to reinforce it. Consequently, positive reinforcement should be used sparingly during positive practice to reduce the likelihood that the practice period will become associated with reinforcement, thereby increasing the inappropriate behavior that preceded it.

An inadvertent reinforcer can be delivered when the offender is rewarded by the proximity, redirecting statements, or graduated guidance of the practitioner.

Measel and Alfieri (1976) provide suggestive evidence that an overcorrection procedure can serve to reinforce the inappropriate behavior targeted for reduction. Their study was designed to decrease the head banging of a 16-year-old adolescent with mental retardation who had been institutionalized for 10 years. Essentially, the procedure involved reinforcing the adolescent for completing simple motor tasks without banging his head; episodes of head banging were ignored. During the reinforcement plus overcorrection condition, if head banging occurred, it was followed by a sharp reprimand ("No, don't bang your head!") and a head movement regimen that required the adolescent to hold his head to the right, left, and straight ahead for 30 seconds each. The head movement regimen was conducted with graduated guidance.

Figure 20.3 shows that during the reinforcement condition head banging increased over baseline levels. Further, when reinforcement

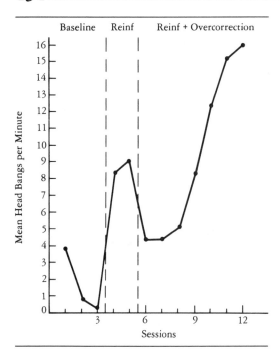

FIGURE 20.3 Mean head bangs per minute by Michael during individual sessions in Study 2. Each point represents the mean for one session. (From "Treatment of Self-Injurious Behavior by a Combination of Reinforcement for Incompatible Behavior and Overcorrection" by C. J. Measel and P. A. Alfieri, 1976, *American Journal of Mental Deficiency,* *81*(2), p. 152. Copyright 1976 by the *American Association on Mental Deficiency.* Reprinted by permission.)

plus overcorrection was introduced, head banging increased dramatically in frequency. Although Measel and Alfieri (1976) readily concede that sufficient data were not available to perform a functional analysis, the existing data combined with anecdotal information from caretakers led them to speculate that elements of the overcorrection procedure (e.g., physical contact with staff) may have served to reinforce head banging.

How is the practitioner to know whether the overcorrection procedure is serving to reinforce undesirable behavior? The best solution is to use direct and daily measurement of the target behavior as well as collateral behaviors if possible. If the behavior increases subsequent to the introduction of the overcorrection procedure, the teacher can conclude that the procedure served as a reinforcer. Also, the teacher can rely on environmental cues to help with the decision. For example, does the individual receive reinforcement from peers as the overcorrection procedure is delivered? If so, these other sources of reinforcement need to be eliminated.

Effects on Collateral Behaviors

There is some empirical research on the effects of overcorrection on collateral behaviors (Marholin et al., 1980). Collateral behaviors should be monitored whenever an overcorrection procedure is applied to determine whether the procedure produces an increase in these behaviors. The practitioner can then use these data to determine whether to introduce overcorrection for the collateral behaviors or initiate a different procedure.

Generalization and Maintenance

The data are mixed with respect to generalized effects of overcorrection. Some studies indicate that generalization did not occur across settings (Townsend & Marholin, 1978; Martin & Matson, 1978); other studies show that overcorrection can be used to reduce inappropriate behavior across settings (Harris & Romanczyk, 1976), and some (e.g., Kelly & Drabman, 1977) have shown that overcorrection reduced self-injurious behavior not only in treatment settings, but also in generalized settings.

The Marholin et al. (1980) analysis of studies in which generalization took place indicates that the more similar the nontreatment setting was to the treatment setting, the more likely the generalization was to occur, echoing the concern of Baer, Wolf, and Risley (1968) and Stokes and Baer (1977) that generalization should be programmed at the time of treatment.

Studies of the maintenance of the suppressive effect of overcorrection fall into three categories: those in which overcorrection was effective in suppressing the behavior permanently; those in which overcorrection needed to be continually applied across time to be effective; and those in which the reductive effect was maintained by a conditioned aversive stimulus (e.g., "No!") established during training (Marholin et al, 1980). On the whole, the results of studies of maintenance have a mixed profile similar to that of generalization. Some studies show that the suppressive effect was maintained (Measel & Alfieri, 1976; Ollendick et al., 1978); others show that it was not (Martin & Matson, 1978; Martin et al., 1977). Maintenance of the suppressive effect seems more likely if overcorrection is used during follow-up or if a verbal warning is conditioned during the treatment (Foxx & Azrin, 1973a).

GUIDELINES FOR USING OVERCORRECTION

Relate Restitutional and/or Positive Practice Overcorrection to the Offense

To the maximum extent possible, the restitutional and/or positive practice components of overcorrection should be directly related to the topography of the misbehavior. If an individual steals another person's food and consumes it, that particular food item cannot be replaced. However, during restitution the offender can return a comparable food item to the victim. Likewise, if a child breaks a priceless family heirloom, he cannot replace it; but he can clean up the broken pieces. The point is that the offender should actively experience the inconvenience created by his action. If a group of juveniles vandalize a school (e.g., break bottles on the playground, write graffiti on the walls, break windows), the restitutional and positive practice components of overcorrection

should be directly related to their inappropriate behavior. To fulfill the restitutional component, the offenders might be required to sweep the entire playground, sand all of the school walls, or fix all of the windows. To complete the positive practice component, they should repeatedly throw empty bottles in trash cans, paint murals on a canvas for display, or check the security of each window. Carey and Bucher (1981) demonstrated that even though restitutional overcorrection and positive practice were effective in suppressing behavior, appropriate behavior was learned only when the positive practice was topographically similar to the inappropriate behavior.

Use Quiet or Relaxation Training If the Individual Is Acting Out and/or Is Disruptive

According to Foxx and Bechtel (1983), quiet training or relaxation should be implemented first when an individual is acting out or is openly disruptive (e.g., having a temper tantrum). Only after the individual is calm should overcorrection by used.

Use Prompts Only As Required

Verbal or physical prompting may be required in an overcorrection procedure, but these prompts should be used sparingly and removed as quickly as possible. For example, if a student repeatedly fails to hang up her coat upon entering the classroom and the teacher decides to use an overcorrection procedure to decrease this behavior, he may tell her (verbal prompt) to hang up her coat and straighten up the rest of the coats on the rack. The teacher may even have to help her hang up her coat (physical prompt) until she does it for herself. However, the teacher should gradually reduce prompting as soon as possible, perhaps using a shadowing technique, so that the behavior comes under the teacher's initial direction or under the control of environmental cues (e.g., entering the classroom). The exception to this guideline occurs when a verbal stimulus (e.g., "No!") is paired with overcorrection as a conditioned aversive stimulus. In this case the verbal warning is designed to maintain the suppressive effect of overcorrection in its absence (see Foxx & Azrin, 1973a).

Use Promps That Are Firm, Directive, and Businesslike; Avoid Debates

When verbal prompts are used, the voice should convey the message being sent: that is, a particular task should be completed promptly (e.g., "Paul, clean your desk and the others in your row"). Abusive language or corporal intimidation is not necessary; just a deliberate, structured message. Also, the word *OK* should not be tacked onto the end of the sentence. (e.g., "Paul, clean your desk and the others in your row, OK?"), indicating a choice where none is intended.

In addition, the practitioner should avoid getting into a debate. If verbal or physical resistance is encountered after the instructions are given, the directions can be repeated once. If compliance is not achieved, the practitioner should initiate a brief time out procedure (see Measel & Alfieri, 1976; Matson & Stephens, 1977). Afterwards, the individual can be returned to the original environment for the continuation of restitution or positive practice training.

Whenever Possible, Reinforce Incompatible Behavior

Like any other form of punishment (e.g., time out or response cost) overcorrection tends to be more effective if it is used in conjunction with reinforcement of alternative behaviors. As Measel and Alfieri's (1976) data suggest, reinforcing behaviors incompatible with the target behavior while simultaneously using an overcorrection procedure is more beneficial in reducing the inappropriate behav-

ior than applying the reinforcement procedure alone. Whenever possible, practitioners should set the occasion for reinforcement of alternative positive behavior.

Keep Records

Records should be kept indicating the level of the individual's performance before, during, and after the overcorrection procedure. Direct and daily measurement of the target behavior is the single most important source of data collection (see Tawney & Gast, 1984). Although informal staff observations can be of some use in evaluating the effectiveness of overcorrection, a direct measure of the individual's performance provides all the data needed to make an appropriate treatment decision. Azrin and Besalel (1980) suggest that a daily record include information such as the date, number of misbehaviors, and anecdotal comments. The comments should be brief statements describing important aspects of the procedure (see Figure 20.4).

Use the Data to Make Instructional Decisions

As stated previously, one of the hallmarks of applied behavior analysis is instructional decisions based on solid evidence, not intuition. If decreased rates of misbehavior are not noted after 3 to 5 days of initial treatment, perhaps another reductive procedure or a combination of procedures should be considered.

Do Not Reinforce Behaviors During Overcorrection

Although it may seem paradoxical not to reinforce appropriate behavior during overcorrection, especially during positive practice overcorrection, the rationale is quite simple. The individual may learn to perform inappropriate or undesirable behavior in order to acquire positive reinforcers (Foxx & Bechtel, 1983). Reinforcement should occur at other times during training—DRI, DRO, and positive

Date	No. of Misbehaviors		Comments
Oct. 22	ЖႵ	5	I picked up the toys each time for him.
Oct. 23	///	3	I picked up the toys each time for him.
Oct. 24	////	4	I picked up the toys each time for him.
Oct. 25	ЖႵ /	6	I picked up the toys each time for him.
Oct. 26	//	2	He picked up the toys and put them in his room. Complained on the first time.
Oct. 27		0	His father also talked to him about overcorrection. Praised for neatness.
Oct. 28	/	1	No complaints by him. Still played with toys but put them away.
Oct. 29		0	Told him I was proud.
Oct. 30		0	Told him I was proud.
Oct. 31		0	Told him I was proud.
Nov. 1		0	Told him I was proud.
Nov. 2		0	Told him I was proud.

FIGURE 20.4   A daily record of misbehavior. Each day should be noted even if no misbehavior occurred. (From *How to Use Overcorrection,* p. 25, by N. H. Azrin and V. A. Besalel, 1980, Austin, TX: Pro-Ed. Reprinted by permission.)

reinforcements are all desirable—but not during overcorrection.

Program for Generalization and Maintenance

Marholin et al. (1980) recommend three strategies to set the occasion for generalization and maintenance. The first is to conduct training under a variety of stimulus settings so that no one setting becomes a discriminative stimulus for responding. Thus, if overcorrection is initiated in a work setting for disruptive behavior, the procedure should also be applied in the home and recreational settings. The second strategy is to condition a verbal stimulus such as "No!" early in the overcorrection program so that this verbal stimulus acquires sufficient reductive properties. A verbal stimulus is also transportable, meaning that it can be used by other staff members in other situations. Finally, a plan should be made to reinforce the occurrence of appropriate behavior in the environment so that increases in desired behavior can be rewarded. As stated previously, reinforcement of desirable behavior is the key to increasing the future probability of appropriate responses.

SUMMARY

Definition of Overcorrection

1   Overcorrection is defined as the response contingent application of restitution and positive practice either singularly or in combination after the occurrence of a behavior; it is designed to reduce the future probability of the occurrence of that behavior.

Rationale and Assumptions for Overcorrection

2 Overcorrection assists the normalization process.

3 With overcorrection a corrective and educative consequence can be applied to the misbehavior.

4 Overcorrection sets the occasion for the offending individual to experience the effort required to restore the environment to the original state.

5 Overcorrection serves as an alternative to other forms of punishment.

6 Overcorrection is an effective deceleration procedure that can be applied across settings and behaviors.

Distinguishing Overcorrection from Other Similar Reductive Approaches

7 In overcorrection, the damaged environment is restored to a condition better than that which existed before the damage. Contingent exercise, forced movement exercises, and negative practice, although reductive, are not synonomous with overcorrection.

8 In a simple correction procedure the environment is returned to its original state.

9 In contingent exercise the individual performs a behavior that is not topographically similar to the misbehavior.

10 Negative practice is the opposite of overcorrection. That is, the individual is required to perform the misbehavior repeatedly.

11 Quiet training, required relaxation, and/or relaxation training should be used initially when the offending individual is agitated.

Types of Positive Practice Overcorrection

12 In forced movement exercises or functional movement training, the individual is guided from one movement to another with a graduated guidance procedure. Usually, forced movement exercises are completed by telling the individual what behavior to perform and guiding her through the movements repeatedly.

13 A habit reversal procedure requires that an individual perform a behavior incompatible with the inappropriate behavior.

Considerations with Overcorrection

14 Overcorrection is potentially difficult to implement because additional staff are usually required to monitor the procedure.

15 Depending upon the behavior to reduce, overcorrection can take a larger amount of staff time to implement than other reductive procedures.

16 Client resistance (physical and/or verbal) can occur with overcorrection. It can be minimized or eliminated by anticipating its occurrence, using supplementary cues or time out, and applying the procedure consistently.

17 Selecting restitutional or positive practice behaviors may be difficult, especially with victimless crimes such as self-stimulation.

18 The attention, physical proximity or guidance, or verbal prompts used in overcorrecting can become positive reinforcers for an individual and thereby reduce the effectiveness of overcorrection as a deceleration procedure.

19 Overcorrection can affect collateral behaviors.

20 Generalization and maintenance of effects are more likely to result from overcorrection contingencies if they are programmed during treatment.

Guidelines for Using Overcorrection

21 Established guidelines can assist the practitioner in implementing an overcorrection procedure.

21

Time Out from Positive Reinforcement

KEY TERMS

Time out from positive
reinforcement

Time out

Nonexclusion time out

Planned ignoring

Peer mediated time out

Withdrawal of a specific
positive reinforcer

Reinforcer isolation

Contingent observation

Time out ribbon

Exclusion time out

Human services professionals must apply the behavior change procedure most appropriate for a particular problem. In some cases a positive reductive procedure is sufficient to increase, strengthen, or maintain desirable behavior. At other times, however, maladaptive behavior must be decreased. Just as there are many procedures to increase or maintain the occurrence of behavior, so too there are a variety of procedures to decrease the occurrence of undesirable, inappropriate, or self-injurious behavior.

This chapter defines and operationalizes time out from positive reinforcement and distinguishes it from extinction and response cost. The two major types of time out (nonexclusion and exclusion) are presented, followed by a description of the desirable aspects of time out.

This chapter was written by Timothy E. Heron.

The chapter concludes with suggestions for using time out in applied settings and identifies the legal and ethical issues involved.

DEFINITION OF TIME OUT

Time out from positive reinforcement, or simply **time out,** is defined as the withdrawal of the opportunity to earn positive reinforcement or the loss of access to positive reinforcers for a specified period of time, contingent upon the occurrence of a behavior; the effect is to reduce the future probability of that behavior (Gast & Nelson, 1977; Heward, Dardig, & Rossett, 1979; Foxx, 1982). Implicit in the definition of time out are three important aspects: (1) the discrepancy between the "time in" in a normal setting and the time out environment (Brantner & Doherty, 1983); (2) the response-contingent loss of access to reinforcement; and (3) a resultant decrease in the future probability of the occurrence of the behavior. Contrary to most thinking, time out is not conducted by simply removing an individual to a secluded setting. Such a removal procedure may accurately describe isolation (Brantner & Doherty, 1983), but it is by no means the only way in which time out can be used. Technically, time out is a Type II punishment procedure; the individual loses the opportunity to acquire additional reinforcers for a specified period of time, the effect of which is a behavior decrease (Foxx, 1982; Nelson & Rutherford, 1983).

Time out can be viewed from a procedural, conceptual, and functional perspective. Procedurally, it is that period of time when the individual is removed from a reinforcing environment (e.g., a student is sent from the classroom to the hallway for 5 minutes) or loses access to reinforcers within an environment (e.g., a student is ineligible to earn reinforcers for 5 minutes). Conceptually, the distinction between the time in and the time out environment is of paramount importance.

The more reinforcing the time in setting, the more effective time out is likely to be as a punisher (Solnick, Rincover, & Peterson, 1977). From a functional perspective time out must involve the reduced likelihood of the future occurrence of the behavior. Without that reduced probability time out is not in effect, even if the individual is procedurally removed from the setting or loses access to reinforcers.

DISTINGUISHING EXTINCTION AND RESPONSE COST FROM TIME OUT

Although the effects of response cost, time out, and extinction are similar—reduction of the future rate of a behavior—the three procedures are different from one another. As defined in chapter 17, the withholding of reinforcement for a previously reinforced behavior is termed extinction. When extinction is in effect, the rate of individual performance has no bearing on access to reinforcement. Consequently, high rates of inappropriate behavior, even higher initial levels that those of baseline, may be evident. Eventually, however, the level of the behavior declines. In time out, on the other hand, access to additional reinforcers is contingent upon the individual's behavior. When time out is in effect, the rate of the individual's behavior does have an effect on access to reinforcement. Each occurrence of the inappropriate behavior brings the individual into contact with the time out contingency. Likewise, in response cost there is a direct relationship between the individual's behavior (response rate) and the availability of reinforcement. With each occurrence of the inappropriate behavior, the individual loses a specific amount of positive reinforcement. Table 21.1 shows the relationship between the target behavior and the reinforcer in each of the three reductive procedures.

TABLE 21.1. Differences between extinction, time out, and response cost.

Procedure	Consequence	Effect on Behavior
Extinction	Withhold S^{R^+}	Gradual decrease
Time out	Lose access to S^{R^+}	Moderate to rapid decrease
Response cost	Withdraw amount of S^{R^+}	Moderate to rapid decrease

There are two basic types of time out—nonexclusion and exclusion. Within each type are several variations that allow the practitioner a degree of flexibility when deciding a course of action for reducing behavior.

NONEXCLUSION TIME OUT

Nonexclusion time out occurs in any one of four ways: planned ignoring, withdrawal of a specific reinforcer, contingent observation, and the time out ribbon. Each variation has a common element: time out is delivered while the individual remains within the original, time in setting.

Planned Ignoring

Planned ignoring occurs when social reinforcers—usually attention, physical contact, or verbal interaction—are removed for a brief period of time, contingent upon the occurrence of an inappropriate behavior. According to Nelson and Rutherford (1983), planned ignoring assumes that the time in setting is reinforcing and that all outside sources of positive reinforcement can be controlled. Operationally, planned ignoring involves systematically looking away from the individual, remaining quiet, and refraining from any interaction whatsoever for a specific period of time. For example, let us suppose that during a group therapy session for drug rehabilitation a client begins to express her fascination with stealing money to buy narcotics. If, at that point, the other members of the group break off contact and do not respond to her verbalizations in any way until her comments are more

consistent with the group's discussion, then planned ignoring is in effect. In this case, since the members of the group participated in the reductive procedure, it would be termed **peer mediated time out** (Kerr & Nelson, 1983).

Planned ignoring can be distinguished from extinction in that extinction withholds reinforcement for previously reinforced behavior, and no time element is involved. Planned ignoring occurs only within the context of time: when the inappropriate behavior is no longer evident, reinforcement resumes. Although planned ignoring has the advantage of being a nonintrusive time out procedure that can be applied quickly and conveniently, its effectiveness as a powerful behavior reduction procedure has not been conclusively demonstrated in the literature (Nelson & Rutherford, 1983).

Withdrawal of a Specific Positive Reinforcer

Bishop and Stumphauzer (1973) demonstrated that the **withdrawal of a specific positive reinforcer** contingent upon an inappropriate behavior decreased the level of that behavior. In their study the contingent termination of television cartoons successfully reduced the frequency of thumb sucking in three young children. Unknown to the children, a remote on/off switch was attached to the television. Baseline data indicated that each child emitted a high rate of thumb sucking while viewing the cartoons. During time out the television was immediately turned off when thumb sucking occurred and was turned back on when thumb sucking stopped. The procedure was effective in reducing thumb sucking not only in the treatment location (an office), but also during a story period at school.

In a group application of this nonexclusionary time out procedure, Ritschl, Mongrella, and Presbie (1972) demonstrated that the out-of-seat behavior of 25 mentally retarded students on a school bus could be suppressed when music was turned off, contingent upon out-of-seat behavior. Music remained available as long as the students were in their seats, but it was switched off for 5 seconds after each episode of out-of-seat behavior. Under this group time out procedure the inappropriate behavior was reduced. Figure 21.1 shows that when group time out was in effect, the mean number of out-of-seat occurrences for the group during the afternoon ride was 2.6. When group time out was not in effect, the out-of-seat behaviors occurred at a frequency of 7.5.

The Ritschl et al. study points out several of the advantages of this approach that are cited by Foxx (1982). First, this approach can be used in an existing environment; special provisions for removing students are not needed. Second, "the presence or absence of the reinforcers provides a clear signal as to when time out is in effect" (p. 81). And students soon

recognize that continued inappropriate behavior results in additional loss of reinforcers.

Mansdorf (1977) used **reinforcer isolation,** a term synonomous with withdrawing a reinforcer, as a time out procedure to decrease the incidence of noncompliant behavior of an institutionalized person. The procedure involved removing personal items from the individual, turning off the television or radio, or removing pillows or bedding from the client's room, contingent upon occurrences of noncompliant behavior. If the woman complied with a request, her personal items were returned, the television or radio was reinstated, and so on. If noncompliant behavior persisted, reinforcer isolation continued. Figure 21.2 shows the number of noncompliant episodes per week. Under the reinforcer isolation procedure the number of compliant incidents was markedly reduced, and the reduction was maintained at a 6-month follow-up.

Contingent Observation

In **contingent observation** the individual is placed in a different part of the setting for a specified period of time with access to rein-

FIGURE 21.1 Daily total frequency of out-of-seat behaviors during afternoon bus rides. Reprinted with permission of authors and publisher from : Ritschl, C., Mongrella, J. & Presbie, R. J. Group time-out from rock and roll music and out of seat behavior of handicapped children while riding a school bus. *Psychological Reports,* 1972, 31, p. 967–973. Fig. 1.)

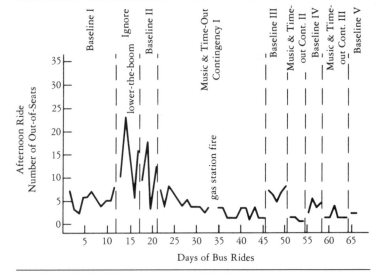

FIGURE 21.2 Number of non-compliant episodes per 5-day work week for each experimental condition. (From "Reinforcer Isolation: An Alternative to Subject Isolation in Time Out from Positive Reinforcement" by I. J. Mansdorf, 1977, *Journal of Behavior Therapy and Experimental Psychiatry, 8,* p. 392. Copyright 1977 by Pergamon Press, Ltd. Reprinted by permission.)

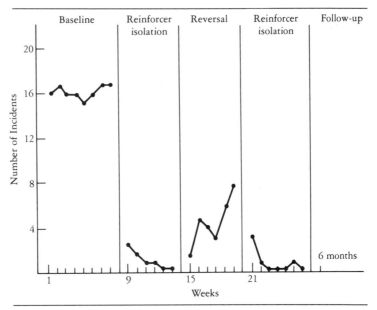

forcement curtailed but with observation of ongoing group activities still possible. A special education teacher who tells one of his students to sit several feet from the group, contingent upon the occurrence of an undesirable behavior, is using contingent observation. Presumably, after being removed from the group and seeing the teacher reinforce other students for appropriate behavior, the student will begin to imitate that appropriate behavior and earn reinforcement when she later returns to the group.

In an often-cited study Porterfield, Herbert-Jackson, and Risley (1976) used contingent observation with 26 preschoolers, aged 21 to 34 months, to reduce five types of disruptive behavior (i.e., aggression, crying, tantrums, destructive use of toys, and creating a dangerous situation). Essentially the contingent observation procedure used in the study required that each time a disruptive action occurred, a day care worker would (1) tell the child what he had done inappropriately (e.g., "No, you cannot take toys from others while they are playing"); (2) remove the child to the side of the room where toys were not located

and tell the child to sit and watch the other children play and ask for things; and (3) return after a minute to see whether the child was ready to rejoin the group. Readiness to rejoin the group was determined by having the day care worker ask the child, "Are you ready to return?" If the child said yes, the caretaker escorted the child back to the group and reinforced him for appropriate behavior immediately. If, however, the child said that he was not ready to return or if he was crying or yelling, the caretaker told the child to continue to sit on the periphery of the activity until he could ask for the toy in a correct way.

In this study contingent observation was compared with a redirection phase in which the caretaker told the child that he had done something wrong, like taking someone's toy, but helped the child to find another toy to play with. The results of the study are shown in Figure 21.3. The data indicate that under the contingent observation condition there were one-half fewer disruptions than under the redirection condition. Also, ratings by parents and other caretakers at the center indicate that

FIGURE 21.3 Number of disruptions and aggressions per child per hour for 50 days in a toddler day care center with follow-up at 1 and 2 months. (From "Contingent Observation: An Effective and Acceptable Procedure for Reducing Disruptive Behavior of Young Children in a Group Setting" by J. K. Porterfield, E. Herbert-Jackson, and T. R. Risley, 1976, *Journal of Applied Behavior Analysis, 9*(1), p. 61. Copyright 1976 by the Society for the Experimental Analysis of Behavior, Inc. Reprinted by permission.)

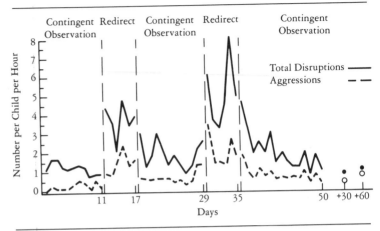

contingent observation was socially acceptable to them as a behavior reduction procedure.

A distinguishing feature of this study was that the end of the time out period was not determined by the passage of time. Rather, time out was over when the child indicated that he was ready to ask for a toy appropriately. Porterfield et al. indicate that excessive time outs were not observed, but they offered no suggestion on dealing with a child who repeatedly said that he was not ready. Although contingent observation has been shown to be effective in reducing inappropriate social behavior, noncompliance, and aggressiveness (Porterfield et al., 1976; Tyroler & Lahey, 1980; Fleece, O'Brien, & Drabman, 1981), its effectiveness with older students, adult populations, or severe behavior problems awaits further investigation.

The Time Out Ribbon

Foxx and Shapiro (1978) used a novel, non-exclusionary time out procedure that they termed the **time out ribbon**. The time out ribbon was a colored ribbon that had become a conditioned reinforcer by being paired with the opportunity to be positively reinforced (e.g., praised) by the teacher. As a conditioned

reinforcer, the ribbon became discriminative for receiving reinforcement. Contingent upon inappropriate behavior, the ribbon was removed from the student, and all forms of social interaction with the offender were terminated for 3 minutes. The student was permitted to remain in the room, however. If inappropriate behavior was still occurring after 3 minutes, the time out was extended until the misbehavior was finished. Figure 21.4 shows that when the time out ribbon plus reinforcement was in effect, the mean percentage of disruptive behavior was markedly reduced for the four students.

EXCLUSION TIME OUT

The distinguishing feature of **exclusion time out** is that the individual is physically removed from the environment for a specified period of time, contingent upon the occurrence of an inappropriate behavior. According to Foxx (1982), exclusion time out can be conduced in classroom settings in three ways: (1) the student can be removed to a special time out room; (2) the student can be separated from the rest of the group by a partition; or

FIGURE 21.4 The mean percent of time spent in disruptive classroom behavior by four subjects. The horizontal broken lines indicate the mean for each condition. The arrow marks a one-day probe (Day 39) during which the time out contingency was suspended. A follow-up observation of the teacher-conducted program occurred on Day 63. (From "The Timeout Ribbon: A Nonexclusionary Timeout Procedure" by R. M. Foxx and S. T. Shapiro, 1978, *Journal of Applied Behavior Analysis, 11*(1), p. 131. Copyright 1978 by the Society for the Experimental Analysis of Behavior, Inc. Reprinted by permission.)

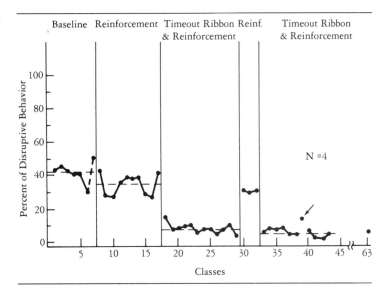

Time Out Room

(3) the student can be placed in the hallway. Each of these variations offers the practitioner one option for operationalizing time out in applied settings.

A time out room is any room outside the individual's normal educational or treatment environment that is devoid of positive reinforcers and in which the individual can be safely placed for a temporary period of time. The time out room should preferably be located near the time in setting and should have a chair and perhaps a table for the individual. It should have adequate lighting and ventilation but should not have other furnishings and features (e.g., pictures on the wall, telephone, breakable windows). Gast and Nelson (1977) provide specific suggestions on the arrangement of time out locations.

The time out room has several advantages that make it attractive to practitioners. First, after a few exposures to the time out room, some students learn to discriminate this room from other rooms in the total setting. The room assumes conditioned aversive properties, thus increasing the probability that the time in setting will be viewed as more desirable. Second, the risk of a student's hurting other students in the time in setting is reduced when the offending student is removed for a period of time. Third, the opportunity to acquire reinforcement during time out is reduced because the environment is physically constructed to minimize such an occurrence.

However, there are several disadvantages that must also be weighed by the practitioner. Foremost is the necessity of taking the student to the time out room. Resistance can be encountered at any step in the removal process, from the time the individual is told to the time she is actually placed in the setting. Practitioners should be prepared to deal with resistant behavior and emotional outbursts when using this approach. In addition, unlike the nonexclusion options mentioned previously, removing an individual from the time in environment prohibits that individual from having access to any of the ongoing instruction. For many individuals in treatment programs or in educational settings, missed instructional time should be minimized. A final disadvantage of the time out room is that the individual can engage in behaviors that should be stopped but that go undetected unless the room is monitored (e.g., self-destructive, self-stimulatory behaviors). Using a partition in the classroom helps to eliminate this disadvantage.

Using a Partition

According to Foxx (1982), time out using a partition is similar to time out in a self-contained classroom, except that the opportunity to obtain reinforcement illegitimately is greater when the individual remains within the time in setting. To the extent that the individual is able to obtain reinforcement while behind the partition, the powerfulness of this variation is compromised. For example, if a teacher tells a student to go behind the partition in the classroom for 5 minutes because of his disruptive verbal behavior and the student continues to make his disruptive verbalizations from behind the partition, he is likely to continue to receive attention from either the teacher or other students. If he does receive reinforcement from one of these sources, it is unlikely that the disruptive verbalizations will decrease.

Hallway Time Out

Teachers, in particular, have long used the approach of sending students out into the hallway, contingent upon disruptive behavior. Although it shares the advantages of the variations just mentioned, this approach is not highly recommended for two reasons: (1) the student can obtain reinforcement from a multitude of sources (e.g., students in other rooms, individuals walking in the hallway) and (2) there is increased likelihood that the student will try to escape if she was combative on her way to time out. Even with the door of the classroom open, teachers are often too busy with activities in the time in setting to effectively monitor the student in time out. This approach might be effective with younger children who follow directions, but it is clearly inappropriate for any child who cannot follow the teacher's directives.

DESIRABLE ASPECTS OF TIME OUT

Ease of Application

Time out, especially the nonexclusion variation, can be easily applied in most settings. Even physically removing a student from the environment can be accomplished with relative ease if the teacher acts in a businesslike fashion and does not attempt to embarrass the student. Issuing a direction privately (e.g., "Sarah, you have disrupted Bob twice; do not do so again") (O'Leary, Kaufman, Kass, & Drabman, 1970) can help the teacher handle a student who has misbehaved but who does not want to leave the room. If the behavior warrants time out, the teacher must insist that the student leave; however, that insistence should be communicated at close range so that the student is not placed in a position of challenging the teacher openly in order to save face with a peer group. Gast and Nelson (1977) describe the administration of time out.

> Verbal instruction is the preferred method, as this tactic avoids the necessity of teachers modeling aggressive behaviors, is less disruptive, and requires less adult-child interaction. Furthermore, this method places more responsibility for self control on the child. The actual method of administration will be a function of the degree of resistance offered by the child. In the case of such high intensity behaviors as kicking, hitting, or scratching, immediate physical removal may be dictated. (p. 459)

Still, the practitioner must be cognizant of the fact that verbal interaction can inadvertently reinforce the behavior it was intended to terminate.

> It is possible that rather than terminating a particular aversive behavior the prompts may serve to reinforce those same aversive behaviors. Thus, a behavioral chain may develop: that is, to receive

attention a client performs deviant or antisocial behavior. Subsequently the deviant behavior sets the occasion for a response in the form of a prompt.... The prompt itself, as well as the social interaction following, may then reinforce the initial response in the chain which occasioned the prompt. (Burleigh & Marholin, 1977, p. 112)

Acceptability

According to Kazdin (1980b), the acceptability of time out refers to the judgments that professionals and nonprofessionals make regarding its appropriateness, fairness, effectiveness, and ease of application. The results of Kazdin's (1980b) study show that on each of these dimensions time out has met the criterion of acceptability, especially when compared to other forms of reductive treatment (e.g., drug therapy, shock therapy). In another study Kazdin (1980a) found that nonexclusion time out and DRI were preferable to exclusion time out, but the acceptability of the latter could be improved by presenting it with a contingency contract or as a backup to other forms of previously administered time out.

Despite the data on acceptability Brantner and Doherty (1983) recommend that public acceptability be assessed prior to implementing time out because of its potential for determining the overall effectiveness of the technique.

Rapid Suppression of Behavior

Time out, when effectively implemented, usually suppresses the target behavior rapidly. Sometimes only a few applications are needed to achieve an acceptable level. Other reductive procedures (e.g., extinction, DRL) also produce decreases in behavior, but they are time-consuming. Many times the practitioner does not have the luxury of waiting several days or a week for a behavior to decrease. In such instances time out merits consideration.

Generalizable

There is some evidence to indicate that the effects of time out administered in one setting

or to one group will also be observed in other settings or with other groups. Bishop and Stumphouzer (1973) demonstrated that when thumb sucking was reduced with time out in a treatment office, it also decreased for the same children during story time in a nursery school. Wilson, Robertson, Herlong, and Haynes (1979) found that when time out was applied to one child's aggressive behavior, the aggressive behavior of untreated children was reduced concomitantly. Figure 21.5 shows the percentage of aggressive behavior for the target child and his 13 kindergarten classmates. The data indicate reduced percentages of aggressive behavior for both sets of children under time out.

Combined Applications

Time out is easy to combine with other procedures. When it is combined with behavior-strengthening procedures, desirable behavior can be increased simultaneously with the decrease in misbehavior. As Baer, Rowbury, and Baer (1973) found, differential reinforcement for compliance coupled with time out for noncompliance increased compliant responses to nearly 100%.

More recently, Wahler and Fox (1980) demonstrated that a treatment approach using reinforcement for solitary play was more effective than one stressing reinforcement for social interaction; but in reducing oppositional and aggressive behavior in four young children, the positive effects were short-lived. When reinforcement for solitary play was combined with time out, toy play increased and oppositional behavior decreased. Also, when the combined contingency was in effect, the parents' ratings of their children's behavior improved.

Fleece, O'Brien, and Drabman (1981), in a replication of the Porterfield et al. (1976) study, compared contingent observation time out coupled with general modeling instructions and contingent observation coupled with specific modeling instructions, in an attempt to reduce the noncompliant behavior of a 5-year-old inner city child. The results of the study

FIGURE 21.5 Percentage of intervals of aggressive behavior for the target child and untreated classmates across the four phases. Missing data points at Days 8, 13, and 14 represent absences on the part of the target child. (From C. C. Wilson, S. J. Robertson, L. H. Herlong, and S. N. Haynes, "Vicarious Effects of Time-Out in the Modification of Aggression in the Classroom," *Behavior Modification,* Vol. 3, No. 1 (January, 1979), p. 105. Copyright © 1979 by Sage Publications, Inc. Reprinted by permission of Sage Publications, Inc.)

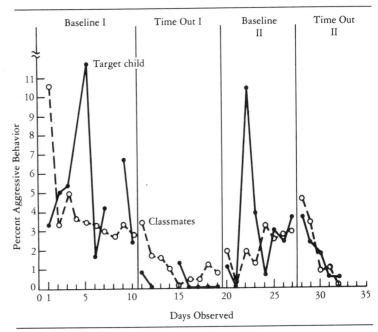

show that contingent observation can be successfully combined with other procedures to produce desirable effects.

USING TIME OUT EFFECTIVELY IN APPLIED SETTINGS

Effective implementation of time out requires the practitioner to make several decisions prior to, during, and after using time out. Figure 21.6 shows a time out implementation checklist designed by Powell and Powell (1982) to aid in the decision-making process. This section expands on the major points underlying some of the decisions.

Consider Other Options

Although time out has been shown to be effective in reducing behavior, it should not be the method of first choice. Practitioners faced with the task of reducing behavior should first consider techniques such as extinction or posi-

tive reductive procedures (e.g., DRO, DRI). Only when these less intrusive procedures have failed should time out be considered (Powell & Powell, 1982).

Decide on Nonexclusion or Exclusion Time Out

Institutional constraints or school board policy help the practitioner decide on the type of time out that should be used. In addition, a lack of building space may prohibit exclusionary forms of time out. One rule of thumb in deciding which type to use is again to use the least intrusive approach first, usually a nonexclusionary procedure.

Obtain Permission

Without question one of the more important tasks that a practitioner must perform is to obtain permission prior to using time out, especially the exclusionary variations. Because the potential for abuse of time out is high (e.g., leaving the individual in time out too long,

Step	Task	Date Completed	Teacher's Initials
1.	Try less aversive techniques and document results.	_____	_____
2.	Operationally define disruptive behaviors.	_____	_____
3.	Record baseline on target behaviors.	_____	_____
4.	Consider present levels of reinforcement (strengthen if necessary).	_____	_____
5.	Decide on timeout procedure to be used.	_____	_____
6.	Decide on timeout area.	_____	_____
7.	Decide on length of timeout.	_____	_____
8.	Decide on command to be used to place child in timeout.	_____	_____
9.	Set specific criteria that will signal discontinuance of timeout.	_____	_____
10.	Set dates for formal review of the timeout procedure.	_____	_____
11.	Specify back-up procedures for typical timeout problems.	_____	_____
12.	Write up the entire procedure.	_____	_____
13.	Have the procedure reviewed by peers and supervisors.	_____	_____
14.	Secure parental/guardian approval and include the written program in the child's IEP.	_____	_____
15.	Explain procedure to the student and class (if appropriate).	_____	_____
16.	Implement the procedure, take data, and review progress daily.	_____	_____
17.	Formally review procedure as indicated.	_____	_____
18.	Modify the procedure as needed.	_____	_____
19.	Record results for future teachers/programs.	_____	_____

FIGURE 21.6 Time out implementation checklist. (From "The Use and Abuse of Using the Timeout Procedure for Disruptive Pupils" by T. H. Powell and I. Q. Powell, 1982, *The Pointer, 26*(2), p. 21. Copyright 1982 by *The Pointer*. Reprinted by permission.)

continuing to use time out when it is not effective), practitioners must obtain administrative approval before using it. However, interactions happen so fast in most applied settings that obtaining permission instance-by-instance would be unduly cumbersome. A preferred method is for the practitioner, in cooperation with administrators, to decide beforehand the type of time out that will be used (e.g., nonexclusion or exclusion) and the behaviors for which it will be used.

Define Behaviors Leading to Time Out

Before time out is implemented, all of the appropriate parties must be informed of the behaviors that will lead to time out. If a teacher decides to use time out, she should describe in specific, observable terms those behaviors that will be timed out: not "disruptive behavior" but "out-of-seat" or "calling out."

Explain the Time Out Rules

In addition to posting the behaviors that will lead to time out, the teacher should also state the rules. These rules should focus on the initial duration of time out and the exit criteria (i.e., rules that determine when time out is over and what happens if ongoing inappropriate behavior is occurring when time out is over).

In most applied settings such as schools, treatment centers, and institutions the initial duration of time out should be short. A period of 2 to 10 minutes is sufficient, although a short duration may be ineffective initially if an individual has had a history of longer time out periods. Gast and Nelson (1977), in their review of the time out literature, indicate that time out periods exceeding 15 minutes are not likely to be effective; but if they are already implemented, the practitioner should consult with supervisory staff to determine the advisability of continuing them.

Long periods of time out are counterproductive for several reasons. First, some individuals develop a tolerance for the longer duration and find ways to obtain reinforcement during time out. This situation is likely to occur with individuals with a history of self-stimulatory behavior. The longer the duration of time out, the more opportunity there is to engage in reinforcing activities (e.g., self-stimulation) and the less effective time out becomes. Also, long periods of time out keep the individual away from the educational, therapeutic, or family time in environment in which the opportunity to earn reinforcers is available. Thus, although the data appear to be mixed on the optimum duration of time out to use in a given situation, Brantner and Doherty's (1983) observation seems to have sound merit. That is, short durations of time out have been shown to be effective; and given the undesirable practical, legal, and ethical aspects of longer periods of time out (perhaps in excess of 30 minutes), a prudent initial course of action is for the practitioner to use relatively short time out periods, which are implemented consistently (Burchard & Barrera, 1972).

There seems to be consensus among applied behavior analysts with respect to exit criteria: if an individual misbehaves at the point of scheduled termination of time out, the contingency should be continued until the inappropriate behavior ceases (Mansdorf, 1977; Foxx, 1982; Brantner & Doherty, 1983). Thus, the decision to terminate a time out should not be based exclusively on the passage of time; an improved behavioral condition should also be used as a criterion for ending time out. Under no conditions should an individual be removed from time out if any inappropriate behavior is occurring.

If the practitioner suspects that the inappropriate behavior that led to time out may occur at the point of scheduled termination, two strategies can be tried. First, the practitioner can tell the individual that the scheduled time out period (e.g., 5 minutes) will not begin until the inappropriate behavior has ceased. The second alternative is to simply extend the time period. Clark, Rowbury, Baer, and Baer (1973) suggest that a "changeover delay"—a short extension of time (perhaps 15 seconds) that permits the inappropriate behavior to cease—can serve a useful purpose.

Apply Consistently

Each occurrence of the undesirable behavior should lead to time out. If a teacher, parent, or therapist is not in a position to deliver the time out consequence after each occurrence of the target behavior, it may be better to use an alternative reductive technique. Using time out only on occasion leads to student or client confusion about which behaviors are acceptable and which are unacceptable.

Reinforce the Time In Environment

The time in environment must be reinforcing if time out is to be effective (Nelson & Rutherford, 1983); but as Plummer, Baer, and LeBlanc (1977) have shown, simply having some reinforcers in the setting does not guarantee that the total environment is positive. Solnick et al. (1977) showed that enriched time in settings are more effective than impoverished ones in reducing inappropriate behavior.

Reinforce Appropriate Behavior

In making the time in environment reinforcing, the practitioner should seek ways to reinforce behaviors that are incompatible with behaviors that lead to time out. Appropriate behaviors will increase only with reinforcement.

Obtain Reliability Data

Most applied researchers recommend that reliability data be obtained periodically throughout an intervention to determine whether changes observed by the experimenter are independently recorded by observers (Tawney & Gast, 1983). Reliability is often thought of as the independent assessment of the dependent variable (e.g., the amount of behavior, its duration, its frequency, and so on). However, as Nelson and Rutherford (1983) indicate, time out can be applied incorrectly in at least two ways (i.e., using time out alone and applying it so late that other operants, like tantrums, surface). Consequently, the practitioner must also obtain reliability data for the independent variable as well. Procedural reliability data tell whether the treatment was implemented as it was designed to be implemented. Only with these data can there be assurance that the procedure will not continue unnecessarily or incorrectly.

Evaluate Effectiveness

Universally educators and researchers call for the regular evaluation of the use of time out in applied settings (Gast & Nelson, 1977; Foxx, 1982; Brantner & Doherty, 1983). At the very least data need to be obtained on the inappropriate behavior that initially led to time out. If time out was effective, the level of that behavior should be substantially reduced, and that reduction should be noticed by other persons in the environment (Wolf, 1978). For legal and ethical reasons it is suggested that additional records be kept documenting the use of time out and the duration of each time out procedure and describing the individual's behavior before, during, and after time out (Stolz, 1978; Nelson & Rutherford, 1983; Foxx, 1982). Powell and Powell (1982) indicate that a formal review

should be conducted 1 week after time out is instituted to determine whether it is being as effective as it should be.

In addition to the target behavior, it is sometimes beneficial to collect data on collateral behaviors. An improvement in another behavior that was not targeted for treatment but that coincided with intervention for a related behavior would give evidence of the generalizability of the intervention. As Wilson et al. (1979) demonstrated, it is possible for collateral changes to occur either within or across subjects. Data might also be collected on any unexpected or side effects of time out. For instance, it is possible for time out to produce emotional operants (i.e., crying, aggressiveness, withdrawal) that might overshadow any positive gains intended.

LEGAL AND ETHICAL ISSUES OF TIME OUT

The use of time out in applied settings has been much discussed. Although litigation surrounding the use of this procedure has focused primarily on institutionalized populations (e.g., *Wyatt v. Stickney,* 1972; *Morales v. Turman,* 1973), the rulings in these cases have had a profound effect on the use of time out in other settings. It should be noted that the issue before the court in these cases was the protection of client rights and the degree of public acceptability of the time out procedure (Budd & Baer, 1976; Kazdin, 1980a). Because both cases have ruled on the legality of time out, particularly the exclusion variation (termed *seclusion* in these cases), each case will be briefly discussed.

In *Wyatt v. Stickney* (1972), a class action suit on behalf of mentally retarded residents in an Alabama institution, the court ruled in part that an individual's rights to treatment include a right to be free from isolation. However, the ruling also included language that permitted the use of time out in a behavioral shaping program as long as the program was closely monitored. According to Budd and Baer (1976), the court appeared to be ruling that seclusion, the legal analogue to exclusionary time out, was unconstitutional because it denied an individual her right to treatment; but the court simultaneously sanctioned its use under professional supervision.

In *Morales v. Turman* (1973), a case involving an incarcerated juvenile delinquent, the court distinguished between dormitory confinement, leaving a resident alone in a locked room within his own domicile; solitary confinement, leaving a resident alone in a locked room outside his domicile; and seclusion, leaving a resident alone in a locked building. The court ruled that dormitory confinement was permissible to suppress behaviors that were imminently destructive to persons or property or that created substantial disruption; but the

court set a 50-minute limit on confinement (Gast & Nelson, 1977).

At least two conclusions have been drawn from the rulings in these two landmark court cases. First, removing an individual to a locked room is now considered illegal unless it can be demonstrated that the seclusion is part of an overall treatment plan and unless the program is carefully and closely monitored. Second, the duration of time out has been clearly defined by both rulings to extend no longer than 1 hour. Extensions of this time limit can be obtained but only from a duly constituted review committee.

According to Gast and Nelson (1977) many states have adopted a set of procedural guidelines for time out authored by May et al. (1975). On the whole, these guidelines indicate the practitioner should assess, prior to using time out, its effectiveness, public acceptability, social impact, and potential for abuse or mismanagement (Brantner & Doherty, 1983).

SUMMARY

Definition of Time Out

1 Time out from positive reinforcement, or simply time out, is defined as the withdrawal of the opportunity to earn reinforcement or the loss of access to positive reinforcement for a specified period of time, contingent upon the occurrence of a behavior; the effect is to reduce the future probability of that behavior.

2 Time out from positive reinforcement is a Type II punisher.

Distinguishing Extinction and Response Cost from Time Out

3 Extinction, response cost, and time out reduce behavior. In time out, access to additional reinforcers is contingent upon the individual's behavior; the rate of behavior does affect access to reinforcement.

Nonexclusion Time Out

4 Nonexclusion time out occurs in any one of four ways: planned ignoring, withdrawal of a specific positive reinforcer, contingent observation, or the time out ribbon. In each of these variations the individual remains within the original setting.

Exclusion Time Out

5 Exclusion time out occurs in any one of three ways: a time out room, a partition, or hallway time out.

Desirable Aspects of Time Out

6 Time out has several desirable aspects. It is easy to apply, it is acceptable to the public in some forms, it rapidly suppresses behavior,

its effects are generalizable to other individuals or behaviors, and it can be combined with other procedures.

Using Time Out Effectively in Applied Settings

7   When using time out in applied settings, the practitioner should (1) consider other reductive procedures first; (2) decide on non-exclusion or exclusion time out; (3) obtain permission; (4) define the behavior(s) that will lead to time out; (5) explain the time out rules; (6) apply time out consistently; (7) examine the quantity and quality of reinforcers in the time in setting; (8) reinforce appropriate behavior; (9) obtain reliability data; and (10) evaluate the effectiveness of time out.

Legal and Ethical Issues of Time Out

8   Time out can be a legitimate procedure to use to reduce behavior if it is used in conjunction with a behavioral shaping program and is closely monitored and reviewed.

9   The duration of time out should not exceed 1 hour. In most cases 5 to 10 minutes are sufficient.

10   Guidelines for using time out, which are now widely adopted by the states, indicate that the practitioner should assess, before using time out, its effectiveness, public acceptability, social impact, and potential for abuse or mismanagement.

22

Response Cost

KEY TERMS

Response cost
Bonus response cost

Inappropriate behavior often needs to be suppressed quickly. Teachers who need to reduce an inappropriate social behavior in the classroom may find response cost a functional alternative to time out from positive reinforcement because confrontations with students are avoided. Also, response cost may be a treatment option when other reductive procedures would take too long or when the practitioner is constrained by the type of punishment that can be used.

This chapter defines response cost, lists its desirable aspects, suggests how to implement it efficiently and effectively, states criteria for using it, and presents considerations for using it in applied settings. The chapter concludes with guidelines for using this procedure.

DEFINITION OF RESPONSE COST

Response cost is a form of punishment in which the loss of a specific amount of reinforcement occurs, contingent upon the performance of an inappropriate behavior, and results in the decreased probability of the future occurrence of the behavior. According to Foxx (1982), response cost can be classified as a Type II punisher and is defined in the same probabilistic sense as other reductive procedures. If the future probability of the punished behavior is reduced by the response-contingent withdrawal of positive reinforcers, then response cost is in effect. However, if the removal of the reinforcer increases the level of the behavior, response cost has not been

---

This chapter was written by Timothy E. Heron.

executed even though procedurally it may have been implemented. This distinction between procedural correctness and functional effect is the key aspect in the definition of response cost.

There are many examples of the use of response cost in applied settings (Walker, Hops, & Fiegenbaum, 1976; Walker, Hops, & Greenwood, 1981; Rapport, Murphy, & Bailey, 1982; Sindelar, Honsaker, & Jenkins, 1982). The teacher who reduces the length of recess time contingent upon disruptive behavior is using a response cost procedure. The psychiatric nurse who removes already-earned tokens from a patient contingent upon the occurrence of work refusal is also using a response cost procedure. Each occurrence of the inappropriate behavior results in the loss of a specific amount of positive reinforcement already held by the individual.

DESIRABLE ASPECTS OF REPONSE COST

Response cost has several features that make it a desirable procedure to use in applied settings. First, like other forms of punishment, response cost usually produces a moderate to rapid decrease in behavior. The practitioner does not have to wait a long time to access the relative effects of response cost. If the procedure is going to be effective, it will show an effect after a fair trial—usually within 3 to 5 days (cf. Lovitt, 1977).

In addition, response cost is a convenient approach to use, especially in the classroom. Leonardi, Duggan, Hoffheins, and Axelrod (1972) used response cost effectively in the classroom by listing the number of minutes of free time to be lost after each occurrence of the inappropriate behavior. Such a procedure has the obvious advantage of avoiding a direct confrontation with a student or a group of students. Students know beforehand via classroom rules or contracts what behavior will

produce "fines."[1] And the teacher does not have to constantly reprimand students. Each fine that is levied indicates that a positive reinforcer has been lost and serves to remind students that future occurrences of the same behavior will result in the same consequence. Furthermore, a response cost chart with associated rules can be positioned anywhere in the classroom, making it convenient for teachers to use.

Figure 22.1 shows a sample response cost chart as it might be used in a classroom or tutorial setting. To implement the response cost procedure, the teacher can simply write a column of decreasing numbers on the board. Whenever a disruptive behavior occurs, the teacher crosses off the highest remaining number. If the teacher places the numbers 15 through 0 on the board and five disruptive behaviors occur, the students have 10 minutes of free time left that day. According to Axelrod (1983), the teacher can identify the offending student per occurrence by placing her initials or name next to the stricken number.

Hall and Copeland (1972) found that the response-contingent removal of slips of paper bearing the student's name had a reductive effect on the number of complaints an emotionally disturbed boy emitted. Prior to reading and math the teacher placed five slips of colored paper bearing the boy's name on his desk. Each time the boy complained during reading or math, a slip of paper was removed. Figure 22.2 shows that when the response cost approach was in effect, complaining decreased markedly; and when response cost was not in effect, this behavior increased.

One final desirable aspect of response cost is that it can be combined with other procedures in a comprehensive behavior change program. For example, Walker et al. (1978) and Walker et al. (1981) incorporated response

---

[1]Readers interested in learning more about posting classroom contingencies and rules are referred to Kerr and Nelson (1983).

15 T.H.
14 W.H.
13 J.O.
12
11
10
9
8
7
6
5
4
3
2
1
0

FIGURE 22.1 A sample response cost chart showing the total number of minutes of free time remaining after three rule infractions.

cost into their social skills training program. Included in the program, in addition to response cost, were rule statements and reinforcers at school and at home to reduce aggressive behavior in primary-grade children. Walker et al. (1983) incorporated response cost into a package including positive reinforcement, modeling, and direct instruction for acceptable social behavior and then incorporated the package into the ACCEPTS curriculum (A Curriculum for Children's Effective Peer and Teacher Skills) to improve the social behavior skills of handicapped students.

Even though response cost can be combined with other procedures, the relative contribution of these procedures in reducing certain classes of undesirable behavior remains unclear. Gresham (1979) compared response cost and time out, both alone and in combination, with a group of developmentally handicapped students. Figure 22.3 shows the daily average of noncompliance with teacher commands. Baseline data indicate that 48% of teacher commands resulted in noncompliance. During the response cost (RC) condition, in which students lost a token contingent upon noncompliance, the percentage of noncompliance decreased to 11%. When response cost was combined with time out (RC and TO), a condition in which the student was removed from the classroom for 1 minute and also lost the token, noncompliance occurred 13% of the time. In the replication of each of these conditions—RC and RC plus TO—the percentage of noncompliance was 5% and 12%, respectively. Follow-up conducted 3 months later in another classroom showed the percentage of noncompliance at 11%. The author concludes that time out was not necessary for reducing certain classes of behavior, although analysis of the data did not permit specification of those classes. Thus, it remains an empirical question whether combining response cost with other reductive procedures produces sufficient decreases in behavior to warrant that combination.

Response cost can also be combined with reinforcement. Axelrod (1973) reports the results of a study conducted at the secondary level that combined response cost and token reinforcement. During baseline the teacher counted the number of derogatory comments made by the class. Because students had been earning credit points that were later exchanged for grades, the teacher decided to remove credit points during intervention for each derogatory verbalization made by a class member. And because one particular student's remarks were especially offensive, the teacher placed an additional contingency on him. If the entire class period passed without a derogatory remark from that student, the whole class would earn an extra credit point. Thus, a dual point system was in effect: students lost points for derogatory remarks (reponse cost) but were

FIGURE 22.2 The frequency of Billy's complaints during the 30-minute reading and arithmetic periods. (From "Modification of Disrupting and Talking-Out Behavior with the Teacher as Observer and Experimenter" by R. V. Hall, R. Fox, D. Williard, L. Goldsmith, M. Emerson, M. Owen, E. Porcia, and R. Davis, 1970, paper presented at the American Educational Research Association Convention, Minneapolis. Reprinted with permission.)

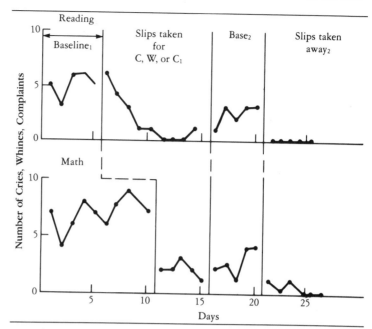

able to earn points contingent upon the absence of derogatory remarks by one individual student (reinforcement). The results were impressive. Derogatory remarks decreased from an average of 18 during baseline to 2.6 during the points conditions. In addition, the student for whom the individual contingency was implemented improved his report card grade.

Phillips (1968) and Phillips, Phillips, Fixsen, and Wolf (1971) describe how token reinforcement and token response cost were used jointly to modify the predelinquent behaviors of adolescent boys at Achievement Place, a community-based treatment facility. The boys earned tokens in varying amounts for appropriate behavior, such as good grooming, completed homework, household chores, reading, punctuality, and watching the news on television. Points were lost for such behaviors as arguing, speaking aggressively, stealing, cheating, and receiving failing grades. Points were exchanged weekly for reinforcers that could be obtained in the facility (e.g., games, TV allowance, permission to stay up late). The token system was structured so that the boys could obtain all of the reinforcers each week if they

performed their tasks and had a minimal loss of tokens resulting from fines.

The series of Achievement Place studies conducted by Phillips and his associates show convincingly that token reinforcement plus token response cost can be successful in improving academic and self-help behaviors and in decreasing inappropriate social behaviors. According to Phillips et al., the token system is the work horse of the Achievement Place program. It is one means to teach functional independent skills that can be maintained after discharge by naturally occurring community reinforcers.

Combining token response cost and token reinforcement has not been restricted to school-aged populations or predelinquent adolescents. Winkler (1970) demonstrated how these two conditions could be combined to manage the behavior of 31 adult chronic psychiatric patients. Patients earned tokens for performing a wide variety of appropriate physical and self-help behaviors (e.g., exercising, bed making, dressing). Tokens were lost for noisy and violent behavior. The results of the reversal design study show that acceptable behavior

FIGURE 22.3 Daily average of noncompliance with teacher commands. (From "Comparison of Response Cost and Time out in a Special Education Setting" by F. M. Gresham, 1979, *Journal of Special Education, 13*(2), p. 204. Copyright 1979 by Buttonwood Farms. Reprinted by permission.)

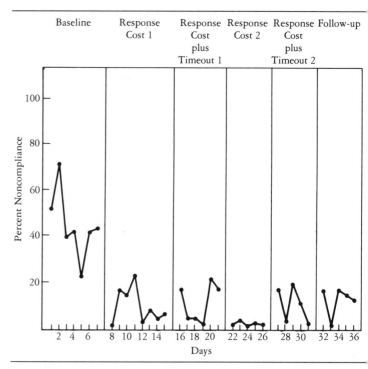

improved when tokens were made contingent upon it; and violent behavior decreased when tokens were removed because of it.

Likewise, Reisinger (1972) demonstrated that a combination of token acquisition and response cost was effective in increasing smiling and decreasing crying in a 20-year-old institutionalized female. In a reversal design study the patient, who had been diagnosed as anxiety depressive, received one token for each occurrence of smiling and lost one token for each crying episode. Under this contingency smiling increased and crying decreased markedly. In a later phase of the study, the tokens were gradually removed, and previous gains were successfully maintained by socially reinforcing smiling and ignoring crying.

Kaufman and O'Leary (1972) compared token reinforcement, response cost, and self-evaluation procedures with 16 disruptive students residing in a psychiatric hospital. The students began each of three 15-minute rating periods with no tokens. They could earn a maximum of 10 tokens during each period by following the classroom rules, which related to unauthorized movement, vocalizations, or off-task behaviors. In the response cost class students began each of three 15-minute periods with 10 tokens, which they could keep if they did not violate a rule. Each rule infraction resulted in the loss of 1 token; a maximum of 10 tokens could be lost each period. The results indicate that both procedures—the reinforcer alone and the reinforcer plus response cost—were effective in reducing disruptive behavior. In both conditions the students made significant advances in academic areas, gaining one-half year in reading over the course of the 10-week study. No measurable differences were found between the two procedures.

McLaughlin and Malaby (1972) conducted a similar study comparing the differential effects of response cost and reinforcement with 25 ifth- and sixth-grade students. In the first condition of the study, students lost points for inappropriate verbalizations in class. In the next condition they earned points for quiet behavior. These two conditions were successively reinstated, and the data were analyzed using an A-B-A-B reversal design. The results indicate that fewer inappropriate verbalizations occurred when students earned points for quiet behavior than when they lost points. In other words, the number of inappropriate verbalizations was lower under positive reinforcement conditions than under response cost conditions.

Finally, Iwata and Bailey (1974) compared the effects of positive reinforcement and response cost procedures on the social and academic behavior of two groups of elementary special education students. Their study gave students in one condition the opportunity to choose either reinforcer or cost consequences: students could start the class session with either zero tokens and a chance to earn them or a given number of tokens and a chance to lose them. The results show no differential effects as a function of either contingency; students found the response cost consequence to be as desirable as the reinforcer contingency. The teacher's use of approval statements with students may have been slightly higher under the reinforcer conditions, but Iwata and Bailey indicate that such a conclusion must be reached cautiously because of the low rates of teacher approval throughout the study.

In sum, the findings of studies comparing response cost and reinforcement have been mixed. Several other factors may have to be considered before a final determination can be made as to whether either procedure is more efficacious than the other. For example, negative side effects (e.g., emotional outbursts, aggressiveness) were generally not found by Kaufman and O'Leary (1972), McLaughlin and Malaby (1972), or Iwata and Bailey (1974). Such side effects might become evident, however, if procedural changes are made in the removal of more powerful reinforcers or the shortening of the delay between occurrence of an inappropriate behavior and removal of a token. In almost all reported studies, with the exception of Sindelar et al. (1982), there was a considerable time lag between the occurrence of the inappropriate behavior and token removal. In the Sindelar et al. study response cost occurred immediately after the undesirable behavior; and one finding was that the more temporally precise the application of the response cost was, the more effective it was. As a general rule, we recommend that reinforcement of appropriate behavior be paired with a response cost procedure. However, response cost should not be used as the sole approach to modifying behavior because a Type II punishment procedure is not able to teach new behavior. We suggest combining any response cost procedure with DRI or DRO.

IMPLEMENTING A RESPONSE COST CONTINGENCY

Procedurally, response cost can be implemented in any one of four ways. First, as discussed previously, response cost can be used in tandem with a reinforcement contingency. For example, a student might earn points for improved academic performance and simultaneously lose points for instances of inappropriate behavior. A student could receive a point for each of 10 academic assignments completed during the morning but lose a point for each of six occurrences of calling out. The student would net a total of four points.

The second way that response cost can be implemented is by fining the individual a specific amount. A residential client who loses minutes of free time for each occurrence of noncompliant behavior is an example. In this case response cost is applied to reinforcers the individual already has access to (e.g., minutes of free time). There are situations in which removing basic reinforcers (e.g., food, free time) from an individual would be considered legally and ethically inappropriate and/or undesirable. To avoid any potential problems, practitioners can obtain permission from the appropriate human rights review committee or can modify the response cost contingency using a third option.[2]

In the third variation of response cost, the practitioner makes additional reinforcers available to the individual noncontingently, specifically for removal via response cost. For example, if a teacher normally schedules 15 minutes of recess each morning for his class of emotionally disturbed adolescents, in a **bonus response cost** variation (Sulzer-Azaroff & Mayer, 1977) he would make an additional 15 minutes of recess available, subject to removal in prespecified amounts if classroom rules are violated. The students retain the regularly scheduled recess, but any bonus time depends on the number of rule infractions.

There are at least two advantages of this third procedural variation of response cost: (1) if all of the tokens are not lost, the remaining ones can be traded for backup reinforcers, thus adding a reinforcement component that is incorporated into many programs (e.g., Walker, 1983); and (2) existing reinforcers are not removed, thereby lessening legal and ethical concerns. The following vignette illustrates how a father might implement a bonus response cost procedure with his two sons to reduce their fighting at dinner time.

Father: Boys, I'd like to talk to you.

Tom and *Pete:* OK.

Father: We have got to find a way to stop the fighting and squabbling at dinner time. The way you two go at each other upsets everyone in the family, and I can't eat my dinner in peace.

Tom: Well, Pete usually starts it.

Pete: I do not!

Tom: You do, too . . .

---

[2]Budd and Baer (1976) and Stolz and Associates (1978) provide an excellent discussion of the legal and ethical considerations of using punishment procedures, especially with institutionalized or residential populations.

Father: (Interrupting) That's enough! This is just what I mean, nit-picking at each other. It's ridiculous and it's going to stop. I've given it some thought, and here's what we're going to do. Since each of you earns an allowance of $3.00 per week for doing household chores, I was tempted to take it away from you the next time either of you got into a fight. But I've decided against doing that. Instead, I'm going to make an additional $3.00 available to each of you, but for each sarcastic comment or squabble you get into at the dinner table, you'll lose $.50 of that extra money. So if you act properly, you'll get an additional $3.00. If you have two fights, you'll lose $1.00 and only get $2.00. Do you understand?

Pete: How about if Tom starts something and I don't?

Father: Whoever does any fighting or squabbling loses $.50. If Tom starts something and you ignore him, only he loses. Tom, the same thing holds true for you. If Pete starts something and you ignore him, only Pete loses. One more thing. Dinner time starts when you are called to the table; it ends when you are excused from the table. Any other questions?

Tom: When do we begin?

Father: We'll begin tonight.

It is important to note here that the father described the contingencies completely to his sons. He told them what would happen if no fights occurred, and he told them what would happen if one brother attempted to start a fight but the other ignored him. In addition, he clearly defined when dinner time would begin and end. Each of these explanations was necessary for a complete understanding of behavioral consequences. Presumably, the father will also praise his sons for their appropriate mealtime behaviors so that they are reinforced and strengthened.

The final variation of the use of response cost involves group consequences. That is, contingent upon the inappropriate behavior of any member of a group, the whole group loses a specific amount of reinforcement. Barrish, Saunders, and Wolf's (1969) Good Behavior Game and Axelrod's (1973) study serve as illustrations of how response cost can be applied to groups. Chapter 25, which discusses group contingencies, presents this variation of response cost in more depth.

CRITERIA FOR USING RESPONSE COST OR BONUS RESPONSE COST

Which variation of response cost would be the most effective in an initial behavior reduction program is usually an empirical question. However, three criteria can help the practitioner decide. First, the least aversive procedure should be attempted initially. The third variation described, bonus response cost, may be the least aversive of the variations because the reinforcers are not deducted directly from the individual; instead they are lost from a pool of potentially available (i.e., bonus) reinforcers.

The second criterion is similar to the first and can be stated in the form of a question: What is the potential for aggressive, emotional outbursts? Students would probably find it more agreeable to lose reinforcers from an available reserve than from their earnings. Consequently, a bonus response cost procedure might be less likely to induce aggressive or emotional outbursts, side effects to be aware of with any punishment procedure (Pazulinec, Meyerrose, & Sajwaj, 1983).

A third criterion is the need to reduce the behavior quickly. Combative or noncompliant behavior may be more appropriately suppressed with response cost consequences because the contingency directly reduces the subject's available reinforcers. The response-contingent withdrawal of reinforcers in this case might serve to reduce the behavior quickly and markedly.

CONSIDERATION IN THE USE OF RESPONSE COST IN APPLIED SETTINGS

Increased Aggression

Response-contingent withdrawal of positive reinforcers can increase verbal and physical aggressiveness. The student who loses several tokens within a short time period may verbally or physically assault the teacher. According to Walker (1983), emotional behaviors should be ignored whenever possible if they accompany the implementation of a response cost contingency.

Avoidance

The setting in which response cost occurs or the person who administers it can become a conditioned aversive stimulus. If this situation occurs in school, the student may avoid the classroom or teacher by being absent or tardy. A teacher can reduce the likelihood of becoming a conditioned aversive stimulus by contingently delivering positive reinforcement for appropriate behavior.

Spillover

The response-contingent withdrawal of positive reinforcers for one behavior can affect the performance of other behaviors as well. If the teacher fines Sally 1 minute of recess for each call out she makes during math class, the response cost procedure may reduce not only call outs but also math productivity. Sally may say to the teacher, "Since I lost my recess time for calling out, I am not going to do my math."

Calls Attention to the Punished Behavior

A response cost procedure, unlike an extinction procedure, calls attention to the undesirable behavior; and if the behavior is followed by a reinforcing consequence (like attention), it may increase the probability of the behavior's occurring again in the future. For instance, a teacher who uses the Good Behavior Game (Barrish, Saunders, & Wolf, 1969) may have difficulty with some students because every mark against their teams, indicating that a positive reinforcer has been lost, calls attention to the undesirable behavior and inadvertently reinforces it. In such a situation the teacher should change his tactic for the offending students, perhaps combining response cost with time out.

To counteract the possibility of calling attention to inappropriate behavior too frequently, several researchers (e.g., Walker, 1983; Pazulinec et al., 1983) recommend that response cost be used with positive reinforcement. Including positive reinforcement increases the likelihood that the ratio of punishment to reinforcement will be small and the problems of overusage noted by Bassett and Blanchard (1977) will be minimized.

Unpredictability

As with other forms of punishment, the effects of response cost are often unpredictable. The primary and secondary effects of response cost seem to be related to a number of variables that have been addressed in the literature but have not been fully investigated across subjects, settings, or behaviors. These variables include the magnitude of the fine, the previous punishment and reinforcement history of the individual, the frequency with which behaviors are fined, and the availability of alternative responses that are eligible for reinforcement.

GUIDELINES

Clearly Define the Behaviors and the Amounts of the Fine

Walker (1983) suggests that defining the behavior and the amount of the fine is a precondition for using response cost effectively. A teacher should not assume that her students will recognize calling out as a disruptive behavior. The rules for appropriate behavior and the behaviors that will lead to a fine should be explained fully.

Included in the definition of target behaviors should be the corresponding point loss for each behavior. Typically, one point is deducted for each occurrence of an undesirable behavior. However, in situations where multiple behaviors are subject to the response cost contingency or where the degree or severity of the behavior determines the response cost, correspondingly greater fines should be associated with more severe behavior (cf. Phillips et al., 1971).

According to Weiner (1962)—the originator of the term *response cost*—and Sajwaj (1968), the magnitude of the response cost fine is important. Sajwaj, for example, found that as the magnitude of the fine increased from one to five points, larger reductions in the rate of the undesirable behavior occurred. Losses beyond five points, however, did not seem to affect the rate of the reduction. As a general rule, it is important that the fine be sizable enough to suppress the future occurrence of the behavior but not so large as to bankrupt the individual or cause the system to lose its effectiveness. If a client loses tokens or other reinforcers at a high rate, he is likely to give up, and the procedure will become ineffective. Furthermore, fines should not be changed arbitrarily. If a 1-minute loss of recess is imposed on each noncompliant behavior in the morning, the teacher should not impose a 5-minute fine on the same noncompliant behavior in the afternoon.

Determine the Immediacy of the Fines

Ideally, the fine should be imposed immediately after the occurrence of each undesirable behavior (Sindelar et al., 1983). The more quickly the response cost contingency is applied subsequent to the occurrence of the behavior, the more powerful the procedure becomes.

Ensure Reinforcement Reserve

Positive reinforcers cannot be removed from individuals who no longer have any. Prior to using a response cost procedure, the practitioner must ensure a sufficient reinforcement reserve, without which the procedure is unlikely to be successful. For example, if a teacher used response-contingent withdrawal of free time for each occurrence of inappropriate behavior in a highly disruptive class, the students could exhaust all of their available free time before the first hour of class was over, leaving the teacher wondering what to do for the remainder of the day. Deducting free time for succeeding days would hardly be beneficial.

Walker (1983) offers two suggestions to reduce the likelihood of having no reinforcers available. First, the ratio should be controlled between points that are earned or issued noncontingently and points that are lost. If baseline data indicate that the inappropriate behavior occurs at a high rate, more reinforcers should be available for removal. Also, the magnitude of the fines should be determined and stated beforehand. Minor infractions may warrant relatively small fines, whereas major infractions may warrant substantially higher fines. Walker's second suggestion is that if all reinforcers are lost and another inappropriate behavior occurs, time out should be applied. After that, when reinforcers have again been earned, response cost can be reinstituted.

To establish the initial number of reinforcers that should be available, baseline data should be collected on the occurrence of inappropriate behavior during the day or session. The mean baseline figure should be increased for the number of reinforcers to be sure that all reinforcers are not lost when response cost is in effect. Although no empirically verifiable guidelines are available (Walker, 1983), a prudent approach is to increase the number of reinforcers 25% above the mean number of occurrences during baseline. For example, if baseline data indicate that the mean number of disruptions per day is 20, the teacher should establish 25 minutes of free time (the positive reinforcer) as the initial level

(20 × 1.25). If the practitioner calculates points instead of percentages, Walker (1983) found that having 35 points, which could be fined in increments of one to five points across responses, was sufficient to conduct his response cost program.

Keep Records

Each occurrence of response cost and the behavior that occasioned it should be recorded. Minimally, the analyst should record the number of times fines are imposed, the persons to whom fines are issued, and the effects of the fines. Daily, or at least regular, data collection helps to determine the efficacy of the response cost procedure. By graphing the effects of the program, the behavior analyst can determine the suppressive effect of the procedure. Under a response cost procedure the occurrence of inappropriate behavior should be less frequent than under baseline conditions.

Recognize the Potential for Unplanned or Unexpected Outcomes

Two situations may require the implementation of a contingency plan. One occurs when the repeated imposition of response cost serves to reinforce, rather than punish, the undesirable behavior. When this situation arises, the practitioner should stop using response cost and switch to another reductive procedure. The second situation occurs when the individual refuses to give up her positive reinforcers. To reduce the likelihood of this situation, the practitioner should clarify the consequences of such refusal beforehand and (1) impose an additional penalty fine for not giving up the tokens; (2) reimburse the individual with some fractional portion of the fine for complying with token payment immediately; (3) allow the individual who owes substantial fines to repay his debts in installments (Doty, McInnis, & Paul, 1974; or (4) make sure that an adequate supply of backup reinforcers are available.

Do Not Overuse Response Cost

If every inappropriate behavior leads to a loss of positive reinforcers, appropriate behavior may never by noticed. Response cost should be saved for those major undesirable behaviors that call attention to themselves and need to be suppressed quickly. Primary attention should be focused on positive responses, and response cost should be combined with DRI to build adaptive behavior.

SUMMARY

Definition of Response Cost

1 Response cost is defined as the loss of a specific amount of a positive reinforcer, contingent upon the performance of an inappropriate behavior; it results in the decreased probability of that behavior's occurring in the future.

2 Response cost is a Type II punishment procedure and is defined in terms of its effect on the future probability of the behavior that preceded it.

Desirable Aspects of Response Cost

3 Response cost is quick, convenient, and able to be combined with other procedures in a comprehensive behavior reduction and/or behavior development program. It requires that an ongoing positive reinforcement program be in effect.

Implementing a Response Cost Contingency

4 Response cost can be conducted in four ways: (1) the individual can earn reinforcers for one behavior and lose them for another; (2) the individual can be fined a specific number of reinforcers for each inappropriate behavior; (3) after receiving noncontingent reinforcers, the individual can lose reinforcers from that pool (bonus response cost); and (4) groups can lose reinforcers contingent upon the inappropriate behavior of any member of the group.

Criteria for Using Response Cost or Bonus Response Cost

5 Four criteria were proposed: (1) the least aversive form of response cost should be used initially; (2) the individual reserve of reinforcers should not be exhausted too quickly; (3) the potential for aggressive side effects should be assessed; and (4) the speed with which the behavior needs to be changed should be evaluated.

Considerations in the Use of Response Cost in Applied Settings

6 Response cost can produce aggression, avoidance, and spillover effects. It can also call attention to the punished behavior and is generally unpredictable.

Guidelines

7 Before using response cost, the practitioner should clearly define the behavior and the amount of the fine, ensure a reinforcement reserve, determine the frequency of the fines, prepare to keep records, recognize the potential for unplanned or unexpected outcomes, and commit to not overusing response cost.

PART NINE

Special Applications

Parts Four through Eight describe the basic principles of behavior and the major behavior change procedures that have been derived from those principles. Part Nine presents four special applications of behavior-change technology. Each of these four applications—contingency contracting, token economy, group-oriented contingencies, and self-management—is given chapter-length treatment because it is represented by a significant literature demonstrating its effectiveness across a wide range of subjects, settings, and behaviors. Each of the four applications is best conceived as an overall strategy for changing behavior and is composed of various specific procedures and tactics, depending upon the situation.

23

Contingency Contracting

KEY TERMS

Contingency contract   Rule-governed behavior

Behavioral contract   Self-contract

Behavior therapists, marriage counselors, social workers, teachers, and others in the helping professions, as well as parents and children themselves, have used contingency contracting to successfully change a wide range of behaviors. In fact, in some clinics, classrooms, and homes contracting is the primary system used to manage the therapist-client relationship or the selection and completion of academic assignments or important interactions between parent and child. Although the popularity of contingency contracting can be associated with the literature describing its effectiveness, it is also widely used because it is straightforward, logical, and relatively easy to implement. However, effective contingency contracting is not so simple as it may first appear. Contracting is not a single procedure, but rather an intervention package that makes use of several behavior principles and techniques.

DEFINITION AND COMPONENTS OF A CONTINGENCY CONTRACT

A **contingency contract,** also called a **behavioral contract,** is a document that specifies a contingent relationship between the completion of a specified behavior and access to, or delivery of, a specified reward, such as a treat, an *A,* or a favorite activity. Typically, contracts specify how two or more people will

---

This chapter was written by William L. Heward.

behave toward each other. Such quid pro quo agreements make one person's behavior (e.g., preparing dinner) dependent upon the other person's behavior (e.g., washing and putting away the dishes by a prescribed time the night before). Many contingency contracts used in family settings are of this behavior exchange type (Dardig & Heward, 1977). Although verbal agreements may be considered contracts in the legal sense, they are not contingency contracts as the term is used here. The specification necessary in a contingency contract is unlikely to occur in a verbal agreement; in addition, the act of signing the contract and the document itself are integral parts of contingency contracting as a behavior modification procedure.

What Should Be Included in a Contingency Contract?

There are two major parts in every contract—a description of the task and a description of the reward. The contract illustrated in Figure 23.1 was implemented by the parents of a 10-year-old learning disabled boy to help him learn to get up and get ready for school each day. The contract is divided into the characteristic two parts—task and reward.

Task   The task side of the contract consists of four parts. *Who* is the person that will be performing the task and getting the reward—in this case, Mark. *What* is the task or behavior the person must perform—in this example, getting

---

CONTRACT

TASK	REWARD
Who: Mark	Who: Mom and Dad
What: Get ready for school	What: Jimmy staying over and treat
When: Every school day	When: Friday night after perfect week
How Well: Mark will get out of bed, get dressed and finish his cereal by 7:15 each school morning. No more than 1 reminder from Mom or Dad. Must be ready for bus all 5 days to get reward.	How Much: Jimmy can come home with Mark after school and stay overnight. Boys can have night snack of pizza and ice cream.

Sign Here: *Mark Davidson*   Date: Feb. 12, 1987
Sign Here: *Belinda Davidson*   Date: Feb. 12, 1987

TASK RECORD

M	T	W	TH	F	M	T	W	TH	F	M	T	W	TH	F
★	★		★	★	★	★	★	★	★	★	★	★	★	★
		oops!	Great work, Mark			reward!!								reward

FIGURE 23.1   Contingency contracting form. (From *Sign Here: A Contracting Book for Children and Their Parents* (2nd ed., p. 31) by J. C. Dardig and W. L. Heward, 1981, Bridgewater, NJ: Fournies and Associates. Copyright 1981 by Fournies and Associates. Reprinted by permission.)

ready for school. *When* identifies the time that the task must be completed—every school day. *How well* is the most important part of the task side and perhaps of the entire contract. It calls for the specifics of the task. Sometimes it is helpful to list a series of steps or subtasks so that the person can use the contract itself as a checklist of what must be done. Any exceptions should be written in this part.

Reward Some people are very good at specifying the task side of a contract; they know what they want the other person to do. When it comes to the reward side, however, specificity is sometimes lost and problems can arise. Reward statements such as "Can watch some television" or "Will play catch when I get a chance" are not specific and are thus not fair to the person completing the task. The reward side of a contract must be as complete and as accurate as the task side.

On the reward side *Who* is the person that will be judging task completion and controlling delivery of the reward. With Mark's getting-ready-for-school contract, those persons are his parents. *What* is the reward. *When* specifies the time that the reward can be received by the person earning it. With any contract it is crucial that the reward come *after* successful task completion. However, many rewards cannot be delivered immediately, especially certain activities or outings. In addition, some rewards have a built-in limited availability; they can be delivered only at certain times. For example, it is impossible to take a child to a weekend doubleheader on Wednesday. Mark's contract specifies that his reward must be received on Friday nights. *How much* is the amount of reward that can be earned by completing the task. Any bonus contingencies should be included; for example, "By making her contract Monday through Friday, Eileen is allowed an extra reward on Saturday and Sunday without doing the task."

Task Record Including a place to record the progress of a contract right on the contract

itself serves two purposes. First, recording task completion and reward delivery on the contract sets the occasion for both parties to look at and be reminded of the contract regularly. Second, if a certain number of task completions are required to earn the reward (e.g., if a child must dress herself each morning before school for 5 days in a row), a checkmark, smiling face, or star can be placed on the task record each time the task is completed successfully. Marking the contract in this manner can help the individual remain on task until the assignment is completed and the reward is earned. Mark's parents used the top row of boxes in the task record to mark the days of the work week. In the middle row of boxes they placed gummed stars each day Mark met his contract. In the bottom row Mark's parents wrote comments about the progress of his contract.

How Do Contracts Work?

At first glance the principles of behavior behind contingency contracts seem deceptively simple: a behavior is followed by a contingent reward—surely a case of positive reinforcement. Yet in most contracts the reward, although contingent, is much too delayed to reinforce the specified behavior directly; and many successful contracts specify a reward that would not, in fact, function as a reinforcer for the task even if it was presented immediately after the task completion. So how do contracts work? Certainly reinforcement is involved, but not in as simple or direct a fashion as it might seem at first. **Rule-governed behavior** may also be involved (Skinner, 1969). A contract constitutes a statement of a strong rule: a specified behavior will produce a specified (and reasonably immediate) consequence. The contract itself serves as a cue to perform the specified behavior and enables the effective use of consequences (e.g., going to the movies Saturday night) too delayed in themselves to reinforce certain behaviors (e.g., practicing the trumpet on Tuesday). Delayed consequences can help exert control over behaviors performed hours and even days before if they are associated with and linked by verbal behavior to the rule (e.g., "I've just finished my trumpet practice—that's another checkmark toward the movies on Saturday"), or to interim token reinforcers (e.g., the checkmark on the contract after practicing). Malott (1981) has suggested that the reward stated in a behavioral contract may have little, if any, control over the performance of the specified task; the real control is a function of the contract's "making it public," resulting in performance of the specified task to escape "feeling guilty." Certainly, a behavioral contract is not a simple, positive reinforcement contingency loosely based on the Premack principle (see chapter 11), as has been suggested by some; instead it represents a more complex intervention package of related positive and negative reinforcement contingencies that operate together as an effective behavior change strategy (O'Banion & Whaley, 1981).

APPLICATIONS OF CONTINGENCY CONTRACTING

Contingency contracting has been used successfully as a behavior change technique by teachers, parents, and therapists. This section describes some of those applications as well as a method for using contracting to teach self-management skills to children.

Contingency Contracting in the Classroom

Contracting has become a widely used and fairly well understood method for motivation and instructional management in the classroom.

> The method can be used at any grade level and with any subject. The method—or variations of it—has been applied successfully with normal children in regular public school classrooms,

> with children suffering from severe emotional disturbances, by parents within their own families, and in many other situations. As a matter of fact, the successes achieved with behavior management systems of this kind during the past few years have established it as one of the most significant developments of the twentieth century in applied psychology. (Homme, Csanyi, Gonzales, & Rechs, 1970, p. ix)

Homme et al. (1970), in their book *How to Use Contingency Contracting in the Classroom,* provide a detailed description of how to design and implement a classroom contingency contracting program. Students contract to complete specified academic tasks, the reward for which is access for a specified period of time to a reinforcement area that consists of games, puzzles, magazines, records, and other age-appropriate activities. Initially, students contract for short task-reward cycles (e.g. "Complete one workbook page with no more than one error and have 5 minutes in the RE area"). As the child's skill levels and work habits increase, he gradually contracts for larger amounts of work, but reward periods generally remain frequent and immediately follow task completion throughout the day.

Classroom teachers have used contracting to solve specific discipline or performance problems of individual students. For example, White-Blackburn, Semb, and Semb (1977) report a sixth-grade teacher's use of daily contracts with four students who were disruptive and seldom completed assignments. Each morning the teacher negotiated an individual contract with each student, based on a list of assignment completion goals and rewards along with a list of penalties for specified disruptive behaviors. After fixed work periods of 15 minutes, each student met with the teacher to determine whether a reward or penalty had been earned. Throughout the study the students were in agreement with the teacher on whether a reward or penalty had been earned. On-task behavior, daily assignment completion, and weekly grades increased, while disruptive behavior decreased for all four students. When the contracts were in effect, the performance of the four experimental students compared favorably with three model students chosen for comparison.

Kelley and Stokes (1982) used contingency contracts to improve the academic productivity of students enrolled in a vocational/educational training program for disadvantaged high school dropouts. The participants in the program, aged 16 to 21, had dropped out of the regular junior or senior high school for various reasons, including disinterest in school, family problems, pregnancy, and poor relations with school authorities. The program, consisting of 2.5 hours of vocational training and 2.5 hours of basic academic skills training each day, was designed to prepare students for their high school diploma equivalency (GED) examination. Students received $2.35 per hour for each hour they attended school. Before the study began, the students' program administrator complained of having minimal control over the students' behavior during the academic skills portion of the day; the students completed little or no academic work despite the administrator's frequent and coercive attempts to motivate them. Prior to the study the researchers obtained permission to alter the manner in which the participants received their pay, which normally had been on a bimonthly schedule with a 2-week delay. The dependent variable in the study was the number of academic items completed correctly by each student.

During the baseline phases students completed exercises in the self-paced workbooks used in the program. At the end of the day, the workbooks were turned in to the teacher, who scored the work before the next day and allowed students to review their work after it was graded. Students were paid every Friday, based on their attendance during the preceding week. During Contracting I and II students were told that they could earn the same amount of money as before except that their pay would now be contingent upon correct completion of

an agreed-upon number of academic items. The teacher met weekly with each student to negotiate a contract specifying daily and weekly goals for the number of items to be completed.

> Students earned more money each day they reached their goals. For example, on the first day of the week students reached their goals they earned $3; the second day $4; and so on. Students also were rewarded for weekly goal achievement. Rewarding students for weekly goal achievement was included so that students were rewarded for "catching up" on their work when they had been absent or had failed to complete a daily goal. While negotiating a contract for the first time, the teacher suggested a figure that represented at least a 10% increase over the student's current level of productivity. . . . the teacher and the student usually agreed on a number that represented a compromise between his suggested workload and the workload proposed by the student. (Kelley & Stokes, 1982, p. 450)[1]

Figure 23.2 shows the results for the seven students who were enrolled in the program during the entire experiment. As an example, Bill completed an average of 20 and 16 correct items during Baseline I and II, respectively; during Contracting I and II, he completed an average of 68 and 103 correct items. His item completion frequency showed an upward trend during both Contracting phases. Attendance during the four experimental phases averaged 85% during Baseline I, 91% during Contracting I, 82% during Baseline II, and 94% during Contracting II. The teacher reported that the weekly contracting sessions took approximately 10 minutes per student and provided a designated opportunity to evaluate and monitor student progress. The students reported a preference for contracting because they knew exactly how much work they had to accomplish each day and could not be

[1]From "Contingency Contracting with Disadvantaged Youth: Improving Classroom Performance" by M. L. Kelley and T. F. Stokes, 1982, *Journal of Applied Behavior Analysis, 15,* p. 450. Copyright 1982 by the Society for the Experimental Analysis of Behavior, Inc. Reprinted by permission.

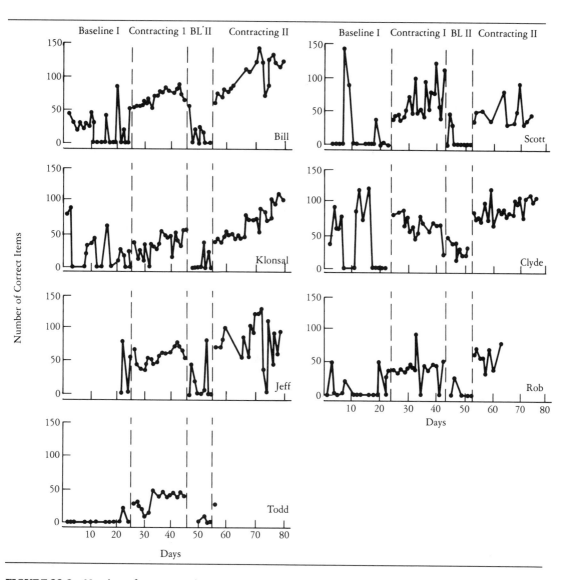

FIGURE 23.2 Number of correct academic items completed by vocational school students during baseline and contracting conditions. Missing data points represent student absences. (From "Contingency Contracting with Disadvantaged Youths: Improving Classroom Performance" by M. L. Kelley and T. F. Stokes, 1982, *Journal of Applied Behavior Analysis, 15,* p. 452. Copyright 1982 by the Society for the Experimental Analysis of Behavior, Inc. Reprinted by permission.)

reprimanded for wasting time after they had completed their work.

Home-School Contracts

Teachers and parents together can develop and implement a home-school contract to help a student improve social and/or academic skills. In the typical home-school contract tasks completed in school (e.g., academic assignments) earn rewards delivered at home (e.g., extra allowance). Several advantages can be cited for home-school contracts. First, they enable teachers to take advantage of rewards not typically available in the classroom; for example, money, use of the family car, special privileges or activities such as staying up late to watch a TV movie (Cantrell, Cantrell, Huddleston, & Woolridge, 1969). Second, when parents are participating with the teacher in the systematic specification and rewarding of desired behaviors, the student's two most important environments—home and school— are working together in a consistent effort to support learning. Indirect benefits of home-school contracting are the possibility of more positive parent-child interactions as the parent recognizes and rewards the child's efforts in school (and hopefully in the home as well) and increased parent involvement in the child's school program (Heward & Dardig, 1978; Heward, Dardig, & Rossett, 1979).

Rewards delivered by parents can be helpful in bringing a student's problem behavior under control in school, where typical rewards available in the classroom have failed. Home-based rewards can also be used to supplement or enhance an already-effective in-school program. Trovato and Bucher (1980) found that elementary students participating in an in-school peer tutoring program and a home-school contract made almost double the gains in oral reading and comprehension that students made. who participated in the same peer tutoring program without the home-school contract.

Contingency Contracting in Family Settings

Contingency contracts have been used in family settings to deal with parent-child interaction problems, juvenile delinquency, and marital discord. Dardig and Heward (1981a) developed a contracting approach that families of varied backgrounds have used successfully to manage a wide array of parent-child problems. Stuart (1971), Tharp and Wetzel (1969), and Weathers and Liberman (1975) report limited success with contingency contracts with the families of juvenile delinquents. Tharp and Wetzel (1969) encountered many parents who could not talk productively with their children. Because parent-child interactions were largely aversive, the researchers sought to depersonalize them and minimize the need for parent-child verbalizations with behavioral contracts negotiated through a third party. On the other hand, Stuart's (1971) use of contracts with the families of delinquents suggests that contracts can function as catalysts to more positive parent-child interactions. Stuart believes that one cause of juvenile delinquency is a lack of positive reinforcement in the home. He advocates contracts for families as a means of structuring the exchange of positive reinforcement, delayed as it might be, when the reciprocal pattern of appropriate exchanges has broken down.

Although some contracting success has been noted with juvenile delinquents, the success rate seems to depend on various factors. Stuart and Lott (1972) suggest three important influences, based on their research. First, families with histories of constructive negotiation are more likely to implement a contract successfully. Second, the more immediate and critical the conflict, the more the families are willing to negotiate. Third, the more skillful the therapist in helping the parents and child reach a compromise in which no one loses face, the more successful the contract is apt to be. In summarizing the research on contingency contracting with families of juvenile delinquents, Burchard and Harig (1976) warn, "Thus it appears that while behavioral contracts are indeed useful, their implementation should not be oversimplified. The tactics of inducing a compromise using a contract rivals, in Stuart's opinion, the intervention mechanisms themselves" (p. 441).

The warning against oversimplification of contracting is important. Contracting is not as simple as it is often presented, whether it is used with delinquent teenagers or well-behaved third graders. The negotiation/compromise process is not an adjunct to, but rather an integal component of contingency contracting as a behavior change intervention.

Contingency contracting is one of the major intervention strategies employed by behavioral marriage counselors (Gambrill, 1977; Stuart, 1969). Sometimes referred to as reciprocity counseling, contracting emphasizes the notion of reciprocal, or mutually reinforcing, consequences—an ideal dimension of the happy marriage. Figure 23.3 shows one of three contracts negotiated and implemented with the help of a counselor to assist a married couple in communicating with one another (Weiss, 1975). Prior to implementing the contracts, the therapist engaged the couple in discussions that revealed the causes of their interaction difficulties. However, in spite of this new knowledge, the usual inappropriate behavior recurred when they returned home. The contract, when implemented, provided new cues and positive consequences for more amiable, supportive responses toward one another.

Contracting in Behavior Theory

Clinicians have used contingency contracting to treat problems such as smoking (Tighe & Elliot, 1968), obesity (Mann, 1972), and alcoholism (Miller, 1972; Miller, Hersen, & Eisler, 1974). By employing a version of the "deposit contract" first described by Tighe and Elliot (1968), Wysocki, Hall, Iwata, and Riordan (1979) increased the amount and regularity of physical exercise of seven adults. Each subject deposited six items of personal value with the experimenters (e.g., jewelry, clothing, books, checks made out to charitable associations) with the chance to earn two items back each week by attaining a contracted amount of aerobic points (Cooper, 1970) and by observing and recording the exercise of other participants. However, before the two earned items were returned each week, the subjects were required to deposit two more personal items of value with the experimenters, to ensure a constant source of deposited items to maintain the program. Withdrawal from the program resulted in loss of all deposited items. A multiple baseline design across two groups of subjects was used to evaluate the contracting program. One subject did not meet her contracted amount of exercising and dropped from the program after 4 weeks, forfeiting her deposited items. All seven other participants met or exceeded their weekly exercise contracts during the 2-month program. Figure 23.4 shows the mean number of aerobic points earned each week by the two groups of subjects. All seven subjects reported higher-than-baseline rates of exercise in a 1-year follow-up.

Using Contracting to Teach Self-Management to Children

Correctly applied, contingency contracting involves the active participation of the child throughout the development, implementation, and evaluation of the contract. For many children, contracting is a first experience in identifying specific ways in which they would like to act and then arranging certain aspects of their environment to set the occasion for and reward those acts. If more and more of the decision making, monitoring, and evaluation of the contracting process is gradually and systematically turned over to children, they can become skilled at self-contracting. A **self-contract** is a contingency contract that an individual makes

Conversation Alone and With Others

Wife	Husband

Accelerate:

1. Initiates 3 ten-minute conversations with husband about husband's feelings, thoughts, and so on. Conversation begins with an open-ended question by wife.
2. During the conversation wife keeps eye contact and makes comments on topic.
3. If child interrupts the conversation, wife acknowledges the interruption (for example, "I want to finish hearing this but . . ."), attends to child, then returns to the conversation. If the interruption is long, wife brings up the conversation later (for example, "I want to finish hearing about _____")

Accelerate:

1. During one occasion when company is present, husband will bring wife into conversation, make positive statements about her (for example, "That was interesting." "That was a good idea") and do affectional things with her (for example, touch her hair, hold her hand, put his arm around her).
2. Husband will do each of the above behaviors at least once for a total of five.

Reward:
Two games of cards of wife's choosing.

Reward:
During three consecutive mornings wife makes coffee or tea for husband.

Penalty:
Wife picks up children's room and living room for 3 consecutive days.

Penalty:
Husband does laundry once.

We the undersigned agree to the conditions of the above contract. We further agree to accept the partner's initiation of the above activities or suggest a more convenient alternate time.

Wife _____ Husband _____

Therapists:

_____ _____

Date _____

FIGURE 23.3 Contingency contract between wife and husband. (From R. L. Weiss, "Contracts, Cognition, and Change: A Behavioral Approach to Marriage Therapy," *The Counseling Psychologist,* Vol. 5, No. 3, p. 23. Copyright © 1975 by Division 17, The Division of Counseling Psychology of the American Psychological Association. Reprinted by permission of Sage Publications, Inc.)

with herself, incorporating a self-selected task and reward as well as personal monitoring of task completion and self-delivery of the reward. (The self-management of behavior change is examined in chapter 26.)

Kabler (1976) taught self-contracting skills to 41 students in three different fourth-grade

classrooms. Using a multiple baseline across subjects (classrooms) design, Kabler demonstrated a functional relationship between exposure to an instructional package on contracting and students' skills in writing self-contracts. Kabler's study directly taught children to write self-contracts following an initial 5-day

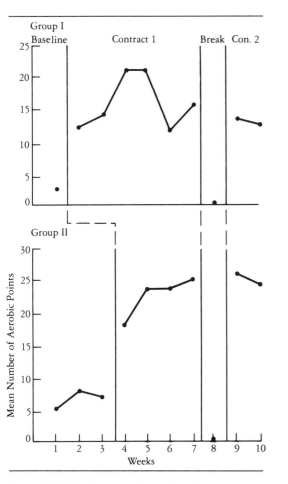

FIGURE 23.4 Mean number of aerobic exercise points earned per group during baseline and contingency contracting. (From "Behavioral Management of Exercise: Contracting for Aerobic Points" by T. Wysocki, G. Hall, B. Iwata, and M. Riordan, 1979, *Journal of Applied Behavior Analysis, 12,* p. 60. Copyright 1979 by the Society for the Experimental Analysis of Behavior, Inc. Reprinted by permission.)

experience with completely teacher-controlled contracts.

Kabler, Dardig, and Heward (1977) describe a procedure for teaching children self-contracting skills that involves a gradual shift from adult-controlled to child-controlled contracts. This five-phase procedure can be used in class-room or family settings in which an ongoing contracting program is operating.

1 *Adult-Controlled Contract.* The adult identifies and specifies both the task and reward in cooperation with the child. The adult monitors the task, records the child's performance, and delivers the reward.

2 *Shared Control I.* The adult identifies and specifies both the task and reward in cooperation with the child. The adult trains the child to monitor his own task performance, proceeds to monitor it jointly with the child until the child's monitoring is accurate, then turns over control of the monitoring to the child. The adult continues to deliver the reward.

3 *Shared Control II.* The adult identifies and specifies both the task and reward in cooperation with the child. The child continues to monitor his own task performance. Delivery of the reward is now child-controlled.

4 *Shared Control III.* The adult shifts control of the reward identification and specification to the child, while the child continues monitoring his task performance. The child is now free to select a reward of his or her choosing. It is recommended that a "reward menu" be developed with the child, from which selections can be made. Task selection remains under the control of the adult.

5 *Self-Controlled Contract.* The child is now ready to move to the final phase where he or she will select both the task and the reward and write the contract. The adult and child should jointly review the initial contracts; when the child writes three acceptable contracts consecutively, the adult may terminate the evaluation. However, periodic checks may still be appropriate. (Kabler, Dardig, & Heward, pp. 30–31)

Teachers and parents who wish to maintain a degree of control and to focus attention on behaviors they want the child to modify can develop and post a mutually developed list of tasks and rewards with the child. The child can then be instructed to write his self-contracts, using tasks and rewards from this list. Homme et al. (1970) also describe a procedure for moving gradually from adult- to child-controlled contracts.

DEVELOPING BEHAVIORAL CONTRACTS

Although it is possible for teachers, parents, or therapists to unilaterally determine a contract for a child or client, contracting is usually more effective when all of the parties involved play an active role in developing the contract. Several methods have been proposed for developing behavioral contracts (Dardig & Heward, 1981a; DeRisi & Butz, 1975; Hall & Hall, 1980; Homme et al., 1970; O'Banion & Whaley, 1981). Contract development involves the specification of tasks and rewards in a fashion agreeable and beneficial to each party. Dardig and Heward (1977) describe a five-step procedure for task and reward identification. Originally developed for use by families, the procedure has been adapted and used by many classroom teachers. It is designed to be carried out by the entire family together; each family member completes three forms prior to the actual writing of the contract.

Step 1: Hold a Family Meeting

To get the entire family involved in the contracting process, a family meeting should be held. At this meeting the family can discuss how contracts work, how they can help the family cooperate and get along better, and how contracts can help individuals meet personal goals. Parents should emphasize that they will participate in all of the steps leading up to and including implementation of contracts. It is important that children view contracting as a behavior exchange process shared by all members of the family, not as something adults do to them. The list-making procedures described in the following steps provide a simple and logical framework for the selection of tasks and rewards for family contracts. Most families can complete the procedure within 1 to 2 hours.

Step 2: Fill Out List A

List A, Figure 23.5, is designed to help each family member identify not only those tasks she can perform within the context of a contract, but also those tasks she already does to help the family. In this way positive attention can be focused on appropriate behaviors that individuals are now completing satisfactorily.

Each family member should be given a copy of List A. Everyone should be careful to describe all tasks as specifically as possible. Then the completed lists can be put aside, and the family can proceed to the next step. If there is a family member who does not write, the parents can talk with him about this list (as well as Lists B and C) and complete it for him.

Step 3: Fill Out List B

List B, Figure 23.6, is designed to help family members focus not only on possible contracting target behaviors, but also on helpful behaviors currently being completed. List B can also identify areas where disagreement exists as to whether certain tasks are actually being completed properly and regularly.

Each family member should be given a copy of List B and asked to write her name in all three blanks at the top. These lists can then be passed around the table so that everyone has a chance to write at least one behavior on each side of everyone else's list. Everyone writes on every List B except her own. And each person should be required to write at least one positive behavior on everyone else's List B. Once completed, these lists should be put aside before moving to the next step.

Step 4: Fill Out List C

List C, Figure 23.7, identifies potential rewards for each family member. Individuals should list not only everyday favorite things and activities, but also special items and activities they may have wanted for a long time. It is all right if two or more people put down the same reward. Once List C is completed, each person

LIST A:	My Name: _Mark_
Things I Do to Help My Family	**Other Ways I Could Help My Family and Myself**

1. Help Dad clean the garage.	1. Not fight with everybody in the morning
2. Clean up my bedroom (sometimes)	2. Work better at school
3. Nice to my sister Mary	3. Homework
4. Take garbage out	4. Take care of Mugsie without being yelled at
5. Mow the lawn	5. Write to Grandma
6. Dry dishes	6.
7.	7.

FIGURE 23.5 A form for self-identification of possible tasks for behavioral contracts. (From *Sign Here: A Contracting Book for Children and Their Parents* (2nd ed., p. 111) by J. C. Dardig and W. L. Heward, 1981, Bridgewater, NJ: Fournies and Associates. Copyright 1981 by Fournies and Associates. Reprinted by permission.)

should collect his two other lists and read them carefully, talking over any items he does not understand.

Step 5: Write Contracts

The final step begins with choosing a task for each person's first contract. Discussion should move around the group with family members trying to help each other decide which task is the most important to start doing first. Everyone should write *who* is going to perform the task, exactly *what* the task is, *how well* and *when* it has to be done, and any possible exceptions. Everyone should also look at List C and choose a reward that is neither excessive nor insignificant but is fair for the selected task. Each member should write *who* will control

the reward, *what* the reward is, *when* it is to be given, and *how much* is to be given. Everyone in the family should write one contract during the first meeting so that contracting becomes a family activity.

EVALUATING CONTRACTS

Evaluation of a contingency contract, like that of all behavioral procedures, must focus on objective measurement of the target behavior. The simplest, most straightforward way to evaluate a contract is to record the frequency of task completion while the contract is in effect; including a task record on the contract iself helps make evaluation a natural by-product of

LIST B:

My Name: Mark

Things _Mark_ **Does**
to Help the Family

Other Ways _Mark_
Could Help the Family

1. Keeps his bedroom neat

2. Helps Mom with dishes

3. Helps Dad around the house

4. Mows the lawn

5. Eats all his vegetables

6. _____

7. _____

1. Get up in time for school

2. Go to bed at night at bedtime

3. Play more with Mary

4. Take care of the dog

5. _____

6. _____

7. _____

FIGURE 23.6 A form for identifying potential contracting tasks for others. (From *Sign Here: A Contracting Book for Children and Their Parents* (2nd ed., p. 113) by J. C. Dardig and W. L. Heward, 1981, Bridgewater, NJ: Fournies and Associates. Copyright 1981 by Fournies and Associates. Reprinted by permission.)

the contracting process. By comparing that record with a precontract baseline of task completion, an objective determination can be made as to whether improvement has occurred. In this sense a good contract is one that results in the specified task being completed more often than it was before the contract.

Such a before-and-after comparison is, of course, only an A-B design. To demonstrate whether a functional relationship exists between the observed behavior change and the contract, an experimental analysis must be undertaken. Reversal and multiple baseline designs are commonly used to evaluate experimentally the effects of contingency contracting (e.g., Kelley & Stokes, 1982; Wysocki et al., 1979). In most classrooms, family, and self-management situations, however, an A-B (baseline-intervention) comparison con-

stitutes a satisfactory evaluation of a contingency contract.

Sometimes the data indicate that the task is being completed more often and more consistently than it was before the contract, but the parties involved are still not happy with it. Either the original problem or goal that prompted development of the contract in the first place is not being attained, or one or more of the participants do not like the way in which the contract is being carried out. The first possibility results from selecting the wrong behavior for the task part of the contract. For example, let us suppose that John, a ninth grader, wants to improve on the *D*s and *F*s he has been getting in algebra and writes a contract with his parents specifying as the task "studying his math" for 1 hour each school night. After several weeks John has failed to

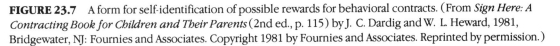

LIST C:	My Name: Mark

My Favorite Things, Activities, and Special Treats

1. Play catch with Dad
2. Battlestar Galactica
3. Staying up late
4. Ice cream
5. Cupcakes
6. Helping Mom cook
7. Cartoons
8. Pizza
9. Skateboard
10. Jimmy staying over
11. Roller skating
12.
13.
14.
15.

FIGURE 23.7 A form for self-identification of possible rewards for behavioral contracts. (From *Sign Here: A Contracting Book for Children and Their Parents* (2nd ed., p. 115) by J. C. Dardig and W. L. Heward, 1981, Bridgewater, NJ: Fournies and Associates. Copyright 1981 by Fournies and Associates. Reprinted by permission.)

study the required 1 hour on only two nights, but his in-school algebra performance remains unchanged. Has John's contract worked? The correct answer is both yes and no. John's contract was successful in that he was consistently completing the specified task—1 hour of study each day. Still, in terms of his original objective—better algebra grades—the contract was a failure. John's contract helped him change the behavior he specified, but he specified the wrong task. Studying for 1 hour, for John at least, was not directly related to his goal. By changing his contract to require that he correctly solve 10 new algebra equations each night (the behavior required to get good grades on algebra tests), his goal may become a reality.

It is also important to consider the participants' affective reactions to the contract. A con-

tract that produces desired change in the specified target behavior but causes other maladaptive responses may be an unacceptable solution. Such a situation can usually be avoided by including the client in the negotiation, developing the contract jointly, and holding regular, subsequent sessions in which the contractee's progress is evaluated by all concerned.

Evaluating a Contract's Components

Contingency contracts can also be evaluated before they are initiated. Kabler, Dardig, and Heward (1977) developed a rating form for scoring the presence or absence of nine elements essential to a well-written contingency contract (see Figure 23.8), and they elaborate on those nine elements.

Contract Elements	Present	
1. Task description is present.	Yes _____	No _____
2. Described task is observable.	Yes _____	No _____
3. When the task will be accomplished is indicated.	Yes _____	No _____
4. How much of the task or how well a task will be performed is indicated.	Yes _____	No _____
5. Reward description is present.	Yes _____	No _____
6. When the reward will be delivered is indicated.	Yes _____	No _____
7. How much of the reward will be delivered is indicated.	Yes _____	No _____
8. Reward is indicated to occur at a time after the task has been completed.	Yes _____	No _____
9. Amount of reward is appropriate for the task.	Yes _____	No _____
Total number of elements present: _____		

FIGURE 23.8 A rating form for scoring the presence or absence of nine key elements in a contingency contract. (From *A Leader's Manual for Sign Here: A Contracting Book for Children and Their Parents*, p. 18, by M. L. Kabler, J. C. Dardig, and W. L. Heward, 1977, Kalamazoo, MI: Behaviordelia. Copyright 1977 by Behaviordelia. Reprinted by permission.)

1 A statement about the task is present. The contract describes what the person will do in order to earn a reward. Any description of a task meets the requirements for this element. Examples: "do my work," "do better in arithmetic," "pay attention," "be good in class," etc.

2 The described task is observable. Examples: "hand in my daily homework assignments," "feed the class hamster," "complete 10 arithmetic problems." Statements such as "I'll be good" do not meet the requirements of this element.

3 The contract states when the task will be accomplished. Any mention of time satisfactorily meets the requirements of this element. Examples: "when I get home," "each day," "during class," "on time," etc.

4 The contract states how much of a task, or how well a task, will be performed. Any mention of quantity or quality is adequate. Examples: "all my spelling," "all my work," "during the whole math class period," "do all my arithmetic correctly," "pay attention by looking at the teacher," "get an A on my spelling assignments," etc. (Note: Adjectives such as more, a lot, some, better and very well, do not meet the requirements of this element.)

5 A statement describing a reward is present in the contract. Any description of a reward

which follows the task meets the requirements of this element. The use of a punisher is scored negatively. This would occur only when the contract was written as a punishing contract. Example: "When I talk-out in class, Ms. Smith will take away one of my points."

6 When the reward will be awarded is indicated. Any indication of time is adequate. Examples: "after school," "each day when I get home," "at noon each day," "on Saturday," etc.

7 How much of the reward is to be given is indicated. Any mention of quantity meets this requirement. When the amount of a reward is clear, it is not necessary that a numeral be stated in the contract. For example, "eat a candy bar each day" is adequate. An unacceptable description of the amount reward would be "watch TV each day." In this example, there is no indication of how much TV watching will be allowed. An acceptable description would be "watch TV from when I get home after school until supper," or "watch 'The Electric Company' each day."

8 The contract shows a relationship between reward and task which indicates that the reward occurs after the task is completed. The time indicated for the task and for the reward reflect the proper relationship (i.e., task occurs before the reward is awarded).

For example, "Jeff will get a special surprise after he gets a *B* in arithmetic on his report card." In contracts where the time for task and reward are merely stated as "each day," this element would not be present. However, the use of the phrase "after school" in a contract involving a school task would be adequate.

9 The amount of reward is appropriate for the task. This element is to be scored positively, unless the reward is ridiculously out-of-proportion to the task. Examples of un-acceptable rewards for tasks are "When I complete one math assignment, I will buy myself a candy bar each day for a week"; or "When I get *A*s on my weekly spelling, history, and science quizzes for one month, I will treat myself to a penny piece of candy." When the quantity of either the task or the reward is not specified clearly, this element is to be scored negatively. (pp. 15–17)

Evaluating contracts with a preimplementation checklist like that in Figure 23.8 can lead to the identification and correction of inadequacies in the written document before it takes effect, thereby avoiding problems after the contract is implemented.

DESIRABLE ASPECTS OF CONTINGENCY CONTRACTING

Contingency contracting as a behavior change intervention has many advantages to recommend it.

1 Contracting is a positive reward-based management system (although response cost contingencies can be built into the contracts).

2 Contracting is a way for teachers to individualize instructional contingencies (Homme et al., 1970; Kelley & Stokes, 1982; Langstaff & Volkmor, 1975).

3 Contracts help teachers and parents remain consistent by stipulating how and when specified behaviors must be rewarded (Gambrill, 1977; Tharp & Wetzel, 1969).

4 Contracting is a good method for involving parents and significant others in the student's/client's program (Heward, Dardig, & Rossett, 1979; Trovato & Bucher, 1980).

5 Contracting encourages active participation and self-determination by the student/client (Munro, 1981; White-Blackburn, Semb, & Semb, 1977).

6 Contracting can be used to teach independence and self-control (Homme et al., 1970; Kabler, 1976).

7 Contracting is a fairly simple behavior change intervention that can be implemented by nonprofessionals with a modest amount of training (Kabler, 1976; Norman, 1977; Shrewsberry, 1977; Upper, Lochman, & Aveni, 1977).

8 Participants usually like contingency contracting (Munro, 1981; Shrewsberry, 1977).

CONSIDERATIONS IN IMPLEMENTING CONTINGENCY CONTRACTS

In determining whether contingency contracting is an appropriate intervention, the practitioner must consider the nature of the desired behavior change, the verbal and conceptual skills of the individual, and the individual's relationship with the person(s) with whom the contract will be made. The target behavior to be changed by a contingency contract must already be in the individual's repertoire and must typically be under proper stimulus control in the environment in which the response is desired. Contracting is most effective with responses that produce permanent products (e.g., completed math assignment, clean bedroom) or that occur in the presence of the person who is to deliver the reward (e.g., positive comments to one's spouse).

Reading skills are not a prerequisite for successful contracting, but the individual must be able to come under the control of the visual or oral statements (rules) of the contract. These rules mediate the delay between performance of the response and delivery of the reward. This requirement rules out contracting as an effective intervention for many individuals with severe/profound mental retardation.

Implementing contingency contracts with nonreaders presents certain challenges. Although a contingency contract has been defined as a written product describing the contingent relationship between a task and a reward, a contract can be written without words. Contracting with nonreaders involves three types of clients: (1) preschoolers with good verbal skills; (2) school-aged children with limited reading skills; and (3) adults with adequate language and conceptual skills but without reading and writing skills as a result of some handicapping condition. Contracts using key words, symbols, pictures, photographs, clock hands to indicate time, audiotapes, and so on can be developed to suit the individual skills of children and adults in all three nonreader groups (Heward, Dardig, & Rossett, 1979). Figure 23.9 shows a contract for a nonreader that clearly indicates the task, the reward, and the contingency.

Contracting may also be less effective with certain subject populations. Weathers and Liberman (1975) report the unsuccessful use of contingency contracting with juvenile delinquents from six families. They suggest that

attainment of many important behavioral goals by these adolescents would require direct, massive intervention. In describing a contracting program with another group of delinquents, Burchard and Harig (1976) report success with most youth aged 9 to 13 but poor results with older youths. The authors speculate that failures with the older delinquents were caused by the adult mediators' (parents, relatives) not controlling the most powerful reinforcers. Undoubtedly, the success of a contingency contract is dependent to some degree on the value of the stated reward in relation to the reinforcers currently maintaining behaviors incompatible with the task specified in the contract.

Individuals who refuse to enter into a contingency contract are another consideration. Even though most children are eager, or at least willing, to try a contract—most children like the fact that a contract specifies exactly what is expected of them and requires an adult to "put it on the line"—some children want nothing to do with the whole idea. Dardig and Heward (1981a) suggest several approaches that parents have found effective with nonsigners. These techniques are (1) modeling successful contracting with a sibling, spouse, or friend; (2) letting the nonsigner begin by controlling the reward for a contract that specifies a task the parent must complete; (3) letting the nonsigner who believes contracting will not be honest or fair try a self-contract; (4) systemati-

FIGURE 23.9 A mealtime contingency contract for a nonreader. (From *Working with Parents of Handicapped Children*, p. 149, by W. L. Heward, J. C. Dardig and A. Rossett, 1979, Columbus, OH: Charles E. Merrill. Copyright 1979 by Charles E. Merrill. Reprinted by permission.)

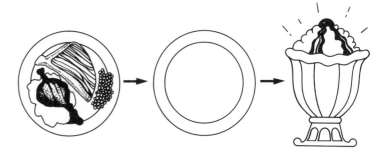

cally using positive attention and praise for any signs of interest in contracting by the non-signer (shaping) and ignoring all of her negative statements such as "Contracts are stupid" or "You'll never get me to sign a contract! (extinction); and (5) for the nonsigner who claims he does not need a contract (yet he has not been completing the task in question), cutting out the task record portion of a contract, taping it in a conspicuous place, recording the frequency of task completion, and praising the child if he can do the task without the contract. Even after all of these approaches, some nonsigners may still not agree to participate in a contingency contract. In such cases more direct behavior change strategies must be considered for dealing with the target behavior.

GUIDELINES FOR EFFECTIVE CONTRACTING

Numerous lists of rules and guidelines for using contingency contracting have been published, with most authors making similar recommendations. Many factors must be considered in the planning and implementation of a contingency contract, but there are only three rules of contracting that must be followed.

Rule 1: Contracts Must Be Fair

There must be a fair relationship between the difficulty and amount of the task and the quality and amount of the reward. Behavioral contracts are not documents to be forged like many contracts between industry and organized labor in which each party seeks maximum advantage.

Rule 2: Contracts Must Be Clear

In many instances a contract's biggest contribution is that it specifies each person's expectations exactly. When a teacher's or parent's expectations are clearly stated, the performance of many children automatically improves. However, it seems that children are often more

willing to be specific than are adults, who perhaps enjoy the privilege of changing their minds (i.e., the contingencies). In any event contingency contracts must say what they mean and mean what they say.

Rule 3: Contracts Must Be Honest

An honest contract exists if the reward is delivered at the time and in the amount specified when the task is completed as specified. In an honest contract the reward is *not* delivered when the task is not completed as specified. A dishonest contract exists when the task is completed and the reward is not delivered or when the task is not completed, but the reward is delivered anyway. The honesty rule is broken more often than the fairness or clarity rules. It is not broken because teachers and parents write bad deals or try to swindle children. On the contrary, it is most often broken because teachers and parents promise too much. For example, a teacher wants her students to be really motivated to be productive and writes a big reward into the contract—a trip to the zoo on Friday. The children perform beautifully; but on Friday the teacher is informed of a last-minute curriculum committee assignment, and the trip is off. The result is a dishonest contract. Of course, disappointments are a reality, and children must learn to handle them; but a child's first contract designed to change an important behavior is not the place for such learning to occur.

Similarly, adults do a child a disservice by delivering a reward even though the task was not completed as specified in the contract. When this occurs, the child is being rewarded for unsatisfactory performance. If the task requirements seem too high after the child has tried but missed, the contract can be rewritten; but failing to complete the contracted task should not be rewarded. Adults must specify rewards they are prepared to deliver or withhold depending upon the child's behavior; this is the essence of an honest contract.

In addition to these three rules, a number of suggestions can be made for effective contingency contracting. The guidelines that follow come from several authors who have conducted, researched, and written about contingency contracting (Dardig & Heward, 1981a; DeRisi & Butz, 1975; Hall & Hall, 1980; Heward, Dardig, & Rossett, 1979; Homme et al., 1970; O'Banion & Whaley, 1981; Stuart, 1969, 1971).

- Use frequent, small rewards.
- Do not write a contract that might eliminate an individual early. For example, if Mary must perform some chore every morning and every afternoon for a week to earn her reward on Saturday, what is her motivation for the rest of the week if she misses once on Tuesday?
- Build in several layers of rewards (e.g., bonus rewards for a certain number of days of consecutive performance).
- Add a response cost contingency if needed (see chapter 22).
- Post the contract in a visible place.
- If a series of contracts is used, write them on a standard form to save time and make it easy for participants to locate particular elements.
- To avoid a quid pro quo contract in which one person must change before the other (who is going to go first?), write a contract with parallel rewards independent of the behavior the contracting partner is supposed to change.
- Renegotiate and change a contract when either party is consistently unhappy with it.

Terminating a Contingency Contract

Contingency contracting is a method of arranging special rewards to help a person learn to perform a task or behavior she agrees should be accomplished. When the person has started to receive the naturally occurring reinforcers available for completing the task in question, such as praise from family and peers or the satisfaction of successful performance, the formal contract can be dropped. After several weeks of meeting the terms of a contract, many children state that they no longer need the contract. When this occurs, the adult should drop the formal contract but continue to monitor and praise task performance. Another procedure often effective is to gradually turn over management of the contract to the child in a manner similar to the process described for teaching children self-contracting.

SUMMARY

Definition and Components of a Contingency Contract

1 A contingency contract is a document that specifies the relationship between a task and a contingent reward.
2 A contract consists of two major parts: task and reward. Under task *who, what, when,* and *how well* should be specified. Under reward *who, what, when* and *how much* should be specified.
3 Including a task record assures a place for recording the progress of the contract and providing interim rewards.

4 Contingency contracts are probably effective because of several behavior principles, including positive reinforcement, negative reinforcement, and rule-governed behavior.

Applications of Contracting

5 Contracting is widely used as a classroom instructional management system and in family and behavior therapy settings.
6 By gradually assuming more functions of the contracting process, children can be taught to use self-contracts as a self-management skill.

Developing Contracts

7 A five-step procedure involving a group meeting and completion of three lists can be used to develop contingency contracts.

Evaluating Contracts

8 A contract is effective if it results in a higher frequency of task completion than existed prior to its implementation.

9 A-B designs are typically used in applied settings to evaluate a contract's effectiveness, although a functional analysis is required to determine whether the contract actually caused the change in behavior.

10 Contracts can be evaluated before they are implemented by checking for the presence of nine important elements.

Considerations

11 The contracted task must already be in the person's repertoire and under appropriate stimulus control.

12 Contracting is most effective with behaviors that produce permanent products or occur in the presence of the person controlling the reward.

13 Contracting is usually not effective with severely/profoundly mentally retarded individuals because of deficits in language and comprehension.

14 Contracting with juvenile delinquents has had only mixed success.

15 Contracts can be effective with nonreaders if symbols, pictures, photographs, and/or audiotapes are used.

16 Modeling, adult contracting, self-contracting, and shaping and extinction can be used to get a nonsigner to participate in a contract.

Guidelines for Effective Use

17 Contracts must be fair, clear, and honest.

18 Many successful contracts tend to terminate automatically as naturally occurring reinforcers begin to maintain the task.

19 Gradually turning the management of the contract over to the child is another method of terminating the contract.

24

Token Economy

KEY TERMS

Token economy

Token

Backup reinforcer

Generalized conditioned
reinforcer

Level system

The token economy is a highly developed and
researched behavior change system. It has been
applied successfully in almost all instructional
settings (e.g., homes, classrooms, and residential institutions). The usefulness of a token
economy in changing behaviors that have been
resistant to instruction is well established in
the literature (e.g., Ayllon & Azrin, 1968; Kazdin,
1977b; Kazdin & Bootzin, 1972; O'Leary &
Drabman, 1971). The purpose of this chapter
is to describe and define token economy and
outline effective procedures for using it in
applied settings.

DEFINITION OF TOKEN ECONOMY

Three aspects define a **token economy.** First,
behaviors to be reinforced are identified and
defined. Second, a medium of exchange is
selected; that medium of exchange is a symbol,
called a **token.** Third, **backup reinforcers**
are provided that can be purchased with the
token (Upper, 1977). Trading stamps are
analogous to a token economy. When a cus-
tomer purchases an item from a participating
store, the cashier provides the purchaser with

This chapter was written by John O. Cooper.

trading stamps—the medium of exchange—which serve as the token. The stamps are traded later through a redemption center or catalog for backup items such as sports equipment, clothing, or furniture. Money is another example of a token that can be exchanged at a later time for backup objects and activities (e.g., food, clothing, transportation, entertainment).

Robinson, Newby, and Ganzell (1981) used a token system to improve the reading and vocabulary performance of an 18-member class of third-grade boys with hyperactivity. Red, green, yellow, and white discs of metal-edged cardboard were used as tokens. As they were acquired, students made bracelets of them. Students earned a green token after learning seven vocabulary words, a yellow token for teaching a second student those words, a red token for learning to use the words in sentences, and a white token for teaching a second student to use the words in sentences. After earning the four colored tokens, the students could exchange the tokens for 15 minutes of playing time on an electronic game. In addition, each time students passed a weekly test given by the school's testing supervisor, they were allowed to play seven games on a pinball machine.

Figure 24.1 shows student academic performance in both the presence and absence of the token economy. The 18 students completed an average of 34.8 assignments per day during the first token condition. When tokens were withheld, the average number of completed assignments decreased to 3.8 per day. When tokens were reinstated, the average number of completed assignments increased to 39.57 per day. On the weekly tests given by the school's testing supervisor, the 18 students passed only .85 tests per week for the 20 weeks prior to the token system. During the first token condition, they passed an average of 3.0 tests per week. No tests were passed when the tokens were withheld, but the number of passed tests increased to 6.0 per week when the tokens were reinstated. The data indicate

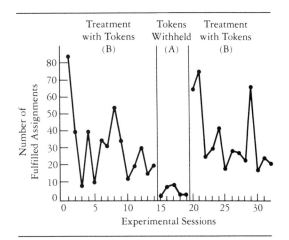

FIGURE 24.1 Total number of completed assignments for an 18-member class of hyperactive students. (From "A Token System for a Class of Underachieving Hyperactive Children" by P. W. Robinson, T. J. Newby, and S. L. Ganzell, 1981, *Journal of Applied Behavior Analysis, 14,* p. 311. Copyright 1981 by the Society for the Experimental Analysis of Behavior, Inc. Reprinted by permission.)

that all 18 students improved their reading and vocabulary performance during the token conditions. Also, it was demonstrated that a token economy system can control academic performance in a large class of hyperactive children.

A conditioned reinforcer was defined in chapter 11 as an event, object, or stimulus that is not initially reinforcing but acquires the properties of a reinforcer after frequent pairing or association with another reinforcer. A token is an example of a conditioned reinforcer; it can be exchanged for a wide variety of backup reinforcers. For instance, one resource room teacher in an elementary classroom for students with learning disabilities used beans as token reinforcement. The teacher dropped a specified number of beans in a glass jar to reinforce appropriate academic and social behaviors. When the jar was filled, the class exchanged the beans for a popcorn party.

All token economies function like the one in this illustration. If tokens are not regularly paired with backup reinforcement (e.g., the popcorn party), they will not function as reinforcement, or they will quickly lose their reinforcement capability. In addition, a conditioned reinforcer is effective only when the individual is deprived of the reinforcer(s) with which it is associated. If trading stamps could be exchanged only for bedroom lamps and an individual had an adequate supply of bedroom lamps, the stamps would not be effective reinforcement. Likewise, if popcorn parties are a regular occurrence at school, the beans (tokens) will probably not function as effective conditioned reinforcement.

Tokens function as a special kind of conditioned reinforcer called a **generalized conditioned reinforcer,** which means that they are paired with a wide variety of backup reinforcers. Trading stamps and money are examples of generalized conditioned reinforcers; they can be exchanged for a host of backup items. Generalized conditioned reinforcers can be independent of specific states of deprivation when they are associated with a wide variety of backup reinforcers. However, generalized conditioned reinforcement is a relative concept: effectiveness depends to a large extent on the extensiveness of the backup reinforcers. Stahl and Leitenberg (1976) state that for a token economy to be maximally effective, as many sources of reinforcement as can possibly be arranged should be contingent on token exchanges. Because money, for example, can be exchanged for many objects, activities, and services, all individuals are likely to be deprived of at least some of the items that can be obtained with money. Because of this independence from reinforcer-specific deprivation, money is effective as a generalized conditioned reinforcer most of the time. Tokens exchangeable for a wide variety of backup reinforcers have considerable utility in schools, hospitals, or clinics, where it is difficult for personnel to control the deprivation states of their clients.

Common Misconceptions About Generalized Conditioned Reinforcement

There are two common misconceptions concerning the use of the technical term *generalized conditioned reinforcers*. Sometimes it is stated that a reinforcer is generalized because it effectively reinforces a wide range of behaviors. Or it is stated that a generalized conditioned reinforcer can be used to effectively reinforce behaviors in a wide range of settings. Both statements misrepresent the concept: *all* reinforcers increase the future probability of occurrence of a wide range of behaviors. For instance, a stimulus or object that is reinforcement for spelling is also likely to be effective reinforcement for reading, math, and social behavior. And even specific reinforcement is effective in a wide range of settings. If a stimulus functions as reinforcement in a clinical setting, chances are good that the same stimulus will be effective in a family or school setting. Thus, the stimulus used as a generalized conditioned reinforcer (i.e., the token) is not generalized to behaviors or settings, but to many backup reinforcers.

Reasons for the Effectiveness of Token Economies

Token economies are often effective for three reasons. First, tokens can bridge the time gap between occurrence of a behavior and delivery of a backup reinforcer. For example, Johnston and Johnston (1972) used a token reinforcement procedure for correcting articulation problems of young children. To reinforce correct speech sounds, children were allowed to choose a special activity during playtime. The time gap between correct speech sounds and playtime was bridged by giving the child a mark or sticker contingent on correct speech sounds. These marks were later exchanged for the activity reinforcer.

In addition, tokens can bridge the setting gap between the behavior and the delivery of the backup reinforcer. Smith and Fowler (1984) awarded children in a kindergarten classroom points contingent on (1) cleaning one area of the classroom, (2) following classroom rules when they went as a group to the restroom, and (3) waiting quietly on their individual mats after returning from the restroom. The children received one point for each activity. Learners with three points could vote for and participate in a daily outdoor activity (e.g., kite flying, Frisbee throwing). Children who earned two points could participate in the activity but could not vote during its selection. The students earning one or no points could not participate in the outdoor activity. Not only was there a time gap between the classroom activities and the outdoor activity, but there was also a setting gap between the two. Tokens, therefore, can bridge not only time gaps but setting gaps between criteria for reinforcement and its delivery.

Finally, as noted above, tokens are generalized conditioned reinforcers, which makes the management of satiation and deprivation less critical for the behavior analyst.

PROCEDURES FOR IMPLEMENTING A TOKEN ECONOMY

Advance Preparation

Selecting Tokens A token is a tangible symbol that can be given immediately after a behavior and exchanged later for known reinforcers. Frequently used tokens include washers, checkers, coupons, poker chips, tally marks, teacher initials, holes punched in a card, and strips of plastic. Criteria to consider in selecting the token itself are important. First, the token should be safe; it should not be harmful to the learners. If a very young child or

an individual with severe learning or behavioral problems is to receive the token, it should not be an item that can be swallowed or used to cause injury. Second, the analyst should control token presentation; learners should not be able to bootleg the tokens. If tally marks are used, they should be on a special card or made with a special marking pen that is available only to the analyst. Likewise, if holes are punched in a card, the paper punch should be available only to the analyst. Most individuals are honest, but the system should not permit counterfeiting.

In addition, tokens should be durable because they may have to be used for an extended period of time, and they should be easy to carry, handle, bank, store, or accumulate. Tokens should also be readily accessible to the analyst at the moment they are to be dispensed. It is important that they be provided immediately after the target behavior. And tokens should be cheap; there is no need to spend a large sum of money to purchase tokens. Rubber stamps, stars, checkmarks, and buttons are all inexpensive items that can be used as tokens. Finally, the token itself should not be a desirable object. One teacher used baseball cards as tokens, but the students spent so much time interacting with the token (e.g., reading about players) that the token itself distracted students from the purpose of the system.

Defining Rules/Behaviors Chapter 3 discussed selection and definition of behavior change targets. The criteria presented in that chapter also apply to the selection and definition of rules and target behaviors for a token economy. Generally, the guidelines for selecting behaviors for a token economy include (1) selecting only measurable and observable behaviors; (2) specifying criteria for successful task completion; (3) starting with a small number of behaviors, including some that are easy for the individual to accomplish; and (4) being sure the individual possesses the prerequisite skills for any targeted behaviors (Heward, Dardig, & Rossett, 1979).

After rules and behaviors are defined that apply to everyone, then criteria and behaviors specific to individual learners should be established. Many token economy failures can be traced to requiring the same behaviors and setting the same criteria for all learners. Token economies usually need to be individualized. For example, in a classroom setting the teacher may want to select different behaviors for each student. Or perhaps the token economy should not be applied to all students in the classroom. Some students may be working well under current classroom procedures, and a token system would be a step backward. Perhaps only the lowest functioning students in the classroom should be included. However, if some students do not need a token system, it is important that they continue to receive other forms of reinforcement.

Selecting Backup Reinforcers Most token economies can use naturally occurring activities and events as backup reinforcers. For example, in a classroom or school setting, tokens can be used to buy time with popular games or materials, or they can be exchanged for favorite classroom jobs such as office messenger, paper passer, teacher assistant, or media operator. Tokens can also be used for schoolwide privileges such as a library or study hall pass, a special period (e.g., physical education) with another class, or special responsibilities such as school patrol, cafeteria monitor, or tutor. Phillips, Phillips, Fixsen, and Wolf (1971) used naturally occurring activities and events as backup reinforcers for a token economy in a community-based family-style center for delinquents. Hobbies, games, snacks, TV, allowance, permission to go home or downtown, sports events, and bonds for gifts or special clothing were used as backup reinforcers in this setting.

If naturally occurring activities and events fail, then backup items not ordinarily present in a particular program can be considered (e.g., pictures of movie or sports stars, records, magazines, or edibles). Such items should generally be considered only when more naturally occurring activities have proven ineffective. However, if the naturally occurring backup items have been available to learners non-contingently prior to the introduction of the token economy, Stahl and Leitenberg (1976) recommend that new backup activities and events should be the major items for token exchange.

Selection of backup reinforcers should follow consideration of ethical and legal issues, as well as the policies of state and local education agencies if the system is to be applied in an educational setting. Budd and Baer (1976) have described in detail those privileges to which learners should have free access. Naturally occurring activities and events that should not be used as backup reinforcers include the following: (1) meals—learners should have free access to nutritionally adequate meals in the normal setting; (2) communication—mail and telephone privileges cannot be restricted, and clients should have noncontingent access to all forms of communication; (3) general comforts—all areas related to general comfort are inappropriate to use as backup reinforcers, for example, clean clothing, adequate heating, ventilation, and hot water; and (4) general prerogatives—privileges such as access to religious services, education, medical care, social interaction, and exercise need to be freely available to all individuals. Within these constraints practitioners should plan to use as many backup reinforcers as possible.

Establishing a Ratio of Exchange Initially, the ratio between the number of tokens earned and the price of backup items should be small to provide immediate success for the learners. The ratio of exchange should be adjusted thereafter to maintain the responsiveness of the participants.

Kazdin (1975) states that many behavior analysts attribute the success of a token economy almost entirely to principles of reinforcement. They view any limitation in the system as a result of inadequate application of appropriate reinforcement procedures. However, Kazdin argues that three principles from economic theory need to be considered in addition to principles of reinforcement. First, if an individual earns only a few tokens, only a few are available to spend. If an individual earns a large number of tokens, it becomes possible to exchange only a small portion of the tokens for backup reinforcers, and still have tokens left over. Eventually, token savings can become so great that the individual does not have to acquire additional tokens to have access to sufficient backup items. At high levels of token saving, individuals need not emit behaviors to acquire additional tokens. Kazdin offers the following recommendations to alter the level of earnings when token-earning behaviors and token income and savings increase: the prices of backup items should be increased, and the value of tokens should be decreased. These manipulations will automatically alter the value of the savings. Then the number of backup items available for exchange can be increased. These adjustments should cause more tokens to be spent and should reduce the number of tokens being saved.

The second economic principle to be considered is that as the number of earned tokens increases, the proportion of the tokens used for urgent needs (e.g., recess, using calculator for math) will decrease. It is likely then that the proportion of tokens spent on luxuries (e.g., after-school sports, chewing gum, table monitor) will increase. This principle has a clear implication for token economies when token-earning behaviors and token income are increased. As the number of earned tokens increases, the number of luxury backup activities and events should expand also because of increased demand.

The third principle is that if the number of tokens required to purchase backup items increases, urgent needs should require more

tokens and luxuries should be relatively inexpensive. If the number of tokens required to purchase luxury items is increased substantially, learners may be less likely to emit behaviors that generate additional tokens. Table 24.1 provides an example of a ratio of exchange between tokens and backup reinforcers for a sixth-grade math class (McLaughlin, 1981).

To summarize, there are several general guidelines for establishing the ratio between earned tokens and the price of backup items: (1) keep initial ratios low; (2) as token-earning behaviors and income increase, increase cost of backup items, devalue tokens, and increase number of backup items; (3) with increased earnings increase number of luxury backup items; and (4) increase prices of necessary backup items more than those of luxury items.

One other procedure for establishing a ratio between tokens and backup items is to auction the backup items (Polloway & Polloway, 1979). With this procedure a group of individuals can bid for backup items, but no learner can bid beyond the total number of tokens he has accumulated. The auction takes the guesswork out of determining the value of an activity or item.

Addressing General Procedures Some general procedures need to be addressed prior to implementation of a token economy. These procedures respond to frequently asked questions.

What procedure will be used to dispense tokens? If objects such as tally marks or holes punched in a card are selected as the tokens, the way in which the learner will receive them is obvious. No special considerations are necessary. But if objects such as coupons or poker chips are used, there should be some container for storing the accumulated tokens before they are exchanged for the backup items. Some analysts have learners construct individual folders for storing their tokens. Others place the tokens in a paper cup. Another suggestion is to deposit the tokens through cut

TABLE 24.1. Ratio of exchange between tokens (points) and backup reinforcers.

Behaviors That Earn Points		Activity Reinforcers	
Behaviors	Points per Day	Activities	Point Cost per Week
Assignment completion	7–15	Recess	20
Math problem rates	0–10	Cleaning animal cages	10
Field trips	10	Talking with permission	25
Food and sawdust for animals	5–100	Being on a committee	10
Good behavior in library	10	Going to library during free time	15
Taking notes	5	Line checker at noon*	15
Returning school notices	5	Table monitor in the lunchroom*	30
Being good at convocations	5	After-school sports	60
Study behavior	5	Friday recess	20
Listening	5	Seeing the animals in the room	15
Being good during music	10	Weekend equipment checkout	30
Oral points in science		Special projects	30
discussions	0–15	Using the adding machine during	
		math	30
Behavior during break	5	Chewing gum on Thursdays	30

*These activities were sold on a lottery basis.

SOURCE: From "The Effects of a Classroom Token Economy on Math Performance in an Intermediate Grade School Class" by T. F. McLaughlin, 1981, *Education and Treatment of Children, 4*, p. 141. Copyright 1981 by *Education and Treatment of Children*. Adapted by permission.

slots in the plastic tops of coffee cans. With younger learners tokens can be chained to a necklace or bracelet.

How will the tokens be exchanged? A "menu" of the backup items should be provided with a given price for each item. Individuals can then select from the menu. Many teachers have a table "store" with all the items displayed (e.g., games, balloons, toys, certificates for privileges). To avoid noise and confusion at shopping time, Sulzer-Azaroff and Mayer (1977) recommend using order blanks; individual orders can be filled by writing in or checking off the items to be purchased. Those items are then placed in a bag with the order form stapled to the top and are returned to the purchaser. Initially, the store should be open frequently, perhaps once in the morning and once in the afternoon. Learners with lower functioning may need even more frequent exchange periods. Later, exchange periods might be available only on Wednesdays and Fridays, or only on Fridays. As quickly as possible, token exchange should occur on an intermittent basis.

What will happen if the individual does not meet the requirements to earn a token? One approach is to nag the individual: "You didn't do your homework. You know your homework must be completed to earn tokens. Why didn't you do it?" A better approach is a matter-of-fact reaction to the contingency: "No, I'm sorry. You haven't enough tokens to exchange. Try again." It is important to know whether the individual has the skills required to earn tokens. An individual should always be able to meet the response requirement.

What should be done when a learner tests the system? How should a behavior analyst respond to "I don't want any tokens or backup items"? One approach is to argue, debate, or cajole the learner. A better approach is to say something neutral (e.g., "That is your decision") and then walk away, precluding any argument or debate. In this way a confrontation is avoided, and the occasion remains set for token delivery for the learner. The success of a token economy can be enhanced by enlisting the learners' help in planning and administering the system (Stahl & Leitenberg, 1976). Most learners can and should have input in selecting the backup items, generating the rules for the economy, establishing the price for the backup items, and performing general duties in managing the system. A learner can be a salesperson for the store or a bookkeeper to record who has how many tokens and what items are purchased. When learners are involved and their responsibility for the economy is emphasized, they are less likely to test the system.

Will the token economy include a response cost procedure? The procedures for including response cost with a token economy were presented in chapter 20. Most token economies do include a token loss contingency for inappropriate behaviors and rule infractions. Any behaviors subject to response cost should be defined and stated clearly in the rules. Learners need to be aware of what actions will result in token loss and how much the behavior will cost. The more serious the inappropriate behavior, the greater the token loss should be. Table 24.2 presents the amount of token loss for the occurrence of specified behaviors used by McLaughlin (1981). In this illustration fighting or cheating result in much greater token loss than out-of-seat or talk-outs. Token loss should never be applied to a behavior if the learner does not have tokens. Students should not be allowed to go into debt, which would likely decrease the reinforcement value of the tokens. A learner should always earn more tokens than she loses.

Field Testing the System   The final step before actually implementing a token system is to field test it. For 3 to 5 days token delivery is tallied exactly as if tokens were being earned, but no tokens are actually given out during the field test. Data from the field test are used for assessment. Are learners actually deficient in the targeted skills? Are some learners demonstrating mastery of behaviors targeted for intervention? Are some learners not receiving tokens? Based on answers to questions such as

TABLE 24.2.   Amount of token loss for the occurrence of specified behaviors.

Behaviors	Points Lost
Out-of-seat	15
Talk-outs	15
Fighting	100
Cheating	100
Wasting time	25
Incomplete assignments	Number squared
Failing to take notes	25
Not listening	25
Misbehavior on field trips	100
Swearing	100

SOURCE: From "The Effects of a Classroom Token Economy on Math Performance in an Intermediate Grade School Class" by T. F. McLaughlin, 1981, *Education and Treatment of Children, 4,* p. 141. Copyright 1981 by *Education and Treatment of Children.* Adapted by permission.

these, final adjustments in the system can be made. For some learners more difficult behaviors may need to be defined; others may need less demanding target behaviors. Perhaps more or fewer tokens need to be delivered relative to the price of the backup reinforcers.

Initial Steps in Token Training

Beginning the System   The manner in which initial training is conducted to implement a token economy depends upon the functioning level of the learners. For mildly handicapped or high functioning learners, the initial training might be minimal, relying primarily on verbal instructions or modeling. Usually the initial token training for these individuals can be accomplished in 15 to 30 minutes. Three steps are normally sufficient. First, an example of the system should be given. The analyst might use words like these.

> This is a token and you can earn it by [specify behavior] . I will watch your behavior; and when you accomplish [specify behavior] , you will earn a token. Also, as you continue [specify behavior] , you will earn more tokens. At [specify time period] you will be able to exchange the tokens

you have earned for whatever you want and can afford on this table. Each item is marked with the number of tokens needed for purchase. You can spend only the tokens you have earned. If you want an item that requires more tokens than you have earned, you will have to save your tokens over several [specify time period].

The second step is to model the procedure for token delivery. For instance, each learner might be directed to emit the specified behavior. Immediately following the occurrence of the behavior, the learner should be praised (e.g., "Mary, I'm pleased to see how well you are working by yourself!") and the token delivered.

The third step is to model the procedure for token exchange. Learners should be taken to the store and shown the items for purchase. All of the learners should already have one token, which was acquired during the modeling of token delivery. Several items should be able to be purchased for one token at this time (the price may go up later)—a game, 5 minutes of free time, a pencil sharpening certificate, or teacher helper privilege. Tokens should actually be exchanged for the students.

Lower functioning learners may require several sessions of initial token training before the system is functional for them. Also, many physical or verbal prompts may be needed. Snell (1983a) suggests an eight-step procedure for token training with low functioning clients. Almost all initial token training for these learners follows the procedure suggested by Snell or one similar to it.

1 A behavior or class of behaviors, easily performed by the individual, is selected (e.g., imitation of movements, following simple commands—"Show me the baby," "Comb your hair," "Look at me").

2 A choice of known backup reinforcers (arranged on a tray or cupcake pan), a token container (one-pound coffee can), and a uniform set of at least 30 tokens (poker chips, washers, checkers, etc.) are readied at a training table.

3 The individual is requested to perform the behavior and

    a is reinforced immediately following the behavior with a single token placed into the individual's hand with enthusiastic praise.

    b is prompted if the behavior is not forthcoming, and then is reinforced with a token and praise immediately following the behavior.

4 Immediately, the trainer holds out a hand to collect the token (with prompting if necessary) and presents the reinforcer tray from which the individual is prompted to select one reinforcer.

5 This cycle—request for the behavior, praise and token reinforcement, and immediate exchange—is repeated until the individual, without any prompts, shows evidence of making an association between tokens and token exchange. For example, an individual may reach for the tokens after a respnse as an attempt to "speed up" the exchange process. Then the exchange schedule is increased gradually from one token to an accumulation of four or five tokens before exchange.

6 While remaining at four or five tokens, the token container is introduced to facilitate the collection and exchange process. Tokens are then dropped into the can by the teacher and the individual is shown how to lift and empty the contents during exchange time.

7 The exchange ratio is increased gradually over the remainder of the token training session, which should not last beyond 15 to 20 minutes.

8 At this point, tokens may be used during actual teaching sessions as the method of reinforcement. Initially, a brief review (a few immediate or low ratio exchanges) may be necessary to remind the individual of the tokens' exchange value. (pp. 119–120)

Ongoing Token Reinforcement During ongoing token reinforcement it is necessary to follow the rules for effective use of reinforcement, as presented in chapter 11. Tokens should be dispensed contingently and immediately after the occurrence of the desired behavior. Procedures for delivery and exchange should be clear and should be followed consistently. Finally, the focus should be on building and increasing desirable behaviors through token delivery rather than decreasing undesirable behaviors through token response cost.

The behavior analyst may choose to take part in the token economy. For example, the analyst could pinpoint a self-behavior to be increased and could then model how to act when one does not get a token, how to save, how to keep track of progress. After 2 to 3 weeks a revision in the token economy system may be needed. It is usually desirable to have learners discuss behaviors they want to change, the backup items they would like to have available, or the schedule of exchange. If some individuals rarely earn tokens, it may be necessary to revert to a simpler response or prerequisite skill. On the other hand, some individuals may always earn all possible tokens, and requirements may need to be changed to a more complex skill.

Removing the Token Economy

Before the initial program is applied, analysts should plan how they will remove the token system. The goal of the token program should be to have the descriptive verbal praise that is delivered simultaneously with the token acquire the reinforcing capability of the token. Thus, even from the beginning, a systematic goal of the token economy should be to withdraw the program. Such an approach, aside from having functional utility for the analyst (i.e., he will not have to issue tokens forever), also has advantages for the learner. For example, if a special education teacher is using a token economy with one of the students scheduled to be mainstreamed into a regular fourth grade, the teacher wants to be certain that the student's responses can be maintained in the absence of the token economy. It is unlikely that the student would encounter a similar token system in the regular fourth-grade class.

Various methods have been used to withdraw token reinforcers gradually after criterion levels of behavior have been reached. The following six guidelines allow the practitioner to develop, and later withdraw, token rein-

forcers effectively. First, the token presentation should always be paired with social approval (e.g., verbal praise). This should increase the reinforcing effect of the social approval and serve to maintain behaviors after token withdrawal. Second, the number of responses required to earn a token should be gradually increased. For instance, if a student receives a token initially after reading only one page, more pages should be read later for token delivery. Third, the length of time the token economy is in effect should be gradually decreased. For example, during September the system might be in effect all day; in October the time might be 8:30 A.M. to 12:00 P.M. and 2:00 P.M. to 3:00 P.M.; in November, 8:30 A.M. to 10:00 A.M. and 2:00 P.M. to 3:00 P.M.; in December the times might be the same as those in November but on only 4 days a week; and so on.

Fourth, the number of activities and privileges that serve as backup items and are likely to be found in the untrained setting should be gradually increased. For example, the analyst should start taking away tangible items in the store that might not be present in the regular classroom. Are edibles available at the store? They are usually not available for reinforcement in regular classrooms. Gradually, items should be introduced that would be common in a regular class (e.g., special award sheets, gold stars, positive notes home). Fifth, the price of more desirable items should be gradually increased while keeping a very low price on undesirable items for exchange. For example, in a token system with institutionalized adolescent girls with moderate to severe mental retardation, the price of candy bars and trips to the canteen and grooming aids (e.g., comb, deodorant) was initially about the same. Gradually, the cost of items such as candy bars was increased to such a high level that the girls no longer saved tokens to purchase them. More girls used their tokens to purchase grooming aids, which cost substantially less than candy.

Sixth, the physical evidence of the token should be gradually faded. The following sequence illustrates how the physical evidence of the token can be faded.

- ☐ Learners earn physical tokens such as poker chips or washers.
- ☐ The physical tokens are replaced with slips of paper.
- ☐ The slips of paper are replaced with tally marks on an index card that is kept by the learners.

- ☐ In a school setting the index card can now be taped to the learner's desk.
- ☐ The index card is removed from the learner and is kept by the analyst, but individuals can check their balance at any time.
- ☐ The analyst keeps tallies, but no checking is allowed during the day. Totals are announced at the end of the day, every other day.

Level One:	Each student begins the school year in Level One where tokens such as poker chips are given approximately every 15 minutes for appropriate academic and social behavior. Every morning and afternoon each student is allowed to rent games, materials, or activity privileges during a 15-minute free time period. Prices of rentals vary according to demand. Upon reaching a specified level of successful performance (e.g., 90% academic success for 10 consecutive days with no major rule infraction), a student may move to Level Two.
Level Two:	In Level Two, tokens are replaced with a card which is marked with checks for correct academic and social behavior every half hour. The checkmarks are exchanged at the end of the day for listed classroom privileges for the following day (e.g., office messenger, paper passer, teacher assistant, media operator). In addition, students on Level Two can use previously purchased activity, material, or game items from Level One free of charge. In effect, it becomes attractive to attain Level Two because more privileges are available but the frequency of reinforcement is decreased and the "concreteness" of tokens (e.g., poker chips) is reduced to checkmarks. Upon reaching another specified criterion of successful performance (e.g., 90% academic success for 10 consecutive days with no major rule infraction) a student may move to Level Three.
Level Three:	In Level Three, checkmarks are replaced by contracts which cover each morning and afternoon. At the end of each session, the teacher reviews each student in Level Three and determines if the contract was met. The students meeting criterion earn schoolwide privileges such as library pass, study hall pass, special period with another class such as P.E. or other appropriate privileges involving increased responsibility. Level One and Level Two privileges are now free for students at Level Three.
Level Four:	Following another successful 10 days, students at Level Three may attain Level Four, in which weekly report cards determine whether goals are met. In Level Four, special responsibilities are encouraged such as school patrol, cafeteria monitors, tutoring others.
Summary:	Each level contains a minimum performance criterion for academic and social behavior. As the student advances in level, a failure to meet the minimum criterion at the advanced level causes the student to move back one level and necessitates working back through demonstrated success. This criterion for backward movement enables those who need more help to be identified quickly and returned to an appropriate level.

FIGURE 24.2 Illustration of a level system with a token economy. (From "Suggestions for Phasing Out Token Economy Systems in Primary and Intermediate Grades" by L. J. La Nunziata, Jr., K. P. Hunt, and J. O. Cooper, 1984, *Techniques, 1*, pp. 153, 155. Copyright 1984 by *Techniques*. Reprinted by permission.)

□ The token system is no longer operative. The behavior analyst does not announce totals even though they are still kept.

In each of the six guidelines presented here, tokens become fewer and fewer and are taken over by procedures more natural to the setting. Another procedure for gradual token withdrawal is the tiered or **level system.** The procedure uses levels through which learners move by demonstrating appropriate behavior for specified time periods. Privileges are increased at each level while frequency of reinforcement is decreased. LaNunziata, Hunt, and Cooper (1984) describe the use of a level system in a school setting (see Figure 24.2).

Considerations

Before implementing a token economy, one should consider the possible disadvantages.

Token systems should be implemented only when desirable aspects outweight disadvantages and plans for withdrawing the token system have been made.

Intrusive Token systems are frequently intrusive. Most natural environments do not reinforce individuals' behaviors with tokens. One noticeable exception is a job in which work behaviors produce money payment.

Self-Perpetuating A token economy can be an effective procedure for managing behavior, and analysts can be so encouraged by the results that they do not want to remove the system. Learners then continue working for reinforcement that is not normally available in the natural environment.

Cumbersome Initially token economies are usually cumbersome to implement and may require additional time and effort from both the learner and the behavior analyst.

SUMMARY

Definition of a Token Economy

1 Three aspects define a token economy: (1) behaviors are specified; (2) a medium of exchange is selected (e.g., tokens); and (3) backup items are purchased with the medium of exchange.
2 Tokens are generalized conditioned reinforcers that are paired with a wide variety of backup reinforcers.
3 Generalized reinforcers are commonly misperceived as generalized because (1) they can reinforce behaviors in a wide variety of settings or (2) they reinforce many different behaviors. All reinforcers function in this way.

Effectiveness of Token Economies

4 Tokens can bridge the time gap between the behavior and the delivery of the backup reinforcer.
5 Tokens can bridge the setting gap between the behavior and the delivery of the backup reinforcer.

6 Management of satiation and deprivation becomes less critical for the behavior analyst.

Procedures for Implementing a Token Economy

Advance Preparation
7 Select a token. It should be safe, controllable, durable and easy to carry, accessible, and cheap.
8 Define rules/behaviors for which tokens will be given.
9 Select backup items that can be bought with the tokens. Whenever possible use normally occurring activities and events as the backup items and as wide a variety of items as possible.
10 Establish the ratio of exchange. Initially, the ratio between the number of tokens earned and the price of backup items should be low to provide immediate success for the learners.
11 Field test the system before starting. For 3 to 5 days before the token economy is actually implemented, keep records of who would have

earned how many tokens. The data are used to assess the selection of behaviors and the ratio of exchange.

Initial Steps in Token Training

12 For mildly handicapped or high functioning learners, the initial token training can be minimal and can rely primarily on verbal instructions and some modeling. However, for low functioning learners, more extensive initial training is required.

13 It is necessary to follow the rules for effective use of reinforcement as presented in chapter 11.

14 Behavior analysts implementing a token system should decide in advance how they will remove the system.

Considerations

15 Token systems are frequently intrusive.

16 A token system can perpetuate itself.

25

Group-Oriented Contingencies

KEY TERMS

Group-oriented contingency

Hero procedure

Dependent group-oriented contingency

Independent group-oriented contingency

Interdependent group-oriented contingency

Good Behavior Game

Thus far in the text we have focused primarily on how contingencies of reinforcement can be applied to individuals to increase the future probability of occurrence of certain behaviors. Experimental work has also demonstrated how contingencies can be applied to groups, and behavior analysts have increasingly turned their attention toward group-oriented contingencies in areas such as energy consumption (Geller, Winett, & Everett, 1982), student performance in classrooms (Baer & Richards, 1980), and

dental hygiene (Swain, Allard, & Holborn, 1982). Each of these applications has shown that group-oriented contingencies, properly managed, can be an effective and practical approach to changing the behavior of many individuals simultaneously.

This chapter defines a group-oriented contingency, provides a rationale for its use, addresses ethical considerations associated with group-oriented contingencies, cites a classification scheme for categorizing group-oriented

This chapter was written by Timothy E. Heron.

contingencies, and provides guidelines for implementing group-oriented contingencies in applied settings.

DEFINITION OF A GROUP-ORIENTED CONTINGENCY

A **group-oriented contingency** is one in which the presentation, or loss, of a reinforcer is contingent upon the behavior of an individual within the group, a segment of the group, or the group as a whole. According to Litow and Pumroy (1975), a useful distinction is made between the terms *group contingency* and *group-oriented contingency*. In their view a group contingency cannot exist because groups do not perform behaviors; only individuals do. A group-oriented contingency, on the other hand, connotes the performance of a behavior by individuals within the group. Although this distinction may appear trite, it does serve to focus attention on the behavior of individuals within a group. We recognize that both terms are used interchangeably in the literature.

RATIONALE

There are a number of reasons for using a group-oriented contingency in applied settings. First of all, it can save time during administration (Gresham, 1983). Instead of repeatedly administering a consequence to each member of a group, the practitioner can apply one consequence to all members of the group. From a logistical perspective, a practitioner's workload may be reduced. And the group contingency has been shown to be as effective as an individual contingency in producing behavior change (Solomon & Tyne, 1979). Thus, a group-oriented contingency can be effective and economical, requiring fewer persons or less time during implementation.

Another advantage is that a practitioner can use a group-oriented contingency in a situation where it is impractical to initiate an individual contingency. For example, a teacher attempting to reduce a large number of disruptive student behaviors might find it difficult to administer a reductive program for each pupil in the classroom. A substitute teacher, in particular, might find the use of a group-oriented contingency a practical alternative because her knowledge of the students' previous histories of reinforcement would be limited, and the group-oriented contingency could be applied across a variety of behaviors, settings, or students.

A group-oriented contingency can also be used in cases where the practitioner must resolve a problem quickly, as when serious disruptive behavior occurs on a regular basis. The practitioner might be interested not only in decreasing the disruptive behavior rapidly, but also in building improved levels of appropriate behavior. A group-oriented contingency is useful in this regard (Axelrod, 1983; Gresham & Gresham, 1982).

Furthermore, a practitioner can use a group-oriented contingency to capitalize on peer influence or peer monitoring because this type of contingency sets the occasion for peers to act as change agents (LaRowe, Tucker, & McGuire, 1980; Gresham & Gresham, 1982). Admittedly, peer pressure can have a detrimental effect on some individuals; they may become scapegoats. But this potentially harmful outcome can be minimized by structuring the contingency carefully. Scapegoating is discussed in more detail later in the chapter.

Finally, a practitioner can establish a group-oriented contingency to facilitate positive social interaction among a group of students. For example, a teacher might establish a group-oriented contingency for a student with a learning disability (LD). The student might be integrated into the regular classroom in such a way that the entire class would be awarded free time, contingent on the performance of the LD student (see Gresham, 1983). Awarding the free time to the class could serve as a discriminative stimulus for a "natural community of reinforcers" (Strain, Shores, & Kerr, 1976). That is, the nonhandicapped students might provide additional reinforcement for the LD student by saying, "Thanks for earning more free time for us."

When an individual earns a reinforcer for a group, the contingency is referred to as the **hero procedure.** According to Kerr and Nelson (1983), the hero procedure facilitates positive interaction between students because the class as a whole benefits from the improved behavior of the student targeted for the group-oriented contingency.

ETHICAL CONSIDERATIONS

Despite the fact that group-oriented contingencies have been demonstrated to be practical, effective, and economical, their wholesale endorsement must be tempered by a consideration of several points of ethics. First, one of the distinguishing features of a group-oriented contingency is that peers act as change agents by monitoring or providing consequences for specific behaviors. According to Sapon-Shevin (1979), the use of undefined peer pressure to set the occasion for behavior change, particularly without recording the nature of the peers' interactions, is an ethical matter of paramount importance. Baer and Richard (1980) agree: "It is possible that some group members may exert harmful group pressure (e.g., ridicule, teasing, etc.) on those who fail to improve" (p. 193)

Specific instances in the literature have shown that when an individual or group does not receive a reinforcer, an increased likelihood of covert verbal statements or threats may follow (Axelrod, 1973; LaRowe, Tucker, & McGuire, 1980). The essential issue is not necessarily that of peer pressure, which already

exists in the classroom. The ethics of the issue relate to the planned use of peer pressure to meet prescribed ends (i.e., improved behavior) when the means (i.e., the process by which students monitor each other's behavior) are not equally well studied or manipulated by the practitioner. Sapon-Shevin (1979) has another view of the problem.

> Since we are concerned with a functional analysis of group contingencies, that is, an evaluation of what actually happened under the control of various arrangements of the environment (by the teacher), then the occurrences of undesirable behaviors among children during the operation of group contingencies must be viewed as a *component* of group contingencies. (p. 21)

Practitioners considering a group-oriented contingency must use direct and daily measures of student performance (assessment), coupled with frequent measures of social validity, to determine whether a group-oriented contingency should be initiated or continued.

> In situations where there is concern that group contingencies may (a) induce potentially damaging peer pressure to those who deter the attainment of the group goal; (b) reduce the students' personal control over the consequences of their behavior, and (c) constrain individual incentives, an individual contingency system may be more appropriate. (Solomon & Tyne, 1979, p. 198)

Practitioners must be alert to occurrences of covert peer pressure or coercion that could produce undesirable effects and might go unrecorded if limited observation and analysis techniques are used.

A second ethical concern exists when the implementation of the group-oriented contingency specifies that the offender(s) be announced publicly in some manner (e.g., addressing the student verbally, writing the student's name on the blackboard). Figure 25.1(a) shows a blackboard chart that visually identifies students responsible for the loss of 1-minute increments of class free time. Such a publicly posted chart may increase the like-

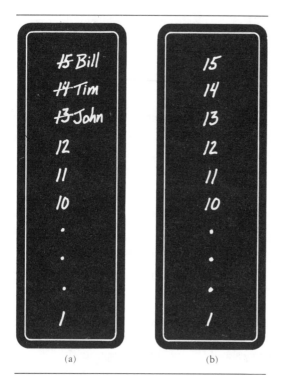

(a)   (b)

FIGURE 25.1

lihood of covert peer pressure and scapegoating. As an alternative, a group-oriented contingency can produce the intended result—for example, reduced disruptive behavior—without the potential side effect of scapegoating by eliminating the offender's name from the chart, as in Figure 25.1(b). Another functional way to reduce the likelihood of scapegoating is to adjust the criterion for the group-oriented contingency (Kerr & Nelson 1983). A contingency can be established whereby the whole class receives the reinforcer if 75% of the group achieves a criterion level of 85% or above. Thus, an individual's occasional minor infraction does not preclude the group from ultimately meeting the established criterion.

The presumed advantage of using a class or group as the unit of analysis raises another ethical issue, that of reporting data showing an overall improvement for the group when, in fact, some of the students did not improve or even did more poorly under the group-oriented contingency. Because scores for a group are averaged, the performance of these students is masked under the group-oriented contingency. This situation can lead the practitioner to continue what seems to be an effective approach when actually a certain percentage of students or clients are getting worse (Sapon-Shevin, 1979).

If the practitioner is unable to observe the behavior of individuals within the group periodically to determine whether the desired effect is produced, the group-oriented contingency should probably not be used. According to Sapon-Shevin (1979), it is irresponsible to initiate a procedure in which the likelihood of success is not equally high for each individual and for which a data collection system does not exist that can provide sufficient opportunity for the teacher to judge the merits of the program. Responsible practitioners can avoid this situation by collecting data on a regular basis and performing reliability checks frequently (cf. Vogler & French, 1983). Both of these procedures increase the likelihood that believable data will be obtained for all individuals within the group.

A final ethical problem can occur when a group-oriented contingency is established with some members of the group unable to complete the requisite behaviors specified in the contingency (Stolz, 1978). In this situation the individual is placed under the constraints of a contingency that cannot be met or avoided. To avoid this situation, the practitioner should assess the limits of student performance (i.e., the range of student behavior) before establishing the criterion for a group-oriented contingency and should set the initial criterion according to a minimum standard. As student performance improves, the criterion can be raised.

CLASSIFICATION SCHEMES FOR GROUP-ORIENTED CONTINGENCIES

Litow and Pumroy (1975) propose a categorization scheme for group-oriented contingencies. In their view group-oriented contingencies can be divided into three categories: dependent group-oriented contingencies, independent group-oriented contingencies, and interdependent group-oriented contingencies. Because a comprehensive examination of all the studies associated with each type of contingency can be found elsewhere (see Litow & Pomroy, 1975; Hayes, 1976), the following section presents only a few representative studies within each category.

Dependent Group-Oriented Contingencies

Under a **dependent group-oriented contingency** the reinforcer for the group is dependent upon the performance of an individual student or small group. Kazdin's (1980c) term for such a contingency is consequence sharing. Regardless of the terminology, the contingency operates like this: if an individual (or small group) performs a behavior to a specific criterion, the group shares the reinforcer. Thus, the group's access to the reinforcer is entirely dependent upon the individual's (or small group's) performance. If the individual performs below the criterion, reinforcement is not delivered. Figure 25.2 illustrates the dependent group-oriented contingency as a three-term contingency.

Walker and Buckley (1972) conducted a dependent group-oriented contingency study as part of an overall strategy to program for generalization and maintenance across time and settings. In their study 48 elementary-aged students in Grades 3 through 6 served as subjects. After receiving 2 months of training in an experimental classroom in which improved academic

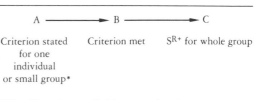

(E.g., "Joe, when you finish your math assignment, the class will have 5 minutes of free time.")

FIGURE 25.2 A dependent group-oriented contingency.

and social behavior was reinforced with tokens, the students were divided into three experimental groups and a control group. The three experimental groups were (1) peer reprogramming with a dependent group-oriented contingency in which appropriate behavior earned a reinforcer for the group; (2) equating stimulus conditions, in which the post treatment setting was structured to resemble the treatment setting; and (3) teacher training, in which the regular teacher was taught behavior modification strategies. Results indicated that peer reprogramming and equating stimulus conditions produced the greatest maintenance and generalization. The dependent group-oriented contingency produced the most stable changes in student performance and required less time than teacher training.

Gresham (1983) conducted a dependent group-oriented contingency study in which the contingency was applied at home, but the reinforcer was delivered at school. In this study an 8-year-old boy who was highly destructive at home (i.e., set fires, destroyed furniture) earned good notes for nondestructive behavior at home. "Billy" received a good note—a daily report card—each day that no destructive acts took place. Each note was exchangeable for juice, recess, and 5 tokens at school the next day. After Billy received 5 good notes, the whole class received a party, and Billy served as the host. Gresham reports that the dependent group-oriented contingency reduced the amount of destructive behavior and represented the first application of a dependent group-oriented contingency in combined home-school settings.

Allen, Gottselig, and Boylan (1982) used an interesting variation of the dependent group-oriented contingency. In their study eight disruptive third graders from a class of 29 students served as target students. On the first day of intervention the teacher posted and explained classroom rules for hand raising, leaving a seat, disturbing others, and getting help. Contingent upon reduced amounts of disruptive behavior—being out-of-seat, calling-out, disturbing others—during 5-minute intervals in math and language arts, the class as a whole earned 1 extra minute of recess time. If a disruptive behavior occurred during the 5-minute interval, the teacher cited the disrupter for the infraction (e.g., "James, you disturbed Sue") and reset the timer for another 5-minute interval. The teacher also posted the accumulated time on an easel in full view of the class. The results of this multiple baseline study indicate that reduced disruptive behavior occurred under the dependent group-oriented contingency (see Figure 25.3).

Independent Group-Oriented Contingencies

According to Litow and Pumroy (1975), the **independent group-oriented contingency** is an arrangement in which a contingency is presented to all members of a group, but reinforcement is delivered only to those individuals who meet the criterion outlined in the contingency. In other words, some individuals may earn reinforcement; others may not. Figure 25.4 illustrates the independent group-oriented contingency as a three-term contingency.

Hopkins, Schutte, and Garton (1971) provide an example of an independent group-oriented contingency that improved the rate at which elementary students completed daily copying assignments. Data were collected on

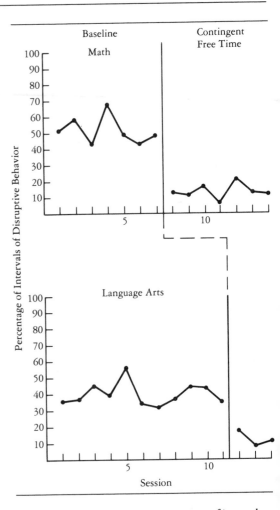

FIGURE 25.3 Daily mean percentage of intervals of disruptive behavior during baseline and contingent free time phases for the group. (From "A Practical Mechanism for Using Free Time as a Reinforcer in the Classroom" by L. D. Allen, M. Gottselig, and S. Boylan, 1982, *Education and Treatment of Children*, 5(4), p. 351. Copyright 1982 by *Education and Treatment of Children*. Reprinted by permission.)

the mean number of letters per minute and the mean number of errors per letter during a daily copying assignment. During baseline conditions the class was given a chalkboard assignment and told to copy it within 50 minutes. The 24 children in two grades were told that as

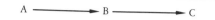

A $\longrightarrow$ B $\longrightarrow$ C

Criterion stated   Criterion met S^{R+} For *each* member
for all   achieving criterion
group members*

*(E.g., "Each student who spells 9 out of 10 words correctly on the test Friday will earn 10 extra points.")

FIGURE 25.4   An independent group-oriented contingency.

soon as their assignment was completed and was scored by the teacher, they were to return to their desks and remain seated until the last child finished the copying task. During the next condition, Playroom 50-Minutes, the children were told that as soon as their paper was completed and scored, they could spend the remainder of the 50-minute period in the playroom. Thus, the faster a student finished his work, the longer he could be in the playroom. Subsequently, baseline conditions were reinstituted, followed by Playroom 50, 45, 40, and 35. Each of these successive conditions replicated the Playroom 50 condition, except that progressively fewer minutes were allocated to completing the copying assignment (i.e., 45 minutes, 40 minutes, and 35 minutes, respectively).

The results indicate that during the independent group-oriented contingency (Playroom 50, 45, 40, and 35) reliable increases in writing rates and reliable decreases in errors occurred. The authors suggest that the typical procedures used in classrooms to gain access to free time (e.g., waiting until everyone has completed an assignment) are inefficient and perhaps produce poorer student performance. An independent group-oriented contingency that provides reinforcement contingent upon speed and accuracy might serve as a more functional alternative (see Figure 25.5).

Two of the more popular uses of the independent group-oriented contingency occur during contingency contracting and token rein-

forcement programs. These programs usually establish reinforcement schedules independent of the performance of other members of the group. Litow and Pumroy (1975) report 42 studies using this group contingency, and chapters 23 and 24 in this text summarize several of those investigations.

Interdependent Group-Oriented Contingencies

An **interdependent group-oriented contingency** is one in which all of the individuals of a group must meet the criterion of the contingency (individually *and* as a group) before any member earns reinforcement. Of the three contingencies this one is the most conservative; if only one member fails to meet the criterion, reinforcement is not delivered to any member of the group.

Procedurally, the interdependent group-oriented contingency can be delivered in four ways: (1) the group as a whole meets the criterion (Gola, Holmes, & Holmes, 1982; Zwald & Gresham, 1980; Packard, 1970); (2) reinforcement is delivered on the achievement of a mean group score (Baer & Richards, 1980; Hamblin, Hathaway, & Wodarski, 1971); (3) a single student is designated or randomly selected to earn the reinforcer for the group (Speltz, Shimamur, & McReynolds, 1982; Drabman, Spitalnik, & Spitalnik, 1974; and (4) the Good Behavior Game can be used (Barrish, Saunders, & Wolf, 1969). Figure 25.6 illustrates the interdependent group-oriented contingency as a three-term contingency.

Total Group Meets Criterion   Gola, Holmes, and Holmes (1982) applied an interdependent group-oriented contingency, which required the total group to meet criterion, to a profoundly retarded population. In their study a group of four females were initially reinforced (praise and candy were delivered) when two, then three, and finally all four of the women sat in a chair for 15 consecutive seconds (DRH schedule). In a second

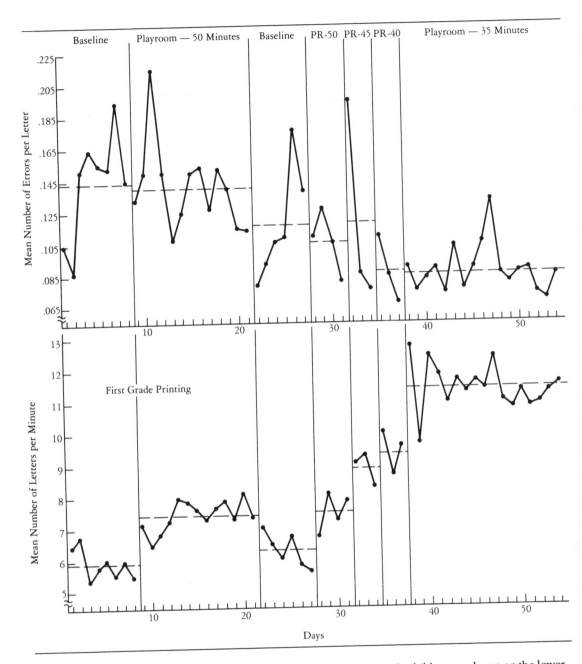

FIGURE 25.5 The mean number of letters printed per minute by first grade children are shown on the lower coordinates and the mean proportion of letters scored as errors. Each data point represents the mean, averaged over all children for that day. The horizontal dashed lines are the means of the daily means averaged over all days within the experimental conditions noted at the top of the figure. (From "The Effects of a Playroom on the Rate and Quality of Printing and Writing of First and Second-Grade Students" by B. L. Hopkins, R. C. Schutte, and K. L. Garton, 1971, *Journal of Applied Behavior Analysis, 4,* p. 81. Copyright 1971 by the Society for the Experimental Analysis of Behavior, Inc. Reprinted by permission.)

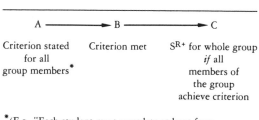

*(E.g., "Each student must complete at least four science projects by the 6th week in the term in order for the class to go on the field trip.")

FIGURE 25.6 An interdependent group-oriented contingency.

phase of the study, the group not only had to sit for an increased amount of time, 30 seconds, but also had to be engaged in a prevocational task. The results of this multiple baseline study show improved prevocational behavior, and the teacher reported anecdotally that the women were less aggressive and more tolerant of being next to one another.

Zwald and Gresham (1982) combined differential reinforcement of lower rates of behavior (DRL) with an interdependent group-oriented contingency to decrease the negative verbal interactions (e.g., name calling, teasing) of three adolescents who attended a special education resource room. Specifically, the three students were told that they could earn reinforcement (e.g., drinks, free reading, or access to a radio) if there were five or fewer incidents of teasing or name calling during a 50-minute class period (DRL 5). The total group had to meet the criterion before reinforcement was delivered. Each incident of name calling or teasing was tallied by the teacher on the blackboard in full view of the students. If five or more negative verbal statements occurred during the day, students could still earn 20 minutes of free time on Friday if there were 9 or fewer incidents on any given day. This secondary contingency was established to reduce the likelihood of excessive negative verbalizations on days when the students did not meet the criterion.

In a second phase of the study, essentially the same procedures were employed, but a DRL 3 contingency was introduced, and the teacher recorded the name calling episodes in her notebook, not on the blackboard. The students were informed of their performance at the end of the class period. Figure 25.7 shows the results of this changing criterion design study. Compared to the baseline condition, which also shows a descending trend, the level of negative verbal statements under the DRL 5 and the DRL 3 group-oriented contingency decreased. Anecdotally, the teacher reported a corresponding decrease in movement throughout the classroom and a corresponding increase in the level of cooperation.

Group Averaging Baer and Richards (1980) used a group averaging interdependent group-oriented contingency to improve the math and English performance of 5 elementary-aged students. In their study all of the students in a class of 10, including the 5 target students, were told that they would earn 1 extra minute of recess for each point of class improvement beyond the previous weekly average. Also, all students were given a contract stating this same contingency. The extra recess was awarded every day of the following week. For example, if the students' weekly average exceeded their previous weekly average by 3 points, they would receive 3 minutes of extra recess every day of the following week. The results of this 22-week study show that all students improved when the group-oriented contingency was in effect (See Figure 25.8). Anecdotal data indicate that all students participated and received reinforcement during the course of the study. The authors reported that the teachers were so excited about the results that they decided to implement the program the following year on their own.

Designated or Randomly Selected Student Speltz, Shimamura, and McReynolds (1982) conducted a study comparing procedural variations of group contingencies, including rein-

FIGURE 25.7 The rate of name calling and teasing during a 50-minute period by three junior high school students. (From "Behavioral Consultation in a Secondary Class: Using DRL to Decrease Negative Verbal Interactions" by L. Zwald and F. M. Gresham, 1982, *School Psychology Review, 11*(4), p. 431. Copyright 1982 by *School Psychology Review.* Reprinted by permission.)

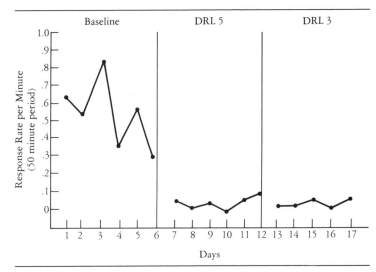

forcement based on a designated or randomly selected student. Four academically delayed students with learning disabilities served as target subjects. The study was conducted in six phases. During Baseline 1 all 12 students enrolled in the class worked as a group on a math assignment for 10 minutes without receiving feedback or reinforcement. This phase served to identify the four lowest students in the group. During Baseline 2 students worked in four groups at small tables in a room across the hall from the classroom. Then, an individual contingency was introduced whereby each student in a group received one point for each math problem solved correctly. Subsequently, during the whole group contingency students received points for the group's average number of correctly completed problems. Each student in the group received an equal share of points based on the average of the group. During the identified responder contingency reinforcement was awarded for the number of problems completed correctly by one of the low performing LD students. Before this condition was implemented, all group members were told the identity of the target student. Reinforcement for the group was based on that target student's performance. Finally, during the un-

identified responder contingency the name of one student from each group was randomly drawn from a hat after the work period ended. All group members were awarded points based on the number of math problems solved correctly by this student.

The results of this counterbalanced, Latin square design show that all group-oriented contingencies were equally effective in improving math performance. With respect to the number of positive social interactions in each group, the identified responder and unidentified responder produced higher levels of positive interaction than baseline conditions produced (see Figure 25.9). According to Speltz et al. (1982), three of the four target students achieved their highest level of positive, social interaction during the identified responder contingency, and they reported anecdotally that this contingency was more acceptable to them than the others. Also, it was reported that during the identified responder contingency not a single instance of verbal abuse occurred. Reports show that students used problem-oriented prompts such as "Do this one" "Now, do this one" to assist the identified responder. This absence of verbal threats directed toward the identified student

FIGURE 25.8 Mean arithmetic and English scores for all students according to baseline and program conditions. (From "An Interdependent Group-Oriented Contingency System for Improving Academic Performance" by G. G. Baer and H. C. Richards, 1980, *School Psychology Review, 9,* p. 192. Copyright 1980 by *School Psychology Review.* Reprinted by permission.)

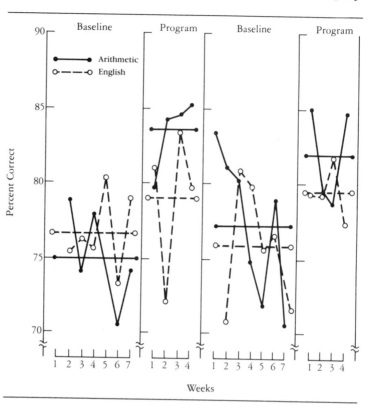

contrasts with reports of other researchers (cf. Gresham, 1981; Hayes, 1976).

Good Behavior Game Barrish, Saunders, and Wolf (1969) used the interdependent group-oriented contingency known as the **Good Behavior Game.** In this game a group is divided into two or more teams. The teams are told that whichever team has the fewest marks against it at the end of the game wins a class privilege. Each team is also told that it can win a privilege if it has fewer than a specified number of marks (a DRL schedule). The advantage of the Good Behavior Game is that competition is encouraged within groups, and against the criterion, rather than across groups. Data reported by the authors show that this strategy can be an effective method of reducing disruptive behavior in the class-

room. When game conditions were in effect during math or reading, talking-out and out-of-seat behaviors occurred at low levels. When game conditions were not in effect, disruptive behaviors occurred at much higher levels (see Figure 25.10).

In a replication Swain, Allard, and Holborn (1982) conducted the Good Toothbrushing Game with first- and second-grade children to improve oral hygiene by reinforcing students in school for a behavior performed at home (i.e., toothbrushing). After baseline data on oral hygiene scores had been collected, the game was initiated with the first graders. Eight sessions later, the game was initiated with the second graders. Results show that a reduction in mean oral hygiene scores was evident for first and second graders, indicating improved oral hygiene while the game condition was in effect. Improved hygiene was still evident at

FIGURE 25.9 Percentage of negative and positive/neutral social interaction in each group directed at a target student. Numbers in parentheses indicate actual order of presentation. (From "Procedural Variations in Group Contingencies: Effects on Children's Academic and Social Behavior" by M. L. Speltz, J. W. Shimamura, and W. T. McReynolds, 1982, *Journal of Applied Behavior Analysis, 15*(4), p. 542. Copyright 1982 by the Society for the Experimental Analysis of Behavior, Inc. Reprinted by permission.)

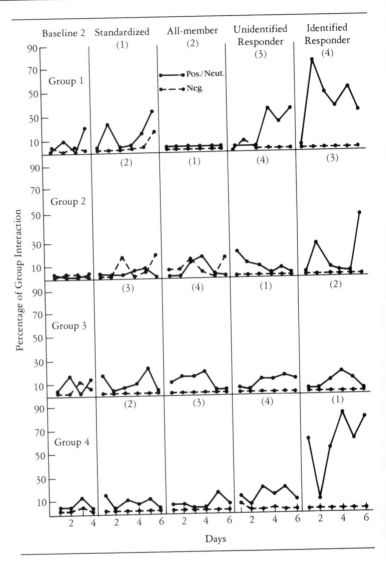

the time of follow-up, 9 months later (see Figure 25.11).

IMPLEMENTING A GROUP-ORIENTED CONTINGENCY

Implementing a group-oriented contingency requires as much preplanning as any other behavior change procedure. Presented here are six guidelines to follow before and during application of a group-oriented contingency.

Choose a Powerful Reinforcer

One of the more important aspects of a group-oriented contingency is the strength of the reinforcer; it must be strong enough to serve as a consequence. Practitioners are advised to use generalized conditioned reinforcers and/or reinforcer menus at every opportunity. Both of these strategies individualize the contingency, thereby increasing its power, flexibility, and applicability.

FIGURE 25.10 Percent of 1-minute intervals containing talking-out and out-of-seat behaviors in a classroom of 24 fourth-grade children during math and reading periods. (From "Good Behavior Game: Effects of Individual Contingencies for Group Consequences on Disruptive Behavior in a Classroom" by H. H. Barrish, M. Saunders, and M. M. Wolf, 1969, *Journal of Applied Behavior Analysis, 2*(2), p. 122. Copyright 1969 by the Society for the Experimental Analysis of Behavior, Inc. Reprinted by permission.)

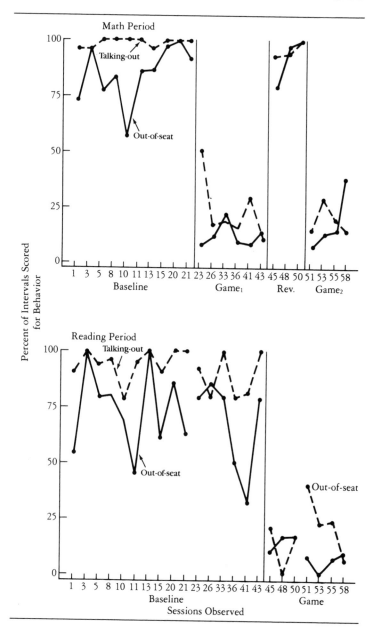

Determine the Behavior to Change and Any Collateral Behaviors That Might Be Affected

Let us suppose a dependent group-oriented contingency is established in which a class receives 10 minutes of extra free time, contingent upon the improved academic performance of a student with developmental disabilities. Obviously, the teacher will need to collect data on the student's academic performance. However, data might also be collected on the frequency of positive interactions between the student and her nonhandicapped

FIGURE 25.11 The effects of the Good Toothbrushing Game on oral hygiene. Missing data points are the result of intervening activities. The assessment setting was shifted prior to the sixth baseline measurement for each class, as indicated by the arrow. (From "The Good Toothbrushing Game: A School Based Dental Hygiene Program for Increasing the Toothbrushing Effectiveness of Children" by J. J. Swain, G. B. Allard, and S. W. Holborn, 1982, *Journal of Applied Behavior Analysis,* *15*(1), p. 175. Copyright 1982 by the Society for the Experimental Analysis of Behavior, Inc. Reprinted by permission.)

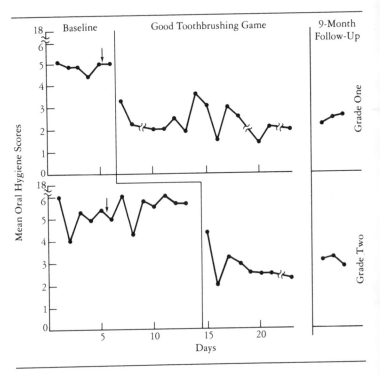

classmates within and outside the room. An additional benefit of using a group-oriented contingency might be the additional reinforcement of the student with developmental disabilities by her fellow students.

Set Appropriate Performance Criteria When Using Group-Oriented Contingencies

If a group-oriented contingency is used, the individuals for whom the contingency is applied must have the prerequisite skills to perform the specified behaviors. Otherwise, the person will not be able to meet the criterion and could be subject to ridicule or abuse (Stolz, 1978).

According to Hamblin, Hathaway, and Wodarski (1971), the criteria for a group-oriented contingency can be established by using the average, high, or low performance levels of the groups as the standard. In the average-performance group-oriented contingency the mean performance of the group is averaged, and reinforcement is made contingent on the achievement of that mean score or a higher score. If the average score for a math exercise was 20 correct problems, students with a score of 20 or above would be reinforced. In the high-performance group-oriented contingency the high score determines the level of performance needed to receive the reinforcer. If the high score on a spelling test was 95%, only students achieving a score of 95% or better would be reinforced. In the low-performance group-oriented contingency the low performance score determines the reinforcer. If the low score on a social studies term paper was *C*, then students with a *C* or better would receive the reinforcer.

Hamblin et al. (1971) indicate that differential effects can be noted with these performance contingencies. Their data show that slow students performed worse under a high-performance contingency, whereas gifted students performed best under this contingency. The data of Hamblin et al. suggest that a group-oriented contingency can be effective in improving behavior, but it should be applied with the understanding that effectiveness will vary for different members of the group.

Combine with Other Procedures When Appropriate

According to LaRowe, Tucker, and McGuire (1980), a group-oriented contingency can be used alone or in combination with other procedures to systematically change performance. The LaRowe et al. study was designed to reduce the excessive noise levels in an elementary school lunchroom; their data suggest that differential reinforcement of low rates of behavior (DRL) can be incorporated easily into a group-oriented contingency. In situations where higher levels of group performance are desired, differential reinforcement of high rates of behavior (DRH) can be used. With either DRL or DRH the use of a changing criterion design will facilitate the analysis of treatment effects.

Select the Most Appropriate of the Group-Oriented Contingencies

The selection of a specific group-oriented contingency should be based on the overall programmatic goals of the practitioner, the parents (or guardian), and the individual or group whenever possible. For instance, if the group-oriented contingency is designed to improve the behavior of one person or a small group of individuals, then perhaps a dependent group-oriented contingency should be employed. If the practitioner wants to differentially reinforce students for appropriate behavior, then an independent group-oriented contingency should be considered. But if the practitioner wants each individual within a group to perform at a certain level, then an interdependent group-oriented contingency should be chosen. Regardless of which group-oriented contingency is selected, the ethical issues discussed earlier in the chapter must be addressed.

Monitor Individual and Group Performance

With a group-oriented contingency it is necessary to observe both group and individual performance. It is possible that the group's performance will improve but that some members within the group may not improve, or at least may not improve as fast. Some members of the group might even attempt to sabotage the group contingency, preventing the group from achieving the reinforcement. In this case individual contingencies should be arranged for the saboteurs, in combination with the group-oriented contingency.

SUMMARY

Definition of a Group-Oriented Contingency

1 A group-oriented contingency is one in which the presentation, or loss, of a reinforcer is contingent upon the behavior of an individual within the group, a segment of the group, or the group as a whole.

Rationale

2 A group-oriented contingency can save time, is at least as effective, and is perhaps more economical than an individual contingency.
3 A group-oriented contingency is useful when it is impractical to initiate an individual contingency.

4 A group-oriented contingency can be used when the practitioner needs to resolve a serious disruptive behavior quickly.

5 A group-oriented contingnecy may be able to capitalize on peer influence or peer monitoring.

6 A group-oriented contingency can be combined with an individual contingency.

Ethical Considerations

7 Some group-oriented contingencies may exert harmful peer pressure on individuals.

8 A group-oriented contingency may increase the likelihood of scapegoating.

9 If performance measures of a group-oriented contingency are averaged, the behavior of individual students can be masked. If individual data cannot be collected during a group-oriented contingency, a different procedure should be implemented.

10 Before establishing the criterion for a group-oriented contingency, the practitioner should assess the limits of student performance.

Classification Schemes for Group-Oriented Contingencies

11 There are three categories of group-oriented contingencies: dependent, independent, and interdependent.

12 A dependent group-oriented contingency is one in which the reinforcer is dependent upon the performance of an individual or small group.

13 An independent group-oriented contingency is one in which the reinforcer is delivered to all members of the group who meet the criterion.

14 The interdependent group-oriented contingency is one in which all of the individuals of the group must meet the criterion of the contingency before any member receives reinforcement.

Implementing a Group-Oriented Contingency

15 Six guidelines can assist the practitioner in implementing a group-oriented contingency.

26

Self-Management

KEY TERMS

Self-management   Self-monitoring

This chapter is about self-management—someone making responses to alter the probability that he will emit self-specified responses in the future. We begin by detailing the rationale for and advantages of self-management. Then specific self-management strategies and tactics are described and classified according to their emphasis in the three-term contingency. A discussion of the theoretical implications of self-control follows, and suggestions are offered for teaching self-management skills to children. The chapter concludes with guidelines for successful self-management.

WHAT IS SELF-MANAGEMENT AND WHY IS IT IMPORTANT?

A Definition of Self-Management

At times the causes of behavior (even the functional ones) are readily apparent to anyone observing the action in question. A mother picks up and cuddles her crying infant, and the crying stops. A highway worker quickly leaps off the road when he sees a fast-approaching car not slowed by the flagman and warning signs. A fisherman casts his line as close as

This chapter was written by William L. Heward.

possible to the spot where his last cast produced a strike. Escape, avoidance, and positive reinforcement contingencies such as these are easy to spot; and although the nonbehaviorist might offer a variety of explanations for each response, most would correctly identify the functional stimuli.

In each example an important change occurred in the person's environment just before the response of interest was emitted: a baby cried; a speeding car approached; a fish took the bait. And an analysis of the three occurrences would no doubt reveal that the immediately preceding events had functional roles—the first two as discriminative stimuli, the third as a powerful reinforcer. But much human behavior is not functionally related to preceding variables that are so easily observed by others. Nonetheless, society has a long history of assigning causal status to events that immediately precede the behavior in question. "We tend to say, often rashly, that if one thing follows another, it was probably caused by it— following the ancient principle of *post hoc, ergo propter hoc* (after this, therefore because of this)" (Skinner, 1974, p. 7). Skinner (1974) goes on to explain:

> The person with whom we are most familiar is ourself; many of the things we observe just before we behave occur within our body, and it is easy to take them as the causes of our behavior. . . . Feelings occur at just the right time to serve as causes of behavior, and they have been cited as such for centuries. We assume that other people feel as we feel when they behave as we behave. (pp. 7, 8)

Our culture is replete with literature, customs, everyday idioms, and, more important, contingencies of reinforcement that help maintain the belief that the primary causes of behavior lie within the person. The tendency to point to internal causes of behavior is particularly strong when immediate causes in the surrounding environment are not readily apparent. Why does one student begin her major term paper early in the semester, maintaining regular study and writing periods, while her roommates spend night after night partying? And when a group of people join a weight-loss or a stop-smoking program in which each member of the group is exposed to the same intervention, why do some meet their initial goals and some do not? Why does a high school basketball player with limited physical attributes consistently outperform his more physically gifted teammates?

In the absence of experimental investigation, everyday observations often assume the role of mentalistic explanations. Our hard-working student is said to have more willpower than her less serious roommates; group members who lose weight or stop smoking possess more desire than their peers who drop out or fail; the athlete's superior play is a result of his above-average drive. Traditional psychological theory has supported the layperson's reasoning, giving terms such as *willpower, desire,* and *drive* causal status.

Skinner was the first to apply the philosophy and theory of radical behaviorism to actions typically considered to be under the control of the self. In his classic book, *Science and Human Behavior,* Skinner (1953) devotes a chapter to self-control.

> When a man controls himself, chooses a course of action, thinks out the problem, or strives toward an increase in self-knowledge, he is *behaving.* He controls himself precisely as he would control the behavior of anyone else— through manipulation of variables of which behavior is a function. His behavior in so doing is a proper object of analysis, and eventually it must be accounted for with variables lying outside the individual himself. (pp. 228–229)

Skinner (1953) continues by characterizing self-control as a two-response phenomonon.

> The *controlling response,* affects variables in such a way as to change the probability of the other, the *controlled response.* The controlling response may manipulate any of the variables of which the controlled response is a function; hence there are a good many different forms of self-control. (p. 231)

Thus, self-control, or self-management, involves at least two responses: (1) the response to be controlled (e.g., eating, smoking, saving money); and (2) the response(s) emitted in order to control the rate of the target behavior (e.g., recording everything eaten during the day, throwing away one's cigarettes, signing up for a payroll deduction plan).

We prefer the term **self-management** since it is somewhat "less value-laden" and not so "inherently misleading" (Brigham, 1980). Self-control implies that the ultimate functional control of behavior lies within the individual. The theoretical discussion of self-control near the end of this chapter will help to explain our preference for the term *self-management.* However, since self-control has been used in the behavioral literature more often than self-management, the two terms are used interchangeably here and should be viewed as synonomous.

How is self-management to be distinguished from other behavior since many of the responses that a person emits each day play an important role in influencing the probability of other responses? Thoresen and Mahoney (1974) speak of self-control when, in the "relative absence" of immediate external controls, a person emits a response designed to control the behavior of interest. According to this criterion, self-control is not evident when immediate and obvious external contingencies set the occasion for and reinforce the controlling response. Thus, the dieter who, when home alone, rides his exercise bike before going to bed, instead of having his usual popcorn and beer, is using self-control. The dieter would not be credited with self-control if he passed up his nightly snack because his wife was there reminding him of his overeating, praising him for riding the exercise bike, and marking a chart with his time and mileage.

However, what if the dieter was responsible for his wife's actions in the first place? One problem with Thoresen and Mahoney's concept of self-control is that it excludes those situations in which an individual designs and arranges external contingencies to control a behavior of concern. An additional problem with the concept of "relative absence of external controls" is that it suggests a distinction between internal and external controlling variables when, in fact, all of the causal variables for behavior ultimately reside in the environment outside the self.

Kazdin's (1975) definition of self-control as "the application of behavioral principles to modify one's own behavior" (p. 189) is more functional for applied behavior analysis. With this definition self-control can occur whenever a person purposely emits behavior that changes the environment so as to modify another behavior in her repertoire. Self-control is considered purposeful in the sense that an individual labels her responses as designed for a specified result (e.g., to reduce the number of cigarettes smoked each day). The self-management responses themselves are a function of the person's reinforcement history (i.e., they are caused by events outside the person) and thus, like any other behaviors, they are subject to experimental analysis.

We define *self-management* as the personal and systematic application of behavior change strategies that result in the desired modification of one's own behavior. Given this definition, self-management includes the one-time response in the morning that results in the target response that evening (e.g., taping a note to the bathroom mirror to remind oneself to put the garbage out that evening). Self-management also includes more complex and long-running behavior change programs in which a person plans and implements one or several contingencies designed to change his behavior, (e.g., a self-designed program to increase one's rate of physical exercise, involving the systematic use of various cues as well as reinforcing and punishing contingencies). This definition of self-management is a functional one: if the desired change in the target behavior does not occur, self-management has not been demonstrated; and self-management has not occurred if the change in the target behavior would have taken place without the self-management responses.

Rationale for and Advantages of Self-Management

It is not surprising that both the identification and evaluation of self-management strategies and the development of effective methods for teaching self-management skills to others have become important areas of research in applied behavior analysis.

Instances of Important Behavior Can Be Missed by External Change Agents In most applied settings, particularly in group situations such as classrooms, many important responses go unnoticed by the person responsible for applying behavior change procedures. There is simply too much behavior being emitted for one person to be everywhere at once. In the classroom students invariably miss opportunities to respond, or respond and receive no feedback, because in the behavioral sense the teacher wasn't there.

Self-Management Can Be an Effective Method for Extending the Generality of a Behavior Change A behavior change that lasts over time, occurs in settings other than the one in which it was originally taught, and/or spreads to other related behaviors is said to have generality (Baer, Wolf, & Risley, 1968). Important behavior changes without generality are often of little utility.[1] As soon as the subject is no longer in the setting in which a behavior change was learned, she may no longer emit the desired response. Sometimes certain stimuli in the original teaching environment or the external agent (teacher, parent) who administered the teaching program become discriminative stimuli for the newly learned response

(Redd & Birnbrauer, 1969), thereby enabling the learner to easily discriminate the presence or absence of certain contingencies across settings (Kazdin, 1975). Often, however, the contingencies in the nonteaching environment do not reinforce the desired behavior change or may even set the occasion for and reinforce an undesired response.

Baer and Fowler (1984) pose and answer a pragmatic question related to the problem of generality.

> "What behavior change agent can go with the student to every necessary lesson, at all times, to prompt and reinforce every desirable form of the behavior called for by the curriculum? The student's own "self" can always meet these specifications. (p. 148)

Certain Kinds of Behavior Do Not Lend Themselves to External-Agent Control Sometimes the behavior a person wishes to change must be cued, monitored, evaluated, and/or reinforced or punished on a day-to-day or even minute-to-minute basis in all of the situations and environments that the person encounters. Even though a person can sign up to participate in a behavior change program planned and directed by others, most successful smoking, weight loss, and exercise programs rely heavily on training participants to use self-management techniques. Many behavior problems brought to the clinician pose the same challenge: how can a working contingency be arranged that follows the client wherever he goes? Appropriate target behaviors designed to increase a secretary's self-esteem and assertiveness can be identified and defined in the therapist's office, but implementation of an active contingency in the workplace is apt to require self-management techniques.

A self-management strategy may also be indicated for target behaviors with topographies that make them inaccessible to observation by others. Thoughts of self-doubt, obsessive thoughts, and feelings of depression are examples of private events for which a self-management approach may be needed.

---

[1]Producing behavior changes with generality is a major goal of applied behavior analysis and is the subject of chapter 27.

Students with Self-Management Skills Can Help Operate a More Efficient Classroom, Giving the Teacher More Time to Teach Classroom teachers have traditionally assumed the responsibility of evaluating students' academic performances, delivering consequences relative to those performances, and managing the social behavior of the children. The time required for these functions is considerable. To the extent that students themselves can self-score their own work, generate their own feedback, and behave appropriately without teacher assistance, the teacher is freed to attend to other aspects of the curriculum and perform other instructional duties (Lovitt, 1973).

When Hall, Delquadri, and Harris (1977) conducted observations of elementary classrooms and found low levels of active student response, they surmised that higher rates of academic productivity might actually be punishing to teachers. Even though there is considerable evidence linking high rates of student opportunity to respond with academic achievement (Greenwood, Delquadri, & Hall, 1984), in most classrooms generating more student academic responses results in even more teacher time being spent grading papers. The time savings produced by students with even the most simple self-management skills can be significant. In one study a class of five elementary special education students completed as many arithmetic problems as they could during a 20-minute session each day (Hundert & Batstone, 1978). When the teacher graded the papers, an average of 50.5 minutes was required to prepare and conduct the session and score and record each student's performance. When the students scored their own papers, the total teacher time needed to conduct the arithmetic period was reduced to an average of 33.4 minutes, resulting in a 50% savings of teacher time.

Self-Management Techniques Can Sometimes Be Used to Control Behaviors Not Affected by Weak Outcomes Malott (1980) uses the generic term *outcome* to include all events that serve as consequences for behavior. He refers to effective behavioral consequences, both reinforcers and punishers, as strong outcomes and calls consequent events that are too delayed, too improbable, or too small and only of a cumulative importance in affecting behavior weak outcomes. Malott contends that the difficulty we have with modifying many of the personal behaviors that give us trouble—improper diet, insufficient exercise, smoking—is caused by ineffective, weak outcomes succumbing to the power of immediate, strong consequences. The deleterious effect of any one cigarette is small, so small that it is not even noticed. Poor health, lung cancer, or even an early death are probably years and thousands of puffs away. A delayed outcome, even one as major as dying, is no match for the smaller but immediate reinforcers that maintain smoking.

Self-management strategies can be used to arrange strong outcomes—immediate consequences designed to counteract the contingencies currently maintaining the self-destructive behavior. The smoker who immediately follows the first puff on a cigarette, or better yet the thought of lighting up, with self-recording on a small card that she either did or did not smoke is attempting to provide herself with immediate behavioral consequences that will work to decrease her smoking rate.

Some People Perform Better Under Self-Selected Standards Most studies that have compared self-selected and other-selected reinforcement contingencies have found that self-selected contingencies can be as effective in maintaining behavior as contingencies determined by others (e.g., Bandura & Perloff, 1967; Felixbrod & O'Leary, 1973, 1974; Glynn, Thomas, & Shee, 1973). However, a frequently cited study by Lovitt and Curtiss (1969) demonstrated in three brief experiments with a single student that pupil-selected contingencies can sometimes be more effective than teacher-selected performance standards. In the first phase of Experiment 1, the subject, a

12-year-old boy in a special education class-room, earned a teacher-specified number of minutes of free time based on the number of math and reading tasks he completed correctly. In the next phase of the study, the student was allowed to specify the number of correct math and reading items needed to earn each minute of free time. During the final phase of the study the original teacher-specified ratios of academic production to reinforcement were again in effect. The student's median academic response rate during the self-selected contingency phase was 2.5 correct responses per minute (math and reading tasks reported together), compared to correct rates of 1.65 and 1.9 in the two teacher-selected phases.

A later experiment published by Dickerson and Creedon (1981) employed a yoked-control (Sidman, 1960) and between-group comparison design with 30 second and third graders and found that pupil-selected standards resulted in significantly higher academic production of both reading and math tasks. Both the Lovitt and Curtiss and the Dickerson and Creedon studies demonstrate that self-selected reinforcement contingencies *can* be more effective than teacher-selected contingencies. However, research in this area also shows that simply letting children determine their own performance standards does not guarantee high levels of performance; some studies have found that children select too-lenient standards when given the opportunity (Felixbrod & O'Leary, 1973, 1974). More research is needed to determine the conditions under which students can be taught to self-select and maintain appropriate standards of performance (Dickerson & Creedon, 1981; Rosenbaum & Drabman, 1979).

Self-Management Is One of the Ultimate Goals of Education
When asked to describe what education should accomplish for its students, most people—educators and laypersons alike—include the development of independent, self-directed, or self-achieving citizens, persons capable of behaving appropriately and constructively without the supervision of others. John Dewey (1939), one of this country's most influential educational philosophers, said that "the ideal aim of education is the creation of self-control" (p. 75). A student's ability to be self-directed, with the teacher as a guide or facilitator, and his ability to self-evaluate his performance are considered cornerstones of humanistic education (Gage & Berliner, 1975). As Lovitt (1973) has noted, the fact that systematic instruction of self-management skills is *not* a regular part of most schools' curriculum is a paradox since "one of the expressed objectives of the educational system is to create individuals who are self-reliant and independent" (p. 139).

Teaching Students Self-Management Skills Supports and Gives Meaningful Practice for Other Parts of the Curriculum
When students learn to define and measure behavior and to graph, evaluate, and analyze their own responses, they are practicing various math and science skills in a relevant way (Lovitt, 1977).

Self-Management Feels Good
A final, but by no means trivial, reason for learning self-management skills is that being in control is rewarding. A person who systematically arranges her environment in ways that support and maintain the behaviors she both should and would like to do is not only going to be productive, but will also feel good about it. Malott (1981) notes his personal feelings about a successful self-management program that got him exercising, flossing his teeth, practicing his drums, writing, and doing certain household chores at the rates he desired.

> It really feels good to get your life under control.... I feel much better when my day is organized and I have innocent little contingencies that keep me going and productive; I like that better than when I simply sit around numbed, overwhelmed by how behind I am in everything and only escaping the aversiveness of it all by losing myself in a copy of RUNNER'S WORLD. (Volume III, No. 5)

SELF-MANAGEMENT STRATEGIES

In most behavior change programs one person (teacher, therapist, parent) manipulates environmental events in order to modify the behavior of another person (student, client, child). Another person defines the target behavior, arranges specific discriminative stimuli, offers verbal and/or physical prompts, administers reinforcing and punishing consequences, and records the occurrence or nonoccurrence of the target behavior. When any or all of these behavior change functions are performed by the individual to modify his own behavior, some degree of self-management is involved.

There are few pure self-management strategies that involve only one specific principle of behavior. Our discussion of various self-management techniques is organized according to each technique's relative emphasis on the elements of the three-term contingency. Thus, stimulus control strategies for self-management include environmental manipulations that alter some critical aspect of the antecedent conditions associated with the target behavior. Self-monitoring, although technically a consequence, focuses on the middle component of the three-term contingency—the target behavior itself. Finally, there are numerous strategies for self-delivery of consequences that a person can employ to ensure contingent reinforcement and/or punishment.

Stimulus Control Techniques for Self-Management

When the probability is greater that a given operant will be emitted in the presence of one stimulus configuration rather than another, the behavior is said to be under stimulus control. Many everyday behaviors are emitted only in the presence of certain stimuli; some are obvious (the telephone rings and we pick it up), and others are not so obvious (the long hours a person spends watching television may be partly a function of the location of a favorite chair). Although operant behavior is developed and maintained by its consequences, many operants can be functionally controlled on a trial-to-trial basis by the presentation or removal of discriminative stimuli. When a person arranges the antecedent stimulus conditions in her environment to increase or decrease a given behavior, her self-management effort involves a stimulus control strategy.

Stimulus control strategies are sometimes called environmental planning in the self-management literature (Bellack & Hersen, 1977; Thoresen & Mahoney, 1974). Procedurally, stimulus control techniques for self-management include (1) providing extra cues in the environment to set the occasion for the desired response; (2) confronting oneself with stimuli that successfully control the desired behavior; (3) altering the environment to make an undesired behavior less likely; and (4) restricting the stimulus conditions for an undesired behavior.

Providing Extra Cues for the Desired Behavior When a person writes a note that says, "Call Bob tonight," and tapes it on her closet door, where she is sure to see it when she hangs up her coat after work, she is providing herself an extra cue. Dieters often put pictures of overweight people, or perhaps even unattactive pictures of themselves, on the refrigerator door, near the ice cream, in the cupboard—everywhere that they might get food. Seeing the pictures can set the occasion for other controlling responses, such as going for a walk, telephoning a friend, or giving oneself a point on an I-didn't-eat chart. Parents who want to increase the number of times they praise their children might cut out reminders like those in Figure 26.1 and place them around their home where they are likely to see them routinely—on the bathroom mirror, on the television channel selector, as a bookmark, on a lampshade (Heward, Dardig, & Rossett,

FIGURE 26.1 Example of cues used by parents to remind themselves to emit self-specified parenting behavior. (Originally developed by Charles Novak. From *Working with Parents of Handicapped Children*, p. 26, by W. L. Heward, J. C. Dardig, and A. Rossett, 1979, Columbus, OH: Charles E. Merrill. Copyright 1979 by Charles E. Merrill. Reprinted by permission.)

Instructions: Cut out the decorative ZAP reminders below and place them in conspicuous locations throughout your house or apartment, for example, on the refrigerator, bathroom mirror, and television set.

1979). Each time a parent sees one of the cues, he is reminded to look for some behavior for which to praise his child.

Confronting Oneself with Stimuli That Successfully Control the Desired Behavior

A self-management strategy similar to but more direct than adding additional prompts to the environment is to behave so that your future behavior makes contact with a powerful discriminative stimulus for the desired behavior. Most human behaviors can be analyzed as chains of many simpler responses; the component responses are performed in a given sequence to produce a more complex behavior chain (see chapter 15). Each response in a behavior chain must be under reliable stimulus control (i.e., it must occur reliably in the presence of its related discriminative stimulus) in order for the chain to be completed successfully. By performing part of a behavioral chain at one point in time (the self-management response), a person can manipulate her environment so that she is later confronted with the discriminative stimu-

lus that will set the occasion for the desired (self-managed) response. Skinner (1983b) provides an excellent example of this self-management strategy.

> Ten minutes before you leave your house for the day you hear a weather report: It will probably rain before you return. It occurs to you to take an umbrella (the sentence means quite literally what it says: The behavior of taking an umbrella occurs to you), but you are not yet able to execute it. Ten minutes later you leave without the umbrella. You can solve that kind of problem by executing as much of the behavior as possible when it occurs to you. Hang the umbrella on the doorknob, or put it through the handle of your briefcase, or in some other way start the process of taking it with you. (p. 240)

Using Situational Inducement

Another stimulus control self-management strategy is to change one's environment in such a way that an undesired response is less likely. The smoker who throws out his cigarettes and the overeater who cleans all of the ice cream and snack foods out of the house have, at least for the short run, effectively controlled their smoking and junk food eating behaviors.

Restricting the Stimulus Conditions for an Undesired Behavior An individual can reduce the rate of an undesired behavior by limiting the stimulus conditions under which she will emit the behavior. If effective, stimulus control can be acquired by the new situation and if access to this situation is infrequent or otherwise not reinforcing, a reduction in the target behavior will occur. Nolan (1968) reported on a woman who wished to quit smoking and who used this type of stimulus control strategy. The woman noted that she most often smoked when other people were around or when she watched television, read, or lay down to relax. It was decided that she would only smoke in a prescribed place and would eliminate from that place the potentially reinforcing effects of other activities. She chose a specific chair as her smoking chair and positioned it so that she could not watch TV or easily engage in conversation while sitting in it. She asked other family members not to approach her or talk to her while she was in her smoking chair. From a baseline average of 30 cigarettes per day, her smoking dropped to 12 per day as she faithfully followed the procedure. Nine days after beginning the program, the woman decided to try to reduce her smoking even further by making her smoking chair less accessible. She put the chair in the basement, and her smoking dropped to 5 cigarettes per day. A month after beginning the smoking chair program, she quit smoking altogether. Martin and Pear (1983) report the successful use of this strategy by another smoker who limited his smoking to the bathroom. After one month he also had given up smoking altogether.

Goldiamond (1965) used a similar tactic to help a man who continually sulked when interacting with his wife. The husband was instructed to limit his sulking behavior to his sulking stool, which was placed in the garage, to go there whenever he wished, to sulk as long as he wanted, and to leave when he was finished sulking. The man found that his sulk-ing behavior decreased considerably when he did it only on the stool in the garage.

This strategy can also be used to increase a desired behavior that is not being emitted at an acceptable rate because of competing behaviors. In one case an adult insomniac reportedly went to bed about midnight but did not fall asleep until 3:00 or 4:00 A.M. Before falling asleep, he worried about several mundane problems and turned on the television (Bootzin, 1972). Treatment consisted of instructing the man to go to bed when he felt tired, but he was not to stay in bed if he was unable to sleep. Instead of thinking about his problems or watching television, he was to get out of bed and go into another room, where he could do whatever he wanted. When he again felt sleepy, he was to return to bed and try again to go to sleep. If he still could not sleep, he was to leave the bedroom again. The man reported getting up four or five times a night for the first few days of the program, but within 2 weeks he went to bed, stayed there, and fell asleep.

In a similar manner students have improved their study habits when they have selected a specific place in which to study, free of other distractions, and have not engaged in any other behaviors such as daydreaming or letter writing in that place (Goldiamond, 1965). Skinner (1981b) suggests this kind of stimulus control strategy when he instructs aspiring writers.

> Equally important are the conditions in which the behavior occurs. A convenient place is important. It should have all the facilities needed for the execution of writing. Pens, typewriters, recorders, files, books, a comfortable desk and chair. . . . Since the place is to take control of a particular kind of behavior, you should do nothing else there at any time. (p. 2)

Conclusions Self-management efforts that incorporate principles of stimulus control can be effective in controlling behavior. When the cigarettes have been destroyed, none will be smoked. However, powerful contingencies are often needed to set the occasion for and reinforce the controlling response. The desk may now effectively control good study behavior, but the response of regularly getting to the desk must be emitted. If these powerful contingencies can be set in motion, the controlling response is probable, and the self-management objective is often met. However, stimulus control techniques of self-mangement may be only temporary solutions to a behavioral problem (e.g., a friend may come over and offer a cigarette).

Self-Monitoring

Self-monitoring, self-recording, self-observation, and self-assessment all refer to an individual's systematically observing his own behavior and responding to the occurrence or non-occurrence of a specified target response. Self-monitoring has been called "the lifeblood of effective self-control methods" (Thoresen & Mahoney, 1974) and has been the subject of more research and clinical application than any other self-management strategy.

Self-monitoring was originally conceived as a method of clinical assessment for collecting data on behaviors which only the client could observe and record (e.g., eating, smoking, fingernail biting). However, because of the reactive effect often produced by self-monitoring, it has become a major therapeutic intervention in its own right. Reactivity refers to the effects on a subject's behavior produced by an assessment or measurement procedure. In general, the more obtrusive an observation and measurement method, the greater the likelihood of reactivity (Kazdin, 1974). When the subject of a behavior change program is also the observer/recorder, obtrusiveness is complete and reactivity is likely.

If measured changes in the target behavior are to be functionally related to manipulations of the independent variable, other sources of variability must be eliminated. In applied behavior analysis, reactivity is an uncontrolled

and therefore undesirable variable that must be minimized to the greatest extent possible. In order to verify the effects of self-monitoring as an intervention, the behavior analyst must use an unobtrusive data collection procedure, independent of the self-observation and self-recording efforts of the subject. Self-monitoring must then be manipulated according to the features of an intrasubject research design, with evaluation of its effects based on the data gathered across the conditions of the experiment—that is, in the presence and absence of self-monitoring. (See, for example, the Broden, Hall, & Mitts, 1971, study that follows in this same section.)

From a clinical standpoint, however, the reactive effects of self-monitoring have proven very useful. Not only does self-monitoring often change behavior, but the change is almost always in the desired direction. Behavior therapists have had clients use self-monitoring to reduce overeating, decrease smoking (Lipinski, Black, Nelson, & Ciminero, 1975; McFall, 1977), stop biting their nails (Maletzky, 1974), and drink less alcohol. Self-monitoring has helped students pay more attention in the classroom (Broden, Hall, & Mitts, 1971; Kneedler & Hallahan, 1981), decrease talk outs and aggression (Lovitt, 1973), and improve their academic performances in a variety of subject areas (Hundert & Bucher, 1978; James, Trap, & Cooper, 1977). Sometimes, however, self-monitoring alone has no apparent effect on the target behavior (see, for example, Ballard & Glynn, 1975, and Foxx & Rubinoff, 1979).

In one of the first published accounts of self-monitoring in the classroom, Broden, Hall, and Mitts (1971) analyzed the effects of self-recording on the behavior of two eighth-grade students. Liza was the subject of the first experiment; she was earning a $D-$ in history and exhibited poor study behavior during the lecture format class. Using 10-second momentary time sampling for 30 minutes each day, an observer seated in the back of the classroom—

Liza was not told she was being observed—produced a 7-day baseline showing that Liza, on the average, exhibited study behaviors (e.g., faced the teacher, took notes when appropriate) only 30% of the time, despite two conferences with the school counselor in which she promised to "really try." Prior to the eighth session, the counselor gave Liza a piece of paper with three rows of 10 squares (see Figure 26.2) and told her to record her study behavior whenever she thought of it during history class. She was to mark a + in the square if she was studying and a − if she was not studying at that time.

Figure 26.3 shows the results of Liza's self-monitoring. Her level of study behavior increased to 78% (as measured by the independent observer) and stayed at approximately that level during Self-Recording$_1$, quickly fell to baseline levels when self-management was terminated during Baseline$_2$, and averaged 80% during Self-Recording$_2$. During Self-Recording Plus Praise Liza's teacher attended to Liza whenever he could during history class and praised her for study behavior whenever possible. Liza's level of study behavior under this condition increased to 88%.

The bottom part of Figure 26.3 shows the number of times per session the observer recorded teacher attention toward Liza. The fact that the frequency of teacher attention did not correlate in any apparent way with Liza's study behavior during the first four phases of the experiment, suggests that teacher attention—which often exerts a powerful influence on student behavior—was not a confounding variable and that the improvements in Liza's study behavior can be attributed to the self-recording procedure. However, the effects of self-monitoring may have been confounded by the fact that Liza turned her self-recording slips into the counselor before the end of each school day and at weekly student-counselor conferences received praise from the counselor for recording slips with a high percentage of plus marks.

In the second experiment self-monitoring was used with Stu, an eighth-grade student who

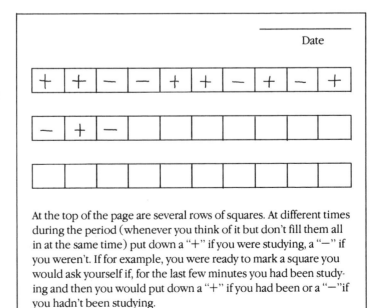

FIGURE 26.2 Example of a self-recording form used by an eighth-grade girl. (From "The Effect of Self-Recording on the Classroom Behavior of Two Eighth-Grade Students" by M. Broden, R. V. Hall, and B. Mitts, 1971, *Journal of Applied Behavior Analysis, 4*, p. 193. Copyright 1971 by the Society for the Experimental Analysis of Behavior, Inc. Reprinted by permission.)

Date

+	+	−	−	+	+	−	+	−	+

−	+	−							

At the top of the page are several rows of squares. At different times during the period (whenever you think of it but don't fill them all in at the same time) put down a "+" if you were studying, a "−" if you weren't. If for example, you were ready to mark a square you would ask yourself if, for the last few minutes you had been studying and then you would put down a "+" if you had been or a "−"if you hadn't been studying.

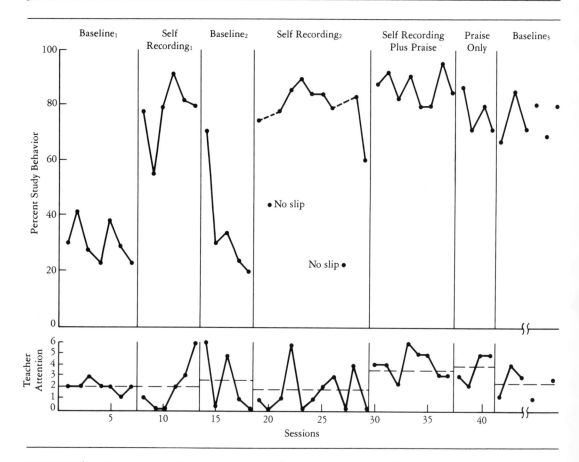

FIGURE 26.3 Percentage of observed intervals in which an eighth-grade girl paid attention in a history class. (From "The Effect of Self-Recording on the Classroom Behavior of Two Eighth-Grade Students" by M. Broden, R. V. Hall, and B. Mitts, 1971, *Journal of Applied Behavior Analysis, 4,* p. 194. Copyright 1971 by the Society for the Experimental Analysis of Behavior, Inc. Reprinted by Permission.)

continually talked out in class. Using a 10-second partial interval recording procedure to calculate the rate of talk outs per minute, an independent observer recorded Stu's behavior during both parts of a math class that met before and after lunch. Self-recording was begun first during the portion of the math class before lunch. The teacher handed Stu a piece of paper on which was marked a 2″ × 5″ rectangular box with instructions to record a mark very time he talked out without permission (see Figure 26.4). Stu was told to use the recording slip and turn it in after lunch.

No other instructions were given. Self-recording was later implemented during the second half of the math class. Figure 26.5 shows the results. During the prelunch portion of the math class, Stu's baseline rate of talk outs was 1.1 per minute followed by a rate of 0.3 when he self-recorded his talk outs. After lunch Stu talked out an average rate of 1.6 times per minute before self-recording and 0.5 during self-recording.

The combination reversal and multiple baseline across environments design clearly shows a functional relationship between Stu's rate of

PUT A MARK DOWN EVERY TIME YOU TALK OUT

FIGURE 26.4 Example of a self-recording form used by an eighth-grade boy. (From "The Effect of Self-Recording on the Classroom Behavior of Two Eighth-Grade Students" by M. Broden, R. V. Hall, and B. Mitts, 1971, *Journal of Applied Behavior Analysis, 4,* p. 196. Copyright 1971 by the Society for the Experimental Analysis of Behavior, Inc. Reprinted by permission.)

talking out and the self-monitoring procedure. However, during the final phase of the experiment Stu's talk outs occurred at rates equal to or above initial baseline levels, even though self-recording was in effect. Broden, Hall, and Mitts suggest that the lack of effect produced by self-recording during the final phase may have resulted from the fact that "no contingencies were ever applied to differential rates of talking out and the slips thus lost their effectiveness" (p. 198). Although, as the authors point out, further research is necessary to determine whether this was actually the case, it is a behaviorally sound conclusion. However, if teacher-administered reinforcement contingencies were needed to maintain the reduced rates of talking out, the initial decreases in talk outs attributed to self-recording may have been con-

founded by the subject's expectations of some form of teacher reinforcement.

As can be seen from an examination of these two frequently cited self-recording experiments by Broden, Hall, and Mitts (1971), self-monitoring is extremely difficult to isolate as a straightforward, "clean" procedure; it almost always entails other contingencies. Nevertheless, the various and combined procedures that can best be labeled as self-monitoring have often proved to be effective in changing behavior.

Some studies have shown self-monitoring to be an effective initial behavior change strategy, whereas other research has found it effective only after a period of external evaluation, for example by a teacher or parent (Santogrossi et al., 1973; Turkewitz et al., 1975). O'Brien, Riner, and Budd (1983) found a self-monitoring procedure coupled with self-delivery of a token reward more effective for a noncompliant 5-year-old boy immediately after a period in which the boy's mother administered the procedure than after a baseline phase. Their data suggest that in some instances self-monitoring can be more effective in maintaining behavior change first brought about by external agents than in bringing about initial changes in behavior.

Why Does Self-Monitoring Work? Some behavior theorists believe that self-monitoring is effective in changing behavior because it produces self-evaluative statements that serve either to reinforce desired behaviors or to punish undesired behaviors. Cautela (1971) has hypothesized that a child who records on a chart that he has completed his chores may emit covert verbal responses (e.g., "I am a good boy") that serve to reinforce chore completion. Malott (1981) suggests that self-monitoring improves performance because of what he calls guilt control. Self-monitoring less-than-desirable behavior produces covert guilt statements that can be escaped only by better performance. Novelist Anthony Trollope, writing in his 1883 autobiography, apparently agreed.

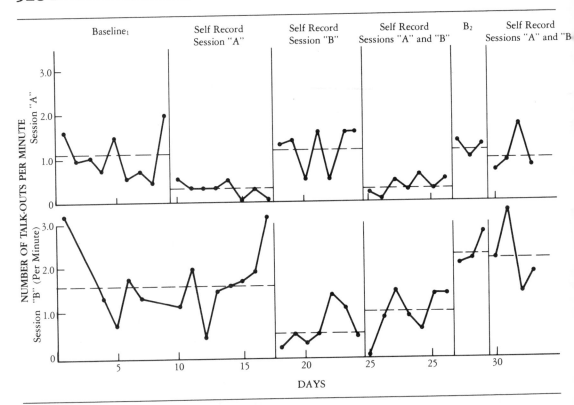

FIGURE 25.5 Record of an eighth-grade boy's talking-out behavior during two parts of a daily math class. (From "The Effect of Self-Recording on the Classroom Behavior of Two Eighth-Grade Students" by M. Broden, R. V. Hall, and B. Mitts, 1971, *Journal of Applied Behavior Analysis, 4,* p. 197. Copyright 1971 by the Society for the Experimental Analysis of Behavior, Inc. Reprinted by Permission.)

When I have commenced a new book, I have always prepared a diary, divided into weeks, and carried on for the period which I have allowed myself for the completion of the work. In this I have entered, day by day, the number of pages I have written, so that if at any time I have slipped into idleness for a day or two, the record of that idleness has been there staring me in the face, and demanding of me increased labour, so that the deficiency might be supplied. . . . I have allotted myself so many pages a week. The average number has been about 40. It has been placed as low as 20, and has risen to 112. And as a page is an ambiguous term, my page has been made to contain 250 words; and as words, if not watched, will have a tendency to straggle, I have had every word counted as I went. . . . There has ever been the record before me, and a week

passed with an insufficient number of pages has been a blister to my eye and a month so disgraced would have been a sorrow to my heart. (Wallace, 1977, p. 518)

Exactly what principles of behavior are operating when self-monitoring results in a change in the target behavior is not known because much of the self-monitoring procedure consists of private, covert events. In addition to the problem of access to these private events, another major difficulty is that self-monitoring is usually confounded by other variables. Self-monitoring is often part of a self-management package in which contingencies of reinforcement and/or punishment are included, either explicitly (e.g., "If I run 10 miles this week, I can go to the movies") or implicitly (e.g., "I've got to show my record of calories consumed to my wife"). Regardless of the principles of behavior involved, however, self-monitoring is often an effective procedure for changing one's behavior.

How Is Self-Monitoring Done? Each of the methods of measuring behavior described in chapter 4 can be used for self-monitoring: event, permanent product, duration, and the various time sampling procedures. Event recording has probably been used the most in self-monitoring. With personal behaviors that can be counted as discrete responses, it is important to immediately record each occurrence of the behavior when it is emitted. By marking a tally on a slip of paper, advancing a wrist counter, or moving a penny from one pocket to another as soon as the target behavior has been emitted (or in some cases even before), a person is more likely to produce accurate self-monitoring data, and the individual can deliver self-evaluative statements (e.g., "I'm doing well") that may serve as effective behavioral consequences in altering the future probability of the behavior.

In addition, by emitting a self-recording response early in a behavioral chain, an individual may be more effective in changing the target behavior in the desired direction. Rozensky (1974) reports that when a woman who had been a heavy smoker for 25 years recorded the time and place of each cigarette after she smoked it, there was little change in her rate of smoking. She then began to record the same information each time she noticed herself beginning the chain of behaviors that would lead to smoking: reaching for her cigarettes, removing a cigarette from the pack, and so on. She stopped smoking within a few weeks of self-monitoring in this fashion.

Event recording can be aided by a prompt to self-monitor the target behavior. Lovitt (1984) describes the use of "countoons," which remind young children of not only what behavior to record, but also what consequences to provide for themselves. Figure 26.6 shows a countoon that was taped to an elementary student's desk, showing her what behavior to record (finger snapping), how to record it (by putting an X through the next number on the countoon), and what her self-delivered consequence would be each time (solving 25 arithmetic problems).

FIGURE 26.6 A countoon that can be taped to a student's desk as a reminder of the target behavior, the need to self-record it, and the consequence. (From *Tactics for Teaching*, p. 202, by T. C. Lovitt, 1984, Columbus, OH: Charles E. Merrill. Copyright 1984 by Charles E. Merrill. Reprinted by permission.)

When the behavior of interest reliably produces a permanent product available for inspection and measurement by no later than the end of the session, permanent product recording can be used for self-monitoring. For example, elementary children have successfully self-recorded their own performances on arithmetic assignments (Hundert & Bucher, 1978), handwriting (Johns, Trap, & Cooper, 1977), and written compositions (Ballard & Glynn, 1975). Even experienced writers have found self-monitoring the products of their efforts beneficial. Describing the self-management techniques used by famous authors, novelist Irving Wallace (1977) quotes from an article by George Plimpton about the legendary Ernest Hemingway.

> He keeps track of his daily progress—"so as not to kid myself"—on a large chart made out of the side of a cardboard packing case and set up against the wall under the nose of a mounted gazelle head. The numbers on the chart showing the daily output of words differ from 450, 575, 462, 1250, back to 512, the higher figures on days Hemingway put in extra work so he won't feel guilty spending the following day fishing on the gulf stream. (p. 518)

Data on the duration of behavior can also be obtained via self-monitoring. Skinner (1981a) describes a reliable method for measuring the amount of time he spends writing. He attached an electric clock to his desk lamp so that time was measured cumulatively only when he was at his writing desk. However, some target behaviors do not lend themselves to event or duration recording. The class of operants best described as on-task or working behaviors is not made up of easily observed and counted individual responses, and attempting to record the cumulative time that one stays on-task usually interferes with the task. Other behaviors may not normally be noticed, and watching for occurrences of these behaviors could interrupt a person's usual routine. Habitual behaviors such as hair pulling, tooth grinding, or finger biting fall in this category. Time

sampling recording procedures have been successfully used for self-monitoring such behaviors.

For example, second graders in a study by Glynn, Thomas, and Shee (1973) placed a check mark in the next of a series of squares if they thought they were on-task at the moment they heard a tape-recorded beep. A total of 10 beeps occurred at random intervals during a 30-minute class period. Using a similar procedure, Hallahan, Lloyd, Kosiewicz, Kauffman, and Graves (1979) had an 8-year-old boy place a check next to Yes or No under the heading "Was I paying attention?" when he heard a tone played at random intervals by a tape recorder. Persons can produce their own cues as well. Malott (1981) set an electronic calculator to sound a beep every 5 minutes cueing him to self-monitor his work behavior while writing.

How Accurate Is Self-Monitoring? Although some studies have shown that young children can accurately self-record their own behavior without specific external contingencies for accuracy (e.g., Ballard & Glynn, 1975; Glynn, Thomas, & Shee, 1973; Thomas, 1976), other researchers have reported low agreement between the self-recordings of children and the data collected by independent observers (Kaufman & O'Leary, 1972; Turkewitz, O'Leary & Ironsmith, 1975). One factor that seems to affect the accuracy of self-scoring is the use of self-reported scores as a basis for reinforcement. Santogrossi, O'Leary, Romanczyk, and Kaufman (1973) found that when children were allowed to evaluate their own work and those self-produced evaluations were used to determine levels of token reinforcement, the accuracy of self-monitoring deteriorated over time. Similarly, Hundert and Bucher (1978) found that students who previously had accurately self-scored their arithmetic assignments greatly exaggerated their scores when higher scores resulted in points that could be exchanged for prizes.

Rewarding children for producing self-recorded data that match the data of an independent observer and spot-checking students' self-scoring reports are two procedures that have been used successfully to increase the accuracy of self-monitoring by young children. Drabman, Spitalnik, and O'Leary (1973) used the first procedure in teaching behavior disordered children to self-evaluate their own classroom behavior.

> Now something different is going to happen. If you get a rating within plus or minus one point of my rating, you can keep all your points. You lose all your points if you are off my rating by more than plus or minus one point. In addition, if you match my rating exactly you get a bonus point. (O'Leary, 1977, p. 204)

After the children demonstrated that they could evaluate their own behavior reliably, the teacher began checking only 50% of the children's self-ratings by pulling names from a hat at the end of the period, then 33%, then 25%, then 12%. During the last 12 days of the study she did not check any child's self-rating. Throughout this period of reduced checks and finally no checks at all, the children continued to self-evaluate accurately. Wood and Flynn (1978) used a similar faded matching technique to train predelinquent juveniles to accurately evaluate their own room cleaning behaviors. Hundert and Bucher (1978) publicly checked all students' self-reported scores on arithmetic assignments, awarding bonus points or assessing penalties for scores that matched or differed from the teacher's score. This procedure (called Maximum Checks) greatly reduced exaggerated scores. Then a Minimum Checks procedure was instituted in which only one randomly selected student was checked each day, and the students continued to self-score accurately

Hundert and Batstone (1978) employed only the threat of surveillance and punishment to increase students' accuracy in self-scoring arithmetic work. Here is their caution to five elementary special education students:

"From now on, I shall be collecting your workbooks after you score them and check them for myself. If I find evidence that you were exaggerating, I shall have to take action" (p. 99). Although this threatened surveillance procedure effectively reduced the number of exaggerated scores, it is not recommended. First, it is easy to randomly check a few students' self-reported data each day, thereby gaining an opportunity to reinforce accurate self-monitoring. In addition, at some point it is likely that a student will exaggerate her score and will discover that no action follows. This discovery can only undermine the teacher's future effectiveness as a behavior change agent and could lead to other problems with the student. And finally, the ethics of giving students a false rule are questionable.

Although accuracy in self-monitoring is desirable, it is not a sufficient or even necessary condition for behavior change (O'Leary & Dubey, 1979; Rosenbaum & Drabman, 1979). Several studies have found little correlation between the accuracy of self-monitoring and its effectiveness in changing the behavior being recorded. For example, in the Hundert and Bucher (1978) experiment, even though the students became highly accurate in self-scoring their arithmetic, their performance on the arithmetic itself did not improve. On the other hand, the self-recorded data of neither student in the Broden, Hall, and Mitts (1971) study matched the data from independent observers, yet both students' behavior improved. In reviewing a series of studies evaluating the use of self-monitoring of on-task behavior by learning disabled children, Kneedler and Hallahan (1981) also found that accuracy was not a necessary requirement for improved performance.

Conclusions Sometimes self-monitoring is an effective behavior change technique, and sometimes it is not. One variable that probably plays a part in determining whether self-monitoring is effective is the desire of the individual to change the behavior being self-recorded (Bellack & Schwartz, 1976; O'Leary & Dubey, 1979). When self-monitoring does produce a reactive effect, it is usually in the educationally or therapeutically desired direction. However, the effects of self-monitoring on the target behavior are sometimes temporary and may require the implementation of reinforcement contingencies to maintain the desired behavior changes. The role of accuracy in self-monitoring is unclear; there is little correlation in the literature between accuracy and effectiveness.

Self-Delivery of Consequences

Arranging to have one's own behavior receive specified consequences according to self-planned contingencies of reinforcement and/or punishment is one of the fundamental approaches to self-management. Some of the techniques that have been used to self-reinforce and self-punish are reviewed in this section.

Strengthening Behavior The probability that a given behavior will occur again in the future can be increased in a self-management program, as in any behavior change program with both positive and negative reinforcement. Most of the self-reinforcement studies with school children have involved positive reinforcement in which students have self-determined the number of tokens, points, or minutes of free time they should receive, based on a self-assessment of their performance (Ballard & Glynn, 1975; Bolstad & Johnson, 1972; Glynn, 1970).

Evaluating the effects of self-reinforcement procedures is difficult because of the confounding of the self-monitoring, which is a necessary precursor to self-reinforcement. However, in the Ballard and Glynn (1975) study third graders were taught after a baseline condition to self-score and self-record several aspects of their writing—number of sentences, number of describing words, and number of action words. Self-monitoring proved to have no effect on any of the variables measured even

though the students handed in their counting sheet with their writing each day (see Figure 26.7). The children were then given a notebook in which to record their points, which could be exchanged at the rate of one point per minute for each student's choice of activities during an earned-time period each day. The self-reinforcement procedure resulted in large increases with each of the three dependent variables.

Negative reinforcement can also play a role in self-management programs through self-determined escape and avoidance contingencies. Malott (1981) describes a simple but effective self-management effort in which he wrote a behavioral contract that required him to practice his drums each morning for 15 minutes or pay his secretary $1. Malott (1981) advocates the use of mild aversive control in self-management programs.

> Our everyday life is full of such avoidance procedures, and yet they don't make us miserable. You don't have an anxiety attack every time you walk through a doorway, even though you might hurt yourself if you don't avoid bumping into the door jamb. And you don't break out in a cold sweat every time you put the leftovers in the refrigerator, and thereby avoid leaving them out to spoil.... Don't hesitate to use an avoidance procedure to get yourself to do something you want to do anyway. Just be sure the penalty is small and the response is easy to make. (Volume 111, No. 4)

Weakening Behavior The probability that a behavior will occur less frequently in the future can be increased in self-management programs with the contingent self-delivery of punishing consequences. Powell and Azrin (1968) designed a special cigarette case that delivered a 1-second electric shock when opened (the controlling response in this kind of self-management program is carrying the case and smoking only those cigarettes one has personally removed from it). Mahoney (1971) reported a case study in which a man beleaguered by obsessional throughts wore a heavy rubber band around his wrist. Whenever

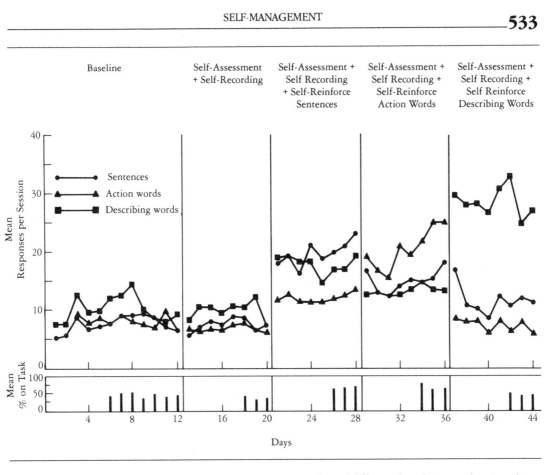

FIGURE 26.7   Mean number of sentences, different action words, and different describing words written by elementary students during baseline, self-recording, and self-reinforcement. (From "Behavioral Self-Management in Story Writing with Elementary School Children" by K. D. Ballard and T. Glynn, 1975, *Journal of Applied Behavior Analysis, 8,* p. 393. Copyright 1975 by the Society for the Experimental Analysis of Behavior, Inc. Reprinted by permission.)

he experienced an obsessive thought, he snapped the rubber band, delivering a brief, painful sensation to his wrist. A 15-year-old girl who had been compulsively pulling her hair for 2½ years, to the point of creating bald spots, also used contingent self-delivered snaps of a rubber band on her wrist to stop her habit (Mastellone, 1974). Another woman stopped her hair pulling by performing 15 sit-ups each time she pulled her hair or had the urge to do so (MacNeil & Thomas, 1976).

Punishment can also be self-determined and/or self-delivered by arranging the contin-

gent loss of reinforcers or a denial of access to reinforcement for a specified period of time. Response cost and time out contingencies are widely used self-management strategies. Individuals have reduced their rate of smoking by tearing up a dollar bill each time they light up (Axelrod, Hall, Weis, & Rohrer, 1971). Response cost procedures have also been used effectively with elementary children who have self-determined the number of tokens they should lose for both social behavior (Kaufman & O'Leary, 1972) and academic work (Humphrey, Karoly, & Kirschenbaum, 1978).

James (1981) taught an 18-year-old man who had stuttered severely since the age of 6 to use a time out from speaking procedure. Whenever he observed himself stuttering, the young man immediately stopped talking for at least 2 seconds, after which he could begin speaking again. His frequency of disfluencies decreased markedly.

Conclusions Self-reinforcement and self-punishment can and do often work, sometimes in powerful fashion.[2] However, sometimes self-management programs are completely effective with just stimulus control and/or self-monitoring strategies. Bellack and Schwartz (1976) warn against designing elaborate self-reinforcement/self-punishment contingencies for self-management programs if they are not needed.

> First, therapeutic strategy suggests that the least complicated yet effective intervention should be employed. Adding complicated procedures where they are not required is more likely to have negative than positive effects. Second, our experience indicates that many individuals find explicit self-reinforcement procedures to be tedious, childish, and "gimmicky." (p. 137)

On the other side of that perspective, there is no need for self-reinforcement procedures to be complicated, and probably just as many people find them fun as find them tedious or childish.

Other points should be considered when developing contingencies for self-delivery of consequences: (1) the intended rewards must be readily accessible for immediate delivery, (2) bootleg or unintended reinforcers that can be attained even though the self-determined objective has not been met must be eliminated, and (3) punishing consequences should not

be so severe that the individual will not be consistent in applying them.

Other Self-Management Strategies

Other self-management strategies have been the subject of behavior analysis research but are not so easily classified according to the three-term contingency.

Verbal Mediators People talk to themselves all the time, offering self-encouragement (e.g., "You can do this; you've done it before"), specific instructions (e.g., "Pull the bottom rope through the middle"), congratulations (e.g., "All right! I really crushed that tee shot!"), and admonishment (e.g., "Don't say that anymore; you hurt her feelings"). Such verbal self-statements can function as controlling responses that affect the occurrence of other behaviors.

One study that has been frequently cited and reprinted as evidence of the positive and lasting effects of self-instruction is that by Bornstein and Quevillon (1976). They taught three hyperactive preschool boys a series of self-instructions designed to keep them on-task with classroom activities. During a 2-hour session the children were taught to use self-instructions via a sequence of steps that had been previously developed by Meichenbaum and Goodman (1971): (1) the experimenter modeled the task while talking aloud to himself; (2) the child performed the task while the experimenter provided the verbal instructions; (3) the child performed the task while talking aloud to himself with the experimenter whispering the instructions softly; (4) the child performed the task while whispering softly to himself with the experimenter moving his lips but making no sound; (5) the child performed the task while making lip movements but no sound; and (6) the child performed the task while guiding his performance with covert instructions.

The specific self-instructions Bornstein and Quevillon taught the children were of four

---

[2]Although it is not clear exactly what principles of behavior operate when someone self-reinforces or self-punishes his behavior, most behaviorists agree that these self-management strategies involve more than a simple application of reinforcement or punishment. Self-reinforcement is further discussed later in this chapter.

types: (1) questions about the assigned task (e.g., "What does the teacher want me to do?"), (2) answers to the self-directed questions (e.g., "I'm supposed to copy that picture"), (3) verbalizations to guide the child through the task at hand (e.g., "OK, first I draw a line through here . . ."), and (4) self-reinforcement (e.g., "I really did that one well"). During the training session a variety of classroom tasks were used, ranging from simple motor skills such as copying lines and figures to more complex situations such as block design and grouping tasks.

Figure 26.8 shows the percentage of observed intervals in which each of the three subjects was judged to be on-task in the classroom before and after the self-instructional training. This study is significant not only because the children showed a marked increase in on-task behavior immediately after receiving self-instructional training, but also because their improved behavior was maintained over a considerable period of time. The authors suggest that the generality obtained from the training setting to the classroom may have been the result of telling the children during training to imagine that they were working with their teacher, not the experimenter. The authors hypothesize that a behavioral trapping phenomenon (Baer & Wolf, 1970) may have been responsible for the maintenance of on-task behavior; that is, the self-instructions may have initially produced better behavior, which in turn produced teacher attention, which maintained the on-task behavior.

Two experiments have been published in the behavior analysis literature that failed to reproduce the impressive results obtained by Bornstein and Quevillon. Friedling and O'Leary (1979) report a failure to obtain similar results in using the self-instructional training procedure with second- and third-grade hyperactive children, although the researchers did find an improvement in accuracy on easy math by three of the four experimental subjects. Billings and Wasik (1985) also attempted to reproduce the results of Bornstein and Quevillon, con-

ducting their replication with the same age, sex, and type of subjects and following the training procedures as closely as possible. They could not produce any significant improvements in classroom behavior as a function of self-instructional training.

Nevertheless, other studies have produced some positive results with self-instructional training. Burgio, Whitman, and Johnson (1980) found that a similar self-instructional training program did result in use of the self-instructions in the classroom as well as a decrease in off-task behavior. Additional studies investigating self-instructions with children have also produced generally encouraging results (Barkley, Copeland, & Sivage, 1980; Robin, Armel, & O'Leary, 1975; Kosiewicz, Hallahan, Lloyd, & Graves, 1982; Peters & Davies, 1981). However, given the varied results, definitive statements about the effects of self-instructional training must await further research. O'Leary and Dubey (1979) summarize their review of self-instructional training with children by suggesting four factors that appear to influence its effectiveness.

> In summary, self-instructions appear to be effective self-controlling procedures if the children actually implement the instructional procedure, if the children use them [the self-instructions] to influence behavior at which they are skilled, if children have been reinforced for adhering to their self-instructions in the past, and if the focus of the instructions is the behavior most subject to consequences. (p. 451)

Alternative Responses In his early discussion of self-control, Skinner (1953) included "doing something else" as a strategy for self-management. Azrin and Nunn (1973) later developed a habit reversal program in which clients are taught to self-monitor their nervous habits, interrupting the behavioral chain as early as possible by emitting an incompatible response. For example, a nail biter might squeeze her hand into a tight fist for 2 or 3 minutes each time she observes herself beginning to bite her fingernails. Robin, Schneider,

FIGURE 26.8 Percent of on-task behavior of three overactive preschool boys before and after training in the use of self-instructions (B). (From "The Effects of a Self-Instructional Package on Overactive Preschool Boys" by P. H. Bornstein and R. P. Quevillon, 1976, *Journal of Applied Behavior Analysis, 9*, p. 184. Copyright 1976 by the Society for the Experimental Analysis of Behavior, Inc. Reprinted by permission.)

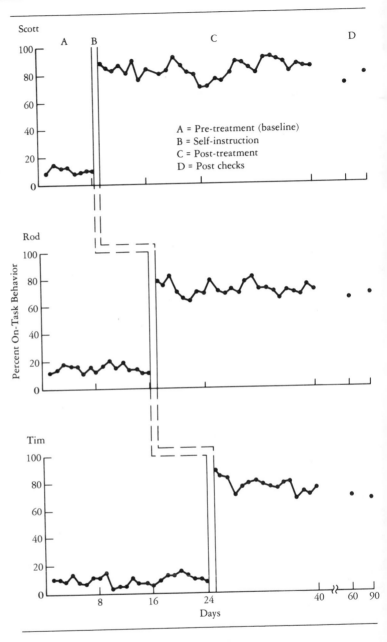

and Dolnick (1976) taught 11 primary-aged students enrolled in a special classroom for emotionally disturbed children to control their aggressive behaviors by using the turtle technique; the children pulled their arms and legs close to their bodies, put their heads down on their desks, relaxed their muscles, and imagined they were turtles. The children were taught to use the turtle response whenever they believed an aggressive exchange was about to take place with someone else, when they were angry with themselves and felt they were about to have a tantrum, or when the teacher or a classmate called out "Turtle."

Systematic desensitization is a widely used behavior therapy treatment for anxieties, fears, and phobias that also involves an alternative response strategy. Originally developed by Wolpe (1958), systematic desensitization involves the substitution of one response, generally muscle relaxation, for the unwanted behavior—the fear and anxiety. The client develops a hierarchy of situations from the least to the most fearful and then learns to relax while imagining these anxiety-producing situations, first the least fearful, then the next, and so on. Wenrich, Dawley, and General (1976) have written a manual describing a self-directed systematic desensitization process in which a person learns how to develop his own anxiety-stimulus hierarchies, how to attain deep muscle relaxation, and how to visualize scenes from the hierarchy while deeply relaxed. Here is an anxiety-stimulus hierarchy from Wenrich et al. that a person might develop in attempting to control a fear of cats.

Fear of Cats

1   You're sitting in a comfortable chair in the safety of your home watching T.V.
2   You're watching a commercial for cat food—no cat is visible.
3   The commercial continues and a cat is now eating the food.
4   A man is now petting the cat.
5   A man is holding the cat and fondling it.
6   A woman is holding the cat, and the cat is licking her hands and face.
7   You're looking out the window of your home and you see a cat on the lawn across the street.
8   You're sitting in front of your house, and you see a cat walk by on the sidewalk across the street.
9   You're sitting in your yard, and you see a cat walk by on your sidewalk.
10 A cat walks within 15 feet of you.
11 A friend of yours picks the cat up and plays with it.
12 Your friend is ten feet away from you, and the cat is licking his face.
13 Your friend comes within five feet of you while he's holding the cat.
14 Your friend stands two feet away and plays with the cat.
15 Your friend asks if you'd like to pet the cat.

16 Your friend reaches out and offers you the cat.
17 He puts the cat on the ground, and it walks over to you.
18 The cat rubs up against your leg.
19 The cat walks between your legs purring.
20 Your reach down and touch the cat.
21 You pet the cat.
22 You pick up the cat and pet it. (p. 71)

As soon as a person is able to go completely through his hierarchy, imagining each scene in detail while maintaining deep relaxation and feeling no anxiety, he begins to expose himself gradually to real-life situations.

Massed Practice   Sometimes forcing oneself to engage in an undesired behavior over and over will decrease its future rate. Wolff (1977) reports an interesting case of such a massed practice treatment by a 20-year-old woman who engaged in a compulsive, ritualized routine of 13 specific security checks every time she entered her apartment (e.g., looking under beds, checking the closets, looking in the kitchen). She began her program by deliberately going through the 13 steps in exact order and then repeating the ritual five times. After doing this for 1 week, she permitted herself to check the apartment if she wanted to but made herself go through the entire routine five times whenever she did any checking all. She soon quit performing her compulsive checking behavior.

TEACHING SELF-MANAGEMENT TO STUDENTS

Self-control is a social skill expected and valued by society, yet until recently it was seldom addressed directly by the school curriculum (Stephens, 1980). Teaching self-management as part of the curriculum requires that students learn a fairly sophisticated sequence of skills, as opposed to simply learning how to self-score one's arithmetic or handwriting, for example. However, systematic teaching of self-management skills, if successful, is worthy of the effort required; students will have an effective means of dealing with situations in which there is little, if any, external control.

When taught as a social skill in its own right, self-management can be organized into five elements: (1) self-selection and definition of the target behavior to be managed; (2) self-observation and recording of the target behavior; (3) specification of the behavior change procedures; (4) implementation of those procedures; and (5) evaluation of the self-management program (Heward, 1979).

Selection of Target Behavior

It is important that students be allowed to choose their own target behaviors when learning self-management. Even though the behaviors they select may not be those the teacher feels are the most important to change, the essence of self-control must be maintained. The teacher must remember that the goal of this operation is to teach self-management skills, not to remediate a student's specific behavior problem. The teacher can make input into the student's selection by making suggestions or by providing a list of possible choices; but it is important that the student be motivated to change the target behavior, and self-selection helps validate that desire.

If the teacher does present a list of possible behaviors to help students select targets for initial self-management projects, the list should not consist of problem behaviors only , which might make self-management appear somewhat negative and limited. By including behaviors such as learning to play the guitar, saving money for a special purchase, or asking someone for a date, self-management can be presented as an effective way to help attain personal goals. Throughout the self-management curriculum the teacher should use at least as many examples of these positive personal-objective target behaviors as there are examples of problem behaviors.

Students should be encouraged to select target behaviors for initial self-management projects that lend themselves to easy monitoring and recording. If a student is equally interested in changing two or more behaviors, the teacher should encourage her to select the behavior that appears to be the easiest to change. Again, the goal is to teach self-management skills, not to remake the child on her first self-control project. As with any new skill, every attempt should be made to introduce it in as successful and rewarding a way as possible. Harder-to-change, more socially relevant behaviors can be dealt with in subsequent projects.

Self-Monitoring

Even though several studies cited earlier showed that the accuracy of self-monitoring is not necessarily related to its effectiveness in changing behavior, accuracy is an important consideration in a self-management training program. It is important because students will also be learning how to decide which behavior change techniques to use, how to set appropriate criteria for reinforcement, how to determine whether modifications are necessary in an ongoing self-management program, and how to evaluate their self-control projects. As in any applied behavior analysis effort, all of these decisions should be based on direct, repeated measures of the target behavior. In a self-management project these decisions are made on the basis of self-collected data; therefore, inaccurate data can lead to poor decisions.

Two procedures can be used to help students learn to become accurate in self-monitoring. The first is the faded matching technique described earlier, in which students are rewarded for producing self-monitoring data that closely match the data obtained by the teacher (Drabman, Spitalnik, & O'Leary, 1973). As students become more accurate in their self-observations, the matching contingencies are gradually withdrawn.

The second approach is to teach students how to obtain and calculate measures of inter-observer agreement. Students trained in obtaining and computing reliability data have a method for checking the accuracy of data from any self-management project, inside or outside the classroom. Students can serve as second observers for one another, conducting either overt or covert observations and then comparing their results. A complete self-management curriculum should probably include a carefully faded matching procedure for target behaviors that occur in the classroom, followed by instruction and practice in how to employ reliability observers. Students should also be taught how to construct simple graphs from the data they collect and how to interpret those graphs.

Planning the Intervention

Although self-monitoring alone is sometimes effective in changing behavior, many self-management projects are more successful if reinforcing or punishing consequences are contingent upon the target behavior. The ability to plan effective self-reinforcement contingencies involves at least three components: (1) a working knowledge of the principle of reinforcement; (2) skill in identifying potentially effective reinforcers; and (3) setting appropriate criteria for reinforcement.

It is important that the examples and activities designed to teach students about reinforcement include a discussion of bootleg reinforcement; that is, access to the specified reward, or to other equally reinforcing stimuli, without meeting the response requirements of the self-management contingency. Bootleg reinforcement is perhaps the most common downfall of self-control projects. Teaching students how to add a response cost feature to their self-management programs is often a good method of overcoming the effects of bootleg reinforcement (e.g., "Not only do I not get a dollar today because I did not meet my

objective, but I have to take two previously earned dollars from the jar and give them to my roommate").

As with the selection of target behaviors, teachers can suggest possible reinforcers for students' self-management projects, perhaps providing a menu of rewards that students can select from. Again, however, teachers must let students choose their own rewards to whatever extent possible. One advantage of teaching self-management in a class setting is that peers are often a source of powerful reinforcement for one another, and students can interrelate their self-management projects so that they are in a position of monitoring and perhaps even dispensing rewards for one another.

A key to the effectiveness of any reinforcement contingency is the level at which the initial response requirement is set. The self-management curriculum should instruct students in setting criteria for rewarding their own behavior. Otherwise students are apt to make the same two kinds of mistakes that teachers often make when they plan reinforcement strategies without accurate baseline data—setting expectations so low that improvements in the current level of performance are not necessary to contact the reinforcement contingency or making the initial criterion for reinforcement too high, thereby effectively programming an extinction contingency that will not help improve performance and may cause the student to give up on self-management altogether. The criterion-setting formula (Heward, 1980) described on page 271 is easy for students to learn and should be included in this part of the self-management training program.

Implementing Self-Management Contingencies

Will students carry out self-management contingencies consistently and honestly, especially if a planned response cost feature requires them to punish themselves? What keeps anyone from cheating on a self-control project?

Many people have consistently implemented contingencies that require them to withhold rewards and, sometimes, even to carry out a response cost requirement for not meeting a self-selected objective. Two variables play important roles in determining how faithfully a person will carry out self-management procedures. First, the student must be motivated to change his behavior; and second, the student is more likely to be consistent with other self-control efforts if he has had success with self-management projects in the past. The teacher may have only marginal influence on a student's relative motivation to alter one behavior or another. However, teachers can exert considerable control over the second variable by making the learning of self-management skills as enjoyable and rewarding as possible and by seeing that the majority of a student's first self-control projects are successful.

Nevertheless, the temptation to deliver unearned rewards or to overlook a response cost contingency is often very great, regardless of how much the person wants to change. Teachers can help students who really want to change a behavior but have difficulty, or are afraid they will have difficulty, carrying out a planned intervention by suggesting the following procedure. After the student has planned the intervention strategy, including the criteria for reinforcement, she then turns over the actual implementation of the strategy—delivery of the reward and/or response cost procedure—to someone else. It is still self-management—the student has arranged her environment to help herself achieve a self-selected goal.

Evaluation of Self-Management Projects

Students who have learned to define, observe, record, and graph their own behavior can easily be taught how to evaluate their self-management efforts. A simple A-B design provides a straightforward accounting of the results in a before-and-after fashion that is usually sufficient for self-evaluation. In most instances

a person is interested in achieving his behavioral goal, and an experimental analysis of the program components is less important. However, the changing criterion design (Hartmann & Hall, 1976) lends itself nicely not only to the stepwise increments in performance that are often a part of improving personal performance but also to a more clear evaluation of the relationship between the intervention and the target behavior.

In addition to data-based evaluation, students should learn to evaluate their self-management projects in terms of social validity dimensions (Wolf, 1978). Providing students with a checklist of questions covering such things as how practical their intervention was, whether they felt the program affected their behavior in any unmeasured ways, and whether they enjoyed the project can aid them in making this kind of evaluation.

Teaching Self-Management to Incarcerated Youth

An example of systematically teaching self-management skills as a component of a school curriculum was provided by Marshall and Heward (1979). Eight boys 16 to 17 years old who were enrolled in a residential facility for juvenile offenders participated in the program. They met for 13 sessions over a period of 5 weeks, with instruction taking place in a specially designed classroom in which students responded on overhead projectors built into their desks (Heward, 1978c). The self-management training program followed this sequence; numerals indicate session numbers.

1   Introduction to the Visual Response System
2   Introduction to self-management course and pretest
    Selection of target behaviors
    Definition of target behaviors
3   Measurement of behavior
    Recording of behavior

4 Review of defining, measuring, and recording behavior
Baseline—definition and rationale

5 Graphing of behavior

6 Rewards (positive reinforcement) and setting standards (changing criterion design)

7 Relief rewards (negative reinforcement)

8 Interobserver agreement

9 Punishers

10 Tokens and backup rewards

11 Less frequent rewards (intermittent reinforcement)

12 Review of rewards, relief rewards, and punishers

13 Posttest

A total of 90 overhead transparencies were developed to present concepts to the students and to set the occasion for student responses. Each student carried out assignments that required him to plan, implement, and evaluate a self-management project in conjunction with the material covered in class. Starting with Session 4, the first part of each class period was devoted to students' presenting the data from their self-management projects and discussing their progress. As the program progressed, more class time was used for the sharing of student projects.

A 35-item pre- and posttest was used to evaluate the students' acquisition of verbal knowledge about principles of self-management. The group averaged 36% correct on the pretest and 81% correct on the posttest. In addition, each student's self-management project was judged on 20 different criteria (see Table 26.1), although students were not aware that their projects were being rated. Results showed the student projects to be, for the most part, technically correct, with definition of the target behavior showing the greatest weakness. At the conclusion of the study, seven of the eight students felt they had successfully changed their self-selected target behaviors.

Figure 26.9 shows the results of one of the students' self-management projects. This student consistently experienced trouble interacting properly with others. He felt that one reason for his difficulty was his tendency to "dip," or interrupt, the conversations of others. When he counted his self-selected target behavior, he discovered a baseline average of 15.9 interruptions per day. His self-designed intervention consisted of a self-delivered reward of a small box of raisins at the end of each day in which he had committed eight or fewer dips. He changed the criterion necessary to earn the reward twice during his project, first to six, then to four or fewer dips per day. He interrupted others an average of only 4.6 times per day during his intervention and, at the conclusion of the program, reported that he felt he had significantly improved his interactions with others and could use the skills learned in the class to change other behaviors.

Another student wanted to take more responsibility for the direction of his life, especially by finding a job after release from the institution (he was scheduled to be released 6 weeks after the study). The target behavior he chose was writing and mailing letters to potential employers, requesting employment applications and possible interviews. Figure 26.10 shows the results of this student's self-management project. He wrote no letters over a 15-day baseline. He chose two candy bars as his reward for meeting his initial criterion of one letter per day. On the eighth day of intervention he raised his response requirement to two letters per day. He wrote and mailed a total of 21 letters during the 15 days of his intervention; a staff member who covertly checked the outgoing mail each day confirmed his total.

THEORETICAL CONCERNS WITH SELF-CONTROL

A fundamental assumption of radical behaviorism is that the causes of behavior are

TABLE 26.1.   Evaluation of student self-management projects.

Student	Topic	Target Behavior	Definition		Measuring		Recording		Graphing				Consequences				Interobserver			Results		Total
		Relevant to Institutional Goals	Observable	Specific	Timing or Counting	Recommended Procedure	Missed 2 or Fewer Days	Days Labelled	Behavior Labelled	Plotted Correctly	Baseline	Connect Pts. Correctly	Practical	Appropriate Amount	Initial Criterion	2 Increases or More	Attempted	Computed Correctly	80% or Better	Graph	Questionnaire	
1		X	X	O	X	X	X	X	O	X	X	X	X	X	X	X	X	X	X	X	X	17
2		X	O	O	X	X	X	X	X	X	X	X	X	X	O	O	O	O	O	X	O	12
3		O	O	O	X	X	X	X	X	O	X	X	X	X	X	X	X	O	X	X	X	15
4		X	X	X	X	O	X	X	X	X	X	X	X	X	X	X	X	X	X	X	X	19
5		X	X	O	X	X	X	X	O	X	X	X	X	X	X	O	O	O	X	X	X	16
6		X	X	X	X	O	X	X	O	X	X	X	X	X	X	O	X	O	O	X	X	14
7		O	O	O	X	X	X	X	O	X	X	X	X	X	X	X	X	X	X	X	X	16
8		X	X	O	X	X	X	X	X	X	O	X	X	X	X	O	X	X	X	X	X	17
% Rec. Credit		75	62.5	25	100	75	100	100	50	87.5	100	87.5	100	100	87.5	50	75	50	75	100	87.5	X̄ = 15.8
% By Topic		75	43.8		87.5		100		85				84.4				66.7			93.8		

X—judged acceptable
O—judged unacceptable

SOURCE: From "Teaching Self-Management to Incarcerated Youth" by A. E. Marshall and W. L. Heward, 1979, *Behavioral Disorders, 4,* p. 220.
Copyright 1979 by *Behavioral Disorders.* Reprinted by permission.

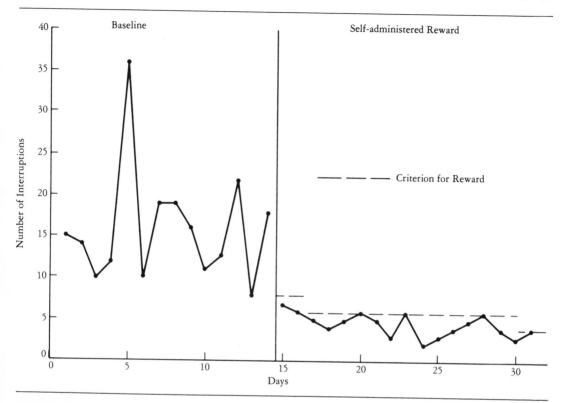

FIGURE 26.9 Number of verbal interruptions during baseline and self-administered reward by an incarcerated youth. (From "Teaching Self-Management to Incarcerated Youth" by A. E. Marshall and W. L. Heward, 1979, *Behavioral Disorders, 4,* p. 222. Copyright 1979 by *Behavioral Disorders.* Adapted by permission.)

to be found in the environment (Skinner, 1974). Throughout the evolution of the human species, causal variables found in the contingencies of survival have been passed on through genetic endowment. During the lifetime of an individual other causes of behavior are found in the contingencies of reinforcement that describe behavior-environment interaction. What role, then, does the self play? The concept and language of self-control have been the subject of increasing theoretical debate as the procedures and techniques that are called self-control have become better understood from an applied perspective. This section describes behaviorists' major theoretical concerns with self-control in an effort to make clear the advantages of a functional analysis of this important area of human behavior.

Behavior Analysis of Self-Control

As noted earlier, when Skinner (1953) first wrote about self-control, he made it clear that he believed a person can exhibit control over her life by emitting behaviors that successfully manipulate variables that, in turn, control the probability of other behaviors. He further discussed the ultimate control of behavior.

A man may spend a great deal of time designing his own life—he may choose the circumstances in which he is to live with great care, and he may manipulate his daily environment on an extensive scale. Such activity appears to exemplify a high order of self-determination. But it is also behavior, and we account for it in terms of other variables in the environment and history of the individual. It is these variables which provide the ultimate control. (p. 240)

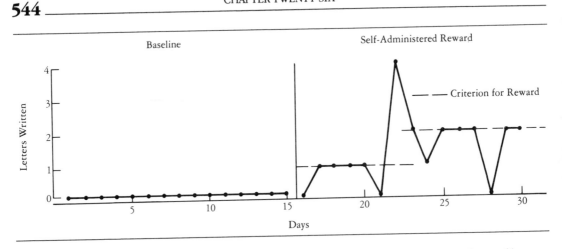

FIGURE 26.10   Number of letters of application written during baseline and self-administered reward by an incarcerated youth. (From "Teaching Self-Management to Incarcerated Youth" by A. E. Marshall and W. L. Heward, 1979, *Behavioral Disorders, 4,* p. 222. Copyright 1979 by *Behavioral Disorders.* Adapted by permission.)

The behavioristic position has not changed since Skinner's discussion of self-control more than 30 years ago. Ultimately, the causes of behavior must be found outside the person. And ultimately, it is the controlling response that must be functionally analyzed if a fuller understanding and an applied technology of self-management are to be developed.

At the center of the debate between external and internal control is the concept of self-reinforcement. Skinner (1953) was the first to point out that what we call self-reinforcement should not be considered synonymous with operant reinforcement.

> The place of operant reinforcement in self-control is not clear. In one sense, all reinforcements are self-administered since a response may be regarded as "producing" its reinforcement, but "reinforcing one's own behavior" is more than this. . . . Self-reinforcement of operant behavior presupposes that the individual has it in his power to obtain reinforcement but does not do so until a particular response has been emitted. This might be the case if a man denied himself all social contacts until he had finished a particular job. Something of this sort unquestionably happens, but is it operant reinforcement? It is roughly parallel to the procedure in conditioning the behavior of another person. But it must be remembered that the individual may at any moment drop the work in hand and obtain the

reinforcement. We have to account for his not doing so. It may be that such indulgent behavior has been punished—say, with disapproval—except when a piece of work has just been completed. (pp. 237–38)

Goldiamond (1976) continues with Skinner's example in his discussion of self-reinforcement, stating that the fact that the individual "does not cheat, but engages in the task, cannot be explained simply by resort to *his* self-reinforcement by social contact, which he makes available contingent on his finishing the job" (p. 510). In other words, the variables influencing the controlling response—in this case not allowing oneself social contact until the job is complete—must still be accounted for; simply citing self-reinforcement as the cause is an explanatory fiction.

The issue is not whether self-reinforcement or self-control works; it most certainly does, as the many examples cited in this chapter demonstrate. But Goldiamond (1976) and others (e.g., Brigham, 1980; Catania, 1975; Rachlin, 1977) have pointed out that a careful examination of instances of self-reinforcement reveal that something is involved that is more than, or different from, a straightforward, simple application of positive reinforcement. The term *self-reinforcement* is a misnomer, but the issue is not merely a semantic one, as some writers have suggested, (e.g., Mahoney, 1976). By assigning the effectiveness of a clinical technique called self-reinforcement to a well-understood principle of behavior with clear and specific defining conditions (i.e., operant reinforcement) when something other than or more than that principle is at work, we ignore the presence of relevant variables. If the analysis of a behavioral episode is considered complete because it was identified as a case of self-reinforcement, further search for other relevant variables will be curtailed (Jones, Nelson, & Kazdin, 1977).

Theoretical vs Applied Self-Control

Theoretically, self-reinforcement has been defined as occurring when, "in the relative absence of external controlling influences, an individual has full control over available reinforcers but freely imposes certain contingencies for the self-administration of the reinforcing stimuli" (Jones, Nelson, & Kazdin, 1977, p. 151). But this definition is fraught with problems: When are external controls relatively absent? How does an individual freely do anything? Rosenbaum and Drabman (1979) concluded that the sources of external control evident in the classroom self-control research they reviewed meant that theoretical self-reinforcement was as yet undemonstrated. However, at the same time these reviewers and others (e.g., O'Leary & Dubey, 1979) found evidence of powerful and systematic effects as a result of self-control procedures.

From a terminology standpoint *self-management* is a less misleading and less value-laden term than *self-control* (Brigham, 1980). Early in this chapter self-management was defined as the personal and systematic application of behavior change strategies that result in the desired modification of one's own behavior. However, such a definition is not explanatory; it is only descriptive in a broad sense. And even though various self-management strategies can

be classified according to their emphasis on a given component of the three-term contingency, as has been done here, it is likely that all self-management strategies involve multiple principles of behavior. When self-management strategies are described, a detailed statement of the exact procedures used in each specific situation should be given (Goldiamond, 1976). And behavior analysts must be careful in ascribing the effects of self-management programs to specific principles of behavior in the absence of an experimental analysis demonstrating such relationships. Only through such research can a more complete understanding be attained of the complex and promising area called self-management.

GUIDELINES FOR MORE EFFECTIVE SELF-MANAGEMENT

In their review of the self-management literature, Bellack and Schwartz (1976) note that "it is considerably easier to develop faulty programs than effective ones" (p. 111). Incorporating the five suggestions that follow into the design and implementation of self-management programs should increase the likelihood of success. None of these guidelines has been rigorously examined through experimental analyses—research on self-management has a long way to go—but each represents a "best practice" commonly reported in the self-management literature, and each is consistent with procedures proven effective in other areas of applied behavior analysis. Most of these self-management guidelines have been discussed by Malott (1980–81) in his *Notes from a Radical Behaviorist.*

Convert Hard-to-Follow Weak Rules into Easy-to-Follow Strong Rules

Malott (1984) describes weak rules as those with delayed, incremental, and/or unpredictable outcomes. An example of a hard-to-follow weak rule is "I'd better not smoke or I might get cancer some day and die." Even though the potential consequence—cancer and death—is a major one, it is far off in the future and is not a sure thing even then (we all know someone who smoked two packs a day since the age of 15 and lived to be 85), which severely limits its effectiveness as a behavioral consequence. So the rule "Don't smoke or you might get cancer" is hard to follow. What will one more puff hurt?

By setting up an easier-to-follow minirule—that is, a contingency with more immediate, definite consequences that are delivered each time the target behavior is emitted or not emitted—a person can greatly increase the probability of obtaining a previously elusive self-management goal. In our example a rule/contingency that requires the individual to self-record each cigarette and report that number to her spouse each evening will result in more immediate and definite consequences for her smoking behavior than the threat of lung cancer at some point in the future. The basis for all self-management efforts is arranging effective, immediate consequences for desired behavior that are more powerful than the contingencies currently maintaining the undesired behavior.

Build in Periodic Accountability

Let us suppose that a graduate student has a 30-page paper to write by the end of the semester, which is 15 weeks away—no problem. Then, all of a sudden, there are only 4 weeks left, and she decides to implement a self-management program. She follows the first self-management guideline and breaks down the large task into smaller, day-by-day increments with immediate consequences: she will write two pages on each of 5 days each week, putting one quarter into a jar each day she meets the two-page criterion and taking two quarters out of the jar whenever she fails to meet the criterion.

With her self-management program in effect, our student sits down at her desk each day with good intentions; sometimes she makes her two pages, but just as often, she does not. She finds that even with the prospect of losing two more quarters, she has great difficulty staying on-task. Instead of working steadily on the job at hand, she thinks about other things, gets caught up in reading interesting but irrelevant material, gets up from her desk, and takes too many breaks.

Our student realizes that even her two-pages per-day contingency is not immediate enough to control her writing behavior from moment to moment. Consequently, she gets out her cassette tape recorder and on a blank 45-minute tape records the words "Are you working?" at 10 random intervals. Each time she sits down to write, she starts the tape. When she hears her recorded voice, she tells herself how well she is doing if she is working, and she gets back on-task immediately if she is not working. By building this periodic accountability into her self-management program, the student can self-monitor her on-task behavior in an effective way and, in all likelihood, will meet her two-pages-per-day criterion.

The student in this example is using an accountability tactic with frequent monitoring (10 times every 45 minutes). Other self-management programs can be successful with less frequent monitoring. Malott (1981) reports that calling his secretary each morning by 9:00 A.M. and telling her that he was at his desk ready to begin writing was effective in keeping him from "goofing off or reading *Organic Gardening*." The frequency of an accountability check should be determined empirically in each individual situation. If once per day proves ineffective, perhaps once per hour will work; if not, a system of self-monitoring every few minutes may be necessary to get the desired behavior going.

Make It Public

The effectiveness of a self-management effort can be enhanced by publicly sharing the intentions of the program. Malott (1981) calls this the Public Spotlight Principle of Self-Management. When a person shares a goal or makes a prediction to others about his future behavior, he has arranged potential consequences—praise or condemnation—for his success or failure in meeting that goal.

> A public statement of goals improves performance. But just how do the social contingencies engaged by public commitment produce change? They increase the rewarding value of success and the aversive value of failure, I presume. But those outcomes are probably too delayed to directly reinforce problem solving. Instead they must be part of the rules the student self-states at crucial times: "If I don't make my goal, I'll look like a fool; but if I do make it, I'll look pretty cool." Such rules then function as cues for immediate self-reinforcement of on-task behavior and self-punishment of off-task behavior. (Malott, 1981, Volume II, No. 18)

Skinner (1953) also theorizes about the principles of behavior that operate when a person shares his self-management goal with important others.

> By making it in the presence of people who supply aversive stimulation when a prediction is not fulfilled, we arrange consequences which are likely to strengthen the behavior resolved upon. Only by behaving as predicted can we escape the aversive consequences of breaking our resolution. (p. 237)

Set Up a Self-Management Exchange with Someone Else

Setting up a self-management exchange is a good way to involve another person whose differential feedback about how a self-management project is going can be effective as a behavioral consequence. Two people, each of whom has a long-range job or a regular series of tasks to do, can agree to talk to one another on a daily or weekly basis, as determined by the target behaviors and by each person's progress. They can share the data from their self-monitoring and exchange verbal praise and/or admonishments and perhaps

even more tangible consequences contingent on individual performance. Malott (1981) reports a successful self-management exchange in which he and a colleague paid each other $1 each time either failed to complete any one of a series of self-determined daily exercise, housekeeping, and writing tasks. Each morning they spoke on the telephone, reporting their performance during the previous 24 hours.

Turn Over Operation of the Contingency to Someone Else

What keeps an individual from failing to deliver her self-planned aversives or from rationalizing that she did most of the behaviors she was supposed to and engaging in the rewarding event anyway? Unfortunately, in most unsuccessful self-management programs the contingencies for the controlling responses are not sufficiently strong. If a person really wants to change her behavior but has difficulty following through with her self-management program, she should enlist the cooperation of another person (Heward, 1979).

Kanfer (1976) calls this kind of self-management decisional self-control: the individual makes the initial decision to alter her behavior and plans how that will be accomplished but then turns over the procedure to a second party so as to avoid the possibility of not emitting the controlling response. Kanfer makes the distinction between decisional self-control and protracted self-control, in which an individual consistently engages in self-deprivation in order to effect the desired behavior change. Bellack and Hersen (1977) state that decisional self-control "is generally considered to be less desirable than protracted self-control as it does not provide the individual with an enduring skill or resource" (p. 111).

However, a self-management program that uses the assistance of another person is not necessarily less desirable. A self-designed behavior change program in which the contingencies are turned over to someone else may be more effective because that someone is more consistent in applying the consequences. In addition, as a result of experiencing successful self-management programs in which he has chosen the target behavior, set the criteria for reinforcement, determined a self-monitoring/evaluation system, and designed the contingencies of reinforcement and punishment, an individual can build a considerable repertoire of self-management skills for future use.

SUMMARY

A Definition of Self-Management

1   Self-management involves at least two responses:(a) the response to be controlled and (b) the response(s) emitted in order to control the identified response.
2   The controlling (self-management) responses themselves are a function of the person's history of reinforcement and thus, like any other behavior, are subject to experimental analysis.
3   Self-management is defined as the personal and systematic application of behavior change strategies that result in the desired modification of one's own behavior.
4   This definition of self-management is a functional one: (a) if the desired change in the target behavior does not occur, self-management has not been demonstrated; and (b) self-management has not occurred if the change in the target behavior would have occurred without the self-management responses.

Rationale for and Advantages of Self-Management

5   Without self-management, instances of important behavior can be missed by external change agents.
6   Self-management can be an effective method of extending the generality of a behavior change.
7   Some behaviors do not lend themselves to external-agent control.
8   Students with self-management skills can help operate a more efficient classroom.
9   Self-management techniques can sometimes be used to control behaviors not affected by weak outcomes.
10   Some people perform better under self-selected standards.
11   Self-management is one of the ultimate goals of education.

12   Teaching self-management skills to students supports and gives meaningful practice for other parts of the curriculum.
13   Self-management can be fun; it feels good.

Stimulus Control Techniques for Self-Management

14   One strategy is to provide extra cues for the desired behavior.
15   Another technique is to confront oneself with stimuli that successfully control the behavior.
16   Situational inducement can be used.
17   The stimulus conditions for the behavior can be restricted.

Self-Monitoring

18   Self-monitoring requires a person to observe and respond to, usually by recording, the behavior he is trying to change. Originally developed as a data collection technique, self-monitoring has evolved into the most widely used and studied self-management strategy because it often results in desired behavior change.
19   Self-monitoring is sometimes more effective when it follows a period in which the person's behavior is monitored and reinforced or punished by someone else.
20   It is difficult to determine exactly how self-monitoring works because the procedure necessarily includes, and is therefore confounded by, private events (covert verbal behavior); it often includes either explicit or implicit contingencies of reinforcement.
21   Self-monitoring is likely to be more effective if (a) the behavior is recorded immediately upon its occurrence, (b) the behavior is recorded early in a response chain, (c) effective prompts cue the person to observe and record regularly,

and (d) a permanent product of the behavior or a record of its occurrence is made for evaluation.

22 Children can be taught to accurately self-monitor and self-record their behavior by means of a faded matching technique, in which the child is rewarded initially for producing data that match the teacher's or parent's data. Over time the child is required to match the adult's record less often, eventually monitoring the behavior independently.

23 Some research has found that accuracy of self-monitoring is not necessary for the strategy to improve the behavior being monitored.

Delivery of Consequences

24 Behavior can be changed by the use of self-delivered consequences. Contingencies resembling positive and negative reinforcement, punishment by contingent presentation of an aversive stimulus, response cost, and time out can be incorporated into self-management programs.

25 When designing self-management programs involving self-delivery of consequences, persons should be sure that (a) the intended rewards are readily accessible for immediate delivery, (b) bootleg or unintended reinforcers that can be attained even though the self-determined objective has not been met are eliminated, and (c) punishing consequences are not so severe that the individual will not be consistent in applying them.

Other Self-Management Strategies

26 Teaching children to use covert self-instructions can be effective in controlling future behavior if (a) the children actually use the self-instructions, (b) they use the self-instructions for behaviors at which they are skilled, (c) they have been reinforced for adhering to self-instructions in the past, and (d) the focus of the instructions is a behavior subject to consequences.

27 The controlling response in a self-management program might consist of an alternative response that is incompatible with the response the individual desires to control. Habit reversal and systematic desensitization are two self-management procedures that involve an alternative response.

28 Massed practice, performing an undesired behavior repeatedly, can also be an effective self-management strategy for ultimately reducing the frequency of an undesired behavior.

Teaching Self-Management to Students

29 When taught as a curriculum component in its own right, self-management can be organized into five elements; (a) self-selection and definition of the target behavior to be managed, (b) self-observation and recording, (c) specification of the procedures for changing the target behavior, (d) implementation of the self-management strategy, and (e) evaluation of the self-management program.

Theoretical Concerns with Self-Control

30 Although a person can exhibit control over her life by emitting behaviors that in turn control the probability of other behaviors, the controlling behaviors must also come under analysis if a full understanding of self-management is to be achieved.

31 An analysis of the controlling behaviors in self-management reveals that they, like all other behaviors, are ultimately a function of variables found in the environment and in the history of the individual.

32 What is called self-reinforcement should not be considered a straightforward example of operant reinforcement. The variables influencing the controlling response must still be accounted for. Simply citing self-reinforcement as being responsible for the phenomenon is an explanatory fiction that is likely to preclude further search for the relevant variables.

Guidelines for More Effective Self-Management

33 Convert hard-to-follow weak rules into easy-to-follow strong rules.

34 Build in periodic accountability.

35 Make a public commitment to change the target behavior.

36 Set up a self-management exchange with someone else.

37 If necessary, turn over operation of the contingency to someone else.

PART TEN

Generality of Behavior Change

The preceding chapters describe basic principles of behavior and show how various behavior-change procedures derived from those principles can be used to increase behavior, achieve desired stimulus control, teach new behaviors, and decrease behavior. Part Nine illustrates how various procedures are combined to form the special applications of contingency contracting, token economy, group contingencies, and self-management. The literature of applied behavior analysis is clear: socially important behavior can be changed. However, achieving desired changes in behavior often requires the use of procedures that are intrusive or costly, or which for a variety of other reasons cannot or should not be continued indefinitely. Yet, it is almost always desirable for newly wrought behavior changes to continue. Similarly, in many instances the teaching necessary for producing new patterns of responding cannot be carried out in all of the environments and stimulus configurations in which the learner must use the new behavior. Nor is it possible in certain skill areas to teach directly all of the specific responses the learner may need. Therefore, a major challenge to the applied behavior analyst is to design and implement teaching programs that produce behavior changes with generality. A behavior change with generality is one that continues over time after the contingencies that produced it are no longer operating, appears in environments other than those in which the instructional program was conducted, and/or spreads to other related behaviors that were not taught directly. Chapter 27 describes the social importance of producing behavior changes with generality, briefly traces the history of generality in applied behavior analysis, provides definitions and examples of the major types of generality, and outlines several strategies for achieving generality.

27

Promoting the Generality of Behavior Change

KEY TERMS

Generality of behavior change
Stimulus generality
Maintenance
Response generality

Generalization across subjects
Percentage of generalization
General case analysis/strategy

When the staff at a group home implemented an instructional program to teach the women how to select articles of clothing that matched in style and color, Bonnie learned to choose coordinated outfits. Now, just 6 months later, Bonnie wears clothes as "loud" and inappropriate as those she wore before the program.

Ricky was placed in a special education resource room for a large part of each school day because of his distractibility and inability to work on his own in the regular classroom. In the resource room Ricky learned to complete assignments independently; but each time he is returned to the regular sixth-grade classroom, his conduct and academic performance are as poor as ever.

Jim is 10 years old and is enrolled in a program for children with severe handicaps. Functional communication skills are one of the major goals for Jim. His teacher, with a great deal of effort, has taught Jim to say, "Hello, how are you?" as a greeting. Now, whenever he meets anyone, Jim invariably says, "Hello, how are you?" Although Jim's parents are happy that he is beginning to talk, they are concerned that their son's language is stilted and parrotlike.

This chapter was written by William L. Heward.

Bonnie has seemingly lost her ability to select appropriate clothing; Ricky has learned to be a productive student in the special education classroom but still acts out in the regular classroom; and Jim's greeting behavior is limited. Each of these three situations typifies a particular kind of teaching failure—one of the most important and most difficult challenges facing the applied behavior analyst. If a behavior change is to be truly worthwhile and effective, it must last and be useful to the individual in different settings and in various ways. The student who has learned to count money and make change in the classroom today should be able to count and make change in the supermarket and at the drugstore tomorrow, next week, and next year. Likewise, the beginning writer who has been taught to write a few good sentences should be able to write many more meaningful sentences. Behavior changes that meet these expectations are said to have generality. This chapter describes the strategies most commonly used to plan for and promote generalized behavior change. But first, it presents a brief history of generality in applied behavior analysis and gives an explanation of terminology.

GENERALITY AND THE DEVELOPMENT OF BEHAVIOR CHANGE TECHNOLOGY

Emergence of Behavior Change Technology (1949-1967)

In 1949 Fuller published a study demonstrating the operant reinforcement and extinction of arm raising in a profoundly retarded individual who had been considered unable to learn. For the better part of the next two decades researchers and practitioners alike experimented with the application of basic principles of behavior to the problems of people in clinic, school, home, and work environments. From the few basic principles of behavior, numerous techniques were discovered and developed for changing human behavior in applied settings. Successful applications of shaping, token reinforcement, extinction, and punishment procedures were regularly reported. There was much excitement over the relative power and reliability of the new approach—and behavior modification was born.

Of the many criticisms that behavior modification attracted during this period, one was particularly troublesome. It was at the empirical level and was directed at the primary purpose espoused by applied behavior analysts—making changes in behavior that have real significance for the individual. The criticism went something like this: "Yes, behavior modification techniques can be used to produce positive changes in behavior, sometimes even dramatic changes. But the improvements are only temporary and often seem to be limited to the settings in which treatment took place."

Unfortunately, the criticism was not effectively countered. Early behavior modification literature contains few studies with significant follow-up data or probes in nontraining environments to assess the generality of the behavior changes produced. This lack does not suggest that the pioneers of behavior analysis did not know or did not care about the existence or extent of any generalized effects of their efforts. Rather, the field was in its infancy with much of its measurement and analysis methodology and many of its strategies and tactics still to be developed. The problem of generality was just one of many that had to be solved.

Increased Awareness of Generality's Critical Importance (1968-1976)

The year 1968 was cited in chapter 1 as the official beginning of applied behavior analysis. In that year the first volume of the *Journal of Applied Behavior Analysis* was published, and in the journal's first issue Baer, Wolf, and Risley

(1968) defined the new field in their article "Some Current Dimensions of Applied Behavior Analysis." They included **generality of behavior change** as one of the seven defining characteristics of applied behavior analysis.

> A behavior change may be said to have generality if it proves durable over time, if it appears in a wide variety of possible environments, or if it spreads to a wide variety of related behaviors. (p. 96)

After several examples Baer et al. indicated their belief that the importance of generality was not widely understood.

> That generality is a valuable characteristic of applied behavior analysis which should be examined explicitly apparently is not quite that obvious, and is stated here for emphasis. (p. 96)

By this time basic strategies for behavior change had been demonstrated and replicated across various subject populations and settings, and the measurement and analysis methodology of the young field was becoming more sophisticated. An increasing number of published studies in the applied behavior analysis literature contained direct measures designed to assess generality, although relatively few experimenters actively sought to produce or analyze it.

Generality Becomes a Major Issue/Area of Research (1977-1986)

The publication of Stokes and Baer's 1977 paper, "An Implicit Technology of Generalization," placed the generality of behavior change at the forefront as a major issue and an unresolved challenge for applied behavior analysis. Based on a review of 270 published studies relevant to generality (generalization), Stokes and Baer made the following points:

1 Generalization had been treated primarily as a passive phenomenon.
2 Whereas discrimination was fairly well understood as an active process, gen-

eralization was seen only as a failure to practice discrimination technology adequately. As a result, generalization had remained a passive concept, almost devoid of a technology.

3 The importance of generality in therapeutic behavior change was widely accepted, but its analysis was seldom pursued. Researchers and practitioners pointed with pride to instances in which behavior changes showed generality; but when generality did not occur, its absence was lamented. Seldom were specific strategies employed to produce it.

4 An "informal germ of a technology for generalization" (p. 350) already existed in the applied behavior analysis literature. Stokes and Baer organized this implicit technology into nine general strategies or approaches for promoting generalizable behavior changes.

5 The generalization of behavior change is best approached from a pragmatic orientation, in terms of both definition and procedure. Furthermore, applied behavior analysts should act as if there was no such thing as "free" generalization. Instead, they should always plan and program for it.

The production and analysis of the generality of behavior change is a critical issue in the continued development of applied behavior analysis. The direct assessment and discussion (if not actual analysis) of the extent of generality of any behavioral improvement is now viewed as an essential element of good research in applied behavior analysis. The importance of producing socially important improvements that are maintained and extended beyond the treatment conditions can even be viewed from an ethical perspective.

> Often, elaborate behavioral procedures and data collection systems are imposed on the subjects and those around them in order to obtain experimentally meaningful results. A question arises concerning the ethics involved in soliciting the

cooperation and trust of those in need of professional assistance without attempting to discover methods to prevent beneficial treatment effects from disappearing when the behavioral program is withdrawn. (Drabman, Hammer, & Rosenbaum, 1979, p. 204)

TERMINOLOGY

Before strategies can be described for promoting generality in behavior changes, several key terms must be clarified and defined. Various terms have been used to refer to the generality of behavior change. The word *generalization* has been used most often in the applied behavioral literature to indicate behavior changes that occur in nontraining conditions. *Stimulus generalization* and *transfer of training* have also been used to refer to generality across settings, people, and conditions. The terms *response generalization* and *concomitant behavior change* have been used to indicate the development of related behaviors not directly trained. *Maintenance, response maintenance,* and *resistance to extinction* are terms that have been used to refer to behavior changes that persist over time. To complicate matters further, the term *generalization* itself has been used often in recent years as a catchall to refer to all three types of generality.

Stokes and Baer (1977) use the term *generalization* to refer to the generality of behavior change, defining it as

> the occurrence of relevant behavior under different, nontraining conditions (i.e., across subjects, settings, people, behaviors, and/or time) without the scheduling of the same events in those conditions. Thus, generalization may be claimed when no extratraining manipulations are needed for extratraining changes; or may be claimed when some extra manipulations are necessary, but their cost is clearly less than that of the direct intervention. Generalization will not be claimed when similar events are necessary for similar effects across conditions. (p. 350)

Stokes and Baer's definition of generality is a good one for applied behavior analysis. They

have purposely taken a pragmatic orientation, stating simply that if the trained behavior occurs at other times or in other places without being retaught completely, or if it results in the occurrence of other related behaviors not requiring complete training, then a behavior change with generality has taken place. Generality, therefore, is a relative concept. A program can result in a lot of generality—the client uses the newly learned skill, as well as several related behaviors previously not observed in his repertoire, at every appropriate opportunity without the programming of any additional prompts or consequences. At the other end of the generality continuum are behavior change programs that produce only a small amount of generality—the client uses the new skill in other situations, but only after some additional procedure is applied.

A difficulty arises in using the term *generalization* to refer to all aspects of the generality of behavior change. Generalization is comprised of two behavioral processes (Sidman, 1960). *Stimulus generalization,* examined in chapter 13, refers to the phenomenon in which a response that has been reinforced only in the presence of a given stimulus occurs with an increased frequency in the presence of different but similar stimuli. *Response generalization* describes the situation in which a given stimulus, previously paired with reinforcement for a particular response, evokes similar but different responses. Both stimulus generalization and response generalization are technical terms referring to specific behavioral processes, and their use should be restricted to those instances (Johnston, 1979). Stokes and Baer (1977) clearly indicate their awareness of the differences in definitions.

> The notion of generalization developed here is an essentially pragmatic one; it does not closely follow the traditional conceptualizations (Keller and Schoenfeld, 1950; Skinner, 1953). In many ways, this discussion will sidestep much of the controversy concerning terminology. (p. 350)

Baer (1981a) explains his preference for the term *generalization* while discussing the use of natural communities of reinforcement to maintain and extend programmed behavior changes.

> It is the best of the techniques described here and, interestingly, it does not deserve the textbook definition of "generalization." It is a reinforcement technique, and the textbook definition of generalization refers to unreinforced behavior changes resulting from other directly reinforced behavior changes. . . . remind yourself that we are dealing with the pragmatic use of the word, generalization, not the textbook meaning. We reinforce each other for using the word pragmatically , and it serves us well enough so far, so we shall probably maintain this imprecise usage. (p. 32)

Johnston (1979) criticizes the use of the term *generalization* (a specific behavioral process) to describe any desirable behavioral change in a nontraining setting (a characteristic of behavior change—generality).

> This kind of usage is misleading in that it suggests that a single phenomenon is at work when actually a number of different phenomena need to be described, explained, and controlled. . . . Carefully designing procedures to optimize the contributions of stimulus and response generalization would hardly exhaust our repertoire of tactics for getting the subject to behave in a desirable way in non-training settings. Our successes will be more frequent when we realize that maximizing behavioral influence in such settings requires careful consideration of *all* behavioral principles and processes. (p. 1–2)

Indeed, the strategies and techniques described here for promoting the generality of behavior change, many of which are based on the contributions of Stokes and Baer (1977) and Baer (1981a), incorporate numerous behavior principles in addition to stimulus and response generalization. Therefore, in an effort to encourage precise usage of the technical terminology of behavior analysis and as a reminder that the phenomenon at hand can be a product of a variety of behavior principles, the term *generality of behavior change* is used in this chapter, and the terms *stimulus generality, maintenance,* and *response generality* are

used to refer to the three primary forms that the generality of behavior change can take.

Stimulus Generality

When a target behavior is emitted in the presence of stimulus conditions other than those in which it was directly trained, stimulus generality has occurred. Following Stokes and Baer's (1977) conceptualization of generality, we define **stimulus generality** as the extent to which the learner improves her performance of the target behavior in environments different from the original training environment. The setting in which stimulus generality is desired can contain some components of the behavior change program that was implemented in the training environment, but not all of the components. If the complete program is required to produce behavior change in a different environment, then no stimulus generality can be claimed. However, if some component(s) of the training program result in desired behavior change in a nontraining setting, then stimulus generality can be claimed, provided it can be shown that the component(s) used in the generality setting were not sufficient to produce the behavior change alone in the training environment. For example, cards with pictures of food items and the amount of money necessary for their purchase might not enable a young adult with severe mental retardation to buy those items independently. However, if an instructional program that included modeling, imitation, guided assistance, role-playing, token reinforcement, and the picture cards produced the desired behaviors in the teaching setting, and thereafter the student correctly made purchases by herself, aided only by the cards, stimulus generality has occurred.

Stimulus generality was assessed in two ways in a study by van den Pol et al. (1981). They evaluated the effectiveness of classroom instruction in teaching three mentally retarded young adults to eat independently in fast food restaurants. All three students had previously eaten in restaurants but could not order or pay for a meal without assistance. The experimenters began by constructing a task analysis of the steps required to order, pay for, and eat a meal appropriately in a fast food restaurant. Classroom instruction consisted of students role-playing each of the steps during simulated customer-cashier interactions and responding to questions about photographic slides showing customers at a fast food restaurant performing the various steps in the sequence. The 22 steps in the task analysis were divided into four major components: locating, ordering, paying, and eating and exiting. After students had mastered the steps in each consecutive component in the classroom, a probe was conducted at a MacDonald's restaurant. Observers were stationed inside the restaurant and recorded each student's performance of the various steps. Figure 27.1 shows the results of these generality probes before, during, and after instruction. In addition to assessing the degree of generality from the classroom training environment, which was based on the specific MacDonald's restaurant used for most of the probes, van den Pol et al. conducted follow-up probes in a Burger King restaurant (also a measure of maintenance).

All of the probes represented by the data points in Figure 27.1 can be considered measures of stimulus generality. All instruction—repeated trials, prompts, reinforcement, and a specific remediation procedure for incorrect responses—was conducted in the classroom. During the generality probes students were simply given a randomly determined amount of money (between $2 and $5) and instructed to go to lunch. Even though each student was aware that his performance was being recorded during the probes and the observers' presence may have served as a discriminative stimulus for the just-trained behaviors, substantial stimulus generality occurred because none of the materials or instructional contingencies from the classroom were operating in the actual

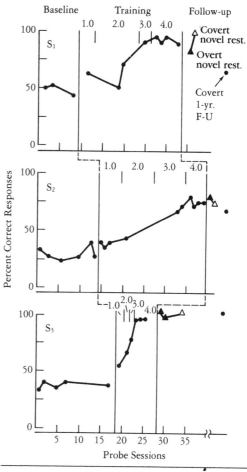

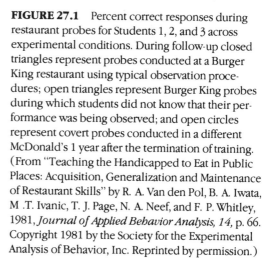

FIGURE 27.1 Percent correct responses during restaurant probes for Students 1, 2, and 3 across experimental conditions. During follow-up closed triangles represent probes conducted at a Burger King restaurant using typical observation procedures; open triangles represent Burger King probes during which students did not know that their performance was being observed; and open circles represent covert probes conducted in a different McDonald's 1 year after the termination of training. (From "Teaching the Handicapped to Eat in Public Places: Acquisition, Generalization and Maintenance of Restaurant Skills" by R. A. Van den Pol, B. A. Iwata, M .T. Ivanic, T. J. Page, N. A. Neef, and F. P. Whitley, 1981, *Journal of Applied Behavior Analysis, 14,* p. 66. Copyright 1981 by the Society for the Experimental Analysis of Behavior, Inc. Reprinted by permission.)

restaurant. In addition, stimulus generality took place from one restaurant chain to another and in the presence of covert observers.

Maintenance

Maintenance is defined as the extent to which the learner continues to perform the target behavior after a portion or all of the intervention has been terminated. From one perspective it might be argued that stimulus generality and maintenance are the same, or are at least inseparable, because by definition any postintervention measurement of stimulus generality must come after training has taken place and under conditions of reduced training contingencies. But the distinction between stimulus generality and maintenance is a functional one, which Whaley and Malott (1971) clarify. A lack of stimulus generality occurs when behavior changes produced in the clinic or the classroom are not emitted in the natural environment. A lack of maintenance occurs when a desired behavior change that begins to be emitted in the nontraining setting meets extinction or punishment contingencies. These are two separate challenges to enduring behavior change.

A study by Koegel and Rincover (1977, Experiment I) clearly demonstrates that stimulus generality and maintenance are different phenomena. Three autistic boys participated in the study; each was mute, echolalic, or displayed no appropriate contextual speech. All training sessions were conducted in a small room by one trainer seated at a table with one of the children. Each child was taught a series of imitative responses (e.g., the trainer raised his arm and said, "Do this," or said, "Touch your [nose, ear]"). Throughout the experiment each 40-minute session consisted of blocks of 10 training trials alternated with blocks of 10 trials conducted by an unfamiliar adult standing outside, surrounded by trees. During these generalization trials the same instructions and imitative prompts were given

to the children, but reinforcement was not provided for correct responses, nor did any other interaction take place between child and adult.

Figure 27.2 shows the percentage of trials in which each of the three children responded correctly in the training and nontraining settings. All three children acquired the imitative behaviors in the training room. Both Child 1 and Child 3 gradually began to respond correctly in the nontraining environment also as their imitative skills improved in the training room; but their generalized responding underwent extinction and was not maintained. The imitative repertoire acquired by Child 2 never showed generality to the outside setting. By the end of the study all three children showed 0% correct responding in the nontraining setting. For Child 2 it was a problem of stimulus generality, but for Child 1 and Child 3 it was a maintenance problem. Koegel and Rincover's experiment supports the validity of the two problems pointed out by Whaley and Malott (1971) and distinguishes between stimulus generality and maintenance. In addition, it demonstrates that both forms of generality can be directly assessed if measurement is continuous.

Response Generality

Response generality is the extent to which the learner performs a variety of functional responses in addition to the trained response; that is, responses for which no specific contingencies have been applied are altered as a function of the contingencies applied to other responses. In the Goetz and Baer (1973) study cited in chapter 8, response generality is illustrated in the block-building behavior of three preschool girls. During baseline the teacher sat by each girl as she played with the blocks, watching closely but quietly, displaying neither enthusiasm nor criticism for any particular use of the blocks. Then the teacher began to reinforce the different forms produced by the

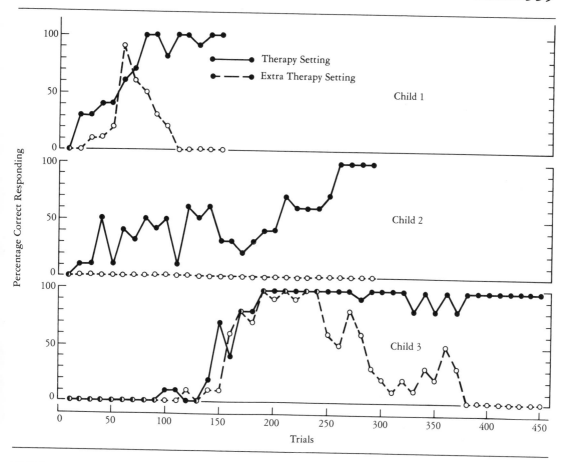

FIGURE 27.2 Percent correct responses for three children undergoing trials in two different settings. (From "Research on the Differences Between Generalization and Maintenance in Extra-Therapy Responding" by R. L. Koegel and A. Rincover, 1977, *Journal of Applied Behavior Analysis, 10,* p. 4. Copyright 1977 by the Society for the Experimental Analysis of Behavior, Inc. Reprinted by permission.)

children by remarking with interest (e.g., "Oh, that's very nice—that's different!") every time the child placed and/or rearranged the blocks to create a new form that had not appeared previously in that session's constructions. Another experimental phase followed in which every repeated construction of a given form in a given session was praised (e.g., "How nice—another arch!"). The study ended with a phase in which descriptive praise was again contingent upon use of different forms. Figure 27.3

shows the results. All three children constructed more new forms with the blocks when form diversity was reinforced than they did under baseline or under the reinforcement-for-the-same-forms condition.

In this study even though specific responses produced reinforcement (i.e., the actual block forms that preceded each instance of teacher praise), other responses sharing that functional characteristic (i.e., difference from previous forms) increased in frequency as a function of

FIGURE 27.3 Form diversity scores of three children engaged in block building. Data points labeled N represent scores produced under a condition of no reinforcement; points labeled D represent scores produced when reinforcement was programmed only for nonrepetitive forms; and points labeled S represent scores produced when reinforcement was programmed only for repetition of forms already constructed during the session. (From "Social Control of Form Diversity and the Emergence of New Forms in Children's Blockbuilding" by E. M. Goetz and D. M. Baer, 1973, *Journal of Applied Behavior Analysis*, 6, p. 213. Copyright 1973 by the Society for the Experimental Analysis of Behavior, Inc. Reprinted by permission.)

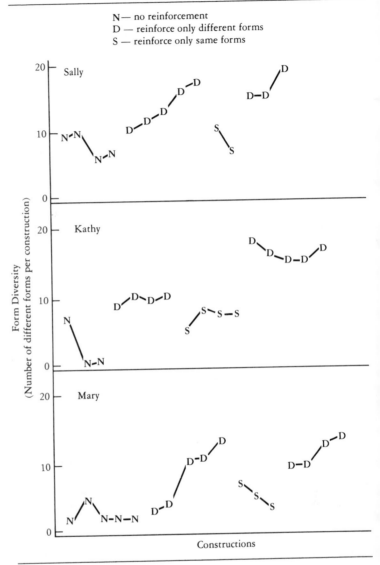

the teacher's praise. As a result, during reinforcement for different forms, new forms were constructed with the blocks even though each new form itself had never before appeared and therefore could not have been reinforced previously. Reinforcing a few members of the response class of new forms resulted in other members of the class being strengthened as well.

Concurrent Assessment of Generality

With many socially important behaviors more than one form of generality—across stimulus conditions, time, and/or responses—must be assessed in order to determine the usefulness of the behavior change program. An excellent example of the concurrent assessment of stimulus generality and response generality is provided in a study comparing two methods of teaching nonvocal language to students with severe physical handicaps that precluded their use of oral speech as a means of communication (Hurlbut, Iwata, & Green, 1982). An alternative language system often used by such persons is the communication board—a flat area, often in the form of a tray or table attached to a wheelchair, on which are pictures or symbols representing various persons, objects, activities, and so on. An advantage of the communication board is that it enables an individual with severely limited motor capabilities to use expressive verbal behavior by pointing to the pictures or symbols. An obvious disadvantage of the communication board is that the vocabulary of the user is restricted to the concepts that can be represented in picture or symbol form and correctly identified by the "speaker."

The two stimulus formats most widely used for representing language on communication boards are Blissymbolics and iconic line drawings. Bliss symbols represent concepts in combinations of geometric shapes. Blissymbolics was created originally to serve as a universal language; it is built on the assumption that the user will acquire a logical language system (e.g., the symbol for *school* is a combination of the symbols *house-gives-knowledge*) (Archer, 1977; Bliss, 1965). As a result, many of the Bliss symbols are highly abstract and do not resemble the objects they represent. In contrast, iconic symbols are simple line drawings that look like the objects they represent (Clark, Davies, & Woodcock, 1974).

Hurlbut et al. compared the effectiveness of expressive language instruction conducted with Bliss and iconic symbols. In addition to measuring the subjects' rates of acquisition of language items with each symbol format, the researchers collected various probe data that revealed the degree of maintenance, stimulus generality, and response generality of expressive language with the two sytems. A pretesting

procedure was used to identify 20 items for both training and generality assessment for each subject. The items were common objects or body parts that each subject could correctly identify when asked (e.g., "Is this a cup?") by vocalizing "uh-huh" or "uh-uh," moving his eyelids in an idiosyncratic yes or no response, or pointing to yes or no cards on a communication board. Then a baseline condition was implemented to verify that the items were not in each subject's expressive language repertoire. Both Bliss symbols and iconic line drawings for each of the 20 items were randomly placed on each subject's communication board. During baseline trials the experimenter presented an item and asked, "What is this?" The student was given 30 seconds to point to the correct symbol for that item (45 seconds was allowed for one of the subjects, whose pointing response consisted of tilting his head to focus a beam of light on various portions of his board). Each item was presented five times during baseline; if a subject pointed to the correct symbol for an item (in either the Bliss or iconic format) on more than one of the five times, the item was not included in the experiment. The 20 items were then divided randomly into two groups, 10 items for training and 10 items for generalization testing. The list of 10 training items was further divided into 5 items for Bliss symbol training and 5 items for iconic symbol training.

Individual training sessions were conducted each school morning and consisted of acquisition and review trials. Acquisition trials were presented for one Bliss symbol and one iconic symbol each session. A maximum of 10 trials for each acquisition item were presented each session, and an item was presented in successive sessions until a criterion of 10 consecutive correct responses was achieved (8 correct responses could be carried over from the previous day's session). Review trials (one of the maintenance measures) consisted of three trials on each of three previously learned items in each symbol format. Another measure of maintenance consisted of one probe trial administered during the afternoon on Bliss and iconic items from each subject's list of learned items.

For assessment of stimulus generality three to seven objects were selected from the same stimulus class as the training item, but with a difference in size, color, and/or shape (e.g., probe stimuli for the item *sock* were socks that differed in colors, sizes, and patterns from the sock used in the training trials). Response generality was measured by conducting one probe trial each day on the 10 untrained items. These probes revealed the extent to which the subjects could emit correct language responses to untrained stimulus-object pairs and also the symbol system selected to make each correct untrained response. In addition, the experimenters obtained data on the subjects' spontaneous usage of their communication boards during the school day, recording the frequency of expressive language responses made with both the trained and untrained Bliss and iconic symbols (the total of 40 symbols/pictures— one Bliss and one iconic for each of the original list of 20 items—remained on the students' communication boards throughout the day). These data provided information on the extent of both stimulus generality and response generality in an applied context.

The results of the study demonstrate a clear superiority of iconic line drawings over Bliss symbols in the acquisition and generality of nonvocal language. Even though all three of the subjects had been receiving training in the use of Bliss symbols for about 1 year prior to the study, each learned the iconic symbols in fewer trials, performed better on the iconic-trained items on review and maintenance trials, exhibited greater stimulus generality and response generality with the iconic symbols, and made more spontaneous language responses during the school day with the iconic symbols. The students required approximately four times more trials to learn the Bliss symbols as to learn the iconic pictures. Figure 27.4 shows the daily number of

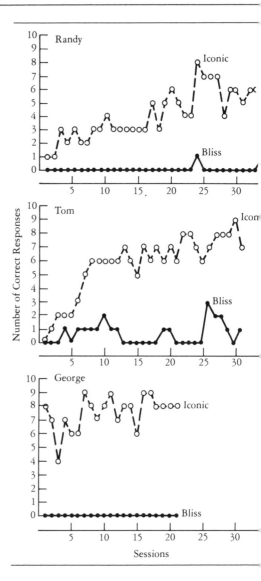

FIGURE 27.4 Number of correct responses in both language systems on the 10 items presented during response generalization probes. (From "Nonvocal Language Acquisition in Adolescents wit Severe Physical Disabilities: Blissymbol Versus Iconic Stimulus Formats" by B. I. Hurlbut, B. A. Iwata, and J. D. Green, 1982, *Journal of Applied Behavior Analysis, 15,* p. 253. Copyright 1982 by the Society for the Experimental Analysis of Behavior, Inc. Reprinted by permission.)

correct responses made to untrained items during the response generalization probes. Although the stimulus items were different from the trained items, these data represent an assessment of response generality because the specific responses measured had not undergone training (i.e., pointing to a symbol or picture of an untrained item). Randy, Tom, and George averaged 4.2, 5.7, and 7.5 correct responses on the response generality probes with the iconic pictures and .06, .65, and 0 correct responses, respectively, with the Bliss symbols.

The data for Randy's spontaneous language usage are shown in Figure 27.5. Randy emitted a total of 148 responses with Bliss symbols during the study (a mean of 2.8 per day), all of which involved one of the 5 trained Bliss symbols. He made a total of 615 spontaneous responses during the study with iconic pictures (a mean of 11.6 per day). A breakdown of this total reveals additional evidence of generality: 162 of the spontaneous responses were of the 5 trained iconic symbols (stimulus generality), 421 spontaneous responses were from the response generalization list (both stimulus and response generality), and 32 of the spontaneous iconic responses consisted of items that had been trained with Bliss symbols (i.e., even though the item had been trained with the Bliss symbol, Randy responded with an iconic picture, indicating both stimulus and response generality). Data for spontaneous language usage by the other two subjects reveal similar patterns in favor of the iconic stimuli.

Not only is the Hurlbut, Iwata, and Green (1982) study important because of the information it provides relative to the design of teaching programs for nonvocal language, but it also serves as a good model of a carefully conceived and well-controlled analysis of the generality of behavior change. As an ever-increasing number of research efforts in applied behavior analysis reach this level of sophistication, a truly effective technology of instruction will be closer at hand.

Generalization Across Subjects

Generality of behavior change is primarily concerned with the three forms already described; that is, the extension of an individual's behavior across settings, time, and responses as a function of previous treatment in another setting and/or for another behavior. However, there is a significant and growing body of literature showing that when behavioral interventions are applied to some persons in a given setting, behavior changes may occur in other persons not directly treated by the contingencies. This phenomenon, which has been described with a variety of related or synonymous terms—for example, "vicarious reinforcement" (Bandura, 1971; Kazdin, 1973, 1977), "ripple effect" (Kouin, 1970), and "spillover effect" (Strain, Shores, & Kerr, 1976)—provides another dimension by which the generality of treatment effects can be assessed. **Generalization across subjects** refers to changes in the behavior of untreated subjects as a function of treatment contingencies that are applied to other subjects.

The term *subject generalization* is used here instead of *subject generality* because the latter phrase often refers to the generality of a functional relationship found in a given study for persons other than those who participated as subjects in the study. For example, the concept of subject generality would be used in a discussion of the degree to which the results of an experiment on reading comprehension with regular classroom third graders in a middle-class, suburban school would be meaningful (i.e., reproducible) with older students, younger students, inner-city students, poor students, and/or special education students.

Fantuzzo and Clement (1981) examined the degree to which behavior changes would generalize from one child who received teacher-administered or self-administered token reinforcement during a math activity to a peer seated next to him. The subjects were 10 second-grade boys from poor families; the

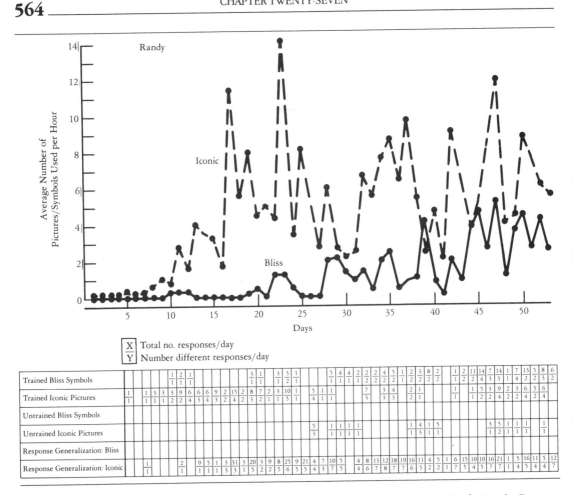

	X	Total no. responses/day
	Y	Number different responses/day

Trained Bliss Symbols						1/1	2/1	1/1						3/1 1/1		3/1 2/1	3/1						5/1 1/1	4/1	4/1 2/2	2/2	2/2	2/2	4/2 2/1	5/2	1/2 2/2	2/2	3/2 8/2	2/2			1/1	2/2 11/4	14/3	7/3 1/1	14/4	1/2	7/2	13/3 5/2	8/3 6/2
Trained Iconic Pictures	1/1	1/1	3/1 3/1	3/2 9/2	6/4 6/3	6/4 9/3	2/2 15/4	2/2 8/3	7/2 2/1	3/1 10/5 1/1		5/1 4/1 1/1		7/3	3/3 4/3	2/1 1/1			1/1	1/1 5/2	3/2 9/4	2/2 3/2	6/4 5/2	6/4
Untrained Bliss Symbols																																														
Untrained Iconic Pictures												5/3		1/1 1/1	1/1 1/1					1/1 1/3	4/1 3/1	1/5 1/1				3/1 1/2	5/1 1/1	1/1 1/1	1/1		1/1
Response Generalization: Bliss																																														
Response Generalization: Iconic	1/1		2/1	9/1 5/1	1/1 3/3	3/1 31/3	3/1 20/5	3/2 9/2	8/5 25/6	9/5 21/5	4/4 7/3	10/7 5/5		4/4 8/6	13/7 12/8	18/7 19/7	16/6 11/5	4/2 5/2	1/1 6/7	15/5 10/4	10/5 16/7	21/7 1/1	5/4 16/5	11/4 5/4	12/7

FIGURE 27.5 Mean number of pictures and symbols used spontaneously per hour per day for Randy. Data are broken down further into six categories, each reflecting the total number of responses per day, as well as the number of different responses per day. (From "Nonvocal Language Acquisition in Adolescents with Severe Physical Disabilities: Blissymbol Versus Iconic Stimulus Formats" by B. I. Hurlbut, B. A. Iwata, and J. D. Green, 1982, *Journal of Applied Behavior Analysis, 15,* p. 254. Copyright 1982 by the Society for the Experimental Analysis of Behavior, Inc. Reprinted by permission.)

boys had a record of unsatisfactory performance in arithmetic, were deficient in sustained attention, and presented behavior problems in the classroom. One of the students, Al, was selected by the experimenters to serve as the "confederate"; the remaining nine students were divided randomly into one of three different experimental sequences. These nine students were the nontreated students whose behavior would be observed and measured to determine the existence and extent of generalization across subjects.

Experimental sessions were conducted in a room containing two student desks and chairs and one desk and chair for the teacher. Al, who behaved in specific ways as requested by the experimenters and who was considered the treated student, participated in every session seated next to one of the other subjects. Sessions consisted of two parts: a 10-minute videotaped math lesson followed by a 10-minute period in which the two boys were instructed to work independently on math worksheets. Data were collected on the students' behavior during the worksheet activity (attending, glancing at one another, and percent correct and completed arithmetic problems).

No consistent generalization across subjects was noted in the students who observed the confederate receiving teacher-administered praise and token reinforcement for on-task behavior; a VI 60-second schedule was used, controlled by a tape recorder that delivered a 1-second tone within a 30- to 90-second range. However, three students who observed the confederate using self-administered token reinforcement for on-task worksheet behavior (on the same VI 60-second schedule) showed subject generalization. That is, changes in the on-task behavior of the nontreated students mirrored changes in the confederate's behavior even though the nontreated students were never given any additional instructions nor were they attended to in any way by the teacher or the confederate during the math activity. Increases in the accuracy of math performance also indicated some response generality across two of the three subjects who observed the confederate using self-administered reinforcement for his attending behavior.

Three of the nontreated students participated in sessions in which the confederate self-administered token reinforcement and in which the nontreated student had an opportunity to self-reinforce. Each nontreated student who experienced this condition had on his desk a control box for delivering points just like that of the confederate, but the teacher gave no instruction on its use and did not respond to the student's proper or improper use. The teacher said simply, "Children, these boxes are not toys. You may use them to help yourself, if you wish." This procedure produced the greatest amount of generalization across subjects.

Figure 27.6 shows the attending behavior for the three students who experienced this opportunity to self-reinforce. Visual inspection reveals a functional relationship between the behavior of the three nontreated students (Ed, Ron, and Fred) and changes in Al's behavior. Fantuzzo and Clement reported the amount of subject generalization as a **percentage of generalization**, which is computed by dividing the amount of change for a nontreated subject by the amount of change for the treated subject. If the behaviors of the treated and nontreated subjects change in opposite directions (i.e., one improves and one deteriorates), the percentage of generalization is reported as negative. The authors reported that the overall mean amount of generalization across subjects for attending behavior was 85% for the three students who participated in the opportunity-to-self-reinforce experimental sequence.

Another measure of generalization across subjects can be found in the nontreated subjects' use of the control box to self-deliver points. The confederate's use of the self-administered reinforcement procedure was 95%, 88%, and 93% accurate in the presence of Ed, Ron, and Fred, respectively. Such high levels of accuracy would be expected from the confederate since he received training in using the self-reinforcement procedure. However, Ed, Ron, and Fred, who never received any information on how to use the control box, self-administered points appropriately 82%, 67%, and 54% of the time. Collapsing the data for all three nontreated students, the authors state, "The accuracy of the reinforcement data indicated that all three nontreated students used the feedback boxes on a contingent basis achieving a mean score for accuracy of 68%. They did this without direct training or reinforcement for equipment use. Since the confederate's mean score for accuracy was 92%, the amount of generalization for this behavior was 74%" (p. 444).

Also, increases in percent of math problems completed correctly were noted in Ed's and

FIGURE 27.6 Percentages of attentive behavior across experimental phases for Al (confederate) and Ed, Ron, and Fred (nontreated students). The phase sequence is as follows: A = baseline; B = self-administered reinforcers for Al's attending plus access to self-reinforcement equipment for nontreated students; A = return to baseline conditions for Al; B = reinstatement of self-administered reinforcement for Al's attending and access to equipment for nontreated students. (From "Generalization of the Effects of Teacher- and Self-Administered Token Reinforcers to Nontreated Students" by J. W. Fantuzzo and P. W. Clement, 1981, *Journal of Applied Behavior Analysis, 14*, p. 443. Copyright 1981 by the Society for the Experimental Analysis of Behavior, Inc. Reprinted by permission.)

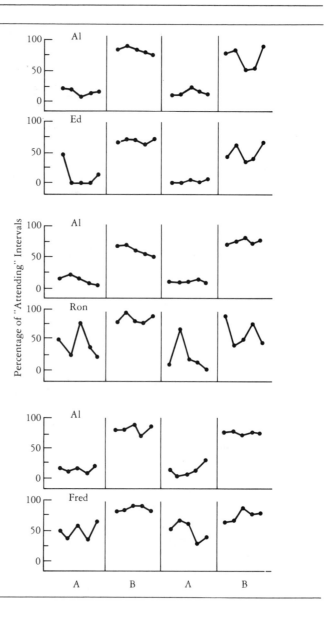

Fred's data during the final phase, whereas Ron's data suggested a clear functional relationship with the self-reinforcement procedures used by Al. Fantuzzo and Clement suggest two implications of their results for classroom practice. First, their data showing a lack of generalization across subjects for the teacher-administered reinforcement condition demonstrate the importance of "not assuming that all behavioral interventions with children will automatically generalize and have positive effects on neighboring students" (p. 445). Second, and more specifically, their results indicate that the opportunity to observe a peer use a successful self-management intervention can result in improvement for the nontreated child.

The Generalization Map

After a review of 188 child behavior modification studies, Drabman, Hammer, and Rosenbaum (1979) concluded that there are four major descriptive categories of the generalization of treatment effects: (1) across time (i.e., maintenance), (2) across settings (i.e., stimulus generality), (3) across behaviors (i.e., response generality), and (4) across subjects. They combined these four basic types of generality into a conceptual framework called the generalization map. By viewing each type of generality as dichotomous (i.e., it is either present or absent) and by combining all the possible permutations of the four categories, Drabman et al. arrived at a total of 16 different kinds of generality of behavior change. The 16 classes of generality included in the generalization map range from maintenance (Class 1) to subject-behavior-setting-time generalization (Class 16). Class 1 generalization is evident if the target behavior of the target subject(s) continues in the treatment setting whenever any "experiment-controlled contingencies" are continued. Class 16, the ultimate form of generality, "includes a change in a nontarget subject's nontarget behavior which endures in a different setting after the contingencies have been withdrawn in the treatment setting" (Drabman et al., 1979, p. 213).

Although Drabman et al., recognize that "with any heuristic technique the classifications may prove arbitrary" (p. 204), they have provided objectively stated rules for determining whether a given behavioral event fits the requirements of each of their 16 classifications. Regardless of whether the generality of behavior change consists of such distinctly separate phenomena as the generalization map suggests, Drabman et al., have provided an objective framework by which the extended effects of behavioral interventions can be described and communicated. And objective description of the various outcomes that are subsumed under the concept of generality of behavior change is a step toward more complete assessment and analysis. For example, Stevenson and Fantuzzo (1984) measured 15 of the 16 classes of generality included in the generalization map in their study of the effects of training a fifth-grade boy to use self-management techniques. They not only measured the effects of the intervention on the target behavior (math performance) in the training setting (school), but they also assessed any effects on math behavior at home, disruptive behavior at home and at school, both behaviors for a nontreated peer in both settings, and maintenance of all of the above.

PLANNING FOR THE GENERALITY OF BEHAVIOR CHANGE

> Teaching one example never automatically instills a concept, a rule, or a habit. Learning one aspect of anything never means that you know the rest of it. Doing something skillfully now never means that you will always do it well. . . . Thus, it is not the learner who is dull, learning disabled, concretized, or immature, because all learners are alike in this: no one learns a generalized lesson *unless a generalized lesson is taught.* (Baer, 1981a, pp. 1–2)

Before an applied behavior analysis program is begun, careful planning should be devoted to the generality of the behavior change to be produced. This preimplementation planning for generality includes identification of (1) all the desired behavior changes, (2) all the environments in which the behavior analyst wants the client to emit the target behavior(s) after direct training has ceased, and (3) all the behaviors required of others in order to support and maintain all of the desired behavior changes. The following steps are adapted from Baer (1981a) for planning behavior changes with generality.

Step 1: List All Desired Behavior Changes

A list should be made of all the forms of the target behavior that need to be changed. This is not an easy task, but it is a necessary one if the behavior analyst is to have a complete picture of the teaching task ahead. For example, if the target behavior is a young handicapped child's feeding herself, must the child display cutting, scooping, piercing, picking up, holding, biting, chewing, drinking? Should she also be able to ask for more, to indicate when she has had enough, and to wipe her mouth with a napkin? Only by having a complete list of all the desired forms of the behavior can the practitioner make meaningful decisions about which behaviors will be taught directly and which will be left to generality.

Step 2: List All the Situations, Settings, and Places Where and Persons with Whom the Desired Behavior Changes Should Occur

A list should be made of all the desired situations and environments in which the newly learned skill(s) should be emitted by the learner if generality of the behavior change is complete. In the example of the handicapped child learning to eat independently, what foods must the child learn to eat: peas, soup, bread, meat, spaghetti, corn on the cob? How about mashed potatoes, baked potatoes, and french fries? And drinking—must she be able to use a cup, a mug, a soft-drink can, and a bottle? (This kind of analysis often adds more behaviors to the list developed in Step 1.) Should she be able to eat independently at home with her parents, with her brother and sister present, with Grandma and Grandpa, with strangers? Will she need to eat at school, seated around a big table with other children? Will she be confronted with opportunities to eat in a restaurant, at a picnic table, or from a TV tray?

When all of the possible situations and settings have been identified, they should be prioritized in order of the most important and the most likely opportunities to use the new skill. Further analysis of the prioritized environments should then be conducted. What discriminative stimuli usually set the occasion for the target behavior in these various settings and situations? What schedules of reinforcement for the target behavior are typical in these nontraining environments? What kinds of reinforcers are likely to be contingent upon emission of the target behavior in each of the settings? Only when answers to all of these questions have been determined, if not through objective observation then at least by considered estimation, can the behavior analyst begin to have a full picture of the teaching task ahead.

Step 3: List All the Behaviors That Must Be Emitted by Everyone Else Involved in or Affected by the Behavior Change

In virtually every behavior change program other persons are involved in addition to the subject and the behavior analyst.

> All persons are potential teachers of all sorts of behavior changes. Just because you are designated as "teacher" or "behavior analyst" does not give you an exclusive franchise on the ability to make deliberate behavior changes. In fact, there is no possibility of such a franchise. Everyone in contact contributes to everyone else's behavior, both to its changes and its maintenance. (Baer, 1981a, p. 12)

Baer goes on to suggest that the behavior of others involved in the proposed behavior change should be classified into two separate lists: a tolerance list and an active-support list. The first list identifies all of the behaviors that must be emitted by those who must merely tolerate the learner's new behavior. The second list includes those behaviors that must be emitted, or *not* emitted, by persons who must actively support the new behavior by providing opportunities to respond, cues and prompts to respond, and various types and schedules of reinforcement.

In the independent eating program the tolerance list would likely include certain members of the child's family, school cafeteria staff, and peers. Beyond the home and school environments the behavior analyst should consider the possible role of the general public with whom the child may find herself sharing a table or dining area in a public restaurant. The learner's initial sloppiness and slowness (she may always be sloppier and slower than most people) as she makes the first attempts beyond the familiar contingencies of home and school might result in various responses from strangers that could punish the new eating skills. Being stared at, laughed at, talked about, told to hurry up, or even offered assistance could reduce the possibility of generality. Certainly, the behavior analyst can inform various school staff and family members of the onging eating program and request that they not interfere with the child's attempts to eat independently. But the public at large is another issue. It is not only impractical but also impossible to inform everyone of the program. Nevertheless, it is important to consider as many of these nontolerant behaviors as possible that the learner may encounter. It may be possible to modify the teaching program to include practice under such nontolerant conditions. Teaching sessions might be contrived to reinforce the learner for ignoring rude remarks and continuing to eat independently.

The active-support list might include one or two key people in the school's cafeteria, a volunteer or aide who works regularly with the child, the child's parents, and an older sibling. These people are vital parts of the teaching team. If optimal generality is to occur, the active supporters must see to it that the learner has many opportunities to use the new skill in the nontraining environments they share, and the natural reinforcers they control in those environments (e.g., praise, touch, smiles, companionship) must be used as consequences for the target behavior. When developing an active-support list, it is not necessary, and probably not desirable, to limit it to school staff, family members, and peers. They may not be regularly available in all the environments and situations identified in Step 2. A person who clears tables at a local fast food restaurant could be recruited to help support the new behavior. A small amount of attention and praise from this new person might be very effectvive in extending the generaliity of the new skill.

Benefits of the Generality Planning Lists

Without question, considerable time and effort must be expended to produce all of the information required by the three planning steps just described. Why not put those resources into direct instruction of the target behavior? In fact, teaching a new behavior without developing and implementing a plan to facilitate the maintenance and extension of the behavior is done so often that it has been labeled the "train and hope" approach to generality (Stokes & Baer, 1977). It is true that many behavior changes do show generality, even though the extension of the trained behavior across time, settings, and other behaviors was unplanned and unprogrammed. When target behaviors have been chosen that are truly functional for the subject and when those behaviors have been brought to a high level of proficiency under discriminative stimuli relevant to nontraining settings, the chances of generality are good. But what constitutes a high level of proficiency for certain behaviors in various settings? What are all of the relevant discriminative stimuli in all of the relevant settings? What are all the relevant settings?

Without developing a systematic plan, one usually does not know the answers to these vital questions. With few behaviors important enough to teach are the generality needs so limited that the answers to such questions are obvious. With only a cursory examination of our independent eating example, numerous variables were cited relative to the behaviors, settings, and people involved. A more complete analysis would produce many more considerations. In fact, a complete plan for generality would reveal more behaviors to be taught, to one person or another, than time or resources would ever allow. And this child in all likelihood needs to learn other skills also, such as dressing, bathing, using language, participating in recreation. Why then create all the lists in the first place when everything cannot be taught anyway? Why not just train and hope? Because . . .

1 The lists allow you to see the full scope of the problem and, therefore, the corresponding scope of your teaching program.
2 If you teach less than the full scope of the problem, you do so knowingly.
3 If less than a complete teaching program results in less than a complete set of behavior changes, you will not be surprised.
4 You can decide to teach less than there is to learn, because of practical considerations. This is almost *always* the case, but with the planning lists you can . . .
5 Decide what the most important aspects are and teach them directly, and in a way that will encourage generality to the other desired behaviors and situations. (Baer, 1981a, pp. 13–14)

STRATEGIES FOR PROMOTING THE GENERALITY OF BEHAVIOR CHANGE

Once the behavior analyst has determined which behaviors will be taught directly and in which environments those behaviors will be taught, the instructional program itself can be planned and implemented. Six general strategies for producing behavior changes with generality are described below (Stokes & Baer, 1977).

Aim for Natural Contingencies of Reinforcement

Behaviors that are not followed by reinforcement are not maintained. Ayllon and Azrin (1968) recommend that the relevance-of-

behavior rule be followed when selecting target behaviors. The rule is a simple one—choose only those behaviors to change that will be maintained by the natural environment, those behaviors that will naturally produce reinforcers in the postintervention environment.

Numerous criteria have been suggested for determining whether a proposed teaching objective is relevant or functional for the learner. Age-appropriateness and a skill's degree of normalization are two criteria typically cited as being important in the selection of target behaviors for instruction to handicapped students. Both are important dimensions and were discussed in chapter 3, along with other considerations in choosing and prioritizing target behaviors. But in terms of the generality of a newly learned behavior, there is only one criterion for functionality: a behavior change is functional (in the operant sense) to the extent that it produces reinforcement for the learner. No matter how much teachers, family, friends, or even the learner himself consider a behavior desirable, it is not functional if it does not result in reinforcement for the learner.

Baer (1981a) believes so strongly in the importance of this criterion that he recommends that practitioners

not make any deliberate behavior changes that will not meet natural communities of reinforcement. Breaking this rule commits you to maintain and extend the behavior changes that you want by yourself, indefinitely. If you break this rule, do so knowingly. Be sure that you are willing and able to do what will be necessary. (p. 16)

Some naturally available contingencies of reinforcement are powerful. Baer and Wolf (1970) refer to these existing contingencies as behavioral traps. Using a mouse trap as an analogy, they describe how a householder has only to exert a relatively small amount of behavioral control over the mouse—getting the mouse to smell the cheese on the set trap—to produce a behavior change with considerable (in this case, complete) generality

"The essence of a trap, in behavioral terms, is that only a relatively simple response is necessary to enter the trap, yet once entered, the trap cannot be resisted in creating general behavior change" (p. 321).

Behavioral trapping is a fairly common phenomenon, experienced by everyone from time to time. For example, a young man is persuaded to fill in as a substitute for a friend's bowling team. He has always regarded bowling as uncool, an activity for persons not like himself. And bowling looks so easy on television that he does not see how it can be considered a real sport. Nevertheless, he is persuaded to go, just to help out this one time. During the evening he finds out that bowling is not nearly so easy as he has always thought (he has a history of being reinforced by athletic challenges) and also that some very nice people whom he would like to get to know are avid bowlers (i.e., it is a mixed doubles league). Within a week he has purchased a custom-fitted bowling ball, a bag, and shoes; has twice practiced on his own; and has signed up for the next league season. Indeed, a great deal of his behavior seems to have been trapped by natural contingencies.

However, for many important behavior changes the existing contingencies of reinforcement are not so powerful or so readily apparent. Yet it must be remembered that all of the behaviors emitted everyday are being reinforced by some schedule of reinforcement sufficient enough to maintain that responding. Baer (1981a) warns that it can be a mistake to think that there are no natural communities of reinforcement for socially important behavior changes: "The everyday environment is full of steady, dependable, hardworking sources of reinforcement for almost all of the behaviors that seem natural to us. That is why they seem natural" (p. 15).

Baer (1981a) identifies two problems commonly made when practitioners attempt to employ natural communities of reinforcement. The first problem is simply that the behavior change has not been taught well enough. The new behavior is not being emitted at a rate, level of accuracy, and/or strength sufficient to make contact with the naturally occurring contingencies of reinforcement. The solution for this kind of generality problem, if not simple, is at least straightforward. The behavior change must be made more fluent: the learner must be taught to emit the target behavior at a higher rate, with more accuracy, within a shorter latency, and/or at a greater magnitude. An assessment of existing natural sources of reinforcement, part of Step 2 in generality planning, should include identification of the levels of performance necessary to access those existing reinforcers.

A second kind of problem with natural communities of reinforcement is that sometimes they are "asleep and need to be waked up and turned on" (Baer, 1981a, p. 17). In other words, there may exist in the natural environment potentially effective contingencies of reinforcement that are not operating in a form available to the learner, no matter how well she performs the target behavior(s). To solve this kind of problem, the behavior analyst must often be creative. For example, Seymour and Stokes (1976) taught delinquent girls to work more productively in the vocational training area of a residential institution. However, observation showed that staff at the institution provided no praise or positive interaction for the girls, regardless of the quality of their work. The much-needed natural community of reinforcement to ensure the generality of the girls' improved work behaviors was not functioning. To get around this difficulty, the experimenters trained the girls to use a simple response that called the attention of staff members to their work. With this strategy, staff praise for good work increased. Thus, teaching the girls an additional response that could be used to recruit reinforcement enabled the target behavior to come into contact with natural reinforcers that would serve to extend and maintain the desired behavior change.

A study by Stokes, Fowler, and Baer (1978) also provides an example of teaching children to recruit reinforcement in an effort to extend and maintain another behavior. They taught eight children in a preschool setting the dimensions of good work; for example, practicing good lines by staying close to the dashed lines, erasing and correcting mistakes, working consistently and quietly. The children were then taught to evaluate their own work and, when they judged the quality to be good, to cue the teacher to evaluate their work. The children were taught a number of different recruiting responses, such as "How is this work?" "Have I been working carefully?" and "Look how careful I've been." The children used the cues appropriately, received higher rates of teacher praise, and performed better academically. The study demonstrated that even very young children can be taught to use a response that effectively awakens an existing but seldom available natural community of reinforcement.

With responses to recruit natural communities of reinforcement, care must be taken to select behaviors that are not counterproductive (Baer, 1981a). A student who disrupts the whole class by shouting out and waving his arms in an attempt to cue his teacher to look at his work will probably experience more aversive consequences than praise. Estimates must also be made of an appropriate rate for the recruiting response (Stokes, Fowler, & Baer, 1978). A student who requests that his teacher look at his work 20 times in a 10-minute work period, no matter how politely he asks, will probably produce more resentment than praise. Although still a largely unexamined strategy, training individuals to emit behaviors designed to bring them into contact with existing but dormant natural communities of reinforcement appears to be an approach to generality that holds great promise.

Teach Enough Examples

The most common mistake that teachers make, when they want to establish a generalized behavior change, is to teach one good example of it and expect the student to generalize from that example. (Baer, 1981a, p. 17)

When a practitioner wishes a newly taught behavior to appear in a wide variety of settings and situations, she must be sure to teach the behavior in a number of different settings and situations. When a practitioner wants many forms of the new behavior to be used, she must be sure to teach a number of different forms of the behavior. Of course, teaching every desired behavior in every desired situation would obviate the need for stimulus generality (maintenance would be the only problem then). But this is seldom a practical, or even a possible, solution. Instead, the practitioner must select a subset of stimulus and response examples to teach and then check for generality. She can teach one example and then probe for generality to other examples. If generality has not yet occurred, she can teach another example, and another, continually assessing the extent of generality to the population of desired stimulus and response variations.

The planning lists of all the desired behavior changes and all the settings and situations in which those behavior changes should occur provide the range of possible examples. As stated earlier, those behaviors and settings of greatest importance should not be left to generality at all but should be taught directly. Within the subset of the most important behaviors and situations, those that are easiest to teach and easiest for the student to learn should be taught first. When generality to a sufficient number of untaught examples is apparent, teaching can be halted. The number of examples that must be taught before significant generality occurs varies considerably. It is a function of such variables as the target behavior(s) being taught, the instructional procedures employed, the subject's opportunities to emit the target behavior under the various conditions, the existing natural contingencies of reinforcement, and the learner's history of reinforcement with regard to generalized responding.

Sometimes, however, as few as two examples are all that are needed to produce significant generality. Stokes, Baer, and Jackson (1974) studied the generality of a greeting response by four severely retarded children to different staff members of the state institution in which they resided. Baseline revealed that the children hardly ever used a greeting response (see Figure 27.7). The senior author, working as a dormitory assistant, used primary reinforcement and praise to shape the greeting response (at least two back-and-forth waves of a raised hand). Then this initial trainer (E1) maintained the hand wave by contriving 3 to 6 contacts per day with each of the subjects in various environments throughout the institution (e.g., playroom, corridor, dormitory, courtyard). Throughout the study as many as 23 different staff members participated by conducting generality probes—passing by the subjects and recording whether they responded with the trained greeting. Approximately 20 generality probes were conducted each day with each subject.

Immediately after learning the greeting response with just one trainer, one of the subjects (Kerry) showed good stimulus generality by using it appropriately in most of her contacts with other staff members. However, the other three subjects failed to greet staff members most of the time, even though they continued to greet the original trainer virtually all of the time. A second staff member (E2) then began to reinforce and maintain the greeting responses of these three subjects. As a result of adding the second trainer, the subjects' greeting behavior showed widespread generality to the other staff members. The Stokes, Baer, and Jackson (1974) study is important for at least two reasons. First, it demonstrates an effective method for continual assessment of stimulus generality across numerous examples (in this case people). Second, the study shows that it is sometimes possible to produce widespread generality by programming only two examples.

Some behaviors must be emitted in the presence of a virtually infinite number of possible stimulus configurations (e.g., reading, mathematics). Surely, teaching programs for such behaviors must include multiple examples, but numerous examples will not automatically produce reliable generality. The behavior analyst must pay close attention to the type of stimulus examples selected if maximum generality is to be attained. Specifically, it has been argued that effective instructional design requires the selection of teaching examples that systematically sample the range of stimulus and response variations that exist in the situations where generalized responding is desired (Becker, Engelmann, & Thomas, 1975; Engelmann & Carnine, 1982).

Horner and his colleagues have empirically tested this assertion in the design and evaluation of several teaching programs for severely handicapped students (Horner & McDonald, 1982; Horner, Sprague, & Wilcox, 1982; Sprague & Horner, 1984). With a set of systematic guidelines called **general case analysis,** these researchers have selected teaching examples that represent the range of stimulus situations and response requirements in the natural environment. For example, Sprague and Horner (1984) evaluated general case instruction as a strategy for facilitating the generalized use of vending machines by six high school students with moderate to severe mental retardation. The dependent variable was the number of vending machines correctly operated by each student during probes of 10 different machines located within the community. In order for a probe trial to be considered correct, the student had to perform a series of five different responses correctly (i.e., insert the proper number of coins, activate the machine for the desired items, and so on). The 10 vending machines used for assessing generality were selected because each student's performance on those machines would serve as an index of his performance "across all vending machines dispensing food

FIGURE 27.7 Percentage of greeting responses by four institutionalized children across two training conditions and multiple generality probes. (From "Programming the Generalization of a Greeting Response in Four Retarded Children" by T. F. Stokes, D. M. Baer, and R. L. Jackson, 1974, *Journal of Applied Behavior Analysis, 7,* p. 603. Copyright 1974 by the Society for the Experimental Analysis of Behavior, Inc. Reprinted by permission.)

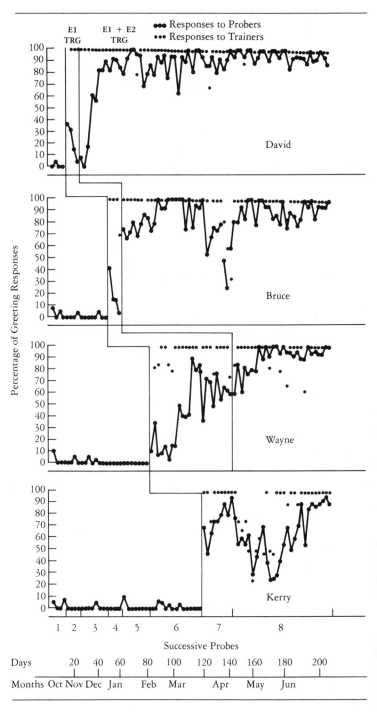

and beverage items costing between $.20 and $.75 in Eugene, Oregon" (p. 274). None of the generality vending machines were identical to the vending machines used during instruction.

After a baseline probe to determine each student's ability to use the 10 vending machines in the community (none of the students correctly operated any of the 10 machines during the baseline probe), single-instance instruction began. Under this condition each student received individual training on a single vending machine located in the school until he performed three consecutive correct trials on each of two consecutive days. The generality probe that followed single-instance instruction (see Probe Session 2 in Figure 27.8) revealed little or no success with the vending machines located in the community, even though each student had learned to reliably operate one machine with no errors. The continued inability of Students 2, 3, 5, and 6 to demonstrate generalized responding in the successive probes following additional instruction with the single-instance training machine shows that overlearning a single example does not necessarily aid generality. Of the eight probe trials correctly perfomed by all students after single-instance training, seven were on Probe Machine 1, which most closely resembled the training machine.

A multiple-instance training strategy was then evaluated with Students 4, 5, and 6. Teaching procedures in this condition exactly replicated those used in the single-instance condition except that each student received training until he reached criterion on three new machines, similar to each other. The training machines used in the multiple-instance condition were purposely selected because they did not sample the range of stimulus and response requirements of the vending machines in the natural environment. The data show that even after reaching training criterion on three additional machines, Students 4, 5, and 6 were unable to operate the machines used to assess generality. They performed correctly only 9 of the 60 total trials that were administered during the six probe sessions under the multiple-instance condition.

The **general case strategy** was then implemented in multiple baseline fashion across subjects. Instruction was conducted in the same manner as before except that three different vending machines were used that, when combined with the single-instance machine, presented the students with the total range of stimulus and response variations found in all machines in the community. None of the training machines, however, were exactly like the machines used to assess generality. After reaching training criterion on the general case machines, all six students showed substantial improvements in their performance on the 10 untrained machines. The authors suggest that Student 3's poor performance immediately after general case instruction may have been the result of a ritualistic pattern of inserting coins that he had developed during previous probe sessions. Between Probe Sessions 5 and 6 Student 3 was given repeated practice on the coin insertion step during the training session. As with all strategies for facilitating generality, much research remains to be done. The general case strategy, however, suggests a promising avenue of investigation.

Program Common Stimuli

The principle of stimulus generalization states that a target response is likely to be emitted in the presence of stimuli with a high degree of similarity to the stimulus conditions under which it was previously reinforced, but the response probably will not be emitted under stimulus conditions that differ significantly from the training stimuli. Stimulus generalization is a relative phenomenon: the more a given stimulus configuration resembles the training stimuli, the greater the probability that the trained response will be emitted and vice versa. A primary reason for planning-stage examination of the settings and situations in

FIGURE 27.8 The number of nontrained probe machines operated correctly by students across phases and probe sessions. (From "The Effects of Single Instance, Multiple Instance, and General Case Training on Generalized Vending Machine Use by Moderately and Severely Handicapped Students" by J. R. Sprague and R. H. Horner, 1974, *Journal of Applied Behavior Analysis, 17,* p. 276. Copyright 1984 by the Society for the Experimental Analysis of Behavior, Inc. Reprinted by permission.)

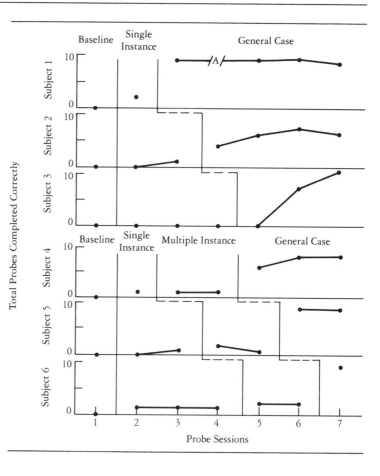

which generality of the target behavior is desired is to identify stimuli important to those environments that can be incorporated into the teaching program. If physical stimuli prominent in the nontraining environments can be included in training, the probability of generalized responding increases.

Walker and Buckley (1972) enhanced the generality of a training program for special education students by having them use the same academic materials in the special classroom that they used when they were reintegrated into the regular classroom. Anderson-Inman (1981) went even further in programming common stimuli by demonstrating the generality of the accurate written and oral spelling responses of a special education student from a resource room to a regular fifth/sixth-grade classroom. Each morning the student was given 15 to 20 minutes of spelling practice in the resource room, using the same materials, procedures, and words she would cover later the same day in the regular classroom. During baseline the student averaged 55% accuracy on her written spelling responses in the regular classroom, compared to a mean of 84% correct for her 20 nonhandicapped peers. During the two phases of special instruction in the resource room, the student increased her spelling accuracy in the regular classroom to the 84% level maintained by the rest of the class. Although less pronounced, the subject's oral responses during spelling also improved as a function of the resource room program that focused on stimuli relevant to the regular classroom.

Some behaviors may still show little generality, even though efforts have been made to include stimuli in the training setting that are common to the nontraining environment(s). Baer (1981a) recommends that in such cases a new stimulus be introduced that can be made functional for the target behavior in the training environment and that can be transported easily to the nontraining setting.

Train Loosely

To the extent that generality of behavior change can be viewed as the opposite of strict stimulus control and discrimination, one strategy for facilitating generality is to vary as many of the noncritical dimensions of the antecedent stimuli as possible during instruction and accept as correct a wide range of responses. Stokes and Baer (1977) note that the behavior analysis literature contains few examples of this approach, not surprisingly since behavioral researchers have purposely attempted to control and standardize their teaching techniques in order that their effects can be interpreted and the procedures replicated. Yet this restriction of teaching procedures to a "precisely repetitive handful of stimuli or formats may, in fact, correspondingly restrict generalization of the lessons being learned" (Stokes & Baer, 1977, p. 358).

Taking the notion of varying teaching procedures to its logical limits, Baer (1981a) offers the following advice:

- Use two or more teachers.
- Teach in two or more places.
- Teach from a variety of positions.
- Vary your tone of voice.
- Vary your choice of words.
- Show the stimuli from a variety of angles, using sometimes one hand and sometimes the other.
- Have other persons present sometimes and not other times.
- Dress quite differently on different days.
- Vary the reinforcers.
- Teach sometimes in bright light, sometimes in dim light.
- Teach sometimes in noisy settings, sometimes in quiet ones.
- In any setting, vary the decorations, vary the furniture, and vary their locations.
- Vary the times of day when you and everyone else teach.
- Vary the temperature in the teaching settings.
- Vary the smells in the teaching settings.
- Within the limits possible vary the content of what's being taught.
- Do all of this as often and as unpredictably as possible. (p. 25)

Of course, neither Baer nor the authors of this text expect any teacher to vary all of these variables for every behavior that is taught. But the point for building in some fair degree of "loose teaching" is an important one. Incorporating a wide variety of stimuli during the training of a new behavior makes it less likely that only one or a small group of stimuli will acquire exclusive control over the behavior and more likely that other settings where generality is desired will contain at least some of the stimuli present during training.

A study by Campbell and Stremel-Campbell (1982) evaluated the effectiveness of programming loose training as a strategy for facilitating the generality of newly acquired language for two students with moderate mental retardation. Each subject received two 15-minute language training sessions conducted within the context of other instructional activities that were part of each child's individualized education program, one during an academic task and the second during a self-help task. The student could initiate a language interaction based on the wide variety of naturally occurring stimuli, and the teacher could try to evoke a statement or question from the student by intentionally misplacing instructional materials or offering indirect prompts. Measurement of the students' language behavior during two daily 15-minute free-play periods revealed substantial generality of the language structures acquired during the loose-training sessions.

Use Indiscriminable Contingencies

Two techniques fall under this general strategy for promoting generality of behavior change: intermittent schedules of reinforcement and delayed reinforcement. Behaviors developed and maintained under continuous schedules of reinforcement (CRF) are not resistant to extinction. When reinforcement is no longer available, the response rate is likely to decrease rapidly to prereinforcement levels. In other words, generality of behaviors across time is poor when the CRF schedules that maintained those behaviors are terminated. On the other hand, behaviors acquired under intermittent schedules of reinforcement often continue to be emitted for relatively long periods of time after reinforcement is no longer available.

Since a defining feature of intermittent schedules is that numerous responses go unreinforced, one possible explanation for the maintenance of responding during extinction of behaviors developed under intermittent schedules is the relative difficulty of discriminating that reinforcement is no longer available. Thus, the unpredictability of an intermittent schedule may account for the maintenance of behavior after the schedule is terminated.

Stokes and Baer (1977) suggest that an analogue to not being able to discriminate when a response will be reinforced is not being able to discriminate in what settings a behavior will be reinforced. They cite an experiment by Schwarz and Hawkins (1970) in which each day after school a sixth-grade girl was shown videotapes of her behavior in that

day's math class and was reinforced for improvements in posture, reductions in face touching, and sufficient voice loudness. Reinforcement was contingent upon behaviors emitted during math class only, but comparable improvements were noted in spelling class as well. The experimental data were taken from videotapes that were made of the girl's behavior in spelling class but were never shown to her. Stokes and Baer hypothesize that since reinforcement was delayed (the behaviors that produced reinforcement were emitted during math class but were not rewarded until after school), it may have been difficult for the student to discriminate when improved performance was required for reinforcement. They suggest that the generality across settings of the target behaviors may have been a result of the indiscriminable nature of the delayed reinforcement contingency.

Teach Self-Management Techniques

Perhaps the most potentially effective approach to producing behavior changes with generality rests with the one element that is common to every training and every nontraining environment—the learner herself. Chapter 26 described a variety of behavior change techniques known collectively as self-control or self-management procedures, which have proved to be effective in modifying behavior in some instances. The logic of self-management relative to the problem of producing generalized behavior changes goes like this: if the learner can be taught a behavior (not the original behavior change itself, but an additional response—a controlling response from a self-management perspective) that serves to prompt and reinforce the desired behavior change in all the necessary settings, at all appropriate times, and in all relevant forms, then the generality of the target behavior is ensured (e.g., Rhode, Morgan, & Young, 1983). But as Baer and Fowler (1984) warn,

Giving a student self-control responses designed to mediate the generalization of some critical behavior changes does not ensure that those mediating responses will indeed by used. They are, after all, just responses: they, too, need generalization and maintenance, just as do the behavior changes that they are meant to generalize and maintain. Setting up one behavior to mediate the generalization of another behavior may succeed—but it may also represent a problem in guaranteeing the generalization of two responses, where before we had only the problem of guaranteeing the generalization of one! (p. 149)

The development and analysis of instructional programs designed to teach individuals to manage their own behavior should continue to be one of the highest priorities for applied behavior analysis.

MODIFYING AND TERMINATING A SUCCESSFUL INTERVENTION TO FACILITATE GENERALITY

By manipulation of certain aspects of a person's environment, large changes in behavior can sometimes be produced. But in most behavior change programs, the environmental manipulations required to bring about the improvements in behavior are impossible, impractical, or undesirable to continue indefinitely. Let us consider the teacher in a special education classroom who uses a powerful token economy to increase the academic production and improve the social skills of his students. Students are placed in the special classroom with the understanding that their placement should be temporary. When they acquire the academic and/or social skills needed to perform satisfactorily in the regular classroom, they will return there on a full-time basis. If the regular classrooms for which the special educator is preparing his students for reentry do not use token reinforcement, it is incumbent upon him to devise an effective procedure for maintaining his students' high

levels of performance as he withdraws components of the token economy until the contingencies more closely resemble those of the regular classrooms.

In other behavior change programs continuation of the intervention may be possible but undesirable. For example, an overweight man joins a behavioral weight loss group and learns a fairly complex set of cueing, self-monitoring, self-charting, and self-reinforcement techniques, all of which combine to effectively reduce his eating behavior. After reaching the weight he originally set as his goal, he must maintain his new habits, but he does not want to have to place a little pocket note pad and calorie counter right next to his plate for the rest of his life.

Withdrawal of a successful intervention should be carried out in a systematic fashion, guided by the client's performance of the target behavior in the most important natural environment(s).

Gradual, systematic movement from the prosthetically assisted training conditions to the typical, everyday environment will increase the likelihood of the child maintaining her new behavior patterns over time and space. This shift from formal intervention procedures to the everyday environment can be made by modifying three components of the training program—antecedent or cue-related stimuli, target behavior or task-related elements, and consequence or reinforcement variables. (Heward, Dardig, & Rossett, 1979, p. 122)

Regardless of the purpose or nature of the intervention, any behaviorally based treatment program can be broken down into one or more of these components, each representing one part of the three-term contingency.

1 Antecedents, prompts, or cue-related stimuli
2 Task requirements and criteria
3 Consequence or reinforcement variables

Variables such as the complexity of the intervention, the amount of behavior change required, the ease or speed of that change, and the availability of existing contingencies of reinforcement for the new behavior, all play a role in how readily program components can be withdrawn. Although the order in which intervention components are withdrawn may make little difference in some programs, certain recommendations can be made. With most programs it is probably best to make all task-related requirements as similar as possible to those of the natural environment before withdrawing significant antecedent or consequence components of the intervention. In this way the learner is emitting the target behavior with the same topography and rate that will be required after the complete intervention is withdrawn. All of the desired changes in behavior should be accomplished before shifting attention to natural cueing and reinforcement conditions.

A program that was carried out by a graduate student in one of the author's classes illustrates how the three components of a behavior change program can be gradually and systematically withdrawn. An institutionalized mentally retarded adult male took an inordinate amount of time to get dressed each morning (40 to 70 minutes during baseline), even though he possessed the skills needed to dress himself. Intervention began with a construction paper clock hung by his bed with the hands set to indicate the time by which he had to be fully dressed in order to receive reinforcement. The subject could not tell time, but he could discriminate whether the position of the hands on the real clock nearby matched those on his clock. To increase the probability of initial success, two task-related variables were introduced. First, he was given fewer and easier clothes to put on each morning (e.g., no belt, slip-ons instead of shoes with laces). Second, based on his baseline performance, he was initially given 30 minutes to dress himself, even though the objective of the program was for him to be completely dressed within 10 minutes. An edible reinforcer paired with verbal praise was used first on a continuous schedule of reinforcement. Figure 27.9 shows

how each of the three aspects of the program was modified and eventually withdrawn completely, so that by the program's end the man was dressing himself completely within 10 minutes without being helped by extra clocks or charts or by additional reinforcement other than a natural schedule of intermittent praise from staff members.

The recommendation to bring the target behavior to criterion or close-to-criterion performance before removing any significant portion of the antecedent or consequent components of an intervention is made primarily on the basis of its logical appeal. Unfortunately, there is little empirical evidence in the behavioral literature to guide the practitioner in this important area. Rusch and Kazdin (1981) have provided a description of how the systematic withdrawal of intervention components might be assessed in terms of its effects on response maintenance. Experimental analyses are needed of the differential effects of withdrawing and terminating interventions in different ways.

A word of caution is in order regarding the termination of successful behavior change programs. A fundamental goal of applied behavior analysis is to make socially significant improvements in behavior. Additionally, those improved behaviors should be maintained and should show generality to other relevant settings and behaviors. If optimal generality of the behavior change is to be approached, most, if not all, of the original intervention must normally be withdrawn. However, at times it seems as if teachers, parents, and others responsible for helping children learn important behaviors are more concerned with how a potentially effective intervention will eventually be withdrawn than they are with whether it will produce the needed behavior change. Consideration of how a proposed intervention will lend itself to eventual withdrawal or blending with the natural environment is certainly important and is consistent with everything recommended here. And clearly, when the choice is between two or more interventions of potentially equal effectiveness, first

FIGURE 27.9 An example of modifying and terminating a program to facilitate maintenance and generality: an independent morning dressing program for an adult with severe handicaps.

Antecedents (Cues, prompts)	Behavior (Task criteria/ modifications)	Consequences (Reinforcers, punishers)
A: Mock clock showing when must be dressed B: No clock	A: Fewer clothes B: Full set of clothes C: Time gradually reduced D: Criterion time limit E: Variety of clothes	A: Edible reinforcer B: Token reinforcer C: Chart (self-record) D: Praise on intermittent schedule

Phase			
1	A	A	A
2	A	A	B
3	A	B	B
4	A	B/C	C
5	A	B/D	C
6	B	B/D	C
7	B	D/E	C
8	B	D/E	D

priority should go to the intervention most like the natural environment and most easy to terminate. But important behavior changes should not go unmade because the intervention required may never be able to be withdrawn completely. Some degree of intervention may always be required to maintain certain behaviors, in which case attempts must be made to continue the necessary programming.

A study by O'Brien and Azrin (1972) provides an illustration. They developed an intensive training program for proper mealtime behaviors; their one-to-one teaching sessions included verbal instructions, reprimands, praise, manual guidance, extinction and time out procedures. The goal of the program was to have institutionalized mentally retarded adults maintain their newly learned eating skills during group meals in the facility's cafeteria. Realizing that the naturally existing contingencies of reinforcement for proper eating in the institution were weak, O'Brien and Azrin designed a maintenance procedure intended to be carried out indefinitely as a regular part of the daily meals. The maintenance procedure required that one staff member systematically monitor each meal, moving among the diners and providing verbal praise for proper mealtime behaviors, saying "No!" when errors occurred, and reminding the resident in error of how to perform the correct behavior. A 3-month followup showed that high levels of proper mealtime behaviors were maintained. Considerable generality was produced in the study, across settings (from one-to-one training sessions to the group meals) and across time. Although some degree of systematic intervention was continued during the maintenance program, it required much less effort and fewer resources than initially teaching each resident the proper mealtime behaviors.

The Sprague and Horner (1984) study on the generality of vending machine use provides another example of this point. The six moderately to severely mentally retarded students who participated in the program were given cue cards to aid them in operating a vending machine without another person's assistance. The cue cards, which had food and drink logos on one side and pictures of quarters paired with prices on the other, were not only used during instruction and generality probes, but were kept by the students at the end of the program. A follow-up 18 months after the study was completed found that five of the six students still carried a cue card and were using vending machines independently. Rather than lament the lack of generality or blame the learner for her inability to show generalizable behavior changes, the behavior analyst should work to arrange whatever socially valid contingencies may be needed to extend and maintain the target behavior.

SUMMARY

Generality and the Development of Behavior Change Technology

1 From 1949 to 1967 researchers and practitioners experimented with applications of the principles of behavior to socially important behaviors. One of the criticisms aimed at behavior modification during this period was that changes in behavior did not always endure after the intervention contingencies were withdrawn.

2 The period from 1968 to 1976 witnessed an increased awareness in applied behavior analysis of the importance of the generality of behavior change.

3 Since 1977 production and analysis of the generality of behavior change have been a critical issue for the continued development of applied behavior analysis.

Terminology

4 Stimulus generalization and response generalization are commonly used to refer to all of the phenomena subsumed under the concept of generality of behavior change. This poses a difficulty because the two terms refer to specific behavioral processes, and quite often multiple behavioral principles and processes are involved in the generality of an applied behavior change.

5 Stimulus generality is defined as the extent to which the learner improves his performance of the target behavior in environments different from the original training environment.

6 Maintenance is defined as the extent to which the learner continues to perform the target behavior after a portion or all of the intervention has been terminated.

7 Response generality is defined as the extent to which the learner performs a variety of functional responses in addition to the trained response(s).

8 Generalization across subjects refers to changes in the behavior of untreated subjects as a function of treatment contingencies that are applied to other subjects.

9 A percentange of generalization is computed by dividing the amount of change in the generalization setting, response, or subject by the amount of change in the target setting, response, or subject.

10 The generalization map is a conceptual framework for combining and categorizing the various types of generality of behavior change (Drabman, Hammer, & Rosenbaum, 1979). According to the generalization map there are 16 different classes of generalization.

Planning for the Generality of Behavior Change

11 Before an applied behavior analysis program is begun, careful attention should be devoted to an examination of several variables relevant to generality. This preplanning should involve a three-step process of identifying (a) all of the desired behavior changes to be acquired by the subject, (b) all of the environments where the behavior changes should be emitted, and (c) the behaviors required by other persons so that the newly acquired behaviors will be maintained by the subject.

12 The benefits of identifying these variables include a better understanding of the scope of the teaching task and an opportunity to prioritize the most important behavior changes and settings for direct instruction.

Strategies for Promoting the Generality of Behavior Change

13 One of the best strategies for promoting generality is to teach behaviors that will make contact with naturally existing communities of reinforcement. Natural communities of reinforcement act like a behavioral trap and help ensure the maintenance and generality of the target behavior.

14 Sometimes existing natural communities of reinforcement are not contacted because the target behavior has not been taught well enough. The subject may need to learn to emit the target behavior at a higher rate, more accurately, within a shorter latency, and/or at a greater magnitude.

15 Sometimes the subject can be taught a separate response for recruiting reinforcement from the natural community for performance of the target behavior.

16 A behavior that must be emitted in the presence of a wide variety of stimuli should be taught with a number of different stimulus examples. Similarly, when many forms of a new behavior are desired, the subject should receive direct instruction on a number of different responses.

17 The general case strategy involves the selection of teaching examples that sample the range of stimulus and response variations in the natural environment(s) where the target behavior is to be used.

18 Stimulus generality from the instructional setting to another environment can be enhanced by programming common stimuli from the generality setting in the teaching setting.

19 Loose training is a strategy for facilitating generality that involves systematically varying as many noncritical stimuli as possible during instruction in order to reduce the likelihood that a single or small group of stimuli will gain exclusive control over the behavior and to make it more likely that other settings where generality is desired will contain at least some of the stimuli present during training.

20 Generality of behavior change can be enhanced by the use of contingencies that make it difficult for the subject to discriminate whether the training contingencies are in effect. Use of intermittent schedules of reinforcement and delayed reinforcement techniques are two tactics for programming indiscriminable contingencies.

21 Teaching subjects self-management techniques is a method for promoting generality; the subject learns to make certain controlling responses that in turn prompt and maintain the target behavior in various settings.

Modifying and Terminating a Successful Intervention to Facilitate Generalization

22 Because it is impossible, impractical, or undesirable in most behavior change programs to continue all of the environmental manipulations that were implemented to bring about initial improvements in behavior, the behavior changes must continue with few or none of the program contingencies in operation.

23 The withdrawal of a successful intervention should be conducted in a systematic fashion to facilitate the maintenance and generality of the behavior changes obtained. The change from formal intervention procedures to a normal everyday environment can be accomplished by gradually modifying the three components of the training program: (a) antecedents, prompts, or cue-related stimuli, (b) task modifications and criteria, and (c) reinforcement variables.

PART
ELEVEN

Communication

Data generated during behavior change programs serve at least three purposes: (1) they help the behavior analyst make decisions during the program; (2) they provide the basis for analysis of treatment effects; and (3) they serve as a source of information for others. Two different sets of individuals have interest in data generated from behavior change efforts. The first includes those with a direct interest in the learners' development (e.g., the learners, their parents, other practitioners). The second includes those individuals who are not directly connected with the intervention but who may be interested in learning about its procedures, results, and implications for similar problems they are trying to solve (e.g., the behavior analysis community).

The purpose of chapter 28 is to describe methods for reporting data to clients, parents, practitioners, administrators, and the behavior analysis community. An emphasis is placed on variables the analyst should consider before sharing data. Additionally, the chapter discusses who should have access to learner data, why data should be shared, and what procedural safeguards need to be followed.

28

Communicating the Results of Behavior Change Efforts

SHARING DATA WITH LEARNERS

Sharing data with learners serves three important functions: it informs learners of their legal right to treatment; it serves as a quality control measure; and it sets the occasion for self-recording.

Information

All learners now have the legal right to access all personal data and records collected during their education or treatment. Beyond legalities, however, professional ethics demand that learners receive full disclosure of practitioners' activities. Practitioners should inform learners to the fullest extent possible, regardless of their level of functioning. When sharing data with learners, practitioners should also be sensitive to the communication skills of their learners.

Bloom and Fischer (1982) developed "A Client's Bill of Rights," which specifies 10 rights that learners have in treatment conditions or educational settings. These rights are summarized in Table 28.1. At a minimum learners have the right to be informed of all target behaviors selected for intervention, all techniques and procedures used in the intervention, frequent performance data, and the probable temporal, physical, and monetary cost of the program. Clearly, the intent of full disclosure of information to learners is to have them know, to the maximum extent possible, all of the implications of a given educational or treatment procedure. To facilitate this understanding, the practitioner must be mindful of the learner's verbal functioning, susceptibility to distraction or disorientation, and physical or sensorimotor problems.

This chapter was written by John O. Cooper.

TABLE 28.1. A learner's Bill of Rights.

Components	Conditions
Behaviors selected for education or treatment	All selected behavior should be described in language that the learner can understand.
Goals and objectives	Whenever possible, the learner should help establish the goals and objectives for education or treatment.
Intervention process	The learner should know what intervention will be applied, who will provide the treatment, and what conditions will prevail.
Amount of time for education or treatment	The learner should know, prior to intervention, the amount of time that may be required to meet the goals and objectives.
Alternative methods of education or treatment	Prior to intervention, the learner should be informed of alternative methods and the likelihood of success of each method.
Cost of education or treatment	Even if the learner does not pay directly for the service, he or she still has a right to know the value of the service being received.
Data collection and records	The learner should know what data will be collected, what records will be kept, and who will have access to these data and records.
Terminal criteria	Before the program begins, the learner should be informed of the criteria for termination of treatment.
Self-management	The learner has the right to assume as much management of the intervention as is possible.
Access to data and records	The learner should have access to performance data and should provide input into data-based program decisions.

Quality Control

Providing learners with performance data can serve as a quality control check for practitioners. Commonly, ineffective treatment procedures are used for too long in applied settings; it is often rationalized that a procedure just has not had enough time to take effect. Yet, research data show that most treatments, if they are effective, will generate a behavior change in a few sessions—perhaps not to criterion, but in the desired direction. When the practitioner gives frequent data reports to the learner, the practitioner may be more likely to try another procedure if the current treatment is not producing a behavior change in a reasonable period of time.

Sharing data with learners also serves to encourage objectivity in evaluating the effects of treatment. At times practitioners may exaggerate or minimize the effects of treatment. This tendency is reduced when learners have access to direct and frequent measurement of target behaviors. On the other hand, learners can become frustrated by what appears to be little progress and may terminate treatment before goals and objectives have been met. Access to direct and frequent measures can help decrease premature termination of treatment.

Occasion for Self-Recording

Self-recording is a skill that many learners can develop. There are a number of important reasons that practitioners should encourage learners to self-record. First, it sets the occasion for a practitioner and a learner to evaluate progress jointly and work together in decision making. Further, with self-recording there is an increased likelihood that the learner will be completely informed of, and aware of, the treatment outcomes. Finally, and perhaps most importantly, self-recording provides a clear demonstration that the practitioner is concerned with the learner's ethical and legal right to full disclosure. The learner's knowledge of results is assured when treatment effects are self-recorded.

SHARING DATA WITH PARENTS AND GUARDIANS

Practitioners have legal and ethical responsibilities to share data with learners, and these responsibilities extend to parents and guardians when the learners are minors and/or dependents. There should be frequent communication between the treatment setting and the learner's home or living unit. An acceptable report to parents or guardians includes not only learner progress and the procedures used, but also an indication of how the learner is being evaluated. Sharing data frequently provides a foundation of common information upon which meetings such as parent-teacher conferences can be based. In some situations performance data can facilitate joint interventions of the treatment setting and the home or living unit.

When sharing information with parents, the behavior analyst should be mindful of a parent's role in the education or treatment process. The analyst should provide information on how the learner performs during the instructional process but should also try to obtain information on how the learner performs at home. Such ecological information (cf. Heron & Heward, 1982) can give both parties a fuller understanding of how the learner's behavior is generalizing to other settings or behaviors.

SHARING DATA WITH PRACTITIONERS

Usually several professionals are involved and concerned with a learner's development. For example, teachers frequently work with an interdisciplinary team (e.g., school psychologists, counselors) in instructional planning conferences. Practitioners working in a residential setting have staff meetings to review learner progress and plan for future treatment. Special educators confer with regular teachers when a student is mainstreamed. In all such situations it is important for behavior analysts to share information with their colleagues directly and frequently. A learner's performance data can facilitate the coordination of goals and objectives, selection of specific target behaviors, and a systematic application of treatment and instruction.

SHARING DATA WITH ADMINISTRATORS

It is common for practitioners to share information with their administrators. Usually practitioners are expected to provide their administrators with program goals and objectives, progress of learners, and information about procedures, such as taking learners on field trips, initiating a punishment contingency, and so on. Practitioners can share information with administrators in a formal written progress report or in an informal conference.

There are several advantages for both practitioners and administrators if frequent direct measures of learner data are shared. First, a well-informed administrator increases the likelihood of support for the practitioner's efforts. Support can take many forms—praise, financial backing, or the provision of additional resources. Second, an administrator informed about the progress of a learner can be in a better position to lend technical assistance, from which both the practitioner and the learner will benefit. Third, frequent and direct measures of learner performance can help the administrator in ways not directly related to treatment. For instance, having access to learner data can help the administrator evaluate the performance of the practitioner objectively and can provide the administrator with substantive information to share with the public.

SHARING RESULTS WITH THE BEHAVIOR ANALYSIS COMMUNITY

Sharing Results at a Professional Conference

Numerous opportunities exist for behavior analysts to give presentations at state, regional, national, and international conferences. Organizations such as the Association for Behavior Analysis, the Association for Advancement of Behavior Therapy, the American Psychological Association, and the Council for Exceptional Children sponsor at least one national or international conference each year, as well as several regional or state meetings. The formats used for presentations at these meetings include reading an original paper, reporting on a research project, presenting a workshop, conducting a poster session, and participating in formal group discussions.

Presentation Opportunities A frequent question asked by beginning behavior analysts is, "How do I hear about conference opportunities?" Usually, there is only one official source of information, and that is an announcement from the professional organization titled a "call for papers." There are a number of important reasons for individuals to join the professional organizations of their discipline (e.g., journals, professional standards), but clearly one important reason is to receive the call for papers.

Without membership in an organization, there are still methods of finding out about presentation opportunities. First, friends and colleagues may belong to organizations and may agree to share their call for papers. Second, the faculty at a local college can be contacted and asked to pass along any call for papers in a particular field. Third, professional organizations can be written and asked directly for information on their conferences.

After receipt of the call for papers, it is necessary to prepare a submission package.

The call for papers specifically states what should be included in that package; there are minor variations from one organization to another. Most require a submission form, which is often included with the call for papers. The submission form usually requests the individual's name, affiliation, address, type of presentation, audiovisual equipment requirements (e.g., 35mm slide projector, overhead transparency projector, chalkboard), and two or three copies of the proposal for presentation. The proposal contains a title, brief abstract, and summary of the presentation. If the submission package is for a workshop, the goals, objectives, instructional methods, and materials for the workshop may also be required. Normally, the sponsoring organization requires all submission packages several months before the actual presentation date. The call for papers includes the dates for submission and may also indicate whether late submissions will be accepted.

A submission package selected for presentation requires final preparations before professional presentation. The best advice is to be thoroughly prepared in advance. Often, late preparation produces a presentation that is disorganized and fails to communicate with the audience. The presentation should be carefully practiced before the convention. If the presentation is scheduled for a national or international conference, perhaps arrangements can be made to give the presentation at the local, state, or regional level, possibly as an inservice activity. At the very least the presentation should be given to colleagues, family, or friends who will provide feedback. Any revisions should be incorporated into the final presentation.

Presentation Formats Several different formats can be used for conference presentations. This section discusses the most common presentation formats.

Two styles can be used for presenting a *research project report*. Some presenters read a manuscript aloud, as if they were reading an article published in a professional journal. Often when the presenter chooses this approach, the only stimuli used in the presentation are occasional transparencies of tables or figures to illustrate the data collected. Other presenters give their research project report in the form of a talk, using a more informal lecture style, which may produce a more attentive audience.

At a *poster session* a short, written, graphic description of the research is attached to poster board. Normally, a poster session is held in a large room where several research reports are simultaneously available for review. Each person in the audience can then move from display to display at his own pace. Typically, the presenter serves as the host and answers questions or elaborates on the research. Often, the host provides the audience with a written summary of the research. Figure 28.1 provides an illustration of a poster display.

There are several advantages of poster sessions. First, they are economical. They permit an audience to receive a large amount of information in a short period of time. Whereas an oral presentation can take anywhere from 15 to 60 minutes to deliver, during a poster session an audience can view as many as 10 to 15 research reports in that same amount of time. Second, poster sessions maximize audience participation. The audience must attend to and read the textual portions on the posters if they are to receive information; they cannot be passive listeners. Third, poster sessions can be the most personal format for formal presentation of research resports. The audience can interact with the host on a one-to-one basis.

Several points should be considered in hosting a poster session. First, the lettering of the narrative should be large enough to be read from about 5 feet away. Hand lettering is more work than a typewritten narrative, but handwritten letters can be made large enough to meet this requirement. Second, the narrative should be kept to a minimum. As much as

FIGURE 28.1 Poster display.

possible, results should be communicated to the audience with visuals, such as pictures, illustrations, and graphs. Third, the poster display should be as portable as possible. Often, there is little time available to set up the display before the presentation.

A *workshop* is an intensive training activity designed to provide the audience with specific skills or knowledge. For example, in recent years the directors of the Association for Behavior Analysis (ABA) have offered workshops in such areas as peer tutoring, verbal behavior, parent training, rule-governed behavior, and personalized systems of instruction. Most major conferences sponsor workshops, which are usually held from 1 to 3 days prior to the start of the actual conference and normally require an additional fee. A workshop must stress active participation. The audience practices skills through role-playing, simulations, and interaction with actual clients in some situations. Some conferences sponsor short workshops (e.g., 1 to 3 hours), but the intent is still to provide skill training in a given area.

A *group discussion* consists of a small number of conference attendees seated around a conference table to engage in informal discussion of a designated topic. Group discussions are given a variety of titles: for example, "a conversational hour" or a "crackerbarrel session." Regardless of the conference title, the sessions are informal discussions.

Two opportunities exist in group discussions for the practitioner to share results with the community. The practitioner can just attend a group discussion and share her data, comments, or experiences that relate to the designated topic. Or the practitioner can submit a request to be a discussion leader.

Selection of topics is critical for good group discussions. Topics can be restricted to new areas of research or application or current issues. They can also be designed to reexamine former issues when new litigation, funding patterns, or social values have the potential to change existing programs. In a good group discussion the leader keeps the conversation active, has a number of prepared questions available if the audience is not responding, and does not let any one person dominate the conversation.

Sharing Results with Journal Publications

Even though conferences do provide an outlet for the practitioner to share results with the professional community, they usually limit that sharing to a relatively small audience. In addition, a conference presentation does not usually produce a permanent record of the research unless the paper is published in the conference proceedings. And most conferences do not publish their proceedings and do not include all presentations even when they do publish.

Another way to share results with the behavior analysis community is through publication in a professional journal. In fact, many believe that a research effort is not complete until it is written in a report and submitted for publication consideration.

Selecting a Journal A number of questions can guide the selection of a journal for publication consideration. Does the journal have a history of publishing research in applied behavior analysis? A particular journal may prefer manuscripts reporting statistical treatments of group effects rather than single-subject experimental analysis. The likelihood of such a journal's accepting research in applied behavior analysis is low. However, there are a number of professional journals that publish almost nothing but research in applied behavior analysis.

Is the topic of this research compatible with that of articles currently being accepted for publication by this journal? Topics of applied behavior analysis manuscripts accepted for publication may vary from journal to journal. Some journals place an editorial priority on research with potential for new understanding or for expansion of principles of behavior or for demonstration of unique applications of those principles. Other journals may be more concerned with publishing research that has direct value to practitioners.

Is the methodology of this research and the effect produced compatible with that of articles currently being published by the journal? Some areas to consider in answering this question include the stability of the data, the number of data points in each condition, the magnitude of effect, the overlap of data points among conditions, and so on.

Submitting the Manuscript Prior to submission of the manuscript, knowledgeable colleagues should have an opportunity to review the research report and to provide feedback on style, completeness, and articulation of the effects of the research. A final revision of the manuscript should be prepared after that input is received. It is important for the manuscript to be typewritten in the editorial format used by the journal, and it should contain no grammatical or spelling errors. Using a word processor with an accompanying dictionary/spelling program not only increases the probability of producing an error-free manuscript, but also greatly reduces the time required for revisions.

Also prior to submission of the manuscript, a recent journal issue should be checked for the current editorial address and the journal's submission requirements. Submission requirements vary, but all editors require (1) a cover letter requesting review for publication, (2) a statement verifying that the manuscript has not yet been published, (3) a statement verifying that the manuscript is not currently under review by another journal, and (4) the author's address and telephone number. Multiple high-quality photocopies of the manuscript are also required; some journals request only two copies of the manuscript, whereas others require as many as five.

The editor usually mails a written acknowledgment of receipt of the manuscript within 2 weeks. Editorial review normally takes a minimum of 2 months. Reviewers evaluate the manuscript and submit their recommendations to the editor. The editor then makes a decision and informs the author of one of four possible outcomes. The author may be told that the manuscript has been accepted without revision; an outright acceptance is unusual. Or the author may be told that the manuscript will be accepted if it is revised according to specific suggestions. Most articles accepted for publication require some revision. A third possibility is that the article is rejected in its current form, but the editor can recommend major revisions. If these revisions are made, the manuscript can be resubmitted and will be reviewed as a new manuscript. Finally, the editor can issue a rejection without an opportunity for revision.

Steps After Acceptance When a manuscript has been accepted for publication, the author still has some tasks to perform. Chances are good that changes in the manuscript will be required by the editor. In that case the author is responsible for making those changes to the editor's specifications and preparing a new typewritten manuscript. When final acceptance is given, the author must sign a copyright waiver to the journal. Finally, the author will receive typeset galley proofs for review. The proofs will need careful inspection, and must usually be returned to the editor within 48 hours. It is a good idea to have colleagues also proofread the journal galleys. After the proofs are returned to the editor, the article is scheduled for publication in an upcoming issue of the journal, and the proofs are sent to the printer.

Steps After Rejection When a manuscript is rejected, it is important not to take the rejection personally, blame the editor and reviewers, and decide not to make other research efforts. Manuscripts are often rejected even when they are written by established researchers. And even the editor and reviewers have had work rejected. The rejection should be viewed as a learning opportunity. The first step in that learning is to study the reviewer's comments and reasons for rejecting the paper. Most editors include the reviewers' comments, and some are very instructive. The reviews may help the author become a better practitioner, as well as a better researcher.

On occasion, the author may feel that the reviewers and the editor were not correct in their evaluation. In that situation the manuscript can be submitted to another journal for review. The author may decide that the manuscript can be improved by addressing the concerns of the first editor and reviewers. If so, the manuscript should be revised prior to submission to the second journal. Since most journals can accept only a small percentage of the manuscripts received, the manuscript may need to be reviewed by several journals before it is accepted for publication.

Regardless of the author's confidence in his work, the time may come to accept a rejection and give up on having the manuscript published. If the manuscript has been revised, has been submitted to appropriate outlets, and yet has received four or five rejections, it is probably time to stop. If any of those aspects (i.e., revision, submission to appropriate outlets, and multiple rejections) have not been accomplished, the author should keep working toward publication.

CRITERIA FOR SHARING DATA WITH OTHERS

Practitioners should always remember that data collected during educational or treatment sessions do not belong exclusively to them. The data also belong to the learner, and in the case of children, to parents/guardians. Consequently, learners must be informed as to who will have access to the performance data and how it will be presented; and the data should be shared only with their consent. Learner rights to privacy and confidentiality are protected by the practice of informed consent. An exception to the requirement of informed consent exists with data presentations at professional conferences or in professional journals. In these presentations the practitioner assures confidentiality by omitting information that could identify the individual by name or even by location. Most often the learner is referred to simply as the subject or a student. The practitioner should also be sure that the data clearly represent learner performance.

SUMMARY

Sharing Data with Learners

1   Sharing data with learners can serve three important functions: it informs learners of their legal rights to treatment; it serves as a quality control measure; and it sets the occasion for self-recording.

2   To fulfill the intent of full disclosure of information, the practitioner must be mindful of the learner's verbal functioning, susceptibility to distraction or disorientation, and physical or sensorimotor problems.

Sharing Data with Parents and Guardians

3   Practitioners' legal and ethical responsibilities to share data extend to parents and guardians, especially when learners are minors and/or dependents.

Sharing Data with Practitioners

4   Data sharing with practitioners facilitates the coordination of goals and objectives, selection of the target behaviors, and systematic application of education and treatment.

Sharing Data with Administrators

5   Sharing data with administrators increases the likelihood of (a) enhanced support for the practitioner's efforts, (b) specific program guidance and help from the administrator, and

(c) objective evaluation of the practitioner's performance.

Sharing Results with the Behavior Analysis Community

6   Opportunities for conference presentations include reporting orally on research projects, developing poster sessions, presenting workshops, and participating in group discussions.

7   At a poster session the research report is displayed as a short, written, graphic description attached to poster board.

8   Poster sessions are economical in terms of time and the amount of coverage; they maximize audience participation; and they permit a personalized format.

9   A workshop is an intensive training activity designed to provide the audience with specific skill(s) or knowledge; it stresses active participation by the audience.

10   A conference group discussion is a small group of individuals engaged in informal discussion on a designated topic.

11   A research effort is not complete until it is written and submitted for publication consideration.

Criteria for Sharing Data with Others

12   Data should be shared with others only after the informed consent of the learner has been obtained and her rights to privacy and confidentiality have been protected.

REFERENCES

ACKERMAN, A. M., & SHAPIRO, E. S. (1984). Self-monitoring and work productivity with mentally retarded adults. *Journal of Applied Behavior Analysis, 17,* 403–407.

AGOSTA, J. N., CLOSE, D. W., HOPS, H., & RUSCH, F. R. (1980). Treatment of self-injurious behavior through overcorrection procedures. *Journal of the Association for the Severely Handicapped, 5,* 5–12.

ALBIN, J. B. (1977). Some variables influencing the maintenance of acquired self-feeding behavior in profoundly retarded children. *Mental Retardation, 15*(5), 49–52.

ALEVIZOS, P., DEPISE, W., LIBERMAN, R., ECKMAN, T., & CALLAHAN, E. (1978). The behavior observation instrument: A method of direct observation for program evaluation. *Journal of Applied Behavior Analysis, 11,* 243–257.

ALEXANDER, D. F. (1985). The effect of study skill training on learning disabled students' retelling of expository material. *Journal of Applied Behavior Analysis, 18,* 263–267.

ALLEN, L. D., GOTTSELIG, M., & BOYLAN, S. (1982). A practical mechanism for using free time as a reinforcer in the classroom. *Education and Treatment of Children, 5*(4), 347–353.

ALLEN, L. D., & IWATA, B. A. (1980). Reinforcing exercise maintenance: Using existing high-rate activities. *Behavior Modification, 4*(3), 337–354.

AMERICAN ASSOCIATION ON MENTAL DEFICIENCY. (1977). *Consent handbook.* Washington, DC: Author.

AMERICAN PSYCHOLOGICAL ASSOCIATION. (1983). *Publication manual of the American Psychological Association* (3rd ed.). Washington, DC: Author.

ANAGONA, J., CASSADY, J., & DRABMAN, R. S. (1975). Treating overweight children through parental training and contingency contracting. *Journal of Applied Behavior Analysis, 8,* 269–278.

ANDERSON-INMAN, L. (1981). Transenvironmental programming: Promoting success in the regular class by maximizing the effect of resource room assistance. *Journal of Special Education Technology, 4,* 3–12.

ARCHER, L. A. (1977). Blissymbolics—a non-verbal communication system. *Journal of Speech and Hearing Disorders, 42,* 568–579.

AXELROD, S. (1971). Token reinforcement programs in special classes. *Exceptional Children, 37,* 371–379.

AXELROD, S. (1973). Comparison of individual and group contingencies in two special classes. *Behavior Therapy, 4,* 83–98.

AXELROD, S. (1976). *Behavior modification for secondary school teachers.* Unpublished manuscript, Temple University, Philadelphia.

AXELROD, S. (1977). *Behavior modification for the classroom teacher.* New York: McGraw-Hill.

AXELROD, S. (1983). *Behavior modification for the classroom teacher.* (2nd ed.). New York: Academic Press.

AXELROD, S., & APSCHE, J. (Eds.). (1983). *The effects of punishment on human behavior.* New York: Academic Press.

AXELROD, S., BRANTNER, J. P., & MEDDOCK, T. D. (1978). Overcorrection: A review and critical analysis. *Journal of Special Education, 12,* 367–391.

AXELROD, S., HALL, R. V., WEIS, L., & ROHRER, S. (1971). *Use of self-imposed contingencies to reduce the frequency of smoking behavior.* Paper presented at the Fifth Annual Meeting of the Association for the Advancement of Behavior Therapy, Washington, DC.

AYLLON, T., & AZRIN, N. H. (1968). *The token economy: A motivational system for therapy and rehabilitation.* New York: Appleton-Century-Crofts.

AYLLON, T., & MICHAEL, J. (1959). The psychiatric nurse as a behavioral engineer. *Journal of the Experimental Analysis of Behavior, 2,* 323–334.

AZRIN, N. H. (1956). Some effects of two intermittent schedules of immediate and nonimmediate punishment. *Journal of Psychology, 42,* 3–21.

AZRIN, N. H., & BESALEL, V. A. (1980). *How to use overcorrection.* Austin, TX: Pro-Ed.

AZRIN, N. H., & FOXX, R. M. (1971). A rapid method of toilet training the institutionalized retarded. *Journal of Applied Behavior Analysis, 4,* 89–99.

AZRIN, N. H., & HOLZ, W. C. (1966). Punishment. In W. K. Honig (Ed.), *Operant behavior: Areas of research and application.* New York: Appleton-Century-Crofts.

AZRIN, N. H., & LINDSLEY, O. R. (1956). The reinforcement of cooperation between children. *Journal of Abnormal and Social Psychology, 52,* 100–102.

AZRIN, N. H., & NUNN, R. G. (1973). Habit-reversal for habits and tics. *Behavior Research and Therapy, 11,* 619–628.

AZRIN, N. H., NUNN, R. G., & FRANTZ, S. E. (1980a). Habit reversal vs. negative practice treatment of nervous tics. *Behavior Therapy, 11*(2), 169–178.

AZRIN, N. H., NUNN, R. G., & FRANTZ, S. E. (1980b). Habit reversal vs. negative practice treatment of nailbiting. *Behavior Research and Therapy, 18*(4), 281–285.

AZRIN, N. H., & WESOLOWSKI, M. D. (1974). Theft reversal: An overcorrection procedure for eliminating stealing by retarded persons. *Journal of Applied Behavior Analysis, 7,* 577–581.

AZRIN, N. H., & WESOLOWSKI, M. D. (1975). Eliminating habitual vomiting in a retarded adult by positive practice and self correction. *Journal of Behavior Therapy and Experimental Psychiatry, 6,* 145–148.

BACHMAN, J. E., & FUQUA, R. W. (1983). Management of inappropriate behaviors of trainable mentally impaired students using antecedent exercise. *Journal of Applied Behavior Analysis, 16,* 477–484.

BACON-PRUE, A., BLOUNT, R., PICKERING, D., & DRABMAN, R. (1980). An evaluation of three litter control procedures—trash receptacles, paid workers, and the marked-item technique. *Journal of Applied Behavior Analysis, 13,* 165–170.

BAER, A. M., ROWBURY, T., & BAER, D. M. (1973). The development of instructional control over classroom activities of deviant preschool children. *Journal of Applied Behavior Analysis, 6,* 289–298.

BAER, D. M. (1960). Escape and avoidance response of preschool children to two schedules of reinforcement withdrawal. *Journal of the Experimental Analysis of Behavior, 3,* 155–159.

BAER, D. M. (1961). Effect of withdrawal of positive reinforcement on an extinguishing response in young children. *Child Development, 32,* 67–74.

BAER, D. M. (1962). Laboratory control of thumbsucking by withdrawal and representation of reinforcement. *Journal of the Experimental Analysis of Behavior, 5,* 525–528.

BAER, D. M. (1971). Let's take another look at punishment. *Psychology Today, 5,* 5–32.

BAER, D. M. (1975). In the beginning, there was the response. In E. Ramp & G. Semb (Eds.), *Behavior analysis: Areas of research and application* (pp. 16–30). Englewood Cliffs, NJ: Prentice-Hall.

BAER, D. M. (1977a). "Perhaps it would be better not to know everything." *Journal of Applied Behavior Analysis, 10,* 167–172.

BAER, D. M. (1977b). Reviewer's comment: Just because it's reliable doesn't mean that you can use it. *Journal of Applied Behavior Analysis, 10,* 117–119.

BAER, D. M. (1981a). *How to plan for generalization.* Austin, TX: Pro-Ed.

BAER, D. M. (1981b). A hung jury and a Scottish verdict: "Not proven." *Analysis and Intervention in Developmental Disabilities, 1,* 91–97.

BAER, D. M. (1982). Applied behavior analysis. In G. T. Wilson & C. M. Franks (Eds.), *Contemporary behavior therapy: Conceptual and empirical foundations* (pp. 277–309). New York: Guilford Press.

BAER, D. M. (1985). [Symposium discussant]. In C. E. Naumann (Chair), *Developing response classes: Why re-invent the wheel?* Symposium conducted at the Annual Conference of the Association for Behavior Analysis, Columbus, OH.

BAER, D. M., & FOWLER, S. A. (1984). How should we measure the potential of self-control procedures for generalized educational outcomes? In W. L. Heward, T. E. Heron, D. S. Hill, & J. Trap-Porter (Eds.), *Focus on behavior analysis in education* (pp. 145–161). Columbus, OH: Charles E. Merrill.

BAER, D. M., PETERSON, R. F., & SHERMAN, J. A. (1967). The development of imitation by reinforcing behavioral similarity of a model. *Journal of the Experimental Analysis of Behavior, 10,* 405–416.

BAER, D. M., & SHERMAN, J. A. (1964). Reinforcement control of generalized imitation in young children. *Journal of Experimental Child Psychology, 1,* 37–49.

BAER, D. M., & WOLF, M. M. (1970a). Recent examples of behavior modification in preschool settings. In C. Neuringer & J. L. Michael (Eds.), *Behavior modification in clinical psychology* (pp. 10–55). Englewood Cliffs, NJ: Prentice-Hall.

BAER, D. M., & WOLF, M. M. (1970b). The entry into natural communities of reinforcement. In R. Ulrich, T. Stachnik, & J. Mabry (Eds.), *Control of human behavior* (Vol. 2, pp. 319–324). Glenview, IL: Scott, Foresman.

BAER, D. M., WOLF, M. M., & RISLEY, T. (1968). Current dimensions of applied behavior analysis. *Journal of Applied Behavior Analysis, 1,* 91–97.

BAER, G. G., & RICHARDS, H. C. (1980). An interdependent group-oriented contingency system for improving academic performance. *School Psychology Review, 9,* 190–193.

BAER, R. A., WILLIAMS, J. A., OSNES, P. G., & STOKES, T. F. (1984). Delayed reinforcement as an indiscriminable contingency in verbal/nonverbal correspondence training. *Journal of Applied Behavior Analysis, 17*(4), 429–440.

BAILEY, D. B. (1984). Effects of lines of progress and semilogarithmic charts on ratings of charted data. *Journal of Applied Behavior Analysis, 17,* 359–365.

BAILEY, D. B., JR., & WOLERY, M. (1984). *Teaching infants and preschoolers with handicaps.* Columbus, OH: Charles E. Merrill.

BAILEY, S. (1983). Extraneous aversives. In S. Axelrod & J. Apsche (Eds.), *The effects of punishment on human behavior* (pp. 247–284). New York: Academic Press.

BAILEY, S. L., & LESSEN, E. I. (1984). An analysis of target behaviors in education: Applied but how useful? In W. L. Heward, T. E. Heron, D. S. Hill, & J. Trap-Porter (Eds.), *Focus on behavior analysis in education* (pp. 162–176). Columbus, OH: Charles E. Merrill.

BALDWIN, J. D., & BALDWIN, J. I. (1981). *Behavior principles in everyday life.* Englewood Cliffs, NJ: Prentice-Hall.

BALL, T. S., MCCRADY, R. E., & TEIXEIRA, J. (1978). Automated monitoring and cuing for positive reinforcement and differential reinforcement of other behavior. *Journal of Behavior Therapy and Experimental Psychiatry, 9,* 33–37.

BALLARD, K. D., & GLYNN, T. (1975). Behavioral self-management in story writing with elementary school children. *Journal of Applied Behavior Analysis, 8,* 387–398.

BANDURA, A. (1968). Social-learning theory of identificatory processes. In D. A. Goslin & D. C. Glass (Eds.), *Handbook of socialization theory and research.* Chicago: Rand McNally.

BANDURA, A. (1969). *Principles of behavior modification.* New York: Holt, Rinehart & Winston.

BANDURA, A. (1971). Vicarious and self-reinforcement processes. In R. Glaser (Ed.), *The nature of reinforcement.* New York: Academic Press.

BANDURA, A. (1977). *Social learning theory.* Englewood Cliffs, NJ: Prentice-Hall.

BANDURA, A., & PERLOFF, B. (1967). Relative efficacy of self-monitored and externally imposed reinforcement systems. *Journal of Personality and Social Psychology, 7,* 111–116.

BANDURA, A., ROSS, D., & ROSS, S. A. (1963). A comparative test of the status envy, social power, and secondary reinforcement theories of identificatory learning. *Journal of Abnormal and Social Psychology, 67,* 527–534.

BARBE, W. B., & SWASSING, R. M. (1979). *Teaching through modality strengths: Concepts and practices.* Columbus, OH: Zaner-Bloser.

BARKLEY, R., COPELAND, A., & SIVAGE, C. (1980). A self-control classroom for hyperactive children. *Journal of Autism and Developmental Disorders, 10,* 75–89.

BARLOW, D. H. (1972). Aversive procedures. In W. S. Agras (Ed.), *Behavior modification: Principles and clinical applications* (pp. 87–125). Boston: Little, Brown.

BARLOW, D. H. (1981). [Editorial]. *Journal of Applied Behavior Analysis, 14,* 1–2.

BARLOW, D. H., & HAYES, S. C. (1979). Alternating treatments design: One strategy for comparing the effects of two treatments in a single behavior. *Journal of Applied Behavior Analysis, 12,* 199–210.

BARNARD, J. D., CHRISTOPHERSEN, E. R., & WOLF, M. M. (1977). Teaching children appropriate shopping behavior through parent training in the supermarket setting. *Journal of Applied Behavior Analysis, 10,* 49–59.

BARRISH, H. H., SAUNDERS, M., & WOLF, M. M. (1969). Good behavior game: Effects of individual contingencies for group consequences on disruptive behavior in a classroom. *Journal of Applied Behavior Analysis, 2,* 119–124.

BARTON, E. S., GUESS, D., GARCIA, E., & BAER, D. M. (1970). Improvement of retardates' mealtime behaviors by timeout procedures using multiple baseline techniques. *Journal of Applied Behavior Analysis, 3,* 77–84.

BARTON, L. E., BRULLE, A. R., & REPP, A. C. (1983). Aversive techniques and the doctrine of least restrictive alternative. *Exceptional Education Quarterly, 3,* 1–8.

BASSETT, J., & BLANCHARD, J. (1977). The effect of the absence of close supervision on the use of response cost in a prison token economy. *Journal of Applied Behavior Analysis, 10,* 375–379.

BAUMAN, K. E., REISS, M. L., ROGERS, R. W., & BAILEY, J. S. (1983). Dining out with children: Effectiveness of a parent advice package on pre-meal inappropriate behavior. *Journal of Applied Behavior Analysis, 16,* 55–68.

BECKER, W. C., ENGELMANN, S., & THOMAS, D. R. (1971). *Teaching: A course in applied psychology.* Chicago: Science Research Associates.

BECKER, W. C., ENGELMANN, S., & THOMAS, D. R. (1975). *Teaching 2: Cognitive learning and instruction.* Chicago: Science Research Associates.

BELLACK, A. S., & HERSEN, M. (1977). *Behavior modification: An introductory textbook.* New York: Oxford University Press.

BELLACK, A. S., & SCHWARTZ, J. S. (1976). Assessment for self-control programs. In M. Hersen & A. S. Bellack (Eds.), *Behavioral assessment: A practical handbook* (pp. 111–142). New York: Pergamon Press.

BELLAMY, G. T., HORNER, R. H., & INMAN, D. P. (1979). *Vocational habilitation of severely retarded adults.* Austin, TX: Pro-Ed.

BIJOU, S. W. (1955). A systematic approach to an experimental analysis of young children. *Child Development, 26,* 161–168.

BIJOU, S. W. (1957). Patterns of reinforcement and resistance to extinction in young children. *Child Development, 28,* 47–54.

BIJOU, S. W. (1958). Operant extinction after fixed-interval schedules with young children. *Journal of the Experimental Analysis of Behavior, 1,* 25–29.

BIJOU, S. W. (1968). Studies in the experimental development of left-right concepts in retarded children using fading techniques. In N. R. Ellis (Ed.), *International review of research in mental retardation.* New York: Academic Press.

BIJOU, S. W., & BAER, D. M. (1961). *Child development: Vol. 1. A systematic and empirical theory.* New York: Appleton-Century-Crofts.

BIJOU, S. W., & BAER, D. M. (1965). *Child development: Vol. 2. Universal stage of infancy.* New York: Appleton-Century-Crofts.

BIJOU, S. W., PETERSON, R. F., & AULT, M. H. (1968). A method to integrate descriptive and experimental field studies at the level of data and empirical concepts. *Journal of Applied Behavior Analysis, 1,* 175–191.

BIJOU, S. W., PETERSON, R. F., HARRIS, F. R., ALLEN, K. E., & JOHNSON, M. S. (1969). Methodology for experimental studies of young children in natural settings. *Psychological Record, 19,* 177–210.

BILLINGS, D. C., & WASIK, B. H. (1985). Self-instructional training with preschoolers: An attempt to replicate. *Journal of Applied Behavior Analysis, 18,* 61–67.

BILLINGSLEY, F. F., & ROMER, L. T. (1983). Response prompting and the transfer of stimulus control: Methods, research and a conceptual framework. *Journal of the Association for the Severely Handicapped, 8,* 3–12.

BILLINGSLEY, F., WHITE, D. R., & MUNSON, R. (1980). Procedural reliability: A rationale and an example. *Behavioral Assessment, 2,* 247–256.

BIRKIMER, J. C., & BROWN, J. H. (1979a). A graphical judgmental aid which summarizes obtained and chance reliability data and helps assess the believability of experimental effects. *Journal of Applied Behavior Analysis, 12,* 523–533.

BIRKIMER, J. C., & BROWN, J. H. (1979b). Back to basics: Percentage agreement measures are adequate, but there are easier ways. *Journal of Applied Behavior Analysis, 12,* 535–543.

BIRNBRAUER, J. S. (1979). Applied behavior analysis, service, and the acquisition of knowledge. *The Behavior Analyst, 2,* 15–21.

BIRNBRAUER, J. S. (1981). External validity and experimental investigation of individual behavior. *Analysis and Intervention in Developmental Disabilities, 1,* 117–132.

BIRNBRAUER, J. S., WOLF, M. M., KIDDER, J. D., & TOGUE, C. E. (1965). Classroom behavior of retarded pupils with token reinforcement. *Journal of Experimental Child Psychology, 2,* 219–235.

BISHOP, B. R., & STUMPHAUZER, J. S. (1973). Behavior therapy of thumbsucking in children: A punishment (time out) and generalization effect—what's a mother to do? *Psychological Reports, 33,* 939–944.

BITTLE, R. G. (1975). Improving parent-teacher communication through recorded telephone messages. *Journal of Educational Research, 69,* 87–95.

BLAKE, B. G. (1965). The application of behavior therapy to the treatment of alcoholism. *Behavior Research and Therapy, 3,* 75.

BLEW, P. A., SCHWARTZ, I. S., & LUCE, S. C. (1985). Teaching functional community skills to autistic children using nonhandicapped peer tutors. *Journal of Applied Behavior Analysis, 18,* 337–342.

BLISS, C. K. (1965). *Semantography.* Sydney, Australia: Semantography Publications.

BLOOM, M., & FISHER, J. (1982). *Evaluating practice: Guidelines for the accountable professional.* Englewood Cliffs, NJ: Prentice-Hall.

BLOUNT, R. L., DRABMAN, R. S., WILSON, N., & STEWART, D. (1982). Reducing severe diurnal bruxism in two profoundly retarded females. *Journal of Applied Behavior Analysis, 15,* 565–571.

BOLSTAD, O., & JOHNSON, S. (1972). Self-regulation in the modification of disruptive classroom behavior. *Journal of Applied Behavior Analysis, 5,* 443–454.

BORING, E. G. (1941). Statistical frequencies as dynamic equilibria. *Psychological Review, 48,* 279–301.

BORNSTEIN, P. H., & QUEVILLON, R. P. (1976). The effects of a self-instructional package on overactive preschool boys. *Journal of Applied Behavior Analysis, 9,* 179–188.

BOSTOW, D. E., & BAILEY, J. (1969). Modification of severe disruption and aggressive behavior using brief time out and reinforcement procedures. *Journal of Applied Behavior Analysis, 2,* 31–37.

BOYKIN, R. A., & NELSON, R. O. (1981). The effects of instructions and calculation procedures on observers' accuracy, agreement, and calculation correctness. *Journal of Applied Behavior Analysis, 14,* 479–489.

BRANTNER, J. P., & DOHERTY, M. A. (1983). A review of timeout: A conceptual and methodological analysis. In S. Axelrod & J. Apsche (Eds.), *The effects of punishment on human behavior* (pp. 87–132). New York: Academic Press.

BRASTED, W. S., & CALLAHAN, E. J. (1984). An evaluation of the electronic fetal monitor as a feedback device during labor. *Journal of Applied Behavior Analysis, 17,* 261–266.

BRIGHAM, T. A. (1980). Self-control revisited: Or why doesn't anyone read Skinner anymore? *The Behavior Analyst, 3,* 25–33.

BRIGHAM, T. A., & SHERMAN, J. A. (1968). An experimental analysis of verbal imitation in preschool children. *Journal of Applied Behavior Analysis, 1,* 151–160.

BRODEN, M., HALL, R. V., & MITTS, B. (1971). The effect of self-recording on the classroom behavior of two eighth-grade students. *Journal of Applied Behavior Analysis, 4,* 191–199.

BROPHY, J. E., & GOOD, T. L. (1969). *Teacher-child dyadic interaction: A manual for coding classroom behavior.* Austin: University of Texas, Research and Development Center for Teacher Education.

BROWN, L., BRANSTON, M. B., HAMRE-NIETUPSKI, S., PUMPIAN, S., CERTO, N., & GRUENEWALD, L. (1979). A strategy for developing chronological age-appropriate and functional curricular content for severely handicapped adolescents and young adults. *Journal of Special Education, 13,* 81–90.

BROWN, L., FALVEY, M., VINCENT, L., KAYE, N., JOHNSON, F., FERRARA-PARRISH, P., & GRUENE-WALD, L. (1980). Strategies for generating comprehensive, longitudinal, and chronological age-appropriate individualized programs for adolescent and young-adult severely handicapped students. *Journal of Special Education, 14,* 199–215.

BROWNING, R. M. (1967). A same-subject design for simultaneous comparison of three reinforcement contingencies. *Behavior Research and Therapy, 5,* 237–243.

BRYANT, L. E., & BUDD, K. S. (1984). Teaching behaviorally handicapped preschool children to share. *Journal of Applied Behavior Analysis, 17,* 45–56.

BUDD, K. S., & BAER, D. M. (1976). Behavior modification and the law: Implications of recent judicial decisions. *Journal of Psychiatry and Law, 4,* 171–244.

BUELL, J., STODDARD, P., HARRIS, F. R., & BAER, D. M. (1968). Collateral social development accompanying reinforcement of outdoor play in a preschool child. *Journal of Applied Behavior Analysis, 1,* 167–173.

BUNKER, L. K., and MOON, S. (1983). Motor skills. In M. E. Snell (Ed.), *Systematic instruction of the moderately and severely handicapped,* (2nd ed., pp. 203–226). Columbus, OH: Charles E. Merrill.

BURCHARD, J. D., & BARRERA, F. (1972). An analysis of timeout and response cost in a programmed environment. *Journal of Applied Behavior Analysis, 5,* 271–282.

BURCHARD, J. D., & HARIG, P. T. (1976). Behavior modification and juvenile delinquency. In H. Leitenberg (Ed.), *Handbook of behavior modification and behavior therapy* (405–452). Englewood Cliffs, NJ: Prentice-Hall.

BURGESS, R. L., BURGESS, J. M., & ESVELDT, K. C. (1970). An analysis of generalized imitation. *Journal of Applied Behavior Analysis, 3,* 39–46.

BURGIO, L. D., WHITMAN, T. L., & JOHNSON, M. R. (1980). A self-instructional package for increasing attending behavior in educable mentally retarded children. *Journal of Applied Behavior Analysis, 13,* 443–459.

BURLEIGH, R. A., & MARHOLIN, D., II. (1977). Don't shoot until you see the whites of his eyes—An analysis of the adverse side effects of verbal prompts. *Behavior Modification, 1,* 109–122.

CAMPBELL, C. R., & STREMEL-CAMPBELL, K. (1982). Programming "loose training" as a strategy to facilitate language generalization. *Journal of Applied Behavior Analysis, 15,* 295–301.

CANTRELL, R. P., CANTRELL, M. L., HUDDLESTON, C. M., & WOOLDRIDGE, R. L. (1969). Contingency contracting with school problems. *Journal of Applied Behavior Analysis, 2,* 215–220.

CARDEN SMITH, L. K., & FOWLER, S. A. (1984). Positive peer pressure: The effects of peer monitoring on children's disruptive behavior. *Journal of Applied Behavior Analysis, 17*(2), 213–227.

CAREY, R. G., & BUCHER, B. (1981). Identifying the educative and suppressive effects of positive practice and restitutional overcorrection. *Journal of Applied Behavior Analysis, 14,* 71–80.

CARNINE, D. W. (1976). Effects of two teachers' presentation rates on off-task behavior, answering correctly, and participation. *Journal of Applied Behavior Analysis, 9,* 199–206.

CARNINE, D. W., & FINK, W. T. (1978). Increasing the rate of presentation and use of signals in elementary classroom teachers. *Journal of Applied Behavior Analysis, 11,* 35–46.

CARR, E. G., & DURAND, V. M. (1985). Reducing behavior problems through functional communication training. *Journal of Applied Behavior Analysis, 18,* 111–126.

CARR, E. G., & KOLOGINSKY, E. (1983). Acquisition of sign language by autistic children: II. Spontaneity and generalization effects. *Journal of Applied Behavior Analysis, 16,* 297–314.

CARR, E. G., & LOVAAS, I. O. (1983). Contingent electric shock as a treatment for severe behavior problems. In S. Axelrod & J. Apsche (Eds.), *The effects of punishment on human behavior* (pp. 221–245). New York: Academic Press.

CARR, E. G., NEWSOM, C. D., & BINKOFF, J. A. (1980). Escape as a factor in the aggressive behavior of two retarded children. *Journal of Applied Behavior Analysis, 13,* 101–117.

CATALDO, M. F., BESSMAN, C. A., PARKER, L. H., PEARSON, J. E., & ROGERS, M. C. (1979). Behavioral assessment for pediatric intensive care units. *Journal of Applied Behavior Analysis, 12,* 83–97.

CATANIA, A. C. (1975). The myth of self-reinforcement. *Behaviorism, 3,* 192–199.

CATANIA, A. C. (1984). *Learning* (2nd ed.). Englewood Cliffs, NJ: Prentice-Hall.

CATANIA, A. C., & HARNAD, S. (Eds.). (1984). Canonical papers of B. F. Skinner. *The Behavioral and Brain Sciences, 7,* 473–724.

CAUTELA, J. R. (1971). Covert conditioning. In A. Jacobs & L. B. Sachs (Eds.), *The psychology of private events: Perspective on covert response systems* (pp. 109–130). New York: Academic Press.

CHIANG, S. J., IWATA, B. A., & DORSEY, M. F. (1979). Elimination of disruptive bus riding behavior via token reinforcement on a "distance-based" schedule. *Education and Treatment of Children, 2,* 101–109.

CHRISTOPHERSEN, E. R., ARNOLD, C. M., HILL, D. W., & QUILITCH, H. R. (1972). The home point system: Token reinforcement procedures for application by parents of children with behavior problems. *Journal of Applied Behavior Analysis, 5,* 485–497.

CIMINERO, A. R., CALHOUN, K. S., & ADAMS, H. E. (Eds.). (1977). *Handbook of behavioral assessment.* New York: Wiley.

CLARK, C. R., DAVIES, C. O., & WOODCOCK, R. W. (1974). *Standard rebus glossary.* Circle Pines, MN: American Guidance Service.

CLARK, H. B., ROWBURY, T., BAER, A., & BAER, D. M. (1973). Time out as a punishing stimulus in continuous and intermittent schedules. *Journal of Applied Behavior Analysis, 6,* 443–455.

CONE, J. D., & HAWKINS, R. P. (Eds.). (1977). *Behavioral assessment: New directions in clinical psychology.* New York: Burner/Mazel.

COOK, J. W., ALTMAN, K., & HAAVIK, S. (1978). Consent for aversive treatment. *Mental Retardation, 16,* 47–51.

COOKE, N. L. (1984). Misrepresentations of the behavioral model in preservice teacher education textbooks. In W. L. Heward, T. E. Heron, D. S. Hill, & J. Trap-Porter (Eds.), *Focus on behavior analysis in education* (pp. 197–217). Columbus, OH: Charles E. Merrill.

COOPER, J. O. (1981). *Measuring behavior* (2nd ed.). Columbus, OH: Charles E. Merrill.

COOPER, K. H. (1970). *The new aerobics.* New York: Bantam Books.

COPELAND, R. E., BROWN, R. E., & HALL, R. V. (1974). The effects of principal-implemented techniques on the behavior of pupils. *Journal of Applied Behavior Analysis, 7,* 77–86.

CROLL, W. L. (1970). Children's discrimination learning as a function of intertrial interval duration. *Psychonomic Science, 18,* 321–322.

CRONIN, K. A., & CUVO, A. J. (1979). Teaching mending skills to mentally retarded adolescents. *Journal of Applied Behavior Analysis, 12,* 401–406.

CROW, R. E., & MAYHEW, G. L. (1976). Reinforcement effects on accuracy of self-reporting behavior of elementary students. In T. A. Brigham, R. P. Hawkins, J. Scott, & T. F. McLaughlin (Eds.), *Behavior analysis in education: Self-control and reading.* Dubuque, IA: Kendall/Hunt.

CSAPO, M. (1981). Comparison of two prompting procedures to increase response fluency among severely handicapped learners. *Journal of the Association for the Severely Handicapped, 6,* 39–47.

CUVO, A. J. (1979). Multiple-baseline design in instructional research: Pitfalls of measurement and procedural advantages. *American Journal of Mental Deficiency, 11,* 345–355.

CUVO, A. J., & DAVIS, P. K. (1980). Teaching community living skills to mentally retarded persons: An examination of discriminative stimuli. *Gedrag, 8,* 14–33.

CUVO, A. J., LEAF, R. B., & BORAKOVE, L. S. (1978). Teaching janitorial skills to the mentally retarded: Acquisition, generalization, and maintenance. *Journal of Applied Behavior Analysis, 11,* 345–355.

DALTON, A. J., RUBINO, C. A., & HISLOP, M. W. (1973). Some effects of token rewards on school achievement of children with Down's syndrome. *Journal of Applied Behavior Analysis, 6,* 251–259.

DAMPF, P. M. (1977). The elimination of an inappropriate response to adult direction. *Education and Treatment of Children, 1,* 19–22.

DANFORD, D. E., & HUBER, A. M. (1982). Pica among mentally retarded adults. *American Journal of Mental Deficiency, 87,* 141–146.

DARDIG, J. C., & HEWARD, W. L. (1977, May). *A simple procedure for the selection of tasks and rewards for family contracts.* Paper presented at the Third Annual Meeting of the Association for Behavior Analysis, Chicago.

DARDIG, J. C., & HEWARD, W. L. (1981a). *Sign here: A contracting book for children and their parents* (2nd ed.). Bridgewater, NJ: Fournies.

DARDIG, J. C., & HEWARD, W. L. (1981b). A systematic procedure for prioritizing IEP goals. *The Directive Teacher, 3,* 6–8.

DAVIS, J. (1984). Headset care and maintenance. In *Bicycling Magazine Precision Tune-Up Guide.* Rodale Press.

DEITZ, D. E. D., & REPP, A. C. (1983). Reducing behavior through reinforcement. *Exceptional Education Quarterly, 3,* 34–46.

DEITZ, S. M. (1977). An analysis of programming DRL schedules in educational settings. *Behavior Research and Therapy, 15,* 103–111.

DEITZ, S. M. (1978). Current status of applied behavior analysis: Science versus technology. *American Psychologist, 33,* 805–814.

DEITZ, S. M. (1982). Defining applied behavior analysis: An historical analogy. *The Behavior Analyst, 5,* 53–64.

DEITZ, S. M., & REPP, A. C. (1973). Decreasing classroom misbehavior through the use of DRL schedules of reinforcement. *Journal of Applied Behavior Analysis, 6,* 457–463.

DEITZ, S. M., REPP, A. C., & DEITZ, D. E. D. (1976). Reducing inappropriate classroom behavior of retarded students through three procedures of differential reinforcement. *Journal of Mental Deficiency Research, 20,* 155–170.

DEITZ, S. M., SLACK, D. J., SCHWARZMUELLER, E. B., WILANDER, A. P., WEATHERLY, T. J., & HILLIARD, G. (1978). Reducing inappropriate behavior in special classrooms by reinforcing average interresponse times: Interval DRL. *Behavior Therapy, 9,* 37–46.

DELQUADRI, J., GREENWOOD, C. R., & HALL, R. V. (1979). *Opportunity to respond: An update.* Paper presented at the Fifth Annual Meeting of the Association of Behavior Analysis, Dearborn, MI.

DEMEYER, M. K., & FERSTER, C. B. (1962). Teaching new social behavior to schizophrenic children. *Journal of the American Academy of Child Psychiatry, 1,* 443–461.

DERISI, W. J., & BUTZ, G. (1975). *Writing behavioral contracts: A case simulation practice manual.* Champaign, IL: Research Press.

DEWEY, J. (1939). *Experience and Education.* New York: Macmillan.

DICKERSON, E. A., & CREEDON, C. F. (1981). Self-selection of standards by children: The relative effectiveness of pupil-selected and teacher-selected standards of performance. *Journal of Applied Behavior Analysis, 14,* 425–433.

DOKE, L. A., & EPSTEIN, L. H. (1975). Oral overcorrection: Side effects and extended applications. *Journal of Applied Behavior Analysis, 20,* 496–511.

DOKE, L. A., & RISLEY, T. R. (1972). The organization of day care environments: Required vs. optional activities. *Journal of Applied Behavior Analysis, 5,* 405–420.

DOLEYS, D. M., MCWHORTER, A. Q., WILLIAMS, S. C., & GENTRY, W. R. (1977). Encopresis: Its treatment in relation to nocturnal enuresis. *Behavior Therapy, 8,* 77–82.

DORSEY, M. F., IWATA, B. A., ONG, P., & MCSWEEN, T. E. (1980). Treatment of self-injurious behavior using a water mist: Initial response suppression and generalization. *Journal of Applied Behavior Analysis, 13,* 343–353.

DORSEY, M. F., IWATA, B. A., REID, D. H., & DAVIS, P. A. (1982). Protective equipment: Continuous and contingent application in the treatment of self-injurious behavior. *Journal of Applied Behavior Analysis, 15,* 217–230.

DOTY, D. W., MCINNIS, T., & PAUL, G. L. (1974). Remediation of negative side-effects of an ongoing response cost system with chronic mental patients. *Journal of Applied Behavior Analysis, 7,* 191–198.

DOWRICK, P. W., & DOVE, C. (1980). The use of self-modeling to improve the swimming performance of spina bifida children. *Journal of Applied Behavior Analysis, 13,* 51–56.

DRABMAN, R. S., HAMMER, D., & ROSENBAUM, M. S. (1979). Assessing generalization in behavior modification with children: The generalization map. *Behavioral Assessment, 1,* 203–219.

DRABMAN, R. S., & SPITALNIK, R. (1973). Social isolation as a punishment procedure: A controlled study. *Journal of Experimental Child Psychology, 16,* 236–249.

DRABMAN, R. S., SPITALNIK, R., & O'LEARY, K. D. (1973). Teaching self-control to disruptive children. *Journal of Abnormal Psychology, 82,* 10–16.

DRABMAN, R. S., SPITALNIK, R., & SPITALNIK, K. (1974). Sociometric and disruptive behavior as a function of four types of token reinforcement programs. *Journal of Applied Behavior Analysis, 7,* 93–101.

DUKER, P. C., MORSINK, H. (1984). Acquisition and cross-setting generalization of manual signs with severely retarded individuals. *Journal of Applied Behavior Analysis, 17,* 93–103.

DUMAS, J. E. (1984). Child, adult-interactional, and socioeconomic setting events as predictors of parent training outcome. *Education and Treatment of Children, 7,* 351–364.

DUNHAM, P. (1977). The nature of reinforcing stimuli. In W. K. Honig & J. E. R. Staddon (Eds.), *Handbook of operant behavior* (pp. 98–124). Englewood Cliffs, NJ: Prentice-Hall.

DUVINSKY, J. D., & POPPEN, R. (1982). Human performance on conjunctive fixed-interval fixed-ratio schedules. *Journal of the Experimental Analysis of Behavior, 37,* 243–250.

DWINELL, M. A., & CONNIS, R. T. (1979). Reducing inappropriate verbalizations of a retarded adult. *American Journal of Mental Deficiency, 84,* 87–92.

DYER, K., CHRISTIAN, W. P., & LUCE, S. C. (1982). The role of response delay in improving the discrimination performance of autistic children. *Journal of Applied Behavior Analysis, 15,* 231–240.

EATON, M. D. (1978). Data decisions and evaluation. In Haring, N. G., Lovitt, T. C., Eaton, M. D., & Hansen, C. L. (Eds.), *The fourth R: Research in the classroom* (pp. 167–190). Columbus, OH: Charles E. Merrill.

EATON, M., & WITTMAN, V. (1982). Leap ups: Acceleration of learning through increasing material difficulty. *Journal of Precision Teaching, 3*(2), 29–33.

ENGELMANN, S., & CARNINE, D. (1982). *Theory of instruction: Principles and applications.* New York: Irvington.

EPSTEIN, L. H., DOKE, L. A., SAJWAJ, T. E., SORREL, S., & RIMMER, B. (1974). Generality and side effects of overcorrection. *Journal of Applied Behavior Analysis, 7,* 385–390.

ETZEL, B. C., LEBLANC, J. M., SCHILMOELLER, K. J., & STELLA, M. E. (1981). Stimulus control procedures in the education of young children. In S. W. Bijou & R. Ruiz (Eds.), *Behavior modification contributions to education* (pp. 3–37). Hillsdale, NJ: Lawrence Erlbaum.

EVANS, I., & MEYER, L. H. (1985). *An educative approach to behavior problems: A practical decision model for interventions with severely handicapped learners.* Baltimore: Paul H. Brookes.

FALK, J. L. (1971). The nature and determinants of adjunctive behavior. *Psysiology and Behavior, 6,* 577–588.

FANTINO, E., & LOGAN, C. A. (1979). *The experimental analysis of behavior: A biological perspective.* San Francisco: W. H. Freeman.

FANTUZZO, J. W., & CLEMENT, P. W. (1981). Generalization of the effects of teacher- and self-administered token reinforcers to nontreated students. *Journal of Applied Behavior Analysis, 14,* 435–447.

FAVELL, J. E., AZRIN, N. H., BAUMEISTER, A. A., CARR, E. G., DORSEY, M. F., FOREHAND, R., FOXX, R. M., LOVAAS, I. O., RINCOVER, A., RISLEY, T. R., ROMANCZYK, R. G., RUSSO, D. C., SCHROEDER, S. R., & SOLNICK, J. V. (1982). The treatment of self-injurious behavior. *Behavior Therapy, 13,* 529–554.

FAVELL, J. E., MCGIMSEY, J. F., & JONES, M. L. (1978). The use of physical restraint in the treatment of self-injury and as positive reinforcement. *Journal of Applied Behavior Analysis, 11,* 225–241.

FAVELL, J. E., MCGIMSEY, J. F., & JONES, M. L. (1980). Rapid eating in the retarded: reduction by nonaversive procedures. *Behavior Modification, 4,* 481–492.

FELIXBROD, J. J., & O'LEARY, K. D. (1973). Effects of reinforcement on children's academic behavior as a function of self-determined and externally imposed systems. *Journal of Applied Behavior Analysis, 6,* 241–250.

FELIXBROD, J. J., & O'LEARY, K. D. (1974). Self-determination of academic standards by children: Toward freedom from external control. *Journal of Educational Psychology, 66,* 845–850.

FERSTER, C. B., & CULBERTSON, S. A. (1982). *Behavior principles* (3rd ed.). Englewood Cliffs, NJ: Prentice-Hall.

FERSTER, C. B., CULBERTSON, S., & BOREN, M. C. (1975). *Behavior principles* (2nd ed., pp. 98–124). Englewood Cliffs, NJ: Prentice-Hall.

FERSTER, C. B., & DEMYER, M. K. (1961). The development of performances in autistic children in an automatically controlled environment. *Journal of Chronic Diseases, 13,* 312–345.

FERSTER, C. B., & DEMYER, M. K. (1962). A method for the experimental analysis of the behavior of autistic children. *American Journal of Orthopsychiatry, 32,* 89–98.

FERSTER, C. B., & PERROTT, M. C. (1968). *Behavior principles.* New York: Appleton-Century-Crofts.

FERSTER, C. B., & SKINNER, B. F. (1957). *Schedules of reinforcement.* Englewood Cliffs, NJ: Prentice-Hall.

FISHBEIN, J. E., & WASIK, B. H. (1981). Effect of the good behavior game on disruptive library behavior. *Journal of Applied Behavior Analysis, 14,* 89-93.

FISHER, R. (1956). *Statistical methods and statistical inference.* London: Oliver & Boyd.

FLANAGAN, B., GOLDIAMOND, I., & AZRIN, N. (1958). Operant stuttering: The control of stuttering behavior through response-contingent consequences. *Journal of Experimental Analysis of Behavior, 1,* 173-177.

FLANDERS, N. A. (1967). Interaction analysis in the classroom: A manual for observers. In A. Simon & E. Gil Boyer (Eds.), *Mirrors for behaviors: An anthology of classroom observation instruments* (Vol. 2). Philadelphia: Research for Better Schools.

FLEECE, L., GROSS, A., O'BRIEN, T., KISTNER, J., ROTHBLUM, E., & DRABMAN, R. (1981). Elevation of voice volume in young developmentally delayed children via an operant shaping procedure. *Journal of Applied Behavior Analysis, 14,* 351-355.

FLEECE, L., O'BRIEN, T., & DRABMAN, R. S. (1981). The use of a contingent observation procedure to reduce disruptive behavior in a preschool child. *Journal of Clinical Child Psychology, 10,* 128-130.

FOSTER, C. D., BILLIONIS, C. S., & LENT, J. R. (1976). *Using a sanitary napkin.* Northbrook, IL: Hubbard.

FOSTER, C. D., & KEILITZ, I. (1983). Empirical bases for program revisions of task analysis. *Journal of Special Education Technology, 6*(3), 13-23.

FOSTER, W. S. (1978). Adjunctive behavior: An underreported phenomenon in applied behavior analysis. *Journal of Applied Behavior Analysis, 11,* 545-546.

FOWLER, S. A., & BAER, D. M (1981). "Do I have to be good today?" The timing of delayed reinforcement as a factor in generalization. *Journal of Applied Behavior Analysis, 14*(1), 13-24.

FOXX, R. M. (1982a). *Decreasing behaviors of severely retarded and autistic persons.* Champaign, IL: Research Press.

FOXX, R. M. (1982b). *Increasing behaviors of severely retarded and autistic persons.* Champaign, IL: Research Press.

FOXX, R. M., & AZRIN, N. H. (1972). Restitution: A method of eliminating aggressive-disruptive behavior of retarded and brain damaged patients. *Behavior Research and Therapy, 10,* 15-27.

FOXX, R. M., & AZRIN, N. H. (1973a). *Toilet training the retarded: A rapid program for day and nighttime independent toileting.* Champaign, IL: Research Press.

FOXX, R. M., & AZRIN, N. H. (1973b). The elimination of autistic self-stimulatory behavior by overcorrection. *Journal of Applied Behavior Analysis, 6,* 1-14.

FOXX, R. M., & AZRIN, N. H. (1973c). Dry pants: A rapid method of toilet training children. *Behavior Research and Therapy, 11,* 435-442.

FOXX, R. M., & BECHTEL, D. R. (1983). Overcorrection: A review and analysis. In S. Axelrod & J. Apsche (Eds.), *The effects of punishment on human behavior* (pp. 133-220). New York: Academic Press.

FOXX, R. M., & MARTIN, E. D. (1975). Treatment of scavenging behavior (coprography and pica) by overcorrection. *Behavior Research and Therapy, 13,* 153-162.

FOXX, R. M., MCMORROW, M. J., & MENNEMEIER, M. (1984). Teaching social/vocational skills to retarded adults with a modified table game: An analysis of generalization. *Journal of Applied Behavior Analysis, 17,* 343-352.

FOXX, R. M., & RUBINOFF, A. (1979). Behavioral treatment of caffeinism: Reducing excessive coffee drinking. *Journal of Applied Behavior Analysis, 12,* 335-344.

FOXX, R. M., & SHAPIRO, S. T. (1978). The timeout ribbon: A non-exclusionary timeout procedure. *Journal of Applied Behavior Analysis, 11,* 125-143.

FREDERICKS, H. D., RIGGS, C., FUREY, T., GROVE, D., MOORE, W., MCDONNELL, J., JORDEN, E., HANSON, W., BALDWIN, V., & WADLOW, M. (1976). *The teaching research curriculum for moderately and severely handicapped.* Springfield, IL: Charles C. Thomas.

FRIEDLING, C., & O'LEARY, S. G. (1979). Effects of self-instructional training on second- and third-grade hyperactive children: A failure to replicate. *Journal of Applied Behavior Analysis, 12,* 211-219.

FULLER, P. R. (1949). Operant conditioning of a vegetative organism. *American Journal of Psychology, 62,* 587-590.

GALLAGHER, P. A., SULZBACHER, S. I., & SHORES, R. E. (1967, March). *A group contingency for classroom management of emotionally disturbed children*. Paper presented at the Kansas Council for Exceptional Children, Wichita, KS.

GAMBRILL, E. D. (1977). *Behavior modification: Handbook of assessment, intervention, and evaluation*. San Francisco: Jossey-Bass.

GAMBRILL, E. D. & RICHEY, C. A. (1976). *It's up to you: Developing assertive social skills*. Millbrae, CA: Les Femmes.

GARCIA, E. E. (1976). The development and generalization of delayed imitation. *Journal of Applied Behavior Analysis, 9,* 499.

GARCIA, E. E., & BATISTA-WALLACE, M. (1977). Parental training of the plural morpheme in normal toddlers. *Journal of Applied Behavior Analysis, 10,* 505.

GAST, D. L., & NELSON, C. M. (1977a). Legal and ethical considerations for the use of timeout in special education settings. *Journal of Special Education, 11,* 457–467.

GAST, D. L., & NELSON, C. M. (1977b). Timeout in the classroom: Implications for special education. *Exceptional Children,* 461–464.

GAST, D. L., & WOLERY, M. (1987). Severe maladaptive behaviors. In M. E. Snell (Ed.), *Systematic instruction of people with severe handicaps* (3rd ed.). Columbus, OH: Charles E. Merrill.

GAY, L. R. (1981). *Educational research: Competencies for analysis and application* (2nd ed.). Columbus, OH: Charles E. Merrill.

GAYLORD-ROSS, R. (1980). A decision model for the treatment of aberrant behavior in applied settings. In W. Sailor, B. Wilcox, & L. Brown (Eds.), *Methods of instruction for severely handicapped students* (pp. 135–158). Baltimore: Paul H. Brookes.

GAYLORD-ROSS, R. J., HARING, T. G., BREEN, C., & PITTS-CONWAY, V. (1984). The training and generalization of social interaction skills with autistic youth. *Journal of Applied Behavior Analysis, 17,* 229–247.

GEIS, G. L., STEBBINS, W. C., & LUNDIN, R. W. (1965). *Reflex and operant conditioning.* New York: Appleton-Century-Crofts.

GELLER, E. S., PATERSON, L., & TALBOTT, E. (1982). A behavioral analysis of incentive prompts for motivating seat belt use. *Journal of Applied Behavior Analysis, 15,* 403–415.

GELLER, E. S., WINETT, R. A., & EVERETT, P. B. (1982). *Preserving the environment: New strategies for behavior change.* New York: Pergamon Press.

GENTILE, J. R., RHODEN, A. H., & KLEIN, R. D. (1972). An analysis-of-variance model for the intrasubject replication design. *Journal of Applied Behavior Analysis, 5,* 193–198.

GERSTEN, R., CARNINE, D., & WHITE, W. A. T. (1984). The pursuit of clarity: Direct instruction and applied behavior analysis. In W. L. Heward, T. E. Heron, D. S. Hill, & J. Trap-Porter (Eds.), *Focus on behavior analysis in education* (pp. 38–57). Columbus, OH: Charles E. Merrill.

GLYNN, E. L. (1970). Classroom applications of self-determined reinforcement. *Journal of Applied Behavior Analysis, 3,* 123–132.

GLYNN, E. L., THOMAS, J. D., & SHEE, S. M. (1973). Behavioral self-control of on-task behavior in an elementary classroom. *Journal of Applied Behavior Analysis, 6,* 105–114.

GOETZ, E. M., AYALA, J. M., HATFIELD, V. L., MARSHALL, A. M., & ETZEL, B. C. (1983). Training independence in preschoolers with an auditory stimulus management technique. *Education and Treatment of Children, 6,* 251–261.

GOETZ, E. M., & BAER, D. M. (1973). Social control of form diversity and the emergence of new forms in children's blockbuilding. *Journal of Applied Behavior Analysis, 6,* 209–217.

GOETZ, E. M, HOLMBERG, M. C., & LEBLANC, J. M. (1975). Differential reinforcement of other behavior and noncontingent reinforcement as control procedures during the modification of a preschooler's compliance. *Journal of Applied Behavior Analysis, 8,* 77–82.

GOLA, T. J., HOLMES, P. A., & HOLMES, N. K. (1982). Effectiveness of a group contingency procedure for increasing prevocational behavior of profoundly mentally retarded residents. *Mental Retardation, 20*(1), 26–29.

GOLD, M. (1976). Task analysis of a complex assembly task by the retarded blind. *Exceptional Children, 43*(2), 78–84.

GOLDFRIED, M. R., & POMERANZ, D. (1968). Role of assessment in behavior modification. *Psychological Reports, 23,* 75–87.

GOLDIAMOND, I. (1965). Self-control procedures in personal behavior problems. *Psychological Reports, 17,* 851–868.

GOLDIAMOND, I. (1966). Perception, language, and conceptualization rules. In B. Kleinmuntz (Ed.),

Problem-solving: Research, method, and theory (pp. 183-224). New York: Wiley.

GOLDIAMOND, I. (1974). Toward a constructional approach to social problems: Ethical and constitutional issues raised by applied behavior analysis. *Behaviorism, 2,* 1-85.

GOLDIAMOND, I. (1976). Self-reinforcement. *Journal of Applied Behavior Analysis, 9,* 509-514.

GRAY, J. A. (1979). *Ivan Pavlov.* New York: Penguin Books.

GREENE, B. F., BAILEY, J. S., & BARBER, F. (1981). An analysis and reduction of disruptive behavior on school buses. *Journal of Applied Behavior Analysis, 14,* 177-192.

GREENWOOD, C. R., DELQUADRI, J. C., & HALL, R. V. (1984). Opportunity to respond and student academic achievement. In W. L. Heward, T. E. Heron, D. S. Hill, & J. Trap-Porter (Eds.), *Focus on behavior analysis in education* (pp. 58-88). Columbus, OH: Charles E. Merrill.

GREENWOOD, C. R., HOPS, H., WALKER, H. M., GUILD, J. J., STOKES, J., & YOUNG, K. R. (1979). Standardized classroom management program: Social validation and replication studies in Utah and Oregon. *Journal of Applied Behavior Analysis, 12*(2), 235-253.

GREER, R. D. (1983). Contingencies of the science and technology of teaching and pre-behavioristic research practices in education. *Educational Researcher, 12,* 3-9.

GREER, R. D., & POLIRSTOK, S. R. (1982). Collateral gains and short-term maintenance in reading and on-task responses by some inner-city adolescents as a function of their use of social reinforcement while tutoring. *Journal of Applied Behavior Analysis, 15,* 123-139.

GRESHAM, F. M. (1979). Comparison of response cost and timeout in a special education setting. *Journal of Special Education, 13*(2), 199-208.

GRESHAM, F. M. (1981). Social skills training with handicapped children: A review. *Review of Educational Research, 51,* 139-176.

GRESHAM, F. M. (1983). Use of a home-based dependent group contingency system in controlling destructive behavior: A case study. *School Psychology Review, 12*(2), 195-199.

GRESHAM, F. M., & GRESHAM, G. N. (1982). Interdependent, dependent, and independent group contingencies for controlling disruptive behavior. *Journal of Special Education, 16*(1), 101-110.

GRIFFITH, R. G. (1983). The administrative issues: An ethical and legal perspective. In S. Axelrod & J. Apsche (Eds.), *The effects of punishment on human behavior* (pp. 317-338). New York: Academic Press.

GRIFFITH, R. G., & HENNING, D. B. (1981). What is a human rights committee? *Mental Retardation, 19,* 61-63.

GROBE, R. P., PETTIBONE, T. J., & MARTIN, D. W. (1973). Effects of lecturer pace on noise level in a university classroom. *Journal of Educational Research, 67,* 73-75.

GROSS, A. M., FARRAR, M. J., & LINER, D. (1982). Reduction of trichotillomania in a retarded cerebral palsied child using overcorrection, facial screening, and differential reinforcement of other behavior. *Education and Treatment of Children, 5,* 133-140.

GRUBER, B., REESER, R., & REID, D. H. (1979). Providing a less restrictive environment for profoundly retarded persons by teaching independent walking skills. *Journal of Applied Behavior Analysis, 12*(2), 285-297.

GUILFORD, J. P. (1965). *Fundamental statistics in psychology and education.* New York: McGraw-Hill.

GUTTMAN, N., & KALISH, H. I. (1956). Discriminability and stimulus generalization. *Journal of Experimental Psychology, 51,* 79-88.

HAKE, D. F. (1982). The basic-applied continuum and the possible evolution of human operant social and verbal research. *The Behavior Analyst, 5,* 21-28.

HALL, M. C., GRINSTEAD, J., COLLIER, H., & HALL, R. V. (1980). Responsive parenting: A preventive program which incorporates parents training parents. *Education and Treatment of Children, 3,* 239-259.

HALL, R. V., AXELROD, S., FOUNDOPOULOS, M., SHELLMAN, J., CAMPBELL, R. A., & CRANSTON, S. (1971). The effective use of punishment to modify behavior in the classroom. *Educational Technology, 11,* 24-26.

HALL, R. V., & COPELAND, R. (1972). The responsive teaching model: A first step in shaping school personnel as behavior modification specialists.

Proceedings of the Third Banff International Conference on Behavior Modification (pp. 125-150). Champaign, IL: Research Press.

HALL, R. V., CRISTLER, C., CRANSTON, S. S., & TUCKER, B. (1970). Teachers and parents as researchers using multiple baseline designs. *Journal of Applied Behavior Analysis, 3,* 247-255.

HALL, R. V., DELQUADRI, J., GREENWOOD, C. R., & THURSTON, L. (1982). The importance of opportunity to respond in children's academic success. In E. B. Edgar, N. G. Haring, J. R. Jenkins, & C. G. Pious (Eds.), *Mentally handicapped children: Education and training* (pp. 107-140). Austin, TX: Pro-Ed.

HALL, R. V., & FOX, R. G. (1977). Changing-criterion designs: An alternative applied behavior analysis procedure. In B. C. Etzel, J. M. LeBlanc, & D. M. Baer (Eds.), *New developments in behavioral research: Theory, method, and application* (pp. 151-166). Hillsdale, NJ: Lawrence Erlbaum.

HALL, R. V., & HALL, M. C. (1980). *How to select reinforcers.* Austin, TX: Pro-Ed.

HALL, R. V., LUND, D., & JACKSON, D. (1968). Effects of teacher attention on study behavior. *Journal of Applied Behavior Analysis, 1,* 1-12.

HALL, R. V., WILLARD, D., GOLDSMITH, S., EMERSON, M., OWEN, M., DAVIS, F., & PORCIA, E. (1971). The teacher as observer and experimenter in the modification of disputing and talking-out behaviors. *Journal of Applied Behavior Analysis, 4,* 141-149.

HALLAHAN, D. P., LLOYD, J. W. KOSIEWICZ, M. M., KAUFFMAN, J. M., & GRAVES, A. W. (1979). Self-monitoring of attention as a treatment for a learning disabled boy's off-task behavior. *Learning Disability Quarterly, 2,* 24-32.

HAMBLIN, R. L., HATHAWAY, C., & WODARSKI, J. S. (1971). Group contingencies, peer tutoring and accelerating academic achievement. In E. A. Ramp & B. L. Hopkins (Eds.), *A new direction for education: Behavior analysis* (Vol. 1, pp. 41-53). Lawrence: University of Kansas.

HAMLET, C. C., AXELROD, S., & KUERSCHNER, S. (1984). Eye contact as an antecedent to compliant behavior. *Journal of Applied Behavior Analysis, 17,* 553-557.

HANSEN, G. D. (1979). Enuresis control through fading, escape, and avoidance training. *Journal of Applied Behavior Analysis, 12*(3), 303-309.

HARING, T. G. (1985). Teaching between-class generalization of toy play behavior to handicapped children. *Journal of Applied Behavior Analysis, 18*(2), 127-139.

HARLOW, H. F. (1959). Learning set and error factor theory. In S. Koch (Ed.), *Psychology: A study of science* (Vol. 2, pp. 492-537). New York: McGraw-Hill.

HARRIS, F. C., & LAHEY, B. B. (1978). A method for combining occurrence and nonoccurrence interobserver agreement scores. *Journal of Applied Behavior Analysis, 11,* 523-527.

HARRIS, F. R., WOLF, M. M., & BAER, D. M. (1966). Effects of adult social reinforcement on child behavior. In R. Ulrich, T. Stachnik, & J. Mabry (Eds.), *Control of human behavior* (pp. 130-137). Glenview, IL: Scott, Foresman.

HARRIS, S. L., & ERSNER-HERSHFIELD, R. (1978). Behavioral suppression of seriously disruptive behavior in psychotic and retarded patients: A review of punishment and its alternatives. *Psychological Bulletin, 85*(6), 1352-1375.

HARRIS, S. L., & ROMANCZYK, R. G. (1976). Treating self-injurious behavior of a retarded child by overcorrection. *Behavior therapy, 7,* 235-239.

HART, B. M., ALLEN, K. E., BUELL, J. S., HARRIS, F. R., & WOLF, M. M. (1964). Effects of social reinforcement on operant crying. *Journal of Experimental Child Psychology, 1,* 145-153.

HART, B., & RISLEY, T. R. (1974). Using preschool materials to modify the language of disadvantaged children. *Journal of Applied Behavior Analysis, 7,* 243-256.

HART, B., & RISLEY, T. R. (1975). Incidental teaching of language in the preschool. *Journal of Applied Behavior Analysis, 8,* 411-420.

HART, B., & RISLEY, T. R. (1982). *How to use incidental teaching for elaborating language.* Austin, TX: Pro-Ed.

HARTMANN, D. P. (1974). Forcing square pegs into round holes: Some comments on an analysis-of-variance model for the intrasubject replication design. *Journal of Applied Behavior Analysis, 7,* 635-638.

HARTMANN, D. P. (1977). Considerations in the choice of interobserver reliability estimates. *Journal of Applied Behavior Analysis, 10,* 103-116.

HARTMANN, D. P., GOTTMAN, J. M., JONES, R. R., GARDNER, W., KAZDIN, A. E., & VAUGHT, R. S.

(1980). Interrupted time-series analysis and its application to behavioral data. *Journal of Applied Behavior Analysis, 13,* 543–559.

HARTMANN, D. P., & HALL, R. V. (1976). The changing criterion design. *Journal of Applied Behavior Analysis, 9,* 527–532.

HAWKINS, R. P. (1975). Who decided *that* was the problem? Two stages of responsibility for applied behavior analysts. In W. S. Wood (Ed.), *Issues in evaluating behavior modification* (pp. 195–214). Champaign, IL: Research Press.

HAWKINS, R. P. (1979). The functions of assessment. *Journal of Applied Behavior Analysis, 12,* 501–516.

HAWKINS, R. P. (1984). What is "meaningful" behavior change in a severely/profoundly retarded learner: The view of a behavior analytic parent. In W. L. Heward, T. E. Heron, D. S. Hill, & J. Trap-Porter (Eds.), *Focus on behavior analysis in education* (pp. 282–286). Columbus, OH: Charles E. Merrill.

HAWKINS, R. P. (1986). Selection of target behaviors. In R. O. Nelson & S. C. Hayes (Eds.), *Conceptual foundations of behavioral assessment* (pp. 331–385). New York: Guilford Press.

HAWKINS, R. P., & DOBES, R. W. (1977). Behavioral definitions in applied behavior analysis: Explicit or implicit? In B. C. Etzel, J. M. LeBlanc, & D. M. Baer (Eds.), *New developments in behavioral research: Theory, method, and application* (pp. 167–188). Hillsdale, NJ: Lawrence Erlbaum.

HAWKINS, R. P., & DOTSON, V. A. (1975). Reliability scores that delude: An Alice in Wonderland trip through the misleading characteristics of inter-observer agreement scores in interval recording. In E. Ramp & G. Semp (Eds.), *Behavior analysis: Areas of research and application* (pp. 359–376). Englewood Cliffs, NJ: Prentice-Hall.

HAWKINS, R. P., & FABRY, B. D. (1979). Applied behavior analysis and interobserver reliability: A commentary on two articles by Birkimer and Brown. *Journal of Applied Behavior Analysis, 12,* 545–552.

HAYES, L. A. (1976). The use of group contingencies for behavioral control: A review. *Psychological Bulletin, 83,* 528–643.

HAYES, S. C., RINCOVER, A., & SOLNICK, J. V. (1980). The technical drift of applied behavior analysis. *Journal of Applied Behavior Analysis, 13,* 275–285.

HAYNES, S. N. (1978). *Principles of behavioral assessment.* New York: Gardner Press.

HELWIG, J. (1973). *Effects of manipulating an antecedent event on mathematics response rate.* Unpublished manuscript, Ohio State University, Columbus, OH.

HELWIG, J. J., JOHNS, J. C., NORMAN, J. E., & COOPER, J. O. (1976). The measurement of manuscript letter strokes. *Journal of Applied Behavior Analysis, 9,* 231–236.

HERON, T. E., & HEWARD, W. L. (1982). Ecological assessment: Implications for teachers of learning disabled students. *Learning Disability Quarterly, 5,* 117–125.

HERON, T. E., HEWARD, W. L., COOKE, N. L., & HILL, D. S. (1983). Evaluation of a classwide peer tutoring system: First graders teach each other sight words. *Education and Treatment of Children, 6,* 137–152.

HERSEN, M., & BARLOW, D. H. (1976). *Single case experimental designs: Strategies for studying behavior change.* New York: Pergamon Press.

HERSEN, M., & BELLECK, A. S. (Eds.). (1976). *Behavioral assessment: A practical handbook.* New York: Pergamon Press.

HEWARD, W. L. (1978a, May). *The delayed multiple baseline design.* Paper presented at the Fourth Annual Convention of the Association for Behavior Analysis, Chicago.

HEWARD, W. L. (1978b, August). How to teach a child to imitate. *The Exceptional Parent,* 50–57.

HEWARD, W. L. (1978c). Visual Response System: A mediated resource room for children with learning problems. *Journal of Special Education Technology, 4,* 11–19.

HEWARD, W. L. (1979). Teaching students to control their own behavior. *Exceptional Teacher, 1*(2), 3–5, 11.

HEWARD, W. L. (1980). A formula for individualizing initial criteria for reinforcement. *Exceptional Teacher, 1*(9), 7, 9.

HEWARD, W. L., & CHAPMAN, J. E. (1981). Improving parent-teacher communication through recorded telephone messages: Systematic replication in a special education classroom. *Journal of Special Education Technology, 4,* 11–19.

HEWARD, W. L., & DARDIG, J. C. (1978). Improving the parent-teacher relationship through contingency contracting. In D. Edge, B. J. Strenecky, & S. I. Mour (Eds.), *Parenting learning-problem children: The professional educator's perspective.* Columbus, OH: Ohio State University Press.

HEWARD, W. L., DARDIG, J. C., & ROSSETT, A. (1979). *Working with parents of handicapped children*. Columbus, OH: Charles E. Merrill.

HEWARD, W. L., & EACHUS, H. T. (1979). Acquisition of adjectives and adverbs in sentences written by hearing impaired and aphasic children. *Journal of Applied Behavior Analysis, 12,* 391–400.

HEWARD, W. L., & ORLANSKY, M. D. (1984). *Exceptional children: An introductory survey of special education* (2nd ed.). Columbus, OH: Charles E. Merrill.

HIERONYMOUS, A. N., & LINDQUIST, E. F. (1978). *Iowa Tests of Basic Skills*. Boston: Houghton Mifflin.

HIGGINS, S. T., & MORRIS, E. K. (1985). A comment on contemporary definitions of reinforcement as a behavioral process. *The Psychological Record, 35,* 81–88.

HOBBS, T. R., & HOLT, M. M. (1976). The effects of token reinforcement on the behavior of delinquents in cottage settings. *Journal of Applied Behavior Analysis, 9,* 189–198.

HOLLAND, J. G. (1978). Behaviorism: Part of the problem or part of the solution? *Journal of Applied Behavior Analysis, 11,* 163–174.

HOLLAND, J. G., & SKINNER, B. F. (1961). *The analysis of behavior: A program for self-instruction*. New York: McGraw-Hill.

HOLT, G. L., & SHAFER, J. N. (1973). Function of intertrial interval in matching-to-sample. *Journal of the Experimental Analysis of Behavior, 19,* 181–186.

HOLZ, W. C., AZRIN, H. N., & AYLLON, T. (1963). Elimination of behavior of mental patients by response-produced extinction. *Journal of the Experimental Analysis of Behavior, 6,* 407–412.

HOMME, L., CSANYI, A. P., GONZALES, M. A., & RECHS, J. R. (1970). *How to use contingency contracting in the classroom*. Champaign, IL: Research Press.

HOPKINS, B. L. (1979). Proposed conventions for evaluating observer reliability: A commentary on two articles by Birkimer and Brown. *Journal of Applied Behavior Analysis, 12,* 561–564.

HOPKINS, B. L., & HERMANN, J. A. (1977). Evaluating interobserver reliability of interval data. *Journal of Applied Behavior Analysis, 10,* 121–126.

HOPKINS, B. L., SCHUTTE, R. C., & GARTON, K. L. (1971). The effects of access to a playroom on the rate and quality of printing and writing of first- and second-grade students. *Journal of Applied Behavior Analysis, 4,* 77–87.

HORNER, R. D. (1971). Establishing use of crutches by a mentally retarded spina bifida child. *Journal of Applied Behavior Analysis, 4,* 183–189.

HORNER, R. D. (1980). The effects of an environmental "enrichment" program on the behavior of institutionalized profoundly retarded children. *Journal of Applied Behavior Analysis, 13,* 473–491.

HORNER, R. D., & BAER, D. M. (1978). Multiple-probe technique: A variation on the multiple baseline design. *Journal of Applied Behavior Analysis, 11,* 189–196.

HORNER, R. D., & KEILITZ, I. (1975). Training mentally retarded adolescents to brush their teeth. *Journal of Applied Behavior Analysis, 8*(3), 301–309.

HORNER, R. H., & MCDONALD, R. S. (1982). A comparison of single instance and general case instruction in teaching a generalized vocational skill. *Journal of the Association for the Severely Handicapped, 7,* 7–20.

HORNER, R. H., SPRAGUE, J. R., & WILCOX, B. (1982). Constructing general case programs for community activities. In B. Wilcox & T. Bellamy (Eds.), *Design of high school for severely handicapped students*. Baltimore: Paul H. Brookes.

HOTT, G. L., & SHAFER, J. N. (1973). Function of intertrial interval in matching-to-sample. *Journal of the Experimental Analysis of Behavior, 19,* 181–186.

HOWELL, K. W., KAPLAN, J. S., & O'CONNELL, C. Y. (1979). *Evaluating exceptional children: A task analysis approach*. Columbus, OH: Charles E. Merrill.

HUMPHREY, L. L., KAROLY, P., & KIRSCHENBAUM, D. S. (1978). Self-management in the classroom: Self-imposed response cost versus self-reward. *Behavior Therapy, 9,* 592–601.

HUNDERT, J., & BATSTONE, D. (1978). A practical procedure to maintain pupils' accurate self-rating in a classroom token program. *Behavior Modification, 2,* 93–112.

HUNDERT, J., & BUCHER, B. (1978). Pupils' self-scored arithmetic performance: A practical procedure for maintaining accuracy. *Journal of Applied Behavior Analysis, 11,* 304.

HURLBUT, B. I., IWATA, B. A., & GREEN, J. D. (1982). Nonvocal language acquisition in adolescents with severe physical disabilities: Blissymbol versus iconic stimulus formats. *Journal of Applied Behavior Analysis, 15,* 241–258.

INGRAHAM v. WRIGHT, 430 U.S. 651 (1977).

ISAACS, C. D., EMBRY, L. H., & BAER, D. M. (1982). Training family therapists: An experimental analysis. *Journal of Applied Behavior Analysis, 15,* 505–520.

ISAACS, W., THOMAS, I., & GOLDIAMOND, I. (1960). Application of operant conditioning to reinstate verbal behavior in psychotics. *Journal of Speech and Hearing disorders, 25,* 8–12.

IVANCIC, M. T., REID, D. H., IWATA, B. A., FAW, G. D., & PAGE, T. J. (1981). Evaluating a supervision program for developing and maintaining therapeutic staff-resident interaction during institutional care routines. *Journal of Applied Behavior Analysis, 14,* 95–107.

IWATA, B. A., & BAILEY, J. S. (1974). Reward versus cost token systems: An analysis of the effects on students and teacher. *Journal of Applied Behavior Analysis, 7,* 567–576.

IWATA, B. A., & LORENTZSON, A. M. (1976). Operant control of seizure-like behavior in an institutionalized retarded adult. *Behavior Therapy, 7,* 247–251.

JACOBS, H. E., FAIRBANKS, D., POCHE, C. E., & BAILEY, J. S. (1982). Multiple incentives in encouraging car pool formation on a university campus. *Journal of Applied Behavior Analysis, 15,* 141–149.

JAMES, J. C., TRAP, J., & COOPER, J. O. (1977). Students' self-recording of manuscript letter strokes. *Journal of Applied Behavior Analysis, 10,* 509–514.

JAMES, J. E. (1981). Behavioral self-control of stuttering using time-out from speaking. *Journal of Applied Behavior Analysis, 14,* 25–37.

JASON, L. A., & LIOTTA, R. F. (1982). Reduction of cigarette smoking in a university cafeteria. *Journal of Applied Behavior Analysis, 15,* 573–577.

JASTAK, J. F., & JASTAK, S. R. (1965). *The Wide Range Achievement Test* (rev. ed.) Wilmington, DE: Guidance.

JOHNSON, S. M., & BOLSTAD, O. D. (1973). Methodological issues in naturalistic observation: Some problems and solutions for field research. In L. A. Hamerlynck, L. C. Handy, & E. J. Marsh (Eds.), *Behavior change: Methodology, concepts, and practices.* Champaign, IL: Research Press.

JOHNSON, T. (1973). *Addition and subtraction math program with stimulus shaping and stimulus fading.* Produced pursuant to a grant from the Ohio Department of Education, BEH Act, P.L. 91–230, Title VI-G; OE G-0-714438(604). J. E. Fisher & J. O. Cooper, project co-directors.

JOHNSTON, J. M. (1979). On the relation between generalization and generality. *The Behavior Analyst, 2,* 1–6.

JOHNSTON, J. M., & JOHNSTON, G. J. (1972). Modification of consonant speech-sound articulation in young children. *Journal of Applied Behavior Analysis, 5,* 233–246.

JOHNSTON, J. M., & PENNYPACKER, H. S. (1980). *Strategies and tactics for human behavioral research.* Hillsdale, NJ: Lawrence Erlbaum.

JOHNSTON, R. J., & MCLAUGHLIN, T. F. (1982). The effects of free time on assignment completion and accuracy in arithmetic: A case study. *Education and Treatment of Children, 5,* 33–40.

JONES, F. H., & EIMERS, R. C. (1975). Role playing to train elementary teachers to use a classroom management "skill package." *Journal of Applied Behavior Analysis, 8,* 421–433.

JONES, F. H., FREMOUW, W., & CARPLES, S. (1977). Pyramid training of elementary school teachers to use a classroom management "skill package." *Journal of Applied Behavior Analysis, 10,* 239–254.

JONES, R. R., VAUGHT, R. S., & WEINROTT, M. R. (1977). Time-series analysis in operant research. *Journal of Applied Behavior Analysis, 10,* 151–166.

JONES, R. T., NELSON, R. E., & KAZDIN, A. E. (1977). The role of external variables in self-reinforcement. *Behavior Modification, 1,* 147–178.

JONES, V. F., & JONES, L. S. (1981). *Responsible classroom discipline: Creating positive learning environments and solving problems.* Boston: Allyn & Bacon.

JORGENSON, H. A. (1972). *Use of a music activity and social reinforcement to increase group attending behavior.* Paper presented at the 50th Annual International Conference of the Council for Exceptional Children, Washington, DC.

Journal of Applied Behavior Analysis. (1968). Lawrence, KS: Society for the Experimental Analysis of Behavior.

Journal of Applied Behavior Analysis. (1976). Preparation of graphs for JABA. Author, *9,* 24.

Journal of Applied Behavior Analysis. (1977). Instruction to authors: Preparation of graphs for JABA. Author, *10,* 688.

Journal of Applied Behavior Analysis, (1982). Preparation of figures. Author, *15,* 414.

Journal of the Experimental Analysis of Behavior. (1958). Bloomington, IN: Society for the Experimental Analysis of Behavior.

Journal of Precision Teaching. (1980). Kansas City, MO: Plain English Publications.

KABLER, M. L. (1976). *Teaching fourth-grade children to use self-contracting as a form of self-control.* Unpublished doctoral dissertation, Ohio State University, Columbus, OH.

KABLER, M. L., DARDIG, J. C., & HEWARD, W. L. (1977). *Leader's manual for Sign here: A contracting book for children and their parents.* Bridgewater, NJ: Fournies.

KADUSHIN, A. (1972). *The social work interview.* New York: Columbia University Press.

KANFER, F. H. (1976). *The many faces of self-control, or behavior modification changes its focus.* Paper presented at the Fifth International Banff Conference, Banff, Alberta, Canada.

KANFER, F. H., & GRIMM, L. G. (1977). Behavioral analysis: Selecting target behaviors in the interview. *Behavior Modification, 1,* 7–28.

KANFER, F. H., & SASLOW, G. (1969). Behavior diagnosis. In C. H. Franks (Ed.), *Behavior therapy: Appraisal and status* (pp. 417–444). New York: McGraw-Hill.

KANNER, L. (1957). *Child psychiatry* (3rd ed.). Springfield, IL: Charles C. Thomas.

KANTOR, J. R. (1950). *Psychology and logic* (Vol. 2). Bloomington, IN: Principia Press.

KANTOR, J. R. (1970). An analysis of the experimental analysis of behavior. *Journal of the Experimental Analysis of Behavior, 13,* 101–108.

KANTOR, J. R., & SMITH, N. W. (1975). *The science of psychology: An interbehavioral survey.* Chicago: Principia Press.

KATZENBERG, A. C. (1975). *How to draw graphs.* Kalamazoo, MI: Behaviordelia.

KAU-TO LEUNG, E., TREBLAS, P. V., COOPER, J. O., & TRAP-PORTER, J. (1982). Effects of training for manuscript handwriting on generalization to cursive handwriting. *Behavioral Psychotherapy, 10,* 311–323.

KAUFMAN, K. F., & O'LEARY, K. D. (1972). Reward, cost, and self-evaluation procedures for disruptive adolescents in a psychiatric hospital school. *Journal of Applied Behavior Analysis, 5,* 293–309.

KAZDIN, A. E. (1973a). The effects of vicarious reinforcement on attentive behavior in the classroom. *Journal of Applied Behavior Analysis, 6,* 77–78.

KAZDIN, A. E. (1973b) Methodological and assessment considerations in evaluating reinforcement programs in applied settings. *Journal of Applied Behavior Analysis, 6,* 517–531.

KAZDIN, A. E. (1974). Self-monitoring and behavior change. In M. J. Mahoney & C. E. Thoresen (Eds.), *Self-control: Power to the person.* Monterey, CA: Brooks/Cole.

KAZDIN, A. E. (1975a). Characteristics and trends in applied behavior analysis. *Journal of Applied Behavior Analysis, 8,* 332.

KAZDIN, A. E. (1975b). *Behavior modification in applied settings.* Homewood, IL: Dorsey Press.

KAZDIN, A. E. (1976). Statistical analyses for single-case experimental designs. In M. Hersen & D. H. Barlow (Eds.), *Single case experimental designs* (pp. 265–316). New York: Pergamon Press.

KAZDIN, A. E. (1977a). Artifact, bias, and complexity of assessment: The ABCs of reliability. *Journal of Applied Behavior Analysis, 10,* 141–150.

KAZDIN, A. E. (1977b). *The token economy: A review and evaluation.* New York: Plenum Press.

KAZDIN, A. E. (1977c). Assessing the clinical or applied importance of behavior change through social validation. *Behavior Modification, 1,* 427–452.

KAZDIN, A. E. (1977d). Vicarious reinforcement and direction of behavior change in the classroom. *Behavior Therapy, 8,* 279–286.

KAZDIN, A. E. (1978a). *History of behavior modification.* Austin: TX: Pro-Ed.

KAZDIN, A. E. (1978b). Methodological and interpretive problems of single-case experimental designs. *Journal of Consulting and Clinical Psychology, 46,* 629–642.

KAZDIN, A. E. (1979). Unobtrusive measures in behavioral assessment. *Journal of Applied Behavior Analysis, 12,* 713–724.

KAZDIN, A. E. (1980a). Acceptability of alternative treatments for deviant child behavior. *Journal of Applied Behavior Analysis, 13,* 259–273.

KAZDIN, A. E. (1980b). Acceptability of time out from positive reinforcement procedures for disruptive child behavior. *Behavior Therapy, 11,* 329–344.

KAZDIN, A. E. (1980c). *Behavior modification in applied settings* (rev. ed.). Homewood, IL: Dorsey Press.

KAZDIN, A. E., & BOOTZIN, R. R. (1972). The token economy: An evaluative review. *Journal of Applied Behavior Analysis, 5,* 343–372.

KAZDIN, A., & ESVELDT-DAWSON, K. (1981). *How to maintain behavior.* Austin, TX: Pro-Ed.

KAZDIN, A. E., & HARTMANN, D. P. (1978). The simultaneous-treatment design. *Behavior Therapy, 9,* 912–922.

KEEFE, F. J., KOPEL, S. A., & GORDON, S. B. (1978). *A practical guide to behavioral assessment.* New York: Springer.

KELLER, F. S. (1973). Behaviorism. In J. L. Morse & W. H. Hendelson (Eds.), *Funk & Wagnalls New Encyclopedia* (Vol. 3). New York: Funk & Wagnalls.

KELLER, F. S., & SCHOENFELD, W. N. (1950). *Principles of psychology: A systematic text in the science of behavior.* New York: Appleton-Century-Crofts.

KELLEY, M. L., JARVIE, G. J., MIDDLEBROOK, J. L., MCNEER, M. F., & DRABMAN, R. S. (1984). Decreasing burned children's pain behavior: Impacting the trauma of hydrotherapy. *Journal of Applied Behavior Analysis, 17,* 147–158.

KELLEY, M. L., & STOKES, T. F. (1982). Contingency contracting with disadvantaged youth: Improving classroom performance. *Journal of Applied Behavior Analysis, 15,* 447–454.

KELLY, J. A., & DRABMAN, R. S. (1977). Generalizing response suppression of self-injurious behavior through an overcorrection punishment procedure. *Behavior Therapy, 8,* 468–472.

KELLY, M. B. (1977). A review of the observational data-collection and reliability procedures reported in the *Journal of Applied Behavior Analysis. Journal of Applied Behavior Analysis, 10,* 97–101.

KENT, R. N., KANOWITZ, J., O'LEARY, K. D., & CHEIKEN, M. (1977). Observer reliability as a function of circumstances of assessment. *Journal of Applied Behavior Analysis, 10,* 317–324.

KERR, M. M., & NELSON, C. M. (1983). *Strategies for managing behavior problems in the classroom.* Columbus, OH: Charles E. Merrill.

KIRCHER, A. S., PEAR, J. J., & MARTIN, G. L. (1971). Shock as a punishment in a picture-naming task with retarded children. *Journal of Applied Behavior Analysis, 4,* 227–233.

KIRIGIN, K. A., BRAUKMANN, C. J., ATWATER, J. D., & WOLF, M. M. (1982). An evaluation of teaching family (Achievement Place) group homes for juvenile delinquents. *Journal of Applied Behavior Analysis, 15,* 1–16.

KNEEDLER, R. D., & HALLAHAN, D. P. (1981). Self-monitoring of on-task behavior with learning disabled children: Current studies and directions. *Exceptional Education Quarterly, 2*(3), 73–82.

KOEGEL, R. L., DUNLAP, G., & DYER, K. (1980). Inter-trial interval duration and learning in autistic children. *Journal of Applied Behavior Analysis, 13,* 91–99.

KOEGEL, R. L., & RINCOVER, A. (1977). Research on the differences between generalization and maintenance in extra-therapy responding. *Journal of Applied Behavior Analysis, 10,* 1–12.

KOENIG, C. H., & KUNZELMANN, H. P. (1980). *Classroom learning screening.* Columbus, OH: Charles E. Merrill.

KOSIEWICZ, M. M., HALLAHAN, D. P., LLOYD, J. W., & GRAVES, A. W. (1982). Effects of self-instruction and self-correction procedures on handwriting performance. *Learning Disability Quarterly, 5*(1), 71–78.

KOUNIN, J. (1970). *Discipline and group management in classrooms.* New York: Holt, Rinehart & Winston.

KRASNER, L. A., & ULLMANN, L. P. (Eds.). (1965). *Research in behavior modification: New developments and implications.* New York: Holt, Rinehart & Winston.

KRATOCHWILL, T. R. (1979). Just because it's reliable doesn't mean it's believable: A commentary on two articles by Birkimer and Brown. *Journal of Applied Behavior Analysis, 12,* 553–557.

KRATOCHWILL, T. R., & LEVIN, J. R. (1978). What time-series designs may have to offer educational researchers. *Contemporary Educational Psychology, 3,* 273–329.

KRATOCHWILL, T. R., & WETZEL, R. J. (1977). Observer agreement, credibility, and judgment: Some considerations in presenting observer data. *Journal of Applied Behavior Analysis, 10,* 133–139.

KRUMBOLTZ, J. D., & KRUMBOLTZ, H. B. (1972). *Changing children's behavior.* Englewood Cliffs, NJ: Prentice-Hall.

KUNZELMANN, H. P. (1970). *Precision teaching.* Seattle: Special Child Publications.

KUNZELMANN, H. P. (Ed.) with COHEN, M. A., HULTEN, W. J., MARTIN, G. I., & MINGO, A. R. (1970). *Precision teaching: An initial training sequence.* Seattle: Special Child Publications.

LAGOMARCINO, A., REID, D. H., IVANCIC, M. T., & FAW, G. D. (1984). Leisure-dance instruction for severely and profoundly retarded persons: Teaching an intermediate community-living skill. *Journal of Applied Behavior Analysis, 17,* 71–84.

LAHEY, B. B. (1971). Modification of the frequency of descriptive adjectives in the speech of head start children through modeling without reinforcement. *Journal of Applied Behavior Analysis, 4,* 19–22.

LAHEY, B. B., MCNEES, M. P., & MCNEES, M. C. (1973). Control of an obscene "verbal tic" through timeout in an elementary classroom. *Journal of Applied Behavior Analysis, 6,* 101–104.

LANG, S. D., & GREEN, D. R. (1979). Managing corridor behaviors. *Education and Treatment of Children, 2,* 185–195.

LANGSTAFF, A. L., & VOLKMOR, C. B. (1975). *Contingency management.* Columbus, OH: Charles E. Merrill.

LANUNZIATA, L. J., HUNT, K. P., & COOPER, J. O. (1984). Suggestions for phasing out token economy systems in primary and intermediate grades. *Techniques, 1,* 151–156.

LAROWE, L. N., TUCKER, R. D., & MCGUIRE, J. M. (1980). Lunchroom noise control using feedback and group contingent reinforcement. *Journal of School Psychology, 18,* 51–57.

LEAHAY, T. H. (1980). *A history of psychology.* Englewood Cliffs, NJ: Prentice-Hall.

LEIGHLAND, S. (1984). On "setting events" and related concepts. *The Behavior Analyst, 7,* 41–45.

LEITENBERG, H. (1973). The use of single-case methodology in psychotherapy research. *Journal of Abnormal Psychology, 82,* 87–101.

LEITENBERG, H . (1976). *Handbook of behavior modification and behavior therapy.* Englewood Cliffs, NJ: Prentice-Hall.

LEITENBERG, H., BURCHARD, J. D., BURCHARD, S. N., FULLER, E. J., & LYSAGHT, T. V. (1977). Using positive reinforcement to suppress behavior: Some experimental comparisons with sibling conflict. *Behavior Therapy, 8,* 168–182.

LELAURIN, K. (1984). Ecobehavioral considerations in developmental research: A review and suggested model of inquiry. *Education and Treatment of Children, 7,* 305–314.

LELAURIN, K., & RISLEY, T. R. (1972). The organization of day-care environments: "Zone" versus "man-to-man" staff assignments. *Journal of Applied Behavior Analysis, 5,* 225–232.

LENNON, J., & MCCARTNEY, P. (1965). *We can work it out.* London: Northern Songs Limited.

LEONARDI, A., DUGGAN, T., HOFFHEINS, J., & AXELROD, S. (1972, March). *Use of group contingencies to reduce three types of inappropriate classroom behaviors.* Paper presented at the meeting of the Council for Exceptional Children, Washington, DC.

LIBERTY, K., & WILCOX, B. (1981). Forum: Slowing down learning. *Newsletter of the Association for the Severely Handicapped, 7(2).*

LINDSLEY, O. R. (1971). An interview. *Teaching Exceptional Children, 3,* 114–119.

LINDSLEY, O. R. (1981). *Current issues facing standard celeration charts.* Paper presented at the Winter Precision Teaching Conference, Orlando, FL.

LINDSLEY, O. R. (1985). *Quantified trends in the results of behavior analysis.* Presidential address at the Eleventh Annual Convention of the Association for Behavior Analysis, Columbus, OH.

LINEHAN, M. (1977). Issues in behavioral interviewing. In J. D. Cone & R. P. Hawkins (Eds.), *Behavioral assessment: New directions in clinical psychology* (pp. 30–51). New York: Bruner/Mazel.

LIPINSKI, D. P., BLACK, J. L., NELSON, R. O., & CIMINERO, A. R. (1975). Influence of motivational variables on the reactivity and reliability of self-recording. *Journal of Consulting and Clinical Psychology, 43,* 637–646.

LITOW, L., & PUMROY, D. K. (1975). A brief review of classroom group-oriented contingencies. *Journal of Applied Behavior Analysis, 3,* 341–347.

LONGO, J., ROTATORI, A. F., KAPPERMAN, G., & HEINZE, T. (1981). Procedures used to modify self-injurious behaviors in visually impaired, mentally retarded individuals. *Education of the Visually Handicapped, 13(3),* 77–83.

LOVAAS, O. I., FREITAS, K., NELSON, K., & WHALEN, C. (1967). The establishment of imitation and its use for the development of complex behavior in schizophrenic children. *Behavior Research and Therapy, 5,* 171–182.

LOVAAS, O. I., KOEGEL, R., SIMMONS, J. Q., & LONG, J. S. (1973). Some generalizations and follow-up measures on autistic children in behavior therapy. *Journal of Applied Behavior Analysis, 6,* 131–166.

LOVAAS, I., SCHAEFFER, B., & SIMMONS, J. Q. (1965). Building social behavior in autistic children by use of electric shock. *Journal of Experimental Research in Personality, 1,* 99–109.

LOVAAS, I., & SIMMONS, J. Q. (1969). Manipulation of self-destruction in three retarded children. *Journal of Applied Behavior Analysis, 2,* 143–157.

LOVITT, T. C. (1973). Self-management projects with children with behavioral disabilities. *Journal of Learning Disabilities, 6,* 138–150.

LOVITT, T. C. (1977). *In spite of my resistance . . . I've learned from children.* Columbus, OH: Charles E. Merrill.

LOVITT, T. C. (1984). *Tactics for teaching.* Columbus, OH: Charles E. Merrill.

LOVITT, T. C., & CURTISS, K. A. (1969). Academic response rates as a function of teacher- and self-imposed contingencies. *Journal of Applied Behavior Analysis, 2,* 49–53.

LUCE, S. C., DELQUADRI, J., & HALL, R. V. (1980). Contingent exercise: A mild but powerful procedure for suppressing inappropriate verbal and aggressive behavior. *Journal of Applied Behavior Analysis, 13,* 583–594.

LUCE, S. C., & HALL, R. V. (1981). Contingent exercise: A procedure used with differential reinforcement to reduce bizarre verbal behavior. *Education and Treatment of Children, 4,* 309–327.

LUISELLI, J. K. (1980). Controlling disruptive behaviors of an autistic child: Parent-mediated contingency management in the home setting. *Education and Treatment of Children, 3,* 195–203.

LUNDIN, R. W. (1969). *Personality: A behavioral analysis.* London: Macmillan.

LUTZKER, J. R., CAMPBELL, R. V., & WATSON-PERCZEL, M. (1984). Using the case study method to treat several problems in a family indicated for child neglect. *Education and Treatment of Children, 7,* 315–333.

LUTZKER, J. R., & WHITE-BLACKBURN, G. (1979). The good productive game: Increasing work performance in a rehabilitation setting. *Journal of Applied Behavior Analysis, 12,* 488.

MACKEY v. PROCUNIER, 447 F. 2nd 877 (9th Cir. 1973).

MACKINTOSH, N. J. (1977). Stimulus control attentional factors. In W. K. Honig & J. E. R. Staddon (Eds.), *Handbook of operant behavior* (pp. 481–513). Englewood Cliffs, NJ: Prentice-Hall.

MACNEIL, J., & THOMAS, M. R. (1976). Treatment of obsessive-compulsive hairpulling (trichotillomania) by behavioral and cognitive contingency manipulation. *Journal of Behavior Therapy and Experimental Psychiatry, 7,* 391–392.

MADLE, R. A. (1978). Alternative residential placements. J. J. Neisworth & R. M. Smith (Eds.), *Retardation: Issues, assessment and intervention* (pp. 466–489). New York: McGraw-Hill.

MADSEN, C. H., JR., BECKER, W. C., & THOMAS, D. R. (1968). Rules, praise, and ignoring: Elements of elementary classroom control. *Journal of Applied Behavior Analysis, 1,* 139–150.

MADSEN. C. H., BECKER, W. C., THOMAS, D. R., KOSER, L., & PLAGER, E. (1968). An analysis of the reinforcing function of "sit down" commands. In R. K. Parker (Ed.), *Readings in educational psychology* (pp. 265–278). Boston: Allyn & Bacon.

MAHONEY, M. J. (1971). The self-management of covert behavior: A case study. *Behavior Therapy, 2,* 575–578.

MAHONEY, M. J. (1976). Terminal terminology. *Journal of Applied Behavior Analysis, 9,* 515–517.

MAHONEY, M. J. (1977). Some applied issues in self-monitoring. In J. D. Cone and R. P. Hawkins (Eds.), *Behavioral assessment: New directions in clinical psychology* (pp. 241–254). New York: Brunner/Mazel.

MALETZKY, B. M. (1974). Behavior recording as a treatment: A brief note. *Behavior Therapy, 5,* 107–111.

MALONEY, K. B., & HOPKINS, B. L. (1973). The modification of sentence structure and its relationship to subjective judgments of creativity in writing. *Journal of Applied Behavior Analysis, 6,* 425–433.

MALOTT, R. W. (1973). Contingency management and systems analysis: Summary (part 2). In *An introduction to behavior modification.* Kalamazoo, MI: Behaviordelia.

MALOTT, R. W. (1981). *Notes from a radical behaviorist.* Kalamazoo, MI: Author.

MALOTT, R. W. (1984). In search of human perfectibility: A behavioral approach to higher education. In W. L. Heward, T. E. Heron, D. S. Hill, & J. Trap-Porter (Eds.), *Focus on behavior analysis in education* (pp. 218–245). Columbus, OH: Charles E. Merrill.

MALOTT, R. W., GENERAL, D. A., & SNAPPER, V. B. (1973). *Issues in the analysis of behavior.* Kalamazoo, MI: Behaviordelia.

MALOTT, R. W., TILLEMA, M., & GLENN, S. (1978). *Behavior analysis and behavior modification: An introduction.* Kalamazoo, MI: Behaviordelia.

MALOTT, R. W., & WHALEY, R. (1983). *Psychology.* Holmes Beach, FL: Learning Publications.

MANN, R. A. (1972). The behavior-therapeutic use of contingency contracting to control an adult behavior problem: Weight control. *Journal of Applied Behavior Analysis, 5,* 99–109.

MANSDORF, I. J. (1977). Reinforcer isolation: An alternative to subject isolation in time-out from positive reinforcement. *Journal of Behavior Therapy and Experimental Psychiatry, 8,* 391–393.

MARHOLIN, D., II, LUISELLI, J. K., TOWNSEND, N. M. (1980). Overcorrection: An examination of its rationale and treatment effectiveness. In M. Hersen, R. Eisler, & M. Miller (Eds.), *Progress in behavior modification, 9,* 50–79. New York: Academic Press.

MARHOLIN, D., II, TOUCHETTE, P. E., & STEWART, R. M. (1979). Withdrawal of chronic chlorpromazine medication: An experimental analysis. *Journal of Applied Behavior Analysis, 12,* 159–171.

MARLOWE, R. H., MADSEN, C. H., JR., BOWEN, C. E., REARDON, R. C., & LOGUE, P. E. (1978). Severe classroom behavior problems: Teachers or counsellors. *Journal of Applied Behavior Analysis, 11,* 53–66.

MARSHALL, A. E., & HEWARD, W. L. (1979). Teaching self-management to incarcerated youth. *Behavioral Disorders, 4,* 215–226.

MARTIN, G., & PEAR, J. (1983). *Behavior modification: What it is and how to do it.* Englewood Cliffs, NJ: Prentice-Hall.

MARTIN, J. A. (1975). Generalizing the use of descriptive adjectives through modeling. *Journal of Applied Behavior Analysis, 8,* 203–209.

MARTIN, J., & MATSON, J. L. (1978). Eliminating the inappropriate vocalizations of a retarded adult by overcorrection. *Scandinavian Journal of Behavior Therapy, 7,* 203–209.

MARTIN, J., WELLER, S., & MATSON, J. (1977). Eliminating object transferring by a profoundly retarded female by overcorrection. *Psychological Reports, 40,* 779–782.

MASH, E. J., & TERDAL, L. G. (Eds.). (1976). *Behavior therapy assessment.* New York: Springer.

MASTELLONE, M. (1974). Aversion therapy: A new use of the old rubberband. *Journal of Behavior Therapy and Experimental Psychiatry, 5,* 311–312.

MATSON, J. L. (1980). Preventing home accidents: A training program. *Behavior Modification, 4,* 397–410.

MATSON, J. L., HORNE, A. M., OLLENDICK, D. G., & OLLENDICK, T. H. (1979). Overcorrection: A further evaluation of restitution and positive practice. *Journal of Behavior Therapy and Experimental Psychiatry, 10,* 295–298.

MATSON, J. L., & STEPHENS, R. M. (1977). Overcorrection of aggressive behavior in a chronic psychiatric patient. *Behavior Modification, 1,* 559–564.

MATSON, J. L., STEPHENS, R. M., & HORNE, A. M. (1978). Overcorrection and extinction-reinforcement as rapid methods of eliminating the disruptive behaviors of relatively normal children. *Behavioral Engineering, 4,* 89–94.

MATULICH, M. (1982). *Behavioral code: Interactions between doctor and patient.* Unpublished manuscript, Ohio State University, Columbus, OH.

MAY, J. G., RISLEY, T. R., TWARDOSZ, S., FRIEDMAN, P., BIJOU, S. W., WEXLER, D., BRICKER, W., COX, C., HOPKINS, B. L., KRASNER, L., LOVAAS, I. O., MCALLISTER, J., NASH, M. M., ROOS, P., WALSH, K., & WARREN, S. (1975). Guidelines for the use of behavioral procedures in state programs for retarded persons. *MR Research, 1,* 1–73.

MAYER, G. R., SULZER, B., & CODY, J. J. (1968). The use of punishment in modifying student behavior. *Journal of Special Education, 2,* 323–328.

MAYHEW, G. L., & ANDERSON, J. (1980). Delayed and immediate reinforcement: Retarded adolescents in an educational setting. *Behavior Modification, 4,* 527–545.

MAYHEW, G., & HARRIS, F. (1979). Decreasing self-injurious behavior. *Behavior Modification, 3,* 322–326.

MCALLISTER, L. W., STACHOWIAK, J. G., BAER, D. M., & CONDERMAN, L. (1969). The application of operant conditioning techniques in a secondary school classroom. *Journal of Applied Behavior Analysis, 2,* 277–285.

MCCAIN, L. J., & MCCLEARY, R. (1979). The statistical analysis of the simple interrupted time series quasi-experiment. In T. D. Cook & D. T. Campbell (Eds.), *Quasi-experimentation: Design and analysis issues for field settings.* Chicago: Rand McNally.

MCCUE, L. D. (1981). *Band director's observation code.* Unpublished manuscript, Ohio State University, Columbus, OH.

MCCULLOUGH, J. P., CORNELL, J. E., MCDANIEL, M. H. & MUELLER, R. K. (1974). Utilization of the simultaneous treatment design to improve student behavior in a first-grade classroom. *Journal of Consulting and Clinical Psychology, 42,* 288–292.

MCFALL, R. M. (1977). Parameters of self-monitoring. In R. B. Stuart (Ed.), *Behavioral self-management* (pp. 196–214). New York: Bruner/Mazel.

MCGEE, G. G., KRANTZ, P. J., MASON, D., & MCCLANNAHAN, L. E. (1983). A modified incidental-teaching procedure for autistic youth: Acquisition and generalization of receptive object labels. *Journal of Applied Behavior Analysis, 16,* 329-338.

MCGEE, G. G., KRANTZ, P. J., & MCCLANNAHAN, L. E. (1985). The facilitative effects of incidental teaching on preposition use by autistic children. *Journal of Applied Behavior Analysis, 18,* 17-31.

MCKENZIE, T. L., & RUSHALL, B. S. (1980). Controlling inappropriate behaviors in a competitive swimming environment. *Education and Treatment of Children, 3,* 205-215.

MCLAUGHLIN, T. F. (1981). The effects of a classroom token economy on math performance in an intermediate grade school class. *Education and Treatment of Children, 4,* 139-147.

MCLAUGHLIN, T., & MALABY, J. (1972). Reducing and measuring inappropriate verbalizations in a token classroom. *Journal of Applied Behavior Analysis, 5,* 329-333.

MCLOUGHLIN, J. A., & LEWIS, R. B. (1986). *Assessing special students: Strategies and procedures* (2nd ed.). Columbus, OH: Charles E. Merrill.

MCNEISH, J. L. (1985). *Effects of self-correction on the maintenance and generalization of spelling words with learning disabled students.* Unpublished master's thesis, Ohio State University, Columbus, OH.

MEASEL, C. J., & ALFIERI, P. A. (1976). Treatment of self-injurious behavior by a combination of reinforcement for incompatible behavior and overcorrection. *American Journal of Mental Deficiency, 81,* 147-153.

MEICHENBAUM, D., & GOODMAN, J. (1971). The developmental control of operant motor responding by verbal operants. *Journal of Experimental Child Psychology, 7,* 553-565.

MELIN, L., & GOTESTAM, K. G. (1981). The effects of rearranging ward routines on communication and eating behavior of psycho-geriatric patients. *Journal of Applied Behavior Analysis, 14,* 47-51.

MERBAUM, M. (1973). The modification of self-destructive behavior by a mother-therapist using aversive stimulation. *Behavior Therapy, 4,* 442-447.

MERCATORIS, M., & CRAIGHEAD, W. E. (1974). Effects of nonparticipant observation on teacher and pupil classroom behavior. *Journal of Educational Psychology, 66,* 512-519.

MEYER, V., & CRISP, A. H. (1964). Aversion therapy in two cases of obesity. *Behavior Research and Therapy, 2,* 143.

MEYERS, C. H. (1970). *Handbook of basic graphs: A modern approach.* Belmont, CA: Dickenson.

MEYERS, D. V. (1975). Extinction, DRO, and response-cost for eliminating self-injurious behavior: A case study. *Behavior Research and Therapy, 13,* 189-191.

MICHAEL, J. L. (1970). Principles of effective use. In R. Ulrich, T. Stachnik, & J. Mabry (Eds.), *Control of human behavior* (Vol. 2, pp. 28-35). Glenview, IL: Scott, Foresman.

MICHAEL, J. (1974). Statistical inference for individual organism research: Mixed blessing or curse? *Journal of Applied Behavior Analysis, 7,* 647-653.

MICHAEL, J. (1975). Positive and negative reinforcement, a distinction that is no longer necessary; or a better way to talk about bad things. *Behaviorism, 3,* 33-38.

MICHAEL, J. (1980). The flight from behavior analysis. *The Behavior Analyst, 3,* 1-21.

MICHAEL, J. (1982). Distinguishing between discriminative and motivational functions of stimuli. *Journal of the Experimental Analysis of Behavior, 37,* 149-155.

MILLENSON, J. R. (1967). *Principles of behavioral analysis.* New York: Macmillan.

MILLENSON, J. R., & LESLIE, J. C. (1979). *Principles of behavioral analysis* (2nd ed.). New York: Macmillan.

MILLER, L. K. (1980). *Principles of everyday behavior analysis* (2nd ed.). Monterey, CA: Brooks/Cole.

MILLER, P. M. (1972). The use of behavioral contracting in the treatment of alcoholism: A case report. *Behavior Therapy, 3,* 593-596.

MILLER, P. M., HERSEN, M., & EISLER, R. M. (1974). Relative effectiveness of instructions, agreements, and reinforcement in behavioral contracts with alcoholics. *Journal of Abnormal Psychology, 83,* 548-553.

MILTENBERGER, R. G., & FUQUA, R. W. (1981). Overcorrection: A review and critical analysis. *The Behavior Analyst, 4,* 123-141.

MITCHELL, J. B. (Ed.). (1985). *The ninth mental measurements yearbook.* Lincoln: University of Nebraska Press.

MOORE, J. (1980). On behaviorism and private events. *Psychological Record, 30,* 459-475.

MOORE, J. (1984). On behaviorism, knowledge, and causal explanation. *Psychological Record, 34,* 73–97.

MOORE, J. (1985). Some historical and conceptual relations among logical positivism, operationism, and behaviorism. *The Behavior Analyst, 8,* 53–63.

MOORE, R., & GOLDIAMOND, I. (1964). Errorless establishment of visual discrimination using fading procedures. *Journal of the Experimental Analysis of Behavior, 7,* 269–272.

MORALES v. TURMAN, 364 F. supp. 166 (E. D. Tx. 1973).

MORGAN, Q. E. (1978) *Comparison of two "Good Behavior Game" group contingencies on the spelling accuracy of fourth-grade students.* Unpublished master's thesis, Ohio State University, Columbus, OH.

MORGANSTERN, K. P. (1976). Behavioral interviewing: The initial stage of assessment. In M. Hersen & A. S. Belleck (Eds.), *Behavioral assessment: A practical handbook.* New York: Pergamon Press.

MORRIS, R. J. (1976). *Behavior modification with children: A systematic guide.* Cambridge, MA: Winthrop.

MORRIS, R. J. (1985). *Behavior modification with exceptional children: Principles and practices.* Glenview, IL: Scott, Foresman.

MORSE, W. H., & KELLEHER, R. T. (1977). Determinants of reinforcement and punishment. In W. K. Honig & J. E. R. Staddon (Eds.), *Handbook of operant behavior* (pp. 174–200). Englewood Cliffs, NJ: Prentice-Hall.

MOWRER, O. H. (1960). *Learning theory and behavior.* New York: Wiley.

MOYER, J. R., & DARDIG, J. C. (1978). Practical task analysis for special educators. *Teaching Exceptional Children, 11,* 1–16.

MURPHY, H. A., HUTCHISON, J. M., & BAILEY, J. S. (1983). Behavioral school psychology goes outdoors: The effect of organized games on playground aggression. *Journal of Applied Behavior Analysis, 16,* 29–35.

MURPHY, R. J., RUPRECHT, M. J., BAGGIO, P., & NUNES, D. L. (1979). The use of mild punishment in combination with reinforcement of alternate behaviors to reduce the self-injurious behavior of a profoundly retarded individual. *AAESPH Review, 4,* 187–195.

MYERSON, J., & HALE, S. (1984). Practical implication of the matching law. *Journal of Applied Behavior Analysis, 17,* 367–380.

MYERSON, W. A., & HAYES, S. C. (1977). Controlling the clinician for the client's benefit. In J. E. Krapfl & E. A. Vargas (Eds.), *Behavior and ethics.* Kalamazoo, MI: Behaviordelia.

NEEF, N. A., IWATA, B. A., & PAGE, T. J. (1980). The effects of interspersal training versus high density reinforcement on spelling acquisition and retention. *Journal of Applied Behavior Analysis, 13,* 153–158.

NEFF, S. (1982). *Observation code for in-seat behaviors.* Unpublished manuscript, Ohio State University, Columbus, OH.

NELSON, C. M., & RUTHERFORD, R. B. (1983). Timeout revisited: Guidelines for its use in special education. *Exceptional Education Quarterly, 3,* 56–67.

NELSON, G. L., & CONE, J. D. (1979). Multiple-baseline analysis of a token economy for psychiatric inpatients. *Journal of Applied Behavior Analysis, 12,* 255–271.

NELSON, R. O. (1977). Methodological issues in assessment via self-monitoring. In J. D. Cone & R. P. Hawkins (Eds.), *Behavioral assessment: New directions in clinical psychology* (pp. 217–240). New York: Bruner/Mazel.

NELSON, R. O., & HAYES, S. C. (1979). The nature of behavioral assessment: A commentary. *Journal of Applied Behavior Analysis, 12,* 491–500.

NEW YORK ASSOCIATION FOR RETARDED CITIZENS v. CAREY, No. 72-C-356/357 (E.D. N.Y. April 30, 1975). Approved 393 F. Supp. 715 (E.D. N.Y. 1975).

NOLAN, J. D. (1968). Self-control procedures in the modification of smoking behavior. *Journal of Consulting and Clinical Psychology, 32,* 92–93.

NORMAN, J. E. (1977). *The effects of programmed instructional materials for parent training in contingency contracting.* Unpublished doctoral dissertation, Ohio State University, Columbus, OH.

O'BANION, D. R., & WHALEY, D. L. (1981). *Behavior contracting: Arranging contingencies of reinforcement.* New York: Springer.

O'BRIEN, F. (1968). Sequential contrast effects with human subjects. *Journal of the Experimental Analysis of Behavior, 11,* 537–542.

O'BRIEN, F., & AZRIN, N. H. (1972). Developing proper mealtime behaviors of the institutionalized retarded. *Journal of Applied Behavior Analysis, 5,* 389–399.

O'BRIEN, T. P., RINER, L. S., & BUDD, K. S. (1983). The effects of a child's self-evaluation program on compliance with parental instructions in the home. *Journal of Applied Behavior Analysis, 16,* 69–79.

ODOM, S. L., HOYSON, M., JAMIESON, B., & STRAIN, P. S. (1985). Increasing handicapped preschoolers' peer social interactions: Cross-setting and component analysis. *Journal of Applied Behavior Analysis, 18,* 3–16.

O'LEARY, K. D. (1977). Teaching self-management skills to children. In D. Upper (Ed.), *Perspectives in behavior therapy.* Kalamazoo, MI: Behaviordelia.

O'LEARY, K. D., & DRABMAN, R. (1971). Token reinforcement programs in the classroom: A review. *Psychological Bulletin, 75,* 379–398.

O'LEARY, K. D., KAUFMAN, K. F., KASS, R. E., & DRABMAN, R. S. (1970). The effects of loud and soft reprimands on the behavior of disruptive students. *Exceptional Children, 37,* 145–155.

O'LEARY, K. D., & O'LEARY, S. G. (1977). *Classroom management* (2nd ed.). New York: Pergamon Press.

O'LEARY, S. G., & DUBEY, D. R. (1979). Applications of self-control procedures by children: A review. *Journal of Applied Behavior Analysis, 12,* 449–465.

O'LEARY, S. G., & O'LEARY, K. D. (1976). Behavior modification in the school. In H. Leitenberg (Ed.), *Handbook of behavior modification and behavior therapy* (pp. 475–515). Englewood Cliffs, NJ: Prentice-Hall.

OLLENDICK, T. H., MATSON, J. L., ESVELT-DAW-SON, K., & SHAPIRO, E. S. (1980). Increasing spelling achievement: An analysis of treatment procedures utilizing an alternating treatments design. *Journal of Applied Behavior Analysis, 13,* 645–654.

OLLENDICK, T. H., MATSON, J. L., & MARTIN, J. E. (1978). Effectiveness of hand correction for topographically similar and dissimilar self-stimulatory behavior. *Journal of Experimental Child Psychology, 25,* 396–403.

ORLANSKY, M. D. (1979). Sam's day: A simulated observation of a severely handicapped child's educational program. *American Association for the Education of the Severely/Profoundly Handicapped Review, 4,* 251–258.

PACKARD, R. G. (1970). The control of "classroom attention": A group contingency for complex behavior. *Journal of Applied Behavior Analysis, 3,* 13–28.

PANYAN, M. (1980). *How to use shaping.* Austin, TX: Pro-Ed.

PANYAN, M., BOOZER, H., & MORRIS, N. (1970). Feedback to attendants as a reinforcer for applying operant techniques. *Journal of Applied Behavior Analysis, 3,* 1–4.

PANYAN, M. C, & HALL, R. V. (1978). Effects of serial versus concurrent task sequencing on acquisition, maintenance, and generalization. *Journal of Applied Behavior Analysis, 11,* 67–74.

PARKER, L. H., CATALDO, M. F., BOURLAND, G., EMURIAN, C. S., CORBIN, R. J., & PAGE, J. M. (1984). Operant treatment of orofacial dysfunction in neuromuscular disorders. *Journal of Applied Behavior Analysis, 17,* 413–427.

PARSONSON, B. S., & BAER, D. M. (1978). The analysis and presentation of graphic data. In T. R. Kratochwill (Ed.), *Single subject research: Strategies for evaluating change* (pp. 101–165). New York: Academic Press.

PATTERSON, G. R., JONES, R., WHITTIER, J., & WRIGHT, M. A. (1965). A behavior modification technique for the hyperactive child. *Behavior Research and Therapy, 2,* 217–226.

PAVLOV, I. P. (1927). *Conditioned reflexes: An investigation of the physiological activity of the cerebral cortex* (W. H. Grant, Trans.). London: Oxford University Press.

PAZULINEC, R., MEYERROSE, M., & SAJWAJ, T. (1983). Punishment via response cost. In S. Axelrod and J. Apsche (Eds.), *The effects of punishment on human behavior* (pp. 71–86). New York: Academic Press.

PENNYPACKER, H. S. (1981). On behavioral analysis. *The Behavior Analyst, 4,* 159–161.

PENNYPACKER, H. S., KOENIG, C. H., & LINDSLEY, O. R. (1972). *Handbook of the Standard Behavior Chart.* Kansas City, MO: Precision Media.

PETERS, R., & DAVIES, K. (1981). Effects of self-instructional training on cognitive impulsivity of mentally retarded adolescents. *American Journal of Mental Deficiency, 85,* 377–382.

PETERSON, D. R. (1968). *The clinical study of social behavior.* New York: Appleton-Century-Crofts.

PETERSON, L., HOMER, A. L., & WONDERLICH, S. A. (1982). The integrity of independent variables in behavior analysis. *Journal of Applied Behavior Analysis, 15,* 477–492.

PETERSON, R. F. (1968). Some experiments on the organization of a class of imitative behavior. *Journal of Applied Behavior Analysis, 1,* 225–235.

PETERSON, R. F., & PETERSON, L. R. (1968). The use of positive reinforcement in the control of self-destructive behavior in a retarded boy. *Journal of Experimental Child Psychology, 6,* 351–360.

PHILLIPS, E. L. (1968). Achievement Place: Token reinforcement procedures in a home-style rehabilitation setting for pre-delinquent boys. *Journal of Applied Behavior Analysis, 1,* 213–223.

PHILLIPS, E. L., PHILLIPS. E. A., FIXSEN, D. L., & WOLF, M. M. (1971). Achievement Place: Modification of the behaviors of pre-delinquent boys within a token economy. *Journal of Applied Behavior Analysis, 4,* 45–59.

PIERCE, C. H., & RISLEY, T. R. (1974). Recreation as a reinforcer: Increasing membership and decreasing disruptions in an urban recreation center. *Journal of Applied Behavior Analysis, 7(3),* 403–411.

PIERCE, W. D., & EPLING, W. F. (1980). What happened to analysis in applied behavior analysis? *The Behavior Analyst, 3,* 1–9.

PIERREL, R., & SHERMAN, J. G. (1963). Barnabus, the rat with college training. *Brown Alumni Newsletter,* 8–12.

PINKSTON, E. M., REESE, N. M., LEBLANC, J. M., & BAER, D. M. (1973). Independent control of a preschool child's aggression and peer interaction by contingent teacher attention. *Journal of Applied Behavior Analysis, 6,* 115–124.

PLUMMER, S., BAER, D. M., & LEBLANC, J. M. (1977). Functional consideration in the use of procedural timeout and an effective alternative. *Journal of Applied Behavior Analysis, 10,* 689–705.

POCHE, C., BROUWER, R., & SWEARINGEN, M. (1981). Teaching self-protection to young children. *Journal of Applied Behavior Analysis, 14,* 169–176.

POLING, A., MILLER, K., NELSON, N., & RYAN, C. (1978). Reduction of undesired classroom behavior by systematically reinforcing the absence of such behavior. *Education and Treatment of Children, 1,* 35–41.

POLING, A., & RYAN, C. (1982). Differential-reinforcement-of-other-behavior schedules: Therapeutic applications. *Behavior Modification, 6,* 3–21.

POLLOWAY, E., & POLLOWAY, C. (1979). Auctions: Vitalizing the token economy. *Journal for Special Educators, 15,* 121–123.

POPPEN, R. (1982). The fixed-interval scallop in human affairs. *The Behavior Analyst, 5,* 127–136.

PORTERFIELD, J. K., HERBERT-JACKSON, E., & RISLEY, T. R. (1976). Contingent observation: An effective and acceptable procedure for reducing disruptive behavior of young children in a group setting. *Journal of Applied Behavior Analysis, 9,* 55–64.

POWELL, J. R., & AZRIN, N. (1968). The effects of shock as a punisher for cigarette smoking. *Journal of Applied Behavior Analysis, 1,* 63–71.

POWELL, J., MARTINDALE, A., & KULP, S. (1975). An evaluation of time-sample measures of behavior. *Journal of Applied Behavior Analysis, 8,* 463–469.

POWELL, J., MARTINDALE, B., KULP, S., MARTINDALE, A., & BAUMAN, R. (1977). Taking a closer look: Time sampling and measurement error. *Journal of Applied Behavior Analysis, 10,* 325–332.

POWELL, T. H., & POWELL, I. Q. (1982). The use and abuse of using the timeout procedure for disruptive pupils. *The Pointer, 26,* 18–22.

PREMACK, D. (1959). Toward empirical behavioral laws: I. Positive reinforcement. *Psychological Review, 66,* 219–233.

QUATTROCHI-TUBIN, S., & JASON, L. A. (1980). Enhancing social interactions and activity among the elderly through stimulus control. *Journal of Applied Behavior Analysis, 13,* 159–163.

RACHLIN, H. (1977). *Introduction to modern behaviorism* (2nd ed.). San Francisco: W. H. Freeman.

RAMEY, G. (1974). Use of electric shock in the classroom: The remediation of self-abusive behavior of a retarded child. *Behavioral Engineering, 1(2),* 4–9.

RAPPORT, M. D., MURPHY, H. A., & BAILEY, J. S. (1982). Ritalin vs. response cost in the control of hyperactive children: A within-subject comparison. *Journal of Applied Behavior Analysis, 15,* 205–216.

RATHUS, S. A. (1973). A 30-item schedule for assessing assertive behavior. *Behavior Therapy, 4,* 398–406.

REDD, W. H., & BIRNBRAUER, J. S. (1969). Adults as discriminative stimuli for different reinforcement contingencies with retarded children. *Journal of Experimental Child Psychology, 2,* 249–254.

REESE, D. G., & WOOLFENDEN, R. M. (1973). *Behavioral analysis of everyday life: A program for the generalization of behavioral concepts.* Kalamzaoo, MI: Behaviordelia.

REESE, E. P. (1966). *The analysis of human operant behavior.* Dubuque, IA: William C. Brown.

REID, J. B. (1970). Reliability assessment of observation data: A possible methodological problem. *Child Development, 41,* 1143–1150.

REISINGER, J. J. (1972). The treatment of "anxiety-depression" via positive reinforcement and response cost. *Journal of Applied Behavior Analysis, 5,* 125–130.

REKERS, G. A., & LOVAAS, O. I. (1974). Behavioral treatment of deviant sex-role behaviors in a male child. *Journal of Applied Behavior Analysis, 7,* 173–190.

REPP, A. C., & BARTON, L. E. (1980). Naturalistic observations of institutionalized retarded persons: A comparison of licensure decisions and behavioral observations. *Journal of Applied Behavior Analysis, 13,* 333–341.

REPP, A. C., BARTON, L. E., & BRULLE, A. R. (1983). A comparison of two procedures for programming the differential reinforcement of other behaviors. *Journal of Applied Behavior Analysis, 16,* 435–445.

REPP, A. C., & DEITZ, D. E. D. (1979). Reinforcement-based reductive procedures: Training and monitoring performance of institutional staff. *Mental Retardation, 17,* 221–226.

REPP, A. C., & DEITZ, S. M. (1974). Reducing aggressive and self-injurious behavior of institutionalized retarded children through reinforcement of other behaviors. *Journal of Applied Behavior Analysis, 7,* 313–325.

REPP, A. C., DEITZ, S. M., & DEITZ, D. E. D. (1976). Reducing inappropriate behaviors in classroom and in individual sessions through DRO schedules of reinforcement. *Mental Retardation, 14,* 11–15.

REPP, A. C., DEITZ, S. M., & SPEIR, N. C. (1975). Reducing stereotypic responding of retarded persons through the differential reinforcement of other behaviors. *American Journal of Mental Deficiency, 80,* 51–56.

REYNOLDS, G. S. (1961). Behavioral contrast. *Journal of the Experimental Analysis of Behavior, 4,* 57–71.

REYNOLDS, G. S. (1968). *A primer of operant conditioning.* Glenview, IL: Scott, Foresman.

REYNOLDS, N. J., & RISLEY, T. R. (1968). The role of social and material reinforcers in increasing talking of a disadvantaged preschool child. *Journal of Applied Behavior Analysis, 1,* 253–262.

RHODE, G., MORGAN, D. P., & YOUNG, K. R. (1983). Generalization and maintenance of treatment gains of behaviorally handicapped students from resource rooms to regular classrooms using self-evaluation procedures. *Journal of Applied Behavior Analysis, 16,* 171–188.

RILLING, M. (1977). Stimulus control and inhibitory processes. In W. K. Honig & J. E. R. Staddon (Eds.), *Handbook of operant behavior* (pp. 432–480). Englewood Cliffs, NJ: Prentice-Hall.

RINCOVER, A. (1978). Sensory extinction: A procedure for eliminating self-stimulatory behavior in psychotic children. *Journal of Abnormal Child Psychology, 6,* 299–310.

RINCOVER, A. (1981). *How to use sensory extinction.* Austin, TX: Pro-Ed.

RINCOVER, A., COOK, R., PEOPLES, A., & PACKARD, D. (1979). Sensory extinction and sensory reinforcement principles for programming multiple adaptive behavior change. *Journal of Applied Behavior Analysis, 12,* 221–233.

RINCOVER, A., & KOEGEL, R. L. (1975). Setting generality and stimulus control in autistic children. *Journal of Applied Behavior Analysis, 8,* 235–246.

RIORDAN, M. M., IWATA, B. A., FINNEY, J. W., WOHL, M. K., & STANLEY, A. E. (1984). Behavioral assessment and treatment of chronic food refusal in handicapped children. *Journal of Applied Behavior Analysis, 17,* 327–341.

RISLEY, T. R. (1968). The effects and side effects of punishing the autistic behaviors of a deviant child. *Journal of Applied Behavior Analysis, 1,* 21–34.

RISLEY, T. R. (1969, April). *Behavior modification: An experimental-therapeutic endeavor.* Paper presented at the Banff International Conference on Behavior Modification, Banff, Alberta, Canada.

RISLEY, T. R., & HART, B. (1968). Developing correspondence between the non-verbal and verbal behavior of preschool children. *Journal of Applied Behavior Analysis, 1,* 267–281.

RISLEY, T. R., & REYNOLDS, N. J. (1970). Emphasis as a prompt for verbal imitation. *Journal of Applied Behavior Analysis, 3,* 221–222.

RITSCHL, C., MONGRELLA, J., & PRESBIE, R. L. (1972). Group time out from rock and roll music and out-of-seat behavior of handicapped children while riding a school bus. *Psychological Reports, 31,* 967–973.

ROBIN, A. L., ARMEL, S., & O'LEARY, K. D. (1975). The effects of self-instruction on writing deficiencies. *Behavior Therapy, 6,* 178–187.

ROBIN, A., SCHNEIDER, M., & DOLNICK, M., (1976). The turtle technique: An extended case study of self-control in the classroom. *Psychology in the Schools, 13,* 449–453.

ROBINSON, C. C., & ROBINSON, J. H. (1983). Sensorimotor functions and cognitive development. In M. Snell (Ed.), *Systematic instruction of the moderately and severely handicapped* (2nd ed., pp. 227–266). Columbus, OH: Charles E. Merrill.

ROBINSON, P. W., NEWBY, T. J., & GANZELL, S. L. (1981). A token system for a class of under-achieving hyperactive children. *Journal of Applied Behavior Analysis, 14,* 307–315.

ROGERS-WARREN, A. K. (1984). Ecobehavioral analysis. *Education and Treatment of Children, 7,* 283–303.

ROGERS-WARREN, A., & WARREN, S. F. (Eds.). (1977). *Ecological perspectives in behavior analysis.* Austin, TX: Pro-Ed.

ROLIDER, A., & VAN HOUTEN, R. (1984a). Training parents to use extinction to eliminate nighttime crying by gradually increasing the criteria for ignoring crying. *Education and Treatment of Children, 7,* 119–124.

ROLIDER, A., & VAN HOUTEN, R. (1984b). The effects of DRO alone and DRO plus reprimands on the undesirable behavior of three children in home settings. *Education and Treatment of Children, 7,* 17–31.

ROLIDER, A., & VAN HOUTEN, R. (1985). Movement suppression time-out for undesirable behavior in psychotic and severely developmentally delayed children. *Journal of Applied Behavior Analysis, 18,* 275–288.

ROLLINGS, J. P., BAUMEISTER, A. A., & BAUMEISTER, A. A. (1977). The use of overcorrection procedures to eliminate the stereotyped behaviors of retarded individuals: An analysis of collateral behaviors and generalization of suppressive effects. *Behavior Modification, 1*(1), 29–46.

ROMANCZYK, R. G., KENT, R. M., DIAMENT, C., & O'LEARY, K. D. (1973). Measuring the reliability of observational data: A reactive process. *Journal of Applied Behavior Analysis, 6,* 175–184.

ROSE, T. L. (1978). The functional relationship between artificial food colors and hyperactivity. *Journal of Applied Behavior Analysis, 11,* 439–446.

ROSE, T. L. (1983). A survey of corporal punishment of mildly handicapped students. *Exceptional Education Quarterly, 3,* 9–19.

ROSENBAUM, M. S., & DRABMAN, R. S. (1979). Self-control training in the classroom: A critical review. *Journal of Applied Behavior Analysis, 12,* 467–485.

ROTHOLZ, D. A., & LUCE, S. C. (1983). Alternative reinforcement strategies for the reduction of self-stimulatory behavior in autistic youth. *Education and Treatment of Children, 6,* 363–377.

ROZENSKY, R. H. (1974). The effect of timing of self-monitoring behavior on reducing cigarette consumption. *Journal of Consulting and Clinical Psychology, 5,* 301–307.

RUSCH, F. R., & KAZDIN, A. E. (1981). Toward a methodology of withdrawal designs for the assessment of response maintenance. *Journal of Applied Behavior Analysis, 14,* 131–140.

SAGOTSKY, G., PATTERSON, C. J., & LEPPER, M. R. (1978). Training children's self-control: A field experiment in self-monitoring and goal setting in the classroom. *Journal of Experimental Child Psychology, 25,* 242–253.

SAIGH, P. A., & UMAR, A. M. (1983). The effects of a good behavior game on the disruptive behavior of Sudanese elementary school students. *Journal of Applied Behavior Analysis, 16,* 339–344.

SAJWAJ, T. (1968). *Some parameters of point loss.* Unpublished doctoral dissertation, University of Kansas, Lawrence, KS.

SAJWAJ, T., LIBET, J., & AGRAS, S. (1974). Lemon juice therapy: The control of life-threatening rumination in a six-month-old infant. *Journal of Applied Behavior Analysis, 7*(4), 557–563.

SALEND, S. J. (1984a). Therapy outcome research: Threats to treatment integrity. *Behavior Modification, 8,* 211–222.

SALEND, S. J. (1984b). Integrity of treatment in special education research. *Mental Retardation, 22,* 309–315.

SANDERS, M. R., & GLENN, T. (1981). Training parents in behavioral self-management: An analysis of generalization and management. *Journal of Applied Behavior Analysis, 14,* 223–237.

SANDERS-FISHER, R. W., POOLE, A. D., & DUNN, J. (1980). An empirical method for determining an appropriate interval length for recording behavior. *Journal of Applied Behavior Analysis, 13,* 493–500.

SANTOGROSSI, D. A., O'LEARY, K. D., ROMANCZYK, R. G., & KAUFMAN, K. F. (1973). Self-evaluation by adolescents in a psychiatric hospital school token program. *Journal of Applied Behavior Analysis, 6,* 277–287.

SAPON-SHEVIN, M. (1979). *The ethics of group contingencies.* Paper presented at the Annual Meeting of the Association for Behavior Analysis, Dearborn, MI.

SCHLEIEN, S. J., WEYMAN, P., & KIERNAN, J. (1981). Teaching leisure skills to severely handicapped adults: An age-appropriate darts game. *Journal of Applied Behavior Analysis, 14,* 513-519.

SCHROEDER, G. L., & BAER, D. M. (1972). Effects of concurrent and serial training on generalized vocal imitation in retarded children. *Developmental Psychology, 6,* 293-301.

SCHWARTZ, B., & GAMZU, E. (1977). Pavlovian control of operant behavior. In W. K. Honig & J. E. R. Staddon (Eds.), *Handbook of operant behavior* (pp. 53-97). Englewood Cliffs, NJ: Prentice-Hall.

SCHWARZ, M. L., & HAWKINS, R. P. (1970). Application of delayed reinforcement procedures to the behavior of an elementary school child. *Journal of Applied Behavior Analysis, 3,* 85-96.

SEWELL, E., MCCOY, J. F., & SEWELL, W. R. (1973). Modification of an antagonistic social behavior using positive reinforcement for other behavior. *Psychological Record, 23,* 499-504.

SEYMOUR, F. W., & STOKES, T. F. (1976). Self-recording in training girls to increase work rate and evoke staff praise in an institution for offenders. *Journal of Applied Behavior Analysis, 9,* 41-54.

SHAFTO, F., & SULZBACHER, S. (1977). Comparing treatment tactics with a hyperactive preschool child: Stimulant medication and programmed teacher intervention. *Journal of Applied Behavior Analysis, 10,* 13-20.

SHAPIRO, E. S., BARRETT, R. P., & OLLENDICK, T. H. (1980). A comparison of physical restraint and positive practice overcorrection in treating stereotypic behavior. *Behavior Therapy, 11,* 227-233.

SHERMAN, J. A. (1971). Imitation and language development. In H. W. Reese (Ed.), *Advances in child development and behavior* (Vol. 6, pp. 239-272). New York: Academic Press.

SHINE, L. C., II, & BOWER, S. M. (1971). A one-way analysis of variance for single-subject designs. *Educational and Psychological Measurement, 31,* 105-113.

SHIPP, B. (1979). *A code for recording bus behavior.* Unpublished manuscript, Ohio State University, Columbus, OH.

SHREWSBERRY, R. D. (1977). *Assignment completion in group parent training.* Unpublished doctoral dissertation, Ohio State University, Columbus, OH.

SIDMAN, M. (1960). *Tactics of scientific research.* New York: Basic Books.

SIDMAN, M., & STODDARD, L. T. (1966). Programming perception and learning for retarded children. In N. R. Ellis (Ed.), *International review of research in mental retardation.* New York: Academic Press.

SIEGEL, G. M., LENSKE, J., & BROEN, P. (1969). Suppression of normal speech disfluencies through response cost. *Journal of Applied Behavior Analysis, 2,* 265-276.

SIMPSON, M. J. A., & SIMPSON, A. E. (1977). One-zero and scan method for sampling behavior. *Animal Behavior, 25,* 726-731.

SINDELAR, P. T., HONSAKER, M. S., & JENKINS, J. R. (1982). Response cost and reinforcement contingencies of managing the behavior of distractible children in tutorial settings. *Learning Disability Quarterly, 5,* 3-13.

SINGH, J., & SINGH. N. N. (1985). Comparison of word-supply and word-analysis error-correction procedures on oral reading by mentally retarded children. *American Journal of Mental Deficiency, 90,* 64-70.

SINGH, N. N., DAWSON, M. J., & MANNING, P. (1981). Effects of spaced responding DRL on the stereotyped behavior of profoundly retarded persons. *Journal of Applied Behavior Analysis, 14,* 521-526.

SINGH, N. N., & KATZ, R. C. (1985). On the modification of acceptability ratings for alternative child treatments. *Behavior Modification, 9,* 375-386.

SINGH, N. N., & SINGH, J. (1984). Antecedent control of oral reading errors and self-corrections by mentally retarded children. *Journal of Applied Behavior Analysis, 17,* 111-119.

SINGH, N. N., & WINTON, A. S. (1985). Controlling pica by components of an overcorrection procedure. *American Journal of Mental Deficiency, 90,* 40-45.

SISSON, L. A., & BARRETT, R. P. (1984). An alternating treatments comparison of oral and total communication training with minimally verbal retarded children. *Journal of Applied Behavior Analysis, 17,* 559-566.

SKINNER, B. F. (1938). *The behavior of organisms: An experimental analysis.* New York: Appleton-Century.

SKINNER, B. F. (1948). *Walden two*. New York: Macmillan.

SKINNER, B. F. (1953). *Science and human behavior*. New York: Macmillan.

SKINNER, B. F. (1956). A case history in scientific method. *American Psychologist, 11*, 221–233.

SKINNER, B. F. (1957). *Verbal behavior*. New York: Appleton-Century-Crofts.

SKINNER, B. F. (1963). Behaviorism at fifty. *Science, 140*, 951–958.

SKINNER, B. F. (1966). Operant behavior. In W. K. Honig (Ed.), *Operant behavior: Areas of research and application* (pp. 12–32). New York: Appleton-Century-Crofts.

SKINNER, B. F. (1968). *Technology of teaching*. New York: Meredith.

SKINNER, B. F. (1969). *Contingencies of reinforcement: A theoretical analysis*. New York: Appleton-Century-Crofts.

SKINNER, B. F. (1971). *Beyond freedom and dignity*. New York: Knopf.

SKINNER, B. F. (1974). *About behaviorism*. New York: Knopf.

SKINNER, B. F. (1978). *Reflections on behaviorism and society*. Englewood Cliffs, NJ: Prentice-Hall.

SKINNER, B. F. (1979). *The shaping of a behaviorist: Part two of an autobiography*. New York: Knopf.

SKINNER, B. F. (1981a). How to discover what you have to say—A talk to students. *The Behavior Analyst, 4*, 1–7.

SKINNER, B. F. (1981b). Selection by consequences. *Science, 213*, 501–504.

SKINNER, B. F. (1983a). Can the experimental analysis of behavior rescue psychology? *The Behavior Analyst, 6*, 9–17.

SKINNER, B. F. (1983b). Intellectual self-management in old age. *American Psychologist, 38*, 239–244.

SKINNER, B. F. (1984). *A matter of consequences: Part three of an autobiography*. Washington Square, NY: New York University Press.

SKINNER, M. E. (1978). Using fading to remediate number reversals. *The Directive Teacher, 1*(a), 10, 15.

SKRTIC, T. M., & SEPLER, H. J. (1982). Simplifying continuous monitoring of multiple-response/multiple-subject classroom interactions. *Journal of Applied Behavior Analysis, 15*, 183–187.

SMITH, D. D., SMITH, J. O., & EDGAR, E. B. (1976). A prototypic model for developing instructional materials for the severely handicapped. In N. G. Haring & L. J. Brown (Eds.), *Teaching the severely handicapped* (Vol. 1, pp. 155–176). New York: Gruen & Stratton.

SMITH, L. K. C., & FOWLER, S. A. (1984). Positive peer pressure: The effects of peer monitoring on children's disruptive behavior. *Journal of Applied Behavior Analysis, 17*, 213–227.

SNELL, M. E. (1983a). Implementing and monitoring the IEP: Intervention strategies. In M. E. Snell (Ed.), *Systematic instruction of the moderately and severely handicapped* (2nd ed., pp. 113–145). Columbus, OH: Charles E. Merrill.

SNELL, M. E. (1983b). Self-care skills. In M. E. Snell (Ed.), *Systematic instruction of the moderately and severely handicapped* (2nd ed., pp. 358–409). Columbus, OH: Charles E. Merrill.

SNELL, M. E. (Ed.). (1983c) *Systematic instruction of the moderately and severely handicapped* (2nd ed.). Columbus, OH: Charles E. Merrill.

SNELL, M E., & GAST, D. L. (1981). Applying the time delay procedure to the instruction of the severely handicapped. *Journal of the Association for the Severely Handicapped, 6*, 3–14.

SNELL, M. E., & SMITH, D. D. (1978). Intervention strategies. In M. E. Snell (Ed.), *Systematic instruction of the moderately and severely handicapped*. Columbus, OH: Charles E. Merrill.

SNELL, M. E., & SMITH, D. D. (1983). Developing the IEP: Selecting and assessing skills. In M. E Snell (Ed.), *Systematic instruction of the moderately and severely handicapped* (2nd ed., pp. 76–112). Columbus, OH: Charles E. Merrill.

SOLNICK, J. V., RINCOVER, A., & PETERSON, C. R. (1977). Some determinants of the reinforcing and punishing effects of timeout. *Journal of Applied Behavior Analysis, 10*, 415–424.

SOLOMON, R. L. (1964). Punishment. *American Psychologist, 19*, 239–253.

SOLOMON, R., & TYNE, T. F. (1979). A comparison of individual and group contingency systems in a first-grade class. *Psychology in the Schools, 16*, 193–200.

SPANGLER, P. F., & MARSHALL, A. E. (1983). The unit play manager as facilitator of purposeful activities among institutionalized profoundly and severely retarded boys. *Journal of Applied Behavior Analysis, 16*, 345–349.

SPEIGEL-MCGILL, P., BAMBARD, L. M., SHORES, R. E., & FOX, J. J. (1984). The effects of proximity on socially oriented behaviors of severely multiply handicapped children. *Education and Treatment of Children, 7,* 365–378.

SPELTZ, M. L., SHIMAMURA, J. W., & MCREYNOLDS, W. T. (1982). Procedural variations in group contingencies: Effects on children's academic and social behaviors. *Journal of Applied Behavior Analysis, 15*(4), 533–544.

SPOONER, F. (1984). Comparisons of backward chaining and total task presentation in training severely handicapped persons. *Education and Training of the Mentally Handicapped, 19,* 15–22.

SPOONER, F., SPOONER, D., STIREWALT, C., & ULICNY, G. (1983). *A study of backward chaining: Comparisons of backward and reverse chaining in the skill training of severely retarded learners.* Unpublished manuscript, University of North Carolina at Charlotte.

SPOONER, F., SPOONER, D., & ULICNY, G. R. (1986). Comparisons of modified backward chaining: Backward chaining with leaps ahead and reverse chaining with leaps ahead. *Education and Treatment of Children, 9*(2), 122–134.

SPRADLIN, J. E., & SAUNDERS, R. R. (1984, May). *Probe procedures and the experimental analysis of human behavior.* Address at the annual meeting of the Association for Behavior Analysis, Nashville, TN.

SPRAGUE, J. R., & HORNER, R. H. (1984). The effects of single instance, multiple instance, and general case training on generalized vending machine use by moderately and severely handicapped students. *Journal of Applied Behavior Analysis, 17,* 273–278.

STADDON, J. E. R. (1977). Schedule-induced behavior. In W. K. Honig & J. E. R. Staddon (Eds.), *Handbook of operant behavior* (pp. 125–152). Englewood Cliffs, NJ: Prentice-Hall.

STAHL, J. R., & LEITENBERG, H. (1976). Behavioral treatment of the chronic mental hospital patient. In H. Leitenberg (Ed.), *Handbook of behavior modification and behavior therapy.* Englewood Cliffs, NJ: Prentice-Hall.

STEFFY, R. A., MEICHENBAUM, D., & BEST, J. A. (1964). Aversive and cognitive factors in the modification of smoking behavior. *Behavior Research and Therapy, 2,* 143.

STEPHENS, T. M. (1976). *Directive teaching of children with learning and behavioral handicaps.* Columbus, OH: Charles E. Merrill.

STEVENSON, H. C., & FANTUZZO, J. W. (1984). Application of the "generalization map" to a self-control intervention with school-aged children. *Journal of Applied Behavior Analysis, 17,* 203–212.

STITZER, M. L., & BIGELOW, G. E. (1984). Contingent reinforcement for carbon monoxide reduction: Within-subject effects of pay amount. *Journal of Applied Behavior Analysis, 17,* 477–483.

STITZER, M. L., BIGELOW, G. E., LIEBSON, I. A., & HAWTHORNE, J. W. (1982). Contingent reinforcement for benzodiazepine-free urines: Evaluation of a drug abuse treatment intervention. *Journal of Applied Behavior Analysis, 15,* 493–503.

STOKES, T. F., & BAER, D. M. (1977). An implicit technology of generalization. *Journal of Applied Behavior Analysis, 10,* 349–367.

STOKES, T. F., BAER, D. M., & JACKSON, R. L. (1974). Programming the generalization of a greeting response in four retarded children. *Journal of Applied Behavior Analysis, 7,* 599–610.

STOKES, T. F., FOWLER, S. A., & BAER, D. M. (1978). Training preschool children to recruit natural communities of reinforcement. *Journal of Applied Behavior Analysis, 11,* 285–303.

STOKES, T. F., & KENNEDY, S. H. (1980). Reducing child uncooperative behavior during dental treatment through modeling and reinforcement. *Journal of Applied Behavior Analysis, 13,* 41–49.

STOLZ, S. B. (1978). *Ethical issues in behavior modification.* San Francisco: Josey-Bass.

STRAIN, P. S., SHORES, R. E., & KERR, M. M. (1976). An experimental analysis of "spillover" effects on the social interaction of behaviorally handicapped preschool children. *Journal of Applied Behavior Analysis, 9,* 31–40.

STRAIN, P. S., & TIMM, M. A. (1974). An experimental analysis of social interaction between a behaviorally disordered preschool child and her classroom peers. *Journal of Applied Behavior Analysis, 7,* 583–590.

STRIEFEL, S. (1974). *Behavior modification: Teaching a child to imitate.* Austin, TX: Pro-Ed.

STRIEFEL, S. (1981). *How to teach through modeling and imitation.* Austin, TX: Pro-Ed.

STRIEFEL, S., & WETHERBY, B. (1973). Instruction following behavior of a retarded child and its controlling stimuli. *Journal of Applied Behavior Analysis, 6,* 663–670.

STUART, R. B. (1969). Operant-interpersonal treatment for marital discord. *Journal of Consulting and Clinical Psychology, 6,* 675–682.

STUART, R. B. (1971). Behavioral contracting within the families of delinquents. *Behavioral Therapy and Experimental Psychiatry, 2,* 1–11.

STUART, R. B., & DAVIS, B. (1972). *Slim chance in a fat world: Behavioral control of obesity.* Champaign, IL: Research Press.

STUART, R. B., & LOTT, L. A. (1972). Behavioral contracting with delinquents: A cautionary note. *Journal of Behavior Therapy and Experimental Psychiatry, 3,* 161–169.

STUART, R. B., & STUART, F. M. (1972). *Marriage precounseling inventory and guide.* Champaign, IL: Research Press.

STUMPHAUZER, J. S. (1977). *Behavior modification principles.* Kalamazoo, MI: Behaviordelia.

SULZER B., & MAYER, G. R. (1972). *Behavior modification procedures for school personnel.* Hinsdale, IL: Dryden Press.

SULZER-AZAROFF, B. (1983). A review of Johnston and Pennypacker's *Strategies and tactics of human behavioral research. Journal of Applied Behavior Analysis, 16,* 461–464.

SULZER-AZAROFF, B., & MAYER, G. R. (1977). *Applying behavior-analysis procedures with children and youth.* New York: Holt, Rinehart & Winston.

SURRATT, P. R., ULRICH, R. E., & HAWKINS, R. P. (1969). An elementary student as a behavioral engineer. *Journal of Applied Behavior Analysis, 2,* 85–92.

SWAIN, J. J., ALLARD, G. B., & HOLBORN, S. W. (1982). The good toothbrushing game: A school-based dental hygiene program for increasing the toothbrushing effectiveness of children. *Journal of Applied Behavior Analysis, 15,* 171–176.

SWITZER, E. B., DEAL, T. E., & BAILEY, J. S. (1977). The reduction of stealing in second graders using a group contingency. *Journal of Applied Behavior Analysis, 10,* 267–272.

TANNER, B. A., & ZEILER, M. (1975). Punishment of self-injurious behavior using aromatic ammonia as the aversive stimulus. *Journal of Applied Behavior Analysis, 8,* 53–57.

TARPLEY, H. D., & SCHROEDER, G. R. (1979). Comparison of DRO and DRI on rate of suppression of self-injurious behavior. *American Journal of Mental Deficiency, 84,* 188–194.

TARPY, R. M. & SWABINI, R. L. (1974). Reinforcement delay: A selective review of the last decade. *Psychological Bulletin, 81,* 984–997.

TATE, B. G., & BAROFF, G. S. (1966). Aversive control of self-injurious behavior in a psychotic boy. *Behavior Research and Therapy, 4,* 281–287.

TAWNEY, J., & GAST, D. (1984). *Single subject research in special education.* Columbus, OH: Charles E. Merrill.

TERRACE, H. S. (1963a). Discrimination learning with and without "errors." *Journal of the Experimental Analysis of Behavior, 6,* 1–27.

TERRACE, H. S. (1963b). Errorless transfer of a discrimination across two continua. *Journal of the Experimental Analysis of Behavior, 6,* 223–232.

TERTINGER, D. A., GREENE, B. F., & LUTZKER, J. R. (1984). Home safety: Development and validation of one component of an ecobehavioral treatment program for abused and neglected children. *Journal of Applied Behavior Analysis, 17,* 159–174.

TEST, D. W., & HEWARD, W. L. (1984). Accuracy of momentary time sampling: A comparison of fixed- and variable-interval observation schedules. In W. L. Heward, T. E. Heron, D. S. Hill, and J. Trap-Porter (Eds.), *Focus on behavior analysis in education* (pp. 177–194). Columbus, OH: Charles E. Merrill.

THARP, R. G., & WETZEL, R. J. (1969). *Behavior modification in the natural environment.* New York: Academic Press.

THOMAS, C., HOLMBER, M., & BAER, D. M. (1974). A brief report on a comparison of time sampling procedures. *Journal of Applied Behavior Analysis, 7,* 623–626.

THOMAS, D. R., BECKER, W. C., & ARMSTRONG, M. (1968). Production and elimination of disruptive classroom behavior by systematically varying teacher's behavior. *Journal of Applied Behavior Analysis, 1,* 35–45.

THOMPSON, T. J., BRAAM, S. J., & FUQUA, R. W. (1982). Training and generalization of laundry skills: A multiple probe evaluation with handicapped persons. *Journal of Applied Behavior Analysis, 15*(1), 177–182.

THOMPSON, T., & GRABOWSKI, J. G. (1972). *Reinforcement schedules and multioperant analysis.* New York: Appleton-Century-Crofts.

THORESEN, C. E., & MAHONEY, M. J. (1974). *Behavioral self-control.* New York: Holt, Rinehart & Winston.

THORNDIKE, E. L. (1911). *Animal intelligence: Experimental studies.* New York: Macmillan.

TODD, J. T., & MORRIS, E. K. (1983). Misconception and miseducation: Presentations of radical behaviorism in psychology textbooks. *The Behavior Analyst, 6,* 153–160.

TOPPING, J. S., & CROWE, J. T. (1974). Comparison of three response elimination procedures following FI and VI reinforcement training in humans. *Bulletin of the Psychonomic Society, 3,* 49–52.

TOUCHETTE, P. E., & HOWARD, J. S. (1984). Errorless learning: Reinforcement contingencies and stimulus control transfer in delayed prompting. *Journal of Applied Behavior Analysis, 17,* 175–188.

TOWNSEND, N. M., & MARHOLIN, D., II. (1978). Practice makes perfect: The elimination of stereotypic body-rocking through positive practice. *Scandinavian Journal of Behavior Therapy, 7,* 195–201.

TRAP, J. J., MILNER-DAVIS, P., JOSEPH, S., & COOPER, J. O. (1978). The effects of feedback and consequences on transitional cursive letter formation. *Journal of Applied Behavior Analysis, 11,* 381–393.

TRICE, A. D., & PARKER, F. C. (1983). Decreasing adolescent swearing in an instructional setting. *Education and Treatment of Children, 6,* 29–35.

TROVATO, J., & BUCHER, B. (1980). Peer tutoring with or without home-based reinforcement, for reading remediation. *Journal of Applied Behavior Analysis, 13,* 129–141.

TUCKER, D. J., & BERRY, G. W. (1980). Teaching severely multihandicapped students to put on their own hearing aids. *Journal of Applied Behavior Analysis, 13,* 65–75.

TURKEWITZ, H., O'LEARY, K. D., & IRONSMITH, M. (1975). Generalization and maintenance of appropriate behavior through self-control. *Journal of Consulting and Clinical Psychology, 43,* 577–583.

TYLER, V. O., & BROWN, G. D. (1967). The use of swift, brief isolation as a control device for institutionalized delinquents. *Behavior Research and Therapy, 5,* 1–9.

TYROLER, M. J., & LAHEY, B. B. (1980). Effects of contingent observation on the disruptive behavior of a toddler in a group setting. *Child Care Quarterly, 9,* 265–274.

ULLMANN, L. P., & KRASNER, L. A. (Eds.). (1965). *Case studies in behavior modification.* New York: Holt, Rinehart & Winston.

ULMAN, J. D., & SULZER-AZAROFF, B. (1975). Multi-element baseline design in educational research. In E. Ramp & G. Semb (Eds.), *Behavior analysis: Areas of research and application* (pp. 371–391). Englewood Cliffs, NJ: Prentice-Hall.

UPPER, D. (1977). Token economies in the psychiatric hospital. In D. Upper (Ed.), *Perspectives in behavior therapy.* Kalamazoo, MI: Behaviordelia.

VAN BIERVLIET, A., SPANGLER, P. F., & MARSHALL, A. M. (1981). An ecobehavioral examination of a simple strategy for increasing mealtime language in residential facilities. *Journal of Applied Behavior Analysis, 14,* 295–305.

VAN DEN POL, R. A., IWATA, B. A., IVANIC, M. T., PAGE, T. J., NEEF, N. A., & WHITLEY, F. P. (1981). Teaching the handicapped to eat in public places: Acquisition, generalization and maintenance of restaurant skills. *Journal of Applied Behavior Analysis, 14,* 61–69.

VAN HOUTEN, R. (1979). Social validation: The evolution of standards of competency for target behaviors. *Journal of Applied Behavior Analysis, 12,* 581–591.

VAN HOUTEN R. (1980). *Learning through feedback.* New York: Human Sciences Press.

VAN HOUTEN, R. (1983). Punishment: From the animal laboratory to the applied setting. In S. Axelrod & J. Apsche (Eds.), *The effects of punishment on human behavior* (pp. 13–44). New York: Academic Press.

VAN HOUTEN, R., MALENFANT, L., & ROLIDER, A. (1985). Increasing driver yielding and pedestrian signaling with prompting, feedback, and reinforcement. *Journal of Applied Behavior Analysis, 18,* 103–110.

VAN HOUTEN, R., & NAU, P. A. (1981). A comparison of the effects of posted feedback and increased police surveillance on highway speeding. *Journal of Applied Behavior Analysis, 14,* 261–271.

VAN HOUTEN, R., & NAU, P. A. (1983). Feedback interventions and driving speed: A parametric and comparative analysis. *Journal of Applied Behavior Analysis, 16,* 253–281.

VAN HOUTEN, R., NAU, P. A., MACKENZIE-KEATING, S. E., SAMEOTO, D., & COLAVECCHIA, B. (1982). An analysis of some variables influencing the effectiveness of reprimands. *Journal of Applied Behavior Analysis, 15,* 65–83.

VAN HOUTEN, R., NAU, P. A., & MARINI, Z. (1980). An analysis of public posting in reducing speeding behavior on an urban highway. *Journal of Applied Behavior Analysis, 13,* 383–395.

VOGLER, E. W., & FRENCH, R. W. (1983). The effects of a group contingency strategy on behaviorally disordered students in physical education. *Research Quarterly for Exercise and Sport, 54,* 273–277.

WACKER, D. P., BERG, W. K., WIGGINS, B., MULDOON, M., & CAVANAUGH, J. (1985). Evaluation of reinforcer preferences for profoundly handicapped students. *Journal of Applied Behavior Analysis, 18,* 173–178.

WAHLER, R. G., & FOX, J. J., III. (1980). Solitary toy play and time out: A family treatment package for children with aggressive and oppositional behavior. *Journal of Applied Behavior Analysis, 13,* 23–39.

WAHLER, R. G., & FOX, J. J. (1981). Setting events in applied behavior analysis: Toward a conceptual and methodological expansion. *Journal of Applied Behavior Analysis, 14,* 327–338.

WAHLER, R. G., & MANN, D. M. (1984). The communication patterns of troubled mothers: In search of a keystone in the generalization of parenting skills. *Education and Treatment of Children, 7,* 335–350.

WALKER, H. M. (1979). *The acting-out child: Coping with classroom disruption.* Boston: Allyn & Bacon.

WALKER, H. M. (1983). Application of response cost in school settings: Outcomes, issues and recommendations. *Exceptional Education Quarterly, 3,* 46–55.

WALKER, H. M., & BUCKLEY, N. K. (1972). Programming generalization and maintenance of treatment effects across time and across settings. *Journal of Applied Behavior Analysis, 5,* 209–224.

WALKER, H. M., HOPS, H., & FIEGENBAUM, E. (1976). Deviant classroom behavior as a function of combinations of social and token reinforcement and cost contingency. *Behavior Therapy, 7,* 76–88.

WALKER, H. M., HOPS, H., & GREENWOOD, C. R. (1981). Research and development of a behavior management package for remediating social aggression in the school setting. In P. Strain (Ed.), *The utilization of classroom peers as behavior change agents.* New York: Plenum Press.

WALKER, H. M., MCCONNELL, S., HOLMES, D., TODIS, B., WALKER, J., & GOLDEN, N. (1983). *ACCEPTS: A curriculum for children's effective peer and teacher skills.* Austin, TX: Pro-Ed.

WALKER, H. M., STREET, A., GARRETT, B., CROSSEN, J., HOPS, H., & GREENWOOD, C. R. (1978). *RECESS* (Reprogramming environmental contingencies for effective social skills) consultant manual; teacher manual; consultant trainer manual; supervisor manual. Eugene: University of Oregon. Center at Oregon for Research in the Behavioral Education of the Handicapped.

WALLACE, I. (1977). Self-control techniques of famous novelists. *Journal of Applied Behavior Analysis, 10,* 515–525.

WALLS, R. T., WERNER, T. J., BACON, A., & ZONE, T. (1977). Behavior checklists. In J. D. Cone & R. P. Hawkins (Eds.), *Behavioral assessment: New directions in clinical psychology* (pp. 77–151). New York: Bruner/Mazel.

WALTERS, R. H., PARKE, R. D., & CANE, V. A. (1965). Timing of punishment and the observation of consequences to others as determinants of response inhibition. *Journal of Experimental Child Psychology, 2,* 10–30.

WATSON, J. B. (1913). Psychology as the behaviorist views it. *Psychological Review, 20,* 158–177.

WATSON, J. B. (1924a). *Behaviorism.* New York: W. W. Norton.

WATSON, J. B. (1924b). *Psychology from the standpoint of a behaviorist* (2nd ed.). Philadelphia: J. B. Lippincott.

WEEKS, M., & GAYLORD-ROSS, R. (1981). Task difficulty and aberrant behavior in severely handicapped students. *Journal of Applied Behavior Analysis, 14,* 449–463.

WEIHER, R. G., & HARMAN, R. E. (1975). The use of omission training to reduce self-injurious behavior in a retarded child. *Behavior Therapy, 6,* 261–268.

WEINER, H. (1962). Some effects of response cost upon human operant behavior. *Journal of Experimental Analysis of Behavior, 5,* 201–208.

WEISS, R. L. (1975). Contracts, cognition, and change: A behavioral approach to marriage therapy. *The Counseling Psychologist, 5,* 15–26.

WELLS, K. C., FOREHAND, R., HICKEY, K., & GREEN, K. D. (1977). Effects of a procedure derived from the overcorrection principle on manipulated and nonmanipulated behaviors. *Journal of Applied Behavior Analysis, 10,* 679–687.

WELSCH v. LIKINS, 373 F. Supp. 487 (D. Minn., 1974).

WENRICH, W. W., DAWLEY, H. H., & GENERAL, D. A. (1976). *Self-directed systematic desensitization: A guide for the student, client, and therapist.* Kalamazoo, MI: Behaviordelia.

WHALEN, C. K., HENKER, B., COLLINS, B. E., FINCK, D., & DETEMOTO, S. (1979). A social ecology of hyperactive boys: Medication effects in structured classroom environments. *Journal of Applied Behavior Analysis, 12,* 65–81.

WHALEY, D. L., & MALOTT, R. W. (1971). *Elementary principles of behavior.* Englewood Cliffs, NJ: Prentice-Hall.

WHALEY, D. L., & SURRATT, S. L. (1968). *Attitudes of science.* Kalamazoo, MI: Behaviordelia.

WHEELER v. GLASS, 473 F. 2d. 983 (7th Cir. 1973).

WHITE, G. D. (1977). The effects of observer presence on the activity level of families. *Journal of Applied Behavior Analysis, 10,* 734.

WHITE, G. D., NIELSEN, G., & JOHNSON, S. M. (1972). Time out duration and the suppression of deviant behavior in children. *Journal of Applied Behavior Analysis, 5,* 111–120.

WHITE, M. A. (1975). Natural rates of teacher approval and disapproval in the classroom. *Journal of Applied Behavior Analysis, 8,* 367–372.

WHITE, O .R. (1971a). *A glossary of behavioral terminology.* Champaign, IL: Research Press.

WHITE, O. R. (1971b). *The "split-middle": A "quickie" method of trend estimation* (working paper No. 1). Eugene: University of Oregon, Regional Center for Handicapped Children.

WHITE, O. R., & HARING, N. G. (1980). *Exceptional teaching* (2nd ed.). Columbus, OH: Charles E. Merrill.

WHITE-BLACKBURN, G., SEMB, S., & SEMB, G. (1977). The effects of a good-behavior contract on the classroom behaviors of sixth-grade students. *Journal of Applied Behavior Analysis, 10,* 312.

WILCOX, B., & BELLAMY, G. T. (1982). *Design of high school programs for severely handicapped students.* Baltimore: Paul H. Brookes.

WILLIAMS, A. M. (1979) The quantity and quality of marital interaction related to marital satisfaction. *Journal of Applied Behavior Analysis, 12,* 665–678.

WILLIAMS, C. D. (1959). The elimination of tantrum behavior by extinction procedures. *Journal of Abnormal and Social Psychology, 59,* 269.

WILLIAMS, J. L. (1973). *Operant learning: Procedures for changing behavior.* Monterey, CA: Brooks/Cole.

WILSON, C. C., ROBERTSON, S. J., HERLONG, L. H., & HAYNES, S. N. (1979). Vicarious effects of time-out in the modification of aggression in the classroom. *Behavior Modification, 3,* 97–111.

WILSON, P. G., REID, D. H., PHILLIPS, J. F., & BURGIO, L. D. (1984). Normalization of institutional mealtimes for profoundly retarded persons: Effects and noneffects of teaching family-style dining. *Journal of Applied Behavior Analysis, 17*(2), 189–201.

WINETT, R. A., & WINKLER, R. C. (1972). Current behavior modification in the classroom: Be still, be quiet, be docile. *Journal of Applied Behavior Analysis, 5,* 499–504.

WINKLER, R. C. (1970). Management of chronic psychiatric patients by a token reinforcement system. *Journal of Applied Behavior Analysis, 3,* 47–55.

WINKLER, R. C. (1971). Reinforcement schedules for individual patients in a token economy. *Behavior Therapy, 2,* 534–537.

WITT, J. C., & ADAMS, R. M. (1980). Direct and observed reinforcement in the classroom: The interaction between information and reinforcement for socially approved and disapproved behaviors. *Behavior Modification, 4,* 321–336.

WODARSKI, J. W., FELDMAN, R. A., & PEDI, S. J. (1974). Objective measurement of the independent variable: A neglected methodological aspect in community based behavioral research. *Journal of Abnormal Child Psychology, 2,* 239–244.

WOLERY, M., & Gast, D.L. (1984). *Effective and efficient procedures for the transfer of stimulus control.* Unpublished manuscript, University of Kentucky, Lexington, KY.

WOLF, M. M. (1978). Social validity: The case for subjective measurement or how applied behavior analysis is finding its heart. *Journal of Applied Behavior Analysis, 11,* 203–214.

WOLF, M. M., RISLEY, T. R., & MEES, H. L. (1964). Application of operant conditioning procedures to the behavior problems of an autistic child. *Behavior Research and Therapy, 1,* 305–312.

WOLFENSBERGER, W. (1972). *The principle of normalization in human services.* Toronto: National Institute on Mental Retardation.

WOLFF, R. (1977). Systematic desensitization and negative practice to alter the afterfacts of a rape attempt. *Journal of Behavior Therapy and Experimental Psychiatry, 8,* 423–425.

WOLPE, J. (1958). *Psychotherapy by reciprocal inhibition.* Stanford, CA: Stanford University Press.

WOOD, F. H., & BRAATEN, S. (1983). Developing guidelines for the use of punishing interventions in the schools. *Exceptional Education Quarterly, 3,* 68–75.

WOOD, R., & FLYNN, J. M. (1978). A self-evaluation token system versus an external evaluation token system alone in a residential setting with pre-delinquent youths. *Journal of Applied Behavior Analysis, 11,* 503–512.

WORTHY, R. C. (1968). A miniature, portable timer and audible signal-generating device. *Journal of Applied Behavior Analysis, 1,* 159–160.

WYATT v. STICKNEY, 344 F. Supp. 387, 344 F. Supp. 373 (M.D. Ala. 1972), 344 F. Supp. 1341, 325 F. Supp. 781 (M.D. Ala. 1971), aff'd sub nom, Wyatt v. Aderholt, 503 F. 2d. 1305 (5th Cir. 1974).

WYSOCKI, T., HALL, G., IWATA, B., & RIORDAN, M. (1979). Behavioral management of exercise: Contracting for aerobic points. *Journal of Applied Behavior Analysis, 12,* 55–64.

YEATON, W. H., & BAILEY, J. S. (1983). Utilization analysis of a pedestrian safety training program. *Journal of Applied Behavior Analysis, 16,* 203–216.

YEATON, W. H., & SECHREST, L. (1981). Critical dimensions in the choice and maintenance of successful treatments: Strength, integrity, and effectiveness. *Journal of Consulting and Clinical Psychology, 49,* 156–167.

YELTON, A. R. (1979). Reliability in the context of the experiment: A commentary on two articles by Birkimer and Brown. *Journal of Applied Behavior Analysis, 12,* 565–569.

ZEILBERGER, J., SAMPEN, S. E., & SLOANE, H. N. (1968). Modification of a child's problem behaviors in the home with the mother as a therapist. *Journal of Applied Behavior Analysis, 1,* 47–54.

ZIMMERMAN, E. H., & ZIMMERMAN, J. (1962). The alteration of behavior in a special classroom situation. *Journal of the Experimental Analysis of Behavior, 5,* 59–60.

ZWALD, L., & GRESHAM, F. M. (1982). Behavioral consultation in a secondary class: Using DRL to decrease negative verbal interactions. *School Psychology Review, 11*(4), 533–544.

INDEX TO KEY TERMS

NAME INDEX

SUBJECT INDEX

WE VALUE YOUR OPINION—PLEASE SHARE IT WITH US

Merrill Publishing and our authors are most interested in your reactions to this textbook. Did it serve you well in the course? If it did, what aspects of the text were most helpful? If not, what didn't you like about it? Your comments will help us to write and develop better textbooks. We value your opinions and thank you for your help.

Text Title _____ Edition _____

Author(s) _____

Your Name (optional) _____

Address _____

City _____ State _____ Zip _____

School _____

Course Title _____

Instructor's Name _____

Your Major _____

Your Class Rank _____ Freshman _____ Sophomore _____Junior _____ Senior

_____ Graduate Student

Were you required to take this course? _____ Required _____Elective

Length of Course? _____ Quarter _____ Semester

1. Overall, how does this text compare to other texts you've used?

_____ Superior _____Better Than Most _____ Average _____Poor

2. Please rate the text in the following areas:

	Superior	Better Than Most	Average	Poor
Author's Writing Style	_____	_____	_____	_____
Readability	_____	_____	_____	_____
Organization	_____	_____	_____	_____
Accuracy	_____	_____	_____	_____
Layout and Design	_____	_____	_____	_____
Illustrations/Photos/Tables	_____	_____	_____	_____
Examples	_____	_____	_____	_____
Problems/Exercises	_____	_____	_____	_____
Topic Selection	_____	_____	_____	_____
Currentness of Coverage	_____	_____	_____	_____
Explanation of Difficult Concepts	_____	_____	_____	_____
Match-up with Course Coverage	_____	_____	_____	_____
Applications to Real Life	_____	_____	_____	_____

3. Circle those chapters you especially liked:
1   2   3   4   5   6   7   8   9   11   12   13   14   15   15   16   17   18   19   20
What was your favorite chapter? _____
Comments:

4. Circle those chapters you liked least:
1   2   3   4   5   6   7   8   9   11   12   13   14   15   15   16   17   18   19   20
What was your least favorite chapter? _____
Comments:

5. List any chapters your instructor did not assign. _____

6. What topics did your instructor discuss that were not covered in the text? _____

_____

7. Were you required to buy this book? _____ Yes _____ No

Did you buy this book new or used? _____ New _____ Used

If used, how much did you pay? _____

Do you plan to keep or sell this book? _____ Keep _____ Sell

If you plan to sell the book, how much do you expect to receive? _____

Should the instructor continue to assign this book? _____ Yes _____ No

8. Please list any other learning materials you purchased to help you in this course (e.g., study guide, lab manual).

_____

9. What did you like most about this text? _____

_____

10. What did you like least about this text? _____

_____

11. General comments:

May we quote you in our advertising? _____ Yes _____ No

Please mail to: Boyd Lane
                  College Division, Research Department
                  Box 508
                  1300 Alum Creek Drive
                  Columbus, Ohio 43216

Thank you!